Principles of Econometrics

Principles of Econometrics

A Modern Approach Using EViews

Sankar Kumar Bhaumik

OXFORD
UNIVERSITY PRESS

OXFORD
UNIVERSITY PRESS

Oxford University Press is a department of the University of Oxford.
It furthers the University's objective of excellence in research, scholarship,
and education by publishing worldwide. Oxford is a registered trademark of
Oxford University Press in the UK and in certain other countries

Published in India by
Oxford University Press
22 Workspace, 2nd Floor, 1/22 Asaf Ali Road, New Delhi 110002, India

ISBN-13: 978-0-19-809853-9
ISBN-10: 0-19-809853-7

Typeset in 11/13 Arno Pro
by Excellent Laser Typesetters, Pitampura, Delhi 110 034
Printed in India by Repro Books Limited, Thane.

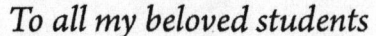

To all my beloved students

Contents

Tables, Figures, and Screenshots

FIGURES

SCREENSHOTS

Preface

Econometrics as a subject that provides tools for analysis of economic data has become immensely popular now. The process actually started since the availability of many user-friendly (Windows-based) econometric software packages late 1990s onwards.[1] There is virtually no field in economics where econometric tools are not applied to rigorously verify the validity or otherwise of the established wisdom (hypotheses). Even in other subjects like commerce and management, the tools of econometrics have found wide applications. Students and researchers these days are thus required to learn econometrics for application purposes. In the corporate and government sectors and research institutions, econometricians are needed to perform data analysis and forecasting-related works where application of tools of statistics and econometrics becomes necessary. So, learning econometrics for a typical student of economics has become almost unavoidable.

Recognizing the ever-increasing importance of econometrics, the University Grants Commission of India in early 2000s proposed the introduction of econometrics as a separate paper at the undergraduate honours level for economics. Following this, many universities responded by including econometrics as one of the papers in their undergraduate curricula for Economics Honours. Even for those who have not done so, a compulsory paper on econometrics is now offered in the very first year of the master's course in order to acquaint the students with the essentials of econometrics. The present book covers the syllabi usually followed under both the courses. Additionally, the book introduces some advanced topics like panel data models, models with qualitative dependent variable, and time series econometrics, which are important for applied researchers in economics and other branches of social sciences.

The main features of the book are the following:

- It has been written keeping in view the requirements of beginners in econometrics both at the levels of undergraduate and post-graduate studies.
- The main thrust of this book is upon building an intuitive understanding of the most modern tools and techniques of econometrics. So, without sacrificing necessary analytical rigour, we kept the usage of mathematics at the minimum possible level.

---

[1] 1995 is a landmark year towards the development of user-friendly statistical and econometric software packages. In this year, the Windows software was launched, which encouraged development of Windows-based versions of other software packages by the companies engaged in software development.

Even where simple algebra has been used to establish the results, we have provided as many steps as possible for the benefit of the students.

- The book makes extensive use of data sets drawn from Indian sources to illustrate econometric issues.

- Besides discussing various econometric issues from theoretical standpoints, we explain their applications to analyse real-life problems, mostly drawn from the Indian economy. This is how the book seeks to generate enthusiasm among the young scholars about econometrics.

- To help the students learn applications of EViews (one of the most user-friendly econometric software packages), the book clearly describes the steps to be followed in such applications, and also explains interpretations of econometric results. This will help young scholars to learn applications of EViews independently and develop skills for empirical research.

I am grateful to many people for their help and encouragement. First and foremost, I would like to convey my gratitude to two of my most revered teachers, G.K. Chadha (Jawaharlal Nehru University) and Chandan Mukhopadhyay (North Bengal University), who not only introduced the subject to me three and half decades back but also helped in many different ways to nurture my interest in it till date. It is they who had set the perspective for me, which is to use econometrics judiciously, not mechanically, to analyse economic and other data. I have religiously followed their advice all along in my own research and tried to convey the same message through this book. I must also acknowledge the help received from Professor Mukhopadhyay who, despite his frail health, took pains to read a rather lengthy chapter on time series econometrics and provided extremely useful suggestions for its improvement.

As always, all my colleagues in the Department of Economics, University of Calcutta, have been supportive and helpful. I am grateful to all of them.

Several other persons have helped me in the process of writing this book. The help and encouragement received from P.S. Das and Soumyen Sikdar, my ex-colleagues, has been extraordinary. Dipankor Coondoo helped me with his brief but useful comment on the chapter on time series econometrics. Arpita Dhar and Panchanan Das also read parts of the same chapter and offered useful suggestions. Nachiketa Chattopadhayay helped me with his detailed comments on two chapters on regression analysis. I received useful suggestions from Sidhartha Kundu on the chapter on dummy variables and from Tusher Nandi on panel data regression. Soumyadip Chattopadhayay read almost the entire manuscript and made very useful observations. Sibabrata Das, a dear friend of mine, was always ready to help me with his expertise in EViews applications. Sayantan Majumder supplied some data used in time series econometrics chapter. I am highly indebted to all of them.

I must also admit that the basic inspiration in writing this book has been drawn from several batches of students of my department. In fact, I have always considered myself fortunate in having an opportunity of teaching and interacting with such bright students as we have in the Economics department of Calcutta University. Not only they provided patient hearing to my classroom presentations over the years, but they were also rightfully critical about my approaches, which made me more serious about the subject. If I have managed to accomplish anything by writing this book, full credit must go to them. So, I dedicate this book to all my beloved students.

The comments received from three anonymous referees of Oxford University Press (OUP) were very helpful. I also received extremely useful help and advice from the members of the editorial and production teams of OUP at various stages of development of this book. I am thankful to all of them. I must also thank Ankita De Sarker, my research student, for helping me in the preparation of statistical tables and index for the book. Indrani Chakraborty, the librarian of our department library, has always been very prompt to locate necessary books and journal articles for me. I am thankful to her.

Finally, I must say that I would not have reached my present position without the sacrifice and blessings of my parents. My wife, Bidisha, and daughter, Jayini, kept constant vigil over me so that the time schedule for the work is maintained. It is because of their love, affection, and encouragement that I could finish the work on my part. It is now up to the students and researchers to assess its usefulness and indicate the deficiencies that remain. I sincerely invite comments and suggestions from everybody for future improvement of the book.

1 Scope and Methodology of Econometrics

As far as the laws of mathematics refer to reality they are not certain, and as far as they are certain they do not refer to reality.

—**Albert Einstein**
(Famous theoretical physicist who won the 1921 Nobel Prize in Physics)

We need a special field called econometrics, and textbooks about it, because it is generally accepted that economic data possess certain properties that are not considered in standard statistics texts or are not sufficiently emphasized there for use by economists.

—**Clive W.J. Granger**
(Co-recipient of 2003 Nobel Prize in Economic Sciences)

1.1. WHAT IS ECONOMETRICS?

Econometrics is a neologism formed by combining two Greek words: *oikonomia* (meaning economics) and *metron* (meaning measure) (Tintner 1953, 33). Thus, the literal meaning of econometrics appears to be 'measurement in economics'. However, although measurement is indeed an important component of econometrics, the scope of econometrics is much wider than that. This becomes clear from various definitions of econometrics[1] provided by leading econometricians over the years. A few of those definitions are presented below.

The method of econometric research aims, essentially, at a conjunction of economic theory and actual measurements, using the theory and technique of statistical inference as a bridge pier. (Haavelmo 1944, iii)

[I]t is better to restrict econometrics to investigations which utilize mathematics, economics and statistics. These will be different from investigations in quantitative economics, which frequently use no mathematics. They will also be distinguished from work in mathematical economics, which is quantitative, but not empirical and uses no statistics. Finally, it will be distinct from theoretical work in statistics, which uses mathematics but is in general unrelated to economic theory. (Tintner 1953, 37)

---

[1] The term 'econometrics' appears to have been first used by Pawel Ciompa as early as 1910 although Ragnar Frisch is credited for coining the term and establishing it as a subject in the sense in which it is known today.

[E]conometrics is the science which deals with the determination by statistical methods of concrete quantitative laws occurring in economic life. (Lange 1962, 13)

Econometrics attains even broader meaning if mathematics and statistics are defined in the following broad sense: mathematics teaches how to derive propositions from other propositions; statistics teaches how to derive propositions from observed facts. Mathematics would then coincide with deductive logic, and statistics with inductive logic .... Econometrics would then be simply the application of rules of logic to economics. (Marschak 1948, 1)

[E]conometrics may be defined as the quantitative analysis of actual economic phenomenon based on the concurrent development of theory and observation, related by appropriate methods of inference. (Samuelson, Koopmans, and Stone 1954, 142)

Econometrics may be defined as the social science in which tools of economic theory, mathematics, and statistical inference are applied to the analysis of economic phenomena. (Goldberger 1964, 1)

[T]he discipline in which one studies theoretical and practical aspects of applying statistical methods to economic data for the purpose of testing economic theories (represented by carefully constructed models) and of forecasting and controlling the future path of economic variables. (Sowey 1983, 257)

Econometrics is the field of economics that concerns itself with the application of mathematical statistics and the tools of statistical inference to the empirical measurement of relationships postulated by economic theory. (Greene 2003, 1)

Broadly speaking, econometrics aims to give empirical content to economic relations for testing economic theories, forecasting, decision making, and for ex post decisions/policy evaluation. (Geweke, Horowitz, and Pesaran 2008, 609)

It clearly emerges from above definitions that econometrics as a branch of economics differs from other branches like mathematical economics, economic statistics, and mathematical statistics. While mathematical economics expresses economic theory in formal algebraic language without bothering about measurability or empirical verification of the theory, the econometrician often uses mathematical equations proposed by the mathematical economist but puts these equations in a form so that they lend themselves to empirical testing. The economic statistics is concerned with collecting, processing, and presenting economic data in the form of charts and tables; the econometrician uses these data to test economic theories. Further, mathematical statistics provides many tools used by econometrics. However, the econometrician needs different methods because of the special nature of economic data, which is that data are rarely generated through controlled experiments.

In brief, we can say that the objective of econometrics is to provide empirical content to economic theory. The three ingredients of econometrics are: economic theory, economic data, and statistical methods. Neither 'theory without measurement' nor 'measurement without theory' is sufficient to explain economic phenomenon. It is precisely their union that is important, as emphasized by Ragnar Frisch in the editorial note to the inaugural issue of *Econometrica*, the journal of the Econometric Society, published in 1933 (Frisch 1933).

1.2. BRIEF HISTORY OF ECONOMETRICS

Although quantitative economic analysis is a good three centuries old, econometrics as a recognized branch of economics began to emerge only in the 1930s and 1940s with the foundation of the Econometric Society, the Cowles Commission in the United States, and the Department of Applied Economics (DAE) in Cambridge, England. In the initial years of its development, these institutions emphasized on the development of econometric methods.

The first major methodological debate in econometrics appears to have taken place over the issue of applicability of the probability calculus and the sampling theory to the analysis of economic data. Frisch himself was highly sceptical of the usefulness of these tools as his primary concern was the problems of 'multicollinearity' and 'measurement errors' which he believed were pervasive in economics. However, his approach was not accepted by the econometricians at large. Instead, it was the probabilistic rationalizations of regression analysis that formed the basis of modern econometrics. In fact, acceptance of Haavelmo's (1944) probabilistic approach marked the beginning of a new era in econometrics, and paved the way for its rapid development with the likelihood method gaining importance as a tool for identification, estimation, and inference in econometrics.

In the initial years, the researchers at the Cowles Commission were mostly busy in providing a formal solution to the problems of 'identification' and developing methods for estimation of simultaneous equations models. On the other hand, the researchers at the DAE were mostly engaged in understanding various problems of time series data and obtaining a satisfactory solution to the problem of 'spurious correlation'. Their contributions during that period helped to better analyse the economic time series data and eventually laid down the basis of what is now known as the 'time series econometrics' approach.

Several other areas where econometrics witnessed significant developments over the years are dynamic specification, latent variables, expectation formation, limited dependent variables, discrete choice models, random coefficient models, disequilibrium models, nonlinear estimation, panel data models, forecasting and forecast evaluation, non-parametric and semi-parametric estimation, bootstrapping, programme evaluation methods, integration and simulation methods, Bayesian econometrics, and so on.

All in all, the development of econometrics and the impact it has made on both theoretical and empirical researches in economics over the past seven to eight decades have been phenomenal.[2] This is corroborated by the fact that already six volumes of *Handbook of Econometrics* (Engle and McFadden 1994; Griliches and Intriligator 1983, 1984, 1986; Heckman and Leamer 2001, 2007) have been published, which include as many as 77

---

[2] Spanos (2006) provides a retrospective, but self-critical, account of the development of econometrics.

chapters covering diverse aspects of theoretical and empirical issues in econometrics. Another dazzling fact is that out of 44 Nobel Memorial Prizes in Economic Sciences given to 71 scholars till 2012, 5 awards have gone to 8 scholars for their contributions to the field of econometrics[3] (see Table 1.1 for the list of awardees), which is second highest among all branches of economics.[4] Thus, Geweke et al. (2008, 631) rightly observed:

> Econometrics has come a long way over a relatively short period. Important advances have been made in the compilation of economic data and in the development of concepts, theories and tools for the construction and evaluation of a wide variety of econometric models. Application of econometric methods can be found in almost every field of economics…. In both theory and practice econometrics has already gone well beyond what its founders envisaged.

Table 1.1   List of Nobel Laureates from Econometrics and the Rationale behind the Award

Year	Laureate	Country	Rationale
1969	Ragnar Frisch	Norway	For having developed and applied dynamic models for the analysis of economic processes.
	Jan Tinbergen	Netherlands	
1980	Lawrence Klein	United States	For the creation of econometric models and the application to the analysis of economic fluctuations and economic policies.
1989	Trygve Haavelmo	Norway	For his clarification of the probability theory foundations of econometrics and his analyses of simultaneous economic structures.
2000	James J. Heckman	United States	For his development of theory and methods for analysing selective samples.
	Daniel L. McFadden	United States	For his development of theory and methods for analysing descrete choice.
2003	Robert F. Engle	United States	For methods of analysing economic time series with time-varying volatility (ARCH)*.
	Clive W.J. Granger	United Kingdom	For methods of analysing economic time series with common trends (cointegration).

* See Chapter 10, Section 10.9, for the meaning of ARCH.

1.3. METHODOLOGY OF ECONOMETRICS

By methodology of econometrics, we mean the steps which are followed in an econometric study. Broadly speaking, an econometric analysis proceeds along the following steps.

(i)   The statement of economic theory or formation of hypothesis
(ii)   Specification of the econometric model to test the theory or hypothesis
(iii)   Estimation of parameters of the specified model

[3] Apart from these scholars, the Nobel Prize for 2011 was awarded to Thomas J. Sargent and Christopher A. Sims of the United States 'for their empirical research on cause and effect in the macro-economy'. It is to be noted that in their empirical research on macro-economics, they used econometric tools innovatively. Moreover, Christopher A. Sims advanced the 'structural VAR' which many experts consider as an extremely significant contribution in the field of macroeconometric modelling.

[4] The highest number of awards (seven) has been bagged by the macroeconomists.

(iv)   Verification or statistical inference
(v)   Forecasting and policy formulation

Hypothesis

Hypothesis is that aspect of economic theory which is to be tested for empirical validity. Suppose we want to examine validity of the Keynesian consumption theory that postulates that consumption is a function of income. So if we frame the statement 'consumption is a function of income', it represents a hypothesis.

Model Specification

The model is an algebraic representation of a real world process. At the stage of model speci-fication, we decide on the precise form of functional relationship between consumption and income. For this, we may take guidance from the mathematical economist. Suppose the mathematical economist suggests the following form of relationship between consumption and income

$$Y_i = \alpha + \beta X_i \qquad (1.1)$$

where

Y = consumption and X = income. The subscript i refers to the case of a particular individual ($i = 1, 2, \ldots, n$).

Two features of the above relationship become apparent.

(i)   There is *one-way causation* between consumption and income. This means that consumption changes with change in income and not the other way around; and

(ii)   The relationship between consumption and income is *exact* and *deterministic*. This means that given the values of parameters α and β, we obtain only one value of Y for each value of X.

However, the reality is that the relationship between consumption and income is not *exact* but a *typical* one. This becomes clear when we look at the data which show that for each value of X (income) there is a whole distribution of the values of Y (consumption). In other words, persons with same income level are found to have different levels of consumption. This type of a situation calls for a stochastic specification of the consumption function, which is done by writing our model as

$$Y_i = \alpha + \beta X_i + \varepsilon_i \qquad (1.2)$$

Here ε_i is called the *stochastic term* or *disturbance term*, or *error term*. Equation (1.2) rep-resents an econometric specification of the consumption–income relationship as against mathematical specification of such relationship provided by (1.1). The consumption–income relationship represented by (1.2) is also stochastic because of inclusion of the stochastic term ε_i. The term 'stochastic' here means that for each value of X, there is a whole distribution of the values of Y so that it is not possible to forecast the value of Y exactly. This uncertainty concerning Y arises precisely because of the presence of stochastic term ε_i. Since ε_i is a random variable, Y_i in (1.2) is also a random variable.

The above discussion suggests that we make stochastic specification of relationship between the variables in econometrics, which is possible only with the inclusion of the stochastic or disturbance term ε_i in our model. Otherwise, the relationship will continue to remain *exact* or *deterministic*. In fact, inclusion of the disturbance term or our preference for a stochastic specification may be justified at least in three important ways (Kennedy 2008, 3).

(i)   *Human indeterminacy*: It is believed that human behaviour is such that actions taken even under ideal circumstances will differ in a random way. In that case, the disturbance term helps to capture random or unpredictable behaviour of human beings.

(ii) *Influence of omitted variables*: Although income might be the major determinant of consumption, it is not the only determinant. Other variables like individuals' caste, sex, education, liquid asset holdings, etc., may also have a systematic influence on their consumption levels. However, in model (1.1), we have explicitly recognised income as the only determinant of consumption although we cannot rule out the possibility of these 'omitted' factors determining individuals' consumption levels. It is here the disturbance term helps by capturing the net influence of such omitted factors/variables on the dependent variable of our model, which is consumption.

(iii) *Measurement error*: It is possible that the variable being explained (which is consumption in our example) cannot be measured accurately in some cases either because of data collection difficulties or because of it being unmeasurable. In such a situation, the disturbance term can be thought of representing the measurement errors.

Estimation

Our objective here is to obtain estimates or numerical values of the unknown parameters of model (1.2) by using any one of the estimation techniques. Some popular estimation techniques used by the econometricians are Ordinary Least Squares (OLS), Maximum Likelihood (ML), Moment, etc.

Verification or Inference

In this stage, we develop suitable criteria to examine whether the estimates obtained are in conformity with the expectations of the theory that is being tested. For this purpose, we depend on the branch of statistical theory known as statistical inference.

Forecasting and Policy Formulation

This is the final stage where we utilize the estimated model for the purpose of forecasting and/or policy formulation.

1.4. NECESSARY ASSUMPTIONS FOR ESTIMATION

Once we have specified the behavioural relationship between Y and X as in model (1.2), our next task is to estimate the values of two unknown parameters of our model which are α and β. For this purpose, we need data on variables Y and X and also the disturbance term ε. But the difficulty is that ε is not observable like Y and X. Hence, to estimate the above model, we guess the values of ε. In other words, we make some reasonable assumptions about the shape of the distribution of each ε. Specifically, we make the following assumptions.

(i)   *The mean or expected value of disturbance term ε is zero*. This is algebraically expressed by writing

$$E(\varepsilon_i) = 0 \text{ for all } i$$

This assumption means that for any given X, ε may have different values, but on an average it is zero. This assumption is important in that violation of it leads to the 'biased intercept' problem.[5]

(ii)   *The disturbances have uniform variance* which is known as the assumption of *homoskedasticity*. Algebraically,

$$Var(\varepsilon_i) = E[\varepsilon_i - E(\varepsilon_i)]^2$$
$$= E(\varepsilon_i^2) \qquad [\because E(\varepsilon_i) = 0]$$
$$= \sigma^2 \text{ constant for all } i$$

In plain language, this assumption means that every disturbance has the same variance, which is unknown. It also implies that the variance of ε would not be higher for higher values of X than for lower values. The violation of this assumption creates an econometric problem called *heteroskedasticity*.

(iii)   The *disturbances are uncorrelated* which is known as the assumption of *serial independence* or *non-autocorrelation*. Algebraically,

$$Cov(\varepsilon_i, \varepsilon_j) = E[\{\varepsilon_i - E(\varepsilon_i)\}\{\varepsilon_j - E(\varepsilon_j)\}]$$
$$= E(\varepsilon_i \varepsilon_j)$$
$$= 0 \text{ for } i \neq j$$

This assumption implies that ε is independent such that different values of ε are not correlated. The violation of this assumption creates the problem of *serial correlation* or *autocorrelation*.

(iv)   *ε is normally distributed*. This assumption is necessary for conducting statistical tests of significance of the parameters estimated. It can be justified by invoking

---

[5] For the meaning of bias of an estimate, refer to Chapter 2, Section 2.5.

the Central Limit Theorem. We suppose that ε captures the impact of all omitted variables, and we have many such variables which are minor but are independently distributed random variables. Then, the distribution of the sum of such independently distributed random variables tends to be normal as the number of such variables increases independently. It is obvious that violation of this assumption will render the usual tests of significance (e.g., the t-test) for the estimated coefficients inapplicable.

(v) X *is a non-stochastic variable with fixed values in repeated samples.* This implies that the values of X are either controllable or fully predictable. Violation of this assumption creates problems like *errors in variables* and *autoregression.*

Probability Distribution of Y_i

Given the above assumptions, we may now look at the probability distribution of the dependent variable Y_i. As Y_i is a linear function of ε_i which is normally distributed, it follows that Y_i is also normally distributed. Further, the mean and variance of Y_i are

$$E(Y_i) = E(\alpha + \beta X_i + \varepsilon_i)$$
$$= E(\alpha + \beta X_i) + E(\varepsilon_i)$$
$$= \alpha + \beta X_i \quad [\because E(\varepsilon_i) = 0 \text{ and the concept of expectation does}$$
$$\text{not relate to } \alpha, \beta, \text{ and } X_i]$$

$$Var(Y_i) = E[Y_i - E(Y_i)]^2$$
$$= E(\varepsilon_i^2) \quad (\because Y_i = \alpha + \beta X_i + \varepsilon_i)$$
$$= \sigma^2$$

So we can write the probability distribution of Y_i as

$$Y_i \sim N(\alpha + \beta X_i, \sigma^2)$$

1.5. DATA FOR ECONOMETRIC ANALYSIS

For empirical analysis of economic problems using the tools of econometrics, we use various types of data. While some econometric tools can straightaway be applied to all types of data, we may require specialized tools for analysing data sets having special features. The three types of data used are cross-sectional data, time series data, and panel data.

Cross-Sectional Data

Cross-sectional data, also known as micro-data, are those collected for different entities in a single time period. Thus, a cross-sectional data set may consist of a sample of individuals, households, firms, regions, countries, or any other type of units at a specific time point. The cross-sectional variables are usually denoted by subscript i with $i = 1, 2, ..., N$, where

N is the number of cross-sectional units from which data have been collected. Among the important fields where cross-sectional data are extensively used are agricultural economics, industrial economics, labour economics, health economics, urban economics, demography, etc. Recently, a new branch of econometrics has emerged that deals with tools specifically required for analysing cross-sectional data or micro-data. This is called *microeconometrics*.

Time Series Data

Time series data, also called macro-data, are those that are collected for the same entity for different time periods. Thus, a time series data set consists of observations on one or more variables over time. The examples of time series data are GDP, money supply, exports, imports, government expenditure, exchange rates, stock prices, etc. The issue of *data frequency* is important in the context of time series data. For economic variables, the most common data frequencies are annual, quarterly, monthly, weekly, and daily. The time series data are denoted by subscript t with $t = 1, 2, ..., T$, where T is the number of time points for which data have been collected. The branch of econometrics that deals with specialized tools for analysis of time series data is popularly known as *macroeconometrics* or *time series econometrics*.[6]

Panel Data

Panel data, also called *longitudinal data*, are data collected for multiple entities where each entity is observed in two or more time points. For instance, if we collect data on some macroeconomic variables (GDP, money supply, exports, etc.) for some countries for two or more years, and arrange these data in a systematic manner, then our data set is called the panel data set. Thus, the panel data set has both cross-sectional and time series dimensions. The panel data are denoted by both i and t subscripts that we used earlier for cross-sectional and time series data, respectively. If the GDP data have been collected from N number of countries and for each country data have been recorded for T number of years, then the GDP variable (labelled as GDP_{it}) would have NT observations. Apart from having enhanced number of observations, the panel data are found to be useful to tackle many econometric problems and analysing specific issues which are otherwise difficult to understand using only cross-sectional or time series data. That is why panel data have been gaining wide applications in recent years in many econometric analyses so that another new branch has emerged which is known as *panel data econometrics*.

Experimental and Non-experimental Data

While discussing the types of data, it is important to note that in econometrics, we use non-experimental data. In fact, econometrics evolved as a discipline separate from mathematical statistics to analyse the non-experimental data. While the experimental data generated in laboratory environments are used in the natural sciences, the econometrician uses non-experimental data (e.g., data collected through sample surveys) that are generated not

---

[6] Some scholars described *microeconometrics* and *macroeconometrics* as the twin sisters in econometrics.

through controlled or laboratory experiments. Of course, the econometrician draws upon the tools from mathematical statistics whenever necessary, but uses separate (econometric) methods developed to analyse the non-experimental data.

Sources of Data

The data to be used for econometric analysis may be obtained from published sources or collected through field surveys. The former is called *secondary* data and the latter as *primary* or field data. Secondary data are mostly available from government departments and international organizations, such as International Monetary Fund (IMF), World Bank, United Nations Development Programme (UNDP), Food and Agricultural Organization (FAO), and International Food Policy Research Institute (IFPRI). These organizations publish both cross-sectional and time series data which are extensively used by the researchers especially for inter-country comparison. In India, important sources of secondary data are the Reserve Bank of India (RBI), Central Statistical Organisation (CSO), Census of India, National Sample Survey Organisation (NSSO), Planning Commission, and different central and state government ministries. Nowadays, a lot of secondary data on diverse aspects of the Indian economy are collated and sold by many private organizations [e.g., Centre for Monitoring Indian Economy (CMIE), Indiastat.com, EPW Research Foundation]. To analyse different developmental issues, the researchers in India depend heavily on data available from these sources. However, it is to be remembered that data available from the secondary sources should not be utilized without criticism. In particular, one should look into the methodology of data collection and ascertain the quality/reliability of data before they are put to final use.

While secondary data are already published, which the researcher merely gathers as per her/his requirements, quite often such data are found inadequate to analyse the problems under consideration. So the researcher might like to collect more data through field surveys which are called primary data. Here again several methodological issues, such as questionnaire design, sample selection, determination of sample size, time frame for survey, and so on, need to be settled before going to the field for actual collection of data.[7] Needless to mention, data collected following scientifically designed sampling procedure would be more reliable and suitable for the purpose of econometric analysis.

1.6. ABOUT EVIEWS SOFTWARE PACKAGE

To illustrate application of various tools of econometrics discussed in this book, we have used the EViews software package. The full form of EViews is 'Econometric Views'. It is developed by Quantitative Micro Software (QMS), USA. EViews version 1.0 was launched in March 1994 replacing its predecessor, MicroTSP. The latest version is EViews 8, released in March 2013. The exercises carried out in this book are based on this latest version. However, as the dialogues and commands for version 8 are almost the same as the previous two versions

---

[7] For detailed discussions on these issues, one may refer to Desai and Porter (2006); Devereux and Hoddinott (1993); and Rudra (1989).

(EViews 6 and 7), scholars using the previous version will not find any difficulty in following the illustrative examples contained in this book.

An important feature of EViews is that it is a very simple and user-friendly econometric software package that runs on Windows machines.[8] It takes advantage of the visual features of the modern Windows software so that one can just use the mouse to guide the operations with standard Windows menus and dialogues. For input and output, it supports various formats, including Excel, PSPP/SPSS, DAP/SAS, Stata, RATS, and TSP. Although EViews is specially designed to work with time series data, it is also extensively used for econometric analyses of cross-sectional and panel data. So it is a very versatile software package.

Some important basic capabilities of EViews 8 are as follows.

- Reading and writing of data files in standard spreadsheet formats
- Computing a new series, based on a formula of any complexity
- Obtaining plots of data series, scatter diagrams, bar graphs, pie charts, etc.
- Descriptive statistics: correlations, covariances, autocorrelations, cross-correlations, and histograms
- Ordinary least squares regression, least squares with autoregressive correction and two-stage least squares
- Non-linear least squares
- Robust least squares
- Tests for various econometric problems: heteroskedasticity, autocorrelation, multicollinearity, model specification error, etc.
- Estimating quintile regression
- Breakpoint testing (both for single and multiple breakpoints)
- Breakpoint regression (automatic selection and user-specified)
- Probit and logit estimation of binary choice models
- Linear and non-linear estimation of systems of equations
- Pooled cross-sectional–time series estimation and forecasting
- Various tests of stationarity of time series data
- Causality tests including panel causality testing
- ARCH-GARCH estimation and forecasting
- Estimation and analysis of vector autoregressive (VAR) systems
- Bayesian VARs
- State space models and Kalman filter
- Forecasts based on regression

[8] Agung (2011, xv), who worked with several software packages and has written useful books on software applications, observed that not only is EViews the most user-friendly among the available statistical/econometric software packages but is also equally competent to analyse all kinds of data sets—cross-sectional, panel, and time series. It may also be noted that the EViews software package is quite economical in relation to other statistical/econometric software packages. For instance, one unit of the student version of EViews 8 is currently available for $39.95 only. This software is marketed by IHS Global Inc., USA.

- Error-trend seasonal exponential smoothing
- Solution and estimation of simultaneous equations models
- Advanced time series analysis: Johansen cointegration test, panel cointegration test, etc.
- Factor analysis
- Panel regressions
- Panel cointegration estimation
- Panel series principal components
- Heckman selection models with support for maximum likelihood and two-step estimation

There are many other things that can be performed using EViews. A fuller idea about the econometric tools that can be applied using this software package may be obtained from EViews 8 User's Guides I and II provided with the package.

A Glimpse of the Main Window of EViews 8

As we double-click on the EViews 8 icon (Screenshot 1.1), which is usually displayed on the desktop of the computer as a shortcut after installation of the software, the main EViews window (as in Screenshot 1.1) opens. There are five main areas of the main window of EViews, marked with arrows in Screenshot 1.1. These are the title bar, main menu, command window, work area, and status line.

1.7. QUESTIONS

A. Multiple-Choice Questions
Tick ($\sqrt{}$) the correct answer.

(i)   Who among the following scholars is credited for coining the term econometrics?
    (a)   Carl Friedrich Gauss
    (b)   Francis Galton
    (c)   Trygve Haavelmo
    (d)   Ragner Frisch

(ii) Who among the following scholars provided the probabilistic foundation to econometrics?
    (a)   Ragnar Frisch
    (b)   Trygve Haavelmo
    (c)   Jan Tinbergen
    (d)   Lawrence Klein

(iii) The GDP data collected for the current year for a number of countries are called
    (a)   Experimental data
    (b)   Cross-section data
    (c)   Time-series data
    (d)   Panel data

Screenshot 1.1 Eviews 8 Icon (Top) and Main Window of EViews 8 (Down)

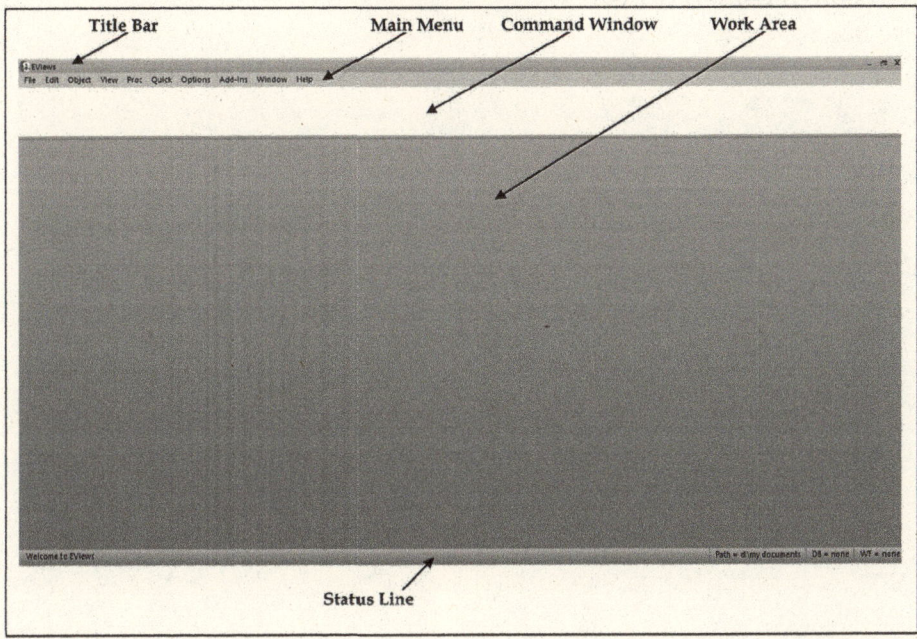

(iv) Non-fulfilment of the zero-mean assumption for the disturbance term leads to the problem of
    (a) Biased intercept
    (b) Biased slope
    (c) Biased intercept and slope
    (d) None of the above

B. General Questions
    (i) Define econometrics.
    (ii) Write briefly about the evolution of econometrics as a branch of economics.
    (iii) How does an econometric model differ from a mathematical model?

(iv)   Explain why the disturbance term is included in an econometric relationship. State the assumptions made with regard to the disturbance term.

(v)   What is the difference between experimental data and non-experimental data?

(vi)   Define cross-section data, time-series data, and panel data.

(vii) Distinguish between secondary data and primary data.

(viii) What are major sources of secondary data in India?

Answers to Multiple-Choice Questions

(i) (d); (ii) (b); (iii) (b); (iv) (a).

2 The Simple Linear Regression Model

This chapter begins with discussion on regression technique, the main workhorse in the toolkit of any researcher, especially in the social sciences. We discuss the issues connected with the two-variable or simple linear regression model (SLRM) in this chapter. The issues specifically dealt with are specification and assumptions of the SLRM, estimation of such a model, hypothesis testing or inference, measuring the quality or goodness of fit of the estimated model, and so on. We also describe the steps involved in estimation of the SLRM using the EViews software package, and clarify the interpretation of EViews regression output.

2.1 DEFINITION

Regression analysis is one of the most important tools at the disposal of any researcher.[1] In very general terms, regression is concerned with describing and evaluating the functional/causal relationship among variables.[2] For instance, if we are interested to know the relationship between consumption expenditure of the individuals and their levels of income, education, sex, caste, and so on, we can do so in terms of regression analysis. In regression analysis, we begin by expressing the relationship among the variables in the form of an equation or a model. In such a model, one of the variables is taken as the dependent variable[3] and all other variables are independent variables.[4] If we are interested to study the relationship between two variables only, our model involves one dependent variable and one independent variable. Such a model is called the simple regression model. On the other hand, we examine the relationship between dependent variable and more than one explanatory variable together in a multiple regression model.

The main issues that concern a researcher employing regression technique to study the relationship among variables are specification and assumptions of the regression model, estimation of such a model, hypothesis testing or inference, and measuring the quality or

---

[1] The term 'regression' was coined by Francis Galton, an accomplished scientist of nineteenth century and a cousin of Charles Darwin.

[2] While regression shows causal/functional relationship between the variables, correlation shows degree of association between them.

[3] Alternative names of dependent variable are: explained variable, response variable, and regressand.

[4] Independent variable is also called explanatory variable, control variable, and regressor.

goodness of fit of the estimated model. In this chapter, we discuss these and a few other issues in the context of simple regression model while the next chapter discusses these issues in the context of multiple regression model.

2.2 SPECIFICATION AND ASSUMPTIONS

Let us suppose that consumption expenditure depends only on income. A sensible first step to test if at all there is any relation between consumption expenditure and income would be to collect some data on these two variables and display such data in a scatter diagram. Table 2.1 presents data on two variables—annual per capita consumption expenditure and annual per capita NSDP (net state domestic product—which proxies for income)—for 22 major states of India. When we plot these data in a scatter diagram, it appears that there is an approximate linear and positive relationship between per capita consumption expenditure (Y_i) and per capita NSDP (X_i) (see Figure 2.1). This means that increases in Y_i are usually accompanied by increases in X_i, and such a relation between the two variables can be described approximately by a straight line. Then the question is: how to draw such a line? Of course, we could draw such a line by hand and see the intercept and slope of it to form an understanding about the relation between consumption and income. However, in practice such a method is likely to be inaccurate and laborious. Therefore, it would be of interest to determine the extent to which the relationship between Y_i and X_i can be described by an algebraic equation that can be estimated using a defined procedure. Here we may consider using the following equation that 'best fits' our data.

$$Y_i = \alpha + \beta X_i \tag{2.1}$$

However, the problem is that equation (2.1) is an 'exact' one which means, given the values of the intercept (α) and slope (β), we can determine with certainty the value of Y for each value of X. But our scatter diagram suggests that for each value of X, there could be different values of Y. In other words, the relationship between Y and X is not exact, and hence the above model appears inadequate to describe the relationship between Y and X as suggested by the data. In this situation, to make the model realistic, we add a stochastic disturbance term or error term (ε_i) to our model and write it as

$$Y_i = \alpha + \beta X_i + \varepsilon_i \tag{2.2}$$

A model such as (2.2) is called the two-variable or simple linear regression model (SLRM).[5] As noted in the previous chapter, the stochastic disturbance term ε_i serves several functions. Most notably, it captures the effects of factors other than income on consumption expenditure, corrects for errors in the measurement of Y_i, captures the effects of random and unpredictable events on Y_i, and so on.

---

[5] The linearity of this model implies that (a) one-unit change in X has the same effect on Y irrespective of the initial value of X (this is so because $\Delta Y_i = \beta \Delta X_i$ when $\Delta \varepsilon_i = 0$) and (b) the highest power of the two parameters α and β is 1.

Table 2.1 Annual Per Capita Consumption Expenditure (PCEXP) and Annual Per Capita NSDP (PCNSDP) in Major States of India

State	PCEXP	PCNSDP
Andhra Pradesh	18,166	51,025
Assam	14,088	27,197
Bihar	10,162	16,119
Chhattisgarh	12,708	38,059
Gujarat	16,093	63,961
Haryana	19,958	78,781
Himachal Pradesh	21,272	50,365
Jammu & Kashmir	15,833	30,582
Jharkhand	12,542	30,719
Karnataka	16,530	50,676
Kerala	21,664	59,179
Madhya Pradesh	13,454	27,250
Maharashtra	20,090	74,027
Orissa	12,854	33,226
Punjab	19,330	62,153
Rajasthan	14,538	34,189
Sikkim	17,653	48,937
Tamil Nadu	16,969	62,499
Tripura	15,595	35,799
Uttar Pradesh	12,778	23,132
Uttarakhand	17,458	55,877
West Bengal	15,424	41,469

Sources: PCEXP (in rupees) for year 2009–10 from NSSO (2011) and PCNSDP (in rupees) for 2009–10 from RBI (2011).

Having specified the relation between Y and X as above, our next task is to estimate the unknown parameters α and β of the model. There are various methods of estimation such as ordinary least squares (OLS) method, maximum likelihood method, moment method, etc. However, we focus on the OLS method as it is the most popular method to estimate a linear model.

The OLS method presupposes fulfilment of the following set of assumptions (which are also referred to as the Gauss-Markov assumptions).

(i)   Zero mean of disturbances (ε_i): Using notations, $E(\varepsilon_i) = 0$ for all i.

(ii) Homoskedasticity or constant variance of ε_i: $Var(\varepsilon_i) = E(\varepsilon_i^2) = \sigma^2 = $ constant for all i.

(iii) Serial independence of ε_i: $Cov(\varepsilon_i, \varepsilon_j) = E(\varepsilon_i \varepsilon_j) = 0$ for all $i \neq j$.

(iv) Non-stochasticity of X_i: This means the series for X_i is fixed in repeated samples.

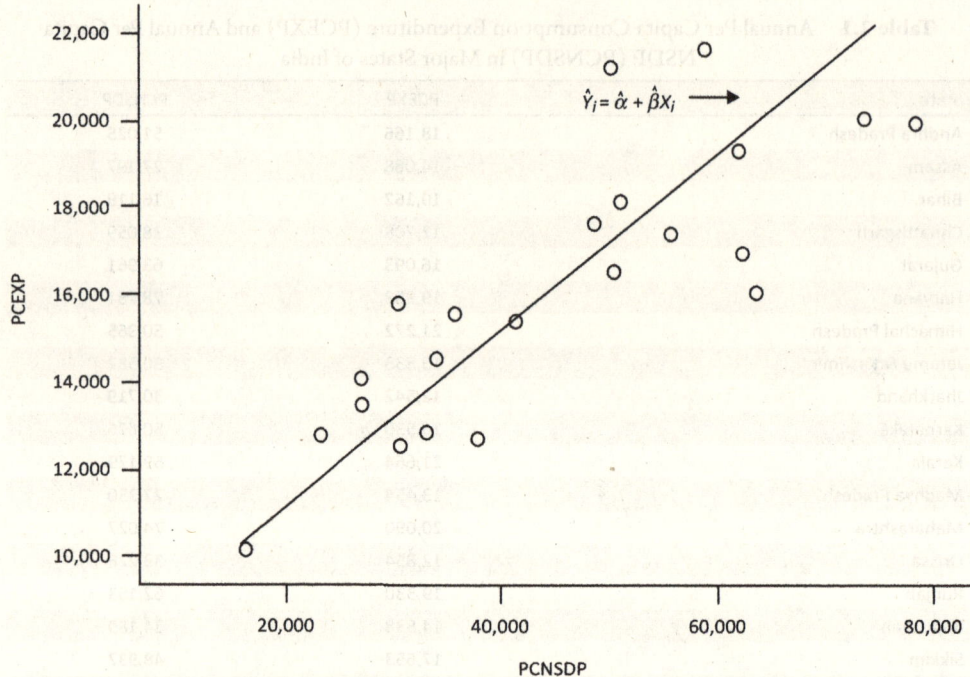

Figure 2.1   Scatter Plot of Data on PCEXP and PCNSDP in Indian States

Source: Author's own.

(v)   Exogeneity: This means that the disturbance term ε_i and the explanatory variable X_i are independently distributed, i.e., they are not correlated with each other.

(vi)   Linearity: The model must be linear in parameters because the OLS is a linear estimation technique.

(vii) The number of observations (n) is greater than number of parameters in the model, i.e., $n > 2$.

(viii) Normality: Apart from above assumptions, we make the normality assumption for the disturbance term, ε_i, which is actually required to conduct tests of hypotheses after OLS estimation of the model.

2.3 OLS ESTIMATION

Before discussing the OLS method for estimating the above model (2.2), let us note the difference between the terms 'estimator' and 'estimate'. An 'estimator' is a formula or method to estimate some unknown parameter of the model. The 'estimate' is the numerical value obtained after applying such a formula to a given data set.

The model such as (2.2) is called the population regression model as it refers to the relationship between consumption and income with reference to the population data. Here α and β are called 'true' population parameters. Our objective is to obtain numerical values (which are called estimates) for these unknown parameters by using sample data on Y_i and X_i. Suppose the numerical estimates of α and β are $\hat{\alpha}$ and $\hat{\beta}$, respectively. Using these estimates, we can write our estimated regression line as

$$\hat{Y}_i = \hat{\alpha} + \hat{\beta} X_i \qquad (2.3)$$

Here the series $\hat{Y}_i$ gives the estimated or predicted values of Y_i for different values of X_i, given the values of $\hat{\alpha}$ and $\hat{\beta}$. So given the data on Y_i and X_i, our objective is to compute the values of $\hat{\alpha}$ and $\hat{\beta}$. Once this is done, we say that estimation is complete and the estimated line has been determined. Figure 2.1 shows one such estimated line.

Now the question is to what extent our estimated line is appropriate to describe the relation between consumption and income that emerges from our sample data set? This is an important question because whichever line is considered, some data points will lie above the line and some below the line. In other words, we have some residuals (e_i) from the line, which are defined as

$$e_i = Y_i - \hat{Y}_i = Y_i - \hat{\alpha} - \hat{\beta} X_i \qquad (2.4)$$

Here, $i = 1, 2, ..., n$ so that we have n sample residuals. In this situation, we may think of choosing the estimated line (i.e., choosing the values of $\hat{\alpha}$ and $\hat{\beta}$) in such a way that the residuals are small. One possible criterion here is to select $\hat{\alpha}$ and $\hat{\beta}$ to make $\sum e_i = 0$. This implies:

$$\sum(Y_i - \hat{\alpha} - \hat{\beta} X_i) = 0 \qquad (2.5)$$

which, on dividing through n, gives

$$\bar{Y} = \hat{\alpha} + \hat{\beta}\bar{X} \qquad (2.6)$$

Equation (2.6) implies that $\hat{\alpha}$ and $\hat{\beta}$ should be chosen in such a way that the estimated line passes through $(\bar{X}, \bar{Y})$. However, the problem of choosing an appropriate estimated line is not solved yet. This is because we could pass a line with any slope whatsoever through $(\bar{X}, \bar{Y})$ which would satisfy the condition that the algebraic sum of the residuals is zero (i.e., $\sum e_i = 0$). Therefore, this criterion is inadequate to determine a specific estimated line.

In this situation, we apply the *least-squares criterion* which requires that the values of $\hat{\alpha}$ and $\hat{\beta}$ are chosen in such a way that $\sum e_i^2$ is minimized.[6]

---

[6] There is a controversy as to who first developed the method of least squares to fit a line. One view is that in the late 1700s and early 1800s Carl Friedrich Gauss in Germany, Adrien-Marie Legendre in France, and Robert Adrain in the United States independently developed the method of least squares. However, Stigler (1986) opined that Gauss probably possessed the method well before others, but he failed to communicate it to his contemporaries.

Using (2.4), we can write:

$$\sum e_i^2 = \sum (Y_i - \hat{\alpha} - \hat{\beta} X_i)^2 \qquad (2.7)$$

The necessary conditions of minimization of $\sum e_i^2$ are

$$\frac{\partial \sum e_i^2}{\partial \hat{\alpha}} = 0 \text{ and } \frac{\partial \sum e_i^2}{\partial \hat{\beta}} = 0$$

Applying these conditions, we obtain

$$\sum Y_i = n\hat{\alpha} + \hat{\beta} \sum X_i \qquad (2.8a)$$

$$\sum X_i Y_i = \hat{\alpha} \sum X_i + \hat{\beta} \sum X_i^2 \qquad (2.8b)$$

These are termed as the OLS 'normal equations'.

It follows that given data on Y_i and X_i to estimate the line implied by equations 2.8a and 2.8b, which is called the estimated regression line, we have to compute five quantities from the sample data, which are

$$n, \sum X_i, \sum Y_i, \sum X_i Y_i, \text{ and } \sum X_i^2$$

Substitution of these into equations (2.8a) and (2.8b) gives two simultaneous equations which can be solved for the two unknowns, $\hat{\alpha}$ and $\hat{\beta}$. Using the values of $\hat{\alpha}$ and $\hat{\beta}$ in (2.3) we obtain the estimated regression line as

$$\hat{Y}_i = \hat{\alpha} + \hat{\beta} X_i$$

2.4 PROPERTIES OF OLS REGRESSION LINE

Some important properties associated with the OLS regression line are as follows:

(i)   As previously mentioned, the *OLS regression line passes through the point of means* $(\overline{X}, \overline{Y})$. This follows directly from the first normal equation (2.8a), which, on dividing by n, gives

$$\overline{Y} = \hat{\alpha} + \hat{\beta}\overline{X}$$

(ii)   *The residuals e_i have zero covariance with the sample X_i values, and also with $\hat{Y}_i$, which represents the estimated or predicted values of Y_i. These can be proved as follows.*

By definition,

$$Cov(X_i, e_i) = \frac{1}{n} \sum (X_i - \overline{X})(e_i - \overline{e})$$

$$= \frac{1}{n} \sum (X_i - \overline{X}) e_i \quad (\because \overline{e} = 0)$$

$$= \frac{1}{n} \sum X_i e_i - \frac{1}{n} \overline{X} \sum e_i$$

$$= \frac{1}{n} \sum X_i e_i \quad (\because \sum e_i = 0)$$

The condition $\dfrac{\partial \sum e_i^2}{\partial \hat{\beta}} = 0$ implies

$$\frac{\partial}{\partial \hat{\beta}} \sum (Y_i - \hat{\alpha} - \hat{\beta} X_i)^2 = 0$$

$$\Rightarrow -2 \sum X_i (Y_i - \hat{\alpha} - \hat{\beta} X_i) = 0$$

$$\Rightarrow -2 \sum X_i e_i = 0 \quad [\because Y_i - \hat{\alpha} - \hat{\beta} X_i = Y_i - (\hat{\alpha} + \hat{\beta} X_i) = Y_i - \hat{Y}_i = e_i]$$

$$\Rightarrow \sum X_i e_i = 0$$

Thus,

$$Cov(X_i, e_i) = \frac{1}{n} \sum X_i e_i = 0$$

Again, $\hat{Y}_i = \hat{\alpha} + \hat{\beta} X_i$ implies that $\hat{Y}_i$ is a linear function of X_i so that

$$Cov(\hat{Y}_i, e_i) = 0$$

(iii) The estimated coefficients $\hat{\alpha}$ and $\hat{\beta}$ may also be computed sequentially using the following formulae.

$$\hat{\beta} = \frac{\sum x_i y_i}{\sum x_i^2} \tag{2.9a}$$

$$\hat{\alpha} = \overline{Y} - \hat{\beta} \overline{X} \tag{2.9b}$$

where

$$x_i = X_i - \overline{X}$$

and

$$y_i = Y_i - \overline{Y}$$

Note that (2.9b) is a mere rearrangement of equation (2.8a). Equation (2.9a) follows from substitution of equation (2.9b) into (2.8b). This is shown below.

$$\sum X_i Y_i = (\overline{Y} - \hat{\beta}\overline{X})\sum X_i + \hat{\beta}\sum X_i^2$$

$$\Rightarrow \sum X_i Y_i = \overline{Y}\sum X_i - \hat{\beta}\overline{X}\sum X_i + \hat{\beta}\sum X_i^2$$

$$\Rightarrow \hat{\beta}\left[\sum X_i^2 - \overline{X}\sum X_i\right] = \sum X_i Y_i - \overline{Y}\sum X_i$$

$$\Rightarrow \hat{\beta}\left[\sum X_i^2 - \frac{1}{n}(\sum X_i)^2\right] = \sum X_i Y_i - \frac{1}{n}\sum X_i \sum Y_i$$

$$\Rightarrow \hat{\beta}\sum x_i^2 = \sum x_i y_i$$

$$\Rightarrow \hat{\beta} = \frac{\sum x_i y_i}{\sum x_i^2}$$

Alternatively, using the definitions of $Cov(X_i, Y_i)$ and $Var(X_i)$, we can write

$$\hat{\beta} = \frac{\sum x_i y_i / n}{\sum x_i^2 / n} = \frac{\left[\sum(X_i - \overline{X})(Y_i - \overline{Y})\right]/n}{\sum(X_i - \overline{X})^2 / n} = \frac{Cov(X_i, Y_i)}{Var(X_i)} \qquad (2.10)$$

(iv)   *The total variation in Y_i may be expressed as sum of two components—the variation 'explained' by the estimated regression line and the variation not explained or 'unexplained' by the estimated regression line.*

To illustrate this properly, consider Figure 2.2, where we have drawn the estimated regression line $\hat{Y}_i = \hat{\alpha} + \hat{\beta}X_i$. Since the least squares regression line passes through the point of means, we take $(\overline{X}, \overline{Y})$ as the new origin. Now consider point P with co-ordinates (X_i, Y_i).

The first co-ordinate can also be expressed as x_i, while the second co-ordinate can be represented as y_i. Now, as shown in the figure, y_i can be split into two components so that

$$y_i = \hat{y}_i + e_i \qquad (2.11)$$

where

$$\hat{y}_i = \hat{Y}_i - \overline{Y}.$$

Now squaring and summing over all observations,

$$\sum y_i^2 = \sum(\hat{y}_i + e_i)^2$$
$$= \sum \hat{y}_i^2 + \sum e_i^2 + 2\sum \hat{y}_i e_i$$
$$= \sum \hat{y}_i^2 + \sum e_i^2 \qquad [\because Cov(\hat{y}_i, e_i) = 0]$$

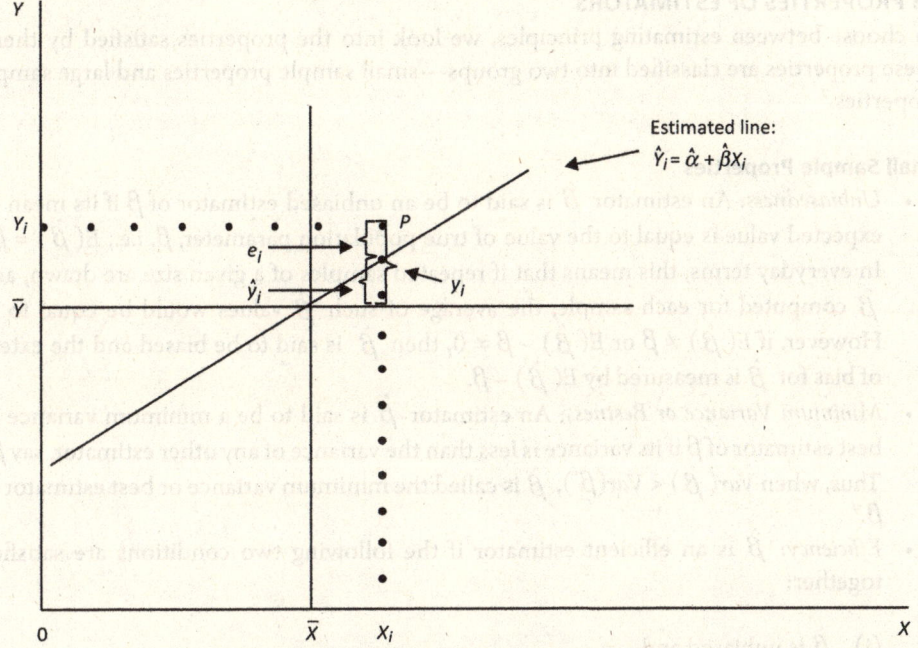

Figure 2.2   Decomposition of Total Sum Squares

Source: Author's own.

We call $\sum y_i^2$ as total sum squares (TSS), $\sum \hat{y}_i^2$ as explained sum squares (ESS), and $\sum e_i^2$ as residual sum squares (RSS). Thus,

$$TSS = ESS + RSS$$

From this result, we may also derive an alternative expression to compute ESS.

$$ESS = TSS - RSS$$
$$= \sum y_i^2 - \sum e_i^2$$
$$= \sum \hat{y}_i^2$$
$$= \sum (\hat{\beta} x_i)^2$$
$$= \hat{\beta}^2 \sum x_i^2$$
$$= \left(\frac{\sum x_i y_i}{\sum x_i^2} \right)^2 \sum x_i^2$$
$$= \hat{\beta} \sum x_i y_i$$

2.5 PROPERTIES OF ESTIMATORS

To choose between estimating principles, we look into the properties satisfied by them. These properties are classified into two groups—small sample properties and large sample properties.[7]

Small Sample Properties

- *Unbiasedness*: An estimator $\hat{\beta}$ is said to be an unbiased estimator of β if its mean or expected value is equal to the value of true population parameter, β, i.e., $E(\hat{\beta}) = \beta$.[8] In everyday terms, this means that if repeated samples of a given size are drawn, and $\hat{\beta}$ computed for each sample, the average of such $\hat{\beta}$ values would be equal to β. However, if $E(\hat{\beta}) \neq \beta$ or $E(\hat{\beta}) - \beta \neq 0$, then $\hat{\beta}$ is said to be biased and the extent of bias for $\hat{\beta}$ is measured by $E(\hat{\beta}) - \beta$.

- *Minimum Variance or Bestness*: An estimator $\hat{\beta}$ is said to be a minimum variance or best estimator of β if its variance is less than the variance of any other estimator, say β^*. Thus, when $Var(\hat{\beta}) < Var(\beta^*)$, $\hat{\beta}$ is called the minimum variance or best estimator of β.[9]

- *Efficiency*: $\hat{\beta}$ is an efficient estimator if the following two conditions are satisfied together:

  (i) $\hat{\beta}$ is unbiased and
  (ii) $Var(\hat{\beta}) \leq Var(\beta^*)$

An efficient estimator is also called as a minimum variance unbiased estimator (MVUE) or best-unbiased estimator.

- *Linearity*: An estimator is said to have the property of linearity if it is possible to express it as a linear combination of sample observations.[10]

- *Mean-Squared Error* (MSE): Sometimes a difficult choice problem arises while comparing two estimators. Suppose we have two different estimators of which one has lower bias, but higher variance, compared with the other. In other words, when

$$(bias\,\hat{\beta}) > (bias\,\beta^*)$$

---

[7] There is no hard and fast rule to distinguish between small and large samples. However, a working definition is that a small sample has 30 or less observations while the large sample has more than 30 observations.

[8] The unbiasedness property reflects on the *accuracy* of the estimator. Thus, when an estimator is unbiased, we say that it is able to provide an accurate estimate of its true population parameter.

[9] Minimum variance is associated with *reliability* dimension of the estimator. Obviously, the estimator that has lower variance is more reliable than the estimator which has higher variance.

[10] Put differently, linearity is associated with linear (i.e., additive) calculation rather than multiplicative or non-linear calculation.

but

$$Var(\hat{\beta}) < Var(\beta^*)$$

then how to choose between the two estimators? In this situation, where one estimator has a larger bias but a smaller variance than the other estimator, it is intuitively plausible to consider a trade-off between the two characteristics. This notion is given a precise, formal, expression in the mean-squared error.

The mean-squared error for $\hat{\beta}$ is defined as

$$
\begin{aligned}
MSE(\hat{\beta}) &= E[\hat{\beta} - \beta]^2 \\
&= E[\{\hat{\beta} - E(\hat{\beta})\} + \{E(\hat{\beta}) - \beta\}]^2 \\
&= E\{\hat{\beta} - E(\hat{\beta})\}^2 + E\{E(\hat{\beta}) - \beta\}^2 + 2E[\{\hat{\beta} - E(\hat{\beta})\}\{E(\hat{\beta}) - \beta\}] \\
&= Var(\hat{\beta}) + (bias\,\hat{\beta})^2
\end{aligned}
$$

This is so because the cross-product term vanishes, as shown below.

$$
\begin{aligned}
E[\{\hat{\beta} - E(\hat{\beta})\}\{E(\hat{\beta}) - \beta\}] &= E\{\hat{\beta}E(\hat{\beta}) - \hat{\beta}\beta - E(\hat{\beta})E(\hat{\beta}) + E(\hat{\beta})\beta\} \\
&= E(\hat{\beta})E(\hat{\beta}) - E(\hat{\beta})\beta - E(\hat{\beta})E(\hat{\beta}) + E(\hat{\beta})\beta \\
&= 0
\end{aligned}
$$

Now, according to the mean-squared error property, if $MSE(\hat{\beta}) < MSE(\beta^*)$, we say that $\hat{\beta}$ has lower mean-squared error, and accept it as an estimator of β.

Large Sample or Asymptotic Properties

These properties relate to the distribution of an estimator when the sample size is large, and approaches to infinity. The important properties here are the following.

- *Asymptotic Unbiasedness*: $\hat{\beta}$ is an asymptotically unbiased estimator of β if

$$\lim_{n \to \infty} E(\hat{\beta}) = \beta$$

This means that the estimator $\hat{\beta}$, which is otherwise biased, becomes unbiased as the sample size approaches infinity. It is to be noted that if an estimator is unbiased, it is also asymptotically unbiased, but the reverse is not necessarily true.

- *Consistency*: Whether or not an estimator is consistent is understood by looking at the behaviour of its bias and variance as the sample size approaches infinity. If the increase in sample size reduces bias (if there were one) and variance of the estimator, and this continues until both bias and variance become zero, as $n \to \infty$, then the estimator is said to be consistent. Thus, $\hat{\beta}$ is a consistent estimator if

$$\lim_{n \to \infty} [E(\hat{\beta}) - \beta] = 0$$

and

$$\lim_{n \to \infty} Var(\hat{\beta}) = 0$$

2.6 PROPERTIES OF OLS ESTIMATORS

The ordinary least-squares estimators are best, linear, and unbiased. In brief, we say that they are BLUE.[11] The BLUE properties for the least-squares estimators are proved below.

Recall the two-variable linear model

$$Y_i = \alpha + \beta X_i + \varepsilon_i$$

where ε_i satisfies the OLS assumptions:

$$\left. \begin{array}{l} E(\varepsilon_i) = 0 \\ E(\varepsilon_i^2) = \sigma_\varepsilon^2 \\ E(\varepsilon_i \varepsilon_j) = 0 \quad \text{for } i \neq j \end{array} \right\} \text{ for all } i$$

We know that

$$\hat{\beta} = \frac{\sum x_i y_i}{\sum x_i^2}$$

and

$$\hat{\alpha} = \overline{Y} - \hat{\beta} \overline{X}$$

where

$$x_i = X_i - \overline{X}$$

and

$$y_i = Y_i - \overline{Y}$$

[11] BLUE—best, linear and unbiased estimator. The BLUE property of the OLS estimators is also known as the Gauss-Markov theorem.

Unbiasedness of $\hat{\beta}$

$$\hat{\beta} = \frac{\sum x_i y_i}{\sum x_i^2}$$

$$= \frac{\sum x_i (Y_i - \bar{Y})}{\sum x_i^2}$$

$$= \frac{\sum x_i Y_i - \bar{Y} \sum x_i}{\sum x_i^2}$$

$$= \frac{\sum x_i Y_i}{\sum x_i^2} \qquad [\because \sum x_i = \sum(X_i - \bar{X}) = 0]$$

$$= \sum w_i Y_i \tag{2.12}$$

where

$$w_i = \frac{x_i}{\sum x_i^2} \tag{2.13}$$

It follows from (2.13) that

$$\sum w_i = \frac{\sum x_i}{\sum x_i^2} = 0 \tag{2.14}$$

$$\sum w_i X_i = \frac{\sum x_i X_i}{\sum x_i^2}$$

$$= \frac{\sum (X_i - \bar{X}) X_i}{\sum (X_i - \bar{X})^2}$$

$$= \frac{\sum X_i^2 - \bar{X} \sum X_i}{\sum X_i^2 - 2\bar{X} \sum X_i + n\bar{X}^2}$$

$$= \frac{\sum X_i^2 - n\bar{X}^2}{\sum X_i^2 - 2n\bar{X}^2 + n\bar{X}^2}$$

$$= \frac{\sum X_i^2 - n\bar{X}^2}{\sum X_i^2 - n\bar{X}^2}$$

$$= 1 \tag{2.15a}$$

$$\sum w_i^2 = \frac{\sum x_i^2}{(\sum x_i^2)^2} = \frac{1}{\sum x_i^2} \tag{2.15b}$$

From (2.12), we have

$$\hat{\beta} = \sum w_i Y_i$$
$$= \sum w_i (\alpha + \beta X_i + \varepsilon_i)$$
$$= \alpha \sum w_i + \beta \sum w_i X_i + \sum w_i \varepsilon_i$$
$$= \beta + \sum w_i \varepsilon_i \qquad (\because \sum w_i = 0 \text{ and } \sum w_i X_i = 1) \qquad (2.16)$$

Taking expectations,

$$E(\hat{\beta}) = E(\beta + \sum w_i \varepsilon_i)$$
$$= \beta + \sum w_i E(\varepsilon_i)$$
$$= \beta \qquad [\because E(\varepsilon_i) = 0]$$

This proves that $\hat{\beta}$ is unbiased.

Linearity of $\hat{\beta}$
From (2.12),

$$\hat{\beta} = \sum w_i Y_i$$

Since w_i's are a set of fixed values, we may write

$$\hat{\beta} = w_1 Y_1 + w_2 Y_2 + \dots + w_n Y_n$$

This shows that $\hat{\beta}$ is a linear combination of sample values of Y_i, the dependent variable. Thus, $\hat{\beta}$ has the property of linearity.

Minimum Variance or Bestness for $\hat{\beta}$
In order to prove minimum variance or bestness property for $\hat{\beta}$, we shall compute the variance of $\hat{\beta}$ and show that it is lower than the variance of some other estimator.

From (2.16), we have

$$\hat{\beta} = \beta + \sum w_i \varepsilon_i$$
$$\Rightarrow \hat{\beta} - \beta = \sum w_i \varepsilon_i$$
$$\Rightarrow \hat{\beta} - E(\hat{\beta}) = \sum w_i \varepsilon_i \qquad [\because E(\hat{\beta}) = \beta]$$

Thus,

$$Var(\hat{\beta}) = E[\hat{\beta} - E(\hat{\beta})]^2$$
$$= E\left(\sum w_i \varepsilon_i\right)^2$$

$$= E\left(\sum w_i^2 \varepsilon_i^2 + 2\sum_{i<j} w_i w_j \varepsilon_i \varepsilon_j \right)$$

$$= \sum w_i^2 E(\varepsilon_i^2) + 2\sum_{i<j} w_i w_j E(\varepsilon_i \varepsilon_j)$$

$$= \sigma^2 \sum w_i^2 \qquad [\because E(\varepsilon_i^2)=\sigma^2 \text{ and } E(\varepsilon_i \varepsilon_j)=0 \text{ for } i \neq j]$$

$$= \frac{\sigma^2}{\sum x_i^2} \qquad \left(\because \sum w_i^2 = \frac{1}{\sum x_i^2} \right) \tag{2.17}$$

Let us now consider some other estimator, say β^*, such that

$$\beta^* = \sum c_i Y_i$$

where c_i $(i = 1, 2, \dots, n)$ represents a set of weights
Then,

$$\beta^* = \sum c_i (\alpha + \beta X_i + \varepsilon_i)$$
$$= \alpha \sum c_i + \beta \sum c_i X_i + \sum c_i \varepsilon_i \tag{2.18}$$

Taking expectations,

$$E(\beta^*) = \alpha \sum c_i + \beta \sum c_i X_i \quad [\because E(\varepsilon_i)=0]$$

It is clear that we require the weights to be such that β^* is an unbiased estimator. This imposes the conditions

$$\sum c_i = 0 \text{ and } \sum c_i X_i = 1 \Rightarrow \sum c_i x_i = 1 \tag{2.19}$$

Let us now compute $Var(\beta^*)$ accepting these conditions. Under these conditions, equation (2.18) reduces to

$$\beta^* = \beta + \sum c_i \varepsilon_i \Rightarrow (\beta^* - \beta) = (\beta^* - E(\beta^*)) = \sum c_i \varepsilon_i$$

Thus,

$$Var(\beta^*) = E[\beta^* - E(\beta^*)]^2$$
$$= E\left(\sum c_i \varepsilon_i \right)^2$$
$$= E\left(\sum c_i^2 \varepsilon_i^2 + 2\sum_{i<j} c_i c_j \varepsilon_i \varepsilon_j \right)$$
$$= \sum c_i^2 E(\varepsilon_i^2) + 2\sum_{i<j} c_i c_j E(\varepsilon_i \varepsilon_j)$$
$$= \sigma^2 \sum c_i^2 \qquad [\because E(\varepsilon_i^2)=\sigma^2 \text{ and } E(\varepsilon_i \varepsilon_j)=0 \text{ for } i \neq j] \tag{2.20}$$

To compare $Var(\hat{\beta})$ with $Var(\beta^*)$, consider the expression

$$c_i = w_i + (c_i - w_i)$$
$$\Rightarrow \sum c_i^2 = \sum w_i^2 + \sum (c_i - w_i)^2 + 2\sum w_i (c_i - w_i) \qquad (2.21)$$

Note that

$$\sum w_i (c_i - w_i)$$
$$= \sum w_i c_i - \sum w_i^2$$
$$= \frac{\sum c_i x_i}{\sum x_i^2} - \frac{1}{\sum x_i^2} \qquad \left(\because w_i = \frac{x_i}{\sum x_i^2} \right)$$
$$= \frac{1}{\sum x_i^2} - \frac{1}{\sum x_i^2} \qquad \left[\because \sum c_i x_i = 1, \text{as shown in (2.19) above} \right]$$
$$= 0$$

Thus,

$$Var(\beta^*) = \sigma^2 \left[\sum w_i^2 + \sum (c_i - w_i)^2 \right]$$
$$= \frac{\sigma^2}{\sum x_i^2} + \sigma^2 \sum (c_i - w_i)^2 \qquad \left(\because \sum w_i^2 = \frac{1}{\sum x_i^2} \right)$$
$$= Var(\hat{\beta}) + \sigma^2 \sum (c_i - w_i)^2$$

Since $\Sigma(c_i - w_i)^2 > 0$ unless $c_i = w_i$ for all i, $Var(\hat{\beta}) < Var(\beta^*)$, and we conclude that $\hat{\beta}$ is a minimum variance or best estimator.

2.7 STATISTICAL INFERENCE IN SLRM

After estimating the population parameters (α and β) of our regression model, our next task is to examine statistical significance of the estimated coefficients ($\hat{\alpha}$ and $\hat{\beta}$) by applying our knowledge of statistical inference.[12] Examination of statistical significance of the estimated coefficients specifically requires the knowledge about their sampling distributions. In this regard, it may be noted that

$$\hat{\alpha} \sim N \left[\alpha, \left(\frac{1}{n} + \frac{\overline{X}^2}{\sum x_i^2} \right) \right] \qquad (2.22)$$

[12] In layman's language, testing statistical significance of an estimated coefficient (say $\hat{\beta}$) enables us to understand the usefulness of X_i as a predictor of Y_i.

$$\hat{\beta} \sim N\left[\beta, \frac{\sigma^2}{\sum x_i^2}\right]\qquad(2.23)$$

Expression (2.22) states that $\hat{\alpha}$ has a normal distribution with mean equal to α and

variance $\frac{1}{n} + \frac{\overline{X}^2}{\sum x_i^2}$. Similarly, (2.23) states that $\hat{\beta}$ also follows a normal distribution with

mean equal to β and variance $\sigma^2 / \sum x_i^2$. However, these results are useful when the variance of the disturbance term (σ^2) is known. Unfortunately, in practice, σ^2 is not known and has to be estimated as

$$\hat{\sigma}^2 = \frac{RSS}{n-2} = \frac{\sum e_i^2}{n-2}\qquad(2.24)$$

where $\hat{\sigma}^2$ is the estimate of σ^2.[13]

Hypothesis Testing

We formalize the object of testing statistical significance of $\hat{\beta}$ (also $\hat{\alpha}$) by stating that we want to test the validity of the null hypothesis (H_N)[14] that the value of true population parameter β is zero against the alternative hypothesis (H_A)[15] that it is different from zero. In the present context, we set our hypotheses as

$H_N: \beta = 0$
$H_A: \beta \neq 0$ (under two-tailed test)

However, if we have any prior knowledge about the sign of β (say positive), then the hypotheses are set as

$H_N: \beta = 0$
$H_A: \beta > 0$ (one-tailed test)

---

[13] Note that $\sqrt{\hat{\sigma}^2} = \hat{\sigma}$ is called the *standard error of regression*. It provides an estimate of standard deviation of the regression error (or disturbance term) ε_i.

[14] In simple language, null hypothesis is what we are going to test.

[15] The alternative hypothesis represents our conclusion if the experimental test indicates that the null hypothesis is false.

Having set the hypotheses to be tested, our next task is to compute one t-value, which is denoted by t^*. The formula used for computation of t^* is:[16]

$$t^* = \frac{\hat{\beta} - \beta}{SE(\hat{\beta})}$$

$$= \frac{\hat{\beta}}{SE(\hat{\beta})} \quad (\text{under } H_N : \beta = 0) \qquad (2.25)$$

where $SE(\hat{\beta})$ is the standard error of $\hat{\beta}$.[17]

Having computed the value of t^* in the manner stated above, we compare it with critical (or theoretical) t-value obtained from the t-table for level of significance[18] $\lambda/2$ (under

---

[16] The reason behind calculation to t^* in this manner lies in the following: As $\hat{\beta}$ is normally distributed, $(\hat{\beta} - \beta)/\sqrt{Var(\hat{\beta})} \sim N(0, 1)$, which means that $(\hat{\beta} - \beta)/\sqrt{Var(\hat{\beta})}$ has a standard normal distribution. Again, it has been be shown that RSS/σ^2 follows a χ^2 distribution with degrees of freedom $k = n - 2$, where n = number of observations. Now there is a theorem which states if we have two variables (X_1 and X_2) which are independent but $X_1 \sim N(0, 1)$ and $X_2 \sim \chi^2$ with degrees of freedom k, then $X_1 / \sqrt{X_2/k} = standardised\ normal / \sqrt{independent\ averaged\ \chi^2}$ follows a t-distribution with degrees of freedom k. Using this theorem, we write

$$t^* = \frac{\hat{\beta} - \beta}{\sqrt{Var(\hat{\beta})}} \bigg/ \sqrt{\frac{RSS}{\sigma^2(n-2)}} \quad \text{with degrees of freedom } k = n - 2$$

Thus,

$$t^* = \frac{\hat{\beta} - \beta}{\sqrt{\sigma^2 / \Sigma x_i^2}} \bigg/ \sqrt{\frac{\hat{\sigma}^2(n-2)}{\sigma^2(n-2)}} \quad [\because Var(\hat{\beta}) = \sigma^2 / \Sigma x_i^2 \text{ and } RSS = \hat{\sigma}^2(n-2)]$$

$$= \frac{\hat{\beta} - \beta}{\sqrt{\hat{\sigma}^2 / \Sigma x_i^2}}$$

$$= \frac{\hat{\beta} - \beta}{SE(\hat{\beta})}$$

Similarly, we can say that $\dfrac{\hat{\alpha} - \alpha}{SE(\hat{\alpha})}$ also has a t-distribution with degrees of freedom $n - 2$.

---

[17] The standard error of an estimator is nothing but the standard deviation of the sampling distribution of the estimator and the sampling distribution of the estimator is a probability or frequency distribution of the set of values of the estimator obtained from all possible samples of the same size from a given population.

[18] Level of significance is the probability of rejecting the null hypothesis (H_N) when it is actually true, i.e., it is the probability of committing a Type I error.

two-tailed test) and degrees of freedom[19] $n-2$. The following *decision rules* are followed here.

- If $\left|t^*\right| > t_{\lambda/2}(n-2)$, i.e., absolute value of computed-t is greater than the value of critical-t at level of significance $\lambda/2$ and degrees of freedom $n-2$, then reject the H_N and conclude that $\hat{\beta}$ is statistically significant at significance level $\lambda/2$ and the regression is meaningful.
- On the other hand, if $\left|t^*\right| \leq t_{\lambda/2}(n-2)$, then accept the H_N and conclude that $\hat{\beta}$ is statistically insignificant at significance level $\lambda/2$ and the regression is meaningless.

The same procedure and decision rules apply when we test statistical significance of $\hat{\alpha}$.

One-Tailed Test

The one-tailed test reduces the critical-t value for a given degrees of freedom, which increases the possibility of obtaining significant regression result. Application of the one-tailed test is justifiable when we are certain about the sign (positive/negative) of the slope parameter β. For instance, the Keynesian consumption theory suggests that the marginal propensity of consume (represented by β) is positive so that our hypotheses, while estimating consumption–income relationship, may be written as

$$H_N: \beta = 0$$
$$H_A: \beta > 0$$

In this situation, we apply the one-tailed test procedure in order to examine statistical significance of $\hat{\beta}$. The *decision rules* here are

- If $\left|t^*\right| > t_{\lambda}(n-2)$, i.e., absolute value of computed-t is greater than the value of critical-t at level of significance λ and degrees of freedom $n-2$, then reject the H_N and conclude that $\hat{\beta}$ is statistically significant at the level of significance λ.
- On the other hand, if $\left|t^*\right| \leq t_{\lambda}(n-2)$, then do not reject the H_N and conclude that $\hat{\beta}$ is statistically insignificant at the level of significance λ.

Likewise, when we are certain that $\beta < 0$ (e.g., in investment-rate of interest model), we may continue with the one-sided test. In this situation, the hypotheses are

$$H_N: \beta = 0$$
$$H_A: \beta < 0$$

and the *decision rules* are the same as mentioned above.

---

[19] The term degrees of freedom means the total number of observations in the sample (n) less the number of independent (linear) constraints put on them. In other words, it is the number of independent observations out of total n observations. In the context of the two-variable model, the degrees of freedom is $n-2$ (not n); for the k-variable model, it is $n-k$. The general rule is that degrees of freedom = n minus number of parameters estimated.

It needs mention that in practice researchers apply one-sided tests more frequently. This is primarily because, compared with two-tailed tests, the critical-t value for rejecting the H_N is lower for the one-sided test, so it is easier to refute the H_N and establish the relationship between the variables (dependent and explanatory) statistically significantly. However, the one-sided test should not be applied mechanically and should be justified beforehand on the basis of theory, previous experience, or common sense.

Confidence Intervals

There is an alternative way of drawing inferences about our null hypothesis (H_N: $\beta = 0$). This is by constructing a confidence interval (CI). The CIs give the numerical region in which we would have some degree of confidence that our H_N: $\beta = 0$ is true.[20] Thus, the CIs capture the region in which H_N: $\beta = 0$ would not be rejected. The formula for the CI for β is given by

$$\hat{\beta} \pm SE(\hat{\beta})t_{\lambda/2} \tag{2.26}$$

where $t_{\lambda/2}$ is the critical value of t with $\lambda/2$ level of significance and $n-2$ degrees of freedom.

The *decision rule* is that if β falls within the CI, we do not reject H_N. On the other hand, we reject the H_N when β falls outside the CI. Alternatively, we may say that when the CI includes the value of 0 (zero), we accept the H_N and conclude that $\hat{\beta}$ is statistically insignificant. However, if 0 doesn't fall within the CI, we reject the H_N and conclude that $\hat{\beta}$ is statistically significant.

The *p*-value Approach

The output from many econometric software packages (including EViews), apart from providing computed-t statistics for the estimated coefficients, also provide the p-values which can be used as an alternative approach in assessing the significance of the estimated coefficients (and hence validity of the H_N). The p-value is the smallest significance level at which the H_N could be rejected, based on the test statistic actually observed.[21] The p-value approach is more informative than the 'choice of significance levels and obtain critical values' approach because one can see exactly the level of significance of the estimated coefficient.[22] For example, if $p = 0.03$, it implies that the H_N would be rejected at 3% level of significance. Similarly, $p = 0.15$ implies that the H_N would be rejected at 15% level of significance. It is customary to reject the H_N and conclude that the estimated coefficient under consideration is statistically significant if the p-value is less or equal to 0.10.

---

[20] Thus, confidence intervals are *interval estimates* as they provide a range of likely values for the population parameter.

[21] The p-value also represents the probability of committing a Type-I error that occurs when we reject a true H_N.

[22] Regression output from almost all econometrics software packages display p-values alongside the estimated coefficients and their standard errors and computed-t values. It is to be noted that the p-value reported by EViews is computed for a two-tailed test. So when we are interested in a one-tailed test, we will have to look up the critical value ourselves.

2.8 MEASURING GOODNESS OF FIT

In the context of the simple regression model, we measure the goodness of fit of the estimated equation by using the *squared-r* (i.e., r^2) statistic, where r is the value of simple correlation coefficient between Y_i and X_i. r^2, being the ratio of *ESS* to *TSS*, shows the proportion of total variation in the dependent variable which is explained by the independent/explanatory variable of the model. Thus,

$$r^2 = \frac{ESS}{TSS} = 1 - \frac{RSS}{TSS} = 1 - \frac{\sum e_i^2}{\sum y_i^2}$$

This may be proved as follows.

$$r = \frac{Cov(X_i, Y_i)}{\sqrt{Var(X_i)}\sqrt{Var(Y_i)}}$$

$$= \frac{\sum x_i y_i}{n S_x S_y} \quad (S_x \text{ and } S_y \text{ are standard deviations of } X_i \text{ and } Y_i \text{ respectively})$$

$$= \frac{\sum x_i y_i}{\sqrt{\sum x_i^2}\sqrt{\sum y_i^2}}$$

Therefore,

$$r^2 = \frac{(\sum x_i y_i)^2}{\sum x_i^2 \sum y_i^2}$$

$$= \hat{\beta}\frac{\sum x_i y_i}{\sum y_i^2}$$

$$= \frac{ESS}{TSS} \qquad (\because \hat{\beta}\sum x_i y_i = ESS \text{ and } \sum y_i^2 = TSS \text{ as noted earlier})$$

$$= 1 - \frac{RSS}{TSS}$$

$$= 1 - \frac{\sum e_i^2}{\sum y_i^2} \qquad\qquad\qquad\qquad (2.27)$$

The value of r^2 always lies between 0 and 1. When the value of r^2 is 0, no part of variation in the dependent variable is explained by the variation in explanatory variable of the model. On the other hand, when the value of r^2 is 1, the entire part of variation in dependent variable is explained by the variation in explanatory variable. However, these are extreme cases. In reality, the value of r^2 is found somewhere between 0 and 1. When it is close to 1, we conclude that we have a good fit estimated line; if it is close to 0, we conclude that the estimated line does not provide a good fit.

2.9 ANALYSIS OF VARIANCE ON OLS REGRESSION

We can also set out the test of significance discussed above in an Analysis of Variance (ANOVA) framework. This is more useful in the context of multiple regressions. As before, our null hypothesis here is $H_N: \beta = 0$. Under this approach, we actually test the significance of the ESS as against RSS from regression. This is done in the manner described below.

We know that

$$TSS = ESS + RSS$$

$$TSS = \sum y_i^2$$

$$ESS = \hat{\beta}^2 \sum x_i^2 = \hat{\beta} \sum x_i y_i$$

$$RSS = \sum e_i^2$$

Then,

$\dfrac{RSS}{\sigma^2}$ follows a χ^2 distribution with degrees of freedom $n-2$; and

$\dfrac{ESS}{\sigma^2}$ also follows a χ^2 distribution with degrees of freedom 1.

Now assuming that the H_N is true and that these two χ^2s are independent, their ratio divided by respective degrees of freedom gives an F-statistic, which is

$$F = \frac{\dfrac{ESS}{\sigma^2} \Big/ 1}{\dfrac{RSS}{\sigma^2} \Big/ n-2}$$

$$= \frac{ESS/1}{RSS/(n-2)}$$

$$= \frac{\hat{\beta} \sum x_i y_i / 1}{\sum e_i^2 / (n-2)}$$

To compute the value of F using this formula, we need some information which are obtained from the following ANOVA table.

After computing the value of F, using the information contained in the ANOVA table, we set the *decision rules* as follows.

(i)   If $F^* > F_\lambda (1, n-2)$, then reject $H_N: \beta = 0$; and

(ii)   If $F^* \leq F_\lambda (1, n-2)$, then do not reject $H_N: \beta = 0$

Table 2.2   ANOVA Table: To Compute F

Source of Variation	Sum Squares	Degrees of Freedom	Mean Squares
X_i	$ESS = \hat{\beta}^2 \sum x_i^2 = \hat{\beta} \sum x_i y_i$	1	$ESS/1$
Residuals	$RSS = \sum e_i^2$	$n-2$	$RSS/(n-2)$
Total	$TSS = \sum y_i^2$	$n-1$	

Source: Author's own compilation.

2.10 SOME IMPORTANT RELATIONS IN THE CONTEXT OF SLRM

Relation between Regression Slope and Correlation Coefficient

There is a relation between the regression slope ($\hat{\beta}$) and correlation coefficient (r) between X_i and Y_i which is demonstrated as follows.

$$r = \frac{\sum x_i y_i}{\sqrt{\sum x_i^2}\,\sqrt{\sum y_i^2}} \qquad (x_i = X_i - \overline{X} \text{ and } y_i = Y_i - \overline{Y})$$

$$= \frac{\sum x_i y_i}{\sum x_i^2}\frac{\sqrt{\sum x_i^2}}{\sqrt{\sum y_i^2}}$$

$$= \frac{\sum x_i y_i}{\sum x_i^2}\frac{\sqrt{\sum x_i^2/n}}{\sqrt{\sum y_i^2/n}}$$

$$= \hat{\beta}\frac{S_x}{S_y} \qquad (S_x \text{ and } S_y \text{ are standard deviations of } X_i \text{ and } Y_i \text{ respectively})$$

Thus, the relation between the regression slope and correlation coefficient is given by

$$\hat{\beta} = r\frac{S_y}{S_x} \tag{2.28}$$

Relation between F-statistic and r^2
We know that

$$TSS = ESS + RSS$$

$$TSS = \sum y_i^2$$

$$ESS = \hat{\beta}\sum x_i y_i = r^2 \sum y_i^2 \qquad \left(\because r^2 = \hat{\beta}\frac{\sum x_i y_i}{\sum y_i^2} \right)$$

$$RSS = TSS - ESS = \sum y_i^2 - r^2 \sum y_i^2 = (1-r^2)\sum y_i^2$$

Thus,

$$
\begin{aligned}
F &= \frac{ESS/1}{RSS/(n-2)} \\
&= \frac{r^2 \sum y_i^2 / 1}{(1-r^2) \sum y_i^2 / (n-2)} \\
&= \frac{(n-2)r^2}{1-r^2}
\end{aligned}
\tag{2.29}
$$

The implication of this relation is that if we have computed the value of r^2, we may use it to compute the value of F and skip computations involved in the ANOVA table.

Relation between F and t^2

In the two-variable model,

$$
\begin{aligned}
F &= \frac{ESS/1}{RSS/(n-2)} \\
&= \frac{\sum(\hat{Y}_i - \bar{Y})^2}{\sum e_i^2 / (n-2)} \\
&= \frac{\sum\left[(\hat{\alpha}+\hat{\beta}X_i)-(\hat{\alpha}+\hat{\beta}\bar{X})\right]^2}{\hat{\sigma}^2} \qquad [\because \hat{\sigma}^2 = \sum e_i^2 / (n-2)] \\
&= \frac{\hat{\beta}^2 \sum(X_i - \bar{X})^2}{\hat{\sigma}^2} \\
&= \frac{\hat{\beta}^2}{\hat{\sigma}^2 / \sum x_i^2} \qquad (x_i = X_i - \bar{X}) \\
&= \frac{\hat{\beta}^2}{[SE(\hat{\beta})]^2} \\
&= t^2
\end{aligned}
\tag{2.30}
$$

This result implies that in the simple regression or two-variable model, the F-test and the two-tailed t-test on the slope coefficient both have the null and alternative hypotheses as: $H_N: \beta = 0$ and $H_A: \beta \neq 0$.[23] Thus, these tests lead to the same conclusion here. Hence there is no point in performing both the tests in simple regression analysis. However, it will be clear from our discussion in the next chapter that in the multiple regression analysis, the F and t tests have different roles to perform, and they test different null hypotheses.

---

[23] It is also to be noted that the critical value of F at any given level of significance here is equal to the square of the critical value of t. We refrain from proving this result as such details are beyond our scope.

Relation between r^2 and t-statistic

We can derive the relation between r^2 and t-statistic using (2.29) and (2.30).

$$t^2 = \frac{(n-2)r^2}{1-r^2}$$

$$\Rightarrow r^2 = \frac{t^2}{t^2 + (n-2)} \qquad (2.31)$$

2.11 REGRESSION WITHOUT INTERCEPT TERM

Sometimes the two-variable regression model may not have the intercept term. Such a model is called *no-intercept model* or *regression through the origin*. An example of no-intercept model is the one that examines relation between output and variable cost. Other examples of no-intercept model abound in economics. For the no-intercept model, the formula for obtaining the estimate for the slope coefficient would not have 'mean corrections'. The formulas for obtaining estimated variance of the disturbance term, variance of estimated slope and r^2 coefficient are also different. These are given below.

Suppose our no-intercept population regression model is

$$Y_i = \beta X_i + \varepsilon_i \qquad (2.32)$$

and the estimated model is

$$\hat{Y}_i = \hat{\beta} X_i \qquad (2.33)$$

This is obtained by minimizing $\sum e_i^2 = \sum (Y_i - \hat{\beta} X_i)^2$.

Application of the necessary condition of minimization here yields

$$\frac{d\sum e_i^2}{d\hat{\beta}} = 2\sum (Y_i - \hat{\beta} X_i)(-X_i) = 0$$

$$\Rightarrow \sum (Y_i - \hat{\beta} X_i)(X_i) = 0$$

$$\Rightarrow \hat{\beta} \sum X_i^2 = \sum X_i Y_i$$

$$\Rightarrow \hat{\beta} = \frac{\sum X_i Y_i}{\sum X_i^2} \qquad (2.34)$$

This is the formula used for computation of $\hat{\beta}$ in the context of no-intercept model. The variance of $\hat{\beta}$ for the no-intercept model is obtained as follows. From (2.34),

$$\hat{\beta} = \frac{\sum X_i Y_i}{\sum X_i^2}$$

$$= \frac{\sum X_i (\beta X_i + \varepsilon_i)}{\sum X_i^2}$$

$$= \beta + \frac{\sum X_i \varepsilon_i}{\sum X_i^2} \qquad (2.35)$$

Taking expectations,

$$E(\hat{\beta}) = \beta \Rightarrow \hat{\beta} \text{ is unbiased}$$

Therefore,

$$Var(\hat{\beta}) = E(\hat{\beta} - \beta)^2$$

$$= E\left(\frac{\sum X_i \varepsilon_i}{\sum X_i^2}\right)^2$$

$$= \frac{E(\varepsilon_i^2)}{\sum X_i^2}$$

$$= \frac{\sigma^2}{\sum X_i^2} \qquad (2.36)$$

Here σ^2 is unknown but can be estimated as

$$\hat{\sigma}^2 = \frac{RSS}{n-1}$$

Now, the standard error of $\hat{\beta}$ is

$$SE(\hat{\beta}) = \sqrt{\frac{\hat{\sigma}^2}{\sum X_i^2}}$$

Hypothesis Testing

The t-test procedure to test $H_N: \beta = 0$ against $H_A: \beta \neq 0$ holds in the context of no-intercept model, but the formula for computation of $SE(\hat{\beta})$ is different. Here computed-t (i.e., t^*) is calculated as

$$t^* = \frac{\hat{\beta}}{SE(\hat{\beta})} = \hat{\beta} \Bigg/ \sqrt{\frac{\hat{\sigma}^2}{\sum X_i^2}} \qquad (2.37)$$

The *decision rules* are same as in the intercept-present model.

Goodness of Fit

For the model without the intercept term, the sum of residuals (i.e., Σe_i) do not necessarily add up to zero like the model with intercept term. Further, the 'fundamental identity' (i.e., $TSS = ESS + RSS$) is no longer true in general for the no-intercept model. For this reason, the conventional r^2 formula used for the intercept-present model is not appropriate to understand the goodness of fit of the no-intercept model. Using the conventional r^2 formula for the no-intercept model may produce negative value of r^2 in some cases (when $RSS > TSS$) and we are unable to interpret properly the value of r^2. To rule out such a possibility, it is essential to use an appropriate r^2 formula for the no-intercept model, which is obtained by modifying the expression of the fundamental identity in the following manner.

For the intercept-present model,

$$TSS = ESS + RSS$$

i.e.,

$$\Sigma(Y_i - \overline{Y})^2 = \Sigma(\hat{Y}_i - \overline{Y})^2 + \Sigma(Y_i - \hat{Y}_i)^2$$

For the no-intercept model, we replace $\overline{Y}$ by zero (as the regression line here passes through the origin) so that the expression for the fundamental identity becomes

$$\Sigma Y_i^2 = \Sigma \hat{Y}_i^2 + \Sigma e_i^2$$

Therefore,

$$r^2 = \frac{\Sigma \hat{Y}_i^2}{\Sigma Y_i^2} = 1 - \frac{\Sigma e_i^2}{\Sigma Y_i^2} \tag{2.38}$$

This is the appropriate formula to compute the value of r^2 when intercept term is absent in the model.[24]

2.12 REVERSE REGRESSION

Until now, we considered the regression of Y_i on X_i. This is called *direct regression*. However, sometimes we may have to consider the regression of X_i on Y_i as well. This is called *reverse regression*. Let us write our reverse regression model as

$$X_i = \alpha^* + \beta^* Y_i + v_i$$

---

[24] The r^2-*statistic* for the no-intercept model is also called the *raw-r^2* as the sum-squares here are not mean-corrected. Although the *raw-r^2* satisfies the condition $0 < r^2 < 1$, it is not directly comparable to the conventional r^2 and the interpretations of the two r^2s (for intercept-present and intercept-absent models) are different. For this reason, some scholars do not report the value of r^2 while working with the no-intercept model.

where v_i is the disturbance term of the *reverse regression* model that satisfies assumptions similar to the *direct regression* model. Here the formulas for obtaining $\hat{\alpha}^*$ and $\hat{\beta}^*$ may be obtained by interchanging X_i and Y_i.

$$\hat{\beta}^* = \frac{\sum x_i y_i}{\sum y_i^2} \text{ and } \hat{\alpha}^* = \overline{X} - \hat{\beta}^* \overline{Y}.$$

where, as before, $x_i = X_i - \overline{X}$ and $y_i = Y_i - \overline{Y}$.

An Important Result

$$\hat{\beta}\hat{\beta}^* = \frac{(\sum x_i y_i)^2}{\sum x_i^2 \sum y_i^2} = \left(\frac{\sum x_i y_i}{\sqrt{\sum x_i^2} \sqrt{\sum y_i^2}} \right)^2 = r_{XY}^2 \qquad (2.39)$$

This implies that when the value of r_{XY}^2 is 1, the two regression lines coincide. The two lines become close to each other when r_{XY}^2 is close to 1.

2.13 OUTLIERS

Sometimes the data that we use to fit some relationship between the variables may contain one or more outliers. *An outlier is an extreme observation that does not follow the pattern of the other data points.* The presence of an outlier in the data may cause substantial change in the estimated regression. In fact, using the OLS estimation method, we may arrive at wrong conclusion about the relation between the dependent and explanatory variable of our model when an outlier is present in the data.

Outliers can arise due to a mistake committed while recording data into the computer. Outliers can also arise when sampling from a small population if one or several members of the population are very different in some relevant aspect from the rest of the population.

In the context of simple regression, the presence of an outlier can be detected easily by plotting data on a scatter diagram. However, in case of multiple regressions, such plotting would not be possible and we have to analyse the series for estimated residuals ($\hat{\varepsilon}_i = e_i$). Some diagnostic tests are also available to detect the presence of outliers.[25]

To obtain more meaningful relationship between the variables, the researchers often delete the outlier, if present in the data set. However, such an approach is not considered to be satisfactory. Sometimes, the outlying observation(s) can provide important information by increasing variation in the data series. In any case, if outliers are present, the researcher should explore the reason behind their occurrence. If these are found to be bona fide and valuable, then a robust estimator should be used instead of the OLS method.[26]

---

[25] For some idea about these tests, refer to Chatterjee and Hadi (2006, Chapter 4).

[26] Different types of robust estimators have been proposed in this context. We have not discussed those as that is outside the scope of this book. For some introductory idea about robust estimators, refer to Kennedy (2008, Chapter 21).

2.14 ESTIMATION OF SLRM USING EVIEWS

In this section, we discuss the method of estimating the SLRM using the EViews software package. To illustrate this, suppose we want to estimate a consumption function using data on per capita consumption expenditure (PCEXP) and per capita net state domestic product (PCNSDP) for 22 major states of India, as presented in Table 2.1. The steps involved are the following.

Step 1: The first step is to obtain data in EViews workfile. If data have been put in an Excel workfile, then we can easily import such data in the EViews workfile. This is done through the following steps.

(i)   Launch EViews by double-clicking on its icon on the desktop.
(ii)   From the main menu, click **File/Open/Foreign Data as Workfile...**
(iii) In the 'Look in' window, put the file name and click **Open**.
(iv)   Click **Next/Next/Finish**.

Screenshot 2.1 shows the 'Workfile' window that opens through these steps when data are imported in the EViews workfile.

Screenshot 2.1   Workfile Window in EViews

Step 2: We now proceed to estimate the regression model. There are several ways to do this, but the easiest is to select **Quick/Estimate Equation…** from the main menu, which will open the 'Equation Estimation' dialog box as shown in Screenshot 2.2.

Screenshot 2.2   Equation Estimation Dialog Box in EViews

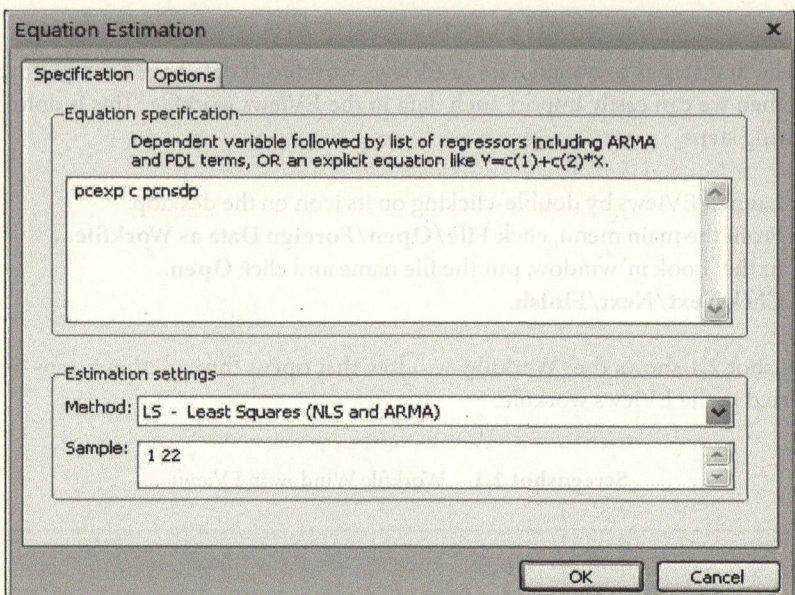

Step 3: In the 'Equation specification' edit box of 'Equation Estimation' dialog box, we have to insert list of variables to be used, with the dependent variable (pcexp) first and including a constant or intercept (c) and then the explanatory variable (pcnsdp). So we write **pcexp c pcnsdp**. Further, note that in the 'Estimation settings' edit box, the default estimation method is OLS [LS – Least Squares (NLS and ARMA)] and the default sample is the whole sample, which may be modified if required (for our present purpose, these are left unchanged).

Step 4: Click **OK** in the above dialog box to obtain the OLS regression output, as displayed in Screenshot 2.3.

Presentation of Regression Results

Usually, the researchers prefer reporting the results of regression in a summary form, highlighting only the key information. The most common way is to write the estimated equation with computed-t values[27] in parentheses beneath the estimated coefficients and include

---

[27] Note that EViews computes the t-value against the null hypothesis that $\beta = 0$. So if we need to test a different hypothesis (say $\beta = 1$), then we are required to calculate the value of t manually by the $t^* = (\hat{\beta} - \beta)/SE(\hat{\beta}) = (\hat{\beta} - 1)/SE(\hat{\beta})$ formula. In this case, it will not be appropriate to use the t-statistics reported by EViews output.

Screenshot 2.3   OLS Regression Output Using EViews

| View | Proc | Object | | Print | Name | Freeze | | Estimate | Forecast |

Dependent Variable: PCEXP
Method: Least Squares
Date: 08/23/13   Time: 22:20
Sample: 1 22
Included observations: 22

Variable	Coefficient	Std. Error	t-Statistic	Prob.
C	9311.181	1099.563	8.468077	0.0000
PCNSDP	0.151035	0.022803	6.623385	0.0000

R-squared	0.686860	Mean dependent var		16143.59
Adjusted R-squared	0.671203	S.D. dependent var		3114.002
S.E. of regression	1785.594	Akaike info criterion		17.89940
Sum squared resid	63766904	Schwarz criterion		17.99858
Log likelihood	-194.8934	Hannan-Quinn criter.		17.92276
F-statistic	43.86923	Durbin-Watson stat		1.674720
Prob(F-statistic)	0.000002			

some other important statistics like r^2, computed-F, D-W statistic, etc. The significance levels of the estimated coefficients and computed-F are also marked by asterisks put on them.[28] This is shown below.

$$\widehat{PCEXP} = 9311.181^* + 0.151035^* \, PCNSDP$$
$$(8.468077) \quad (6.623385)$$
$$r^2 = 0.686860 \quad F = 43.86923^*$$
$$D\text{-}W = 1.674720 \quad n = 22$$

Notes: Figures in parentheses are computed-t values
* indicates significance at 1% level

[28] While examining statistical significance of estimated coefficients using t-test, the following rules are generally applied.

(i) $0.00 \leq p\text{-value} \leq 0.01 \Rightarrow$ the estimated coefficient is statistically significant at 1% level.

(ii) $0.01 < p\text{-value} \leq 0.05 \Rightarrow$ the estimated coefficient is statistically significant at 5% level.

(iii) $0.05 < p\text{-value} \leq 0.10 \Rightarrow$ the estimated coefficient is statistically significant at 10% level.

(iv) $p\text{-value} > 0.10 \Rightarrow$ the estimated coefficient is statistically insignificant.

On the other hand, for F-test, statistical significance up to 5% level is considered. Thus, while conducting F-test, when $p\text{-value} > 0.05$, we conclude that the computed-F is statistically insignificant.

Interpretation of Regression Results

On the basis of the results of regression, it appears that per capita consumption expenditure (PCEXP) is positively related to per capita net state domestic product (PCNSDP). Such a relation appears to be statistically significant at the 1% level, which becomes clear from statistical significance of the estimated slope coefficient. Further, the value of r^2 indicates that nearly 69% of total variation in PCEXP has been explained by PCNSDP alone, which is quite satisfactory. The fact that computed-F is also statistically significant indicates statistical significance of computed-r^2.[29]

2.15 QUESTIONS AND ASSIGNMENTS

A. Multiple-Choice Questions

Tick ($\sqrt{}$) the correct answer.

(i) The term 'regression' has been coined by
 (a) Karl Pearson
 (b) Carl Friedrich Gauss
 (c) Francis Galton
 (d) Ragner Frisch

(ii) The accuracy of an estimator is assessed in terms of
 (a) Unbiasedness property
 (b) Minimum variance property
 (c) Minimum mean-squared error property
 (d) None of the above

(iii) The reliability of an estimator is assessed in terms of its
 (a) Mean
 (b) Variance
 (c) Coefficient of variation
 (d) Ease of computation

(iv) The method of 'least squares' was developed first by
 (a) Adrien-Marie Lagendre
 (b) R.A. Fisher
 (c) Jan Tinbergen
 (d) Carl Friedrich Gauss

(v) The method of least squares gives
 (a) Residual equations
 (b) Normal equations
 (c) Exponential equations
 (d) Quadratic equations

(vi) In method of least squares, the principle is to minimize
 (a) Sum of errors

[29] This point would become further clear in the next chapter.

      (b) Product of errors

      (c) Squares of errors

      (d) Sum of squares of errors

(vii) In usual notations, if $\hat{\beta}_{XY} = -1.8$ and $\hat{\beta}_{YX} = -0.2$, then r_{XY} is equal to

      (a) 0.6

      (b) ± 0.6

      (c) -0.6

      (d) 0.36

(viii) The regression coefficients are affected by change of

      (a) Only origin

      (b) Only scale

      (c) Both origin and scale

      (d) None of the above

(ix) Consistency property requires that

      (a) The bias of the estimator moves towards zero as sample size approaches infinity

      (b) The variance of the estimator moves towards zero as sample size approaches infinity

      (c) Both bias and variance of the estimator move towards zero as sample size approaches infinity

      (d) None of the above

(x) The standard error of regression is

      (a) An estimate of standard deviation of the regression error term

      (b) Standard deviation of the estimated intercept

      (c) Standard deviation of the estimated slope coefficient

      (d) An estimate of standard deviation of the dependent variable of the model

(xi) The appropriate statistic to examine goodness of fit of a two-variable regression model is

      (a) F-statistic

      (b) t-statistic

      (c) r^2-statistic

      (d) Chi-square statistic

(xii) For a no-intercept model, the value of r^2 is

      (a) Always zero

      (b) Always positive

      (c) Always negative

      (d) Can be both positive and negative

(xiii) Which of the following statements sounds like a null hypothesis?

      (a) The coin is not fair

      (b) The coin seems to be fair

      (c) There is a correlation in the population

      (d) There is no difference between male and female incomes in the population

(xiv) The estimated regression equation is given by $y = -12 + 0.5x$. What is the value of the residual at the point $x = 50, y = 70$?

    (a)   −57

    (b)   0

    (c)   57

    (d)   None of the above

B. General Questions

  (i)   Define the following terms.

    (a)   Population parameters

    (b)   Estimated coefficients

    (c)   Least-squares criterion

    (d)   Bestness

    (e)   Efficiency

    (f)   Consistency

    (g)   Mean-squared error

    (h)   BLUE properties

    (i)   Standard error of estimator

    (j)   Standard error of regression

    (k)   Total sum squares (TSS)

    (l)   Goodness of fit

    (m)   Analysis of variance (ANOVA)

    (n)   Outliers

  (ii)   Distinguish between

    (a)   Parameter and estimate

    (b)   True model and estimated model

    (c)   Standard error of an estimator and standard error of regression

    (d)   Null hypothesis and alternative hypothesis

    (e)   Explained sum squares (ESS) and residual sum squares (RSS)

    (f)   One-tailed test and two-tailed test

    (g)   Type-I error and Type-II error

 (iii)   What is regression? State the assumptions necessary for OLS estimation of the two-variable population regression model.

 (iv)   What are the desirable properties of an estimator?

  (v)   In the context of a two variable linear model, prove that the OLS estimators are BLUE.

 (vi)   Show how total variation in dependent variable of a linear regression model can be decomposed into two parts—'explained variation' and 'unexplained variation'.

 (vii)   What is the difference between one-tailed and two-tailed tests of significance? When would you prefer the former? Why?

(viii)   Explain how you would assess goodness of fit of an estimated model.

(ix)   State the relation between regression slope and correlation coefficient.

(x)   Prove that for the two-variable linear regression model, $F = t^2$.

(xi)   State the relation between F and r^2 in the context of a two-variable linear regression model.

(xii)   Formulate a two-variable population regression model without the intercept term. How would you estimate the slope parameter of such a model? What will be your r^2 formula to assess goodness of fit of the estimated model?

(xiii) What is 'reverse regression'?

(xiv)   When does the regression line of Y on X coincide with that of X on Y?

(xv)   What are outliers? What will be the likely effect of outliers on the estimated regression line?

(xvi)   We have the following results from a regression exercise.

$$\hat{Y}_i = 0.7264 + 1.0598 X_i$$
$$(0.3001) \quad (0.0728)$$
$$r^2 = 0.4710 \quad F_{1,238} = 211.895 \quad df = 238$$

(figures in parentheses are standard errors)

(a)   Test the null hypothesis of the coefficient of X_i greater than 1.

(b)   Is the intercept coefficient greater than 0?

(c)   What does the value of r^2 imply? Is it statistically significant?

(xvii) Suppose you estimated the consumption function

$$\hat{C}_t = \alpha_1 + \alpha_2 Y_t + u_t$$

and the savings function

$$\hat{S}_t = \beta_1 + \beta_2 Y_t + v_t$$

where C, S, and Y are consumption, savings, and income respectively, and $C + S = Y$ holds.

(a)   What is the relation between α_2 and β_2?

(b)   Will the residual sum squares (RSS) be the same for the two models? Explain.

(xviii) You obtained the following regression result.

$$\hat{Y}_t = 50 - 2978.5 X_t \qquad r^2 = 0.6149$$
$$(629.3)$$

(the figure in the bracket is the standard error)

Find out the sample size (n) underlying this result. Also interpret the regression result.

(xix) A sample of 12 observations corresponding to a two-variable linear model $Y_i = \alpha + \beta X_i + \varepsilon_i$ provided the following results.

$$\sum X_i = 4200 \qquad \sum(X_i - \bar{X}) = 46509.96$$
$$\sum Y_i = 3861 \qquad \sum(Y_i - \bar{Y}) = 40068.24$$
$$\sum(X_i - \bar{X})(Y_i - \bar{Y}) = 43145.04$$

Using this data, estimate α and β and the variances of your estimates. Also obtain 95% confidence intervals for $\hat{\alpha}$ and $\hat{\beta}$.

(xx) A tabular ANOVA representation gives

	Value	df
ESS	5,602	1
RSS	698	10
TSS	6,300	11

Test the hypothesis that there is no relationship between Y and X in the regression. (Note: At 5% level of significance, $F_{1,10} = 4.96$, $F_{1,11} = 4.84$, and $F_{10,11} = 2.85$).

(xxi) Indicate whether the following statements are true (T), false (F), or uncertain (U), and give brief explanation.

(a) In a two-variable population regression model, when the slope coefficient is zero, the intercept is estimated by the sample mean of the dependent variable.

(b) A high p-value means that the coefficient is significantly different from zero.

(c) The OLS estimate of the slope is adversely affected if an extreme observation is present in the data set.

(d) The OLS estimator cannot be BLUE unless the disturbance term is normally distributed.

(e) Type-I error occurs when we accept a false null hypothesis.

(f) The p-value shows the probability of committing a Type-II error.

(g) The regression line of Y on X coincides with that of X on Y, if and only if, $r^2 = 0$.

(h) Even though the disturbance term in the linear regression model is not normally distributed, the OLS estimators are still unbiased.

C. Computer Assignments

(i) The health economists examining variation in infant mortality rate (IMR) in the states of India hypothesised that it is negatively related to female literacy rate (FLIT), percentage of children immunized (CIMMU), and level of development of the states, which is represented by per capita net state domestic product (PCNSDP). To examine the validity of these hypotheses, you formulated the following regression models.

$$IMR_i = a_1 + a_2 FLIT_i + u_i$$
$$IMR_i = b_1 + b_2 CIMMU_i + v_i$$
$$IMR_i = c_1 + c_2 PCNSDP_i + w_i$$

Estimate the aforementioned models using data presented in Table 2.3. Are FLIT, CIMMU, and PCNSDP statistically significant determinants of IMR in India? Do the estimated slope coefficients have expected signs? Interpret the r^2 values obtained for three estimated models. Can you rank these determinants in terms of their importance to reduce IMR in India?

(ii) The labour economists hypothesised that the incidence of child labour in an underdeveloped economy like India is positively related to school drop-out rate

Table 2.3 Infant Mortality Rate (IMR), Female Literacy Rate (FLIT), Percentage of Immunized Children (CIMMU), and Per Capita Net State Domestic Product (PCNSDP) in Major States of India

State	IMR	FLIT	CIMMU	PCNSDP
Andhra Pradesh	49	59.7	46.0	51,025
Assam	61	67.3	31.4	27,197
Bihar	52	53.3	32.8	16,119
Chhattisgarh	54	60.6	48.7	38,059
Delhi	33	80.9	63.2	116,886
Gujarat	48	70.7	45.2	63,961
Haryana	51	66.8	65.3	78,781
Himachal Pradesh	45	76.6	74.2	50,365
Jammu & Kashmir	45	58.0	66.7	30,582
Jharkhand	44	56.2	34.2	30,719
Karnataka	41	68.1	55.0	50,676
Kerala	12	92.0	75.3	59,179
Madhya Pradesh	67	60.0	40.3	27,250
Maharashtra	31	75.5	58.8	74,027
Orissa	65	64.4	51.8	33,226
Punjab	38	71.3	60.1	62,153
Rajasthan	59	52.7	26.5	34,189
Tamil Nadu	28	73.9	80.9	62,499
Uttar Pradesh	63	59.3	23.0	23,132
West Bengal	33	71.2	64.3	41,469

Sources: (i) IMR from *SRS Bulletin*, January 2011, (ii) FLIT from *Census of India 2011*, (iii) CIMMU from NFHS-3 Survey 2005–06 and (iv) PCNSDP from RBI, *Handbook of Statistics on Indian Economy 2010–11*.

Note: Data for IMR relate to 2009, FLIT to 2011, CIMMU to 2005–06 and PCNSDP to 2009–10.

and poverty, but inversely related to the level of economic development. To examine the validity of these hypotheses, you gathered data on incidence of child labour (CHILDLAB), school dropout rate (DROPOUT), headcount poverty ratio (POV), and per capita net state domestic product (PCNSDP) (which is a proxy for economic development) for 19 major states of India. Such data have been presented in Table 2.4. Estimate three different two-variable regression models to examine the validity of these hypotheses. What are the significant determinants of child labour in India?

(iii) Table 2.5 presents data on foodgrains yield, percentage of gross irrigated area, fertilizers consumption, and credit advanced by the commercial banks in some

Table 2.4 Incidence of Child Labour (CHILDLAB), School Dropout Rate (DROPOUT), Headcount Poverty Ratio (POV), and Per Capita NSDP (PCNSDP) in Major States of India

State	CHILDLAB	DROPOUT	POV	PCNSDP
Andhra Pradesh	6.6	24.0	15.8	25,321
Assam	1.8	44.3	19.7	16,782
Bihar	1.4	51.6	41.4	7,914
Chhattisgarh	4.6	25.3	40.9	18,559
Gujarat	2.5	25.7	16.8	32,021
Haryana	1.7	9.3	10.0	37,842
Himachal Pradesh	2.7	6.8	14.0	32,564
Jharkhand	2.5	41.9	40.3	18,510
Karnataka	4.7	11.9	25.0	26,804
Kerala	0.2	0.0	15.0	31,871
Madhya Pradesh	2.8	29.6	38.3	15,442
Maharashtra	3.4	2.6	30.7	35,915
Orissa	4.9	27.8	46.4	17,380
Punjab	1.7	9.9	8.4	33,103
Rajasthan	4.9	40.7	22.1	18,565
Tamil Nadu	1.5	8.0	22.5	30,062
Uttar Pradesh	3.9	31.1	32.8	12,950
Uttarakhand	2.6	18.6	39.6	24,726
West Bengal	3.5	30.1	24.7	22,649

Sources: (i) CHILDLAB compiled from NSSO, *Report on Employment/Unemployment*, 61st Round, 2004–05; (ii) DROPOUT from EPWRF, *India: A Pocket Book of Data Series 2010–11*; (iii) POV from Planning Commission, *India Human Development Report 2011*; and (iv) *PCNSDP* (*Base: 2004–05*) from *RBI website*.

Note: All data except DROPOUT relate to 2004–05; DROPOUT (I–V classes) data for 2005–06/2006–07.

Table 2.5 Foodgrains Yield (kg/ha) (FGN), Percentage of Gross Cropped Area Irrigated (IIRI), Fertilizers Consumption (kg/ha) (FERT), and Credit Advanced by Commercial Banks to Agriculture (Rs/ha) (CREDIT) in Major States of India in 2008–09

State	FGN	IRRI	FERT	CREDIT
Andhra Pradesh	2,742	48.7	222	21,138
Assam	1,378	3.8	55.4	3,376
Bihar	1,546	61	174	8,700
Chhattisgarh	1,238	27.1	81.4	4,544
Gujarat	1,544	45.6	148.4	18,929
Haryana	3,420	85.3	198.8	17,040
Himachal Pradesh	1,918	19.7	61.3	15,316
Jammu & Kashmir	1,711	41.4	92.4	8,693
Jharkhand	1,709	9.7	87.2	8,139
Karnataka	1,548	31.9	148.1	19,805
Kerala	2,221	17	96.8	44,761
Madhya Pradesh	1,069	32.5	68.9	6,709
Maharashtra	977	19	116.1	11,996
Orissa	1,484	35	59	5,260
Punjab	4,255	97.6	223.4	19,370
Rajasthan	1,180	34.7	46.2	7,016
Tamil Nadu	2,125	58.3	217.2	45,603
Uttar Pradesh	2,206	76.4	157.9	11,247
Uttarakhand	1,785	48	128.6	14,670
West Bengal	2,493	56.2	155	9,592

Sources: (i) CMIE, *Agriculture*, June 2010 and (ii) Government of India, Ministry of Agriculture and Cooperation.

states of India in 2008–09. Estimate separate bi-variate regression models using these data and comment on the determinants of foodgrains yield in India. What policies you would recommend to increase yield of foodgrains in India?

(iv) Table 2.6 presents time-series data on Cropping Intensity (CRIN), Percentage of Gross Irrigated Area (IRRI), Fertilizers Consumption per hectare (FERT), and Percentage of HYV Area (HYV) in India for the period 1970–71 to 1998–99. Use these data to estimate separate two-variable regression models to find out statistically significant determinants of cropping intensity. Interpret your regression results. Do your results support commonly held perception that cropping intensity rises following expansion of irrigated area, HYV area, and fertilizers use?

Table 2.6 Cropping Intensity (CRIN), Percentage of Gross Irrigated Area (IRRI), Fertilizers Consumption (kg) per Hectare (FERT), and Percentage of HYV Area (HYV) in India

Year	CRIN	IRRI	FERT	HYV
1970–71	118.19	23.04	13.13	9.28
1971–72	118.23	23.26	16.08	11.00
1972–73	118.24	24.09	17.07	13.77
1973–74	119.27	23.71	16.71	15.33
1974–75	119.16	25.42	15.67	16.65
1975–76	120.93	25.31	16.89	18.62
1976–77	119.97	26.03	20.38	20.06
1977–78	121.33	26.75	24.89	22.60
1978–79	122.25	27.64	29.27	22.96
1979–80	122.10	29.02	30.99	22.63
1980–81	123.31	28.84	31.95	24.96
1981–82	124.53	29.09	34.31	26.30
1982–83	123.20	30.00	36.98	27.49
1983–84	125.71	29.97	42.94	29.93
1984–85	125.15	30.92	46.57	30.70
1985–86	126.66	30.42	47.48	31.05
1986–87	126.39	31.61	49.01	31.84
1987–88	127.33	32.82	51.45	31.69
1988–89	128.47	33.54	60.57	32.98
1989–90	128.05	33.93	63.47	33.56
1990–91	129.89	33.63	67.55	34.98
1991–92	128.67	36.04	69.84	35.51
1992–93	130.11	35.95	65.46	35.22
1993–94	131.08	36.58	66.28	35.90
1994–95	131.54	37.57	72.13	37.72
1995–96	131.84	38.06	74.02	38.46
1996–97	132.58	40.12	75.50	40.32
1997–98	133.86	39.69	85.19	40.00
1998–99	134.27	40.88	87.63	40.87

Source: www.indiastat.com

Answers to Multiple-Choice Questions

(i) (c); (ii) (a); (iii) (b); (iv) (d); (v) (b); (vi) (d); (vii) (c); (viii) (b); (ix) (c); (x) (a); (xi) (c); (xii) (d); (xiii) (d); (xiv) (c).

3 The Multiple Linear Regression Model

This chapter extends the discussion of the previous chapter. It is concerned with issues relevant to multiple regression analysis. Specifically, we discuss specification and assumptions of multiple regression model, its estimation, goodness of fit measures, and various problems of inference in the context of multiple regression models. We have added a brief discussion on the LR, Wald, and LM tests which are nowadays widely applied to handle a variety of inference and other problems in multiple regressions. Empirical applications of these tools and techniques have been explained using data set and EViews software package.

3.1 DEFINITION

Sometimes the two-variable regression model may appear to be inadequate as one independent/explanatory variable alone may not adequately explain variation in the dependent variable. In other words, it may appear that there are more than one determinants of the dependent variable. Thus, when we consider more than one determinants or independent variables, it becomes the case of multiple regression models. For instance, if we hypothesise that monthly consumption expenditure of the people is determined by their income, age, education, sex, etc., we have to specify a multiple regression model. In brief, a multiple regression model is the one where two or more independent variables are considered to explain variation in the dependent variable.[1]

Obviously, the easiest example of a multiple regression model is where only two independent variables or regressors are considered. In this chapter, we consider such a model while in the appendix to this chapter we present the multiple regression model involving more than two independent variables.

---

[1] Geweke et al. (2008, 610) observed that R. Benini, the Italian statistician, was the first to make use of the method of multiple regression in economics in the decade beginning 1900. However, Henry Moore was the first to place the statistical estimation of economic relations at the centre of quantitative analysis of economics in the 1910s. Moore is also credited for laying the foundation of 'statistical economics', the precursor of econometrics.

3.2 SPECIFICATION AND ASSUMPTIONS

The three-variable population regression model involving the dependent variable Y_i and independent/explanatory variables X_{1i} and X_{2i} is specified as:

$$Y_i = \alpha + \beta_1 X_{1i} + \beta_2 X_{2i} + \varepsilon_i \qquad (3.1)$$

Here ε_i is the stochastic disturbance term and the subscript i denotes the ith observation. As in the case of two-variable model, we make the following assumptions in context of the above multiple regression model.

(i)   Zero mean of ε_i: $E(\varepsilon_i \mid X_{1i}, X_{2i}) = 0$ for each i
(ii)   Homoskedasticity: $Var(\varepsilon_i) = \sigma^2$ constant
(iii)   Non-autocorrelation: $Cov(\varepsilon_i, \varepsilon_j) = 0$ where $i \neq j$
(iv)   Normality: ε_i is normally distributed.
(v)   Non-stochastic Xs, which implies that the values of the X-variables are same in repeated samples.
(vi)   Zero covariance between ε_i and X variables, i.e., $Cov(\varepsilon_i, X_{1i}) = Cov(\varepsilon_i, X_{2i}) = 0$.
(vii)   No exact linear relationship exists between the X variables, i.e., Xs are not correlated.

3.3 OLS ESTIMATION

To obtain the OLS estimates of parameters of the population regression model (3.1), let us write the corresponding sample regression model as

$$Y_i = \hat{\alpha} + \hat{\beta}_1 X_{1i} + \hat{\beta}_2 X_{2i} + e_i \qquad (3.2)$$

where e_i represents estimated residual values, and $\hat{\alpha}$, $\hat{\beta}_1$, and $\hat{\beta}_2$ are estimates of population parameters α, β_1, and β_2, respectively. As in the two-variable model, we apply the 'least-squares criterion' to obtain these estimates. Following this criterion, we select the values of $\hat{\alpha}$, $\hat{\beta}_1$, and $\hat{\beta}_2$ which minimize $\sum e_i^2$.

Here

$$\sum e_i^2 = \sum (Y_i - \hat{\alpha} - \hat{\beta}_1 X_{1i} - \hat{\beta}_2 X_{2i})^2$$

The necessary conditions of minimization of $\sum e_i^2$ are

$$\frac{\partial \sum e_i^2}{\partial \hat{\alpha}} = \frac{\partial \sum e_i^2}{\partial \hat{\beta}_1} = \frac{\partial \sum e_i^2}{\partial \hat{\beta}_2} = 0$$

Applying these conditions, the following 'normal equations' are obtained.

$$\sum Y_i = n\hat{\alpha} + \hat{\beta}_1 \sum X_{1i} + \hat{\beta}_2 \sum X_{2i} \qquad (3.3a)$$

$$\sum X_{1i}Y_i = \hat{\alpha}\sum X_{1i} + \hat{\beta}_1 \sum X_{1i}^2 + \hat{\beta}_2 \sum X_{1i}X_{2i} \qquad (3.3b)$$

$$\sum X_{2i}Y_i = \hat{\alpha}\sum X_{2i} + \hat{\beta}_1 \sum X_{1i}X_{2i} + \hat{\beta}_2 \sum X_{2i}^2 \qquad (3.3c)$$

It is clear that with the given data on Y_i, X_{1i}, and X_{2i}, we have to compute the following quantities to obtain the values of the estimates.

$$n, \sum Y_i, \sum X_{1i}, \sum X_{2i}, \sum X_{1i}Y_i, \sum X_{2i}Y_i, \sum X_{1i}X_{2i}, \sum X_{1i}^2, \text{ and } \sum X_{2i}^2$$

Putting these values in the aforementioned 'normal equations' and solving, we have solutions for values of $\hat{\alpha}$, $\hat{\beta}_1$, and $\hat{\beta}_2$. Using these values, we write the estimated three-variable multiple regression model as

$$\hat{Y}_i = \hat{\alpha} + \hat{\beta}_1 X_{1i} + \hat{\beta}_2 X_{2i}$$

An alternative way to compute the estimates is to use the following formulas that can be derived by solving the 'normal equations'.

$$\hat{\alpha} = \overline{Y} - \hat{\beta}_1 \overline{X}_1 - \hat{\beta}_2 \overline{X}_2 \qquad (3.4)$$

$$\hat{\beta}_1 = \frac{\sum x_{1i}y_i \sum x_{2i}^2 - \sum x_{2i}y_i \sum x_{1i}x_{2i}}{\sum x_{1i}^2 \sum x_{2i}^2 - (\sum x_{1i}x_{2i})^2} \qquad (3.5)$$

$$\hat{\beta}_2 = \frac{\sum x_{2i}y_i \sum x_{1i}^2 - \sum x_{1i}y_i \sum x_{1i}x_{2i}}{\sum x_{1i}^2 \sum x_{2i}^2 - (\sum x_{1i}x_{2i})^2} \qquad (3.6)$$

Here $\overline{Y}, \overline{X}_1$, and $\overline{X}_2$ denote sample mean values for the three variables and the lowercase letters denote deviation from these sample means.

It is also easy to compute the variances of $\hat{\alpha}$, $\hat{\beta}_1$, and $\hat{\beta}_2$ by using the following formulas.

$$Var(\hat{\alpha}) = \left[\frac{1}{n} + \frac{\overline{X}_1^2 \sum x_{2i}^2 + \overline{X}_2^2 \sum x_{1i}^2 - 2\overline{X}_1\overline{X}_2 \sum x_{1i}x_{2i}}{\sum x_{1i}^2 \sum x_{2i}^2 - (\sum x_{1i}x_{2i})^2}\right]\sigma^2 \qquad (3.7)$$

$$Var(\hat{\beta}_1) = \left[\frac{\sum x_{2i}^2}{(\sum x_{1i}^2)(\sum x_{2i}^2) - (\sum x_{1i}x_{2i})^2}\right]\sigma^2 = \frac{\sigma^2}{\sum x_{1i}^2(1 - r_{12}^2)} \qquad (3.8)$$

$$Var(\hat{\beta}_2) = \left[\frac{\sum x_{1i}^2}{(\sum x_{1i}^2)(\sum x_{2i}^2) - (\sum x_{1i}x_{2i})^2}\right]\sigma^2 = \frac{\sigma^2}{\sum x_{2i}^2(1 - r_{12}^2)} \qquad (3.9)$$

In the above formulae, r_{12} is the sample coefficient of correlation between X_{1i} and X_{2i}, σ^2 is variance of the disturbance term ε_i, which is estimated as

$$\hat{\sigma}^2 = \frac{\sum e_i^2}{n-3} \tag{3.10}$$

where 3 is the number of parameters in the population regression equation estimated in the model.

3.4 PROPERTIES OF OLS ESTIMATORS

As in two-variable linear model, the least-squares estimators ($\hat{\alpha}$, $\hat{\beta}_1$, and $\hat{\beta}_2$) in the three-variable model are also BLUE, i.e., best, linear and unbiased estimators of population parameters (α, β_1, and β_2). It is easy to prove these properties. However, we skip this exercise here as Appendix 3.1 provides proof of BLUE properties in context of the general linear multiple regression model.

3.5 MEASURING GOODNESS OF FIT

After estimating the multiple regression model, we may be interested to assess the goodness or quality of fit of our estimated model. In other words, our objective is to know how well the estimated line fits the sample observations.

The goodness of fit of the estimated model in the context of a two-variable model is understood in terms of the value of r^2-statistic. To recapitulate, r^2-statistic provides a measure of proportion of total variation in the dependent variable that is explained by the independent/explanatory variable of the model. We can extend this concept further to obtain a measure of goodness of fit of the estimated model in the context of estimated multiple regression model. This is done as follows.

In the two-variable model,

$$r^2 = \frac{(\sum x_i y_i)^2}{\sum x_i^2 \sum y_i^2}$$

$$= \frac{\hat{\beta} \sum x_i y_i}{\sum y_i^2}$$

$$= \frac{ESS}{TSS}$$

Let us rewrite the above relation supposing that the variables considered are Y_i and X_{1i}. Then,

$$r^2 = \frac{\hat{\beta}_1 \sum x_{1i} y_i}{\sum y_i^2}$$

Now if we suppose that there are two explanatory variables, X_{1i} and X_{2i}, then

$$R^2 = \frac{\hat{\beta}_1 \sum x_{1i} y_i + \hat{\beta}_2 \sum x_{2i} y_i}{\sum y_i^2}$$

The above formula can be extended further by adding terms in the numerator, when we have more than two explanatory variables. If we have k number of explanatory variables in the model, then the R^2 formula becomes

$$R^2 = \frac{\hat{\beta}_1 \sum x_{1i} y_i + \hat{\beta}_2 \sum x_{2i} y_i + \ldots + \hat{\beta}_k \sum x_{ki} y_i}{\sum y_i^2} \qquad (3.11)$$

Usefulness of R^2-statistic

R^2-statistic (in brief, R^2) provides a measure of goodness of fit of the estimated multiple regression model to sample data. It also helps to understand the relevance of explanatory variables in the estimated model. The value of R^2 lies between 0 and 1. When the value of R^2 is close to 0, the explanatory variables have not explained much of the variation in the dependent variable of the model and we have a 'bad fit' estimated equation. In other words, we have not considered the explanatory variables that are relevant to explain variation in the dependent variable. On the other hand, when the value of R^2 is high and close to 1, we have a 'good fit' estimated equation, which explains a large part of variation in the dependent variable and the explanatory variables considered in the model are quite relevant.

Misuse of R^2-statistic

In spite of above-mentioned usefulness of the R^2-statistic, one must be cautious about its possible misuses. In particular, it is to be remembered that it is dangerous to play the game of maximizing the value of R^2. Some researchers do this by gradually increasing the number of explanatory variables in the model. However, in empirical research, quite often we come across a situation where the value of R^2 is high but very few of the estimated coefficients are statistically significant and/or they have expected signs. Therefore, the researchers should be more concerned about the logical/theoretical relevance of the explanatory variables to the dependent variable and also their statistical significance. If in this process, a high value of R^2 is obtained, well and good. On the other hand, if R^2 is low, it does not mean that the model is necessarily bad, particularly when a good number of the estimated coefficients have expected signs and are statistically significant.

To illustrate the above point further, let us consider an interesting example given by Rao and Miller (1972, 14–16) which clarifies the difficulty of choosing between two different models solely on the basis of their computed R^2 values. Rao and Miller estimated both the consumption and savings functions using the same time series data on consumption (C_t) and income (Y_t).[2] The estimated equations were

Consumption function:

$$\hat{C}_t = -0.34 + 0.76Y_t + 0.30Y_{t-1} \qquad R^2 = 0.99$$

Savings function:

$$\hat{S}_t = 0.34 + 0.24Y_t - 0.30Y_{t-1} \qquad R^2 = 0.64$$

It is found that estimated consumption model explains 99% of total variation in the dependent variable while the savings model explains 64% of the same. On the basis of this result, it would be incorrect to conclude that the consumption model provides a better causal relation. The reason for this is as follows.

We know that

$$R^2 = 1 - \frac{RSS}{TSS} = 1 - \frac{\sum e_t^2}{\sum y_t^2}$$

In the case of consumption model,

$$R_c^2 = 1 - \frac{\sum e_t^2}{\sum c_t^2} \text{ where } c_t = C_t - \overline{C}.$$

For the savings model,

$$R_s^2 = 1 - \frac{\sum e_t^2}{\sum s_t^2} \text{ where } s_t = S_t - \overline{S}.$$

Now, since marginal propensity to consume (MPC) is greater than the marginal propensity to save (MPS),[3] $\sum c_t^2 > \sum s_t^2 \Rightarrow R_c^2 > R_s^2$. Thus, as long as MPC $\neq$ MPS, the two R^2 values ought to differ. So, it would not be appropriate to conclude that the estimated consumption model with higher R^2 provides a better-fit estimated equation compared with the estimated savings model.

[2] The data series on savings (S_t) has been generated by taking a difference of income and consumption.

[3] This is shown by the values of estimated coefficients for income variable (Y_t) in the consumption and savings models, which are 0.76 and 0.24, respectively.

Adjusted R² (or R̄²)

An important property of the R^2-statistic is that it is a non-decreasing function of the number of explanatory variables in the model. Therefore, the computed R^2 values of two models having unequal number of explanatory variables are not comparable. This point can be further explained by considering the following expression.

$$R^2 = 1 - \frac{\sum e_i^2}{\sum y_i^2}$$

Here $\sum y_i^2 = \sum (Y_i - \overline{Y})^2$ is independent of the number of explanatory variables in the model. However, $\sum e_i^2$, which is the residual sum squares, depends on the number of explanatory variables in the model. As the number of explanatory variables increases, $\sum e_i^2$ falls and hence R^2 rises.

Therefore, to compare the two R^2s corresponding to two different models, we must take into account the number of explanatory variables present in them. In other words, we have to adjust the two R^2s for difference in number of explanatory variables between them.[4] This is done in the following manner.

$$Adjusted\ R^2\ (\text{or }\overline{R}^2) = 1 - \frac{\sum e_i^2 / (n-k-1)}{\sum y_i^2 / (n-1)} \tag{3.12}$$

where n is the number of observations and k is the number of explanatory variables in the model.

It is clear that while computing $\overline{R}^2$, we make adjustment for degrees of freedom, which is done by dividing $\sum e_i^2$ and $\sum y_i^2$ by their respective degrees of freedom, which are $n-k-1$ and $n-1$, respectively.[5]

A simple manipulation of the above expression shows that the value of $\overline{R}^2$ for a given estimated model can also be computed in terms of the value of R^2.

$$
\begin{aligned}
\overline{R}^2 &= 1 - \frac{\sum e_i^2 / (n-k-1)}{\sum y_i^2 / (n-1)} \\
&= 1 - \left(\frac{\sum e_i^2}{\sum y_i^2} \cdot \frac{n-1}{n-k-1} \right) \\
&= 1 - \left(\frac{RSS}{TSS} \cdot \frac{n-1}{n-k-1} \right) \\
&= 1 - \left[(1-R^2) \frac{n-1}{n-k-1} \right]
\end{aligned}
\tag{3.13}
$$

---

[4] The adjusted-R^2 has been developed by Henry Theil.
[5] Put differently, $\overline{R}^2$ penalises R^2 for adding additional explanatory variables in the model.

Thus, putting the value of R^2 in the above equation, we obtain the $\bar{R}^2$ value for the estimated model.

Some Other Model Selection Criteria

We have seen that $\bar{R}^2$ penalizes R^2 for adding additional explanatory variables in the model so that $\bar{R}^2$ values of models having different number of explanatory variables become comparable. However, $\bar{R}^2$ is not the only statistic (criterion) used by the researchers to select the best-fit model from a set of alternative models. In fact, there are several other model selection criteria that have found wide applications in empirical research. Three such examples are: Akaike Information Criterion (AIC), Schwarz Bayesian Criterion (SBC), and Hannan-Quinn Criterion (HQC). In the context of linear models which are estimated by applying the OLS method, these are computed as[6]

$$AIC = e^{\frac{2k}{n}} \cdot \left(\frac{RSS}{n} \right) \tag{3.14}$$

$$SBC = n^{\frac{k}{n}} \cdot \left(\frac{RSS}{n} \right) \tag{3.15}$$

$$HQC = (\ln n)^{\frac{2k}{n}} \cdot \left(\frac{RSS}{n} \right) \tag{3.16}$$

In these formulae, RSS = residual sum squares, k = number of parameters estimated (including the intercept), and n = number of observations. It is apparent that computation of values of these criteria is facilitated by taking logarithms. In fact, some programmes like EViews actually report their logarithms.

While selecting a model based on these criteria, we select the one that reports minimum values for all these criteria (statistics) compared to an alternative model. However, in practice, we may have contradictory results as different levels of penalties are imposed by different criteria. For example, compared with AIC, the SBC imposes larger penalty for additional explanatory variables. In general, AIC is most popular as a model selection criterion, especially in time series analysis.

3.6 SOME PROBLEMS OF INFERENCE IN MLRM

We describe below some important problems of inference, which the researchers often face while estimating the multiple regression models.

---

[6] It is to be remembered that for models that are estimated by applying the maximum likelihood method, the formulae for these criteria are different.

Testing Significance of Individual Regression Coefficients

Suppose our estimated multiple regression model is

$$\hat{Y}_i = \hat{\alpha} + \hat{\beta}_1 X_{1i} + \hat{\beta}_2 X_{2i} + \dots + \hat{\beta}_k X_{ki}$$

We want to test the hypotheses relating to significance of individual partial regression coefficients. Specifically, the hypotheses are

$$H_N: \beta_i = 0$$
$$H_A: \beta_i \neq 0$$

Assuming that the disturbance term of the population regression model is distributed normally with 0 mean and constant variance [i.e., $\varepsilon_i \sim N(0, \sigma^2 I)$], we compute

$$t^* = \frac{\hat{\beta}_i}{SE(\hat{\beta}_i)} \tag{3.17}$$

with $n - (k + 1) = n - k - 1$ degrees of freedom where n is number of observations and $(k + 1)$ represents total number of parameters estimated (including the intercept).

The *decision rules* are

- If $|t^*| > t_{\lambda/2}(n - k - 1)$, then reject H_N and conclude that $\hat{\beta}_i$ is statistically significant. In other words, the null hypothesis gets rejected when the absolute value of computed-t is greater than the value of critical-t at level of significance $\lambda/2$ (under the two-tailed test) and degrees of freedom $n - k - 1$.
- On the other hand, if $|t^*| \leq t_{\lambda/2}(n - k - 1)$, we accept H_N and conclude that $\hat{\beta}_i$ is statistically insignificant.

Testing the Overall Significance of Regression

For examining the overall significance of the estimated multiple regression model, we may apply the analysis of variance (ANOVA) technique, which is outlined below.

Suppose the model is

$$Y_i = \alpha + \beta_1 X_{1i} + \beta_2 X_{2i} + \dots + \beta_k X_{ki} + \varepsilon_i$$

and the hypotheses to be tested are

$$H_N: \beta_1 = \beta_2 = \dots = \beta_k = 0$$
$$H_A: \text{Not all } \beta\text{s are simultaneously zero}$$

To test these hypotheses, we construct the following ANOVA table.

Table 3.1   ANOVA Table for Testing the Overall Significance of the Estimated
Multiple Regression Model

Source of Variation	Sum Squares	Degrees of Freedom	Mean Sum Squares
X's	$ESS = \hat{\beta}_1 \Sigma x_{1i}y_i + \hat{\beta}_2 \Sigma x_{2i}y_i + \dots + \hat{\beta}_k \Sigma x_{ki}y_i$	k	ESS/k
Residuals	$RSS = \Sigma e_i^2$	$n-k-1$	$RSS/(n-k-1)$
Total	$TSS = \Sigma y_i^2$	$n-1$	

Source: Author's compilation.

It can be shown that given the assumptions $\varepsilon_i \sim N(0, \sigma^2 I)$ and also that the null hypothesis being

$$H_N: \beta_1 = \beta_2 = \dots = \beta_k = 0$$

we have

$$F^* = \frac{ESS/k}{RSS/(n-k-1)} \tag{3.18}$$

where F^* follows an F-distribution with degrees of freedom $k, (n-k-1)$.[7]

The point to note is that all necessary information for computing F^* are available from the ANOVA table.

The *decision rules* are

- If $F^* > F_\lambda [k, (n-k-1)]$, then reject the H_N and conclude that there is overall significance of the estimated multiple regression model.
- On the other hand, if $F^* \leq F_\lambda [k, (n-k-1)]$, accept the H_N and conclude that there is no overall significance of the estimated regression model.

Relation between R^2 and F

The following relation holds between the R^2 and F statistics.

$$
\begin{aligned}
F &= \frac{ESS/k}{RSS/(n-k-1)} \\
&= \frac{\dfrac{ESS}{TSS}\Big/k}{\dfrac{RSS}{TSS}\Big/(n-k-1)} \\
&= \frac{R^2/k}{(1-R^2)/(n-k-1)}
\end{aligned} \tag{3.19}
$$

[7] Note that the degrees of freedom for the ESS is total number of independent/explanatory variables considered in the model while the degrees of freedom for the RSS is number of observations (or sample size) minus total number of parameters estimated including the intercept term.

It implies that it is possible to obtain computed-F (i.e., F^*) simply by putting the computed-R^2 value in the above expression. It also implies that the above-mentioned F-test not only serves as a measure of overall significance of estimated regression model, but also to test statistical significance of computed-R^2. Thus, if F^* *is statistically significant, it implies that computed-R^2 is also statistically significant.*

Testing Relevance of an Additional Explanatory Variable

Sometimes we may have to introduce a new variable into our regression model. Inclusion of such a variable can be justified if it increases ESS significantly in relation to RSS. *In other words, inclusion of an additional variable is justified if the value of R^2 increases significantly.* In empirical research, this knowledge is very essential because one would not like to include an additional variable if that contributes very little to the ESS or does not reduce RSS significantly.

To test whether ESS rises significantly in relation to RSS after inclusion of an additional variable in the model, we may devise another F-test procedure, which is also built on the ANOVA technique. To understand such a test procedure, let us consider the following models.

Old model:

$$Y_i = \alpha + \beta_1 X_{1i} + \varepsilon_{1i}$$

New model:

$$Y_i = \alpha + \beta_1 X_{1i} + \beta_2 X_{2i} + \varepsilon_{2i}$$

The ANOVA table that we construct here is the following.

Table 3.2 ANOVA Table for Testing the Significance of the Incremental ESS in Relation to RSS

Source of Variation	Sum Squares	Degrees of Freedom	Mean Sum Squares
ESS due to X_1 alone	$ESS_{old} = \hat{\beta}_1 \Sigma x_{1i} y_i$	1	$ESS_{old} / 1$
ESS due to X_1 and X_2	$ESS_{new} = \hat{\beta}_1 \Sigma x_{1i} y_i + \hat{\beta}_2 \Sigma x_{2i} y_i$	2	$ESS_{new} / 2$
ESS due to addition of X_2	$ESS_{new} - ESS_{old} = \hat{\beta}_2 \Sigma x_{2i} y_i$	1	$(ESS_{new} - ESS_{old})/1$
Residual	$RSS_{new} = TSS_{new} - ESS_{new}$	$n-3$	$RSS_{new} / (n-3)$
Total	$TSS_{new} = \Sigma y_i^2$	$n-1$	

Source: Author's compilation.

Now to assess the significance of the incremental contribution of X_2 after allowing for the contribution of X_1, we compute one F-value using the following formula.

$$F^* = \frac{(ESS_{new} - ESS_{old}) / \text{no. of new explanatory variable(s)}}{RSS_{new} / \text{no. of observations minus no. of parameters in the new model}}$$

$$= \frac{(ESS_{new} - ESS_{old})/1}{RSS_{new} / (n-3)}$$

To simplify computation of F^*, we divide both the numerator and denominator by TSS. This gives

$$F^* = \frac{(R^2_{new} - R^2_{old})\,/\,\text{no. of new explanatory variable(s)}}{(1 - R^2_{new})\,/\,\text{no. of observations minus no. of parameters in the new model}} \qquad (3.21)$$

The *decision rule* is: if $F^* > F_\lambda\left[1, (n-3)\right]$, i.e., computed value of F is greater than the critical-F value at chosen level of significance λ and degrees of freedom 1 in the numerator and $n - 3$ in the denominator, we conclude that ESS has improved significantly in relation to RSS after inclusion of X_2 variable. Hence, X_2 is a relevant variable.

When to Add a New Variable?

It is clear from above discussion that we would like to add a new variable in our regression model when inclusion of the variable increases ESS significantly in relation to RSS. In such a situation, the value of adjusted-R^2 (i.e., $\overline{R}^2$) also improves in the new model. Thus, comparing the $\overline{R}^2$ values for the old and new models, one could guess the relevance/importance of the additional variable.

Further, it can be shown that $\overline{R}^2$ increases when the absolute value of computed t-statistic of the newly added variable becomes greater than 1.

Some Important Points to Remember

- As R^2 is a non-decreasing function of the number of independent variables in the model, inclusion of an additional independent variable in the model could not reduce the value of R^2.
- When the absolute value of computed-t corresponding to slope coefficient of an independent variable is greater than 1, dropping that variable from the model would reduce the values of both R^2 and $\overline{R}^2$.
- If the absolute value of computed-t corresponding to slope coefficient of an independent variable is less than 1, dropping that variable from the model would reduce the value of R^2 but improve the value of $\overline{R}^2$.

Testing Validity of Linear Equality Restriction

To illustrate the procedure for testing linear equality restriction(s), let us consider the example of Cobb-Douglas production function in its log-linear form.

$$\log Y_i = \alpha + \beta_1 \log X_{1i} + \beta_2 \log X_{2i} + u_i \qquad (3.22)$$

Here Y_i is output and X_{1i} and X_{2i} are two inputs. Now constant returns to scale implies that $\beta_1 + \beta_2 = 1$. This is an example of linear equality restriction in context of the above production function. Hence, testing the validity of this restriction also implies testing the validity of the assumption of constant returns to scale. Obviously, $\beta_1 + \beta_2 \neq 1$ exemplifies linear inequality restriction or absence of constant returns to scale. So the hypotheses to be tested are

$$H_N: \beta_1 + \beta_2 = 1$$
$$H_A: \beta_1 + \beta_2 \neq 1$$

There are two approaches to test these hypotheses: the t-test approach and the F-test approach.

The t-test
Here we compute

$$t^* = \frac{(\hat{\beta}_1 + \hat{\beta}_2) - (\beta_1 + \beta_2)}{SE(\hat{\beta}_1 + \hat{\beta}_2)}$$

$$= \frac{(\hat{\beta}_1 + \hat{\beta}_2) - 1}{SE(\hat{\beta}_1 + \hat{\beta}_2)} \text{ with } n - 3 \text{ degrees of freedom}$$

where

$$SE(\hat{\beta}_1 + \hat{\beta}_2) = \sqrt{Var(\hat{\beta}_1) + Var(\hat{\beta}_2) + 2Cov(\hat{\beta}_1, \hat{\beta}_2)}$$

The *decision rule*: If $|t^*| > t_{\lambda/2}(n - 3)$, reject the null hypothesis (H_N) and accept that $\beta_1 + \beta_2 \neq 1$, i.e., there is no constant returns to scale.

The F-test
The linear equality restriction is given as $\beta_1 + \beta_2 = 1$, which implies $\beta_1 = 1 - \beta_2$ or $\beta_2 = 1 - \beta_1$. Using either of these quantities, we rewrite the log-linear Cobb-Douglas function as

$$\log Y_i = \alpha + (1 - \beta_2) \log X_{1i} + \beta_2 \log X_{2i} + u_i$$
$$\Rightarrow \log Y_i - \log X_{1i} = \alpha + \beta_2 (\log X_{2i} - \log X_{1i}) + u_i$$
$$\Rightarrow \log\left(\frac{Y_i}{X_{1i}}\right) = \alpha + \beta_2 \log\left(\frac{X_{2i}}{X_{1i}}\right) + u_i \qquad (3.23)$$

Estimating (3.23) by OLS, we obtain $\hat{\beta}_2$, which may be used to obtain $\hat{\beta}_1 = 1 - \hat{\beta}_2$. This procedure is known as 'restricted least-squares'. This method can also be generalized to models containing more explanatory variables and more than one linearity restriction.

How do we test whether the above null hypothesis is valid so that $\beta_1 + \beta_2 = 1$? Here we apply an F-test procedure which is described below.

Suppose

$\sum e_{UR}^2$ = RSS of unrestricted model (3.22);

$\sum e_R^2$ = RSS of restricted model (3.23);

m = number of linear restrictions (which is 1 in our present example);
k = number of parameters in the unrestricted model (3.22); and
n = number of observations.
Now compute

$$F^* = \frac{(\sum e_R^2 - \sum e_{UR}^2)/m}{\sum e_{UR}^2/(n-k)}$$

$$= \frac{(R_{UR}^2 - R_R^2)/m}{(1-R_{UR}^2)/n-k} \quad (3.24)$$

This F^* follows an F-distribution with degrees of freedom $(m, n-k)$.

The *decision rule*: If $F^* > F_\lambda (m, n-k)$, reject the null hypothesis (H_N) and say that there is no constant returns to scale.

3.7 THE LIKELIHOOD RATIO (LR), WALD (W), AND LAGRANGE MULTIPLIER (LM) TESTS

In the above discussion, we have seen how t and F tests are oriented towards examining a variety of hypotheses in multiple regression analyses. One important prerequisite of these tests is that they are applied to linear models. However, it is possible to move beyond this comfortable situation of linear models and develop tests that can examine a variety of hypotheses and restrictions for all types of models—linear and non-linear. There are three important tests here: Likelihood Ratio (LR) test, Wald (W) test, and Lagrange Multiplier (LM) test. The test statistics associated with these tests have unknown small-sample distributions, but each is distributed asymptotically (i.e., in large samples) as a Chi-square (χ^2) with degrees freedom equal to the number of restrictions (r) being tested. As formal derivation of these test procedures is beyond our scope, we provide below a brief idea about them.[8]

It is to be noted that these tests actually seek to examine the difference between an unrestricted (UR) model and restricted (R) version of the same model. If the restriction does not affect the fit of the model very much, then we accept the restriction as being valid; otherwise, we reject the restriction and hence the restricted model. This, of course, means that we must have some concrete measure of how much worse the fit can get and still be insignificant following imposition of a restriction. The three tests follow somewhat different approaches although, as mentioned above, they all are asymptotically equivalent in that the test statistic associated with each of these tests follows a χ^2 distribution.

The Likelihood Ratio (LR) test

This test is based on the maximum likelihood (ML) principle.[9] It actually computes two values of the log-likelihood function—one with a given restriction and the other

---

[8] For detailed discussion on these tests, one may refer to Johnston and Dinardo (1997, 147–51).

[9] In Appendix 3.2, we provide brief exposition of the principle of maximum likelihood, and the maximum likelihood estimation method.

without restriction. Suppose the values of these log-likelihoods are l_R and l_{UR}, respectively. It then computes the value of twice the difference between l_{UR} and l_R which follows a Chi-square (χ^2) distribution with degrees of freedom equal to number of restrictions (r). Thus,

$$LR = 2(l_{UR} - l_R) \sim \chi^2(r)$$

This computed value of LR ($= \chi^{2^*}$) is compared with critical-χ^2 value for chosen level of significance (1% or 5%) and degrees of freedom r to arrive at a decision regarding rejection/acceptance of the restriction (null hypothesis). If $\chi^{2^*} > \chi^2(r)$, we reject the null hypothesis and conclude that the restriction is invalid.

The Wald (W) test

Unlike the LR test, in Wald test we only estimate the unrestricted model and then use a formula to test the validity of the restriction (null hypothesis). So in this test it is not necessary to estimate the complete model subject to the restriction. The test statistic here has an asymptotic Chi-square distribution with degrees of freedom being equal to the number of restrictions being tested. The *decision rule* is the same as that for the LR test.

The Lagrange Multiplier (LM) test

In LM test, we estimate the restricted model and then test for a relaxation of the restriction again by applying a formula, but not actually re-estimating the unrestricted model. The steps followed are:

(i)   Estimate the restricted model and save the residuals ($\tilde{e}_i$) out of it.

(ii)   Regress $\tilde{e}_i$ on all explanatory variables (those included in the restricted model as well as those excluded from it) and compute the value of R^2 out of this regression (also called auxiliary regression model), which is R_e^2 (say).

(iii) Compute $LM = nR_e^2$ where n is number of observations or sample size.

(iv)   The LM statistic also follows a Chi-square distribution with degrees of freedom being equal to the number of explanatory variables excluded from the original (unrestricted) model. The *decision rule* here is the same as before.

Among these tests, the LM test has become immensely popular with the empirical researchers as it allows for testing a model for many possible forms of restrictions and model misspecifications without having to estimate different models. However, the actual choice among these tests is typically made on the basis of computational convenience. It also needs mention that although the LR test is judged to be the best in small samples (Kennedy 2008, 64), the values of the LR, Wald, and LM test statistics become close to each other as the sample size tends towards infinity.

3.8 IMPLICATIONS OF SOME FREQUENTLY OBSERVED CASES IN MLRM

We explain here the econometric significance of some cases frequently observed by the researchers in multiple regression analyses.

(i) R^2 and all β_i significant: This is the most satisfactory result that the researcher could hope for, unless some of the estimated coefficients have unexpected signs.

(ii) R^2 and some but not all β_i significant: This is a very common result obtained by the researcher when a large number of explanatory variables are included in the multiple regression model. In this situation, the researcher would like to drop some insignificant explanatory variables from the model. Specifically, the variables whose estimated coefficients have computed-t values (absolute, i.e., ignoring the sign) less than 1 may be dropped. That will also raise the goodness of fit of the estimated model which would be reflected through increase in the value of $\overline{R}^2$.

(iii) R^2 but none of the β_i significant: In this situation, the explanatory variables as a group are able to explain a significant proportion of variation in dependent variable. As a result, R^2 becomes significant. However, the effect of each variable on the dependent variable could not be measured correctly so that none of the estimated coefficients is statistically significant. Such a result is obtained when there are high correlations between the explanatory variables, termed as the problem of multicollinearity. Obviously, the researcher would have to adopt some corrective measure for multicollinearity problem to obtain regression results in which not only R^2 but also some of the estimated coefficients are statistically significant.

(iv)   Some β_i significant, but not all, nor R^2: This is the most difficult situation as insignificant R^2 would tempt the researcher to drop the equation altogether while a few estimated coefficients being significant would provoke to retain it. Here the researcher could try alternative specification by dropping some insignificant variables, particularly those having computed-t values (absolute) less than 1. The researcher hopes that a relatively better-fit estimated equation is obtained through this process.

(v)   Neither R^2 nor any β_i significant: The implication of this is very clear. As both R^2 and all the estimated coefficients are statistically insignificant, the estimated equation is useless and should not be used for further analysis.

3.9 MULTIPLE REGRESSION EXERCISES USING EVIEWS

Suppose we want to examine the reasons behind interstate variation in total fertility rate (FERT) in India. Following the existing literature on the subject, we hypothesise that the fertility rate is inversely related to factors like female literacy rate (FLIT) and rate of urbanization (URBAN), and positively related to poverty (POV). In order to examine the validity of these hypotheses, we have gathered data on these variables for 20 major states of India which are presented in Table 3.1. We now proceed to estimate a multiple regression model using EViews to see the extent to which these are the determinant(s) of fertility rate in India.

Table 3.3 Total Fertility Rate (TFR), Female Literacy Rate (FLIT), Headcount Poverty Ratio (POV), and Percentage of Urban Population (URBAN) in Major States of India

State	TFR	FLIT	URBAN	POV
Andhra Pradesh	1.8	50.4	27.3	15.8
Assam	2.4	54.6	12.9	19.7
Bihar	4.0	33.1	10.5	41.4
Chhattisgarh	2.6	51.9	20.1	40.9
Gujarat	2.4	57.8	37.4	16.8
Haryana	2.7	55.7	28.9	10.0
Himachal Pradesh	1.9	67.4	9.8	14.0
Jammu & Kashmir	2.4	43.0	24.8	5.4
Jharkhand	3.3	38.9	22.2	40.3
Karnataka	2.1	56.9	34.0	25.0
Kerala	1.9	87.7	26.0	15.0
Madhya Pradesh	3.1	50.3	26.5	38.3
Maharashtra	2.1	67.0	42.4	30.7
Orissa	2.4	50.5	15.0	46.4
Punjab	2.0	63.4	33.9	8.4
Rajasthan	3.2	43.9	23.4	22.1
Tamil Nadu	1.8	64.4	44.0	22.5
Uttar Pradesh	3.8	42.2	20.8	32.8
Uttarakhand	2.6	59.6	25.7	39.6
West Bengal	2.3	59.6	28.0	24.7

Sources: (i) TFR from EPWRF (2010–11); (ii) URBAN and FLIT from Census of India (2001); and (iii) POV from Planning Commission (2011).

Note: Data for TFR are for 2005–06, FLIT, and URBAN for 2001 and POV (under Lakdawala methodology) for 2004–05.

Steps in EViews

Steps 1 and 2: Same as in SLRM.

Step 3: Write **tfr c flit pov urban** in the 'Equation Estimation' dialog box. Note that the options for OLS [LS – Least Squares (NLS and ARMA)] and full sample range are continued with.

Step 4: Click **OK** to obtain the multiple regression output as shown in Screenshot 3.1.

Presentation and Interpretation of Multiple Regression Results

We may present our multiple regression results in a summary form in the following manner.

$$\widehat{TFR} = 4.180 - 0.031 * FLIT + 0.013\, POV - 0.009\, URBAN$$
$$(6.755)(-3.451) \qquad (1.521) \qquad (-0.849)$$
$$R^2 = 0.64 \quad \overline{R}^2 = 0.57 \quad F = 9.36^*$$
$$D - W = 2.07 \quad n = 20$$

Notes: Figures in parentheses are computed-*t* values
* indicates significance at 1% level

Screenshot 3.1   Multiple Regression Output Using EViews

| View | Proc | Object | | Print | Name | Freeze | | Estimate | Forecast |

Dependent Variable: TFR
Method: Least Squares
Date: 08/23/13   Time: 14:58
Sample: 1 20
Included observations: 20

Variable	Coefficient	Std. Error	t-Statistic	Prob.
C	4.180282	0.618835	6.755082	0.0000
FLIT	-0.031433	0.009108	-3.451111	0.0033
POV	0.012902	0.008478	1.521838	0.1476
URBAN	-0.009444	0.011123	-0.849113	0.4083

R-squared	0.637060	Mean dependent var		2.540500
Adjusted R-squared	0.569009	S.D. dependent var		0.644160
S.E. of regression	0.422890	Akaike info criterion		1.293448
Sum squared resid	2.861377	Schwarz criterion		1.492594
Log likelihood	-8.934478	Hannan-Quinn criter.		1.332323
F-statistic	9.361493	Durbin-Watson stat		2.074423
Prob(F-statistic)	0.000827			

It is to be remembered that *each estimated coefficient in the above model represents the partial (or marginal) effect of change in its associated explanatory variable on the dependent variable, holding constant the effect of other explanatory variables. This is why the estimated coefficients in a multiple regression model are called partial regression coefficients.* It is clear from the above results that a one-point increase in the value of FLIT would reduce TFR by nearly 0.031 point. It is also clear that among three factors considered, the marginal effect of FLIT on TFR has been the highest, followed by POV and URBAN.

Further, the above results show that among various determinants of fertility rate, only the female literacy rate appears to be negatively and statistically significantly related to fertility rate in India. Although the estimated coefficients of two other factors (POV and URBAN) have expected signs (as per our hypotheses), they are not found to be statistically significant. The value of R^2 for the estimated model is nearly 0.64 which implies that the three factors (explanatory variables) together explained nearly 64% of total variation in fertility rate. The computed value of R^2 is statistically significant, which is revealed by the statistical significance of computed-F value. This latter aspect further reveals that there is overall significance for our estimated model.

However, it is possible to improve the fit of the estimated model (as revealed by $\bar{R}^2$) by dropping the URBAN variable as the absolute value of computed-t of this variable is less than 1.0. When we re-estimated the model by dropping this variable, the following results were obtained.

$$\widehat{TFR} = 4.046 - 0.034 * FLIT + 0.014\, POV$$
$$(6.819)(-3.959) \qquad (1.679)$$
$$R^2 = 0.62 \quad \overline{R}^2 = 0.58 \quad F = 13.91^*$$
$$D - W = 2.20 \quad n = 20$$

Notes: Figures in parentheses are computed-t values
* indicates significance at 1% level

It is clear that compared with the previous model, this model provides a better fit estimated equation as the value of $\overline{R}^2$ has been improved.

The obvious conclusion that follows from this exercise is that, among all factors, literacy rate of females is most important in reducing fertility rate in India, and any improvement in the literacy rate of females is likely to further reduce fertility rate in the states of India. Although reduction in poverty is also likely to reduce the fertility rate, such a relation does not appear to be statistically significant.

Omitted/Redundant Variables Tests in EViews

We can easily perform omitted/redundant variables test using EViews.

OMITTED VARIABLE TEST

To perform the omitted variable test, we first estimate a model and then make a post facto investigation of whether any (relevant) variable(s) contained in our dataset (workfile) got omitted from the model. To illustrate this test, suppose we regress TFR on POV and URBAN following the steps mentioned above. The resulting regression output is presented in Table 3.4.

Now to test whether a relevant variable like FLIT got omitted from our model, we click **View/Coefficient Diagnostics/Omitted Variables Test—Likelihood Ratio ...** from the output window, which opens a new dialog box where we put the name of the variable **FLIT** and click **OK**.[10] This produces the test output as shown in Table 3.5. It is seen that EViews reports three statistics (i.e., t, F, and LR with their respective p-values) to test the validity of the null hypothesis (H_N) that FLIT is not an omitted variable. The *decision rule* here is that if the computed values of t, F, and LR are statistically significant (which is understood from their p-values), we reject the H_N and conclude that the variable in question is an omitted variable. As per our results, the computed values of t, F, and LR are statistically significant (as p-value = 0.00 for all) and hence, we reject H_N and conclude that FLIT is indeed an

---

[10] Note that we can also test whether two or more relevant explanatory variables are omitted from our model by putting their names in this dialog box (here a space must be provided between two variables). Obviously, in that case, we must first estimate the model excluding these variables and then run the omitted variable test.

Table 3.4   Results of Regression of TFR on POV and URBAN

Dependent Variable: TFR				
Method: Least Squares				
Date: 08/23/13 Time: 15:01				
Sample: 1 20				
Included Observations: 20				
Variable	Coefficient	Std. Error	t-Statistic	Prob.
C	2.532266	0.504325	5.021097	0.0001
POV	0.022157	0.010305	2.150104	0.0462
URBAN	−0.021673	0.013509	−1.604272	0.1271
R-squared	0.366894	Mean dependent var		2.540500
Adjusted R-squared	0.292411	S.D. dependent var		0.644160
S.E. of regression	0.541857	Akaike info criterion		1.749850
Sum squared resid	4.991344	Schwarz criterion		1.899210
Log likelihood	−14.49850	Hannan-Quinn criter.		1.779007
F-statistic	4.925864	Durbin-Watson stat		2.550972
Prob(F-statistic)	0.020538			

Source: This table represents the output obtained by the author after application of the EViews software.

omitted variable and is important in determining the value of the dependent variable (TFR) of our model.

In this situation, to overcome the 'omitted variable bias', we would like to include this variable in the model. The EViews does this by estimating the model again incorporating this variable, the results of which are reported in the lower segment of the test output (Table 3.5 below).

REDUNDANT VARIABLE TEST

Here we first estimate a model by incorporating all explanatory variables and then make an investigation of whether any particular explanatory variable(s) may be considered as redundant and hence unimportant in determining the value of the dependent variable. For instance, from our regression results reported in Screenshot 3.1, it appeared that URBAN is an unimportant variable (which has absolute value of computed-t less than 1) and we will do better by dropping this variable (as this will improve the value of $\bar{R}^2$). In other words, this variable appears to be a redundant variable. In order to confirm this, we may run the redundant variable test.

As already stated, we estimate the complete model by incorporating all the explanatory variables. Now to test whether URBAN is a redundant variable, we click **View/Coefficient Diagnostics/Redundant Variables Test—Likelihood Ratio...** from the output window (Screenshot 3.1), which opens a new dialog box where we put the name of the variable **URBAN** and click **OK**.[11] The resulting test results are displayed in Table 3.6. Here again

---

[11] The redundancy of more than one variable can also be tested simultaneously by putting their names in this dialog box.

Table 3.5   Results of Omitted Variable Test

Omitted Variables Test
Equation: UNTITLED
Specification: TFR C POV URBAN
Omitted Variables: FLIT

	Value	Df	Probability
t-statistic	3.451111	16	0.0033
F-statistic	11.91017	(1, 16)	0.0033
Likelihood ratio	11.12804	1	0.0009

F-test summary:

	Sum of Sq.	Df	Mean Squares
Test SSR	2.129967	1	2.129967
Restricted SSR	4.991344	17	0.293608
Unrestricted SSR	2.861377	16	0.178836
Unrestricted SSR	2.861377	16	0.178836

LR test summary:

	Value	Df
Restricted LogL	−14.49850	17
Unrestricted LogL	−8.934478	16

Unrestricted Test Equation:
Dependent Variable: TFR
Method: Least Squares
Date: 08/23/13   Time: 15:04
Sample: 1 20
Included observations: 20

Variable	Coefficient	Std. Error	t-Statistic	Prob.
C	4.180282	0.618835	6.755082	0.0000
POV	0.012902	0.008478	1.521838	0.1476
URBAN	−0.009444	0.011123	−0.849113	0.4083
FLIT	−0.031433	0.009108	−3.451111	0.0033

R-squared	0.637060	Mean dependent var	2.540500
Adjusted R-squared	0.569009	S.D. dependent var	0.644160
S.E. of regression	0.422890	Akaike info criterion	1.293448
Sum squared resid	2.861377	Schwarz criterion	1.492594
Log likelihood	−8.934478	Hannan-Quinn criter.	1.332323
F-statistic	9.361493	Durbin-Watson stat	2.074423
Prob(F-statistic)	0.000827		

Source: Same as for Table 3.2.

we have three statistics (t, F, and LR) to test the validity of the 'H$_N$: URBAN is a redundant variable'. The *decision rule* is that if the computed values of t, F, and LR are statistically significant, we reject the H$_N$ and conclude that the variable in question is not a redundant variable. Our results show that the computed values of t, F and LR are statistically insignificant (as p-value > 0.10 for all) and hence we accept the H$_N$ and conclude that URBAN is a redundant variable. Obviously, in this situation, we would like to drop this variable from our model. The results of regression excluding this redundant variable have been reported in the lower segment of the redundant variable test output.

Table 3.6   Results of Redundant Variable Test

Redundant Variables Test
Equation: UNTITLED
Specification: TFR C FLIT POV URBAN
Redundant Variables: URBAN

	Value	Df	Probability
t-statistic	0.849113	16	0.4083
F-statistic	0.720992	(1, 16)	0.4083
Likelihood ratio	0.881525	1	0.3478

F-test summary:

	Sum of Sq.	Df	Mean squares
Test SSR	0.128939	1	0.128939
Restricted SSR	2.990316	17	0.175901
Unrestricted SSR	2.861377	16	0.178836
Unrestricted SSR	2.861377	16	0.178836

LR test summary:

	Value	Df
Restricted LogL	−9.375240	17
Unrestricted LogL	−8.934478	16

Restricted Test Equation:
Dependent Variable: TFR
Method: Least Squares
Date: 08/23/13 Time: 15:05
Sample: 1 20
Included observations: 20

Variable	Coefficient	Std. Error	t-Statistic	Prob.
C	4.045980	0.593351	6.818865	0.0000
FLIT	−0.033896	0.008562	−3.958762	0.0010
POV	0.013964	0.008316	1.679092	0.1114

R-squared	0.620706	Mean dependent var	2.540500
Adjusted R-squared	0.576083	S.D. dependent var	0.644160
S.E. of regression	0.419405	Akaike info criterion	1.237524
Sum squared resid	2.990316	Schwarz criterion	1.386884
Log likelihood	−9.375240	Hannan-Quinn criter.	1.266681
F-statistic	13.91004	Durbin-Watson stat	2.195305
Prob(F-statistic)	0.000264		

Source: Same as for Table 3.2.

THE WALD TEST OF COEFFICIENT RESTRICTIONS

Suppose we want to test, in respect of our regression output in Screenshot 3.1, whether the effects of FLIT and POV on TFR are same/identical.[12] Here we may apply the Wald test which can also be performed easily using EViews. For this, we click **View/Coefficient Diagnostics/Wald Test – Coefficient Restrictions…** from output window (Screenshot 3.1), which opens a new dialog box where we write **c(2)=c(3)** and click **OK**.[13] The resulting test output is in Table 3.7. Now as the computed value of *F*-statistic (which is equivalent of Chi-square statistic) is statistically significant (*p*-value = 0.00), we reject the 'H$_N$: c(2)=c(3)' and conclude that this restriction is not valid and hence the effects of FLIT and POV on TFR are not same.

Table 3.7   Results of Wald Test for Equivalence of Two Parameters

Wald Test:			
Equation: Untitled			
Test Statistic	Value	*df*	Probability
t-statistic	−4.306575	16	0.0005
F-statistic	18.54659	(1, 16)	0.0005
Chi-square	18.54659	1	0.0000
Null Hypothesis: C(2)=C(3)			
Null Hypothesis Summary:			
Normalized Restriction (= 0)		Value	Std. Err.
C(2)−C(3)		−0.044335	0.010295
Restrictions are linear in coefficients.			

Source: Same as for Table 3.2.

3.10 QUESTIONS AND ASSIGNMENTS

A. Multiple-Choice Questions
Tick ($\sqrt{}$) the correct answer.
   (i)   The multiple regression technique was first used by
        (a) R. Benini
        (b) Carl Friedrich Gauss
        (c) Francis Galton
        (d) L.R. Klein
   (ii) Adjusted-R^2 is developed by
        (a) G.U. Yule
        (b) L.R. Klein
        (c) Henry Theil
        (d) Trygve Haavelmo

---

[12] This is same as testing equivalence of two parameters in a multiple regression model.

[13] The coefficients of three explanatory variables FLIT, POV, and URBAN are algebraically represented as c(2), c(3), and c(4), respectively; c(1) represents the intercept.

(iii)   The estimated regression models having different number of explanatory variables are compared on the basis of
    (a) r^2-statistic
    (b) R^2-statistic
    (c) $\bar{R}^2$-statistic
    (d) χ^2-statistic

(iv)   Addition of explanatory variables in a regression model increases the value of
    (a) TSS
    (b) ESS
    (c) RSS
    (d) Both TSS and ESS

(v)   The model selection criterion that imposes larger penalty for inclusion of additional explanatory variable in the model is
    (a) Akaike Information Criterion
    (b) Schwartz Bayesian Criterion
    (c) Hannan-Quinn Criterion
    (d) $\bar{R}^2$

(vi)   The overall significance of an estimated multiple regression model is tested by using
    (a) t-test
    (b) Chi-square test
    (c) Wald test
    (d) F-test

(vii)   For $R^2 = 0.60$, k (no. of regressors) = 2 and n (sample size) = 10, the $\bar{R}^2$ is
    (a) 0.56
    (b) 0.55
    (c) 0.54
    (d) 0.53

(viii) If, in a multivariate regression model with significant F-value, all the estimated parameters have computed-t values less than 1, then the model is likely to have
    (a) A problem of multicollinearity
    (b) Some or all the regressors are linearly dependent
    (c) Partial correlation for each regressor is insignificant
    (d) All of the above

B. General Questions
(i)   Define the following.
    (a) Overall significance of estimated multiple regression
    (b) Goodness of fit of multiple regressions
    (c) Adjusted-R^2
    (d) Restricted model
    (e) Unrestricted model
    (f) Wald test

(g) Lagrange Multiplier test
(h) The likelihood function
(i) Likelihood ratio test
(ii)	What is multiple regression? How does it differ from simple regression?
(iii)	Consider the general linear model

$$Y = X\beta + \varepsilon$$

[the symbols have their usual meanings]
State the assumptions that are necessary to estimate β by applying the ordinary least-squares (OLS) method. Also prove that the OLS estimators of β are BLUE.
(iv)	How would you test statistical significance of individual partial regression coefficients in a multiple regression model?
(v)	State the usefulness of the R^2-statistic as a measure of goodness of fit. What is adjusted-R^2? How would you examine overall statistical significance of your estimated regression model?
(vi)	Suppose you estimated a multiple regression model and found the R^2 but none of the βs are significant. How would you interpret this result? What would be your response in this situation?
(vii)	How would you examine the relevance of an additional explanatory variable in the context of multiple regression exercises? Explain the test procedure and the decision rules here.
(viii)	Suppose we increase the number of explanatory variable in a multiple regression model. What will happen to the values of R^2 and Adjusted-R^2?
(ix)	Define the R^2 and $\bar{R}^2$ statistics. State the relation between R^2 and F statistics?
(x)	The following estimated equation was obtained by OLS regression using quarterly data for 1960 to 1975 inclusive ($n = 64$).

$$\hat{Y}_t = 2.20 + 0.104\,X_{1t} + 3.48\,X_{2t} + 0.34\,X_{3t}$$
$$(3.4) \quad (0.005) \quad (2.2) \quad (0.15)$$

Standard errors are in parentheses, the explained sum squares (ESS) was 112.5 and the residual sum squares (RSS) was 19.5.
(a)	Which of the slope coefficients are statistically significantly different from 0 at 5% level of significance?
(b)	Calculate the values of R^2 and $\bar{R}^2$ and interpret.
(c)	Calculate the F-value and interpret it.
(xi)	From the data for 45 developed countries, the following regression results were obtained.

$$\widehat{\log C} = 4.30 - 1.34\,\log P + 0.17\,\log Y$$
$$(0.09) \quad (0.32) \qquad (0.20) \qquad \bar{R}^2 = 0.27$$
(standard errors are in parentheses)

where C = cigarette consumption (packs per year), P = real price of cigarette per pack, and Y = per capita real income.

(a) Interpret the above results.

(b) What is the elasticity of demand for cigarettes with respect to price? Is it statistically significant? If so, is it statistically different from zero?

(c) How would you retrieve R^2 from the value of $\bar{R}^2$?

(xii) The model

$$Y_t = \alpha + \beta_1 X_{1t} + \beta_2 X_{2t} + \beta_3 X_{3t} + U_t$$

was estimated by ordinary least squares from 26 observations. The results were

$$\hat{Y}_t = 2.0 + 3.5\, X_{1t} - 0.7\, X_{2t} + 2.0\, X_{3t} \qquad R^2 = 0.982$$
$$\qquad\quad (1.9) \quad\;\; (2.2) \quad\;\; (1.5)$$

The same model was estimated with the restriction $\beta_1 = \beta_2$. The results were

$$\hat{Y}_t = 1.5 + 3\,(X_{1t} + X_{2t}) + 0.6\, X_{3t} \quad R^2 = 0.876$$
$$\qquad\quad (2.7) \qquad\qquad\quad (2.4)$$

(in both the models, the t-ratios are in parentheses)

(a) Test the significance of the restriction $\beta_1 = \beta_2$.

(b) Suppose X_{2t} is dropped from the equation. Would the $\bar{R}^2$ rise or fall?

(c) Would the R^2 rise or fall if X_{2t} is dropped?

(xiii) The following regression equation represents a production function for Q.

$$\log Q = 1.37 + 0.632 \log K + 0.452 \log L$$
$$\qquad\qquad (0.257) \qquad\quad (0.219)$$
$$R^2 = 0.98 \qquad Cov(\beta_K, \beta_L) = 0.055$$

The sample size is 33 and the standard errors are given in parentheses. Examine the null hypothesis that the capital (K) and labour (L) elasticities of output are identical.

(Some selected t-values for 30 degrees of freedom are: $t_{0.005} = 2.750$; $t_{0.025} = 2.042$; $t_{0.05} = 1.697$; and $t_{0.10} = 1.310$)

(xiv) Your friend gives you the following results of two different regression problems. In which case could you be certain that an error had been committed? Explain.

(a) $R^2_{Y.12} = 0.96$ and $R^2_{Y.123} = 0.94$

(b) $\bar{R}^2_{Y.12} = 0.93$ and $\bar{R}^2_{Y.123} = 0.90$

(xv) You are given the following regression results.

$$\hat{Y}_i = 16899 - 2978.5X_{1i}$$
$$(8.5152)(-4.7280) \qquad R^2 = 0.6149$$
$$\hat{Y}_i = 9734.2 - 3782.2X_{1i} + 2815X_{2i}$$
$$(3.3705)(-6.6070) \quad (2.9712) \qquad R^2 = 0.7706$$

[the figures in parentheses are computed-t values]

(a) Find out the sample size underlying these results.
(b) Interpret the results.
(c) Which model would you prefer? Why?

(xvi) Suppose you want to estimate the following log-linear Cobb-Douglas production function.

$$\log Q = \alpha + \beta_1 \log L + \beta_2 \log K + U$$

where Q = output, L = labour units, K = value of capital, and U is the stochastic disturbance term.

How would you examine equivalence of elasticities of labour and capital in respect of your estimated model? Explain the steps involved and *decision rules* in the test chosen for this purpose.

(xvii) Which test would you employ to examine the redundancy of explanatory variable(s) in respect of your estimated multiple regression model? Explain the steps involved therein.

(xviii) Indicate whether the following statements are true (T), false (F), or uncertain (U) and give brief explanation.

(a) Addition of an explanatory variable in a regression model is justifiable when the absolute value of computed-t of the estimated coefficient of the variable is greater than 1.

(b) The value of R^2 always rises with addition of explanatory variables in the model.

(c) The value of $\bar{R}^2$ always rises with addition of explanatory variables in the model.

(d) The value of R^2 for the restricted model is always greater than the value of R^2 for the unrestricted model.

(e) The coefficient of a variable in an estimated model is significantly different from zero at 20% level. If we drop this variable from the regression, then both R^2 and $\bar{R}^2$ will necessarily fall.

(f) In a multiple regression, it is not possible to have a high R^2 if all the partial slope coefficients are individually statistically insignificant on the basis of the usual t-test.

C. Computer Assignments

(i)   Consider the data in Table 2.3 (Chapter 2) to estimate a multiple regression model to identify the main determinants of infant mortality rate in India. Interpret the results. Which factor(s) do you consider to be most important in reducing infant mortality in India and why?

(ii) Estimate a multiple regression model using data presented in Table 2.4 (Chapter 2) to find out the main determinants(s) of child labour in India. Also perform a 'redundant variable test' to identify presence of redundant variable(s), if any, in your estimated model.

(iii) Estimate the following multiple regression model using data given in Table 2.5 (Chapter 2).

$$\ln(FGN) = \alpha + \beta_1 \ln(IRRI) + \beta_2 \ln(FERT) + \beta_3 \ln(CREDIT) + U$$

Interpret your regression results. Do you think that the elasticities of foodgrains yield (FGN) to irrigation (IRRI) and fertilizers use (FERT) are same in India?

Answers to Multiple-Choice Questions

(i) (a); (ii) (c); (iii) (c); (iv) (b); (v) (b); (vi) (d); (vii) (b); (viii) (d).

APPENDIX 3.1: THE GENERAL LINEAR REGRESSION MODEL

Model Specification

The general population regression model involving the dependent variable Y_i and independent/explanatory variables $X_{1i}, X_{2i}, ..., X_{ki}$ is specified as

$$Y_i = \beta_0 + \beta_1 X_{1i} + \beta_2 X_{2i} + ... + \beta_k X_{ki} + \varepsilon_i$$

This equation gives the following set of simultaneous equations.

$$Y_1 = \beta_0 + \beta_1 X_{11} + \beta_2 X_{21} + ... + \beta_k X_{k1} + \varepsilon_1$$
$$Y_2 = \beta_0 + \beta_1 X_{12} + \beta_2 X_{22} + ... + \beta_k X_{k2} + \varepsilon_2$$
$$\vdots$$
$$Y_n = \beta_0 + \beta_1 X_{1n} + \beta_2 X_{2n} + ... + \beta_k X_{kn} + \varepsilon_n$$

This system of equations may be written in the matrix form as

$$\begin{bmatrix} Y_1 \\ Y_2 \\ . \\ . \\ . \\ Y_n \end{bmatrix} = \begin{bmatrix} 1 & X_{11} & X_{21} & .... & X_{k1} \\ 1 & X_{12} & X_{22} & .... & X_{k2} \\ . \\ . \\ . \\ 1 & X_{1n} & X_{2n} & .... & X_{kn} \end{bmatrix} \begin{bmatrix} \beta_0 \\ \beta_1 \\ . \\ . \\ . \\ \beta_k \end{bmatrix} + \begin{bmatrix} \varepsilon_1 \\ \varepsilon_2 \\ . \\ . \\ . \\ \varepsilon_n \end{bmatrix}$$

More compactly, we write

$$Y = X\beta + \varepsilon \tag{A3.1}$$

where

Y is an $(n \times 1)$ vector of observations on dependent variable.

X is an $[n \times (k + 1)]$ matrix of n observations on k variables, $X_{1i}, X_{2i}, ..., X_{ki}$, and the first column of 1s represents the intercept term.

β is a $[(k + 1) \times 1]$ vector of parameters to be estimated and

ε is an $(n \times 1)$ vector of disturbances.

Assumptions

(1)   *Zero Mean of ε*:
        This implies that

$$E(\varepsilon) = E \begin{bmatrix} \varepsilon_1 \\ \varepsilon_2 \\ . \\ . \\ . \\ \varepsilon_n \end{bmatrix} = \begin{bmatrix} E(\varepsilon_1) \\ E(\varepsilon_2) \\ . \\ . \\ . \\ E(\varepsilon_n) \end{bmatrix} = \begin{bmatrix} 0 \\ 0 \\ . \\ . \\ . \\ 0 \end{bmatrix} = 0$$

(2)   *Constant Variance of ε*:
        Here

$$Var(\varepsilon) = E(\varepsilon\varepsilon') = E \begin{bmatrix} \varepsilon_1 \\ \varepsilon_2 \\ . \\ . \\ \varepsilon_n \end{bmatrix} \begin{bmatrix} \varepsilon_1 & \varepsilon_2 & . & . & . & \varepsilon_n \end{bmatrix}$$

$$= E \begin{bmatrix} \varepsilon_1^2 & \varepsilon_1\varepsilon_2 & . & . & . & \varepsilon_1\varepsilon_n \\ \varepsilon_1\varepsilon_2 & \varepsilon_2^2 & . & . & . & \varepsilon_2\varepsilon_n \\ . & & & & & \\ . & & & & & \\ . & & & & & \\ \varepsilon_1\varepsilon_n & \varepsilon_2\varepsilon_n & . & . & . & \varepsilon_n^2 \end{bmatrix}$$

$$= \begin{bmatrix} E(\varepsilon_1^2) & E(\varepsilon_1\varepsilon_2) & . & . & . & E(\varepsilon_1\varepsilon_n) \\ E(\varepsilon_1\varepsilon_2) & E(\varepsilon_2^2) & . & . & . & E(\varepsilon_2\varepsilon_n) \\ . & & & & & \\ . & & & & & \\ . & & & & & \\ E(\varepsilon_1\varepsilon_n) & E(\varepsilon_2\varepsilon_n) & . & . & . & E(\varepsilon_n^2) \end{bmatrix}$$

Using the assumptions that (i) each ε distribution has the same variance (σ^2), and (ii) all disturbances are pair-wise uncorrelated [i.e., $E(\varepsilon_i\varepsilon_j) = 0$ for $i \neq j$], we can write

$$Var(\varepsilon) = \begin{bmatrix} \sigma^2 & 0 & . & . & . & 0 \\ 0 & \sigma^2 & . & . & . & 0 \\ . & & & & & \\ . & & & & & \\ . & & & & & \\ 0 & 0 & . & . & . & \sigma^2 \end{bmatrix}$$

$$= \sigma^2 \begin{bmatrix} 1 & 0 & . & . & . & 0 \\ 0 & 1 & . & . & . & 0 \\ . & & & & & \\ . & & & & & \\ . & & & & & \\ 0 & 0 & . & . & . & 1 \end{bmatrix}$$

$$= \sigma^2 I \text{ where } I \text{ is an } (n \times n) \text{ identity matrix.}$$

(3)   *Non-stochastic Xs*: This implies that all explanatory variables are non-stochastic and hence, independent of the εs.

(4)   *Linear independence of Xs*: This means that the explanatory variables do not form a linearly dependent set. In other words, rank of X matrix [denoted by $\rho(X)$] must be equal to number of explanatory variables in the model, which is k.

(5)   *The ε vector has a multivariate normal distribution.*

OLS Estimation

Given the population regression model

$$Y = X\beta + \varepsilon$$

the sample regression model is

$$Y = X\hat{\beta} + e$$

Here e is an estimate of ε. It follows that

$$e = Y - X\hat{\beta}$$

The least-squares estimators are obtained by minimizing the sum of error squares which is

$$\sum e_i^2 = e_1^2 + e_2^2 + \; .... \; + e_n^2$$

$$= \begin{bmatrix} e_1 & e_2 & . & . & . & e_n \end{bmatrix} \begin{bmatrix} e_1 \\ e_2 \\ . \\ . \\ . \\ e_n \end{bmatrix}$$

$$= e'e$$

$$= (Y - X\hat{\beta})'(Y - X\hat{\beta})$$

$$= (Y' - \hat{\beta}'X')(Y - X\hat{\beta})$$

$$= Y'Y - Y'X\hat{\beta} - \hat{\beta}'X'Y + \hat{\beta}'X'X\hat{\beta}$$

$$= Y'Y - (\hat{\beta}'X'Y)' - \hat{\beta}'X'Y + \hat{\beta}'X'X\hat{\beta}$$

$$= Y'Y - 2\hat{\beta}'X'Y + \hat{\beta}'X'X\hat{\beta} \qquad (\because \; \hat{\beta}'X'Y \text{ is a scalar})$$

[*The rules of matrix transposition applied are* $(AB)' = B'A'$ *and* $(ABC)' = C'B'A'$.]

For least-squares,

$$\frac{\partial \sum e_i^2}{\partial \hat{\beta}} = 0$$

$$\Rightarrow \frac{\partial}{\partial \hat{\beta}}(Y'Y - 2\hat{\beta}'X'Y + \hat{\beta}'X'X\hat{\beta}) = 0$$

$$\Rightarrow -2X'Y + 2X'X\hat{\beta} = 0$$

$$\Rightarrow (X'X)\hat{\beta} = X'Y \tag{A3.2}$$

[Two rules of differentiation used are : (i) $\dfrac{\partial}{\partial X}(X'A) = A$; and (ii) $\dfrac{\partial}{\partial X}(X'AX) = 2AX.$]

The equations contained in (A3.2) are called OLS 'normal equations' in the context of the general linear model.

Now assumption (4) ensures that $(X'X)$ is non-singular. Thus $(X'X)^{-1}$ exists. Then (A3.2) may be written as

$$\hat{\beta} = (X'X)^{-1}X'Y \qquad\qquad (A3.3)$$

The vector $\hat{\beta}$ contains estimators for all unknown parameters.

BLUE Properties
- Unbiasedness

Given the general linear model

$$Y = X\beta + \varepsilon$$

we know that

$$\hat{\beta} = (X'X)^{-1}X'Y$$

Now substituting $Y = X\beta + \varepsilon$ into the expression for $\hat{\beta}$, we obtain

$$\begin{aligned}
\hat{\beta} &= (X'X)^{-1}X'(X\beta + \varepsilon) \\
&= (X'X)^{-1}(X'X)\beta + (X'X)^{-1}X'\varepsilon \\
&= \beta + (X'X)^{-1}X'\varepsilon
\end{aligned} \qquad\qquad (A3.4)$$

Taking expectations,

$$\begin{aligned}
E(\hat{\beta}) &= E[\beta + (X'X)^{-1}X'\varepsilon] \\
&= \beta + (X'X)^{-1}X'E(\varepsilon) \\
&= \beta \qquad [\because E(\varepsilon) = 0]
\end{aligned}$$

This proves that $\hat{\beta}$ is unbiased.

- Linearity

Since $\hat{\beta} = (X'X)^{-1}X'Y$, it is clear that $\hat{\beta}$s have a linear relation with Y, with the weights being functions of the X data, which are non-stochastic.

- Bestness

From (A3.4), we have

$$\hat{\beta} = \beta + (X'X)^{-1}X'\varepsilon$$
$$\Rightarrow \hat{\beta} - \beta = (X'X)^{-1}X'\varepsilon$$

Thus,

$$
\begin{aligned}
Var(\hat{\beta}) &= E[(\hat{\beta}-\beta)(\hat{\beta}-\beta)'] \\
&= E[\{(X'X)^{-1}X'\varepsilon\}\{(X'X)^{-1}X'\varepsilon\}'] \\
&= E[(X'X)^{-1}X'\varepsilon\varepsilon'X(X'X)^{-1}] \\
&= (X'X)^{-1}X'E(\varepsilon\varepsilon')X(X'X)^{-1} \\
&= \sigma^2(X'X)^{-1}(X'X)(X'X)^{-1} \\
&= \sigma^2(X'X)^{-1}
\end{aligned}
$$

(A3.5)

(*The rules applied are: For two matrices A and B, (i) $(AB)^{-1} = B^{-1}A^{-1}$, (ii) $(A^{-1})' = (A')^{-1}$ and (iii) $A^{-1}A = I$ where I is an identity matrix.*)

To show that $Var(\hat{\beta})$ is minimum, let us consider some other estimator of the form

$$\tilde{\beta} = \hat{\beta} + CY$$

where C is a row vector whose all elements are not zero, i.e., C is not a null vector. Then

$$
\begin{aligned}
\tilde{\beta} &= \beta + (X'X)^{-1}X'\varepsilon + C(X\beta + \varepsilon) \\
&= \beta + CX\beta + [(X'X)^{-1}X' + C]\varepsilon
\end{aligned}
$$

(A3.6)

Taking expectations,

$$E(\tilde{\beta}) = \beta + CX\beta$$

This implies that $\tilde{\beta}$ is unbiased if and only if $CX = 0$. Let us make $\tilde{\beta}$ unbiased by allowing $CX = 0$ so that it becomes comparable with $\hat{\beta}$. Then equation (A3.6) becomes

$$\tilde{\beta} = \beta + [(X'X)^{-1}X' + C]\varepsilon$$
$$\Rightarrow \tilde{\beta} - \beta = [(X'X)^{-1}X' + C]\varepsilon$$

Thus,

$$
\begin{aligned}
Var(\tilde{\beta}) &= E[(\tilde{\beta}-\beta)(\tilde{\beta}-\beta)'] \\
&= E[\{(X'X)^{-1}X'+C\}\varepsilon][\{(X'X)^{-1}X'+C\}\varepsilon]' \\
&= \{(X'X)^{-1}X'+C\}E(\varepsilon\varepsilon')\{(X'X)^{-1}X'+C\}' \\
&= \sigma^2\{(X'X)^{-1}X'+C\}\{X(X'X)^{-1}+C'\} \\
&= \sigma^2\{(X'X)^{-1}(X'X)(X'X)^{-1}+(X'X)^{-1}X'C'+(CX)(X'X)^{-1}+CC'\} \\
&= \sigma^2\{(X'X)^{-1}+CC'\} \qquad [\because CX=0 \text{ and } X'C'=(CX)'=0] \\
&= \sigma^2(X'X)^{-1}+\sigma^2(CC') \\
&= Var(\hat{\beta})+\sigma^2(CC')
\end{aligned}
$$

This proves that $Var(\hat{\beta})<(Var\tilde{\beta})$, by an expression $\sigma^2(CC')$ and hence $\hat{\beta}$ is best or minimum variance estimator.

Measuring Goodness of Fit

To measure goodness of fit, we use R^2-statistic, which is computed as

$$
R^2 = \frac{ESS}{TSS}
$$

In the context of the general linear model,

$$
\begin{aligned}
TSS &= \sum y_i^2 = \sum(Y_i-\bar{Y})^2 = \sum Y_i^2 - n\bar{Y}^2 = Y'Y - n\bar{Y}^2 \\
RSS &= \sum e_i^2 \\
&= e'e \\
&= (Y-X\hat{\beta})'(Y-X\hat{\beta}) \\
&= (Y'-\hat{\beta}'X')(Y-X\hat{\beta}) \\
&= Y'Y - \hat{\beta}'X'Y - Y'X\hat{\beta} + \hat{\beta}'(X'X)\hat{\beta} \\
&= Y'Y - \hat{\beta}'X'Y - (\hat{\beta}'X'Y)' + \hat{\beta}'X'Y \qquad [\because (X'X)\hat{\beta}=X'Y] \\
&= Y'Y - \hat{\beta}'X'Y \qquad\qquad (\because \hat{\beta}'X'Y \text{ is a scalar}) \\
ESS &= Y'Y - n\bar{Y}^2 - Y'Y + \hat{\beta}'X'Y \qquad (\because ESS=TSS-RSS) \\
&= \hat{\beta}'X'Y - n\bar{Y}^2
\end{aligned}
$$

Thus,

$$
R^2 = \frac{\hat{\beta}'X'Y - n\bar{Y}^2}{Y'Y - n\bar{Y}^2} \tag{A3.7}
$$

APPENDIX 3.2: MAXIMUM LIKELIHOOD ESTIMATION METHOD

The likelihood function is defined as the joint probability distribution of the given set of data, treated as a function of some unknown coefficients. The maximum likelihood (ML) estimator of the unknown coefficients consists of the values of the coefficients that maximize the likelihood function. As the ML estimator chooses the unknown coefficients to maximize the likelihood function (which is the joint probability distribution), in effect the ML estimator chooses the values of the parameters to maximize the probability of drawing the data that are actually observed. From this perspective, we can say that the maximum likelihood estimators are the parameter values that are most likely to have generated the data.

To express the ML estimation method formally, suppose Y_i depends on X_i according to the simple relationship[14]

$$Y_i = \alpha + \beta X_i + \varepsilon_i$$

where ε_i is assumed to be normally distributed with zero mean and constant variance σ^2 [i.e., $\varepsilon_i \sim N(0, \sigma^2)$]. Given these assumptions, it can be shown that Y_i is also normally distributed with mean $\alpha + \beta X_i$ and variance σ^2. Then the joint probability density function of $Y_1, Y_2, \dots Y_n$ is written as

$$f(Y_1, Y_2, \dots Y_n \mid \alpha + \beta X_i, \sigma^2)$$

As Ys are independent, this joint probability density function can be written as a product of n individual density functions, shown as follows.

$$f(Y_1, Y_2, \dots, Y_n \mid \alpha + \beta X_i, \sigma^2) = f(Y_1 \mid \alpha + \beta X_i, \sigma^2) \cdot f(Y_2 \mid \alpha + \beta X_i, \sigma^2) \dots$$
$$f(Y_n \mid \alpha + \beta X_i, \sigma^2) \tag{A3.8}$$

where

$$f(Y_i) = \frac{1}{\sigma\sqrt{2\pi}} e^{\left\{-\frac{1}{2}\frac{(Y_i - \alpha - \beta X_i)^2}{\sigma^2}\right\}} \tag{A3.9}$$

This is the density function of a normally distributed variable with given mean and variance.

Substituting (A3.9) for each Y_i into (A3.8), we get

$$f(Y_1, Y_2, \dots Y_n \mid \alpha + \beta X_i, \sigma^2) = \frac{1}{(\sigma\sqrt{2\pi})^n} e^{\left\{-\frac{1}{2}\sum\frac{(Y_i - \alpha - \beta X_i)^2}{\sigma^2}\right\}} \tag{A3.10}$$

---

[14] The discussion that follows for the two-variable model can be easily extended to models involving three or more variables (one dependent and two or more independent).

If $Y_1, Y_2, \ldots Y_n$ are known but α, β, and σ^2 are unknown, then the function in (A3.10) is called the likelihood function (i.e., joint probability of all n sample values), and is denoted by L so that

$$L = \frac{1}{(\sigma\sqrt{2\pi})^n} e^{\left\{-\frac{1}{2}\sum \frac{(Y_i - \alpha - \beta X_i)^2}{\sigma^2}\right\}} \tag{A3.11}$$

The ML method consists of estimating the unknown parameters (α, β, and σ^2) in such a way that the value of L (which represents joint probability of observing given Ys) is maximum. So we have to differentiate the above function with respect to three unknown parameters. However, instead of maximizing the likelihood function, we maximize the logarithm of likelihood function as that is more convenient.[15] Thus, we consider

$$\ln L = -\frac{n}{2}\ln\sigma^2 - \frac{n}{2}\ln(2\pi) - \frac{1}{2}\sum\frac{(Y_i - \alpha - \beta X_i)^2}{\sigma^2} \tag{A3.12}$$

[Note: ln = natural log]

Differentiating (A3.12) partially with respect to α, β, and σ^2, setting the resulting equations equal to zero, and denoting $\tilde{\alpha}$, $\tilde{\beta}$, and $\tilde{\sigma}^2$ as ML estimators of three unknown parameters, we obtain

$$\frac{1}{\tilde{\sigma}^2}\sum(Y_i - \tilde{\alpha} - \tilde{\beta}X_i) = 0 \tag{A3.13}$$

$$\frac{1}{\tilde{\sigma}^2}\sum(Y_i - \tilde{\alpha} - \tilde{\beta}X_i)X_i = 0 \tag{A3.14}$$

$$-\frac{n}{2\tilde{\sigma}^2} + \frac{1}{2\tilde{\sigma}^4}\sum(Y_i - \tilde{\alpha} - \tilde{\beta}X_i) = 0 \tag{A3.15}$$

Simplifying equations (A3.13) and (A3.14), we get

$$\sum Y_i = n\tilde{\alpha} + \tilde{\beta}\sum X_i \tag{A3.16}$$

$$\sum X_i Y_i = \tilde{\alpha}\sum X_i + \tilde{\beta}\sum X_i^2 \tag{A3.17}$$

[15] Maximizing L is equivalent to maximizing the logarithm of L because logarithm is a monotonic increasing transformation, i.e., if $a > b$, then $\ln(a) > \ln(b)$.

These are similar to the least-squares normal equations obtained in Chapter 2. Thus, it is said that the ML estimators of α and β are the same as those for OLS estimators. Substituting the ML (= OLS) estimators into (A3.15), we obtain

$$\tilde{\sigma}^2 = \frac{1}{n}\sum(Y_i - \tilde{\alpha} - \tilde{\beta}X_i)^2$$
$$= \frac{1}{n}\sum(Y_i - \hat{\alpha} - \hat{\beta}X_i)^2$$
$$= \frac{\sum\hat{\varepsilon}_i^2}{n} \qquad\qquad (A3.18)$$

This shows that the ML estimator of σ^2 is the residual sum squares (RSS) divided by n rather than $n - 2$ (as in OLS). It can also be shown that while the OLS estimator of σ^2 (denoted by $\hat{\sigma}^2$) is unbiased, the ML estimator of σ^2 (i.e., $\tilde{\sigma}^2$) is biased. But the bias of $\tilde{\sigma}^2$ tends towards zero as sample size (n) tends towards infinity (∞) so that it is asymptotically unbiased. It can further be shown that $\tilde{\sigma}^2$ is consistent which means that as $n \to \infty$, $\tilde{\sigma}^2$ converges to its true value σ^2.

4 Heteroskedasticity

This chapter discusses the issues connected with one of the important econometric problems, namely, heteroskedasticity, observed mostly in cross-section data. Apart from defining heteroskedasticity, we note some of its possible sources. The consequences of the heteroskedasticity problem on OLS estimators have been discussed. This is followed by a discussion on the tests for heteroskedasticity. Some remedial measures for this problem have also been considered. Finally, applications of EViews software for testing heteroskedasticity and appropriately estimating unknown parameters of the model have been clarified using examples.

4.1 DEFINITION

In the context of linear regression models, one of the necessary assumptions was constancy of variance of the disturbance term for all observations. For example, for the simple two-variable model

$$Y_i = \alpha + \beta X_i + \varepsilon_i \tag{4.1}$$

we assumed that the variance of disturbance term, ε_i, is constant for all observations. This is algebraically expressed by writing

$$Var(\varepsilon_i) = E(\varepsilon_i^2) = \sigma^2 \text{ constant for all } i \tag{4.2}$$

This feature of disturbance term of the regression model is known as homoskedasticity.

However, it is quite common in regression analysis to have cases where the variance of disturbance term becomes variable rather than remaining constant. In this situation, the disturbance term is said to be heteroskedastic.[1] Thus, heteroskedasticity represents the situation where the variance of the disturbance term of the model does not remain constant and turns out to be a variable. We express this algebraically by writing

$$Var(\varepsilon_i) = E(\varepsilon_i^2) = \sigma_i^2 \tag{4.3}$$

[1] Some authors spell this word as 'heteroscedastic'. But McCulloch (1985) observed that this word has Greek origin, and the correct spelling is 'heteroskedastic', which can be split into two parts: hetero and skedastic. Here 'hetero' means unequal or different and 'skedastic' means spread or scatter.

The difference between (4.2) and (4.3) is the subscript i attached to σ^2, which means that the variance of disturbance term can change for every different observation in the sample $i = 1, 2, ..., n$.

To make the above points clearer, let us consider a scatter plot of bivariate data (X_i, Y_i) with a population regression line, as shown in Figure 4.1, and compare it with the same in Figure 4.2. It is observed that although the data points in Figure 4.1 refer to different values of X_i, they are closely concentrated around the regression line with equal spread (represented by the dashed lines) above and below the regression line. This is the situation of homoskedasticity. On the other hand, although the data points in Figure 4.2 again refer to different values of X_i, it is now observed that the higher value of X_i has higher spread of data points around the regression line. An opposite situation is displayed in Figure 4.3 where a higher value of X_i has lower spread of data points around the regression line. Both these cases represent the situation of heteroskedasticity; the former is referred to as increasing heteroskedasticity and the latter as decreasing heteroskedasticity.

Sources of Heteroskedasticity
Heteroskedasticity in data may arise due to several reasons.

(i)   When we are dealing with microeconomic or cross-section data, we are very likely to have a heteroskedasticity problem. For instance, when data are collected from a

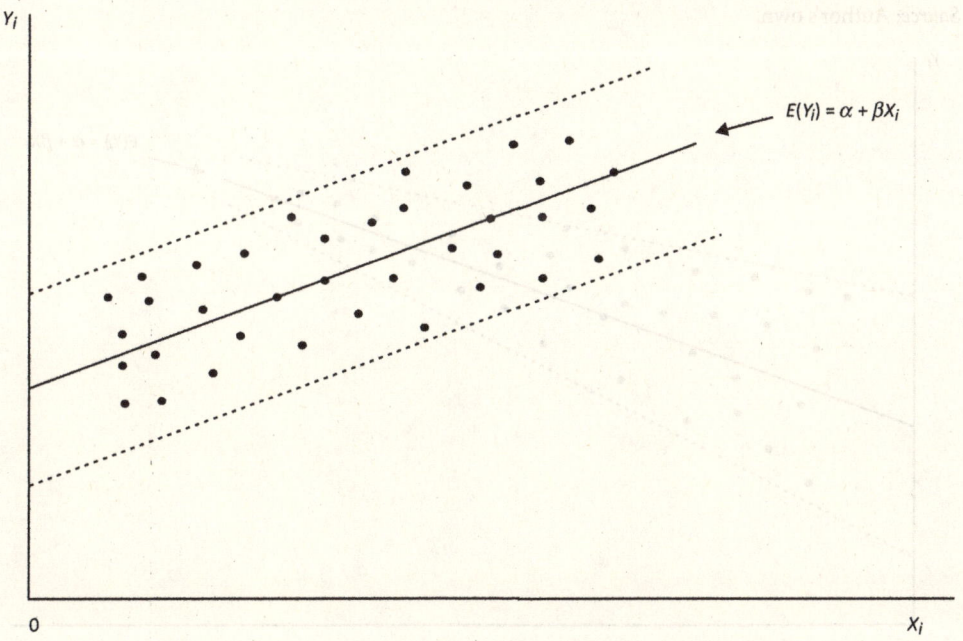

Figure 4.1   Graphical Display of Homoskedasticity Situtation

Source: Author's own.

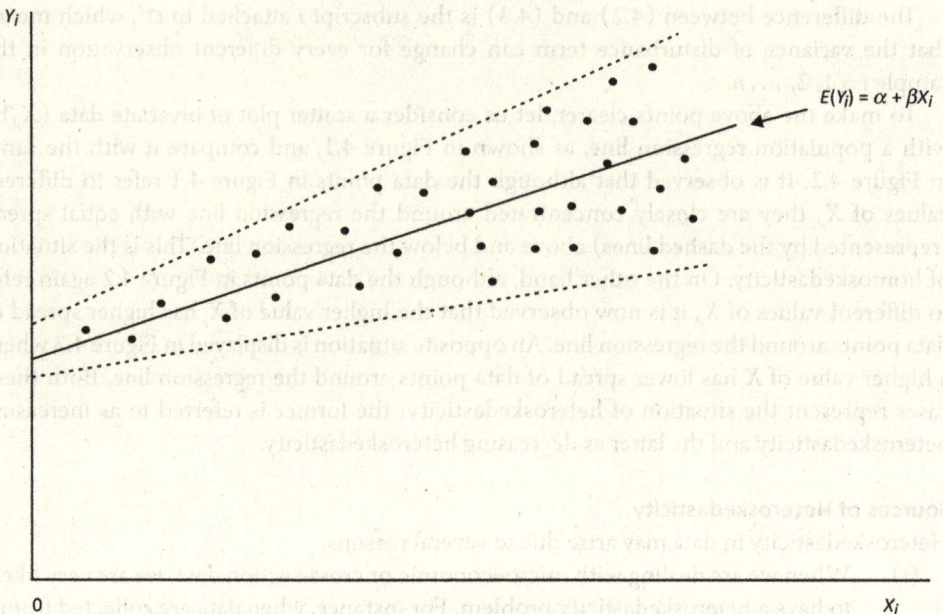

Figure 4.2   Graphical Display of Increasing Heteroskedasticity

Source: Author's own.

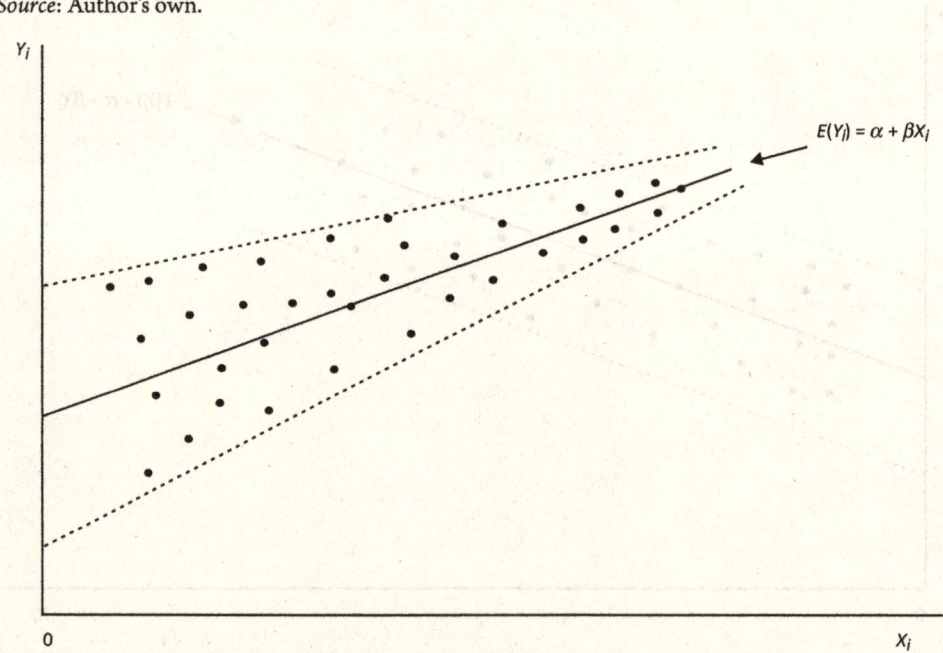

Figure 4.3   Graphical Display of Decreasing Heteroskedasticity

Source: Author's own.

cross-section of individuals on their levels of consumption and income to estimate a consumption function, we are likely to face the heteroskedasticity problem.[2] This is because the variance (or spread) of consumption at low levels of income is much less compared to variance of consumption at higher levels of income. This happens as people with low income levels do not have much flexibility in spending their income; a large proportion of it is spent on food, clothing, and transportation. On the other hand, people with high levels of income have a much wider choice and flexibility in spending; some might consume a lot while others might prefer invest-ing in share market. This will produce high variance of consumption at high levels of income. In any case, this is typically the case of 'increasing heteroskedasticity'. As an example of decreasing heteroskedasticity, we may refer to 'error-learning mod-els'. To take an example, in a regression of score performance by the students on hours taken for preparation, we are likely to observe decreasing heteroskedasticity. This is because, compared to the variance of scores at lower levels of preparation, the variance of scores will be less at higher levels of preparation.

(ii)   Presence of outliers in data may cause heteroskedasticity problem. As we know, an outlying observation is much different from the rest of the observations in the sample. Presence of such an observation, especially when the sample size is small, will create heteroskedasticity problem.

(iii)   Heteroskedasticity may arise if some relevant variables have been mistakenly omitted so that the model is incorrectly specified. For instance, if we do not include the prices of competing or complementary goods in the demand function for a commodity, the residuals obtained from the regression may contain non-constant variance. However, when the omitted variables are included in the model, the non-constancy of variance may disappear.

(iv)   Inclusion of explanatory variables in the model whose distributions are skewed may cause heteroskedasticity problem. The examples of such variables are income, wealth, etc.

(v)   Heteroskedasticity may also arise due to incorrect data transformations (e.g., ratios, first-differences, etc.) and incorrect functional forms (e.g., linear instead of log-linear models).

4.2 CONSEQUENCES OF HETEROSKEDASTICITY

As stated above, heteroskedasticity represents a situation where the variance of the disturbance of the model becomes a variable. To understand the consequences of

---

[2] This is not to say that we never have a heteroskedasticity problem in time-series data. What we are saying is that the possibility of having this problem is less in time-series data compared to cross-sectional data. This is because time series data are of an aggregative nature. For instance, if Y_t represents aggregate consumption level in different years, it is quite possible the level of consumption in recent years is of a similar order of magnitude as the aggregate consumption level, say 20 years ago, and the same is true of X_t (income). Using such data, we are likely to observe constant variance of the disturbance term.

heteroskedasticity, we examine its effects on the properties of the OLS estimators. Specifically, we check whether OLS estimators continue to remain unbiased and minimum-variance or best when the disturbance term of the model is heteroskedastic. For simplicity, let us check these properties using a two-variable linear model. In the appendix to this chapter we clarify the effect of heteroskedasticity on the variance–covariance matrix of disturbance term in the context of the general linear model.

Unbiasedness

We know from Chapter 2 (Section 2.6) that, for the two-variable model like (4.1), the OLS estimator of β is given by

$$\hat{\beta} = \frac{\sum x_i y_i}{\sum x_i^2} \quad \text{where } x_i = X_i - \bar{X} \text{ and } y_i = Y_i - \bar{Y}$$

$$= \beta + \frac{\sum x_i \varepsilon_i}{\sum x_i^2} \tag{4.4}$$

Taking expectations,

$$E(\hat{\beta}) = E\left(\beta + \frac{\sum x_i \varepsilon_i}{\sum x_i^2}\right) = \beta \quad [\because E(\varepsilon_i) = 0]$$

This shows that $\hat{\beta}$ remains unbiased when the disturbance term of the model (ε_i) is heteroskedastic.

Bestness

We know that

$$Var(\hat{\beta}) = E(\hat{\beta} - \beta)^2$$

$$= E\left(\frac{\sum x_i \varepsilon_i}{\sum x_i^2}\right)^2$$

$$= \frac{1}{(\sum x_i^2)^2} E(\sum x_i \varepsilon_i)^2$$

$$= \frac{1}{(\sum x_i^2)^2} E\left(\sum x_i^2 \varepsilon_i^2 + 2\sum_{i<j} x_i x_j \varepsilon_i \varepsilon_j\right)$$

$$= \frac{1}{(\sum x_i^2)^2} \sum x_i^2 E(\varepsilon_i^2) \quad [\because E(\varepsilon_i \varepsilon_j) = 0]$$

$$= \frac{\sum x_i^2 \sigma_i^2}{(\sum x_i^2)^2} \quad [\because E(\varepsilon_i^2) = \sigma_i^2]$$

$$= \frac{\sum x_i^2 k_i \sigma^2}{(\sum x_i^2)^2} \tag{4.5}$$

(Supposing that $\sigma_i^2 = k_i \sigma^2$, where k_i is a variable with unknown values.)

This is different from the situation of homoskedasticity where

$$Var(\hat{\beta}) = \frac{\sigma^2}{\sum x_i^2} \text{ and } \sigma_i^2 = \sigma^2 \text{ for all } i. \tag{4.6}$$

Thus,

$$Var(\hat{\beta})\Big|_{Heteroskedasticity} > Var(\hat{\beta})\Big|_{Homoskedasticity}$$

So, $\hat{\beta}$ is no longer a minimum variance and hence best estimator. Further, as $\hat{\beta}$ is only unbiased and not the best, it becomes inefficient.

Consistency

To prove the consistency property for $\hat{\beta}$ under the presence of heteroskedasticity,[3] suppose that $\theta_i = \sigma_i^2 - \bar{\sigma}^2$, where $\bar{\sigma}^2 = \sum \sigma_i^2 / n$ so that $\sum \theta_i = 0$. Then $Var(\hat{\beta})$ may be written as

$$
\begin{aligned}
Var(\hat{\beta}) &= \frac{\sum x_i^2 \sigma_i^2}{(\sum x_i^2)^2} \\
&= \frac{\sum x_i^2 (\theta_i + \bar{\sigma}^2)}{(\sum x_i^2)^2} \\
&= \frac{\bar{\sigma}^2}{\sum x_i^2} + \frac{\sum x_i^2 \theta_i}{(\sum x_i^2)^2} \\
&= \frac{\bar{\sigma}^2/n}{\sum x_i^2/n} + \frac{(\sum x_i^2 \theta_i/n).\frac{1}{n}}{(\sum x_i^2/n)^2} \\
&= \frac{\bar{\sigma}^2/n}{\sum x_i^2/n} + \frac{Cov(x_i^2, \sigma_i^2)/n}{(\sum x_i^2/n)^2}
\end{aligned}
$$

Note that

(i) $Cov(x_i^2, \sigma_i^2)$ is sample covariance between X_i^2 and σ_i^2, which is a finite number;

(ii) $\lim\limits_{n \to \infty} \left(\sum x_i^2/n \right)$ is a finite number by assumption; and

(iii) $\lim\limits_{n \to \infty} \left(\bar{\sigma}^2/n \right) = 0.$

[3] We prove consistency of $\hat{\beta}$ under heteroskedasticity following Kmenta (1986, 273).

Therefore,

$$\lim_{n \to \infty} Var(\hat{\beta}) = 0 \tag{4.7}$$

This proves that $\hat{\beta}$ is consistent when the disturbance term is heteroskedastic.

On the basis of the above discussion, we can draw the following conclusions, which are also valid in the context of multiple regression models.

- The OLS estimators continue to remain unbiased and consistent under heteroskedasticity. This happens because the explanatory variable(s) is not correlated with the disturbance term of the model. Therefore, a correctly specified model that suffers only from the problem of heteroskedasticity may still be useful.
- Heteroskedasticity increases the variances of the distributions of $\hat{\beta}$s thereby turning the OLS estimators inefficient.
- Heteroskedasticity also affects the variances of OLS estimators and their standard errors. In fact, the presence of heteroskedasticity, in general, causes the OLS method to underestimate the variances and hence standard errors of the estimators.[4] As a consequence, we have higher than expected values of t and F statistics. Thus, heteroskedasticity has a wide impact on hypothesis testing; the conventional t and F statistics are no more reliable for hypothesis testing.
- As the OLS estimators are unbiased under heteroskedasticity, the forecasts generated on the basis of the estimated model will also be unbiased. However, as the OLS estimators are inefficient, the reliability of the forecasts (as measured by their variances) will be inferior to an alternative estimator that is more efficient.

4.3 DETECTION OF HETEROSKEDASTICITY

There are various approaches towards detecting the presence of heteroskedasticity problem in data. We discuss some of these approaches below.

Graphical Approach

We may graphically examine the presence of heteroskedasticity by plotting the squared residuals (ε_i^2) against the explanatory variable (X_i) to which, it is suspected, the disturbance variance is related. Since ε_i and hence ε_i^2 is not observable, we may use $\hat{\varepsilon}_i^2 = e_i^2$ as a proxy for ε_i^2. If it appears that the estimated squared residuals are on average the same regardless the

---

[4] It is to be noted that the OLS standard errors will always be too large for the intercept when the model is heteroskedastic. However, the effect of heteroskedasticity on the slope standard errors will depend on the form of heteroskedasticity. For example, if the variance of the disturbance term is positively related to the square of an explanatory variable (which is the most frequently observed pattern of heteroskedasticity), the slope standard errors will be too low. On the other hand, OLS slope standard errors will be too large when the variance of the disturbance term is inversely related to an explanatory variable (the case of decreasing heteroskedasticity). In any case, the OLS standard errors are distorted when heteroskedasticity is present (Brooks 2008, 135–6).

value of the explanatory variable, then heteroskedasticity probably does not exist. However, if it appears that the value of squared residuals is related (positively or negatively) to the explanatory variable, then heteroskedasticity seems to be present. In that case, a formal check for heteroskedasticity will be needed. It is also to be remembered that the graphical test should be performed for each explanatory variable.

Algebraic Tests

Several algebraic tests have been developed to test the presence of heteroskedasticity in data. Some important ones are discussed below.

Breusch-Pagan-Godfrey Test

Breusch and Pagan (1979) and Godfrey (1978) developed a Lagrange Multiplier (LM) test to examine the presence of heteroskedasticity in data. To understand this test, consider the model

$$Y_i = \beta_0 + \beta_1 X_{1i} + \beta_2 X_{2i} + \dots + \beta_k X_{ki} + \varepsilon_i \qquad (4.8)$$

and suppose that

$$Var(\varepsilon_i) = \sigma_i^2 = f(\gamma_0 + \gamma_1 Z_{1i} + \gamma_2 Z_{2i} + \dots + \gamma_r Z_{ri})$$

This implies that $Var(\varepsilon_i)$ is the function of non-stochastic Zs. Here Zs represent a set of variables that we think determine the variance of the disturbance term, ε_i. Usually, the explanatory variables of (4.8) are used for Zs. The steps involved in the Breusch-Pagan-Godfrey test are the following.

Step 1: Estimate model (4.8) by OLS method and obtain the estimated residuals $e_i = \hat{\varepsilon}_i$.

Step 2: Run the auxiliary regression

$$e_i^2 = \gamma_0 + \gamma_1 Z_{1i} + \gamma_2 Z_{2i} + \dots + \gamma_r Z_{ri} + v_i \qquad (4.9)$$

Step 3: Construct the null and alternative hypotheses

$$H_N : \gamma_1 = \gamma_2 = \dots = \gamma_r = 0 \qquad \text{(Homoskedasticity)}$$

$$H_A : \text{At least one of the } \gamma\text{s is non-zero} \qquad \text{(Heteroskedasticity)}$$

Step 4: Compute the $LM = nR^2$ where n = number of observations used to estimate auxiliary regression model (4.9) and R^2 is the coefficient of determination of this regression. Note that the LM-statistic follows a χ^2-distribution with degrees of freedom r.

Step 5: If $LM^* = \chi^{2*} > \chi^2_\lambda(r)$, reject the H_N and conclude that there is significant evidence of heteroskedasticity in data. An alternative way to arrive at a decision is to see the p-value for computed LM or χ^2 statistics. If it is less than the level of significance $\lambda = 0.05$ (usually chosen), reject the H_N and conclude that heteroskedasticity is present in data.

Glejser Test

Glejser's (1969) test is almost similar to the Breusch-Pagan-Godfrey test except that it estimates a different auxiliary regression, where $|e_i|$ is considered as the dependent variable instead of e_i^2. The steps involved are

Step 1: Estimate model (4.8) by OLS and obtain the residuals $e_i = \hat{\varepsilon}_i$.

Step 2: Run the auxiliary regression

$$|e_i| = \gamma_0 + \gamma_1 Z_{1i} + \gamma_2 Z_{2i} + \; .... \; + \gamma_r Z_{ri} + v_i \qquad (4.10)$$

Step 3: Formulate the null and alternative hypotheses which are same as in Breusch-Pagan-Godfrey test.

Step 4: Compute $LM = nR^2$ where n = number of observations used to estimate auxiliary regression model (4.10) and R^2 is the coefficient of determination of this regression. Here also $LM \sim \chi^2(r)$.

Step 5: If $LM^* = \chi^{2*} > \chi^2_\lambda(r)$, reject H_N and conclude that there is significant evidence of heteroskedasticity in data.

Goldfeld-Quandt Test

Goldfeld and Quandt (1965) proposed a test of heteroskedasticity that may be applied when one of the explanatory variables is suspected to be the heteroskedasticity culprit. The basic idea behind this test is that if the variances of the disturbances are the same across all observations (i.e., homoskedastic), then the variance of one part of the sample should be the same as the variance of another part of the sample. Under this test, we start by assuming that σ_i^2 is proportional to the size of X_i. It is also assumed that the disturbance term of the model (ε_i) is normally distributed and satisfies other regression assumptions.

The hypotheses are

$$H_N : Var(\varepsilon_i | X_i) = \sigma^2 \text{, a constant} \qquad \text{(Homoskedasticity)}$$

$$H_A : Var(\varepsilon_i | X_i) = \sigma_i^2 \text{, a variable} \qquad \text{(Heteroskedasticity)}$$

Given these assumptions, the test is executed through the following steps.

Step 1: Identify the variable to which the variance of disturbance term is suspected to be related.

Step 2: Sort the raw data in ascending order (starting with lowest and going to the highest) of values of X_i.

Step 3: Cut out some central observations (c), breaking data set in two distinct sets—first one with low values of X_i and second one with high values of X_i. Note that there is no clear rule about how many observations to be cut out. Goldfeld and Quandt suggested the value of c as 8 if the sample size is about 30.[5]

---

[5] Judge et al. (1982, 422) suggested that 4 and 10 observations should be cut out when the sample sizes are 30 and 60, respectively. Dougherty (2011, 286) suggested that 11 observations may be cut

Step 4: Fit separate regressions by OLS to the first and last $(n-c)/2$ observations.

Step 5: Compute residual sum squares for the two regressions, which are denoted by RSS_1 and RSS_2, respectively.

Step 6: Compute the F-ratio of two RSSs as

$$F^* = \frac{RSS_2/df_2}{RSS_1/df_1} \tag{4.11}$$

where $df_1 = df_2 = \dfrac{n-c}{2} - k = \dfrac{n-c-2k}{2}$

(Here k is the number of parameters estimated.)

Step 7: Compare F^* with critical-F obtained for level of significance λ and the degrees of freedom (df_2, df_1). The decision rule is that if $F^* > F_\lambda (df_2, df_1)$, we reject H_N and conclude that there is heteroskedasticity in data.

Limitations of Goldfeld-Quandt Test

(i)   The determination of an appropriate value of c sometimes becomes difficult.

(ii) In a model that involves a large number of explanatory variables, there may be difficulty in identifying the X-variable with which to sort the data.

(iii) It does not consider cases where heteroskedasticity is caused by more than one explanatory variable.

White's Test

White (1980) developed a more general test for heteroskedasticity that helps to overcome some of the limitations mentioned above. It is also an LM test, but it has the advantage that it does not require any prior knowledge about the pattern of heteroskedasticity. The assumption of normality is also not required here. For all these reasons, it is considered to be more powerful among the tests discussed so far. This also explains its immense popularity among the researchers.

The basic intuition behind White's test is simple. It focuses on systematic patterns between the residual variance, the explanatory variables, the squares of explanatory variables, and their cross-products. To understand the steps involved in this test, let us consider the following three-variable model

$$Y_i = \beta_0 + \beta_1 X_{1i} + \beta_2 X_{2i} + \varepsilon_i \tag{4.12}$$

Now the steps to be followed are

Step 1: Estimate (4.12) by OLS method and obtain the estimated residuals $e_i = \hat{\varepsilon}_i$.

---

out when the sample size is 30. The point to be remembered here is that the number of observations to be cut out should be so determined that the contrast between the two groups of observations becomes stark. Generally, this happens when 10% to 20% of observations are cut out.

Step 2: Run the following auxiliary regression

$$e_i^2 = \gamma_0 + \gamma_1 X_{1i} + \gamma_2 X_{2i} + \gamma_3 X_{1i}^2 + \gamma_4 X_{2i}^2 + \gamma_5 (X_{1i} X_{2i}) + v_i \qquad (4.13)$$

Step 3: Formulate the null and alternative hypotheses. These are

$H_N: \gamma_1 = \gamma_2 = \ldots = \gamma_5 = 0$ (Homoskedasticity)
$H_A:$ At least one of the γs is non-zero   (Heteroskedasticity)

Step 4: Obtain R^2 from the auxiliary regression and compute $LM = nR^2$ statistic where $n =$ number of observations used to estimate the auxiliary regression. This LM-statistic follows a χ^2-distribution with degrees of freedom 5, the number of slope coefficients in the auxiliary regression.

Step 5: If $LM^* = \chi^{2^*} > \chi_\lambda^2 (5)$, reject the H_N and conclude that there is significant evidence of heteroskedasticity in data. An alternative way to arrive at a decision is to consider the p-value. If p-value < 0.05, reject H_N and conclude that there is significant heteroskedasticity in data.

Limitations of White's test

(i)   When we have a large number of explanatory variables, the number of terms in the auxiliary regression model will be so high that we may not have adequate degrees of freedom.

(ii)   It is basically a large sample test so that, when we work with a small sample, it may fail to detect the presence of heteroskedasticity in data even when such a problem is present.

4.4 REMEDIAL MEASURES

There are two types of measures that can be adopted to correct the problem of heteroskedasticity: (i) measures based on specific idea about the form of heteroskedasticity, and (ii) general measures.

Measures Based on a Specific Idea about the Form of Heteroskedasticity

Here, we require some idea about the form of heteroskedasticity present in our data. Such an idea could be formed while testing the presence of heteroskedasticity. Once we acquire such an idea, it is easy to solve the problem of heteroskedasticity by applying the generalized or weighted least squares method.

Generalized Least Squares (GLS)

Consider the model

$$Y_i = \beta_1 + \beta_2 X_{2i} + \beta_3 X_{3i} + \varepsilon_i \qquad (4.14)$$

and suppose that there is heteroskedasticity so that $Var(\varepsilon_i) = \sigma_i^2$. If we know specifically the form of heteroskedasticity, we may utilize such information to suitably transform our model to overcome the problem of heteroskedasticity and obtain efficient estimates for unknown parameters of our model. Let us illustrate this point by considering some examples.

EXAMPLE 1: SUPPOSE HETEROSKEDASTICITY IS OF THE FORM: $\sigma_i^2 = \sigma^2 Z_i^2$
Here we divide model (4.14) through by $\sqrt{Z_i^2} = Z_i$ so that the transformed model is

$$\frac{Y_i}{Z_i} = \beta_1 \frac{1}{Z_i} + \beta_2 \frac{X_{2i}}{Z_i} + \beta_3 \frac{X_{3i}}{Z_i} + \frac{\varepsilon_i}{Z_i}$$

$$\text{Or } Y_i^* = \beta_1 X_{1i}^* + \beta_2 X_{2i}^* + \beta_3 X_{3i}^* + v_i \tag{4.15}$$

where $Y_i^* = Y_i/Z_i$, $X_{1i}^* = 1/Z_i$, $X_{2i}^* = X_{2i}/Z_i$, $X_{3i}^* = X_{3i}/Z_i$, and $v_i = \varepsilon_i/Z_i$. v_i is the new disturbance term. There is no heteroskedasticity in the transformed model (4.15) because

$$Var(v_i) = E(v_i^2) = E\left(\frac{\varepsilon_i}{Z_i}\right)^2 = \frac{E(\varepsilon_i^2)}{Z_i^2} = \frac{\sigma^2 Z_i^2}{Z_i^2} = \sigma^2 \text{ constant}$$

Thus, estimating model (4.15) by applying OLS method provides efficient estimates for unknown parameters of the original model.

EXAMPLE 2: HETEROSKEDASTICITY IS OF THE FORM: $\sigma_i^2 = \sigma^2 X_{1i}$
In this case, we transform model (4.14) by dividing through $\sqrt{X_{1i}}$.

$$\frac{Y_i}{\sqrt{X_{1i}}} = \beta_1 \frac{1}{\sqrt{X_{1i}}} + \beta_2 \frac{X_{2i}}{\sqrt{X_{1i}}} + \beta_3 \frac{X_{3i}}{\sqrt{X_{1i}}} + \frac{\varepsilon_i}{\sqrt{X_{1i}}}$$

$$\text{Or } Y_i^* = \beta_1 X_{1i}^* + \beta_2 X_{2i}^* + \beta_3 X_{3i}^* + v_i \tag{4.16}$$

where $Y_i^* = Y_i/\sqrt{X_{1i}}$, $X_{1i}^* = 1/\sqrt{X_{1i}}$, $X_{2i}^* = X_{2i}/\sqrt{X_{1i}}$, $X_{3i}^* = X_{3i}/\sqrt{X_{1i}}$, and $v_i = \varepsilon_i/\sqrt{X_{1i}}$. v_i is the new disturbance term. For the transformed model, the variance of the disturbance term is again constant.

$$Var(v_i) = E(v_i^2) = E\left(\frac{\varepsilon_i}{\sqrt{X_{1i}}}\right)^2 = \frac{E(\varepsilon_i^2)}{X_{1i}} = \frac{\sigma^2 X_{1i}}{X_{1i}} = \sigma^2 \text{ constant}$$

Thus, the transformed model (4.16) is free from the problem of heteroskedasticity.

EXAMPLE 3: HETEROSKEDASTICITY IS OF THE FORM: $\sigma_i^2 = \sigma^2 X_{1i}^2$

Here the transformed model is

$$\frac{Y_i}{X_{1i}} = \beta_1 \frac{1}{X_{1i}} + \beta_2 \frac{X_{2i}}{X_{1i}} + \beta_3 \frac{X_{3i}}{X_{1i}} + \frac{\varepsilon_i}{X_{1i}}$$

$$\text{Or } Y_i^* = \beta_1 X_{1i}^* + \beta_2 X_{2i}^* + \beta_3 X_{3i}^* + v_i \tag{4.17}$$

where $Y_i^* = Y_i/X_{1i}$, $X_{1i}^* = 1/X_{1i}$, $X_{2i}^* = X_{2i}/X_{1i}$, $X_{3i}^* = X_{3i}/X_{1i}$, and $v_i = \varepsilon_i/X_{1i}$. The disturbance term of (4.17) also has constant variance.

The above procedures of estimating the transformed model to overcome the heteroskedasticity problem are known as the *generalized least squares*.

Weighted Least Squares (WLS)

These above examples are also referred to as examples of the weighted least squares (WLS) method. This is because we may view $1/Z_i$ in (4.15), $1/\sqrt{X_{1i}}$ in (4.16), and $1/X_{1i}$ in (4.17) as weights (w_i). Then, for instance, model (4.17) may be expressed as

$$(w_i Y_i) = \beta_1 w_i + \beta_2 (w_i X_{2i}) + \beta_3 (w_i X_{3i}) + (\varepsilon_i w_i) \tag{4.18}$$

So the issue is that of finding an appropriate weight (w_i). Once this is found, we can transform the original model in the manner described by (4.18) and estimate the same by applying OLS method to obtain estimates for unknown parameters of the original model, which are efficient and consistent (as the transformed model does not suffer from heteroskedasticity problem). However, we will have to take extra care in interpreting the estimated coefficients of the WLS model like (4.18). This is because while β_1 was the intercept term in the original model, it is now the slope coefficient of the weight variable (w_i). So the researcher interested in the intercept of original model should consider the slope coefficient of this variable. Further, to get $\hat{Y}_i$, we have to multiply the estimated WLS model by X_{1i} (when $1/X_{1i}$ is taken as weight).

The basic intuition behind the WLS/GLS method is that if $Var(\varepsilon_i)$ is a variable, so that the value of it increases with increase in value of one of the explanatory variables (say X_{1i}), then $\hat{Y}_i$ associated with larger values of the explanatory variable are less reliable due to greater divergence between Y_i and $\hat{Y}_i$. Now by dividing each observation through X_{1i} or $\sqrt{X_{1i}}$, depending upon the form of heteroskedasticity, we are giving more weight to observations associated with low values of X_{1i} and less weight to observations associated with high values of X_{1i}. In other words, we are weighing the observations according to reliability to improve accuracy of estimation.

However, the problem is that, in reality, necessary information about the exact form of heteroskedasticity may not be forthcoming so easily. That is why the above methods are often termed as the *infeasible* WLS/GLS. In such a situation, we may follow the *feasible* WLS/GLS approach that runs through the following steps (Wooldridge 2009, 283).

Step 1: Estimate the original model (4.12) by OLS and obtain the residuals e_i.
Step 2: Create the series $\log(e_i^2)$ by squaring the OLS residuals and then taking the natural log.
Step 3: Run the auxiliary regression where you regress $\log(e_i^2)$ on all the explanatory variables.
Step 4: Obtain the fitted values from the above regression, denoted by $\hat{g}_i$.
Step 5: Exponentiate the fitted values as $e^{\hat{g}_i} = \hat{h}_i$.
Step 6: Estimate the original equation using $1/\hat{h}_i$ as weight.

It has been shown that the *feasible* WLS/GLS estimators thus obtained is not unbiased but consistent and asymptotically more efficient.

Heteroskedasticity-Consistent Estimator (HCE)

We observed that application of WLS/GLS is possible when we are able to transform the original model by using a suitable weight. However, if it is impossible to find such a weight or there is more than one explanatory variable appearing to serve as weights as variance of the disturbance term is affected by all of them, then application of WLS/GLS method becomes impossible. In such a situation, if we are compelled to apply the OLS method to estimate the original model, we still have unbiased estimators. But the variance formula [given by (4.6)] derived under the OLS assumptions no longer holds and hence confidence intervals and hypothesis testing procedures become incorrect.

In the above situation, White (1980) proposed the heteroskedasticity-consistent estimation method (HCE). We do not go into the details of this method as that is outside the purview of this book. However, most econometric software packages (including EViews) have an option to apply this method and obtain standard error estimates that have been modified to account for heteroskedasticity following White.

General Measures

- One of the general measures adopted to control heteroskedasticity is log-transformation of data. As log-transformation compresses the scales in which the variables are measured, it helps to reduce intensity of heteroskedasticity problem. Obviously, this method cannot be followed where some variables take on zero or negative values.
- Another method is to use some suitable deflator, if available, to transform the data series. The idea is to estimate the model by using the deflated variables so that more efficient estimates of the parameters are obtained. However, this process might lead to 'spurious relationship' between the variables when a common deflator is used to deflate the variables.
- When heteroskedasticity appears owing to presence of outliers, increasing sample size might be helpful.

4.5 APPLICATIONS USING EVIEWS

Tests of Heteroskedasticity

To understand application of EViews to perform the tests of heteroskedasticity, let us consider the data given in Table 4.1. The table contains data on three variables for 90 countries: (i) per capita carbon dioxide emission (CARBON), (ii) GNI per capita (GNIPC), and (iii) literacy rate (LIT). Our objective is to estimate a regression model to examine the importance of GNIPC and LIT in explaining inter-country differences in carbon dioxide emission (per capita). However, as per capita GNI varies widely among the countries, we suspect the presence of heteroskedasticity in data.[6] So we would like to apply some tests to check if heteroskedasticity is really present in our data.

Using EViews, we perform the heteroskedasticity tests through the following steps:

(i)   Obtain data in EViews workfile.

(ii)   Estimate the model by applying OLS method following the procedure mentioned in Chapter 2. The regression output obtained here is displayed in Table 4.2. It is observed that there is a positive and statistically significant relation between CARBON and GNIPC implying that the rate of carbon emission is high in richer countries. The t-value for the estimated coefficient of GNIPC is significant at 1% level (p-value < 0.01). The relation between CARBON and LIT is positive but statistically insignificant (p-value = 0.76). The F-value for the regression is statistically significant (p-value < 0.01). However, as the t and F-tests will not be reliable if heteroskedasticity is present, we proceed to the next step to apply the heteroskedasticity tests.

(iii)   From the regression output window, click **View/Residual Diagnostics/ Heteroskedasticity Tests…** which will open the 'Heteroskedasticity Tests' dialog box as displayed in Screenshot 4.1.

(iv)   Choose the type of test to perform by clicking on the name of the test in 'Test Type' box (note that several alternatives are available here).

(v)   Click **OK** to obtain test output.

If we choose 'Breusch-Pagan-Godfrey' from 'Test Type' box, the output obtained will be as in Table 4.3. In the same way, if we choose 'Glejser', output will be as in Table 4.4. The output in Table 4.5 is obtained when we choose 'White'.

Our test results show that there is uniformity in the conclusion of these tests for heteroskedasticity. In each case, the computed-χ^2 (i.e., Obs*R-squared) is statistically significant at 1% level (p-value < 0.01). This confirms presence of heteroskedasticity in data used by us for OLS regression.

---

[6] The level of carbon emission is likely to be high for the group of high-income (per capita) countries compared to low-income countries.

Table 4.1 Data on Carbon Dioxide Emissions Per Capita (CARBON) (In Metric Tonnes), GNI Per Capita (GNIPC) (PPP US $) and Literacy Rate (LIT) (In Percentage, for Ages 15 and Above People) in Some Countries

Country	CARBON	GNIPC	LIT	Country	CARBON	GNIPC	LIT
Albania	0.8	5,420	99	Latvia	2.7	13,480	100
Algeria	2.9	6,770	70	Lithuania	3.6	14,220	100
Angola	0.5	2,210	67	Macedonia, FYR	5.1	7,080	96
Argentina	3.5	13,920	97	Madagascar	0.1	880	71
Armenia	1.0	5,060	99	Malawi	0.1	650	64
Azerbaijan	3.4	4,890	99	Malaysia	6.3	10,320	89
Belarus	6.0	7,890	100	Mali	0.0	1,000	19
Benin	0.3	1,110	35	Mauritania	1.1	2,150	51
Bolivia	1.2	2,740	87	Mexico	3.8	10,030	91
Bosnia and Herzegovina	4.7	7,790	97	Moldova	1.6	2,150	98
Brazil	1.8	8,230	89	Mongolia	3.4	2,190	98
Bulgaria	5.3	8,630	98	Morocco	1.5	4,360	52
Burkina Faso	0.1	1,220	22	Namibia	1.1	7,910	85
Burundi	0.0	640	59	Nepal	0.2	1,530	49
Cambodia	0.0	2,490	74	Nicaragua	0.7	3,650	77
Cameroon	0.2	2,150	68	Niger	0.1	800	29
Central African Republic	0.1	1,140	49	Oman	12.1	14,680	81
Chad	0.0	1,470	26	Pakistan	0.7	2,350	50
Chile	3.6	11,470	96	Panama	2.0	7,310	92
China	2.7	6,600	91	Papua New Guinea	0.4	2,370	57
Colombia	1.3	7,420	93	Peru	1.0	5,830	88
Congo, Dem. Rep.	0.0	720	67	Philippines	0.9	5,300	93
Costa Rica	1.4	9,680	95	Romania	4.0	8,940	97
Cote d'Ivoire	0.4	1,490	49	Russian Federation	9.8	10,640	99
Croatia	4.7	12,750	98	Rwanda	0.1	1,320	65
Dominican Republic	2.5	7,150	87	Saudi Arabia	15.0	14,740	79
Ecuador	2.0	4,070	91	Senegal	0.4	1,770	39
Egypt, Arab Rep.	2.1	4,440	71	Sierra Leone	0.1	780	35
Ghana	0.4	2,370	58	Singapore	13.7	29,780	93
Greece	8.5	23,620	96	Slovak Republic	6.8	15,760	100
Guatemala	0.9	4,410	69	South Africa	7.6	12,120	82
Guinea	0.1	2,240	29	Sri Lanka	0.5	4,520	91
Honduras	0.9	2,900	80	Sudan	0.3	2,000	61
India	1.2	3,460	61	Syrian Arab Republic	2.8	3,740	80
Indonesia	1.4	3,720	90	Tajikistan	0.7	1,260	99
Iran, Islamic Rep.	5.5	8,050	77	Tanzania	0.1	730	69
Israel	10.6	25,280	97	Thailand	3.7	8,440	93
Italy	7.5	28,840	98	Togo	0.3	1,550	53
Jamaica	4.1	4,110	80	Tunisia	2.3	7,900	74
Jordan	3.3	5,280	90	Turkey	3.0	8,420	87
Kazakhstan	9.9	7,730	100	Uganda	0.1	1,500	67
Kenya	0.2	1,170	74	Ukraine	6.4	6,720	99
Kuwait	25.6	24,010	93	Venezuela, RB	4.3	6,440	93
Kyrgyz Republic	1.0	1,870	99	Vietnam	0.8	3,010	90
Lao PDR	0.2	2,020	69	Zambia	0.2	950	68

Source: World Bank. Available on the World Bank website at www.worldbank.org.
Note: Data on CARBON relate to 2002; GNIPC and LIT relate to 2004.

Table 4.2   Results of Regression of CARBON on GNIPC and LIT

Dependent Variable: CARBON
Method: Least Squares
Date: 08/23/13 Time: 14:28
Sample: 1 90
Included observations: 90

Variable	Coefficient	Std. Error	t-Statistic	Prob.
C	−0.602291	1.022257	−0.589177	0.5573
GNIPC	0.000504	4.95E-05	10.18622	0.0000
LIT	0.004355	0.014428	0.301838	0.7635
R-squared	0.631308	Mean dependent var		2.947778
Adjusted R-squared	0.622832	S.D. dependent var		4.051279
S.E. of regression	2.488051	Akaike info criterion		4.693642
Sum squared resid	538.5646	Schwarz criterion		4.776969
Log likelihood	−208.2139	Hannan-Quinn criter.		4.727244
F-statistic	74.48471	Durbin-Watson stat		1.895472
Prob(F-statistic)	0.000000			

Source: This table represents the output obtained by the author after application of the EViews software.

Screenshot 4.1   Heteroskedasticity Tests Dialog Box

Heteroskedasticity Tests

Specification

Test type:

Breusch-Pagan-Godfrey
Harvey
Glejser
ARCH
White
Custom Test Wizard...

Dependent variable: RESID^2

The Breusch-Pagan-Godfrey Test regresses the squared residuals on the original regressors by default.

Regressors:

c gnipc lit

Add equation regressors

OK   Cancel

Table 4.3   Results of Breusch-Pagan-Godfrey Test

Heteroskedasticity Test: Breusch-Pagan-Godfrey			
F-statistic	13.85725	Prob. F(2,87)	0.0000
Obs*R-squared	21.74359	Prob. Chi-Square(2)	0.0000
Scaled explained SS	131.2122	Prob. Chi-Square(2)	0.0000

Test Equation:
Dependent Variable: RESID^2
Method: Least Squares
Date: 08/23/13 Time: 14:30
Sample: 1 90
Included observations: 90

Variable	Coefficient	Std. Error	t-Statistic	Prob.
C	1.555753	7.826507	0.198780	0.8429
GNIPC	0.001839	0.000379	4.856930	0.0000
LIT	−0.094168	0.110463	−0.852483	0.3963
R-squared	0.241595	Mean dependent var		5.984051
Adjusted R-squared	0.224161	S.D. dependent var		21.62625
S.E. of regression	19.04878	Akaike info criterion		8.764648
Sum squared resid	31568.47	Schwarz criterion		8.847975
Log likelihood	−391.4092	Hannan-Quinn criter.		8.798250
F-statistic	13.85725	Durbin-Watson stat		1.825967
Prob(F-statistic)	0.000006			

Source: Same as for Table 4.2.

Table 4.4   Results of Glejser Test for Heteroskedasticity

Heteroskedasticity Test: Glejser			
F-statistic	33.76668	Prob. F(2,87)	0.0000
Obs*R-squared	39.33133	Prob. Chi-Square(2)	0.0000
Scaled explained SS	70.34031	Prob. Chi-Square(2)	0.0000

Test Equation:
Dependent Variable: ARESID
Method: Least Squares
Date: 08/23/13 Time: 14:31
Sample: 1 90
Included observations: 90

Variable	Coefficient	Std. Error	t-Statistic	Prob.
C	−0.471959	0.628903	−0.750448	0.4550
GNIPC	0.000196	3.04E-05	6.447277	0.0000
LIT	0.008017	0.008876	0.903213	0.3689
R-squared	0.437015	Mean dependent var		1.400390
Adjusted R-squared	0.424073	S.D. dependent var		2.016968
S.E. of regression	1.530675	Akaike info criterion		3.722059
Sum squared resid	203.8379	Schwarz criterion		3.805386
Log likelihood	−164.4927	Hannan-Quinn criter.		3.755662
F-statistic	33.76668	Durbin-Watson stat		2.020552
Prob(F-statistic)	0.000000			

Source: Same as for Table 4.2.

Table 4.5   Results of White Test for Heteroskedasticity

Heteroskedasticity Test: White			
F-statistic	5.768444	Prob. F(5,84)	0.0001
Obs*R-squared	23.00380	Prob. Chi-Square(5)	0.0003
Scaled explained SS	138.8169	Prob. Chi-Square(5)	0.0000

Test Equation:
Dependent Variable: RESID^2
Method: Least Squares
Date: 08/23/13 Time: 14:32
Sample: 1 90
Included observations: 90

Variable	Coefficient	Std. Error	t-Statistic	Prob.
C	−1.686276	18.37111	−0.091790	0.9271
GNIPC^2	3.68E-08	4.73E-08	0.779068	0.4381
GNIPC*LIT	−6.43E-05	5.45E-05	−1.180364	0.2412
GNIPC	0.006828	0.004553	1.499634	0.1375
LIT^2	0.002379	0.005439	0.437419	0.6629
LIT	−0.230342	0.645547	−0.356817	0.7221
R-squared	0.255598	Mean dependent var		5.984051
Adjusted R-squared	0.211288	S.D. dependent var		21.62625
S.E. of regression	19.20616	Akaike info criterion		8.812679
Sum squared resid	30985.62	Schwarz criterion		8.979333
Log likelihood	−390.5706	Hannan-Quinn criter.		8.879884
F-statistic	5.768444	Durbin-Watson stat		1.883943
Prob(F-statistic)	0.000126			

Source: Same as for Table 4.2.

Estimation of White's Heteroskedasticity-Consistent Standard Errors

As the standard errors from OLS regression become smaller (underestimates) when heteroskedasticity is present, we may like to have heteroskedasticity-consistent standard errors as suggested by White (1980). These may be obtained easily using EViews. The steps to be followed are

(i)   Go to the 'Equation Estimation' window and put specification of the equation in the 'Equation specification' jumbo box.

(ii)   From 'Equation Estimation' window click 'Options' tab and select 'White' from 'Coefficient covariance matrix' box.

(iv)   Click **OK** to obtain the output as shown in Table 4.6.

The results show that the value of standard error of estimated coefficient of GNIPC is expectedly higher and (hence *t*-value is lower) in Table 4.6 compared to the same

Table 4.6   Results of Regression with White Heteroskedasticity-Consistent Standard Errors

Dependent Variable: CARBON
Method: Least Squares
Date: 08/23/13 Time: 14:34
Sample: 1 90
Included observations: 90
White heteroskedasticity-consistent standard errors & covariance

Variable	Coefficient	Std. Error	t-Statistic	Prob.
C	−0.602291	0.526328	−1.144325	0.2556
GNIPC	0.000504	0.000108	4.668332	0.0000
LIT	0.004355	0.012591	0.345889	0.7303
R-squared	0.631308	Mean dependent var		2.947778
Adjusted R-squared	0.622832	S.D. dependent var		4.051279
S.E. of regression	2.488051	Akaike info criterion		4.693642
Sum squared resid	538.5646	Schwarz criterion		4.776969
Log likelihood	−208.2139	Hannan-Quinn criter.		4.727244
F-statistic	74.48471	Durbin-Watson stat		1.895472
Prob(F-statistic)	0.000000	Wald F-statistic		39.70498
Prob(Wald F-statistic)	0.000000			

Source: Same as for Table 4.2.

in Table 4.2. Obviously, in this situation, we shall accept White's heteroskedasticity-consistent standard errors reported in Table 4.6.

Weighted Least Squares Estimation
In the above situation, we may like to estimate our model by following the WLS method. The steps to be followed in EViews are:

(i)   Go to the 'Equation Estimation' window and put specification of the equation in the 'Equation specification' jumbo box.

(ii)   Click 'Options' tab from 'Equation Estimation' window and
  (a)   select 'White' from 'Coefficient covariance matrix' box;
  (b)   select from 'Weights' box the 'Type' of weight and write the name of 'Weight series'.

(iii)   Click **OK** to get the output.

For instance, suppose we select 'Inverse std. dev.' as 'Type' of weight and GNIPC as 'Weight series' (see Screenshot 4.2).[7] The output obtained is presented in Table 4.7.

[7] This is because $Var(\varepsilon_i)$ is assumed to vary with changes in the value of GNIPC.

Screenshot 4.2   Selection of 'Options' from 'Equation Estimation' Window

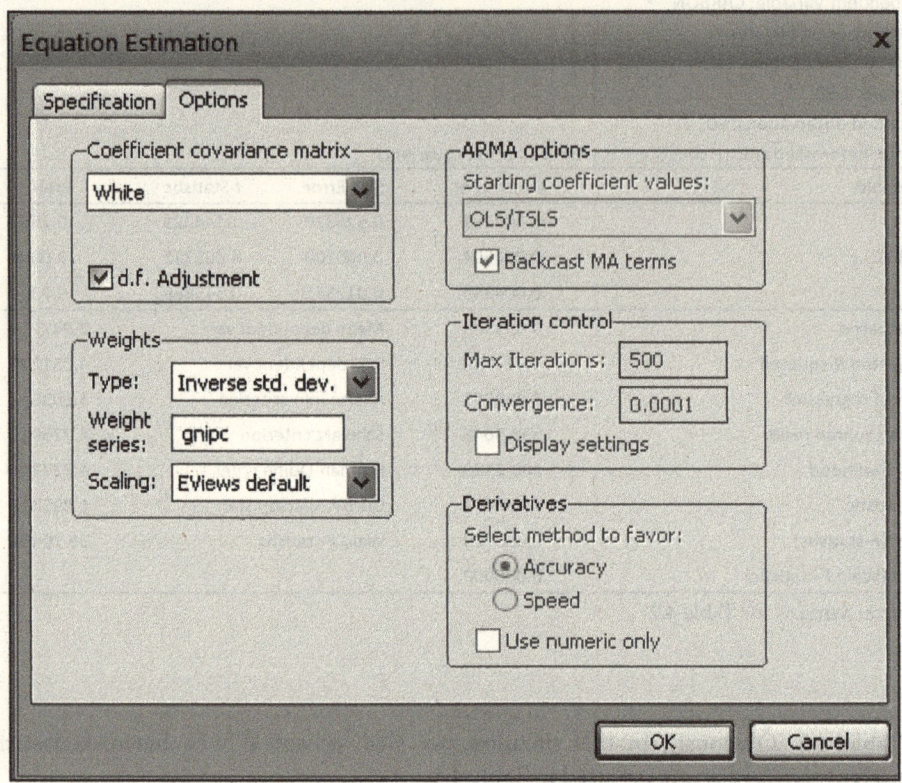

Comparing these results with those in Table 4.2, we find that there is marked improvement in the results of regression. The WLS estimates of both the explanatory variables (GNIPC and LIT) have expected signs and turned statistically significant (at 1% and 2% levels, respectively). The researcher has a valid reason to rejoice in this situation.

4.6 QUESTIONS AND ASSIGNMENTS

A. Multiple-Choice Questions
Tick ($\sqrt{}$) the correct answer.
    (i)   The heteroskedasticity problem arises more in the context of
        (a)   Cross-section data
        (b)   Time-series data
        (c)   Qualitative data
        (d)   Categorical data

Table 4.7   Results of WLS Regression

Dependent Variable: CARBON
Method: Least Squares
Date: 08/23/13 Time: 14:37
Sample: 1 90
Included observations: 90
Weighting series: GNIPC
Weight type: Inverse standard deviation (EViews default scaling)
White heteroskedasticity-consistent standard errors & covariance

Variable	Coefficient	Std. Error	t-Statistic	Prob.
C	15.30675	6.336874	2.415505	0.0178
GNIPC	0.000479	0.000131	3.659033	0.0004
LIT	−0.163924	0.069723	−2.351077	0.0210
Weighted Statistics				
R-squared	0.382761	Mean dependent var		6.086076
Adjusted R-squared	0.368571	S.D. dependent var		14.10554
S.E. of regression	7.093753	Akaike info criterion		6.789071
Sum squared resid	4377.956	Schwarz criterion		6.872398
Log likelihood	−302.5082	Hannan-Quinn criter.		6.822674
F-statistic	26.97512	Durbin-Watson stat		1.889528
Prob(F-statistic)	0.000000	Weighted mean dep.		8.888346
Wald F-statistic	7.457883	Prob(Wald F-statistic)		0.001025
Unweighted Statistics				
R-squared	−0.660285	Mean dependent var		2.947778
Adjusted R-squared	−0.698452	S.D. dependent var		4.051279
S.E. of regression	5.279816	Sum squared resid		2425.252
Durbin-Watson stat	1.429484			

Source: Same as for Table 4.2.

(ii)   Heteroskedasticity problem may arise owing to
    (a)   Presence of outliers in data
    (b)   Model misspecification
    (c)   Incorrect data transformation
    (d)   All of above
(iii)   Heteroskedasticity turns OLS estimators
    (a)   Biased
    (b)   Inefficient
    (c)   Inconsistent
    (d)   All of above

    (iv)   Heteroskedasticity problem may be controlled by
        (a)   Log-transformation of data
        (b)   Using a suitable deflator
        (c)   Both (a) and (b)
        (d)   Cannot be controlled at all

    (v)   Among all tests of heteroskedasticity, the most popular one is
        (a)   Goldfeld-Quandt test
        (b)   Park test
        (c)   Glejser test
        (d)   White test

    (vi)   The appropriate estimation method to follow under heteroskedasticity is
        (a)   Ordinary least-squares
        (b)   Restricted least squares
        (c)   Weighted least squares
        (d)   Any non-linear estimation method

    (vii) When heteroskedasticity is present, the standard errors of the estimated coefficients are
        (a)   Zeros
        (b)   Over-estimated
        (c)   Under-estimated
        (d)   Unchanged

B. General Questions

    (i)   Define the terms 'homoskedasticity' and 'heteroskedasticity'. Give some examples where heteroskedasticity is likely to be present.

    (ii)   Why is heteroskedasticity found more in cross-section data? Give two examples where heteroskedasticity might be present.

    (iii) Distinguish between 'increasing heteroskedasticity' and 'decreasing heteroskedasticity'.

    (iv) Prove that the OLS estimators are inefficient but consistent under heteroskedasticity.

    (v)   Describe how one may understand graphically the presence of heteroskedasticity in data.

    (vi)   Describe the steps involved in the Goldfeld-Quandt test for detection of heteroskedasticity. What are the limitations of this test?

    (vii) Describe White's test for detection of heteroskedasticity. What are its merits and demerits?

    (viii) Suggest some corrective measures for the heteroskedasticity problem.

    (ix)   Show how one can apply the weighted least squares (WLS) method to resolve the problem of heteroskedasticity.

    (x)   What is 'infeasible GLS'? How do we make it 'feasible'?

(xi) What are the 'heteroskedasticity-consistent standard errors'? When are these considered?

(xii) Indicate whether the following statements are true (T), false (F), or uncertain (U) and give a brief explanation.

(a) Heteroskedasticity in the errors leads to biased estimates of the regression coefficients.

(b) Heteroskedasticity leads to overestimation of the t-ratios in a regression.

(c) We need not worry too much about the heteroskedasticity problem so long as the OLS estimates are consistent.

C. Computer Assignments

(i) Using data given in Table 2.3 (Chapter 2), you estimated a multiple regression model by applying the OLS method to understand the determinants of infant mortality rate in India. However, you suspect that your results of regression might not be reliable enough due to presence of heteroskedasticity in data. So apply a suitable test to examine the presence of heteroskedasticity in your data. Does your conclusion in this regard change if you apply alternative tests?

(ii) Table 2.4 (Chapter 2) presented state-level data on incidence of child labour and some of its possible determinants. Estimate a regression model to find out statistically significant determinants of incidence of child labour in India. Does your model suffer from heteroskedasticity problem? Check this in terms of Breusch-Pagan-Godfrey and White tests.

(iii) Use data presented in Table 2.5 (Chapter 2) to estimate the following model.

$$FGN = \alpha + \beta_1 IRRI + \beta_2 FERT + \beta_3 CREDIT + \varepsilon$$

Check for heteroskedasticity using Glejser and White tests.

(iv) Estimate the following multiple regression model using data given in Table 4.8.

$$LEB = \alpha + \beta_1 SCHL + \beta_2 GNIPC + \varepsilon$$

Check for heteroskedasticity using White test. Compute 'White heteroskedasticity-consistent standard errors' for the model and compare those with the standard errors of the initial OLS model. What difference do you find in the values of standard errors? Estimate the WLS model after choosing a suitable weighting series (variable) and interpret the results.

Answers to Multiple-Choice Questions

(i) (a); (ii) (d); (iii) (b); (iv) (c); (v) (d); (vi) (c); (vii) (c).

Table 4.8　Data on Life Expectancy at Birth (LEB), Mean Years of Schooling (SCHL) and GNI Per Capita (GNIPC) (PPP US $) in Some Countries

Sl no.	Country	LEB	SCHL	GNIPC
1	Norway	81.1	12.6	47,557
2	Australia	81.9	12.0	34,431
3	Netherlands	80.7	11.6	36,402
4	United States	78.5	12.4	43,017
5	New Zealand	80.7	12.5	23,737
6	Canada	81.0	12.1	35,166
7	Germany	80.4	12.2	34,854
8	Sweden	81.4	11.7	35,837
9	Switzerland	82.3	11.0	39,924
10	Japan	83.4	11.6	32,295
11	Denmark	78.8	11.4	34,347
12	Austria	80.9	10.8	35,719
13	France	81.5	10.6	30,436
14	Spain	81.4	10.4	26,508
15	Italy	81.9	10.1	26,484
16	Singapore	81.1	8.8	52,569
17	United Kingdom	80.2	9.3	33,296
18	Greece	79.9	10.1	23,747
19	Hungary	74.4	11.1	16,581
20	Poland	76.1	10.0	17,451
21	Uruguay	77.0	8.5	13,242
22	Romania	74.0	10.4	11,046
23	Cuba	79.1	9.9	5,416
24	Bulgaria	73.4	10.6	11,412
25	Mexico	77.0	8.5	13,245
26	Malaysia	74.2	9.5	13,685
27	Libya	74.8	7.3	12,637
28	Ukraine	68.5	11.3	6,175
29	Mauritius	73.4	7.2	12,918
30	Brazil	73.5	7.2	10,162
31	Sri Lanka	74.9	8.2	4,943
32	Fiji	69.2	10.7	4,145
33	China	73.5	7.5	7,476
34	Thailand	74.1	6.6	7,694
35	Mongolia	68.5	8.3	3,391
36	Philippines	68.7	8.9	3,478
37	Namibia	62.5	7.4	62.6
38	Indonesia	69.4	5.8	3,716

(*Contd.*)

Table 4.8 (*Contd.*)

SI no.	Country	LEB	SCHL	GNIPC
39	Iraq	69.0	5.6	3,177
40	India	65.4	4.4	3,468
41	Congo	57.4	5.9	3,066
42	Cambodia	63.1	5.8	1,848
43	Bhutan	67.2	2.3	5,293
44	Kenya	57.1	7.0	1,492
45	Pakistan	65.4	4.9	2,550
46	Bangladesh	68.9	4.8	1,529
47	Myanmar	65.2	4.0	1,535
48	Cameroon	51.6	5.9	2,031
49	Nepal	68.8	3.2	1,160
50	Sudan	61.5	3.1	1,894
51	Zimbabwe	51.4	7.2	376
52	Sierra Leone	47.8	2.9	737
53	Liberia	56.8	3.9	265
54	Mozambique	50.2	1.2	898

Source: UNDP, *Human Development Report 2011*.

APPENDIX 4.1: EFFECT OF HETEROSKEDASTICITY ON THE VARIANCE-COVARIANCE MATRIX OF DISTURBANCE TERM OF THE GENERAL LINEAR MODEL

The general linear model is given by

$$Y = X\beta + \varepsilon \tag{A4.1}$$

Under the classical OLS assumptions, the variance–covariance matrix of the disturbance term (ε) is obtained as

$$E(\varepsilon\varepsilon') = \begin{bmatrix} \sigma^2 & 0 & . & . & . & 0 \\ 0 & \sigma^2 & . & . & . & 0 \\ . & & & & & \\ . & & & & & \\ . & & & & & \\ 0 & 0 & . & . & . & \sigma^2 \end{bmatrix}$$

$$= \sigma^2 \begin{bmatrix} 1 & 0 & . & . & . & 0 \\ 0 & 1 & . & . & . & 0 \\ . & & & & & \\ . & & & & & \\ . & & & & & \\ 0 & 0 & . & . & . & 1 \end{bmatrix}$$

$$= \sigma^2 I \text{ [Here } I \text{ is an } (n \times n) \text{ identity matrix]} \tag{A4.2}$$

However, under the presence of heteroskedasticity, the variance of ε is no longer constant so that

$$E(\varepsilon\varepsilon') = \begin{bmatrix} \sigma_1^2 & 0 & . & . & . & 0 \\ 0 & \sigma_2^2 & . & . & . & 0 \\ . & & & & & \\ . & & & & & \\ . & & & & & \\ 0 & 0 & . & . & . & \sigma_n^2 \end{bmatrix} = \Omega \tag{A4.3}$$

We have variance–covariance matrix of *OLS* estimators $\hat{\beta}$ as

$$\begin{aligned}
Cov(\hat{\beta}) &= E[(\hat{\beta}-\beta)(\hat{\beta}-\beta)'] \\
&= E[\{(X'X)^{-1}X'\varepsilon\}\{(X'X)^{-1}X'\varepsilon\}'] \quad [\because \hat{\beta}=\beta+(X'X)^{-1}\varepsilon \text{ as shown in } (A3.4)] \\
&= E[(X'X)^{-1}X'\varepsilon\varepsilon'X(X'X)^{-1}] \\
&= (X'X)^{-1}X'E(\varepsilon\varepsilon')X(X'X)^{-1} \\
&= (X'X)^{-1}X'\Omega X(X'X)^{-1}
\end{aligned}$$

$$\tag{A4.4}$$

This is different from the classical OLS expression $\sigma^2(X'X)^{-1}$ that is obtained when there is homoskedasticity. In (A4.4), Ω denotes new variance-covariance matrix for the disturbance term, irrespective of the form it takes. So using classical OLS expression to calculate variances, standard errors, and t-statistics of the estimated $\hat{\beta}$s, we are likely to arrive at wrong conclusions. Expression (A4.4) forms the basis for what is known as 'robust' inference, i.e., computing standard errors and t-statistics which are correct even when some of the OLS assumptions (including the assumption of homoskedasticity) are violated.[8] In this situation, what is appropriate is calculating corrected $Cov(\hat{\beta})$ assuming a particular form for Ω.

[8] An example of this is White's 'heteroskedasticity-consistent standard errors'.

5 Autocorrelation

This chapter discusses the issues related to the problem of autocorrelation that is found more in time series data. The issues covered are: meaning and sources of autocorrelation, specification of autocorrelation relationship, different tests for autocorrelation, and methods of estimation when autocorrelation is present. Application of EViews software for testing the presence of autocorrelation and estimation of the regression model under the presence of autocorrelation has been explained using examples.

5.1 DEFINITION

One of the assumptions of the Classical Linear Regression Model (CLRM) is that the disturbance term of the model is independent. Symbolically, it means that, for the model

$$Y_t = \alpha + \beta X_t + \varepsilon_t$$

$$Cov(\varepsilon_t, \varepsilon_s) = E(\varepsilon_t \varepsilon_s) = 0 \text{ for } t \neq s.$$

This feature of regression disturbance is known as serial independence or non-autocorrelation. It implies that the value of disturbance term in one period is not correlated with its value in another period. In other words, the disturbance occurring at one point of time does not carry over into another period.

However, this assumption may not always be fulfilled, particularly when we are dealing with time series data. This is because the disturbance captures the impact of a large number of random and independent factors, which enter into our relationship but are not measurable. Therefore, it is quite possible that the effect of these factors operating in one period would carry over, at least in part, to the following period. Thus, the disturbance term at period t may be related with the disturbance terms at $t - 1, t - 2, \ldots,$ and $t + 1, t + 2, \ldots,$ and so on. In that case, $Cov(\varepsilon_t, \varepsilon_s) \neq 0$ for $t \neq s$ and we say that the disturbances are autocorrelated. So autocorrelation represents lack of independence for the disturbance term of the model as a result of which its value in one period gets correlated with its value in another period.[1]

---

[1] The terms autocorrelation and serial correlation are used interchangeably.

Sources of Autocorrelation

The following are some of the reasons behind the autocorrelation problem.

- *Prolonged influence of shocks*: We have pointed out above that the problem of autocorrelation is found more in time series data. This may happen due to prolonged influence of shocks. In time series data, random shocks or disturbances have effects which persist for a number of time periods. For example, an earthquake, flood, drought, or war affects the performance of the economy in periods following the period of its occurrence. The influences of such shocks become all the more visible when we consider shorter time intervals. It is found more prominently in weekly, monthly, and quarterly data compared to yearly data. Thus, the autocorrelation problem becomes more prevalent when time series data with shorter time intervals are considered.
- *Inertia*: Past actions often have strong influence on current actions owing to inertia or psychological conditioning. Thus, a positive disturbance in one period is likely to influence activities in successive periods resulting in autocorrelation.
- *Spatial autocorrelation*: Although the incidence of the autocorrelation problem is much high in time series data, some cross-sectional data might also suffer from this problem. For example, while working with household-level data, we may observe the disturbances of the households in the same neighbourhood being correlated. Similarly, shocks due to adverse weather conditions might cause error terms of contiguous regions to be related. These are called 'spatial autocorrelation'. However, the presumption that autocorrelation is found in relationships estimated from observations over time is so high that in discussion on autocorrelation, the variables are given a subscript, t (for time) rather than i, that is used in the general case.
- *Model misspecification*: Misspecification of the model might lead to the autocorrelation problem. Exclusion of a relevant explanatory variable from the model, whose successive values are correlated, will make the disturbance term associated with the misspecified model autocorrelated. So when that variable is included in the model, the apparent problem of autocorrelation disappears.[2]

5.2 SPECIFICATION OF AUTOCORRELATION RELATIONSHIP

Supposing that any two successive values of disturbance term are correlated, we may formally express the autocorrelation relationship as

$$\varepsilon_t = \rho \varepsilon_{t-1} + u_t \qquad (5.1)$$

---

[2] However, it may be noted that autocorrelation in the omitted variables need not necessarily imply an autocorrelated disturbance term since individual components may cancel each other out. But, if the autocorrelation in the omitted variables is pervasive and if the omitted variables tend to move in a phase, then the disturbance term will in all likelihood be autocorrelated.

where ρ is a parameter whose absolute value is less than 1, i.e., $|\rho| < 1$ and u_t is the disturbance term of the above autocorrelation relationship, which has the following properties.

$$\left. \begin{array}{l} E(u_t) = 0 \\ Var(u_t) = E(u_t^2) = \sigma_u^2 \end{array} \right\} \text{ for all } t$$

u_t is normally distributed

$$E(u_t u_{t-i}) = 0$$

Equation (5.1) is known as the first-order autoregressive scheme, denoted by AR(1). By successive substitutions for $\varepsilon_{t-1}, \varepsilon_{t-2}, \dots$ in (5.1), we obtain

$$\begin{aligned} \varepsilon_t &= \rho(\rho\varepsilon_{t-2} + u_{t-1}) + u_t \\ &= \rho^2 \varepsilon_{t-2} + \rho u_{t-1} + u_t \\ &= \rho^2(\rho\varepsilon_{t-3} + u_{t-2}) + \rho u_{t-1} + u_t \\ &= \rho^3 \varepsilon_{t-3} + \rho^2 u_{t-2} + \rho u_{t-1} + u_t \\ &= u_t + \rho u_{t-1} + \rho^2 u_{t-2} + \dots \end{aligned} \tag{5.2}$$

This shows that under the first-order autoregressive scheme, the effect of past disturbances wears off gradually, as $|\rho| < 1$.

We may use the expression (5.2) to compute mean, variance, and covariance of disturbances.

Mean of ε_t
The mean of ε_t is

$$\begin{aligned} E(\varepsilon_t) &= E(u_t + \rho u_{t-1} + \rho^2 u_{t-2} + \dots) \\ &= 0 \quad [\because E(u_t) = 0 \text{ for all } t] \end{aligned}$$

Variance of ε_t

$$\begin{aligned} Var(\varepsilon_t) &= E(u_t + \rho u_{t-1} + \rho^2 u_{t-2} + \dots)^2 \\ &= E(u_t^2 + \rho^2 u_{t-1}^2 + \rho^4 u_{t-2}^2 + \dots + 2\rho u_t u_{t-1} + 2\rho^2 u_t u_{t-2} + \dots) \\ &= Var(u_t) + \rho^2 Var(u_{t-1}) + \rho^4 Var(u_{t-2}) + \dots \quad [\because E(u_t u_{t-i}) = 0] \\ &= \sigma_u^2(1 + \rho^2 + \rho^4 + \dots) \quad\quad\quad [\because E(u_t^2) = \sigma_u^2 \text{ for all } t] \\ &= \frac{\sigma_u^2}{1 - \rho^2} \\ &= \sigma_\varepsilon^2 \end{aligned} \tag{5.3}$$

Covariance of ε_t and ε_{t-1}

From (5.2), we have

$$\varepsilon_t = u_t + \rho u_{t-1} + \rho^2 u_{t-2} + ...$$

Lagging this by one period,

$$\varepsilon_{t-1} = u_{t-1} + \rho u_{t-2} + \rho^2 u_{t-3} + ...$$

So the covariance between ε_t and ε_{t-1} is

$$Cov(\varepsilon_t, \varepsilon_{t-1}) = E(\varepsilon_t \varepsilon_{t-1})$$
$$= E[\{u_t + \rho u_{t-1} + \rho^2 u_{t-2} + ...\}\{u_{t-1} + \rho u_{t-2} + \rho^2 u_{t-3} + ...\}]$$
$$= E[\{u_t + \rho(u_{t-1} + \rho u_{t-2} + ...\}\{u_{t-1} + \rho u_{t-2} + \rho^2 u_{t-3} + ...\}]$$
$$= E[u_t u_{t-1} + \rho u_t u_{t-2} + \rho^2 u_t u_{t-3} + ...] + \rho E[u_{t-1} + \rho u_{t-2} + \rho^2 u_{t-3} + ...]^2$$

$$= \rho(\sigma_u^2 + \rho^2 \sigma_u^2 + \rho^4 \sigma_u^2 + ...) \text{ (using assumptions of } u_t \text{ mentioned above)}$$

$$= \frac{\rho \sigma_u^2}{1 - \rho^2}$$

$$= \rho \sigma_\varepsilon^2 \qquad \left[\because \sigma_\varepsilon^2 = \sigma_u^2 / (1 - \rho^2) \right] \qquad (5.4)$$

From (5.4), it follows that

$$\rho = \frac{E(\varepsilon_t \varepsilon_{t-1})}{\sigma_\varepsilon^2} \qquad (5.5)$$

$$\rho^2 = \frac{E(\varepsilon_t \varepsilon_{t-2})}{\sigma_\varepsilon^2}$$

.

.

$$\rho^s = \frac{E(\varepsilon_t \varepsilon_{t-s})}{\sigma_\varepsilon^2} \qquad (5.6)$$

An important observation here is that if we put $s = 0$ in (5.6), then $E(\varepsilon_t^2)/\sigma_\varepsilon^2 = \sigma_\varepsilon^2/\sigma_\varepsilon^2 = 1$, which means that zero-order autocorrelation coefficient is unity.

We can rewrite (5.5) as

$$\rho = \frac{Cov(\varepsilon_t, \varepsilon_{t-1})}{\sqrt{Var(\varepsilon_t)}\sqrt{Var(\varepsilon_{t-1})}}.$$

This means that ρ also represents the correlation coefficient between ε_t and ε_{t-1}. Similarly, ρ^2 is the correlation coefficient between ε_t and ε_{t-2} and ρ^s is the correlation coefficient between ε_t and ε_{t-s}.

Further, it is clear from (5.1) that the strength of autocorrelation problem is determined by the value of ρ. We may have three different cases here.

(i)   When $\rho = 0$, there is no autocorrelation because ε_t becomes equal to u_t which does not suffer from autocorrelation. Such a situation is depicted in Figure 5.1.

(ii)   The strength of autocorrelation becomes high as ρ approaches to unity $(+1)$. Here the value of previous observation of ε_t becomes important to determine its value at the current period and both the values have same sign (both are either positive or negative). This is the case of positive autocorrelation, which is shown in Figure 5.2.

(iii)   If ρ approaches to -1, the strength of autocorrelation becomes high again. Here also the past value of the disturbance term becomes important in determining its value in the current period. But the signs of the disturbance term switch in consecutive observations, as shown in Figure 5.3. This is the case of negative autocorrelation.

Economic examples of negative autocorrelation are relatively uncommon. Sometimes, it is induced by manipulations used to transform the original specification of the model into a form suitable for regression analysis. In our empirical works, in most cases, we are concerned with first-order autocorrelation as described by equation (5.1) although the presence of higher order autocorrelation could not be ruled out altogether in some data sets.

5.3 CONSEQUENCES OF AUTOCORRELATION

To understand the consequences of autocorrelation on the OLS estimators, we examine whether OLS estimators continue to remain unbiased, best, and consistent when this problem

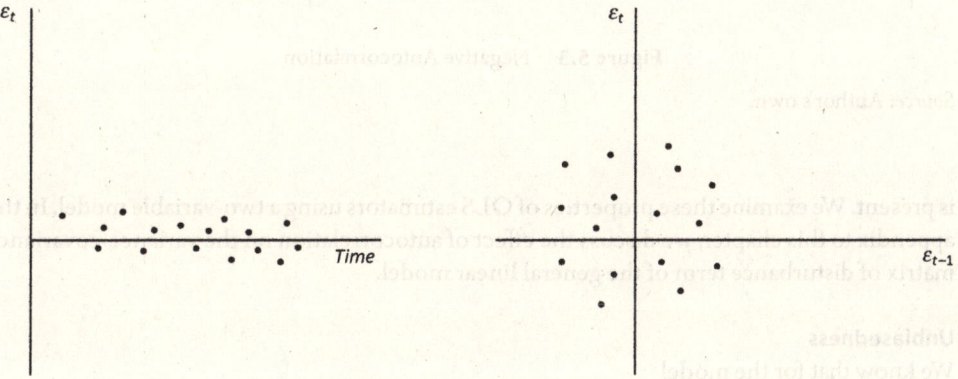

Figure 5.1   Zero Autocorrelation

Source: Author's own.

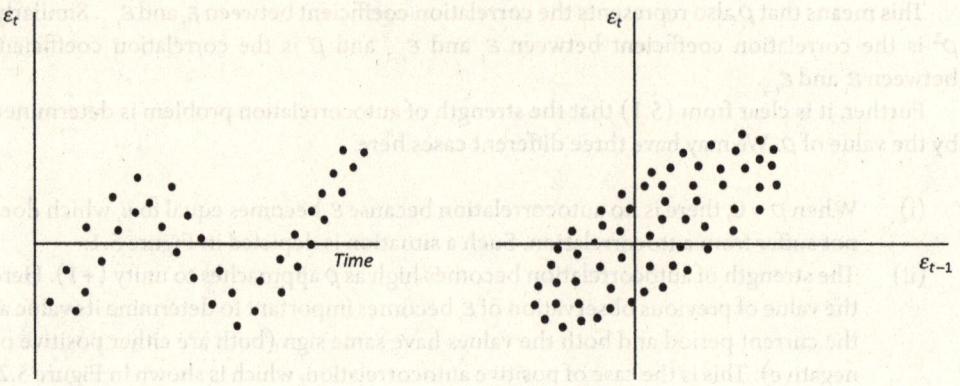

Figure 5.2   Positive Autocorrelation

Source: Author's own.

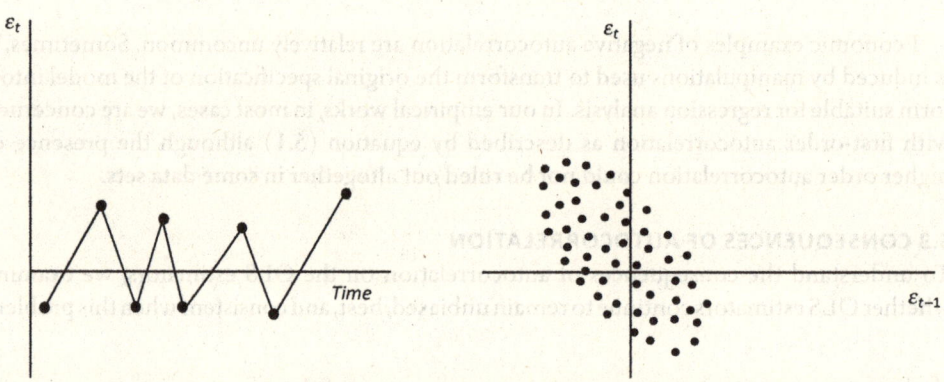

Figure 5.3   Negative Autocorrelation

Source: Author's own.

is present. We examine these properties of OLS estimators using a two-variable model. In the appendix to this chapter, we discuss the effect of autocorrelation on the variance-covariance matrix of disturbance term of the general linear model.

Unbiasedness

We know that for the model

$$Y_t = \alpha + \beta X_t + \varepsilon_t$$

$\hat{\beta}$, the OLS estimator of β, is given by

$$\hat{\beta} = \frac{\sum x_t y_t}{\sum x_t^2}$$

$$= \beta + \frac{\sum x_t \varepsilon_t}{\sum x_t^2}$$

Taking expectations, $E(\hat{\beta}) = \beta$, which implies that $\hat{\beta}$ is an unbiased estimator of β. So, autocorrelation does not remove the unbiasedness property for the OLS estimators.

Bestness

To examine this property, let us compute the variance of $\hat{\beta}$ under autocorrelation, which will be compared with variance of $\hat{\beta}$ when there is no autocorrelation.

$$Var(\hat{\beta}) = E[\hat{\beta} - \beta]^2$$

$$= E\left(\frac{\sum x_t \varepsilon_t}{\sum x_t^2}\right)^2$$

$$= \frac{1}{(\sum x_t^2)^2} E\left(\sum_{t=1} x_t^2 \varepsilon_t^2 + 2\sum_{t=2} x_t x_{t-1} \varepsilon_t \varepsilon_{t-1} + 2\sum_{t=3} x_t x_{t-2} \varepsilon_t \varepsilon_{t-2} + ...\right)$$

$$= \frac{1}{(\sum x_t^2)^2}\left(\sigma^2 \sum x_t^2 + 2\rho\sigma^2 \sum x_t x_{t-1} + 2\rho^2 \sigma^2 \sum x_t x_{t-2} + ...\right)$$

$$\left[\because \frac{E(\varepsilon_t \varepsilon_{t-k})}{\sigma^2} = \rho^k \Rightarrow E(\varepsilon_t \varepsilon_{t-k}) = \rho^k \sigma^2\right]$$

$$= \frac{\sigma^2}{\sum x_t^2}\left(1 + 2\rho\frac{\sum x_t x_{t-1}}{\sum x_t^2} + 2\rho^2\frac{\sum x_t x_{t-2}}{\sum x_t^2} + ...\right) \qquad (5.7)$$

Since ρ is positive and $\sum x_t x_{t-k}$ is also positive (expectedly), the expression in the bracket is greater than 1. Thus, $Var(\hat{\beta})\big|_{AR} > Var(\hat{\beta})$, which means that $\hat{\beta}$ is no longer a minimum variance or best estimator.

Consistency

Here, we have to check whether $\lim_{n \to \infty} Var(\hat{\beta}) = 0$, so that we can say $\hat{\beta}$ is a consistent estimator although it was not a minimum variance or best estimator.

From (5.7), we have

$$Var(\hat{\beta}) = \frac{\sigma^2}{\sum x_t^2}\left[1 + 2\rho\frac{\sum x_t x_{t-1}}{\sum x_t^2} + 2\rho^2\frac{\sum x_t x_{t-2}}{\sum x_t^2} + ...\right]$$

$$= \frac{\sigma^2}{\sum x_t^2} + \frac{2\sigma^2}{(\sum x_t^2)^2}\left[\rho\sum x_t x_{t-1} + \rho^2\sum x_t x_{t-2} + \ ....\right]$$

$$= \frac{\sigma^2}{\sum x_t^2} + \frac{2\sigma^2}{(\sum x_t^2)^2}\left[\rho r_1\sqrt{\sum x_t^2}\sqrt{\sum x_{t-1}^2} + \rho^2 r_2\sqrt{\sum x_t^2}\sqrt{\sum x_{t-2}^2} + \ ....\right]$$

$$\left(\because r_k = \frac{\sum x_t x_{t-k}}{\sqrt{\sum x_t^2}\sqrt{\sum x_{t-k}^2}} \Rightarrow \sum x_t x_{t-k} = r_k\sqrt{\sum x_t^2}\sqrt{\sum x_{t-k}^2}\right)$$

$$= \frac{\sigma^2/n}{\sum x_t^2/n} + \frac{2(\sigma^2/n)}{(\sum x_t^2/n)^2}\left[\rho r_1\sqrt{\sum x_t^2/n}\sqrt{\sum x_{t-1}^2/n} + \rho^2 r_2\sqrt{\sum x_t^2/n}\sqrt{\sum x_{t-2}^2/n} + \ ....\right]$$

Now as $n \to \infty$,

(i) $\sigma^2/n \to 0$;

(ii) $\sum x_t^2/n, \sum x_{t-1}^2/n, \sum x_{t-2}^2/n, \ ....$ approach to some finite number (say θ); and

(iii) $r_1, r_2, \ ....$ approach to numbers with absolute value ≤ 1, say $r_1^*, r_2^*, \ ....$

Therefore,

$$\lim_{n\to\infty} Var(\hat{\beta}) = \frac{\lim\limits_{n\to\infty}(\sigma^2/n)}{\theta} + \frac{2\lim\limits_{n\to\infty}(\sigma^2/n)}{\theta^2}\left(\rho r_1^*\theta + \rho^2 r_2^*\theta + \ ....\right) = 0$$

This proves that $\hat{\beta}$ is a consistent estimator even under autocorrelation.

So our conclusions regarding consequences of autocorrelation are

(i)   The OLS estimators are still unbiased and consistent.

(ii)   The OLS estimators are no longer minimum variance or best estimators. Hence they are not efficient and BLUE.

(iii)   If we disregard the problem of autocorrelation and believe that all usual assumptions are valid, following problems will arise.

      (a)   The estimated variance of disturbance term $[\hat{\sigma}_\varepsilon^2 = \sum\hat{\varepsilon}_t^2/(n-2)]$ will be an underestimate of its true variance σ_ε^2.

      (b)   The standard error of estimated slope coefficient $(\hat{\beta})$ will be much smaller if it is computed using usual OLS formula instead of (5.7) which will provide spurious impression about its statistical significance.

      (c)   The usual t and F tests will become invalid.

5.4 TESTS FOR AUTOCORRELATION

Several tests of autocorrelation are available. We discuss here a few important ones.

Graphical Approach

As autocorrelation is a problem that manifests itself via systematic patterns in residuals from a regression, the simplest way to understand the presence of autocorrelation is through visual inspection of plots of estimated residuals. If a picture like Figure 5.2 emerges when $\hat{\varepsilon}_t$ is plotted against $\hat{\varepsilon}_{t-1}$, we say that positive autocorrelation is present. On the other hand, when a picture like Figure 5.3 is observed, we say that there is negative autocorrelation. Absence of autocorrelation is represented by a picture like Figure 5.1.

Durbin-Watson (1951) Test

This is the simplest and most widely used test for autocorrelation. It is based on following assumptions.

(i)   The regression model includes a constant or intercept term.
(ii) We are examining presence of first-order autocorrelation.
(iii) The regression model does not include a lagged dependent variable as an explanatory variable.

Now to understand how the test is performed, consider the model

$$Y_t = \beta_0 + \beta_1 X_{1t} + \beta_2 X_{2t} + ... + \beta_k X_{kt} + \varepsilon_t \tag{5.8}$$

$$\text{where } \varepsilon_t = \rho \varepsilon_{t-1} + u_t \qquad\qquad |\rho| < 1 \tag{5.9}$$

Under the null hypothesis H_N: $\rho = 0$, the test is performed through the following steps.

Step 1: Estimate model (5.8) by OLS and obtain the estimated residuals $\hat{\varepsilon}_t = e_t$.

Step 2: Compute Durbin-Watson d-statistic as

$$d = \frac{\sum\limits_{t=2}^{n} (\hat{\varepsilon}_t - \hat{\varepsilon}_{t-1})^2}{\sum\limits_{t=1}^{n} \hat{\varepsilon}_t^2}$$

$$= \frac{\sum\limits_{t=2}^{n} (e_t - e_{t-1})^2}{\sum\limits_{t=1}^{n} e_t^2}$$

$$= \frac{\sum\limits_{t=2}^{n} e_t^2 + \sum\limits_{t=2}^{n} e_{t-1}^2 - 2\sum\limits_{t=2}^{n} e_t e_{t-1}}{\sum\limits_{t=1}^{n} e_t^2}$$

For large samples,

$$d \approx \frac{2\sum\limits_{t=1}^{n} e_t^2 - 2\sum\limits_{t=1}^{n} e_t e_{t-1}}{\sum\limits_{t=1}^{n} e_t^2} \approx 2\left(1 - \frac{\sum\limits_{t=1}^{n} e_t e_{t-1}}{\sum\limits_{t=1}^{n} e_t^2}\right)$$

Or

$$d \approx 2(1-\rho) \quad \left(\because \rho = \frac{\dfrac{1}{n}\sum_{t=1}^{n} e_t\, e_{t-1}}{\sqrt{\dfrac{1}{n}\sum_{t=1}^{n} e_t^2}\ \sqrt{\dfrac{1}{n}\sum_{t=1}^{n} e_{t-1}^2}} \right) \tag{5.10}$$

Step 3: Test statistical significance of computed-d (denoted by d^*) by comparing it with the value of theoretical-d, available from Durbin-Watson d-table (given in Statistical Tables A.10 and A.11). The distribution of d depends on number of observations (n) and number of explanatory variables (k) in the model. The Durbin-Watson d-table, in fact, provides upper and lower limits for d, called d_U and d_L values, respectively. The decision rules are summarized in Table 5.1.

Table 5.1   Decision Rules for the Durbin-Watson Test

If →	$0 < d^* < d_L$	$d_L \leq d^* \leq d_U$	$d_U < d^* < 4-d_U$	$4-d_U \leq d^* \leq 4-d_L$	$4-d_L < d^* \leq 4$
Then →	Reject H_N	No decision possible	Do not reject H_N	No decision possible	Reject H_N
Inference →	Positive autocorrelation	–	No significant autocorrelation	–	Negative autocorrelation

Source: Author's own.

Limitations of Durbin-Watson Test
Some limitations of the Durbin-Watson test are:

- It cannot be used for testing higher-order autocorrelation.
- This test is biased towards non-rejection of null hypothesis when a lagged dependent variable is included in the model as an explanatory variable.
- It becomes inapplicable if the model does not contain an intercept term. In this case, one should include an intercept term before applying this test.
- In two cases, when d^* falls between d_L and d_U, and $4-d_U$ and $4-d_L$, the test produces inconclusive result. This is the most troublesome aspect of this test. This happens because the exact distribution of d depends on the sample values of the explanatory variable(s), which change from application to application. One way of dealing with the inconclusive region is to recalculate the relevant part of the distribution for each new set of explanatory variable(s). Using some computer software package one can do this.
- This test is not robust for small samples.

Theil-Nagar Correction to Durbin-Watson d-statistic

To make the Durbin-Watson test suitable for small samples, Theil-Nagar modified the d-statistic. As $d = 2\,(1 - \rho) \Rightarrow \rho = 1 - (d/2)$, Theil-Nagar suggested that, in case of a small sample, ρ should be corrected as

$$\rho_{corrected} = \frac{n^2\left(1-\dfrac{d}{2}\right)+k^2}{n^2-k^2}$$

where n = number of observations and k = number of parameters in the model (including the intercept term).

Durbin's (1970) h-test

In a situation, where lagged dependent variable appeared as an explanatory variable of the model, one can use Durbin's h-test to examine the presence of autocorrelation. This test is outlined below.

Consider the model

$$Y_t = \alpha + \beta X_t + \gamma Y_{t-1} + \varepsilon_t \tag{5.11}$$

$$\text{where } \varepsilon_t = \rho \varepsilon_{t-1} + u_t$$

The hypothesis to be tested is: $H_N: \rho = 0$
We compute the value of h-statistic as

$$h = \left(1 - \frac{d}{2}\right)\sqrt{\frac{n}{1 - n\,s_{\hat{\gamma}}^2}} \tag{5.12}$$

where d = usual Durbin-Watson d-statistic, and $s_{\hat{\gamma}}^2$ = estimated variance of least-squares estimate of γ. The steps involved in computation of h are

(i)   Estimate (5.11) by OLS method.
(ii)   Compute the variance of $\hat{\gamma}$.
(iii) Compute d.
(iv)   Compute $\rho = 1 - (d/2)$.
(v)   Compute h.

Durbin has shown that, for large samples, the h-statistic follows a standard normal distribution with zero mean and unit variance, i.e., $h \sim N(0, 1)$. Therefore, statistical significance of computed h can be tested using the standardized normal distribution table. From normal distribution, we know that

$$\text{Prob}[-1.96 \le h \le 1.96] = 0.95$$

So the *decision rules* are

- If $h > 1.96$, we reject H_N (at 95% level of confidence) and conclude that first-order positive autocorrelation $[AR(1)]$ is present in data.
- If $h < -1.96$, we reject H_N (at 95% level of confidence) and conclude that first-order negative autocorrelation is present in data.
- When $-1.96 \leq h \leq 1.96$, H_N is accepted and the conclusion is that of absence of autocorrelation (positive or negative).

One important limitation of Durbin's h-test is that it cannot be applied if $ns_{\hat{\gamma}}^2 > 1$. In that case, the h-test suffers from 'indeterminacy problem'. Although this situation does not usually arise, we will have to use some other test if it happens.

Breusch-Godfrey Lagrange Multiplier Test

Given the problems of Durbin-Watson test, it is always good to use some other test for autocorrelation. Although there are many alternatives here, the most widely used test is the Breusch-Godfrey Lagrange Multiplier Test (BG test) developed by Breusch (1978) and Godfrey (1978). This test can pick up higher-order autocorrelation and can be performed using many econometrics software packages, including EViews. It is also a more powerful test as it is not biased towards non-rejection of the null hypothesis when a lagged dependent variable is included in the model as an explanatory variable.

To understand the BG test procedure, consider the model

$$Y_t = \beta_0 + \beta_1 X_{1t} + \beta_2 X_{2t} + ... + \beta_k X_{kt} + \varepsilon_t \tag{5.13}$$

where

$$\varepsilon_t = \rho_1 \varepsilon_{t-1} + \rho_2 \varepsilon_{t-2} + ... + \rho_p \varepsilon_{t-p} + u_t \tag{5.14}$$

The null and alternative hypotheses are

$H_N: \rho_1 = \rho_2 = ... = \rho_p = 0$ (No autocorrelation)

H_A: At least one of the ρs is non-zero   (Autocorrelation is present)

Now the BG test is executed through the following steps.

Step 1: Estimate (5.13) by OLS and obtain $\hat{\varepsilon}_t = e_t$.
Step 2: Run the auxiliary regression of e_t on $X_{1t}, X_{2t}, ..., X_{kt}, e_{t-1}, e_{t-2}, ..., e_{t-p}$.
Step 3: To test the validity of above null hypothesis, compute the *LM*-statistic = $(n - p)$. R^2 using the value of R^2 from auxiliary regression (here n is number of observations and p

is the order of autocorrelation we are examining).[3] This LM-statistic follows a Chi-square distribution with degrees of freedom p.

Step 4: Follow the *decision rule* which states that if the value of computed LM-statistic is greater than theoretical value of χ^2 at a chosen level of significance (λ) and given degrees of freedom (p), reject the null hypothesis and conclude that autocorrelation is present. Alternatively, if the p-value associated with computed-χ^2 is less than 0.05, we reject the null hypothesis at 5% significance level.

Note that an F-version of the BG-test may also be constructed. For this, we run the auxiliary regression twice—once by including the terms $e_{t-1}, e_{t-2}, \dots, e_{t-p}$ and again by dropping these terms. The former is the 'unrestricted model' and the latter is the 'restricted model'. Then, we compute the F-value as:

$$F^* = \frac{(R_{UR}^2 - R_R^2)/p}{(1 - R_{UR}^2)/(n - m - 1 - p)} \tag{5.15}$$

where R_{UR}^2 and R_R^2 are values of R^2 from unrestricted and restricted models, respectively; n = number of observations, and m = number of explanatory variables in unrestricted model. Here, the *decision rule* is that if $F^* > F_\lambda(p, n - m - 1 - p)$, we reject the null hypothesis and conclude that autocorrelation is present.

5.5 REMEDIAL MEASURES

We know that the presence of autocorrelation makes the OLS estimators inefficient. So it is necessary to correct this problem. We discuss below two different approaches that may be followed to correct autocorrelation problem.

When the Value of ρ Is Known

The autocorrelation problem can be easily corrected when the value of the autocorrelation coefficient is known. To understand how, consider the model

$$Y_t = \alpha + \beta X_t + \varepsilon_t \tag{5.16}$$

where ε_t is assumed to follow first-order autocorrelation so that

$$\varepsilon_t = \rho \varepsilon_{t-1} + u_t \tag{5.17}$$

Now lagging (5.16) by one period and pre-multiplying it by ρ, we get

$$\rho Y_{t-1} = \rho \alpha + \rho \beta X_{t-1} + \rho \varepsilon_{t-1} \tag{5.18}$$

---

[3] Note that choice of p may sometimes become arbitrary. However, the periodicity of data (monthly, quarterly, yearly, and so on) may guide us to determine the size of p.

Subtracting (5.18) from (5.16) gives

$$(Y_t - \rho Y_{t-1}) = (1-\rho)\alpha + \beta(X_t - \rho X_{t-1}) + (\varepsilon_t - \rho \varepsilon_{t-1}) \qquad (5.19)$$

So

$$Y_t^* = \alpha^* + \beta X_t^* + u_t \quad \left[\because u_t = \varepsilon_t - \rho \varepsilon_{t-1} \ (\text{from } 5.17) \right] \qquad (5.20)$$

where $Y_t^* = (Y_t - \rho Y_{t-1})$, $X_t^* = (X_t - \rho X_{t-1})$ and $\alpha^* = (1-\rho)\alpha$.

It is clear that we lost one observation with this transformation. In order to avoid this loss of observation, it is suggested that Y_1 and X_1 should be transformed for first observation as follows.

$$Y_1^* = Y_1 \sqrt{1-\rho^2} \ \text{ and } \ X_1^* = X_1 \sqrt{1-\rho^2}$$

The transformation that generated Y_t^*, X_t^*, and α^* is known as quasi-differencing or generalized differencing.[4]

It is to be noted that the disturbance term u_t in (5.20) satisfies all usual assumptions of the CLRM. So if ρ is known, we can apply OLS to (5.20) and obtain estimates that are BLUE.

When the Value of ρ Is Unknown

This is the situation that we face in reality. There are two different approaches that can be followed when ρ is not known.

Cochrane-Orcutt (1949) Iterative Procedure

Under this method, we estimate the following equation by OLS method.

$$Y_t = \alpha + \beta X_t + \varepsilon_t$$

Then we obtain $\hat{\varepsilon}_t = e_t$, which is used to calculate $\hat{\rho}$ as

$$\hat{\rho} = \frac{\sum e_t e_{t-1}}{\sum e_t^2}$$

In the next step, use $\hat{\rho}$ to estimate the model

$$(Y_t - \hat{\rho} Y_{t-1}) = \alpha^* + \beta(X_t - \hat{\rho} X_{t-1}) + (\varepsilon_t - \hat{\rho} \varepsilon_{t-1})$$

---

[4] This is known as Prais-Winsten transformation.

Thus, a two-step estimation is involved here.

Suppose α' and β' are Cochrane-Orcutt estimates of α and β in the second step. Use them to obtain a new set of residuals $e'_t = Y_t - \alpha' - \beta' X_t$ and also obtain a new estimate of ρ, say $\hat{\rho}$, as

$$\hat{\rho} = \frac{\sum e'_t e'_{t-1}}{\sum e'^2_t}$$

Again use $\hat{\rho}$ to construct the model

$$(Y_t - \hat{\rho} Y_{t-1}) = \alpha^{**} + \beta(X_t - \hat{\rho} X_{t-1}) + (\varepsilon_t - \hat{\rho} \varepsilon_{t-1})$$

and this procedure is continued until estimated values of α and β converge, i.e., they stop differing by no more than some pre-selected (very small) value, say 0.001.[5]

Hildreth-Lu (1960) Search Procedure

This is a simple approach which is intuitively appealing. Here the OLS method is repeatedly applied to estimate the equation

$$(Y_t - \rho Y_{t-1}) = \alpha^* + \beta(X_t - \rho X_{t-1}) + (\varepsilon_t - \rho \varepsilon_{t-1})$$

by assigning different values to ρ between -1 and $+1$, say

$$\rho = -0.99, -0.98, -0.97, ..., 0.97, 0.98, 0.99$$

From all these estimated models, we select the one that gives the lowest value of the residual sum squares (RSS). Thus, a 'search procedure' is involved here.

It is clear that this search procedure is very hectic and involves a lot of calculations. On the other hand, EViews provides the results of the Cochrane-Orcutt iterative procedure very quickly. While applying the iterative procedure, EViews actually utilizes an iterative non-linear method for estimating generalized differencing results with AR(1) errors (i.e., autoregressive errors of first order) in the presence of autocorrelation. Since the procedure is iterative, it requires a number of repetitions in order to achieve the desired convergence which is reported in the EViews output. This will become clear from the example that we consider in the next section.

Heteroskedasticity and Autocorrelation Consistent (HAC) Standard Errors

When the disturbance term is autocorrelated, instead of using the above methods, we can still apply the OLS method and obtain the corrected standard errors which are known as 'heteroskedasticity and autocorrelation consistent' (HAC) standard errors. The HAC standard errors are standard errors for OLS estimators that are consistent whether or not the disturbance term of the model is homoskedastic and autocorrelated. The method of

---

[5] Usually, such a convergence is attained after 6 to 8 iterations.

obtaining such standard errors has been developed by Newey and West (1987).[6] Most standard software packages, including EViews, enable us to compute the HAC standard errors or Newey-West standard errors. However, it is to be remembered that the HAC standard errors may not be valid (accurate) when the size of the sample is small.

5.6 APPLICATIONS USING EVIEWS

The Durbin-Watson Test

The EViews regression output contains, among other things, the value of Durbin-Watson statistic. To understand its interpretation, let us estimate a multiple regression model using data given in Table 5.2. The table presents time series data for India on three variables: cropping intensity (CRIN), percentage of gross cropped area irrigated (IRRI), and fertilizers consumption (FERT). Our objective is to examine whether IRRI and FERT are important (statistically significant) determinants of CRIN in India.

With the above objective in mind, we estimate a multiple regression model following the EViews command line suggested in Chapter 3. The resulting regression output is presented in Table 5.3. It is found that the computed value of Durbin-Watson statistic (d^*) is 1.566 (approximately). From the Durbin-Watson table, for $n = 58$ and $k = 2$, the values of d_L and d_U are found as 1.514 and 1.652, respectively (at 0.05 level of significance). It is clear that, for our estimated model, $d_L = (1.514) < d^*(= 1.566) < d_U(= 1.652)$. This shows that d^* falls in a zone of indecision. Hence, we cannot conclude anything about presence/absence of autocorrelation in terms of the Durbin-Watson test.

The Breusch–Godfrey (BG) test

Let us now perform the BG test to see if it can detect presence of any autocorrelation in our data. To perform this test in EViews, the steps are the following.

(i)   Estimate the multiple regression model following the command line suggested earlier.

(ii)   From the estimation result window, click **View/Residual Diagnostics/Serial Correlation LM Test...** which will open a small box for specifying the number of lags to be included in the test.

(iii)   Specify the number of lags (this is by default chosen as 2 but can be changed as per our requirement).

(iv)   Click **OK** to obtain the test output.

The BG test output obtained by us (under lag 2) is reported in Table 5.4.[7] It is found that the p-value of the Chi-square statistic (=Obs*R-squared) is 0.0516. So we reject the null

---

[6] We do not discuss the theory underlying the Newey-West methodology as that is beyond the scope of this book.

[7] With lag length 1, we did not find any autocorrelation. That is why we chose lag length 2 to run the test and found presence of autocorrelation of second-order in our data.

Table 5.2 Cropping Intensity (CRIN), Percentage of Gross Irrigated Area (IRRI), and
Fertilizers Consumption (kg) Per Hectare (FERT) in India

Year	CRIN	IRRI	FERT	Year	CRIN	IRRI	FERT
1950–51	111.07	17.11	0.52	1979–80	122.10	29.02	30.99
1951–52	111.58	17.40	0.50	1980–81	123.31	28.84	31.95
1952–53	111.54	16.93	0.48	1981–82	124.53	29.09	34.31
1953–54	112.36	17.10	0.74	1982–83	123.20	30.00	36.98
1954–55	112.70	17.32	0.84	1983–84	125.71	29.97	42.94
1955–56	114.05	17.41	0.89	1984–85	125.15	30.92	46.57
1956–57	114.25	17.20	1.03	1985–86	126.66	30.42	47.48
1957–58	112.98	18.26	1.26	1986–87	126.39	31.61	49.01
1958–59	115.02	17.77	1.48	1987–88	127.33	32.82	51.45
1959–60	114.95	17.96	2.00	1988–89	128.47	33.54	60.57
1960–61	114.69	18.32	1.91	1989–90	128.05	33.93	63.47
1961–62	115.37	18.22	2.16	1990–91	129.89	33.63	67.55
1962–63	114.98	18.79	2.88	1991–92	128.67	36.04	69.84
1963–64	115.01	18.93	3.46	1992–93	130.11	35.95	65.46
1964–65	115.28	19.29	4.85	1993–94	131.08	36.58	66.28
1965–66	114.01	19.90	5.06	1994–95	131.54	37.57	72.13
1966–67	114.67	20.77	7.00	1995–96	131.84	38.06	74.02
1967–68	117.06	20.28	9.40	1996–97	132.58	40.12	75.50
1968–69	116.18	22.24	11.04	1997–98	133.86	39.69	85.19
1969–70	116.93	22.78	12.21	1998–99	134.27	40.88	87.63
1970–71	118.19	23.04	13.13	1999–2000	134.39	41.60	95.38
1971–72	118.23	23.26	16.08	2000–01	131.11	41.11	90.12
1972–73	118.24	24.09	17.07	2001–02	133.80	41.65	92.20
1973–74	119.27	23.71	16.71	2002–03	132.54	41.81	91.66
1974–75	119.16	25.42	15.67	2003–04	135.04	41.11	88.38
1975–76	120.93	25.31	16.89	2004–05	135.69	42.38	96.05
1976–77	119.97	26.03	20.38	2005–06	136.44	43.48	105.36
1977–78	121.33	26.75	24.89	2006–07	138.07	44.77	112.05
1978–79	122.25	27.64	29.27	2007–08	139.02	44.56	115.25

Source: Downloaded from www.indiastat.com

hypothesis of 'no autocorrelation' at 5.16% level of significance and conclude that our data
suffer from second-order autocorrelation.

Estimation of Model Using the Iterative Method

As we found second-order autocorrelation, we follow the iterative procedure and estimate
the model again. For this, as always, we click **Quick/Estimate Equation ...** from the main

Table 5.3   Results of Regression of CRIN on IRRI and FERT

Dependent Variable: CRIN
Method: Least Squares
Date: 08/23/13 Time: 15:10
Sample: 1 58
Included observations: 58

Variable	Coefficient	Std. Error	t-Statistic	Prob.
C	101.3351	1.996316	50.76108	0.0000
IRRI	0.691496	0.105600	6.548236	0.0000
FERT	0.051412	0.026654	1.928868	0.0589
R-squared	0.982796	Mean dependent var		123.1567
Adjusted R-squared	0.982170	S.D. dependent var		8.246756
S.E. of regression	1.101172	Akaike info criterion		3.080966
Sum squared resid	66.69189	Schwarz criterion		3.187540
Log likelihood	−86.34800	Hannan-Quinn criter.		3.122479
F-statistic	1570.956	Durbin-Watson stat		1.566062
Prob(F-statistic)	0.000000			

Source: This table represents the output obtained by the author after application of the EViews software.

Table 5.4   Results of the Breusch–Godfrey Test (under Second Order Autocorrelation)

Breusch–Godfrey Serial Correlation LM Test:

F-statistic	3.017307	Prob. F(2,53)		0.0574
Obs*R-squared	5.928854	Prob. Chi-Square(2)		0.0516

Test Equation:
Dependent Variable: RESID
Method: Least Squares
Date: 08/23/13 Time: 15:12
Sample: 1 58
Included observations: 58
Presample missing value lagged residuals set to zero.

Variable	Coefficient	Std. Error	t–Statistic	Prob.
C	0.820298	1.962794	0.417924	0.6777
IRRI	−0.043507	0.103842	−0.418973	0.6769
FERT	0.010962	0.026209	0.418254	0.6775
RESID(−1)	0.139920	0.134726	1.038552	0.3037
RESID(−2)	0.271390	0.133759	2.028950	0.0475
R-squared	0.102222	Mean dependent var		1.82E−14
Adjusted R–squared	0.034465	S.D. dependent var		1.081681
S.E. of regression	1.062877	Akaike info criterion		3.042099
Sum squared resid	59.87453	Schwarz criterion		3.219724
Log likelihood	−83.22087	Hannan-Quinn criter.		3.111287
F-statistic	1.508654	Durbin-Watson stat		1.926051
Prob(F-statistic)	0.212924			

Source: Same as for Table 5.3.

menu of EViews which opens the 'Equation Estimation' dialog box. Here we write **crin c irri fert ar(2)** as the specification of equation,[8] and click **OK**. The resulting output is presented in Table 5.5.

Table 5.5   Regression Output Using Iterative Procedure

Dependent Variable: CRIN
Method: Least Squares
Date: 08/23/13 Time: 15:15
Sample (adjusted): 3 58
Included observations: 56 after adjustments
Convergence achieved after 8 iterations

Variable	Coefficient	Std. Error	t-Statistic	Prob.
C	105.2278	2.496914	42.14312	0.0000
IRRI	0.501555	0.128186	3.912702	0.0003
FERT	0.094230	0.031235	3.016790	0.0039
AR(2)	0.351718	0.123115	2.856819	0.0061
R-squared	0.985866	Mean dependent var		123.5793
Adjusted R-squared	0.985051	S.D. dependent var		8.075106
S.E. of regression	0.987315	Akaike info criterion		2.881094
Sum squared resid	50.68914	Schwarz criterion		3.025762
Log likelihood	−76.67064	Hannan-Quinn criter.		2.937182
F-statistic	1209.050	Durbin-Watson stat		1.866155
Prob(F-statistic)	0.000000			
Inverted AR Roots	.59		−.59	

Source: Same as for Table 5.3.

It is observed that it required eight iterations to obtain the convergent results. Here, the estimated coefficient of AR(2) is statistically significant. This regression model is also not affected by any autocorrelation. This is so because the Durbin-Watson d fell between d_U and $4 - d_U$.[9] So the results of regression based on iterative procedure is quite satisfactory and acceptable. The absence of autocorrelation in this model may additionally be confirmed by running the BG test again. When we ran this test, the results reaffirmed the conclusion of absence of autocorrelation in respect of the results of iterative procedure.

---

[8] Note that we included ar(2) term in the specification of equation with the expectation that it will correct second-order autocorrelation found previously by applying the BG test.

[9] For $n = 56$ and $k = 3$, the Durbin-Watson table reports the values of d_L and d_U as 1.317 and 1.520, respectively (at 0.01 level of significance). Thus, in respect of regression results in Table 5.5, $d_U(=1.317) < d^*(=1.866) < 4 - d_U(=2.480)$ which imply absence of autocorrelation (positive/negative).

OLS Regression with HAC Standard Errors

Let us consider data given in Table 5.2 and see how to run an OLS regression and yet obtain the HAC standard errors. Using EViews, our steps are as follows.

(i)   Go to the 'Equation Estimation' window and put specification of the equation (which is **crin c irri fert**) in the 'Equation specification' jumbo box.

(ii) From 'Equation Estimation' window click 'Options' tab and select 'HAC(Newey-West)' from 'Coefficient covariance matrix' box.

(iv) Click **OK** to obtain the output as shown in Table 5.6.

Table 5.6   Results of OLS Regression with HAC Standard Errors

Dependent Variable: CRIN
Method: Least Squares
Date: 08/23/13 Time: 15:16
Sample: 1 58
Included observations: 58
HAC standard errors & covariance (Bartlett kernel, Newey–West fixed bandwidth = 4.0000)

Variable	Coefficient	Std. Error	t-Statistic	Prob.
C	101.3351	2.384059	42.50530	0.0000
IRRI	0.691496	0.116153	5.953310	0.0000
FERT	0.051412	0.027215	1.889071	0.0642
R-squared	0.982796	Mean dependent var		123.1567
Adjusted R-squared	0.982170	S.D. dependent var		8.246756
S.E. of regression	1.101172	Akaike info criterion		3.080966
Sum squared resid	66.69189	Schwarz criterion		3.187540
Log likelihood	−86.34800	Hannan-Quinn criter.		3.122479
F-statistic	1570.956	Durbin-Watson stat		1.566062
Prob(F-statistic)	0.000000	Wald F-statistic		825.6740
Prob(Wald F-statistic)	0.000000			

Source: Same as for Table 5.3.

The results show that the values of HAC standard errors of the estimated coefficients of IRRI and FERT are expectedly greater than the standard errors of these coefficients reported in Table 5.3. In spite of that, the two coefficients from OLS regression with HAC standard errors have turned out to be statistically significant at 1% and 6% levels of significance, respectively (which is understood from p–values for t–statistics).

5.7 QUESTIONS AND ASSIGNMENTS

A. Multiple-Choice Questions

Tick ($\sqrt{}$) the correct answer.

(i)   The autocorrelation problem arises more in the context of
(a)   Cross-section data

    (b)   Time-series data

    (c)   Qualitative data

    (d)   Categorical data

(ii)   Spatial autocorrelation is found in

    (a)   Cross-section data

    (b)   Time-series data

    (c)   Qualitative data

    (d)   None of the above

(iii) When autocorrelation is present, standard errors of OLS estimators become

    (a)   Zero

    (b)   Smaller

    (c)   Larger

    (d)   Indeterminate

(iv) An appropriate method to examine presence of higher order autocorrelation is

    (a)   White test

    (b)   Goldfeld-Quandt test

    (c)   Breusch-Godfrey LM test

    (d)   Durbin-Watson test

(v)   Estimation using OLS on autocorrelated data results in the parameters being estimated to be

    (a)   Biased

    (b)   Inconsistent

    (c)   Asymptotically normally distributed

    (d)   Inefficient

(vi) If the value of Durbin-Watson test statistic (d) for the classical linear regression model is close to 2, then

    (a)   The model does not suffer from heteroskedasticity problem.

    (b)   The model does not suffer from autocorrelation problem.

    (c)   The error term does not follow first order autoregressive process.

    (d)   The error term is non-stationary.

(vii) The value of zero-order autocorrelation coefficient is always

    (a)   Zero

    (b)   1

    (c)   −1

    (d)   Unknown

(viii) When autocorrelation is present, compared to standard errors from usual OLS regression, the values of HAC standard errors are found to be

    (a)   Greater

    (b)   Smaller

    (c)   Same

    (d)   Changing signs

B. General Questions

(i)   Explain the following.

    (a)   Spatial autocorrelation

    (b)   Durbin's h-test

    (c)   Hildreth-Lu search procedure

    (d)   Theil-Nagar correction to d-statistic

    (e)   First-difference regression

    (f)   HAC standard errors

(ii)   What is meant by autocorrelation? Which assumption of the CLRM is violated under autocorrelation and why?

(iii) What are different sources of autocorrelation problem?

(iv)   Why is autocorrelation found more in time series data? Give two examples where autocorrelation might be present.

(v)   Explain how the Durbin-Watson test helps to detect the presence of autocorrelation in data. What are the steps involved in this test? What are its limitations?

(vi)   How is the Durbin-Watson d-statistic corrected in the case of a small sample?

(vii) How is the Durbin-Watson test revised when the regression model includes lagged dependent variable as an explanatory variable?

(viii) Explain the steps involved in the Breusch-Godfrey LM test for autocorrelation. What is the main advantage of this test?

(ix)   Suggest a suitable test that can pick up higher order autocorrelation in data.

(x)   Suppose the disturbance term of a linear regression model is autocorrelated but the value of autocorrelation coefficient (ρ) is known. How would you estimate such a model?

(xi)   Assume that the disturbance term in a regression model is autocorrelated but the value of autocorrelation coefficient (ρ) is unknown. Suggest any suitable method to estimate such a model.

(xii) Indicate whether the following statements are true (T), false (F) or uncertain (U) and give a brief explanation.

    (a)   The OLS estimators become biased and inefficient when there is autocorrelation.

    (b)   The exclusion of important variables from the model may give rise to autocorrelation problem.

    (c)   The Durbin-Watson test assumes that the variance of the disturbance term is homoskedastic.

    (d)   The Durbin-Watson test becomes inapplicable when the model includes lagged dependent variable as an explanatory variable.

(xiii) Given a sample of 50 observations and 4 explanatory variables, what can we say about autocorrelation if computed Durbin-Watson d-values are (a) 1.05, (b) 2.50, and (c) 3.97? [Note: For 50 observations and 4 explanatory variables, the $d_L = 1.378$ and $d_U = 1.721$ (at 0.05 significance level)]

(xiv) Suppose you obtained the following results from a multiple regression.

$$\hat{Y}_t = 5.2 + 0.45 X_t + 0.78 Y_{t-1}$$
$$S.E.: (0.6)\,(0.04)\quad(0.05)$$
$$R^2 = 0.99 \quad DW = 1.98$$

Are you fully satisfied with the results where R^2 is exceptionally high and the value of Durbin-Watson d-statistic is very close to 2? If not, why?

(xv) Consider the following estimated demand for money function for India for the period 1978–79 to 1994–95.

$$\ln(\hat{M}_t) = 1.6027 - 0.1024 \ln(R_t) + 0.6869 \ln(Y_t) + 0.5284 \ln(M_{t-1})$$
$$S.E:\quad (1.240)\quad(0.368)\qquad\quad(0.343)\qquad\qquad(0.201)$$
$$R^2 = 0.92 \qquad d = 1.86$$

where M = real cash balances, R = long–term rate of interest and Y = aggregate real national income.

(a) State the reason why for this regression equation, the d-statistic is inappropriate.

(b) Compute the value of h-statistic and use it to test the hypothesis that the regression does not suffer from autocorrelation problem.

C. Computer Assignments

(i) Consider the data in Table 2.1 (Chapter 2 above) and run an OLS regression of per capita consumption expenditure on per capita NSDP. Interpret the value of Durbin-Watson d obtained for your estimated model. Is your conclusion regarding presence of autocorrelation same if you apply the Breusch-Godfrey LM test?

(ii) Using data given in Table 2.3 (Chapter 2), estimate a multiple regression model to find out the determinants of infant mortality rate in India. Find the value of Durbin-Watson d for your estimated model and interpret it.

(iii) Use data in Table 2.4 (Chapter 2) to run a regression of incidence of child labour on school dropout rate, poverty, and per capita NSDP. Is it possible to arrive at any conclusion regarding presence of autocorrelation in terms of Durbin-Watson d-statistic? What result you obtain regarding presence of autocorrelation in terms of the Breusch-Godfrey LM test? If autocorrelation is present, apply the Cochrane-Orcutt iterative method to estimate your model and interpret the results.

(iv) Run an OLS regression of GDP on money supply and rate of interest using data given in Table 10.12 (Chapter 10) and test for presence of autocorrelation by applying both the Durbin-Watson and Breusch-Godfrey LM tests. Are the results same for these tests? Also estimate the OLS model with HAC standard errors. What change you observe in the values of HAC standard errors compared to standard errors of the usual OLS model?

Answers to Multiple-Choice Questions

(i) (b); (ii) (a); (iii) (b); (iv) (c); (v) (d); (vi) (c); (vii) (b); (viii) (a).

APPENDIX 5.1: EFFECT OF AUTOCORRELATION ON THE VARIANCE-COVARIANCE MATRIX OF DISTURBANCE TERM OF THE GENERAL LINEAR MODEL

We know that for the general linear model

$$Y = X\beta + \varepsilon \tag{A5.1}$$

the variance-covariance matrix of the disturbance term (ε), under the classical OLS assumptions, is given by

$$E(\varepsilon\varepsilon') = \begin{bmatrix} \sigma^2 & 0 & . & . & . & 0 \\ 0 & \sigma^2 & . & . & . & 0 \\ . & & & & & \\ . & & & & & \\ . & & & & & \\ 0 & 0 & . & . & . & \sigma^2 \end{bmatrix}$$

$$= \sigma^2 \begin{bmatrix} 1 & 0 & . & . & . & 0 \\ 0 & 1 & . & . & . & 0 \\ . & & & & & \\ . & & & & & \\ . & & & & & \\ 0 & 0 & . & . & . & 1 \end{bmatrix}$$

$$= \sigma^2 I \text{ [Here } I \text{ is an } (n \times n) \text{ identity matrix]} \tag{A5.2}$$

However, when there is autocorrelation, the off-diagonal elements of the variance–covariance matrix of the disturbance term will be non-zero. We also know from (5.6) that $\rho^s = E(\varepsilon_t \varepsilon_{t-s})/\sigma_\varepsilon^2 \Rightarrow E(\varepsilon_t \varepsilon_{t-s}) = \rho^s \sigma_\varepsilon^2$. So the variance-covariance matrix of the disturbances for first-order autocorrelation case (when $s = 1$) will be

$$E(\varepsilon\varepsilon') = \sigma^2 \begin{bmatrix} 1 & \rho & \rho^2 & ... & \rho^{n-1} \\ \rho & 1 & \rho & ... & \rho^{n-2} \\ . & & & & \\ . & & & & \\ . & & & & \\ \rho^{n-1} & \rho^{n-2} & \rho^{n-3} & ... & 1 \end{bmatrix} = \Omega^*$$

Here Ω^* is the variance-covariance matrix of the disturbances when there is first-order autocorrelation.

Now the variance-covariance matrix of OLS estimators $\hat{\beta}$ is given by

$$
\begin{aligned}
Cov(\hat{\beta}) &= E[(\hat{\beta}-\beta)(\hat{\beta}-\beta)'] \\
&= (X'X)^{-1} X'E(\varepsilon\varepsilon')X(X'X)^{-1} \\
&= (X'X)^{-1} X'\Omega^* X(X'X)^{-1}
\end{aligned}
\tag{A5.3}
$$

This is different from the classical OLS expression $\sigma^2 (X'X)^{-1}$, which we obtain when there is both homoskedasticity and serial independence (non-autocorrelation). In (A5.3), Ω^* denotes new variance-covariance matrix for the disturbance term, irrespective of the form it takes. Therefore, using classical OLS expression to calculate variances, standard errors and t-statistics of the estimated $\hat{\beta}$s, we are likely to have wrong conclusions. Expression (A5.3) forms the basis for what is known as 'robust' inference, i.e., computing standard errors and t-statistics which are correct even when some of the OLS assumptions are violated. In this situation, we assume a particular form for the variance-covariance matrix and then use (A5.3) to calculate a corrected covariance matrix.

6 Multicollinearity

This chapter discusses the issues related to multicollinearity which is considered as most difficult among all econometric problems. Beginning with the definition of multicollinearity, we note some possible sources of the multicollinearity problem. Next we explain the theoretical consequences of multicollinearity. Some of the tests for detecting multicollinearity and possible remedial measures for this problem are also discussed. Finally, we describe the procedure for testing multicollinearity in data using EViews software. The interpretation of test results has been clarified using examples.

6.1 DEFINITION

In empirical econometrics, while estimating multiple regression models, quite often we obtain unsatisfactory results in the sense that a good number of the estimated coefficients are found to be statistically insignificant. This happens when variances, and hence standard errors, of the estimated coefficients are large. This is possible when there is little variation in explanatory variables or high intercorrelations among the explanatory variables or both.

Multicollinearity refers to a situation where there are high intercorrelations among the explanatory variables of a multiple regression model.[1] Multicollinearity problem arises only in the context of multiple regressions. It is considered as a problem because when the explanatory variables are highly correlated, most of their variation is common so that there is little variation unique to each variable. In such a situation, although it is possible to estimate unknown parameters of the multiple regression model, we cannot separately measure (understand) the effect of each explanatory variable on the dependent variable. In other words, the estimates become imprecise or unreliable when multicollinearity is present.

It is to be remembered that the possibility of having high intercorrelations among the explanatory variables arises when we are using sample data. The question of having intercorrelations among the explanatory variables does not arise when population data are considered, and we are exploring the *theoretical relationship* between the explanatory variables. That is why it is said that *multicollinearity is a feature of sample data rather than population*. Put differently, when multicollinearity is present, there is lack of independent movement in the sample data on explanatory variables so that there is violation of the assumption of orthogonality (independence) of the explanatory variables.

---

[1] The term multicollinearity was introduced first by Ragnar Frisch in 1934.

6.2 SOURCES OF MULTICOLLINEARITY

In practice, multicollinearity may arise for several reasons.

(i)   Multicollinearity may arise because of faulty data collection method. For example, sampling over a limited range of values of explanatory variables creates this problem.

(ii) Multicollinearity problem arises when the explanatory variables share a common time trend. This is the case in time series regressions. For instance, in a regression of GDP on money supply and prices, the two explanatory variables (money supply and prices) are likely to be highly correlated because when money supply rises in an economy, price level also rises.[2]

(iii) When lagged values of the same variable are included as explanatory variables, we are likely to have multicollinearity problem. For example, in a time series regression of area under cultivation for a crop (say wheat) on its current and past prices,[3] we may have multicollinearity problem because prices of the crop at different time points are generally correlated.

(iv) There are many cross-section regressions where we face high intercorrelations among the explanatory variables. For instance, in a regression of consumption expenditure of persons on their income and education levels, we typically have strong correlation between income and education variables as the persons reporting higher incomes are usually found to be more educated.

(v)   Multicollinearity arises for faulty specification of the model. For example, adding polynomial terms (X and X^2) when X ranges are small will create this problem.

(vi) Multicollinearity arises in the overdetermined model where number of explanatory variables (k) is greater than number of observations (n).

(vii) In a situation of 'dummy variable trap', we have multicollinearity problem. In this situation, the model includes an intercept term and the number of dummies is equal to number of categories.[4]

(viii) As the data used by the economists are mostly collected through sample surveys, the multicollinearity problem becomes a possibility. If data were collected through the controlled experiment, this problem could have been avoided by designing the experiment in such way that the data on explanatory variables are uncorrelated or orthogonal.

6.3 CONSEQUENCES OF MULTICOLLINEARITY

The easiest way to understand the consequences of the multicollinearity problem is to compare simple and multiple regression models. Suppose we have data on dependent variable

---

[2] It may be noted that if the objective of time series regression is to make forecasting about future value of the dependent variable (GDP), then such a correlation does not pose any difficulty as such.

[3] The distributed lag model is one such example, which we discuss in Chapter 8.

[4] This point has been clarified further in Chapter 7.

Y_i and two explanatory variables X_{1i} and X_{2i}. Using these data, we can either estimate two separate simple regression models as

$$Y_i = \alpha_1 + \beta_{Y1} X_{1i} + \varepsilon_{1i} \qquad (6.1)$$

$$Y_i = \alpha_2 + \beta_{Y2} X_{2i} + \varepsilon_{2i} \qquad (6.2)$$

or the multiple regression model

$$Y_i = \alpha + \beta_{Y1.2} X_{1i} + \beta_{Y2.1} X_{2i} + \varepsilon_i \qquad (6.3)$$

Applying the OLS method, we obtain

$$\hat{\beta}_{Y1} = \frac{\sum x_{1i} y_i}{\sum x_{1i}^2} \qquad (6.4)$$

$$\hat{\beta}_{Y2} = \frac{\sum x_{2i} y_i}{\sum x_{2i}^2} \qquad (6.5)$$

$$\hat{\beta}_{Y1.2} = \frac{\sum x_{1i} y_i \sum x_{2i}^2 - \sum x_{2i} y_i \sum x_{1i} x_{2i}}{\sum x_{1i}^2 \sum x_{2i}^2 - (\sum x_{1i} x_{2i})^2} \qquad (6.6)$$

$$\hat{\beta}_{Y2.1} = \frac{\sum x_{2i} y_i \sum x_{1i}^2 - \sum x_{1i} y_i \sum x_{1i} x_{2i}}{\sum x_{1i}^2 \sum x_{2i}^2 - (\sum x_{1i} x_{2i})^2} \qquad (6.7)$$

Here $\hat{\beta}_{Y1}$ and $\hat{\beta}_{Y2}$ are two estimated slope coefficients from simple regression models (6.1) and (6.2), respectively, while $\hat{\beta}_{Y1.2}$ and $\hat{\beta}_{Y2.1}$ are two estimated partial regression coefficients from the multiple regression model (6.3). Further, as always, the lowercase letters denote deviation from sample means for the variables.

Let us define

$$\sum x_{1i} y_i = n \, r_{Y1} \, S_Y \, S_1$$
$$\sum x_{2i} y_i = n \, r_{Y2} \, S_Y \, S_2$$
$$\sum x_{1i} x_{2i} = n \, r_{12} \, S_1 \, S_2$$
$$\sum x_{1i}^2 = n \, S_1^2$$
$$\sum x_{2i}^2 = n \, S_2^2$$

where

S_1 = standard deviation of X_{1i};
S_2 = standard deviations of X_{2i};
S_Y = standard deviation of Y_i;
r_{Y1} = simple correlation between Y_i and X_{1i};
r_{Y2} = simple correlation between Y_i and X_{2i};

r_{12} = simple correlation between X_{1i} and X_{2i}; and

n = number of observations.

Putting the above values into the formulas for OLS estimates, we obtain

$$\hat{\beta}_{Y1} = r_{Y1} \frac{S_Y}{S_1} \qquad (6.8)$$

$$\hat{\beta}_{Y2} = r_{Y2} \frac{S_Y}{S_2} \qquad (6.9)$$

$$\hat{\beta}_{Y1.2} = \left(\frac{r_{Y1} - r_{12}r_{Y2}}{1 - r_{12}^2} \right) \left(\frac{S_Y}{S_1} \right) \qquad (6.10)$$

$$\hat{\beta}_{Y2.1} = \left(\frac{r_{Y2} - r_{12}r_{Y1}}{1 - r_{12}^2} \right) \left(\frac{S_Y}{S_2} \right) \qquad (6.11)$$

We may now visualize three different cases depending upon the value of r_{12}^2.

Case I: Absence of Multicollinearity ($r_{12}^2 = 0$)

Multicollinearity is completely absent when $r_{12}^2 = 0$. In this situation, equation (6.10) collapses to equation (6.8) and equation (6.11) collapses to equation (6.9). This implies that when multicollinearity is absent, we may think of abandoning the multiple regression model and run two separate simple regressions to understand the relation between the dependent variable and the explanatory variables. However, there are two problems here:

(i)   How to obtain $\hat{\alpha}$? This problem is resolved by computing $\hat{\alpha}$ as

$$\hat{\alpha} = \bar{Y}_i - \hat{\beta}_{Y1}\bar{X}_{1i} - \hat{\beta}_{Y2}\bar{X}_{2i}$$

(ii)   In the case of simple regressions, the variances of $\hat{\beta}_{Y1}$ and $\hat{\beta}_{Y2}$ would be upwardly biased (or greater than the variances of $\hat{\beta}_{Y1.2}$ and $\hat{\beta}_{Y2.1}$) (see Kmenta 1986, 432). Therefore, while working with multivariate data, it is advisable to fit multiple regressions so that this problem is avoided.

Case II: Perfect Multicollinearity ($r_{12}^2 = 1$)

We have perfect multicollinearity when $r_{12}^2 = 1$. In this situation, we cannot define equations (6.10) and (6.11). This means that under perfect multicollinearity, it is not possible to compute the values of OLS estimates. In other words, the OLS estimation technique breaks down when perfect multicollinearity is present.

In terms of matrix notation, and for more general case, in a situation of perfect multicollinearity, at least one of the columns of X matrix becomes an exact linear function of one or more of other columns so that the matrix $X'X$ becomes singular. As it is not possible to obtain the inverse of the singular matrix $X'X$, we cannot calculate the OLS estimates as

$\hat{\beta} = (X'X)^{-1}X'Y$. Thus, the OLS estimates become indeterminate in the situation of perfect multicollinearity.

Case III: Imperfect Multicollinearity ($r_{12}^2 < 1$)

The above two are the extreme cases none of which is observed in reality. In practice, some amount of correlation is found between the explanatory variables so that r_{12}^2 is less than unity. If r_{12}^2 is high and close to unity, we say that there is high degree of multicollinearity. In any case, this situation is referred to as imperfect multicollinearity as $r_{12}^2 < 1$. Although imperfect multicollinearity does not pose any problem for estimation of the model by applying OLS method, the problem of obtaining unreliable or imprecise estimates for unknown parameters arises as the estimates will have large sampling variances. This point becomes clear from the formulae used for computation of variances of two partial regression coefficients ($\hat{\beta}_{Y1.2}$ and $\hat{\beta}_{Y2.1}$) for the three-variable model.

$$Var(\hat{\beta}_{Y1.2}) = \frac{\sigma_\varepsilon^2}{\sum x_{1i}^2 (1 - r_{12}^2)}$$

$$Var(\hat{\beta}_{Y2.1}) = \frac{\sigma_\varepsilon^2}{\sum x_{2i}^2 (1 - r_{12}^2)}$$

It is clear that (i) $r_{12}^2 = 1$ makes the variances infinite and (ii) high value of r_{12}^2 (close to 1) makes the variances of the estimated partial regression coefficients very large.

We have considered above the example of a model that contained two explanatory variables. However, when there are more than two explanatory variables, the variance of estimated coefficient of the kth explanatory variable is computed as

$$Var(\hat{\beta}_k) = \frac{\sigma_\varepsilon^2}{\sum x_{ki}^2 (1 - R_k^2)} \tag{6.12}$$

where $\sum x_{ki}^2 = \sum (X_{ki} - \bar{X}_{ki})^2$ and R_k^2 is the squared-multiple correlation between k^{th} explanatory variable (X_{ki}) and all other explanatory variables of the model (or the value of R-squared from an auxiliary regression of kth explanatory variable on all other explanatory variables). It is clear that as $R_k^2 < 1$ in a situation of imperfect multicollinearity, the value of $Var(\hat{\beta}_k)$ is greater than its value when multicollinearity is absent (where $R_k^2 = 0$). Thus, when multicollinearity is present, we face the possibility of the partial regression coefficient ($\hat{\beta}_k$) turning out to be statistically insignificant as its value of computed-t becomes very small.

However, it also needs mention that existence of high value of R_k^2 does not necessarily imply that the value of $Var(\hat{\beta}_k)$ will be large so that computed-t will be small. As clear from (6.12), apart from R_k^2, $Var(\hat{\beta}_k)$ also depends on the variance of X_{ki}, i.e., $\sum x_{ki}^2$, and σ_ε^2. So when there is less variation in the series for X_{ki}, it will provide a low value of $\sum x_{ki}^2$, which will raise the value of $Var(\hat{\beta}_k)$.

Another point to note is that multicollinearity affects not only the variances of the OLS estimates but also their covariances. As a consequence, there might be reversal of signs of some of the estimated coefficients (meaning that we do not have expected signs for the estimated coefficients) when there is high degree of multicollinearity. Further, in a situation of severe multicollinearity, the addition or deletion of just a few observations may substantially alter the estimated coefficients thereby causing instability of OLS estimates.

The above discussion leads to the following conclusions.

- Multicollinearity makes the OLS estimates imprecise or unreliable as they have large variances and hence large standard errors.
- The coefficients affected by multicollinearity will have low t-values (computed) so that their associated variables emerge as statistically insignificant. In this situation, we may be wrongly tempted to drop such variables from our model although, in reality, they substantially contribute in explaining variation of the dependent variable.
- The signs of the estimated coefficients may be reversed under the influence of multicollinearity.
- The addition/deletion of a few observations is likely to substantially alter our regression result when data suffer from high degree of multicollinearity.

6.4 TESTS FOR MULTICOLLINEARITY

Much controversy has surrounded the question of detecting the existence of multicollinearity, i.e., measuring the extent to which data on explanatory variables are collinear. The main reason for this is that many of the methods suggested for this purpose have been found to be inadequate and have justifiably been criticized. Nevertheless, we mention below some of the methods which are often used by the applied researchers.

Correlation Analysis

Since multicollinearity is caused by intercorrelations among the explanatory variables, some idea about this problem may be obtained by computing simple or zero-order correlations between the explanatory variables. To understand these correlations, the researchers usually obtain the correlation matrix by using some software. The next issue is determining significance of computed correlation coefficients so as to conclude about the presence of multicollinearity. This is done either by applying some *rule of thumb*[5] or the *t*-test devised to examine statistical significance of simple correlation coefficients.[6]

---

[5] The commonly used *rule of thumb* is that if $r_{12}^2 > 0.9$, there may be serious problem of multicollinearity in data.

[6] The formula used is: $t^* = r\sqrt{n-2}\big/\sqrt{1-r^2}$ with degrees of freedom $(df) = n-2$. Here $r =$ value of simple correlation coefficient between two explanatory variables and $n =$ number of observations. The *decision rule* is that if the absolute value of computed t is greater than the critical-t value at a chosen level of significance and degrees of freedom $n-2$, then conclude that r is statistically significant at that level of significance.

However, it is to be remembered that using simple correlation coefficient to understand presence of multicollinearity is a valid procedure when the model has only two explanatory variables. When the model includes more than two explanatory variables, instead of simple correlation, we should consider the partial correlations which examine the influence of one variable upon another after eliminating the effects of all other variables. The statistical significance of partial correlation coefficients may also be tested by applying the t-test procedure, but the formula for computation of t is different here.[7]

Klein's Rule of Thumb

Klein (1962) suggested a *rule of thumb* according to which multicollinearity would be regarded as a problem if $R_Y^2 < R_k^2$, where R_Y^2 is the squared multiple correlation coefficient between the dependent variable Y_i and explanatory variables $X_{1i}, X_{2i}, ..., X_{ki}$, and R_k^2 is squared multiple correlation coefficient between k^{th} explanatory variable and other explanatory variables.

The limitation of Klein's rule is that it cannot always correctly diagnose the presence of multicollinearity in data. In fact, it has been found that there are instances where in spite of $R_Y^2 < R_k^2$ we still have small variances of the OLS estimates and hence statistically significant t-ratios.

Variance-Inflation Factor (VIF)

While discussing the consequences of multicollinearity, we observed that its presence generates high variances for the OLS estimates, thereby providing low t-ratios and hence statistically insignificant regression results. Therefore, it is possible to understand the presence of multicollinearity by comparing the variances of OLS estimates for two situations: (i) where multicollinearity is absent (called the 'ideal situation') and (ii) where multicollinearity is present.

As noted previously, when multicollinearity is present, the variance of the estimated coefficient of kth explanatory variable is measured by

$$Var(\hat{\beta}_k) = \frac{\sigma_\varepsilon^2}{\sum x_{ki}^2 (1 - R_k^2)}$$

Under the 'ideal situation', when there is no multicollinearity, $R_k^2 = 0$, so that

$$Var(\hat{\beta}_k) = \frac{\sigma_\varepsilon^2}{\sum x_{ki}^2}$$

---

[7] The t-value corresponding to a partial correlation coefficient is computed as: $t^* = \dfrac{\left(r_{12.3...k}^2\right)\sqrt{n-k}}{\sqrt{1 - r_{12.3...k}^2}}$ with $df = n - k$. Here k = number of explanatory variables and n = number of observations. The *decision rule* is that if the value of computed t is greater than the critical-t value at a chosen level of significance and degrees of freedom $n - k$, then conclude that the partial correlation coefficient is statistically significant at that level of significance.

The VIF compares these two situations by taking a ratio of the two variances. Thus,

$$VIF(\hat{\beta}_k) = \frac{\sigma_\varepsilon^2}{\sum x_{ki}^2 (1 - R_k^2)} \Big/ \frac{\sigma_\varepsilon^2}{\sum x_{ki}^2} = \frac{1}{1 - R_k^2} \qquad (6.13)$$

Now when $VIF(\hat{\beta}_k) = 1$, we say that multicollinearity is completely absent while $VIF(\hat{\beta}_k) > 1$ indicates presence of multicollinearity.

The VIF values are computed for each estimated slope coefficient. Thus, looking at VIF values for different estimated slope coefficients, we can identify the variables that are responsible for generating the multicollinearity problem. We may also apply a *rule of thumb* to conclude about the severity of multicollinearity, which is that when VIF $\geq$ 10 (i.e., $R_k^2 \geq 0.9$) there is severe multicollinearity involving the kth explanatory variable.

Tolerance (TOL)

Tolerance is the reciprocal of VIF. Some statistical packages (e.g., SPSS) present tolerance (TOL_k) in addition to, or instead of, the VIF.

$$TOL_k = \frac{1}{VIF} = 1 - R_k^2 \qquad (6.14)$$

Obviously, closer the value of TOL_k to zero, the greater is the degree of collinearity of kth explanatory variable with other explanatory variables. On the other hand, the closer TOL_k to 1, the greater the evidence that k^{th} explanatory variable is not collinear with other explanatory variables. Here the *rule of thumb* is that tolerance value of 0.10 or less indicates presence of severe multicollinearity.

Limitations of VIF/TOL Measures

The VIF and TOL measures of multicollinearity have been criticized along the following lines.

- As shown in (6.12), $Var(\hat{\beta}_k)$ does not depend on R_k^2 alone; it is also determined by σ_ε^2 and $\sum x_{ki}^2$. Therefore, a high VIF caused by high R_k^2 can be counter-balanced by a low σ_ε^2 or high $\sum x_{ki}^2$. Put differently, a high VIF is neither necessary nor sufficient to get high variances and high standard errors for the estimated coefficients. Therefore, high degree of multicollinearity, as measured by a high VIF, may not necessarily cause high standard errors.

- There is no valid statistical rationale for the choice of any *rule of thumb* threshold value for VIF and TOL to distinguish between 'serious' and 'acceptable' levels of multicollinearity. In fact, in empirical works, quite often the magnitude and direction (sign) of the estimated coefficients are found to change appreciably even at VIF values which are substantially less than the typically suggested threshold value of 10.

Condition Number (CN)

Whereas VIF is computed for each of the estimated coefficients, the condition number provides an overall measure of multicollinearity. It conveys the status or condition of the data matrix X where data on explanatory variables are put in.

The condition number actually decomposes the correlation matrix of k explanatory variables into a set of orthogonal dimensions. Orthogonal dimensions are completely non-overlapping and share no variance in common. When this analysis is performed on the correlation matrix of the k explanatory variables, a set of k eigenvalues or the characteristic roots of the matrix are produced. The proportion of the variance in the explanatory variables accounted for by each orthogonal dimension i is λ/k where λ is the eigenvalue. The eigenvalues are ordered from largest to smallest so that each orthogonal dimension in turn accounts for a smaller proportion of the variance of the explanatory variables. If there are two explanatory variables which are uncorrelated, each eigenvalue will equal 1.0 so that each independent dimension will account for $\lambda_i/2 = 0.50$ of the variance in the set of explanatory variables. As the explanatory variables become increasingly correlated, more and more of the variance in the explanatory variables is associated with the first dimension so that the value of first eigenvalue will become larger and the value of second eigenvalue will become correspondingly smaller. When $r_{12} = 1$ (maximum), $\lambda_1 = 2$ and $\lambda_2 = 0$ so that the first dimension will account for 1.0 of the variance in the explanatory variables, while the second dimension will account for no additional variance in the explanatory variables.

To obtain an overall idea about the condition of the data matrix X, the condition number is computed as the square root of the ratio of largest eigenvalue (λ_{max}) to smallest eigenvalue (λ_{min}). Thus,

$$CN = \sqrt{\frac{\lambda_{max}}{\lambda_{min}}} \qquad\qquad (6.15)$$

The *rules of thumb* here are the following.

- If CN = 1, there is no multicollinearity. So closer the value of CN to unity, the better is the condition of the data matrix X.
- When 1 < CN < 10, multicollinearity is negligible.
- $10 \leq CN \leq 30$ represents the situation of moderate to strong multicollinearity.
- If CN > 30, there is severe multicollinearity.

This measure is also criticized for arbitrary nature of the above *rules of thumb*. Further, it has been shown that CN can change with a reparametrization of the variables. In fact, it can be made equal to 1 with suitable transformation of the variables.

In conclusion, we can say that these measures of multicollinearity only provide some broad idea about its presence and as such are of limited use from practical point of view. To understand the severity of the multicollinearity problem, the researcher should look into all possible aspects, namely, the signs of the estimated coefficients (i.e., whether they have expected signs), standard errors and computed-t values of the estimated coefficients, R^2, F-ratio, and so on, which will also provide an idea about the reliability and usefulness of the estimated multiple regression models.

6.5 REMEDIAL MEASURES

It must be remembered that of all econometric problems, multicollinearity is the most serious one. We do not have any measure that can completely remove multicollinearity when it is present in data. The measures discussed below only attempt to minimize its impact so that reasonable regression results are obtained.

Increasing Sample Size

Increasing sample size helps to reduce some but not all problems associated with multicollinearity. Larger sample sizes will always improve the precision or reliability of the OLS estimates. Hence attempts should be made to work with larger samples. The fact that precision or reliability of the estimates improves with increasing sample size becomes clear from the formulas used for calculation of their variances. It is clear from (6.12) that when sample size increases, $\sum x_{ki}^2$ increases and $Var(\hat{\beta}_k)$ falls, unless additional observations on X_{ki} are equal to $\overline{X}_{ki}$ in all cases, which is most unlikely to happen. Of course, we are unsure about what will happen to R_k^2 when sample size increases. But it is quite possible that with increasing sample size R_k^2 would also fall, which further reduces $Var(\hat{\beta}_k)$. In any case, increasing sample size helps to improve precision of the OLS estimates.

Transformation of Variables

It has been found that the intensity of multicollinearity gets reduced when transformed variables (ratio, first-difference, etc.) are used instead of variables in 'levels'. For example, in a three-variable model, although the levels of X_{1t} and X_{2t} might be correlated, there is no a priori reason to believe that the first difference of these variables, i.e., $(X_{1t} - X_{1t-1})$ and $(X_{2t} - X_{2t-1})$, would also be correlated. However, there might be autocorrelation in the first-difference regression model.

Using Extraneous Estimate

If an extraneous estimate of the coefficient of one of the variables responsible for creating multicollinearity is available, it can be used and a mixed estimation method followed to correct the high-variance problem created by the multicollinearity. However, while applying this method, extra care must be taken to ensure that the extraneous estimate is relevant.

Dropping Variables

A popular method of avoiding the multicollinearity problem is by simply dropping one or more of the collinear variables. Usually, this method becomes effective when a large number of explanatory variables have been included in the model of which all are not important. However, the implication of the dropping variables approach needs to be analyzed properly before taking a decision in this regard. This is because if we drop an explanatory variable whose true coefficient is not zero, a specification error will occur and the estimates of parameters of remaining explanatory variables will be biased. So the real question is whether by dropping a variable we can reduce the variance of remaining estimates by enough to compensate for this bias introduced. This suggests the use of mean-squared-error (MSE) criterion in undertaking a decision to drop a variable. This point is discussed below more formally.[8]

Suppose our three-variable multiple regression model is

$$Y_i = \beta_1 X_{1i} + \beta_2 X_{2i} + \varepsilon_i \qquad (6.16)$$

(We excluded the intercept term for the sake of simplicity of discussion.)

Now assume that X_{1i} and X_{2i} are highly correlated and also that we are interested about X_{1i} and drop X_{2i} to avoid multicollinearity. Then our model becomes

$$Y_i = \beta_1 X_{1i} + v_i \qquad (6.17)$$

We call (6.16) as the 'complete model' and (6.17) the 'omitted variable model'. Let the OLS estimate of β_1 from the complete model be $\hat{\beta}_1$ and that from the omitted variable model be $\tilde{\beta}_1$. As regards $\hat{\beta}_1$, we know that

$$E(\hat{\beta}_1) = \beta \text{ and } Var(\hat{\beta}_1) = \frac{\sigma_\varepsilon^2}{\sum X_{1i}^2 (1 - r_{12}^2)}$$

For $\tilde{\beta}_1$, we have to compute $E(\tilde{\beta}_1)$ and $Var(\tilde{\beta})$.

$$\begin{aligned}
\tilde{\beta}_1 &= \frac{\sum X_{1i} Y_i}{\sum X_{1i}^2} \\
&= \frac{\sum X_{1i} (\beta_1 X_{1i} + \beta_2 X_{2i} + \varepsilon_i)}{\sum X_{1i}^2} \\
&= \beta_1 + \beta_2 \frac{\sum X_{1i} X_{2i}}{\sum X_{1i}^2} + \frac{\sum X_{1i} \varepsilon_i}{\sum X_{1i}^2}
\end{aligned}$$

Thus,

$$E(\tilde{\beta}_1) = \beta_1 + \beta_2 \frac{\sum X_{1i} X_{2i}}{\sum X_{1i}^2} \neq \beta_1 \qquad [\because E(\varepsilon_i) = 0]$$

This implies that $\tilde{\beta}_1$ is a biased estimate.

$$Var(\tilde{\beta}_1) = E[\tilde{\beta}_1 - E(\tilde{\beta})]^2$$

[8] We follow Maddala and Lahiri (2009, 297–300) in our discussion here.

$$= E\left(\frac{\sum X_{1i}\varepsilon_i}{\sum X_{1i}^2}\right)^2$$

$$= \frac{1}{(\sum X_{1i}^2)^2}\sum X_{1i}^2\sigma_\varepsilon^2 \qquad [\because E(\varepsilon_i^2)=\sigma_\varepsilon^2]$$

$$= \frac{\sigma_\varepsilon^2}{\sum X_{1i}^2}$$

It appears that although, $\tilde{\beta}_1$, the OLS estimate of β from the omitted variable model, is biased, it has smaller variance compared to $\hat{\beta}_1$. Moreover, it follows that

$$\frac{Var(\tilde{\beta}_1)}{Var(\hat{\beta}_1)} = \frac{\sigma_\varepsilon^2}{\sum X_{1i}^2}\bigg/ \frac{\sigma_\varepsilon^2}{\sum X_{1i}^2(1-r_{12}^2)} = 1-r_{12}^2 \qquad (6.18)$$

This implies that if r_{12}^2 is very high, $Var(\tilde{\beta}_1)$ will be considerably less than $Var(\hat{\beta}_1)$. Thus, on the basis of unbiasedness property, $\hat{\beta}_1$, the OLS estimate from the complete model seems preferable. But on the basis of minimum variance property, $\tilde{\beta}_1$, the OLS estimate from the omitted variable model seems acceptable, particularly when the two variables are highly correlated.

In a situation where one estimate is unbiased but not having minimum variance, while the other estimate is biased but has minimum variance, we face a difficult choice problem. To get out of this problem, we compare the mean-squared errors (MSE) for the two estimates.

Let us consider the ratio of two mean-squared errors.

$$\frac{MSE(\tilde{\beta}_1)}{MSE(\hat{\beta}_1)} = \frac{(bias\,\tilde{\beta}_1)^2 + Var(\tilde{\beta}_1)}{(bias\,\hat{\beta}_1)^2 + Var(\hat{\beta}_1)}$$

$$= \frac{(bias\,\tilde{\beta}_1)^2}{Var(\hat{\beta}_1)} + \frac{Var(\tilde{\beta}_1)}{Var(\hat{\beta}_1)} \qquad [\because (bias\,\hat{\beta}_1)=0]$$

Here

$$\frac{(bias\,\tilde{\beta}_1)^2}{Var(\hat{\beta}_1)} = \left(\beta_2\frac{\sum X_{1i}X_{2i}}{\sum X_{1i}^2}\right)^2\bigg/ \frac{\sigma_\varepsilon^2}{\sum X_{1i}^2(1-r_{12}^2)}$$

$$= \frac{(\sum X_{1i}X_{2i})^2}{\sum X_{1i}^2\sum X_{2i}^2}\beta_2^2\frac{\sum X_{2i}^2(1-r_{12}^2)}{\sigma_\varepsilon^2}$$

$$= r_{12}^2\beta_2^2\frac{1}{Var(\hat{\beta}_2)}$$

$$= r_{12}^2 t_2^2 \qquad (6.19)$$

Note that t_2 in (6.19) is not estimated but true t-ratio for the slope parameter of X_{2i}. Now using equations (6.18) and (6.19), we can write

$$\frac{MSE(\tilde{\beta_1})}{MSE(\hat{\beta_1})} = r_{12}^2 t_2^2 + (1 - r_{12}^2) = 1 + r_{12}^2(t_2^2 - 1)$$

Thus, if $t_2 < 1$, $MSE(\tilde{\beta_1}) < MSE(\hat{\beta_1})$ and hence $\tilde{\beta_1}$ should be preferred. However, as t_2 is not known, we use $\hat{t}_2$ (which is estimated t-value) from (6.16). Then, as an estimate of β_1, we may use the *conditional-omitted-variable estimator* (denoted by $\tilde{\tilde{\beta_1}}$), which is defined as

$$\tilde{\tilde{\beta_1}} = \begin{cases} \hat{\beta_1} \text{ the OLS estimate if } |\hat{t}_2| \geq 1 \\ \tilde{\beta_1} \text{ the omitted variable estimate if } |\hat{t}_2| < 1 \end{cases} \tag{6.20}$$

The obvious implication of (6.20) is that only when the computed t-value for a variable is less than 1, we might drop that variable and adopt the omitted-variable model. Otherwise, it would be preferable to stick to the complete model.

An important limitation of the dropping variable approach is that when a limited number of variables have been used in the model, this approach doesn't appear to be attractive.

Other Methods

The researchers sometimes apply other techniques such as principal components method, ridge regression, etc., to solve the problem of multicollinearity. Under principal component method, the collinear variables are grouped to form a composite index capable of representing this group of variables by itself. The ridge regression method follows an entirely different approach to the problem of multicollinearity. In ridge regression, a constant is added to the variance of each explanatory variable. This generates bias in the estimates but their variances and hence standard errors are substantially lowered. In a situation of high-degree multicollinearity, it may be reasonable to trade off a small increase in bias for substantial increase in reliability of the estimates obtained through reduction in their standard errors, especially when MSE of ridge estimators becomes smaller than the same for OLS estimators. However, it is to be remembered that these methods are criticized for being ad hoc; so they can at best be used as exploratory tools.[9]

6.6 MULTICOLLINEARITY TESTS USING EVIEWS

To illustrate the tests for multicollinearity, we consider the data presented in Table 6.1. These data were assembled by Longley (1967) and widely used to illustrate the multicollinearity

---

[9] We refrain from detailed discussion of these methods as that is beyond the scope of this book. For useful discussions on these methods, one may refer to Chatterjee and Hadi (2006, Chapter 10), Meyers et al. (2006, part IV) and Ryan (2008).

problem.[10] The table contains data on some macroeconomic variables for the US for 1947 to 1962. These variables are: EMPLOY = employment (thousands), GNP = nominal GNP (millions $), ARMED = size of armed forces, PRICE = GNP deflator, and YEAR = date. Our objective is to estimate a multiple regression model to find out the statistically significant determinants of employment in the US.

Table 6.1 Data on Some Macroeconomic Variables for the US

EMPLOY	GNP	ARMED	PRICE	YEAR
60,323	234,289	1,590	83.0	1947
61,122	259,426	1,456	88.5	1948
60,171	258,054	1,616	88.2	1949
61,187	284,599	1,650	89.5	1950
63,221	328,975	3,099	96.2	1951
63,639	346,999	3,594	98.1	1952
64,989	365,385	3,547	99.0	1953
63,761	363,112	3,350	100.0	1954
66,019	397,469	3,048	101.2	1955
67,857	419,180	2,857	104.6	1956
68,169	442,769	2,798	108.4	1957
66,513	444,546	2,637	110.8	1958
68,655	482,704	2,552	112.6	1959
69,564	502,601	2,514	114.2	1960
69,331	518,173	2,572	115.7	1961
70,551	554,894	2,827	116.9	1962

Source: Longley (1967).

Correlation Matrix

To begin with, let us construct the correlation matrix for the variables to understand the zero-order correlations between different pairs of variables. For this purpose, we first obtain the data in an EViews workfile following Step 1, as mentioned in Chapter 2, Section 2.14. In the next step, from the main menu of EViews workfile window, we click **Quick/Group Statistics/Correlations** which opens the 'Series List' box. We write the names of the variables in this box and click **OK** to obtain the correlation matrix as shown in Table 6.2.

Two points become immediately clear from the correlation matrix: (i) The relation between each explanatory factor and EMPLOY is positive; and (ii) There is a very strong intercorrelation among the explanatory factors. In particular, the pairwise correlations between GNP, PRICE, and YEAR are extremely high (close to 1). This is indicative of presence of high degree of multicollinearity in the data.

[10] See, for example, Greene (2003, 57–8).

Table 6.2   Correlations Matrix for the Variables

	EMPLOY	GNP	ARMED	PRICE	YEAR
EMPLOY	1.000000	0.983552	0.457307	0.970899	0.971329
GNP	0.983552	1.000000	0.446437	0.991589	0.995273
ARMED	0.457307	0.446437	1.000000	0.464744	0.417245
PRICE	0.970899	0.991589	0.464744	1.000000	0.991149
YEAR	0.971329	0.995273	0.417245	0.991149	1.000000

Source: This table represents the output obtained by the author after application of the EViews software.

We now estimate a multiple regression model to see the effect of these correlations on the results of regression. Using EViews, such a model is estimated by performing steps 2 to 4, as mentioned in Chapter 2, Section 2.14.[11] The resulting output is presented in Table 6.3. It is interesting to note that above-mentioned correlations between the variables have produced devastating effect on the results of our regression. It is seen that, contrary to expectation, signs of estimated coefficients of three variables (ARMED, PRICE, and YEAR) are negative, and they are statistically insignificant (p-value being greater than 0.10 in each case). Only the estimated coefficient of GNP has expected sign and statistical significance. All in all, we have a very poor result of regression.

Table 6.3   Results of Multiple Regression Using US Data

Dependent Variable: EMPLOY				
Method: Least Squares				
Date: 08/23/13 Time: 15:20				
Sample: 1 16				
Included observations: 16				
Variable	Coefficient	Std. Error	t-Statistic	Prob.
C	1169088.	835902.4	1.398593	0.1895
GNP	0.064394	0.019952	3.227463	0.0081
ARMED	−0.010145	0.308569	−0.032878	0.9744
PRICE	−19.76807	138.8928	−0.142326	0.8894
YEAR	−576.4643	433.4875	−1.329829	0.2105
R-squared	0.973522	Mean dependent var	65317.00
Adjusted R-squared	0.963893	S.D. dependent var	3511.968
S.E. of regression	667.3371	Akaike info criterion	16.09477
Sum squared resid	4898726.	Schwarz criterion	16.33621
Log likelihood	−123.7582	Hannan-Quinn criter.	16.10714
F-statistic	101.1085	Durbin-Watson stat	1.019480
Prob(F-statistic)	0.000000		

Source: Same as for Table 6.2.

[11] Remember that we now have to write the names of four explanatory variables in the 'equation specification' edit box instead of one variable as in a two-variable model.

Computation of VIFs

As pointed out earlier, in the context of multivariate data, computing zero-order correlations to understand the presence of multicollinearity is not a valid procedure. A more appropriate test of multicollinearity is provided by the variance inflation factors (VIFs) and condition number (CN). Let us, therefore, see how these are computed in EViews.[12]

EViews reports two forms of VIFs—centered and uncentered. The centered VIF is the ratio of the variance of the estimated coefficient from the original equation to the variance of the estimated coefficient when only that explanatory variable and the constant are included. On the other hand, the uncentered VIF is the ratio of the variance of the estimated coefficient from the original equation to the variance of the estimated coefficient when only that explanatory variable is included (no constant). The centered VIF is numerically identical to the VIF formula reported in (6.13). Therefore, for our purpose, we shall consider the centered VIF.

To obtain the VIFs, we first estimate the model by following the steps mentioned earlier. In the next step, from the EViews output window, click **View/Coefficient Diagnostics/Variance Inflation Factors** to obtain the VIFs, as displayed in Table 6.4. It is clear that the VIF values for three of the coefficients (GNP, PRICE, and YEAR) far exceed the threshold value 10 indicating presence of severe multicollinearity.

Table 6.4 VIFs for Estimated Regression Model

Variance Inflation Factors
Date: 08/23/13 Time: 15:21
Sample: 1 16
Included observations: 16

Variable	Coefficient Variance	Uncentered VIF	Centered VIF
C	6.99E+11	25103871	NA
GNP	0.000398	2282.202	132.4638
ARMED	0.095215	24.79732	1.553191
PRICE	19291.20	7241.567	75.67073
YEAR	187911.4	25790300	143.4635

Source: Same as for Table 6.2.

Coefficient Variance Decomposition

EViews also allows us to obtain the Coefficient Variance Decomposition view of an estimated equation, which provides information on the eigenvector decomposition of the coefficient covariance matrix. This decomposition helps to diagnose potential collinearity problem amongst the explanatory variables. This decomposition is done by following Belsley, Kuh, and Welsch (2004). For interpretation of the results, they suggested the following procedure.

- First of all, check the condition numbers of the matrix. A condition number smaller than 1/900 (=0.001) would signify the presence of collinearity.

[12] These tests cannot be performed as built-in procedures using the EViews versions older than 7.

- If there are one or more small condition numbers, then the variance decomposition proportions should be looked into. Two or more variables with values of variance decomposition proportions greater than 0.5 associated with a small condition number indicate possibility of collinearity between these two variables.

To view the Coefficient Variance Decomposition in EViews, we first estimate the model without the intercept or constant term (C). In the next step, from the output window, click **View/Coefficient Diagnostics/Coefficient Variance Decomposition**. This gives the output Table 6.5, which shows the eigenvalues, condition numbers, corresponding Variance Decomposition Proportions, and the eigenvectors.

In the table, the top line provided the eigenvalues, sorted from largest to smallest with the condition number below. The final condition number is always 1.0. It is observed that three of the four eigenvalues have condition numbers smaller than 0.001 which is indicative of a large amount of multicollinearity in data. To derive an overall conclusion regarding the degree of multicollinearity, we may compute the value of CN as per the formula provided in (6.15) above. This works out to be $\sqrt{17208.87/1.88E-07} = 302550.07$, which is abnormally high (far greater than the threshold level 30). This indicates that there is severe multicollinearity so that the matrix containing data on explanatory variables is seriously ill-conditioned.

The second section of Table 6.5 gives the variance decomposition proportions. The proportions associated with the smallest condition number are provided in first column. Three of these values are greater than 0.5. This indicates that there is a high level of collinearity between the three variables, which are YEAR, PRICE, and GNP. This conclusion is similar to the one drawn on the basis of the VIF-test.

An Illustration Using Indian Data

Suppose we want to examine the determinants of cropping intensity in India using data given in Table 2.6 (Chapter 2). We hypothesize that cropping intensity (CRIN) is positively related to percentage of irrigated area (IRRI), fertilizers consumption per hectare (FERT), and percentage of HYV area (HYV). To test this hypothesis, we estimated the multiple regression model using EViews the results of which are presented in Table 6.6.

The regression results show that all the variables have expected signs but the estimated coefficient of an important determinant of cropping intensity, namely irrigation, turned out to be statistically insignificant (p-value > 0.10). To probe further whether this has happened due to the multicollinearity problem, we computed the VIFs corresponding to this regression, the results of which are given in Table 6.7. It emerges that the values of centered VIFs are all greater than 10, implying presence of strong multicollinearity involving the explanatory variables considered in our regression model.

To check whether same conclusion follows in terms of Coefficient Variance Decomposition, we performed this exercise, the results of which are presented in Table 6.8. The first point to note is that the value of condition number as a square-root of the ratio of highest eigenvalue to lowest eigenvalue is $\sqrt{0.226459/0.000202} = 1121.08$ which is much high compared to the threshold level of 30. This suggests the presence of severe

Table: 6.5 Results of Coefficient Variance Decomposition

Coefficient Variance Decomposition
Date: 08/23/13 Time: 15:23
Sample: 1 16
Included observations: 16

Eigenvalues	17208.87	0.208842	0.054609	1.88E-07
Condition	1.09E-11	9.02E-07	3.45E-06	1.000000

Variance Decomposition Proportions

	Associated Eigenvalue			
Variable	1	2	3	4
GNP	0.978760	0.002518	0.017746	0.000975
ARMED	0.037677	0.441984	0.520339	9.31E-11
PRICE	1.000000	9.20E-09	5.75E-10	7.03E-19
YEAR	0.988939	0.010454	0.000607	2.60E-13

Eigenvectors

	Associated Eigenvalue			
Variable	1	2	3	4
GNP	0.000105	−0.001526	0.007921	0.999967
ARMED	0.000434	−0.426303	−0.904557	0.006514
PRICE	−0.999531	0.027528	−0.013451	0.000253
YEAR	0.030636	0.904160	−0.426067	0.004751

Source: Same as for Table 6.2.

Table 6.6 Determinants of Cropping Intensity in India

Dependent Variable: CRIN
Method: Least Squares
Date: 08/23/13 Time: 15:28
Sample: 1970 1998
Included observations: 29

Variable	Coefficient	Std. Error	t-Statistic	Prob.
C	109.5317	2.875326	38.09368	0.0000
IRRI	0.233493	0.146439	1.594477	0.1234
FERT	0.108820	0.031656	3.437601	0.0021
HYV	0.135605	0.055828	2.428980	0.0227

R-squared	0.984079	Mean dependent var	125.5969
Adjusted R-squared	0.982168	S.D. dependent var	5.056923
S.E. of regression	0.675285	Akaike info criterion	2.180078
Sum squared resid	11.40025	Schwarz criterion	2.368671
Log likelihood	−27.61114	Hannan-Quinn criter.	2.239143
F-statistic	515.0684	Durbin-Watson stat	2.763594
Prob(F-statistic)	0.000000		

Source: Same as for Table 6.2.

Table 6.7   The VIFs for Cropping Intensity Regression Model

Variance Inflation Factors
Date: 08/23/13 Time: 15:30
Sample: 1970 1998
Included observations: 29

Variable	Coefficient Variance	Uncentered VIF	Centered VIF
C	8.267498	525.7724	NA
IRRI	0.021444	1363.142	38.16241
FERT	0.001002	167.8890	33.96805
HYV	0.003117	171.7232	16.18116

Source: Same as for Table 6.2.

Table 6.8   Results of Coefficient Variance Decomposition for Cropping Intensity Regression (Without Intercept Term)

Coefficient Variance Decomposition
Date: 08/23/13 Time: 15:31
Sample: 1970 1998
Included observations: 29

Eigenvalues	0.226459	0.012579	0.000202
Condition	0.000891	0.016037	1.000000

Variance Decomposition Proportions

Variable	Associated Eigenvalue		
	1	2	3
IRRI	0.871109	0.128109	0.000782
FERT	0.684784	0.307267	0.007949
HYV	0.994842	0.004926	0.000232

Eigenvectors

Variable	Associated Eigenvalue		
	1	2	3
IRRI	−0.463448	0.754099	−0.465351
FERT	−0.212673	−0.604461	−0.767722
HYV	0.860225	0.256832	−0.440512

Source: Same as for Table 6.2.

multicollinearity in data. Secondly, it is found that the values of variance decomposition proportions are all greater than 0.50 which imply that all the variables are highly collinear. This conclusion is fully consistent with the conclusion drawn earlier on the basis of VIF values.

6.7 QUESTIONS AND ASSIGNMENTS

A. Multiple-Choice Questions
Tick ($\sqrt{}$) the correct answer.
  (i)   The term 'multicollinearity' was introduced by
        (a) Karl Pearson
        (b) Jan Tinbergen
        (c) Ragnar Frisch
        (d) F.M. Fisher
  (ii) An overall understanding about the degree of multicollinearity in a given dataset is
        derived in terms of
        (a) Glejser test
        (b) VIF test
        (c) Condition number
        (d) Chow test
  (iii) Identification of multicollinear variables in the multiple regression model may be
        performed using
        (a) VIF test
        (b) Durbin-Watson test
        (c) White test
        (d) Park test
  (iv) In the regression of Y_i on X_{1i} and X_{2i}, if all values of X_{2i} are identical, then the
        variance of estimated coefficient of X_{2i} will be
        (a) Zero
        (b) Infinite
        (c) Unity
        (d) None of the above
  (v)   If all the estimated parameters have t-values less than 1 in a multivariate regression
        model with significant F-value, then the model is likely to have
        (a) A problem of multicollinearity
        (b) Some or all the regressors are linearly dependent
        (c) Partial correlation for each regressor is insignificant
        (d) All of the above
  (vi) The results of regression change with addition or deletion of a few observations
        when multicollinearity is present—the statement is
        (a) True
        (b) False
        (c) Uncertain
        (d) Irrelevant

B. General Questions
  (i)   Define the term 'multicollinearity'. What are its causes?
  (ii) Distinguish between 'perfect' and 'imperfect' multicollinearity.

(iii)   Is it possible to estimate unknown parameters of a multiple regression model if there is perfect multicollinearity? If not, why?

(iv)   Why, even if multicollinearity is present, one should estimate a multiple regression model rather than simple regression models while working with multivariate data?

(v)   Explain the theoretical consequences of the multicollinearity problem.

(vi)   Explain how the measure based on variance inflation factor (VIF) helps to identify the multicollinear variables. What are the limitations of this measure?

(vii)   What is the difference between the measures of multicollinearity based on 'variance inflation factor' and 'condition number'?

(viii) What is 'tolerance'? How does it help to measure the degree of multicollinearity in data?

(ix)   Suggest some suitable measures to correct the problem of multicollinearity.

(x)   Discuss how you would overcome the multicollinearity problem by following the dropping variable(s) approach. When is this approach justifiable?

(xi)   Explain why increasing sample size helps to reduce adverse effects of multicollinearity. When should this method be followed?

(xii)   Indicate whether the following statements are true (T), false (F), or uncertain (U) and give a brief explanation.

(a)   Multicollinearity problem is unlikely to be present in time series data.

(b)   Multicollinearity makes the standard errors of estimated coefficients small.

(c)   Whether multicollinearity is a problem or not cannot be decided by just looking at the intercorrelations among the explanatory variables.

(d)   The stability of the estimated coefficients of a multiple regression model gets affected by the presence of multicollinearity.

(e)   If all partial slope coefficients are statistically insignificant in an estimated model, the value of R^2 will never be high.

(f)   In cases of high multicollinearity, it is not possible to assess the individual significance of one or more partial regression coefficients.

(g)   Getting more data is always helpful to reduce the variances of estimated coefficients of a multiple regression model.

(h)   The OLS estimators continue to remain unbiased when multicollinearity is present.

(xiii) Suppose in the model

$$Y_i = \beta_1 + \beta_2 X_{2i} + \beta_3 X_{3i} + U_i$$

the coefficient of correlation between X_{2i} and X_{3i} (i.e., r_{23}) is zero. Therefore, someone suggests that you run the following regressions.

$$Y_i = \alpha_1 + \alpha_2 X_{2i} + U_{1i}$$
$$Y_i = \gamma_1 + \gamma_3 X_{3i} + U_{2i}$$

(a)   Will $\hat{\alpha}_2$ equal $\hat{\beta}_2$ and $\hat{\gamma}_3$ equal $\hat{\beta}_3$?

(b)   Will $\hat{\beta}_1$ equal $\hat{\alpha}_1$ or $\hat{\gamma}_1$ or some combination thereof?

(c)   Will $Var(\hat{\beta}_2)$ equal $Var(\hat{\alpha}_2)$ and $Var(\hat{\beta}_3)$ equal $Var(\hat{\gamma}_3)$?

(Answer the above questions intuitively. Proofs are not necessary.)

(xiv) For the general linear model, the OLS estimators are computed as

$$\hat{\beta} = (X'X)^{-1} X'Y$$

(the symbols have their usual meanings)

(a)   What happens to $\hat{\beta}$ when there is perfect multicollinearity?

(b)   How would you know whether perfect multicollinearity exists?

(xv) You estimated a multiple regression model to understand the determinants of total fertility rate in India using data given in Table 3.3 (Chapter 3) the results of which are summarized below.

$$\widehat{TFR} = 4.180 - 0.031 FLIT + 0.013\, POV - 0.009\, URBAN$$
$$(0.619)\,(0.0009) \qquad (0.0008) \qquad (0.011)$$
$$R^2 = 0.637 \qquad F^* = 9.36 \qquad n\ (\text{sample size}) = 20$$
$$\text{(the figures in brackets are standard errors)}$$

(a)   Interpret the above results.

(b)   Do you suspect presence of multicollinearity in the above regression? How do you know?

(c)   Would you like to drop any of the explanatory variables from above regression? If yes, which variable and why?

C. Computer Assignments

(i)   Estimate a multiple regression model, using data given in Table 2.3 (Chapter 2), to explain inter-state variation in infant mortality rate in India. Do your estimated coefficients have expected signs and statistical significance? How would you ensure that the results of regression have not been affected by multicollinearity problem? Can you improve upon your regression result by dropping any variable? Justify your answer.

(ii) Estimate a multiple regression model, using data given in Table 2.4 (Chapter 2), to identify the factors determining the incidence of child labour in India. Are the results of regression up to your expectation? Compute the values of variance inflation factors (VIF) and condition number (CN) to see if your data suffer from multicollinearity problem. Is your conclusion regarding presence of multicollinearity same between tests based on VIF and CN?

(iii) Estimate a multiple regression model, using data given in Table 2.5 (Chapter 2), to find out the main determinants of yield of foodgrains in India. Also perform a coefficient variance decomposition analysis to see if the data on explanatory variables are plagued by multicollinearity problem. What corrective measure would you recommend in case the multicollinearity problem is found to be present?

Answers to Multiple-Choice Questions

(i) (c); (ii) (c); (iii) (a); (iv) (b); (v) (d); (vi) (a).

7 Dummy Variables

This chapter defines dummy variables and provides interpretation of regression coefficients of the model that uses dummy variable(s). We explain the concept of interaction dummy next. The procedure for examining structural stability of estimated regression model has been discussed in terms of both the Chow test as well as the dummy variable approach. This chapter also discusses three important approaches to dealing with dummy/binary dependent variable models, which are Linear Probability Model, Logit Model, and Probit Model. The steps involved in estimation of these models using EViews software have been described. The interpretation of results obtained through estimation of dummy variable models has been clarified using some examples.

7.1 DEFINITION

Sometimes the dependent variable of the regression model may be influenced not only by the variables that can be readily quantified on a well-defined scale, but also by variables that are qualitative in nature. For example, salary of college teachers may depend on their degree qualifications. College teachers with PhD may earn more than their non-PhD counterparts. In this example, the explanatory variable represents an attribute or quality, which is PhD or non-PhD. To quantify such an attribute or quality, we use an artificial variable that is assigned 1 or 0 values; 1 indicating presence of the attribute (PhD) and 0 indicating its absence. The variables that assume such 1 or 0 values are called dummy variables. Alternatively, the dummy variables are called qualitative variables, binary variables, dichotomous variables, etc. Clearly, dummy variables are needed to quantitatively express the qualitative or non-numerical variables the examples of which are in abundance in economics and other disciplines.

7.2 SIMPLE REGRESSION MODEL WITH DUMMY VARIABLE

We can formulate a simple regression model by considering salary of college teachers as the dependent variable and degree qualification as the independent variable. Before we specify the model, let us assume that salary of college teachers is normally distributed with variance σ^2 and mean equal to μ_1 for PhD teachers and μ_0 for non-PhD teachers. The formal model (called population regression model) is

$$Y_i = \alpha + \beta X_i + \varepsilon_i \qquad (7.1)$$

where

Y_i = salary of the ith college teacher
X_i = 1 if the college teacher is a PhD
     = 0 Otherwise

ε_i is the disturbance term with all usual assumptions of the classical linear regression model

In this model,

$$E(Y_i|X_i=0)=\alpha=\mu_0$$
$$E(Y_i|X_i=1)=\alpha+\beta=\mu_1$$

This shows that the intercept (α) of the population regression model (7.1) is the mean salary of the group of non-PhD teachers. It is also called the intercept of the *base* or *reference* category, which is the group of non-PhD teachers. The 'slope coefficient' of the model is the difference of mean salaries of PhD and non-PhD teachers (i.e., $\beta = \mu_1 - \mu_0$). Thus, by testing the null hypothesis, $H_N: \beta = 0$, we can examine whether there exists any statistically significant difference between mean salaries of two groups of teachers.

Dummy Variables for Multiple Categories

The above model considered a dichotomous explanatory variable, i.e., only two possibilities were considered. But we can also think of a model where the explanatory characteristic is trichotomous, i.e., where three possibilities are considered. In that case, we would require more than one dummy variable. Consider an example where we want to explain variation in salaries of school teachers in terms of their degree qualification. We assume that salaries of school teachers is normally distributed with variance σ^2, and mean depending on whether the highest degree attained by a teacher is BA or MA or PhD. Suppose the mean salary for the BA teachers is μ_A, the same for MA teachers is μ_B and for PhD teachers is μ_C. Then the appropriate model is

$$Y_i = \alpha + \beta_1 X_{1i} + \beta_2 X_{2i} + \varepsilon_i \qquad (7.2)$$

where

Y_i = salary of the ith teacher
X_{1i} = 1 if the teacher is a PhD
      = 0 Otherwise
X_{2i} = 1 if the teacher is an MA
      = 0 Otherwise

It follows that

$$E(Y_i|X_{1i}=1, X_{2i}=0)=\alpha+\beta_1=\mu_C$$

$$E(Y_i \mid X_{1i} = 0, X_{2i} = 1) = \alpha + \beta_2 = \mu_B$$
$$E(Y_i \mid X_{1i} = 0, X_{2i} = 0) = \alpha = \mu_A$$
$$\alpha = \mu_A, \beta_1 = \mu_C - \mu_A \text{ and } \beta_2 = \mu_B - \mu_A$$

Thus, for model (7.2), α represents mean salary of the reference category, i.e., BA teachers; β_1 represents difference of mean salaries of PhD and BA teachers; and β_2 represents difference of mean salaries of MA and BA teachers.

Important Points to Remember

Two important points should be remembered while formulating a regression model by incorporating dummy variable(s).

1. *It would be inappropriate to represent a trichotomous situation by using one dummy variable with three different values.* To explain why this is so, consider the following model.

$$Y_i = \alpha + \beta Z_i + \varepsilon_i \tag{7.3}$$

where

$Z_i = 0$ if the teacher is a BA
    $= 1$ if the teacher is an MA
    $= 2$ if the teacher is a PhD

Here

$E(Y_i \mid Z_i = 0) = \alpha = \mu_A$, which is mean salary of BA teachers
$E(Y_i \mid Z_i = 1) = \alpha + \beta = \mu_B$, which is mean salary of MA teachers
$E(Y_i \mid Z_i = 2) = \alpha + 2\beta = \mu_C$, which is mean salary of PhD teachers

It is clear that for model (7.3), $\mu_B - \mu_A = \mu_C - \mu_B = \beta$. This implies that the difference in mean salaries of BA and MA teachers is the same as the difference in mean salaries of MA and PhD teachers. This indeed is a very strong assumption that must hold in the context of model (7.3). Unless we know a priori that this is the pattern of salaries of teachers, we are not justified in making this assumption.

2. *It would be wrong to represent the trichotomy by three dummy variables.* To justify this point, consider the model

$$Y_i = \alpha + \beta_1 X_{1i} + \beta_2 X_{2i} + \beta_3 X_{3i} + \varepsilon_i \tag{7.4}$$

where

$Y_i =$ salary of the ith teacher

X_{1i} = 1 if the ith teacher is a PhD
      = 0 Otherwise
X_{2i} = 1 if the teacher is an MA
      = 0 Otherwise
X_{3i} = 1 if the teacher is a BA
      = 0 Otherwise

It is clear that, as we have used three dummies for three categories of teachers, $X_{1i} + X_{2i} + X_{3i}$ will always be equal to 1. Therefore, these dummies will form an exact linear relationship with the intercept α and we are unable to estimate unknown parameters of the model.[1] This problem is known as the *dummy variable trap*. To avoid this problem, we follow the rule that suggests: *when the explanatory characteristic leads to a classification of G types, G – 1 dummy/binary variables should be used for its representation.*

However, sometimes we may be interested to know the intercept of each of our category, not as such the difference in intercept of a particular category compared with the reference category. In that situation, we have to use separate dummy for each of our categories, i.e., the number of dummies is equal to number of categories. In that case, the intercept α will be dropped from model (7.4) to avoid falling into the *dummy variable trap*.

7.3 INTERACTION DUMMY

To understand the concept of interaction dummy, let us consider an example where we seek to examine variation in annual clothing expenditure of some individuals in terms of their sex status and educational levels. We consider the following model to represent such a situation.

$$Y_i = \alpha + \beta_1 X_{1i} + \beta_2 X_{2i} + \varepsilon_i$$

where
Y_i = annual clothing expenditure of the ith individual
X_{1i} = 1 if the person is a female
      = 0 Otherwise
X_{2i} = 1 if the person is a PhD
      = 0 Otherwise

In this model, X_{1i} and X_{2i} are called the sex and education dummies, respectively. The disturbance term ε_i has all usual OLS assumptions.

An implicit assumption in the above model is that the differential effect of sex dummy (X_{1i}) is constant across the two levels of education and differential effect of education

---

[1] Put differently, as $X_{1i} + X_{2i} + X_{3i} = 1$, the columns of X matrix of the multiple regression model are not independent, which implies that $(X'X)$ is a singular matrix. Hence $(X'X)^{-1}$ could not be defined and estimation of unknown parameters of the model becomes difficult.

dummy (X_{2i}) is constant across the two levels of sex. If this assumption is relaxed, i.e., if we recognise the interaction between the two dummies, then the effect of these dummies on mean clothing expenditure may not be simply additive as above but also multiplicative as well, as in the following model.

$$Y_i = \alpha + \beta_1 X_{1i} + \beta_2 X_{2i} + \delta(X_{1i} X_{2i}) + \varepsilon_i \qquad (7.5)$$

Here $(X_{1i} X_{2i})$ is called the 'interaction dummy', which recognizes interaction between the two dummy variables. To understand the meanings of parameters of the above model, consider the following.

1. $\quad E(Y_i | X_{1i} = 1, X_{2i} = 0) = \alpha + \beta_1$

This gives mean clothing expenditure of the females.

2. $\quad E(Y_i | X_{1i} = 0, X_{2i} = 1) = \alpha + \beta_2$

This is mean clothing expenditure of the PhD persons.

3. $\quad E(Y_i | X_{1i} = 1, X_{2i} = 1) = \alpha + \beta_1 + \beta_2 + \delta$

This is mean clothing expenditure of the PhD females.

Thus, in model (7.5), β_1 measures the differential effect of being a female, β_2 measures the differential effect of being a PhD and δ measures the differential effect of being both PhD and female. This implies that when β_1, β_2, and δ are all positive, the average clothing expenditure of the female is higher than male, that of PhD is higher than the non-PhD, but this is much higher if the female happens to be a PhD. Thus, it is clear that introduction of an interaction dummy modified the effect of the two attributes (sex and education) on clothing expenditure, in comparison to a situation where their effects are considered separately.

7.4. COMPARING TWO REGRESSIONS

To understand how we compare similarity/dissimilarity between two regression models, consider an example where our objective is to know if there exists any difference in consumption behavior of two groups of families (rich and poor) in a locality. With this objective, we collect consumption (C_i) and income (Y_i) data from some sample families in our chosen locality. The sample constitutes two groups of families—rich and poor. The numbers of rich and poor families are n_1 and n_2, respectively. We may now visualize two separate consumption functions for the two groups.

$$C_i = \alpha_1 + \alpha_2 Y_i + \varepsilon_{1i} \qquad (7.6)$$

$$C_i = \beta_1 + \beta_2 Y_i + \varepsilon_{2i} \qquad (7.7)$$

Here equation (7.6) is the consumption function of the rich while equation (7.7) is the consumption function of the poor.

We want to know whether consumption behaviour of the rich is different from that of the poor. Put differently, we are interested to know whether the two groups differ with regard to subsistence consumption level, and also marginal propensity to consume. The former is understood by comparing the two intercept terms (α_1 and β_1) while the latter is known by comparing the two slope coefficients (α_2 and β_2). In other words, we want to test the null hypothesis

$$H_N: \alpha_1 = \beta_1 \text{ and } \alpha_2 = \beta_2$$

This is equivalent to a problem of *testing for structural stability* of the consumption function between the two groups of families.

To test the above hypothesis, two different approaches are followed: one purely statistical, known as the Chow test, and the other an econometric approach that uses dummy variable(s). We discuss these approaches below.

The Chow Test
The test runs through the following steps.
Step 1: Using all ($n_1 + n_2 = n$) observations, estimate the following model (7.8) by OLS and compute the value of residual sum squares from this regression (RSS_n) which has degrees of freedom $df = (n_1 + n_2 - k)$, where k = number of parameters estimated.

$$C_i = \lambda_1 + \lambda_2 Y_i + \varepsilon_i \qquad (7.8)$$

Step 2: Estimate equations (7.6) and (7.7) individually by OLS, and obtain their respective residual sum squares, which are RSS_{n_1} and RSS_{n_2} with degrees of freedom $n_1 - k$ and $n_2 - k$, respectively.
Step 3: Compute the following F-statistic.

$$F^* = \frac{[RSS_n - (RSS_{n_1} + RSS_{n_2})]/k}{(RSS_{n_1} + RSS_{n_2})/(n_1 + n_2 - 2k)} \sim F[k, (n_1 + n_2 - 2k)]$$

Step 4: Follow the *decision rule*: If $F^* > F$ at a chosen level of significance and $df = [k, (n_1 + n_2 - 2k)]$, reject the null hypothesis ($H_N: \alpha_1 = \beta_1$ and $\alpha_2 = \beta_2$), and conclude that the two regressions are not the same. Rejection of the null hypothesis implies that consumption behaviours of the two groups of families differ. In other words, there is no structural stability in the consumption function for the families studied.

The Dummy Variable Approach
Here we follow an econometric approach to estimate the consumption function using consumption and income data collected from two types of families—rich and poor. We

hypothesise that consumption depends on family income and the relationship between consumption and income varies across the rich and poor groups. The difference in consumption behaviour of the two groups may be reflected (i) through the intercept term alone, (ii) through the slope coefficient alone or (iii) through both the intercept term and the slope coefficient. We can examine all these possibilities quite easily following the dummy variable approach.

(i) Model to Examine the Difference of Intercept Term
Here we estimate the model

$$C_i = \alpha + \beta_2 Y_i + \gamma Z_i + \varepsilon_i \tag{7.9}$$

where
$Z_i = 1$ if the ith family belongs to the group of rich
$\quad = 0$ Otherwise[2]

It follows that

$$C_i = (\alpha + \gamma) + \beta_2 Y_i + \varepsilon_i \quad (\text{when } Z_i = 1) \tag{7.10}$$

$$C_i = \alpha + \beta_2 Y_i + \varepsilon_i \qquad (\text{when } Z_i = 0) \tag{7.11}$$

Here equation (7.10) represents consumption function of the rich and (7.11) represents consumption function of the poor. Actually, in this way, we are postulating that for the rich, the intercept (i.e., subsistence level of consumption) changes from α to $(\alpha + \gamma)$ (as shown in Figure 7.1). Whether such a change is statistically significant or not can be examined by estimating equation (7.9) and testing the null hypothesis $H_N : \gamma = 0$.

Here the *decision rule* is: If $\left|t_{\hat{\gamma}}^*\right| > t$ at chosen level of significance and $(n - k)$ degrees of freedom [n denotes the number of observations and k denotes the number of parameters in model (7.9)], reject H_N and conclude that consumption function of the rich families is different from that of poor families and this difference is caused by the difference of intercept term or subsistence level of consumption. This also implies the absence of stability of the consumption function.

(ii) Model to Examine the Difference of Slope Coefficient
The model to be estimated here is[3]

$$C_i = \alpha + \beta_2 Y_i + \delta(Z_i Y_i) + \varepsilon_i \tag{7.12}$$

[2] In this model, Z_i is also called intercept dummy.
[3] Note that here $(Z_i Y_i)$ is the interactive slope dummy. It is obtained by interacting or multiplying the intercept dummy (Z_i) with the explanatory variable (Y_i). The coefficient of this interaction dummy (δ) measures the extent by which the slope (marginal propensity to consume) of rich families' consumption function differs from the slope of consumption function of poor families.

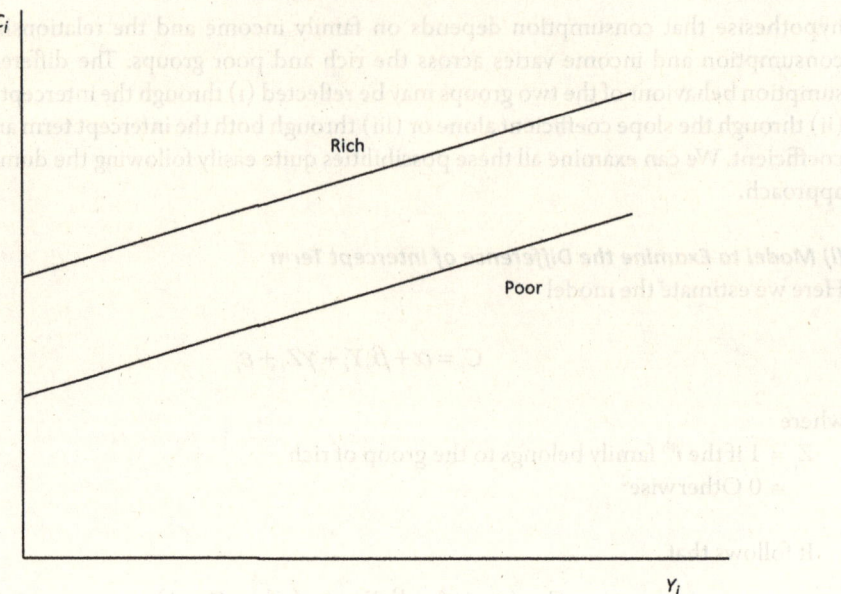

Figure 7.1   Consumption Functions of 'Rich' and 'Poor' With Different Intercepts
Source: Author's own.

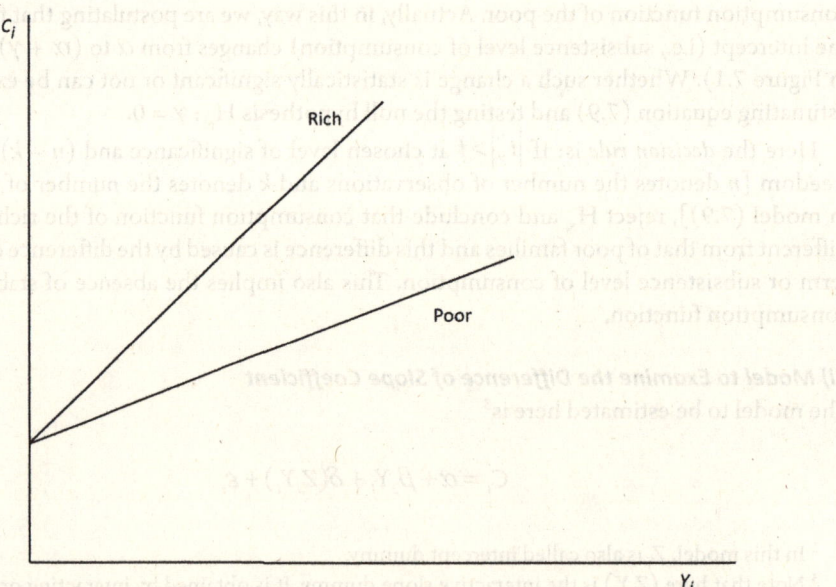

Figure 7.2   Consumption Functions of 'Rich' and 'Poor' With Different Slopes
Source: Author's own.

This gives

$$C_i = \alpha + (\beta_2 + \delta)\,Y_i + \varepsilon_i \quad \text{(when } Z_i = 1) \tag{7.13}$$

$$C_i = \alpha + \beta_2 Y_i + \varepsilon_i \qquad \text{(when } Z_i = 0) \tag{7.14}$$

Thus, we are postulating that the slope coefficient of the rich is higher by the extent of δ compared to the poor (see Figure 7.2). Whether such a difference is statistically significant or not can be understood by estimating equation (7.12) and testing $H_N: \delta = 0$.

The *decision rule* is: If $\left| t_{\hat{\delta}} \right| > t$ at a chosen level of significance and $(n - k)$ degrees of freedom, we reject H_N and conclude that there exists statistically significant difference between the values of slope coefficients, i.e., the marginal propensities to consume of two groups of families. This further signifies that there is no stability of consumption function.

(iii) Model to Examine the Difference of Both Intercept Term and Slope Coefficient

Here the appropriate model is

$$C_i = \alpha + \beta_2 Y_i + \gamma Z_i + \delta(Z_i Y_i) + \varepsilon_i \tag{7.15}$$

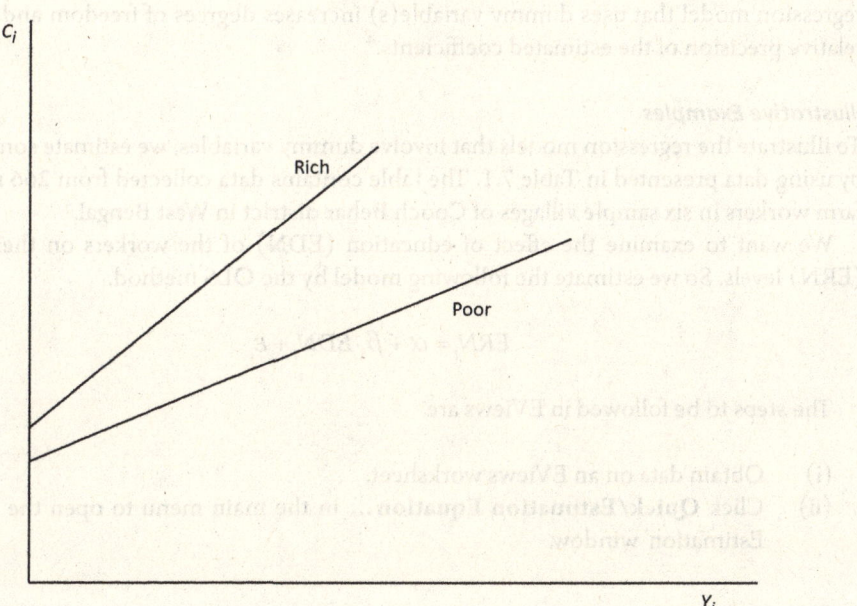

Figure 7.3 Consumption Functions of 'Rich' and 'Poor' With Different Intercepts and Slopes

Source: Author's own.

This gives

$$C_i = (\alpha + \gamma) + (\beta_2 + \delta)Y_i + \varepsilon_i \quad (\text{when } Z_i = 1) \tag{7.16}$$

$$C_i = \alpha + \beta_2 Y_i + \varepsilon_i \qquad (\text{when } Z_i = 0) \tag{7.17}$$

We are postulating here that both the intercept and slope coefficient are different for the two groups of families (Figure 7.3). The hypothesis to be tested is: $H_N : \gamma = 0$ and $\delta = 0$.

The *decision rule* is: if $\left| t_{\hat{\gamma}}^* \right| > t$ and $\left| t_{\hat{\delta}}^* \right| > t$ at chosen level of significance and $(n - k)$ degrees of freedom, we reject H_N and conclude that there is statistically significant difference between both intercepts and slope coefficients of the consumption functions of the rich and poor families. This also implies absence of stability in consumption function for the sampled families.

Advantages of Dummy Variable Approach

As a tool for understanding the stability of regression (i.e., for comparing two separate regressions), the dummy variable approach has some advantages over the Chow test. First, under the dummy variable approach, we may estimate only one equation [e.g., model (7.15)] and specifically identify the source(s) of difference in consumption behavior of the two groups of families, i.e., whether it is due to difference in intercept alone, or slope alone, or both. This is not possible under the Chow test. Secondly, pooling data for two groups in the case of regression model that uses dummy variable(s) increases degrees of freedom and improves relative precision of the estimated coefficients.[4]

Illustrative Examples

To illustrate the regression models that involve dummy variables, we estimate some models by using data presented in Table 7.1. The table contains data collected from 266 rural non-farm workers in six sample villages of Cooch Behar district in West Bengal.[5]

We want to examine the effect of education (EDN) of the workers on their earning (ERN) levels. So we estimate the following model by the OLS method.

$$ERN_i = \alpha + \beta_1 EDN_i + \varepsilon_i \tag{7.18}$$

The steps to be followed in EViews are

(i)   Obtain data on an EViews worksheet.
(ii)   Click **Quick/Estimation Equation…** in the main menu to open the 'Equation Estimation' window.

---

[4] This is so under the assumption that the two groups belong to the same population distribution.
[5] These data form a part of large data set that we generated in course of a study on the rural non-farm sector in two districts (Cooch Behar and Hooghly) of West Bengal in 1999–2000.

Table 7.1   Survey Data on Non-farm Self-Employed and Casual Wage Workers from Cooch
Behar District, West Bengal

S. No.	ERN	MODE	SEX	AGE	EDN	ASSETS	S. No.	ERN	MODE	SEX	AGE	EDN	ASSETS
1	1.73	1	1	14	8	2268	33	1.41	1	1	26	4	1008
2	3.86	1	1	15	1	1008	34	15.12	1	1	26	8	945
3	2.92	1	1	15	6	0	35	10.52	1	1	26	9	2520
4	12.10	1	1	16	5	1739	36	17.90	1	1	27	0	0
5	9.07	1	1	16	9	2898	37	3.02	1	1	27	4	756
6	5.22	1	1	18	1	1008	38	27.22	1	1	27	7	1260
7	3.58	1	1	18	4	0	39	2.75	1	1	27	8	882
8	4.94	1	1	19	11	1260	40	10.08	1	1	28	0	2520
9	19.15	1	1	20	5	1638	41	12.48	1	1	28	1	18900
10	14.18	1	1	21	9	2646	42	1.54	1	1	28	4	630
11	6.43	1	1	22	1	1890	43	7.56	1	1	28	5	0
12	13.61	1	1	22	5	0	44	0.76	1	1	28	6	756
13	6.58	1	1	22	6	1638	45	8.26	1	1	28	8	0
14	10.52	1	1	22	6	2520	46	8.16	1	1	28	8	0
15	4.54	1	1	22	8	0	47	12.60	1	1	28	10	0
16	4.78	1	0	22	9	1260	48	6.30	1	1	29	1	2142
17	9.98	1	1	22	9	630	49	10.30	1	1	30	0	2268
18	25.04	1	1	22	9	65520	50	0.95	1	0	30	0	0
19	11.59	1	1	22	11	2520	51	10.21	1	1	30	0	1512
20	13.29	1	1	24	0	2268	52	11.59	1	1	30	0	1890
21	10.58	1	1	24	0	882	53	3.78	1	0	30	0	1008
22	8.32	1	1	24	0	882	54	12.10	1	1	30	1	0
23	4.41	1	1	24	7	1260	55	7.31	1	1	30	1	1890
24	2.75	1	1	24	8	882	56	15.72	1	1	30	1	0
25	18.82	1	1	25	0	2268	57	12.49	1	1	30	8	504
26	10.58	1	1	25	4	882	58	4.54	1	1	30	9	1512
27	7.27	1	1	25	6	1890	59	5.89	1	1	31	7	630
28	39.83	1	1	25	8	0	60	4.30	1	1	31	14	945
29	1.95	1	0	25	9	1512	61	15.12	1	1	31	14	5859
30	15.47	1	1	26	0	1890	62	21.67	1	1	32	0	0
31	10.58	1	1	26	0	882	63	9.19	1	1	32	2	819
32	5.48	1	1	26	1	0	64	5.04	1	1	32	6	0

(Contd.)

Table 7.1 (*Contd.*)

S. No.	ERN	MODE	SEX	AGE	EDN	ASSETS	S. No.	ERN	MODE	SEX	AGE	EDN	ASSETS
65	19.28	1	1	34	0	0	99	5.82	1	1	40	1	1764
66	6.62	1	1	34	0	2678	100	10.89	1	1	40	1	2268
67	11.34	1	1	34	5	0	101	2.65	1	1	40	5	1008
68	30.24	1	1	34	8	2898	102	4.79	1	1	40	5	378
69	5.04	1	1	34	9	1260	103	5.29	1	1	40	6	504
70	8.47	1	1	35	0	0	104	11.84	1	1	40	8	1386
71	10.66	1	1	35	0	1890	105	10.21	1	1	41	11	882
72	14.26	1	1	35	0	1890	106	8.45	1	1	42	1	0
73	5.86	1	1	35	1	0	107	4.99	1	1	42	5	378
74	8.95	1	1	35	1	1890	108	8.22	1	1	45	1	0
75	16.24	1	1	35	4	1638	109	16.88	1	1	45	1	2520
76	9.83	1	1	35	5	1739	110	1.81	1	1	45	5	0
77	7.69	1	1	35	7	1008	111	6.35	1	1	45	6	1260
78	0.47	1	1	35	8	1008	112	5.44	1	1	45	9	567
79	0.76	1	1	35	8	315	113	5.04	1	1	45	14	8820
80	13.61	1	1	35	8	630	114	24.19	1	1	46	8	630
81	14.82	1	1	35	8	0	115	13.86	1	1	46	9	0
82	10.96	1	1	35	9	0	116	8.91	1	1	48	1	2520
83	9.95	1	1	35	9	1008	117	6.30	1	1	48	9	1260
84	45.36	1	1	35	9	946	118	1.51	1	0	50	0	0
85	13.48	1	1	35	9	0	119	3.34	1	1	50	5	504
86	6.80	1	1	35	9	20160	120	1.51	1	1	55	0	0
87	5.53	1	1	37	1	504	121	3.78	1	1	55	5	0
88	1.26	1	1	37	8	1008	122	7.26	1	1	58	6	1890
89	16.25	1	1	38	0	2016	123	5.67	1	1	59	6	882
90	0.95	1	1	38	1	0	124	18.90	1	1	59	9	65520
91	9.07	1	1	38	1	0	125	5.67	1	1	60	0	756
92	9.45	1	1	38	8	441	126	6.30	1	1	60	0	1512
93	1.76	1	0	40	0	0	127	6.87	1	1	60	0	2016
94	11.64	1	1	40	0	1890	128	1.97	1	1	60	4	756
95	8.95	1	1	40	0	126	129	0.38	1	1	60	4	252
96	5.54	1	1	40	0	504	130	4.23	1	1	64	5	0
97	5.40	1	1	40	1	1890	131	6.80	1	1	65	9	0
98	8.77	1	1	40	1	1890	132	0.76	1	1	65	9	0

(*Contd.*)

Table 7.1 (*Contd.*)

S. No.	ERN	MODE	SEX	AGE	EDN	ASSETS	S. No.	ERN	MODE	SEX	AGE	EDN	ASSETS
133	7.94	1	1	65	9	2520	171	1.89	0	1	20	7	378
134	9.61	1	1	70	1	2268	172	8.69	0	1	20	7	882
135	1.42	0	1	9	0	0	173	9.80	0	1	20	7	1638
136	2.27	0	0	10	0	1890	174	13.23	0	1	20	9	126
137	2.31	0	0	10	0	0	175	4.54	0	1	20	11	756
138	2.38	0	0	10	4	1638	176	11.98	0	1	20	11	1512
139	4.99	0	0	12	0	1890	177	10.89	0	1	21	0	0
140	2.27	0	0	12	3	0	178	11.59	0	1	21	6	756
141	2.38	0	0	13	7	756	179	2.72	0	1	21	9	1260
142	5.03	0	0	14	0	0	180	13.23	0	1	22	0	2016
143	3.02	0	1	15	0	0	181	7.26	0	1	22	1	0
144	9.07	0	1	15	1	756	182	5.76	0	0	22	1	0
145	9.07	0	1	15	5	0	183	10.58	0	1	22	3	630
146	3.39	0	0	15	5	1638	184	11.34	0	1	22	4	126
147	3.29	0	1	15	9	756	185	7.86	0	1	22	9	0
148	9.07	0	1	16	0	1008	186	6.43	0	1	22	11	1008
149	5.15	0	1	16	0	0	187	2.27	0	1	23	2	0
150	16.94	0	1	16	0	0	188	1.89	0	0	23	14	0
151	3.70	0	1	16	4	1638	189	1.54	0	1	24	0	882
152	5.67	0	1	16	5	2520	190	2.12	0	0	24	0	504
153	8.57	0	1	16	5	630	191	10.22	0	1	24	4	378
154	1.89	0	1	17	0	0	192	3.15	0	0	24	6	0
155	9.07	0	0	17	0	1260	193	27.52	0	1	24	9	2520
156	7.26	0	1	17	6	1260	194	6.80	0	1	25	0	0
157	9.07	0	1	18	0	1008	195	23.28	0	1	25	0	756
158	18.87	0	1	18	0	0	196	11.91	0	1	25	0	2016
159	3.97	0	0	18	0	0	197	13.00	0	1	25	1	0
160	9.19	0	1	18	4	1638	198	7.26	0	1	25	1	0
161	11.79	0	1	18	8	0	199	3.45	0	0	25	4	0
162	2.27	0	1	19	3	0	200	22.01	0	1	25	5	0
163	0.79	0	1	19	5	756	201	4.07	0	1	25	6	1890
164	3.02	0	1	20	0	0	202	6.05	0	1	25	8	1134
165	3.48	0	1	20	0	0	203	12.10	0	1	25	8	0
166	14.08	0	1	20	1	882	204	5.92	0	1	25	9	630
167	8.32	0	1	20	2	0	205	13.76	0	1	25	0	0
168	2.87	0	0	20	4	441	206	2.22	0	0	26	0	2520
169	6.89	0	1	20	6	630	207	1.70	0	0	26	0	2678
170	9.58	0	1	20	6	5859	208	11.72	0	1	27	0	882

(*Contd.*)

Table 7.1 (*Contd.*)

S. No.	ERN	MODE	SEX	AGE	EDN	ASSETS	S. No.	ERN	MODE	SEX	AGE	EDN	ASSETS
209	7.98	0	1	27	0	0	238	6.07	0	1	35	5	189
210	9.07	0	1	27	8	0	239	4.63	0	1	35	5	252
211	5.82	0	1	28	0	0	240	40.22	0	1	35	11	0
212	5.67	0	1	28	0	0	241	9.13	0	1	37	0	0
213	10.43	0	1	28	1	252	242	7.06	0	1	37	5	0
214	1.66	0	0	28	1	0	243	9.02	0	1	37	8	1260
215	3.93	0	1	28	7	630	244	17.07	0	1	37	9	0
216	11.62	0	1	28	7	945	245	9.53	0	1	38	0	1386
217	15.61	0	1	29	5	1008	246	15.47	0	1	38	6	882
218	1.89	0	0	30	0	0	247	7.67	0	1	40	1	0
219	0.55	0	1	30	0	0	248	4.99	0	1	40	5	2394
220	9.07	0	0	30	0	693	249	0.63	0	1	40	8	1386
221	2.49	0	0	30	0	1764	250	1.13	0	1	42	1	0
222	6.58	0	0	30	1	756	251	3.78	0	1	44	1	0
223	12.26	0	1	30	3	504	252	1.63	0	0	45	1	441
224	14.72	0	1	30	3	1260	253	10.32	0	1	45	4	0
225	2.12	0	0	30	4	2394	254	3.78	0	1	45	9	0
226	13.06	0	1	30	9	1638	255	12.60	0	1	47	6	756
227	7.06	0	1	31	7	630	256	11.59	0	1	48	0	1260
228	2.09	0	0	32	0	1890	257	3.40	0	1	50	0	1890
229	4.94	0	1	32	0	0	258	15.12	0	1	50	0	1134
230	10.43	0	1	32	1	252	259	3.73	0	1	50	4	0
231	1.71	0	1	32	9	0	260	0.91	0	0	50	5	1890
232	1.51	0	1	33	1	504	261	3.11	0	1	50	7	882
233	18.14	0	1	34	5	0	262	1.36	0	0	52	4	756
234	0.79	0	0	34	9	0	263	1.76	0	1	54	0	0
235	0.25	0	1	35	0	0	264	2.84	0	1	65	6	0
236	2.84	0	1	35	1	151	265	2.27	0	1	67	0	0
237	18.90	0	1	35	1	693	266	2.84	0	1	75	4	0

Source: Field survey by the author, 1999–2000.

ERN: annual earning of the worker (in thousand rupees);

AGE: age of the worker;

SEX: sex of the worker, which is a dummy variable that takes value 1 for male and 0 for female;

EDN: education of the worker (years of schooling);

ASSETS: value of non-farm assets possessed by the worker (in rupees); and

MODE: mode of employment, which is a dummy variable that takes value 1 if the worker is in self-employment and 0 if in casual wage employment.

(iii) Write **ern c edn** in the 'Equation specification' edit box.

(iv) Click **OK**.

The results are shown in Table 7.2. It appears that education is indeed an important determinant of earning of the rural non-farm workers in the surveyed district. The computed t-value for the estimated coefficient of EDU is statistically significant at 5% level of significance (p-value = 0.0367). It is also observed that one-point increase in the level of education (i.e., one year increase in the years of schooling) brings about improvement of earning by 0.226567 point.

Table 7.2 Relation between Earning and Education

Dependent Variable: ERN
Method: Least Squares
Date: 08/23/13 Time: 15:40
Sample: 1 266
Included observations: 266

Variable	Coefficient	Std. Error	t-Statistic	Prob.
C	7.316802	0.601855	12.15709	0.0000
EDN	0.226567	0.107881	2.100166	0.0367
R-squared	0.016433	Mean dependent var		8.254586
Adjusted R-squared	0.012707	S.D. dependent var		6.623694
S.E. of regression	6.581475	Akaike info criterion		6.613885
Sum squared resid	11435.38	Schwarz criterion		6.640829
Log likelihood	−877.6468	Hannan-Quinn criter.		6.624710
F-statistic	4.410697	Durbin-Watson stat		2.018741
Prob(F-statistic)	0.036663			

Source: This table represents the output obtained by the author after application of the EViews software.

Using an Intercept Dummy

We now want to see the effect of both mode of employment (MODE) and education on the earning levels of the rural non-farm workers. This is done by estimating the following model.

$$ERN_i = \alpha + \beta_1 MODE_i + \beta_2 EDN_i + \varepsilon_i \qquad (7.19)$$

In this model, MODE is an intercept dummy and the coefficient associated with it (β_1) measures the extent by which the earnings of the self-employed workers differ from the earnings of the casual wage workers. EDN is a usual quantitative variable.

To estimate this model, we write **ern c mode edn** in the 'Equation specification' edit box of EViews. The results are shown in Table 7.3. It is clear that, holding education constant, the earnings (in thousand rupees) of the casual wage workers become 6.654927, which for the self-employed worker becomes 6.654927 + 1.567777 = 8.222704. Further, as the computed-*t* for estimated coefficient of MODE is statistically significant at 5.5% probability level (*p*-value = 0.0545), it can be said that the intercept of the earnings function of the self-employed workers is different from the same for casual wage workers.

Table 7.3   Earning Function for the Rural Non-farm Workers (Using Intercept Dummy)

Dependent Variable: ERN
Method: Least Squares
Date: 08/23/13 Time: 15:43
Sample: 1 266
Included observations: 266

Variable	Coefficient	Std. Error	t-Statistic	Prob.
C	6.654927	0.689920	9.645945	0.0000
MODE	1.567777	0.811830	1.931162	0.0545
EDN	0.195665	0.108514	1.803138	0.0725
R-squared	0.030185	Mean dependent var		8.254586
Adjusted R-squared	0.022810	S.D. dependent var		6.623694
S.E. of regression	6.547715	Akaike info criterion		6.607324
Sum squared resid	11275.49	Schwarz criterion		6.647739
Log likelihood	−875.7740	Hannan-Quinn criter.		6.623560
F-statistic	4.092843	Durbin-Watson stat		2.040669
Prob(F-statistic)	0.017766			

Source: Same as for Table 7.2.

Using Both Intercept and Slope Dummies

To understand whether both intercept and slope differ between the two categories of workers, we estimate the following model.

$$ERN_i = \alpha + \beta_1 MODE_i + \beta_2 EDN_i + \beta_3 (MODE_i * EDN_i) + \varepsilon_i \qquad (7.20)$$

As before, MODE is an intercept dummy, EDN is a quantitative variable and MODE*EDN is a multiplicative slope dummy. To estimate this model, we write **ern c mode edn mode*edn** in the 'Equation specification' edit box of EViews.

The results are presented in Table 7.4. As $\hat{\beta}_1$ = 2.224366 is statistically significant at 6.6% probability level, we conclude as before that the intercept varies between two categories of workers. However, as $\hat{\beta}_3$ = −0.160869 is statistically insignificant, our conclusion is that the slope coefficient does not differ between the two categories of workers. Thus, the earning functions of the two categories of workers differ only in respect of intercept while the slope is same for the two functions.

Table 7.4   Earning Function for the Rural Non-farm Workers
(Using Both Intercept and Slope Dummies)

Dependent Variable: ERN
Method: Least Squares
Date: 08/23/13 Time: 15:44
Sample: 1 266
Included observations: 266

Variable	Coefficient	Std. Error	t-Statistic	Prob.
C	6.338778	0.812880	7.797925	0.0000
MODE	2.224366	1.205681	1.844904	0.0662
EDN	0.283893	0.161624	1.756504	0.0802
MODE*EDN	−0.160869	0.218243	−0.737113	0.4617
R-squared	0.032192	Mean dependent var		8.254586
Adjusted R-squared	0.021110	S.D. dependent var		6.623694
S.E. of regression	6.553407	Akaike info criterion		6.612771
Sum squared resid	11252.15	Schwarz criterion		6.666658
Log likelihood	−875.4985	Hannan-Quinn criter.		6.634419
F-statistic	2.904936	Durbin-Watson stat		2.024140
Prob(F-statistic)	0.035280			

Source: Same as for Table 7.2.

The Chow Test in EViews

Using EViews, we can conduct the Chow test to examine stability of an estimated regression model. To apply the Chow test, it is necessary to enter data in an EViews worksheet sequentially for the two groups, one after another. This means we have to enter data for 134 self-employed workers first followed by data for 132 casual wage workers.

While conducting the Chow test in EViews, we do not estimate separate regressions for the two groups. Rather we estimate an OLS regression using the entire (pooled) dataset. Our command here is: **ern c edn**. After obtaining the results of estimation, to check the stability of regression, we click **View/Stability Diagnostics/Chow Breakpoint Test…** from the output window. This opens the 'Chow Tests' dialog box (Screenshot 7.1) where we mention the 'break-point' (which is 135 as per our data in Table 7.1), and click **OK** to obtain the test result.

Our test result presented in Table 7.5 shows that computed value of F-statistic is statistically insignificant (as its p-value > 0.05). Thus, on the basis of the Chow test, it may be concluded that the earning function does not differ statistically significantly between the self-employed and casual wage workers. This signifies the presence of stability for the regression model estimated as per the Chow test.

Screenshot 7.1   Chow Tests Dialog Box

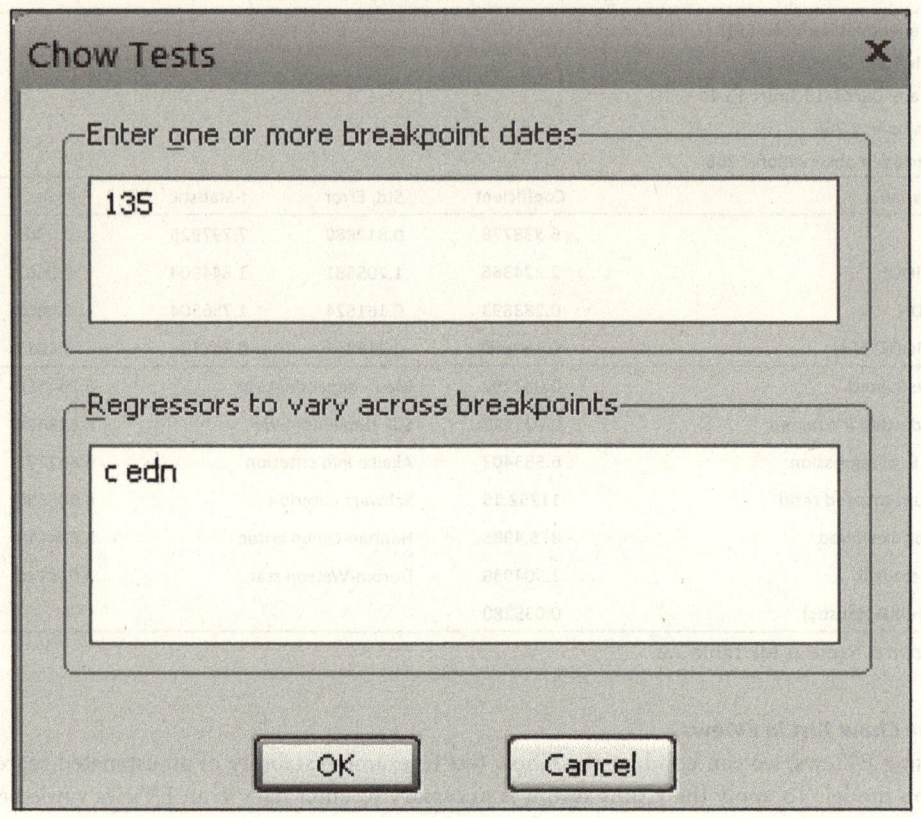

Table 7.5   Results of Chow Breakpoint Test

Chow Breakpoint Test: 135			
Null Hypothesis: No breaks at specified breakpoints			
Varying regressors: All equation variables			
Equation Sample: 1 266			
F-statistic	2.133124	Prob. F(2,262)	0.1205
Log likelihood ratio	4.296495	Prob. Chi-Square(2)	0.1167
Wald Statistic	4.266248	Prob. Chi-Square(2)	0.1185

Source: Same as for Table 7.2.

7.5 MODELS WITH DUMMY DEPENDENT VARIABLE

In the models discussed above, dummy variable(s) appeared as explanatory variables. However, there are circumstances where the dependent variable of the model becomes a dummy or binary variable. The model in which the dependent variable is a binary variable is also called *binary choice model*.[6] In such a model, the dependent variable actually involves only two choices indicating presence or absence of an attribute or quality.

To illustrate the binary choice model, suppose we are interested to know the determinants of choice of occupation by the workers in rural areas. The rural workers usually have two choices—either to work in the farm sector or non-farm sector. What determines the rural workers' choice between farm and non-farm occupations becomes an issue for investigation. Here we may consider a binary choice model that considers workers' occupational choice as the dependent variable and factors like workers' age, sex, education, parental education, etc., as explanatory variables. The dependent variable of such a model (occupational choice) is a qualitative variable, which may be quantified by considering a dummy or binary variable that takes value 1 if a worker is in non-farm occupation and 0 if in farm occupation.

There are three important approaches to dealing with dummy dependent variable models or binary choice models, which are Linear Probability Model, Logit Model, and Probit Model.

7.5.1 Linear Probability Model (LPM)

Suppose we want to know what determines car ownership status of the families in a locality. We hypothesise that car ownership status of the families is determined by their family incomes. To examine the validity of this hypothesis, we collect sample data. In our sample, some families have cars while others don't have. The following points need to be noted here.

(i)   Car ownership status is a qualitative variable.

(ii) However, car ownership status may be quantified by using a binary or dummy variable that is assigned value 1 if the family owns a car and value 0 if the family doesn't own a car.

(iii) Family income is a usual quantitative variable as we have quantitative information on income levels of the sampled families.

The Model

We consider the following model to describe the relationship between car ownership status and income levels of the families.

$$Y_i = \alpha + \beta X_i + \varepsilon_i \tag{7.21}$$

where

X_i = family income.

Y_i = 1 if the family owns a car

= 0 Otherwise, and

ε_i is the disturbance term.

It is an independently distributed random variable, and follows zero mean and serial independence (or non-autocorrelation) assumptions.

---

[6] It is to be noted that the binary choice models also belong to the class of *limited dependent variable models*. This is because the dependent variable here assumes only a limited or countable number of values.

Characteristics of the Model

As Y_i takes on either 1 or 0 values, we can describe the probability distribution of Y_i by letting

$$P_i = Prob\,(Y_i = 1)$$

and

$$1 - P_i = Prob\,(Y_i = 0)$$

Then

$$E(Y_i) = 1.P_i + 0.(1 - P_i) = P_i \qquad (7.22)$$

Again, from (7.21),

$$E(Y_i \mid X_i) = \alpha + \beta X_i \qquad (7.23)$$

Comparing (7.22) and (7.23), we can write

$$E(Y_i \mid X_i) = \alpha + \beta X_i = P_i \qquad (7.24)$$

Since $0 \le P_i \le 1$, we also have

$$0 \le E(Y_i \mid X_i) \le 1$$

It follows from (7.24) that for the model (7.21), the conditional mean of Y_i given X_i, i.e., $E(Y_i \mid X_i)$, is the conditional probability that the event will occur. That is why the model such as (7.21) is called the linear probability model.

Estimation of LPM

Since the linear probability model (7.21) looks like a usual linear regression model, we can estimate this model by applying the ordinary least-squares (OLS) method as a mechanical routine. But we face several problems here.

Problems of LPM

(I) VIOLATION OF NORMALITY ASSUMPTION OF THE DISTURBANCE TERM

The normality assumption for the disturbance term gets violated in the context of the LPM. This can be justified easily. From equation (7.21), we have

$$\varepsilon_i = Y_i - \alpha - \beta X_i$$

Since $Y_i = 1$ or 0, for any given X_i, we have just two values of ε_i, which are

$$\varepsilon_i = 1 - \alpha - \beta X_i \text{ (when } Y_i = 1)$$
$$\varepsilon_i = -\alpha - \beta X_i \text{ (when } Y_i = 0)$$

It is clear that ε_i is not normally distributed; it has a discrete distribution.

(II) HETEROSKEDASTIC DISTURBANCE TERM

The disturbance term of the LPM suffers from the problem of heteroskedasticity. To prove this, let us consider the probability distribution of ε_i which follows from the probability distribution of Y_i.

Y_i	ε_i	$f(\varepsilon_i)$
0	$-\alpha - \beta X_i$	$1 - P_i$
1	$1 - \alpha - \beta X_i$	P_i

Now the variance of ε_i is computed as

$$
\begin{aligned}
Var(\varepsilon_i) &= E(\varepsilon_i^2) \\
&= (-\alpha - \beta X_i)^2 (1 - P_i) + (1 - \alpha - \beta X_i)^2 P_i \\
&= (-\alpha - \beta X_i)^2 (1 - \alpha - \beta X_i) + (1 - \alpha - \beta X_i)^2 (\alpha + \beta X_i) \qquad (\because P_i = \alpha + \beta X_i) \\
&= (1 - \alpha - \beta X_i)[(-\alpha - \beta X_i)^2 + (1 - \alpha - \beta X_i)(\alpha + \beta X_i)] \\
&= (1 - \alpha - \beta X_i)[(-1)(\alpha + \beta X_i)(-\alpha - \beta X_i) + (1 - \alpha - \beta X_i)(\alpha + \beta X_i)] \\
&= (1 - \alpha - \beta X_i)(\alpha + \beta X_i)[\alpha + \beta X_i + 1 - \alpha - \beta X_i] \\
&= (1 - \alpha - \beta X_i)(\alpha + \beta X_i) \\
&= E(Y_i)[1 - E(Y_i)]
\end{aligned}
$$

This proves that ε_i is heteroskedastic because its variance depends on $E(Y_i)$ which in turn depends on X_i. Thus, for model (7.21), $Var(\varepsilon_i) = f(X_i)$.

(III) INVALIDITY OF USUAL TESTS OF SIGNIFICANCE

As the normality and homoskedasticity assumptions are violated in the LPM, the usual procedure of tests of significance (or hypothesis testing) becomes invalid.

(IV) NON-FULFILLMENT OF CONDITION $0 \leq E(Y_i | X_i) \leq 1$

In the LPM, $E(Y_i | X_i)$ is the conditional expectation of Y_i, which is equal to the probability that the event will occur [as shown in (7.24) above]. However, in actual practice, $\hat{Y}_i$, which is the estimated probability of $Y_i = 1$ may lie outside the range $(0,1)$. In other words, $\hat{Y}_i$ may assume impossible values for extreme values of X_i. Such a situation is shown in

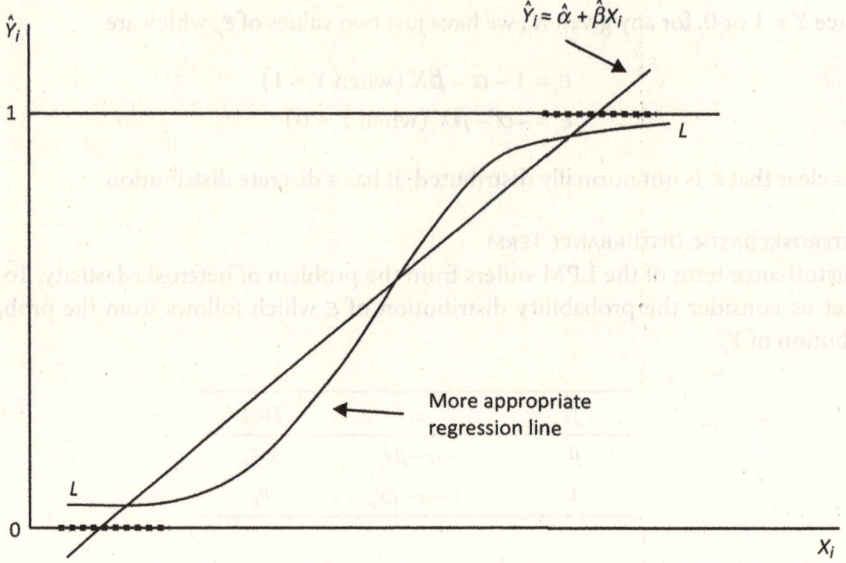

Figure 7.4   Estimated LPM and Predictd Probabilities

Source: Author's own.

Figure 7.4. It is observed that the value of $\hat{Y}_i$ is negative at the lower left end of the line and it is greater than unity at the upper right end.

(V) UNSUITABILITY OF CONVENTIONAL R^2-TYPE MEASURES TO UNDERSTAND GOODNESS OF FIT
Since the value of Y_i is either 0 or 1 corresponding to a given X_i, Y_i values will lie either along the X-axis or along the line corresponding to 1, as shown by the scatter of points in Figure 7.4. Generally, no LPM is expected to fit such a scatter well. Therefore, conventional R^2-type measures are not helpful when the dependent variable Y_i is binary.

7.5.2 Logit Model
The aforementioned discussion on the LPM revealed that when the dependent variable is a binary variable, a non-linear specification of the model appears more appropriate. Specifically, it seems appropriate to fit some kind of an S-shaped or 'sigmoid curve' to the observed data points (e.g., the LL curve in Figure 7.4). The sigmoid curve has following features.

   (i)   It resembles an elongated-S.
   (ii)   The tails of the sigmoid curve level off before reaching $P = 0$ or $P = 1$ so that the problem of impossible values of estimated probability is avoided, and

(iii)   Most importantly, the sigmoid curve resembles the cumulative distribution function (CDF) of a random variable. So, we can choose a suitable CDF to represent the sigmoid curve to capture 0-1 representation for the dependent variable.

The commonly chosen CDFs to represent sigmoid curves are *logistic* and *normal*. The model that uses CDF of a logistic function to represent the binary dependent variable model is named *logit model*. On the other hand, the model that uses CDF of the standard normal distribution to represent the same is called *probit model*.

Specification of Logit Model
The logit model is specified as

$$P_i = P(Y_i = 1) = F(Z_i) = \frac{1}{1+e^{-Z_i}} \tag{7.25}$$

where

P_i is the probability of $Y_i = 1$;
$F(Z_i)$ is the CDF of the cumulative logistic function;
$Z_i = \alpha + \beta X_i$ is a predictor variable; and
e is the base of natural logarithms, equal to 2.71828.

Now,

$$1 - P_i = \frac{1}{1+e^{Z_i}} \qquad [\because P_i + (1-P_i) = 1]$$

and

$$\frac{P_i}{1-P_i} = \frac{1+e^{Z_i}}{1+e^{-Z_i}} = e^{Z_i}$$

So,

$$\ln\left(\frac{P_i}{1-P_i}\right) = Z_i = \alpha + \beta X_i \tag{7.26}$$

Here $\dfrac{P_i}{1-P_i}$ is called the odds-ratio in favour of the event occurring and $\ln\left(\dfrac{P_i}{1-P_i}\right)$ is the log odds-ratio (also called logit of P).

In model (7.26), we considered only one explanatory variable. But, if necessary, more explanatory variables can be added by supposing that Z_i is a linear function of a set of predictor variables. In that case,

$$Z_i = \alpha + \beta_1 X_{1i} + \beta_2 X_{2i} + \dots + \beta_k X_{ki}$$

Estimation of Logit Model

It is not possible to estimate the logit model (7.26) by OLS method for two reasons:

(i)   This is a non-linear model,[7] and

(ii) $\ln\left(\dfrac{P_i}{1-P_i}\right)$ is not a familiar quantity.[8]

In this situation, there are two approaches. The first one uses replicated or grouped data and applies the weighted least squares (WLS) method. The basic idea behind the WLS method as applied here is that we may use our initial (ungrouped) data to form different groups among the sampled families.[9] For each group, we find out the number of families (n) and number of families owing car (f_c). Using these information, we obtain group-wise estimate of P_i, which is $\hat{P}_i = f_c/n$. This enables us to generate the series for $\ln\left(\dfrac{\hat{P}_i}{1-\hat{P}_i}\right)$ and eventually to estimate the model by using the WLS method.[10]

However, a better approach is the one that continues with original (ungrouped) data set and applies the method of maximum likelihood (ML) to estimate the logit model. The procedure involved in ML estimation of logit model is described below.

ML Estimation of Logit Model

For the logit model (7.25), we cannot observe individual P_i values. What we know is whether the first or second choice was selected. If the first choice is made, $Y_i = 1$ and if the second choice is made, $Y_i = 0$. In the maximum likelihood method, our objective is to find out the estimates of unknown parameters α and β such that the choices in the sample would have occurred. With this objective, we construct the likelihood function[11] in the following manner.

Let

n_1 = number of times the first alternative is chosen, and

n_2 = number of times the second alternative is chosen.

$n_1 + n_2 = n$

---

[7] Note that the model is non-linear in variables though it is linear in parameters.

[8] This is because we cannot define $P_i/(1-P_i)$ for those individuals who are car owners, as $P_i = 1$ for them.

[9] For example, the groups may be families earning less than Rs 10, 000 per month, Rs 10,001–20,000 per month, Rs 20,001–30,000 per month, and so on.

[10] The WLS is applied here to avoid the problem of heteroskedasticity which is very likely to happen with grouped data. For discussion on application of WLS method to estimate the logit model using grouped data, refer to Kmenta (1986, 550–3).

[11] The likelihood function gives the joint probability of observing a given set of sample values.

We order the data so that first n_1 observations are associated with the first alternative. Then the likelihood function is

$$L = \text{Prob}\,(Y_1, Y_2, ..., Y_n)$$
$$= \text{Prob}\,(Y_1).\,\text{Prob}\,(Y_2).\,....\,\text{Prob}\,(Y_n)$$

As the probability of the second option being chosen is equal to 1 minus the probability of the first being chosen, we write

$$L = P_1.P_2.\,...\,P_{n_1}.(1-P_{n_1+1}).(1-P_{n_1+2}).\,...\,(1-P_n)$$
$$= \prod_{i=1}^{n_1} P_i \prod_{i=n_1+1}^{n} (1-P_i)$$
$$= \prod_{i=1}^{n} P_i^{Y_i} (1-P_i)^{1-Y_i}$$

(Since $Y_i = 1$ for first n_1 observations and $Y_i = 0$ for last n_2 observations.)
We take logarithms to obtain the following log-likelihood function.

$$\ln L = \sum_{i=1}^{n_1} Y_i \ln P_i + \sum_{i=n_1+1}^{n} (1-Y_i)\ln(1-P_i)$$
$$= \sum_{i=1}^{n_1} Y_i \ln\left[\frac{1}{1+e^{-\alpha-\beta X_i}}\right] + \sum_{i=n_1+1}^{n} (1-Y_i)\ln\left[\frac{1}{1+e^{\alpha+\beta X_i}}\right]$$

Maximizing $\ln L$ with respect to α and β and solving, we obtain ML estimates of unknown parameters α and β.

Features of ML Estimates of α and β

(i)   All parameter estimates are consistent and efficient asymptotically.
(ii)   All parameter estimates are asymptotically normal. Thus, an analogue of the regression t-test can be applied here to test statistical significance of the estimated coefficients.[12]

Computation of Marginal Effects in Logit Model

In the OLS regression, the ith estimated slope coefficient $(\hat{\beta}_i)$ straightway shows the marginal effect of change in the ith explanatory variable (X_i) on the dependent variable. But, in the case of logit model, the marginal effect of change in X_i on P_i needs to be calculated after estimation of the model.[13] This is done in the following manner.

---

[12] Note that some software packages such as EViews, SPSS, and STATA give z-statistics instead of t-statistics. Here, z-statistics are actually approximations to t-statistics and have nothing to do with Z-variable as usually discussed.

[13] It should be noted that in logit (also probit) model the coefficient estimate(s) alone cannot be interpreted as marginal effect(s).

The logit model gives

$$\frac{dP_i}{dZ_i} = \frac{d}{dZ_i}\left[\frac{1}{1+e^{-Z_i}}\right] = \frac{e^{-Z_i}}{(1+e^{-Z_i})^2}$$

This value of dP_i/dZ_i is usually computed at the mean value(s) of the explanatory variable(s). Having obtained the value of dP_i/dZ_i, the marginal effect of change in i^{th} explanatory variable (X_i) on P_i is computed as

$$\frac{dP_i}{dX_i} = \frac{dP_i}{dZ_i} \cdot \frac{dZ_i}{dX_i} = \frac{e^{-\hat{\alpha}-\hat{\beta}\bar{X}_i}}{(1+e^{-\hat{\alpha}-\hat{\beta}\bar{X}_i})^2} \cdot \hat{\beta}_i$$

This marginal effect (dP_i/dX_i) shows change in P_i as a result of a one-point change in X_i.

7.5.3 Probit Model

As mentioned earlier, the probit model also represents a sigmoid curve. It corresponds to the CDF of a standard normal distribution. Here P_i is considered as standard normal CDF, which is evaluated as a linear function of the explanatory variable(s). Thus, the probit model is specified as

$$P_i = P(Y_i = 1)$$
$$= F(\alpha + \beta X_i)$$

Here $F(\alpha + \beta X_i)$ is the CDF of the standard normal distribution so that

$$P_i = F(\alpha + \beta X_i) = \int_{-\infty}^{\alpha+\beta X_i} f(Z)dz$$

where
$f(Z)$ is the density function of $Z \sim N(0, 1)$, i.e.,

$$f(Z) = \frac{1}{\sqrt{2\pi}}e^{\left(-\frac{Z^2}{2}\right)}$$

Estimation of Probit Model

It is same as logit model except that here P_i represents probabilities associated with the cumulative normal function rather than cumulative logistic function.

As in logit model, the log-likelihood function is

$$\ln L = \sum_{i=1}^{n_1} Y_i \ln P_i + \sum_{i=n_1+1}^{n} (1-Y_i)\ln(1-P_i)$$

$$= \sum_{i=1}^{n_1} Y_i \ln F(\alpha+\beta X_i) + \sum_{i=n_1+1}^{n} (1-Y_i)\ln[1-F(\alpha+\beta X_i)]$$

Maximizing $\ln L$ with respect to α and β and solving, we obtain estimates of unknown parameters.

Computation of Marginal Effects in Probit Model

For the Probit model, the marginal effect, i.e., the effect of change in X_i on P_i is computed as

$$\frac{dP_i}{dX_i} = \frac{dP_i}{dZ_i} \cdot \frac{dZ_i}{dX_i} = f(Z).\hat{\beta}_i = \left(\frac{1}{\sqrt{2\pi}} e^{\left(-\frac{Z^2}{2}\right)} \right).\hat{\beta}_i \qquad (\pi=3.14159265)$$

As in the logit model, the value of dP_i/dZ_i is evaluated at the mean value(s) of the explanatory variable(s).

7.5.4 Comparison between Logit and Probit Models

After estimating both the logit and probit models, we face the question: which one of these models should be chosen? Three points are to be noted here specifically.

1. The cumulative distribution functions (CDFs) of logistic and standard normal distributions are similar to the extent that both have domain $(-\infty, \infty)$, zero mean, and are symmetric around the mean. The two CDFs also coincide for a substantial part in the mid-range of the distributions. The difference between the two CDFs is that, compared with the CDF of standard normal distribution, the CDF of logistic function has slightly heavier tails (as shown in Figure 7.5). Therefore, we are unlikely to get very different results using logit and probit models unless the sample is large so that there are enough observations at the tails.

2. Strictly speaking, the values of estimated coefficients of logit and probit models are not comparable. This is precisely because these models differ in specifications as well as interpretation of coefficients. Although the estimated coefficients of logit and probit models are not directly comparable, Amemiya (1981) observed that by multiplying the logit estimates by 0.625, we may obtain corresponding probit estimates. Conversely, multiplication of probit estimates by $1/0.625 = 1.6$ gives corresponding logit coefficients.

3. Amemiya further observed that both the logit and probit models give similar results most of the times, and neither has any particular advantage. As a consequence, the conclusions drawn while using these models do not differ much in most cases.[14]

---

[14] This does not mean that the values of estimated coefficients are identical between these models.

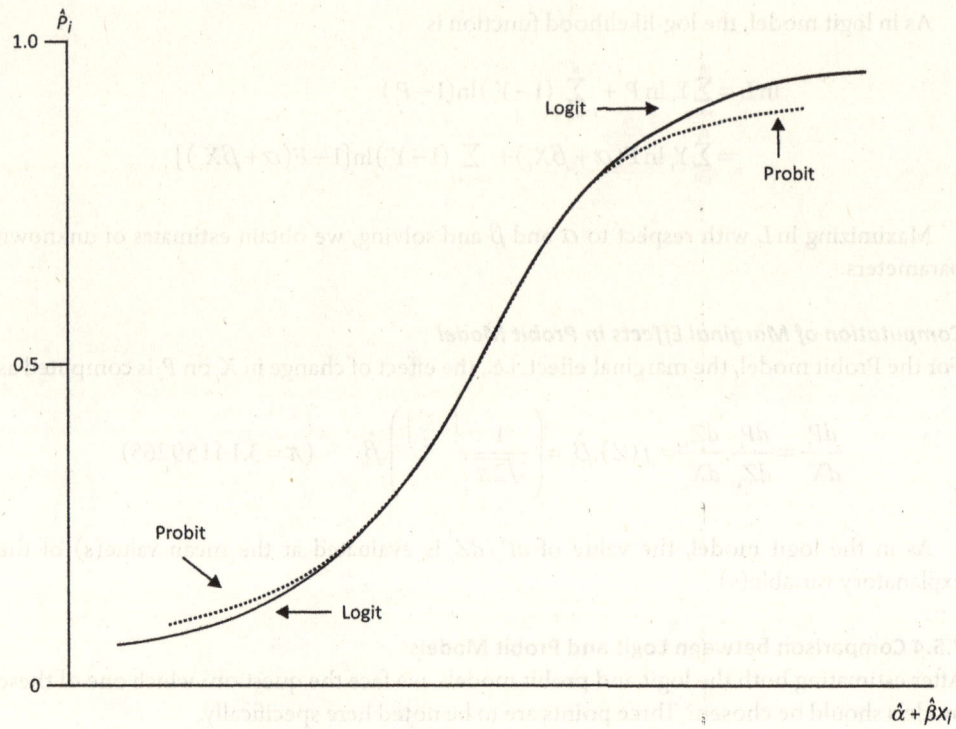

Figure 7.5   Estimated Logit and Probit Models
Source: Author's own creation.

7.5.5 The Problem of Disproportionate Sampling

In many applications of LPM, logit, and probit models, it is found that the number of observations in one sample group is much smaller than the number of observations in the other group. For example, in a study of car ownership status, the number of households possessing a car is much smaller than the number of households not possessing a car. Similarly, in a study of unemployment, the number of unemployed persons is much low compared with the number of employed persons. It is important to note that the slope estimates of the logit model are not affected much in such cases of disproportionate sampling (Maddala and Lahiri 2009, 337). But the intercept term of the logit model needs to be adjusted; it should be decreased by $(\ln n_1 - \ln n_2)$, where n_1 and n_2 are the sampling rates for the two groups for which $Y_i = 1$ and 0, respectively. These observations do not strictly hold for the probit model or the LPM, although, the estimated slope coefficients of such models are also not affected much by unequal sampling rates in most cases.

7.6 MEASURING GOODNESS OF FIT

To understand the goodness of fit of any estimated model, we need a scalar measure. In the case of OLS regression, such a task is performed by R^2 or adjusted-R^2 statistics. However, these measures are not suitable to understand the goodness of fit when the dependent variable of the model is binary. Thus, alternative measures have been proposed to assess goodness of fit of binary-dependent variable models. In fact, there are two different approaches here: (i) revising the existing R^2 formula considering the binary feature of the dependent variable, and (ii) developing alternative measures using the likelihood ratios. We consider one example for each of these approaches below.

Effron's R^2

Effron revised the R^2 formula that is used in the context of OLS regression in such a way that the binary feature of dependent variable is taken cognizance of. This is done in the following manner.

We know that for OLS regression,

$$R^2 = 1 - \frac{RSS}{TSS}$$
$$= 1 - \frac{\sum(Y_i - \hat{Y}_i)^2}{\sum(Y_i - \overline{Y})^2}$$

Here, $\sum(Y_i - \hat{Y}_i)^2$ continues to measure RSS. But since the value of Y_i is either 1 or 0, TSS $= \sum(Y_i - \overline{Y})^2$ reduces to the following form.

$$\sum(Y_i - \overline{Y})^2 = \sum Y_i^2 - n\overline{Y}^2$$
$$= n_1 - n\left(\frac{\sum Y_i}{n}\right)^2$$
$$= n_1 - n\frac{n_1^2}{n^2}$$
$$= \frac{n_1 n_2}{n} \qquad (n_2 = n - n_1)$$

Therefore,

$$\text{Effron's } R^2 = 1 - \frac{n}{n_1 n_2}\sum(Y_i - \hat{Y}_i)^2$$

McFadden's Pseudo-R^2

McFadden's Pseudo-R^2 is a very popular measure of goodness of fit in the context of binary-dependent variable models.[15] It is also known as the log-likelihood ratio index (LRI). It is called Pseudo-R^2 because although there is no measure equivalent to R^2 in the maximum likelihood method, it tends to provide an interpretation similar to R^2 statistic.

---

[15] Almost all econometrics software packages, including EViews, report the Pseudo-R^2 or LRI value in their output sheet.

The Pseudo-R^2 formula is obtained by comparing the value of log-likelihood of initial regression model (call this $\ln L$) with the value of log-likelihood that would have been obtained with only the intercept term in the regression model (call this $\ln L_0$). As likelihood is the joint probability of observing given sample quantities, its value lies between 0 and 1, which implies that log-likelihood is negative. Then,

$$\text{Pseudo-}R^2 = 1 - \frac{\ln L}{\ln L_0}$$

So the minimum value of Pseudo-R^2 is zero when $\ln L = \ln L_0$, and its maximum value is less than one.

7.7 EXAMINING THE OVERALL SIGNIFICANCE OF REGRESSION

For the purpose of examining the overall significance of logit/probit models, we may use the Likelihood Ratio-statistic (LR-statistic). Two important features of LR-statistic are: (i) it uses variations in likelihood as a basis for test, and (ii) it is useful to assess the explanatory power of the model, i.e., to understand overall significance of regression.

The value of LR-statistic is computed as

$$LR = 2\ln\left(\frac{L}{L_0}\right) = 2(\ln L - \ln L_0)$$

It has been shown that $LR \sim \chi^2$ with degrees of freedom k = number of explanatory variables in the model. Thus, our *decision rule* is: If $LR^* = \chi^{2*} > \chi^2_{\lambda,k}$, reject the null hypothesis (H_N) which states that all the coefficients of the estimated model are simultaneously equal to zero, and conclude that there is overall significance of regression.

7.8 ESTIMATION OF LOGIT AND PROBIT MODELS USING EVIEWS

Steps
It is very easy to estimate both logit and probit models using EViews software package. The steps to be followed are the following.

(i)   Obtain data on an EViews worksheet.
(ii)   Click **Quick/Estimation Equation...** in the main menu of EViews, which will open the 'Equation Estimation' window.
(iii) Provide specification of equation in the 'Equation specification' edit box of 'Equation Estimation' window.
(iv)   Select the method of estimation in the 'Estimation settings' edit box. The method to be selected here is 'Binary Choice—(Logit, Probit, Extreme Value)'. Among the

binary choice models, Probit is selected by default. But it can be changed to others just by clicking on other options.

(v)   Click **OK**.

An Illustration

Using data presented in Table 7.1, we seek to identify some factors that determine the choice of mode of employment (MODE) by the rural non-farm workers. This can be done by estimating a binary choice model (logit/probit). We consider following four factors important to determine the choice of mode of employment by the non-farm workers: age of the worker (AGE), sex of the worker (SEX), education of the worker (EDN), and possession of non-farm assets (ASSETS).

Following the steps mentioned above, we estimated both the logit and probit models the results of which are presented in tables 7.6A and 7.6B, respectively. It is found that the relationship between MODE and each of our chosen explanatory variables is positive. This means that in the non-farm sector of our survey areas, the probability of choosing

Table 7.6A   Results of Logit Regression

Dependent Variable: MODE
Method: ML-Binary Logit (Quadratic hill climbing)
Date: 08/23/13 Time: 15:49
Sample: 1 266
Included observations: 266
Convergence achieved after 5 iterations
Covariance matrix computed using second derivatives

Variable	Coefficient	Std. Error	z-Statistic	Prob.
C	−3.679749	0.644852	−5.706344	0.0000
AGE	0.050871	0.012335	4.124267	0.0000
SEX	1.548423	0.494825	3.129235	0.0018
EDN	0.057037	0.037880	1.505734	0.1321
ASSETS	0.000551	0.000165	3.342610	0.0008
McFadden R-squared	0.156476	Mean dependent var		0.503759
S.D. dependent var	0.500928	S.E. of regression		0.452266
Akaike info criterion	1.206919	Sum squared resid		53.38612
Schwarz criterion	1.274278	Log likelihood		−155.5202
Hannan-Quinn criter.	1.233979	Deviance		311.0404
Restr. deviance	368.7393	Restr. log likelihood		−184.3696
LR statistic	57.69891	Avg. log likelihood		−0.584662
Prob(LR statistic)	0.000000			
Obs with Dep=0	132	Total obs		266
Obs with Dep=1	134			

Source: Same as for Table 7.2.

Table 7.6B Results of Probit Regression

Dependent Variable: MODE
Method: ML-Binary Probit (Quadratic hill climbing)
Date: 08/23/13 Time: 15:49
Sample: 1 266
Included observations: 266
Convergence achieved after 5 iterations
Covariance matrix computed using second derivatives

Variable	Coefficient	Std. Error	z-Statistic	Prob.
C	−2.193817	0.358665	−6.116617	0.0000
AGE	0.030837	0.007064	4.365122	0.0000
SEX	0.903840	0.276341	3.270737	0.0011
EDN	0.035249	0.023054	1.528998	0.1263
ASSETS	0.000319	9.26E-05	3.449119	0.0006
McFadden R-squared	0.155729	Mean dependent var		0.503759
S.D. dependent var	0.500928	S.E. of regression		0.452732
Akaike info criterion	1.207955	Sum squared resid		53.49620
Schwarz criterion	1.275314	Log likelihood		−155.6580
Hannan-Quinn criter.	1.235015	Deviance		311.3159
Restr. Deviance	368.7393	Restr. log likelihood		−184.3696
LR statistic	57.42331	Avg. log likelihood		−0.585180
Prob(LR statistic)	0.000000			
Obs with Dep=0	132	Total obs		266
Obs with Dep=1	134			

Source: Same as for Table 7.2.

self-employment goes up if the worker is more aged (experienced), male, educated, and possesses more non-farm assets. All these variables, except education, turned out to be statistically significant. Thus, AGE, SEX, and ASSETS may be viewed as important determinants of choice of mode of employment by the rural non-farm workers. The goodness of fit of the estimated models is shown by the value of McFadden R-squared which is 0.156 in both the models. It is also observed that both the models have got overall significance, which is revealed by statistical significance of LR-statistic. It also needs mention that our conclusions are the same whichever model is chosen—logit or probit.

Computation of Marginal Effects
In EViews, the calculation of marginal effects of the explanatory variables for logit/probit models is not provided as a built-in procedure. However, we may easily compute the marginal effects through some simple arithmetical calculations after estimating the models. This has been done in tables 7.7A and 7.7B for logit and probit models, respectively.

Table 7.7A Calculation of Marginal Effects for Estimated Logit Model

Variable	Mean of the variable	Estimated coefficient	$\left(\begin{array}{c}\text{Mean of the}\\\text{variable}\end{array}\right)*\left(\begin{array}{c}\text{Estimated}\\\text{coefficient}\end{array}\right)$	$\dfrac{dP_i}{dZ_i}$	Marginal effect = $\left(\begin{array}{c}\text{Estimated}\\\text{coefficient}\end{array}\right)*\left(\dfrac{dP_i}{dZ_i}\right)$
AGE	31.45	0.0509	1.600805	0.239647	0.0122
SEX	0.87	1.5484	1.347108	0.239647	0.3711
EDN	4.14	0.0570	0.235980	0.239647	0.0137
ASSETS	1514.28	0.0006	0.908568	0.239647	0.0001
C		−3.6797	−3.679700		
Total (Z_i)			0.412761		

Source: Author's own.

Note: Here $Z_i = -3.6797 + 0.0006 * 1514.28 + 0.0570 * 4.14 + 1.5484 * 0.87 + 0.0509 * 31.45 = 0.412761$ so that $\dfrac{dP_i}{dZ_i} = \dfrac{2.71828^{-0.412761}}{(1+2.71828^{-0.412761})^2} = 0.239647$ ($\because e = 2.71828$)

Table 7.7B Calculation of Marginal Effects for Estimated Probit Model

Variable	Mean of the variable	Estimated coefficient	$\left(\begin{array}{c}\text{Mean of the}\\\text{variable}\end{array}\right)*\left(\begin{array}{c}\text{Estimated}\\\text{coefficient}\end{array}\right)$	$f(Z_i)$	Marginal effect = $\left(\begin{array}{c}\text{Estimated}\\\text{coefficient}\end{array}\right)*f(Z_i)$
AGE	31.45	0.0308	0.968660	0.404158	0.0124
SEX	0.87	0.9038	0.786306	0.404158	0.3653
EDN	4.14	0.0352	0.145728	0.404158	0.0142
ASSETS	1514.28	0.0003	0.454284	0.404158	0.0001
C		−2.1938	−2.193800		
Total (Z_i)			0.161178		

Source: Author's own.

Note: Here $Z_i = -2.1938 + 0.0003 * 1514.28 + 0.0352 * 4.14 + 0.9038 * 0.87 + 0.0308 * 31.45 = 0.161178$ so that $f(Z_i) = \dfrac{1}{\sqrt{2*3.14159265}} 2.71828^{\left(-\frac{0.161178^2}{2}\right)} = 0.404158$ ($\because \pi = 3.14159265$ and $e = 2.71828$)

It is possible to rank different explanatory variables in terms of their respective marginal effect values. On the basis of values of marginal effects, SEX appears to be the most important factor in determining the choice of mode of employment by the rural non-farm workers, followed by EDN, AGE, and ASSETS. The ranking pattern remains the same whichever model is considered.

7.9 QUESTIONS AND ASSIGNMENTS

A. Multiple-Choice Questions
Tick ($\sqrt{}$) the correct answer.
  (i)   Multiplicative dummy is used to assess the change in
         (a)   Intercept of the model
         (b)   Slope of the model
         (c)   Both intercept and slope of the model
         (d)   None of the above
  (ii)   The 'dummy variable trap' arises when
         (a)   Many irrelevant explanatory variables are mistakenly included along with
               dummy variables in the model.
         (b)   The number of dummies included is equal to the number of sub-sample
               categories.
         (c)   The number of dummies included is less than the number of sub-sample
               categories.
         (d)   The number of dummies is equal to the number of other quantitative explana-
               tory variables.
  (iii) The linear probability model is estimated by using
         (a)   OLS method
         (b)   WLS method
         (c)   Restricted least-squares method
         (d)   Maximum likelihood method
  (iv)   The model that follows the cumulative distribution function of the standard
         normal distribution is called
         (a)   Linear probability model
         (b)   Logit model
         (c)   Probit model
         (d)   None of the above
  (v)   The most satisfactory method to estimate a logit/probit model is
         (a)   OLS
         (b)   WLS
         (c)   Ridge regression
         (d)   Maximum likelihood
  (vi)   The overall significance of the estimated logit/probit model is assessed by examin-
         ing statistical significance of
         (a) F-statistic
         (b)   Effron's R^2
         (c)   McFadden R^2
         (d)   Likelihood ratio (LR) statistic

B. General Questions
  (i)   Define the dummy variables. Explain the use of dummy variables.

(ii)   What is an 'interaction dummy'?

(iii) What is 'dummy variable trap'?

(iv) Explain the steps involved in the Chow test for examining stability of estimated regression.

(v)   Explain, with suitable examples, how the dummy variable technique may be applied to examine stability of estimated regression. Why the dummy variable technique is considered superior for this purpose to the Chow test?

(vi) What is a binary variable? Give examples from economics.

(vii) Which method of estimation should one ideally follow when the dependent variable of the model is a binary variable?

(viii) Specify the logit model and state the procedure to estimate such a model by using the method of maximum likelihood. How are the marginal effects computed in a logit model?

(ix) Specify the probit model and state the procedure to estimate such a model by using the method of maximum likelihood. How are the marginal effects computed in a probit model?

(x)   What is the difference between the logit and probit models?

(xi) Why is it inappropriate to examine the 'goodness of fit' of estimated logit/probit models using conventional R^2-statistic? Suggest suitable measures for examining 'goodness of fit' and 'overall significance' of estimated binary choice models.

(xii) Do you think that the results of logit/probit models are affected by the problem of 'disproportionate sampling'? Explain.

(xiii) Consider the following model

$$Y_i = \alpha + \beta X_i + \gamma D_i + u_i$$

where Y_i = annual expenditure on health care of the ith family, X_i = annual income of the ith family, D_i is a dummy variable that takes value 1 if the ith family belongs to urban area and 0 if rural area, and u_i is the disturbance term with all usual OLS assumptions.

Interpret the meanings of α, β, and γ in the above model. How would you test, in terms of above model, whether there is any difference in health care expenditures of the families from urban and rural areas?

(xiv) Suppose you are interested in testing whether the demand for readymade garments (Y_i) as a function of household income (X_i) is stable throughout the year or not. You have two subsamples containing 22 observations each from the festival and regular (non-festival) seasons respectively. The following estimated equations are obtained.

Regression based on 1st sub-sample: $\hat{Y}_i = 20 + 0.50 X_i$ $RSS_1 = 18$

Regression based on 2nd sub-sample: $\hat{Y}_i = 15 + 0.40 X_i$ $RSS_2 = 10$

Regression based on pooled sample: $\hat{Y}_i = 17 + 0.43 X_i$ $RSS_3 = 35$

How would you test the null hypothesis that the entire parameter vector is stable across seasons?

(xv) Indicate whether the following statements are true (T), false (F) or uncertain (U) and give brief explanation.

(a) Dummy variables are needed to proxy for unobservable variables.

(b) Compared with the logit model, the cumulative distribution function of the probit model has a heavier tail.

(c) The results of logit/probit models are drastically affected in the case of disproportionate sampling of two sub-sample categories.

C. Computer Assignments

(i) Estimate a savings function for India using the data given in Table 7.8. Apply both the Chow test and dummy variables technique to examine possible presence of structural break in such a function, beginning with 1980–81.

(ii) Estimate the following earning function using data given in Table 7.9, which have been collected from 120 rural non-farm workers in Cooch Behar district of West Bengal.

$$\text{ERN}_i = \alpha + \beta \text{SEX}_i + \gamma \text{EDN}_i + \delta(\text{SEX}_i * \text{EDN}_i) + \varepsilon_i$$

Here ERN = daily earning (Rs.) of the worker; EDN = education level of the worker measured by years of schooling; and SEX = sex of the worker which is a dummy variable that takes value 1 for male and 0 for female.

Do the intercept and slope coefficients of earning functions of the male and female workers differ? Provide economic interpretation of your results.

Table 7.8   GDP at Factor Cost and Gross Domestic Savings in India
(Base Year: 1999–2000) [Amount in Rupees Crore]

Year	GDP at Factor Cost	Gross Domestic Savings	Dummy
1950–51	224,786	871	0
1951–52	230,034	969	0
1952–53	236,562	845	0
1953–54	250,960	875	0
1954–55	261,615	988	0
1955–56	268,316	1,356	0
1956–57	283,589	1,561	0
1957–58	280,160	1,356	0
1958–59	301,422	1,379	0
1959–60	308,018	1,720	0
1960–61	329,825	1,952	0
1961–62	340,060	2,074	0
1962–63	347,253	2,440	0
1963–64	364,834	2,703	0

(Contd.)

Table 7.8 (*Contd.*)

Year	GDP at Factor Cost	Gross Domestic Savings	Dummy
1964–65	392,503	3,077	0
1965–66	378,157	3,833	0
1966–67	382,006	4,328	0
1967–68	413,094	4,293	0
1968–69	423,874	4,657	0
1969–70	451,496	6,044	0
1970–71	474,131	6,571	0
1971–72	478,918	7,281	0
1972–73	477,392	7,788	0
1973–74	499,120	10,912	0
1974–75	504,914	12,298	0
1975–76	550,379	14,196	0
1976–77	557,258	17,320	0
1977–78	598,885	19,995	0
1978–79	631,839	23,601	0
1979–80	598,974	24,213	0
1980–81	641,921	26,881	1
1981–82	678,033	30,896	1
1982–83	697,861	33,787	1
1983–84	752,669	38,091	1
1984–85	782,484	45,453	1
1985–86	815,049	53,389	1
1986–87	850,217	58,036	1
1987–88	880,267	72,264	1
1988–89	969,702	87,166	1
1989–90	1,029,178	106,092	1
1990–91	1,083,572	130,010	1
1991–92	1,099,072	141,089	1
1992–93	1,158,025	159,682	1
1993–94	1,223,816	189,933	1
1994–95	1,302,076	247,462	1
1995–96	1,396,974	291,002	1
1996–97	1,508,378	313,068	1
1997–98	1,573,263	363,506	1
1998–99	1,678,410	389,747	1
1999–2000	1,786,525	484,256	1
2000–01	1,864,301	499,033	1
2001–02	1,972,606	534,885	1
2002–03	2,048,286	646,521	1
2003–04	2,222,758	820,685	1
2004–05	2,388,768	997,873	1

Source: Reserve Bank of India, Downloaded from www.rbi.org on 12th March 2012.

Table 7.9 Survey Data on Daily Earnings, Sex, and Education of Rural Non-farm Workers in Cooch Behar, West Bengal

ERN	SEX	EDN	ERN	SEX	EDN	ERN	SEX	EDN
2.60	0	4	41.46	0	9	114.24	1	7
3.52	0	0	42.04	0	0	121.33	1	8
4.03	0	5	46.90	0	9	124.19	1	5
4.03	0	6	48.00	0	0	126.00	1	9
12.11	0	0	53.34	0	0	127.26	1	9
15.75	0	1	54.07	0	11	128.49	1	12
17.19	0	7	54.88	0	4	128.49	1	14
17.54	0	0	56.70	0	9	131.04	1	9
17.79	0	0	58.80	0	14	132.62	1	6
20.16	0	14	61.84	0	0	132.62	1	6
20.17	0	0	63.19	0	7	138.87	1	10
21.32	0	0	69.12	0	6	138.87	1	10
22.05	0	0	73.57	0	3	138.87	1	10
22.43	0	0	77.51	0	9	138.87	1	14
24.34	0	1	88.98	0	14	140.00	1	14
24.44	0	6	121.33	0	14	140.00	1	12
24.75	0	0	128.49	0	14	142.38	1	10
25.20	0	1	152.59	0	17	142.38	1	10
25.83	0	7	160.37	0	1	142.38	1	10
28.14	0	4	171.03	0	1	145.44	1	10
29.56	0	5	88.98	1	7	145.44	1	15
29.95	0	0	88.98	1	12	147.42	1	9
30.06	0	0	88.98	1	12	148.62	1	12
32.07	0	12	88.98	1	14	155.65	1	9
32.34	0	4	89.60	1	6	172.80	1	12
33.64	0	6	91.11	1	1	177.66	1	10
34.81	0	9	92.75	1	6	187.32	1	17
34.81	0	6	92.75	1	6	187.32	1	10
35.52	0	0	96.92	1	10	195.30	1	10
35.67	0	0	96.92	1	14	203.96	1	10
36.18	0	0	96.92	1	12	204.16	1	10
36.63	0	0	100.80	1	14	207.59	1	11
36.96	0	0	101.85	1	8	218.40	1	14
37.67	0	1	101.85	1	10	246.96	1	12
38.15	0	3	112.65	1	9	254.02	1	12
38.98	0	4	112.65	1	8	302.40	1	9
38.98	0	1	112.65	1	17	303.66	1	14
39.46	0	1	113.15	1	10	340.14	1	12
39.94	0	0	113.15	1	12	340.14	1	14
41.34	0	0	113.15	1	10	470.56	1	14

Source: Field Survey by the author, 1999–2000.

(iii) Table 7.10 presents data collected through a survey of 180 rural households in
       Hooghly district of West Bengal. The data relate to following four variables.
       PSTAT = poverty status of the household, which is a dummy variable that takes on
       value 1 if the household is 'poor' and 0 if 'non-poor';
       OPAR = land area operated by the household (in acres);
       CASTE = a dummy variable with value 1 for SC/ST households and 0
       otherwise; and
       EDN = average years of education by all working members of the household.

Using these data, estimate both the logit and probit regression models to examine the
importance of variables like OPAR, CASTE, and EDN in determining poverty status of the
households. Interpret your results. Does your conclusion vary between the logit and probit
regressions? Compute the values of marginal effects and rank the variables in terms of their
importance in determining the poverty status of the rural households.

Table 7.10 Survey Data on Poverty of Rural Households in Hooghly, West Bengal

PSTAT	OPAR	CASTE	EDN	PSTAT	OPAR	CASTE	EDN	PSTAT	OPAR	CASTE	EDN
1	1.30	1	8.00	1	1.08	1	0.00	0	1.33	0	6.00
1	0.00	1	0.00	0	0.50	1	0.20	0	1.49	0	11.00
1	0.00	1	4.00	0	0.23	1	2.25	1	0.00	1	0.00
0	0.43	1	3.67	0	0.00	0	10.00	0	0.50	0	5.00
0	1.52	1	1.71	0	3.58	0	6.25	1	0.17	0	7.00
1	0.00	1	0.00	0	2.77	0	9.50	1	0.08	0	11.00
1	0.00	1	4.25	0	0.21	0	3.50	0	1.32	0	8.33
0	0.08	1	0.50	1	0.14	1	6.00	1	0.00	1	0.00
0	1.00	1	5.33	1	0.50	1	1.60	1	0.83	0	7.00
0	0.66	1	6.00	1	0.66	1	2.00	0	2.31	0	7.25
1	0.00	1	1.00	0	0.33	0	6.00	0	0.99	0	8.00
1	0.00	1	0.00	0	0.00	0	7.00	0	0.00	1	13.50
1	0.59	1	4.50	0	4.16	0	8.83	1	0.00	1	0.00
1	0.99	1	1.50	0	0.83	0	6.00	1	0.00	0	0.33
1	0.53	1	3.25	0	3.30	0	7.00	1	0.00	0	6.50
0	1.33	1	9.00	1	0.17	1	0.00	0	0.00	0	1.50
0	0.33	1	0.50	0	5.94	0	9.00	1	0.50	0	3.50
1	0.00	1	0.00	0	0.00	0	8.00	0	0.12	0	0.50
0	0.00	1	0.40	1	1.07	0	2.50	0	1.44	0	7.50
0	0.36	1	2.50	1	0.00	0	8.00	0	0.58	0	7.33
1	0.00	1	2.50	0	2.52	0	14.00	0	0.83	0	5.50
0	0.35	1	2.00	0	2.97	0	12.00	0	1.19	0	6.75
1	0.41	1	4.50	1	0.17	0	0.50	0	0.25	0	5.67
0	0.00	1	1.50	0	1.98	0	6.67	0	0.25	0	2.86

(Contd.)

Table 7.10 (*Contd.*)

PSTAT	OPAR	CASTE	EDN	PSTAT	OPAR	CASTE	EDN	PSTAT	OPAR	CASTE	EDN
1	0.50	1	2.00	0	1.98	0	14.00	0	1.98	0	9.75
1	0.33	1	1.50	1	1.98	0	8.80	1	2.31	0	0.00
1	0.35	1	3.67	0	0.66	0	2.00	0	0.91	0	4.00
1	0.66	1	2.75	1	0.83	0	0.00	0	2.00	0	7.00
0	0.58	1	3.50	0	3.30	0	7.00	1	1.32	0	4.50
1	0.00	1	3.00	1	1.33	0	0.50	1	1.98	0	5.00
1	0.17	1	1.67	0	1.49	0	0.50	0	0.00	0	8.00
1	0.17	1	0.00	0	2.64	1	2.50	1	0.00	0	2.25
1	0.00	1	0.75	0	0.66	0	11.50	1	0.00	1	0.50
1	0.08	1	0.33	0	0.36	0	12.00	1	0.99	0	1.00
1	0.40	1	0.67	1	1.16	0	5.00	0	0.00	0	2.00
1	0.32	1	3.00	0	0.00	1	1.67	1	0.91	0	5.50
1	0.00	1	2.50	0	1.07	1	4.00	0	0.48	0	7.00
1	0.00	1	3.00	0	3.96	0	13.00	1	0.66	0	8.00
0	0.37	1	2.00	1	0.66	0	0.33	1	2.97	0	8.67
1	0.49	1	5.67	0	1.24	0	12.00	0	0.58	0	4.80
0	0.66	1	3.88	0	3.63	0	6.75	0	2.48	0	11.50
1	0.00	1	0.50	0	1.52	0	10.50	0	4.62	0	8.67
1	0.00	1	0.67	0	2.48	0	5.67	0	0.41	0	4.50
1	0.00	1	0.67	0	0.00	1	0.00	0	2.64	0	11.50
0	0.50	1	0.67	0	1.98	0	12.00	1	1.02	0	4.50
1	0.00	1	0.00	0	0.83	0	7.50	0	0.63	0	7.67
0	0.33	1	0.33	0	1.03	0	7.67	0	0.66	0	9.00
0	1.13	1	7.20	0	2.97	0	7.40	0	5.94	0	7.86
1	0.00	1	0.33	0	2.64	0	12.33	1	0.25	0	1.25
1	0.00	1	8.00	0	0.00	0	2.00	1	0.00	1	1.40
1	0.00	1	1.00	0	2.15	0	11.00	1	0.00	1	0.33
1	0.00	1	4.67	0	2.31	0	9.00	1	0.17	0	3.33
0	1.65	1	2.00	0	5.61	0	10.67	1	0.12	0	8.00
1	2.39	1	0.00	1	1.98	0	4.50	1	0.17	1	0.80
1	0.00	1	0.00	0	2.64	0	5.20	1	0.17	1	0.25
1	0.00	1	0.00	0	0.66	0	7.00	1	1.40	0	2.00
1	0.41	1	0.33	0	1.00	0	4.00	1	0.34	1	1.75
0	1.65	0	12.50	0	1.49	0	3.50	1	0.00	1	1.00
1	0.43	1	3.33	0	0.45	0	2.50	1	0.00	1	1.00
1	0.33	1	2.75	0	1.98	0	12.67	1	1.65	0	2.67

Source: Field Survey by the author, 1999–2000.

Answers to Multiple-Choice Questions
(i) (b); (ii) (b); (iii) (a); (iv) (c); (v) (d); (vi) (d).

8 Distributed Lag Models

This chapter discusses the distributed lag models. We consider the distributed lag models that are based on the assumptions of geometric and polynomial lag structures. From the first category, we discuss the Koyck model, adaptive expectations model, and partial adjustment model. We discuss Almon lag model from the second category. The merits and demerits of all these models have been highlighted. Finally, estimation of some of these models using EViews software and interpretation of results are explained by considering examples.

8.1. DEFINITION AND SPECIFICATION

It is often the case that the dependent variable of our model depends not only on the current value of the explanatory variable but also on its past or 'lagged' values. For example, consumption depends not only on current level of income but also on past income levels. This happens due to habit formation or inertia among the consumers. In this situation, to specify the relationship between consumption (Y) and income (X), we consider the following model

$$Y_t = \alpha + \beta_0 X_t + \beta_1 X_{t-1} + \beta_2 X_{t-2} + \dots + \beta_m X_{t-m} + \varepsilon_t \qquad (8.1)$$

In this model, the effect of X-variable on Y-variable is distributed over a number of time periods. A model such as this, which considers the effect of both current and past values of a variable on the dependent variable, is called the distributed lag model. Here m represents lag length, which may be finite or infinite. ε_t is the disturbance term of the model with usual OLS assumptions (zero mean, constant variance, serial independence, normality, etc.).

It will be easy to estimate the above model by applying the OLS method if we have a few terms on the right hand side. However, if the number of terms is large, we suffer heavily in terms of loss of degrees of freedom. Further, there might be multicollinearity problem due to close relationships among the X-variables of this model. To overcome these problems, it is necessary to rationalize the specification of the model. There are two different approaches here: geometric lag approach and polynomial lag approach. Both the approaches make some assumption about the lag-structure so as to avoid these problems.

8.2 GEOMETRIC LAG APPROACH

The basic assumption here is that the weights of lagged explanatory variable are positive and decline geometrically over time. Given this assumption, model (8.1) may be written as

$$Y_t = \alpha + \beta_0 (X_t + \lambda X_{t-1} + \lambda^2 X_{t-2} + \dots) + \varepsilon_t \qquad 0 < \lambda < 1 \qquad (8.2)$$

Two important implications of this model are:

(i)   The effect of explanatory variable on mean of dependent variable, $E(Y_t)$, extends indefinitely into the past (as $m \to \infty$); and

(ii)   The coefficient of X declines in a fixed proportion so that the distant values of X eventually become negligible. In other words, the influence declines in the form of a geometric progression as follows.

$$\left. \begin{array}{l} \lambda \beta_0 = \beta_1 \\ \lambda^2 \beta_0 = \beta_2 \\ \quad \vdots \\ \quad \vdots \\ \lambda^m \beta_0 = \beta_m \end{array} \right\} \quad \text{where } 0 < \lambda < 1$$

Using this geometric lag structure, we can rewrite (8.2) as

$$Y_t = \alpha + \beta_0 X_t + (\lambda \beta_0) X_{t-1} + (\lambda^2 \beta_0) X_{t-2} + \dots + \varepsilon_t \qquad (8.3)$$

8.3. ESTIMATION OF GEOMETRIC LAG MODEL: THE KOYCK METHOD

For estimation of the distributed lag model like (8.3), Koyck (1954) suggested a method that involves transforming the model into a form so that it can be easily estimated by applying the OLS method. This is popularly known as 'Koyck transformation'. There are two steps in Koyck transformation.

Step 1: Lag equation (8.3) by one period and multiply throughout by λ so that

$$\lambda Y_{t-1} = \lambda \alpha + (\lambda \beta_0) X_{t-1} + (\lambda^2 \beta_0) X_{t-2} + (\lambda^3 \beta_0) X_{t-3} + \dots + \lambda \varepsilon_{t-1} \qquad (8.4)$$

Step 2: Subtract (8.4) from (8.3) to obtain

$$Y_t - \lambda Y_{t-1} = \alpha (1 - \lambda) + \beta_0 X_t + (\varepsilon_t - \lambda \varepsilon_{t-1})$$
$$\Rightarrow Y_t = \alpha (1 - \lambda) + \beta_0 X_t + \lambda Y_{t-1} + v_t \qquad (8.5)$$

where $v_t = \varepsilon_t - \lambda \varepsilon_{t-1}$ is the new disturbance term.

It is clear that (8.5) is an autoregressive model as the lagged-dependent variable appears as an explanatory variable of the model.

Advantages of the Koyck Method

The model obtained after applying Koyck transformation has three distinct advantages.

(i) It is easy to estimate as it has been reduced to a three-variable model.

(ii) Estimation of equation (8.5), instead of (8.3), provides maximum economy of degrees of freedom, and

(iii) We are able to avoid the multicollinearity problem as all the lagged Xs have been substituted by a single variable, Y_{t-1}, which is less likely to be correlated with X_t.

Problems of the Koyck Method

In spite of the advantages mentioned above, the Koyck method is not free from blemishes. In fact, while overcoming the problems of losing in terms of degrees of freedom and multi-collinearity, it invited some other econometric problems for the transformed model (8.5), which are as follows.

- *Autocorrelation of the disturbance term*: In the transformed model (8.5), the disturbance term becomes autocorrelated, although this problem was absent in the original model (8.2). This is shown below.

$$
\begin{aligned}
Cov(v_t, v_{t+1}) &= E(v_t v_{t+1}) = E(\varepsilon_t - \lambda\varepsilon_{t-1})(\varepsilon_{t+1} - \lambda\varepsilon_t) \\
&= E(\varepsilon_t \varepsilon_{t+1} - \lambda\varepsilon_{t-1}\varepsilon_{t+1} - \lambda\varepsilon_t^2 + \lambda^2 \varepsilon_t \varepsilon_{t-1}) \\
&= -\lambda\sigma_\varepsilon^2 \qquad\qquad \left[\because E(\varepsilon_t^2) = \sigma_\varepsilon^2 \text{ and } E(\varepsilon_t \varepsilon_s) = 0 \text{ for } t \neq s\right]
\end{aligned}
$$

It is found that $Cov(v_t, v_{t+1}) = -\lambda\sigma_\varepsilon^2 \neq 0$ as $\sigma_\varepsilon^2 \neq 0$ and $\lambda \neq 0$. Therefore, v_t, the disturbance term of the transformed model, is autocorrelated.

- *Dependence of Y_{t-1} on v_t*: One of the explanatory variables of the transformed model (8.5), namely Y_{t-1}, becomes dependent on the disturbance term v_t. This means that $Cov(Y_{t-1}, v_t) \neq 0$. This is simply because Y_t is influenced by v_t and the series for Y_{t-1} is generated out of Y_t. Hence, there is dependence of Y_{t-1} on v_t.

- *Asymptotically biased estimates*: As a result of the above two problems, OLS estimation of the transformed model (8.5) fails to provide unbiased estimators for unknown parameters. Moreover, the bias of the estimators does not vanish even by increasing sample size so that they become asymptotically biased as well. To prove this in a simple manner, let us consider the model

$$
Y_t = \lambda Y_{t-1} + v_t \qquad\qquad (8.6)
$$

where

$$
v_t = \gamma v_{t-1} + u_t \qquad\qquad (8.7)
$$

and u_t is assumed to have all usual OLS assumptions.

While Equation (8.6) admits of the presence of lagged dependent variable as the explanatory variable in the model, Equation (8.7) states that there is first-order autocorrelation for the disturbance term. We now proceed to show that $\hat{\lambda}$, the OLS estimator of λ, is asymptotically biased in this formulation.

Applying OLS method, we have

$$\hat{\lambda} = \frac{\sum Y_t Y_{t-1}}{\sum Y_{t-1}^2} \qquad (8.8)$$

Lagging (8.6) by one period and pre-multiplying throughout by γ,

$$\gamma Y_{t-1} = \gamma \lambda Y_{t-2} + \gamma v_{t-1} \qquad (8.9)$$

Subtracting (8.9) from (8.6),

$$Y_t - \gamma Y_{t-1} = \lambda Y_{t-1} + v_t - \lambda \gamma Y_{t-2} - \gamma v_{t-1}$$
$$\Rightarrow Y_t = (\gamma + \lambda) Y_{t-1} - \lambda \gamma Y_{t-2} + u_t \qquad (\because u_t = v_t - \gamma v_{t-1}) \qquad (8.10)$$

Multiplying (8.10) throughout by Y_{t-1}, summing over all observations, and dividing by $\sum Y_{t-1}^2$, we obtain

$$\frac{\sum Y_t Y_{t-1}}{\sum Y_{t-1}^2} = (\gamma + \lambda) - \lambda \gamma \frac{\sum Y_{t-1} Y_{t-2}}{\sum Y_{t-1}^2} + \frac{\sum u_t Y_{t-1}}{\sum Y_{t-1}^2}$$
$$\Rightarrow \hat{\lambda} = \lambda \left(1 - \gamma \frac{\sum Y_{t-1} Y_{t-2}}{\sum Y_{t-1}^2} \right) + \gamma + \frac{\sum u_t Y_{t-1}}{\sum Y_{t-1}^2} \qquad (8.11)$$

Taking expectations,

$$E(\hat{\lambda}) = \lambda \left(1 - \gamma \frac{\sum Y_{t-1} Y_{t-2}}{\sum Y_{t-1}^2} \right) + \gamma \neq \lambda \qquad [\because E(u_t) = 0]$$

This shows that $\hat{\lambda}$ is a biased estimator.

Let us now see what happens to bias of $\hat{\lambda}$ as sample size (n) approaches to infinity. From Equation (8.11) above,

$$\hat{\lambda} = (\gamma + \lambda) - \lambda \gamma \frac{\sum Y_{t-1} Y_{t-2}}{\sum Y_{t-1}^2} + \frac{\sum u_t Y_{t-1}}{\sum Y_{t-1}^2}$$

Taking probability limits,

$$p\lim_{n\to\infty}\hat{\lambda}=(\gamma+\lambda)-\lambda\gamma\,p\lim_{n\to\infty}\frac{\sum Y_{t-1}Y_{t-2}}{\sum Y_{t-1}^2} \qquad \left(\because\ p\lim_{n\to\infty}\frac{\sum u_t Y_{t-1}}{\sum Y_{t-1}^2}=0\right)$$

Further, as $n\to\infty$, $\sum Y_{t-1}Y_{t-2}\approx\sum Y_t Y_{t-1}$ so that we can write

$$p\lim_{n\to\infty}\hat{\lambda}=(\gamma+\lambda)-\lambda\gamma\,p\lim_{n\to\infty}\hat{\lambda}$$

$$\Rightarrow p\lim_{n\to\infty}\hat{\lambda}=\frac{\gamma+\lambda}{1+\lambda\gamma}$$

Thus,

$$p\lim_{n\to\infty}\hat{\lambda}-\lambda=\text{asymptotic bias of }\hat{\lambda}$$

$$=\frac{\gamma+\lambda}{1+\lambda\gamma}-\lambda$$

$$=\frac{\gamma(1-\lambda^2)}{1+\lambda\gamma}\neq 0$$

This proves that $\hat{\lambda}$ is not only biased but also asymptotically biased.

Median and Mean Lags in Koyck Model

We compute the median and mean lags for the Koyck model to have an idea about the speed with which Y_t responds to a change in X_t. The median lag is the time required for the 50% of the total change in Y_t following a unit change in X_t. It is computed as

$$\text{Median lag}_{\text{Koyck}}=-\frac{\log 2}{\log\lambda} \qquad (8.12a)$$

For example, if $\lambda=0.3$, median lag = 0.58, which means that 50% of the total change in Y_t is accomplished in nearly half a period. On the other hand, if $\lambda=0.9$, median lag = 6.58, which means that much longer time (nearly six and half periods) is required to attain 50% of the total change in Y_t. This shows that higher the value of λ, the lower is the speed of adjustment and vice versa.

The mean lag is computed (provided all β_ks are positive) as

$$\text{Mean lag}_{\text{Koyck}}=\frac{\sum\limits_{k=1}^{m}k\beta_k}{\sum\limits_{k=1}^{m}\beta_k}=\frac{\lambda}{1-\lambda} \qquad (8.12b)$$

which is nothing but the weighted average of all lags involved with the respective β coefficients serving as weights.

Short-Run and Long-Run Multipliers

The lag coefficients (β_ks) represent the short- and medium-run multipliers. On the other hand, the long-run multiplier, which measures total impact of change in X_t on Y_t after taking into account all lagged effects, is computed by taking a sum of the β_ks ($k = 1, 2, ..., m$).

$$
\begin{aligned}
\sum_{k=1}^{m} \beta_k &= \lambda\beta_0 + \lambda^2\beta_0 + ... + \lambda^m\beta_0 \\
&= \beta_0(\lambda + \lambda^2 + ... + \lambda^m) \\
&= \beta_0\left(\frac{1}{1-\lambda}\right)
\end{aligned}
\tag{8.13}
$$

8.4 ADAPTIVE EXPECTATIONS MODEL

Apart from the Koyck model, there are other well-known economic models that also lead to distributed lag formulation, as exemplified by equation (8.2) or (8.3) above. Two such examples are Adaptive Expectations Model (AEM) and Partial Adjustment Model (PAM).

The AEM is based on the 'adaptive expectations hypothesis' formulated by Cagan (1956). The starting assumption of the AEM is that the value of Y_t depends not on the current value of X but on its 'expected' or 'permanent' value, denoted by X_t^*. Thus, we may write

$$
Y_t = \alpha + \beta X_t^* + \varepsilon_t
\tag{8.14}
$$

Since X_t^* is not directly observable, we have to make an assumption about its process of determination. Here we assume that

$$
X_t^* - X_{t-1}^* = \theta(X_t - X_{t-1}^*) \qquad 0 \le \theta \le 1
\tag{8.15}
$$

$$
\Rightarrow X_t^* = \theta X_t + (1-\theta)X_{t-1}^*
\tag{8.16}
$$

Equation (8.15) represents what is known as the *adaptive expectations hypothesis*. Here 'θ' is known as 'adjustment parameter'.

It is clear from (8.16) that if $X_t > X_{t-1}^*$, then X_t^* is revised or adjusted upwards so that $X_t^* > X_{t-1}^*$. The extent of adjustment depends on the size of θ which lies between 0 and 1. Now consider the following cases:

- When $\theta = 1$, $X_t^* = X_t$ and there is complete adjustment.
- When $\theta = 0$, X_t^* remains unchanged and is not influenced by actual value of X. So no adjustment is done here.
- In general, $0 < \theta < 1$, which means some adjustment to X_t^* has been done. Obviously, larger the value of θ, greater is the extent of adjustment.

Let us now see how the AEM leads to a distributed lag model. From (8.15), we have

$$X_t^* = \theta X_t + (1-\theta) X_{t-1}^*$$

Therefore,

$$X_{t-1}^* = \theta X_{t-1} + (1-\theta) X_{t-2}^*$$
$$X_{t-2}^* = \theta X_{t-2} + (1-\theta) X_{t-3}^*$$

.
.
.

Successive substitution in (8.16) for $X_{t-1}^*, X_{t-2}^*, \ldots$ leads to

$$
\begin{aligned}
X_t^* &= \theta X_t + (1-\theta)\theta X_{t-1} + (1-\theta)^2 X_{t-2}^* \\
&= \theta X_t + (1-\theta)\theta X_{t-1} + (1-\theta)^2 \theta X_{t-2} + (1-\theta)^3 X_{t-3}^* \\
&= \theta X_t + (1-\theta)\theta X_{t-1} + (1-\theta)^2 \theta X_{t-2} + (1-\theta)^3 \theta X_{t-3} + \ldots
\end{aligned}
\tag{8.17}
$$

Equation (8.17) implies that while determining X_t^*, the most weight is given to current value of X, which is X_t, and successively declining weights to $X_{t-1}, X_{t-2}, \ldots$.

Now substitution of (8.17) into (8.14) gives:

$$Y_t = \alpha + \beta\theta X_t + \beta\theta[(1-\theta)X_{t-1} + (1-\theta)^2 X_{t-2} + (1-\theta)^3 X_{t-3} + \ldots] + \varepsilon_t \tag{8.18}$$

Equation (8.18) is similar to Equation (8.3) except that $\beta_0 = \beta\theta$ and $\lambda = 1 - \theta$. Thus, we may conclude that the AEM leads to a distributed lag formulation.

Estimation of AEM

As before, we apply 'Koyck transformation' here. Lagging (8.18) by one period, multiplying throughout by $(1 - \theta)$, and subtracting the result from (8.18), we obtain

$$
\begin{aligned}
Y_t - (1-\theta)Y_{t-1} &= \alpha - \alpha(1-\theta) + \beta\theta X_t + \varepsilon_t - (1-\theta)\varepsilon_{t-1} \\
\Rightarrow Y_t &= \alpha\theta + \beta\theta X_t + (1-\theta)Y_{t-1} + \omega_t
\end{aligned}
\tag{8.19}
$$

where $\omega_t = \varepsilon_t - (1-\theta)\varepsilon_{t-1}$

It is now possible to estimate (8.19) by applying the OLS method. However, the disturbance term ω_t is likely to be autocorrelated here. In this situation, straightforward application of the OLS method will not provide unbiased and consistent estimators for unknown parameters. So it would be necessary to apply some alternative methods of estimation in this situation, such as the generalized least squares, instrumental variable method, and so on.

The Other Problem of AEM[1]

The Adaptive Expectations Model became popular during 20 years since World War II. However, the econometricians soon realized its deficiencies to model expectations of economic agents. In particular, it has been observed that *if a variable grows at a constant rate over time, modelling expectations of that variable adaptively leads to irrational behaviour on the part of the economic agents.* We can prove this in the following manner.

Suppose X in (8.15) grows at a constant exponential rate g. This implies that

$$X_{t+1} = (1+g)X_t \qquad \text{for all } t$$
$$g > 0$$

Therefore,

$$\left.\begin{array}{l} X_t = \dfrac{X_{t+1}}{1+g}, \\[2ex] X_{t-1} = \dfrac{X_{t+1}}{(1+g)^2}, \\[2ex] X_{t-2} = \dfrac{X_{t+1}}{(1+g)^3}, \text{ etc.} \end{array}\right\} \tag{8.20}$$

Substituting (8.20) into (8.17),

$$X_t^* = \frac{\theta}{1+g}X_{t+1} + \frac{\theta(1-\theta)}{(1+g)^2}X_{t+1} + \frac{\theta(1-\theta)^2}{(1+g)^3}X_{t+1} + \dots$$

$$= \frac{\theta}{1+g}X_{t+1}\left[1 + \frac{1-\theta}{1+g} + \left(\frac{1-\theta}{1+g}\right)^2 + \dots\right] \tag{8.21}$$

Since $[(1-\theta)/(1+g)] < 1$, the term in square brackets in (8.21) is a convergent geometric series, which may be summed up to obtain

$$X_t^* = \frac{\theta}{1+g}X_{t+1}\left[\frac{1}{1-\dfrac{1-\theta}{1+g}}\right]$$

$$= \frac{\theta}{g+\theta}X_{t+1} \tag{8.22}$$

[1] The discussion here is based on Thomas (1993, 127–8).

It is clear that since $g > 0$, $X_t^* < X_{t+1}$ for all t. Here X_t^* may be interpreted as the economic agent's prediction regarding the value of X in period $t+1$, i.e.,

$$X_t^* = E_t(X_{t+1})$$

where the subscript t on the expected value sign indicates that the expectation is held at period t. Now it follows that

$$X_{t+1} > E_t(X_{t+1}) \text{ for all } t$$

This implies that actual value of X in period $t+1$ always turns out to be higher than the value predicted or forecast in period t. Thus, the economic agent's 'forecast error' is always positive.

Another implication of this result is that forming expectations adaptively under these circumstances would not be rational. The agent would soon realize that he is consistently under-reporting the value of X. The rational agent will take this into account when he makes his predictions. This leads us to a discussion on the hypothesis of 'rational expectations'.[2]

8.5 PARTIAL ADJUSTMENT MODEL

Another model that leads to geometric lag formulation, as in Equation (8.2) above, is the so-called partial adjustment model (PAM), also known as habit persistence model. This model owes its origin to the works on demand analysis done by Nerlove (1958). Under PAM, we suppose that the desired level of Y at time t, denoted by Y_t^*, depends on some explanatory variable X plus a disturbance that has all usual OLS assumptions. We write

$$Y_t^* = \alpha + \beta X_t + \varepsilon_t \tag{8.23}$$

For instance, the mean desired level of inventory held by a firm may be a linear function of sales. Similarly, the mean desired level of consumption may be a linear function of wealth. However, the desired level of Y is not directly observable. Here we just assume that an attempt is being made to bring the actual level of Y to its desired level although such an attempt is likely to be partially successful during any one period. The reasons behind such a *partial adjustment* may be technological constraints, institutional rigidities, persistence of habit, etc.

In PAM, the relationship between actual and desired level of Y is specified as

$$Y_t - Y_{t-1} = \mu(Y_t^* - Y_{t-1}) \qquad 0 < \mu \le 1 \tag{8.24}$$

$$\Rightarrow Y_t = \mu Y_t^* + (1-\mu)Y_{t-1} \tag{8.25}$$

[2] We do not discuss rational expectations hypothesis because that is beyond our scope.

Equation (8.24) implies that if desired Y in period t exceeds actual Y in the previous period $t-1$, then actual Y in period t is increased above its level in period $t-1$, but not by the full extent of difference between Y_t^* and Y_{t-1}. The adjustment in Y is only partial and the extent of adjustment in actual Y towards its desired level depends of the size of μ which is called the 'coefficient of adjustment'.

Substitution of (8.23) into (8.25) gives

$$Y_t = \alpha\mu + \beta\mu X_t + (1-\mu)Y_{t-1} + \mu\varepsilon_t \qquad (8.26)$$

Except for the disturbance term, equation (8.26) is similar to equation (8.19) of the adaptive expectations model, with μ here replacing θ. Also note that the disturbance term in (8.26) is not autocorrelated provided ε_t in (8.23) is not autocorrelated. Hence estimating equation (8.26) by applying OLS method would provide consistent estimators, although presence of Y_{t-1} means that they will be biased. It is also clear that estimation of partial adjustment model (8.26) by OLS method presents fewer problems than that of the adaptive expectations model (8.19).

Let us now see how PAM leads to a geometric lag formulation. Successive substitution of Y_{t-1}, Y_{t-2}, etc., in equation (8.26) gives

$$Y_t = \alpha + \beta\mu[X_t + (1-\mu)X_{t-1} + (1-\mu)^2 X_{t-2} + \dots] + \eta_t \qquad (8.27)$$

where

$$\eta_t = \mu\varepsilon_t + \mu(1-\mu)\varepsilon_{t-1} + \mu(1-\mu)^2\varepsilon_{t-2} + \dots$$

Equation (8.27) is similar to model (8.2) above with $\beta_0 = \beta\mu$ and $\lambda = 1 - \mu$. So we conclude that the PAM, like the AEM, also implies a geometric lag.

8.6 ALMON'S POLYNOMIAL LAG MODEL

The Koyck model discussed above is built upon the assumption of geometrically declining lag structure. It was assumed that β coefficients decline geometrically as the lag length increases. This assumption is restrictive and may not always come true.

The Almon approach, suggested by Shirley Almon, considers a polynomial lag structure to rationalize specification of the distributed lag model (8.1) above. It is assumed that the relationship between β coefficients and lag length i could be approximated by a polynomial. For example, if the relationship between β_i and i follows an inverted-V curve, as in Figure 8.1, we may use a second degree polynomial to represent that relationship and write

$$\beta_i = a_0 + a_1 i + a_2 i^2 \qquad (8.28)$$

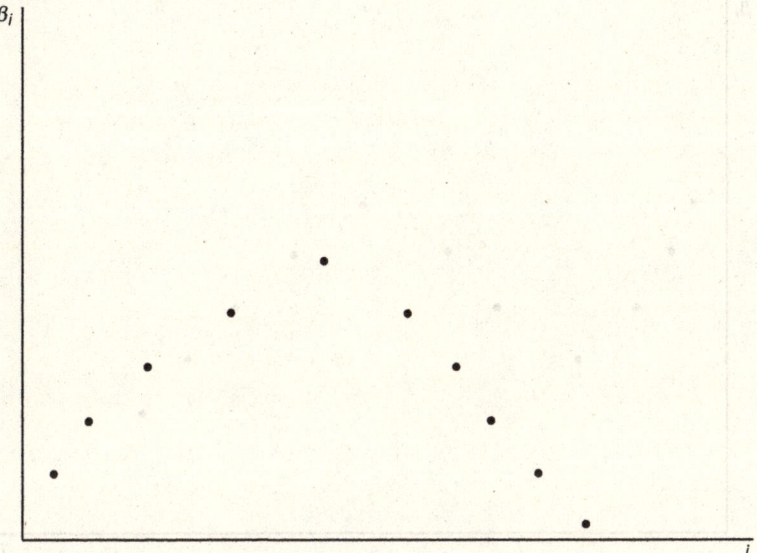

Figure 8.1   Graphical Display of 2nd Degree Polynomial

Source: Author's own.

On the other hand, if the relationship between β_i and i follows a cyclical pattern, having two turning points (shown in Figure 8.2), we may use a third-degree polynomial as given below.[3]

$$\beta_i = a_0 + a_1 i + a_2 i^2 + a_3 i^3 \tag{8.29}$$

Let us see how Almon's polynomial lag structure helps to resolve the problems associated with the distributed lag model (8.1).

We suppose that the relationship between β_i and i follows a second-degree polynomial so that we can approximate all the β coefficients using the polynomial function (8.28). Then, it follows that

$$\beta_0 = a_0$$
$$\beta_1 = a_0 + a_1 + a_2$$
$$\beta_2 = a_0 + 2a_1 + 4a_2$$
$$\cdot$$
$$\cdot$$
$$\cdot$$
$$\beta_m = a_0 + ma_1 + m^2 a_2$$

[3] The general rule is that the degree of polynomial should be at least one more than the number of turning points.

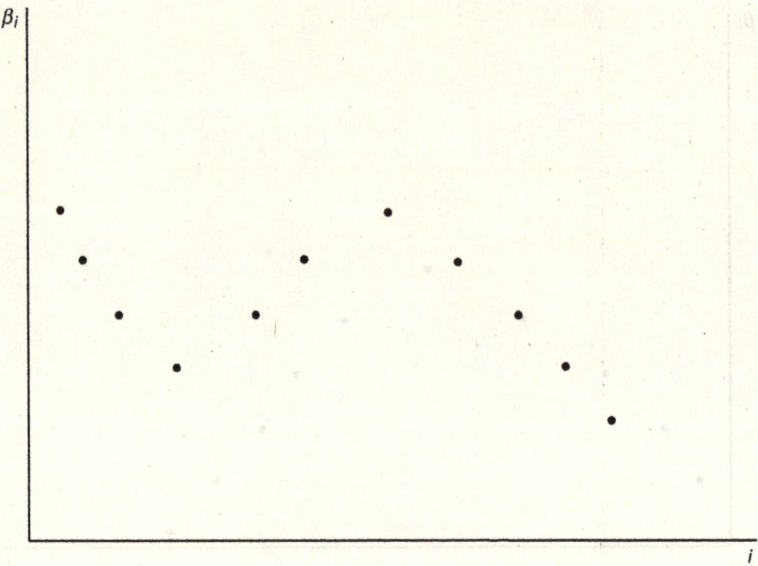

Figure 8.2   Graphical Display of 3rd Degree Polynomial

Source: Author's own.

So, we can write the distributed lag model (8.1) as

$$Y_t = \alpha + a_o X_t + (a_0 + a_1 + a_2)X_{t-1} + (a_0 + 2a_1 + 4a_2)X_{t-2} + \ldots + (a_0 + ma_1 + m^2 a_2)X_{t-m} + \varepsilon_t$$

$$(8.30)$$

Rearranging the terms,

$$Y_t = \alpha + a_0 \sum_{i=0}^{m} X_{t-i} + a_1 \sum_{i=0}^{m} i X_{t-i} + a_2 \sum_{i=0}^{m} i^2 X_{t-i} + \varepsilon_t \qquad (8.31)$$

It is now possible to define three new variables

$$Z_{0t} = \sum_{i=0}^{m} X_{t-i}$$

$$Z_{1t} = \sum_{i=0}^{m} i X_{t-i}$$

$$Z_{2t} = \sum_{i=0}^{m} i^2 X_{t-i}$$

so that we have

$$Y_t = \alpha + a_0 Z_{0t} + a_1 Z_{1t} + a_2 Z_{2t} + \varepsilon_t \qquad (8.32)$$

The parameters of (8.32) can be easily estimated by applying OLS method. Once the estimates of a_0, a_1, and a_2 are obtained, estimates of parameters $\beta_0, \beta_1, \beta_2, ..., \beta_m$ can be computed using the polynomial function (8.28).

However, it is to be noted that, to apply this method, we need to specify an appropriate value of m, which is the maximum lag length.[4] For example, if we suppose that $m = 6$, then the Z variables are constructed as

$$Z_{0t} = X_{t-1} + X_{t-2} + X_{t-3} + X_{t-4} + X_{t-5} + X_{t-6}$$
$$Z_{1t} = X_{t-1} + 2X_{t-2} + 3X_{t-3} + 4X_{t-4} + 5X_{t-5} + 6X_{t-6}$$
$$Z_{2t} = X_{t-1} + 4X_{t-2} + 9X_{t-3} + 16X_{t-4} + 25X_{t-5} + 36X_{t-6}$$

Merits and Demerits of the Almon Approach

The main advantage of the Almon approach is that it helps to overcome some of the problems of distributed lag model. Moreover, a variety of lag distributions could be generated using this approach. However, the difficulty with this approach is that, in practice, we might not have any idea about the maximum lag length or the order of the most appropriate polynomial before estimation. It also needs mention that research applications of polynomial lag models like the Almon model are few compared to the geometric lag models discussed above.

8.7 APPLICATIONS USING EVIEWS

Estimation of the Koyck Model

Consider data given in Table 8.1 on per capita consumption expenditure (PCON) and per capita GDP (PGDP) for India for the period 1960 to 2010. Using these data and EViews software, we want to estimate the Koyck model (Equation 8.5 above). The steps to be followed are

(i)   Obtain data in the EViews workfile.
(ii)   Click **Quick/Estimate Equation...** from the main menu which opens the 'Equation Estimation' dialog box.
(iii) Write **pcon c pgdp pcon(-1)** in 'Equation specification' edit box of 'Equation Estimation' dialog box.
(iv)   Click **OK** to obtain the output presented in Table 8.2.

---

[4] This issue is resolved by estimating models with different lag lengths and then selecting the best one by applying some model selection criterion (AIC, SBC, HQC, etc., which have been discussed in Chapter 3).

Table 8.1 Per Capita Consumption Expenditure (PCON) and Per Capita GDP (PGDP) in India for the Period 1960 to 2010

Year	PCON	PGDP	Year	PCON	PGDP	Year	PCON	PGDP
1960	125.47	145.41	1977	182.88	232.44	1994	271.13	354.07
1961	126.41	147.63	1978	181.32	240.40	1995	286.01	373.48
1962	126.38	148.90	1979	170.44	222.32	1996	305.05	394.06
1963	129.97	154.84	1980	179.70	232.07	1997	310.90	402.38
1964	136.97	162.85	1981	193.35	241.37	1998	333.54	419.05
1965	160.17	193.56	1982	196.79	244.09	1999	337.19	441.91
1966	154.92	189.58	1983	211.52	256.48	2000	346.64	451.60
1967	167.58	199.99	1984	208.88	260.52	2001	357.47	465.57
1968	169.22	201.94	1985	216.35	268.34	2002	350.81	475.78
1969	172.94	210.67	1986	226.30	275.31	2003	377.01	507.92
1970	177.91	216.62	1987	222.43	280.03	2004	374.83	541.38
1971	176.97	214.99	1988	236.56	300.53	2005	399.71	582.73
1972	170.92	208.91	1989	242.94	311.83	2006	422.35	627.68
1973	167.32	211.00	1990	242.03	322.40	2007	446.71	679.61
1974	168.18	208.82	1991	250.43	319.36	2008	500.52	703.24
1975	179.85	222.66	1992	260.17	330.68	2009	522.08	756.78
1976	172.27	221.60	1993	266.94	338.68	2010	546.88	812.31

Sources: (i) World Bank, *National Accounts Data and OECD National Accounts Data File* for consumption expenditure and GDP data; and (ii) RBI website for population data to compute per capita figures.
Note: PCON and PGDP in 2000 US dollar.

Interpretation of Results of the Koyck Model

As regards interpretation of results of estimated Koyck model, the following points may be highlighted, in particular.[5]

(i) The consumption function in Table 8.2 represents the short-run consumption function.

---

[5] It needs mention that whether or not the results of regression here is reliable (i.e., we have drawn correct inference) depends on the presence/absence of autocorrelation problem in the Koyck model which becomes a possibility as it is an autoregressive model. So the value of Durbin-Watson statistic reported in the EViews output should not be relied upon and Durbin's *h*-statistic needs to be computed to draw a conclusion regarding presence/absence of autocorrelation. Alternatively, we may apply the Breusch-Godfrey LM test. In the event of these tests confirming presence of autocorrelation, we will have to employ some method of estimation other than the OLS (which have been discussed in Chapter 5).

Table 8.2   Results of Estimated Koyck Model

Dependent Variable: PCON				
Method: Least Squares				
Date: 08/23/13 Time: 15:52				
Sample (adjusted): 1961 2010				
Included observations: 50 after adjustments				
Variable	Coefficient	Std. Error	t-Statistic	Prob.
C	12.78555	4.649609	2.749812	0.0084
PGDP	0.293855	0.052254	5.623614	0.0000
PCON(−1)	0.581869	0.086757	6.706904	0.0000
R-squared	0.995239	Mean dependent var		254.7168
Adjusted R-squared	0.995036	S.D. dependent var		107.7301
S.E. of regression	7.589962	Akaike info criterion		6.949655
Sum squared resid	2707.554	Schwarz criterion		7.064376
Log likelihood	−170.7414	Hannan-Quinn criter.		6.993341
F-statistic	4912.338	Durbin-Watson stat		2.264665
Prob(F-statistic)	0.000000			

Source: This table represents the output obtained by the author after application of the EViews software.

(ii)   Using estimated values of β_0 ($=0.293855$) and λ ($=0.581869$), we can compute the distributed lag coefficients, which are: $\hat{\beta}_1 = (0.293855)(0.581869) = 0.170987$, $\hat{\beta}_2 = (0.293855)(0.581869)^2 = 0.099492$, $\hat{\beta}_3 = (0.293855)(0.581869)^3 = 0.057891$, and so on.

(iii)   The long-run multiplier is

$$\sum_{k=1}^{m} \hat{\beta}_k = \hat{\beta}_0 \left(\frac{1}{1-\hat{\lambda}} \right) = 0.702782$$

It implies that a sustained increase of a dollar in PGDP will lead to 0.702782 dollar increase in PCON as opposed to immediate (or short-run) increase of 0.293855 dollar.

(iv)   To derive the long-run consumption function, we divide the estimated coefficients of short-run consumption function in Table 8.2 by $1-\hat{\lambda} = 0.418131$ and drop the lagged PGDP term. So the long-run consumption function is

$$\widehat{PCON}_t = 30.57786 + 0.702782 \, PGDP_t$$

(v)   It is found that the long-run marginal propensity to consume (0.702782) is greater than short-run marginal propensity to consume (0.293855). The difference between these two marginal propensities to consume may be explained in terms of median and mean lags. Given $\hat{\lambda} = 0.581869$, the median lag is $-\log(2)/\log \hat{\lambda} = 1.280053$ and the mean lag is $[\hat{\lambda}/(1-\hat{\lambda})] = 1.391595$. As the median lag is smaller than mean lag, it is clear that PCON adjusts slowly to changes in PGDP. Hence the value of marginal propensity to consume is smaller in the short-run than the same in the long-run.

Estimation of Partial Adjustment Model

Consider the data given in Table 8.3. The table contains data on three variables for India: (i) real GDP (Rs crore) (labeled as Y), (ii) real money balances (M), which is monetary aggregate M_2 divided by the consumer price index, and (iii) long-term rate of interest (R) (proxied by the long-term lending rate of the State Bank of India). Using these data, we want to estimate the money demand function

$$M_t^* = \alpha Y_t^{\beta_1} R_t^{\beta_2} e^{u_t} \tag{8.33}$$

where

M_t^* = desired or long-run demand for money (real cash balances),

R_t = long-term rate of interest rate (%), and

Y_t = real GDP

Taking logarithms, we get

$$\ln M_t^* = \ln \alpha + \beta_1 \ln Y_t + \beta_2 \ln R_t + u_t \tag{8.34}$$

The partial adjustment hypothesis can be written as

$$\frac{M_t}{M_{t-1}} = \left(\frac{M_t^*}{M_{t-1}}\right)^\mu \tag{8.35}$$

In log form, this becomes

$$\ln M_t - \ln M_{t-1} = \mu(\ln M_t^* - \ln M_{t-1}) \tag{8.36}$$

Substituting (8.34) into (8.36), we get

$$\ln M_t - \ln M_{t-1} = \mu \ (\ln \alpha + \beta_1 \ln Y_t + \beta_2 \ln R_t + u_t - \ln M_{t-1}) \tag{8.37}$$

$$\Rightarrow \ln M_t = \mu \ln \alpha + \mu \beta_1 \ln Y_t + \mu \beta_2 \ln R_t + (1-\mu) \ln M_{t-1} + \mu u_t \tag{8.38}$$

$$\Rightarrow \ln M_t = \gamma_1 + \gamma_2 \ln Y_t + \gamma_3 \ln R_t + \gamma_4 \ln M_{t-1} + v_t \tag{8.39}$$

Table 8.3   Real GDP (Y), Real Monetary Aggregate (M), and Rate of Interest (R) in India

Year	Y	M	R	Year	Y	M	R
1970–71	474,131	423	7.75	1990–91	1,083,572	1,289	16.50
1971–72	478,918	473	8.50	1991–92	1,099,072	1,330	16.50
1972–73	477,392	498	8.50	1992–93	1,158,025	1,284	19.00
1973–74	499,120	474	8.75	1993–94	1,223,816	1,508	19.00
1974–75	504,914	377	11.25	1994–95	1,302,076	1,718	15.00
1975–76	550,379	437	14.00	1995–96	1,396,974	1,733	16.50
1976–77	557,258	609	14.00	1996–97	1,508,378	1,831	14.50
1977–78	598,885	495	13.00	1997–98	1,573,263	1,976	14.00
1978–79	631,839	608	13.00	1998–99	1,678,410	2,054	13.00
1979–80	598,974	644	16.50	1999–2000	1,786,525	2,175	12.00
1980–81	641,921	661	16.50	2000–01	1,864,301	2,423	11.50
1981–82	678,033	626	16.50	2001–02	1,972,606	2,665	11.50
1982–83	697,861	681	16.50	2002–03	2,048,286	2,891	10.75
1983–84	752,669	715	16.50	2003–04	2,222,758	3,405	10.25
1984–85	782,484	853	16.50	2004–05	2,388,768	3,722	10.25
1985–86	815,049	900	16.50	2005–06	2,616,101	4,559	10.25
1986–87	850,217	1,003	16.50	2006–07	2,871,120	4,961	12.25
1987–88	880,267	1,037	16.50	2007–08	3,129,717	5,504	12.25
1988–89	969,702	1,051	16.50	2008–09	3,339,375	5,452	12.25
1989–90	1,029,178	1,210	16.50	2009–10	3,605,108	5,654	11.75

Source: RBI, *Handbook of Statistics on Indian Economy 2010–11.*
Note: Y = Real GDP at factor cost (Rs crore, Base Year: 1999–2000 = 100); M = the M_2 monetary aggregate (Rs crore) divided by consumer price index (Base 1993–94 = 100), and R = long-term lending rate of the State Bank of India.

where

$$\gamma_1 = \mu \ln \alpha, \; \gamma_2 = \mu \beta_1, \; \gamma_3 = \mu \beta_2, \; \gamma_4 = (1 - \mu) \text{ and } v_t = \mu u_t.$$

To estimate model (8.39) using EViews, our steps are

(i)   Obtain data in EViews workfile.
(ii)   Transform three series Y, M, and R in logs one after another. For this, click on 'Genr' on the main menu of 'Workfile' window, which will open the 'Generate Series by Equation' window. In the 'Enter equation' box of the 'Generate Series by Equation' window, **write ly = log(y)** and click **OK**. This will generate the series for ln$Y$ (labeled as *ly*), which will be added in the list of variables in 'Workfile' window. Repeat the same procedure to log-transform two other variables, namely,

M and R, which are labeled as lm and lr and added in the list of variables in 'Workfile' window.

(iii) Now to estimate model (8.39), write **lm c ly lr lm(−1)** in 'Equation specification' edit box and click **OK** which will give output as displayed in Table 8.4.

Table 8.4 Results of Estimated Short-Run Money Demand Function for India

Dependent Variable: *LM*
Method: Least Squares
Date: 08/23/13 Time: 15:55
Sample (adjusted): 240
Included observations: 39 after adjustments

Variable	Coefficient	Std. Error	t-Statistic	Prob.
C	−7.509927	1.721435	−4.362596	0.0001
LY	0.892069	0.204286	4.366764	0.0001
LR	−0.026777	0.063126	−0.424188	0.6740
LM(−1)	0.328410	0.157703	2.082455	0.0447
R-squared	0.990043	Mean dependent var		7.191684
Adjusted R-squared	0.989189	S.D. dependent var		0.805933
S.E. of regression	0.083796	Akaike info criterion		−2.023946
Sum squared resid	0.245763	Schwarz criterion		−1.853324
Log likelihood	43.46694	Hannan-Quinn criter.		−1.962728
F-statistic	1160.023	Durbin-Watson stat		1.955056
Prob(F-statistic)	0.000000			

Source: Same as for Table 8.2

Interpretation of Results of Partial Adjustment Model

The important points to be noted are the following.

(i)   All the estimated coefficients have expected signs. Except the coefficient of LR, all estimated coefficients are also statistically significant.

(ii)   The value of R^2 is very high mainly because of inclusion of $LM(−1)$ as an explanatory variable.

(iii) From the results, we find that $\hat{\gamma}_4 = 0.328410$ so that $\hat{\mu} = 1 - \hat{\gamma}_4 = 0.67159$. This implies that about 67% of difference between the desired and actual demand for money is eliminated each year.

(iv)   The short-run elasticities of demand for money (M) with respect to income (Y) and rate of interest (R) are 0.892069 and −0.026777, respectively.

(v)   To obtain long-run demand for money function, we divide each of short-run coefficients by $\hat{\mu} = 0.67159$ (the estimate of the adjustment coefficient) and drop the $LM(−1)$ term. Thus, the long-run demand for money function is

$$\widehat{LM}_t = -11.18231 + 1.328294\, LY_t - 0.03871\, LR_t$$

It is observed that the long-run income elasticity of demand for money is quite high (1.328294) compared to the short-run income elasticity of demand for money (0.892069). The long-run elasticity of demand for money with respect to rate of interest is also higher than the same in the short-run.

(vi) The value of Durbin-Watson d-statistic is 1.955056 which is very close to 2. This is because the model (8.39) is an autoregressive model. So this value of d-statistic is not trustworthy and we have to confirm absence of autocorrelation in model (8.39) by applying either Durbin's h-test or Breusch-Godfrey LM test. Only after confirmation of absence of autocorrelation by applying any one of these tests, we shall accept the results reported in Table 8.4.

8.8 QUESTIONS AND ASSIGNMENTS

A. Multiple-Choice Questions

Tick ($\sqrt{}$) the correct answer.

(i)   An autoregressive model is the one
   (a) that is used to avoid the problem of autocorrelation.
   (b) that helps to draw valid inference regarding relationship between the variables.
   (c) where the dependent variable is a lagged variable.
   (d) where one of the explanatory variables is lagged-dependent variable.

(ii) Which of the following problems is overcome by Koyck transformation?
   (a) Autocorrelation
   (b) Heteroskedasticity
   (c) Multicollinearity
   (d) Model misspecification error

(iii) The Koyck model produces estimators that are
   (a) Biased only
   (b) Asymptotically biased
   (c) Both (a) and (b)
   (d) Unbiased

(iv) Under adaptive expectations, an economic agent's 'forecast error' is
   (a) Positive
   (b) Negative
   (c) Zero
   (d) Indeterminate

(v)   The 'partial adjustment model' is advanced by
   (a) Phillips Cagan
   (b) Marc Nerlove
   (c) Shirley Almon
   (d) L.M. Koyck

B. General Questions

(i)   Explain the following.
    (a) Koyck transformation
    (b) Geometric lag structure
    (c) Polynomial lag structure
    (d) Adaptive expectations hypothesis

(ii) What is the Koyck approach to estimating a distributed lag model? What are the merits and demerits of such an approach?

(iii) Show how the Koyck transformation transforms an infinite distributed lag model to an autoregressive model.

(iv) How you calculate the mean and median lags for the Koyck model? What do they imply?

(v)   How do you obtain short-run and long-run multipliers for the Koyck model? What do they imply?

(vi) Explain the adaptive expectations model and show that such a model leads to a geometric lag formulation. What are the limitations of the adaptive expectations model?

(vii) Discuss the partial adjustment model and show that such a model leads to a geometric lag formulation. What is the advantage of this model over the adaptive expectations model?

(viii) Describe Almon's polynomial lag model. How does it differ from Koyck's lag model? What are the advantages and disadvantages of Almon's polynomial lag model?

(x)   Indicate whether the following statement is true (T), false (F), or uncertain (U) and give a brief explanation:
Estimation of the partial adjustment model by OLS method presents more problems than that of the adaptive expectations model.

C. Computer Assignments

(i)   Use data in Table 8.1 above to estimate by OLS the partial adjustment model for per capita consumption expenditure in India and interpret the results. What are the values of short-run and long-run elasticities of per capita consumption expenditure with respect to per capita GDP?

(ii) Use data presented in Table 8.5 to estimate by OLS the Koyck model for industrial production in India. What are the values of short-run and long-run price elasticities of industrial production, and what do they mean? Test the presence of autocorrelation in the Koyck model that you have estimated.

Table 8.5   Indices of Industrial Production and Wholesale Prices for India

Year	IIP	WPI	Year	IIP	WPI
1981–82	47	40	1996–97	131	127
1982–83	49	42	1997–98	140	133
1983–84	52	46	1998–99	145	141
1984–85	56	48	1999–2000	155	145
1985–86	61	51	2000–01	162	156
1986–87	67	54	2001–02	167	161
1987–88	72	58	2002–03	177	167
1988–89	78	62	2003–04	189	176
1989–90	85	67	2004–05	211	187
1990–91	92	74	2005–06	229	196
1991–92	92	84	2006–07	259	209
1992–93	94	92	2007–08	299	218
1993–94	100	100	2008–09	307	236
1994–95	109	113	2009–10	323	245
1995–96	123	122	2010–11	349	268

Source: RBI, *Handbook of Statistics on Indian Economy 2011–12*.

Note: IIP = Index of industrial production (annual) (Base: 1993–94 = 100); and WPI = wholesale price index (Base: 1993–94 = 100) for all commodities, annual.

Answers to Multiple-Choice Questions

(i) (d); (ii) (c); (iii) (c); (iv) (a); (v) (b).

9 Panel Data Regression Models

This chapter provides an introductory idea about panel data regression models, which are being used increasingly in empirical research in social sciences, thanks to the availability of many panel data sets from various sources and user-friendly computer software packages to estimate such models. We begin by defining panel data, and explain the usefulness of such data. We discuss some important models of panel data regression. The tests that are applied to choose between alternative panel regression models are discussed. We also describe the procedure/steps for estimating panel regression models using the EViews software. The interpretation of results obtained through application of the EViews software has been clarified with examples.

9.1 DEFINITION AND USEFULNESS

The panel data have both the cross-sectional and time series dimensions. Cross-sectional dimension of panel data implies that the data have been collected from a number of cross-sectional units. The cross-sectional units may be any one of the categories such as countries, states, districts, cities, villages, firms, individuals, and so on. The time series dimension of panel data is reflected by the fact that data have been collected for chosen cross-sectional units for more than one time point. The time point may refer to year or month or week or even day. Thus, to generate a panel data set, we are required to collect data (either from secondary sources or through primary surveys) for a number of time points for a set of cross-sectional units. The data so collected are presented in a systematic manner to generate the panel data set. Some alternative names of panel data are pooled data (obtained through pooling of time series and cross-sectional observations), micro panel data (which refer specifically to individuals, firms, and households), longitudinal data (these are data generated from study over time of a variable or group of subjects), etc.

As examples of panel data, we may consider macroeconomic variables such as GDP, unemployment rate, money supply, and interest rate for which cross-country data for different years are available. Similarly, a researcher examining inter-state variation in the incidence of rural poverty in India may collect state-level data for as many years as possible on rural head-count poverty ratio (RPOV), and some of its determinants like percentage of rural workers in non-farm employment (RNFW), rural literacy rate (LIT) and so on.[1]

---

[1] In the existing literature, among various factors, RNFW and LIT are considered important to determine the incidence of rural poverty.

Likewise, to study changes in production efficiency in the manufacturing sector in India or any other country, we are required to estimate a production function for which a cross-section of manufacturing units are to be surveyed for a number of years to record data on their output levels and levels of various inputs.[2]

Table 9.1A represents a panel data set. The table contains data on three variables mentioned above (RPOV, RNFW, and LIT) for 17 major states of India at three different time points.

Types of Panel Data

In the context of panel data analysis, we make a distinction between *balanced* and *unbalanced* panels. In a balanced panel, each cross-sectional unit has same number of time series observations while the number of time series observations differs between the cross-sectional units in an unbalanced panel. Clearly, Table 9.1A represents a balanced panel data set. It should be noted that having an unbalanced panel as such does not cause any major conceptual difficulty except that data handling in the computer becomes a bit complex.

Sometimes a distinction is also made between the *short* and *long* panels. In a short panel, the number of cross-sectional units (N) is greater than the number of time points (T). On the other hand, in a long panel, the number of time points exceeds the number of cross-sectional units. On this basis, the data presented in Table 9.1A below represents a short panel.

Another important point to note is that *panel data estimation has been applied traditionally to short panels* where the number of cross-sectional units (N) is very large (Greene 2003, 283). For a short panel, the Random Effects Model (discussed below) becomes more appropriate. On the other hand, the Fixed Effects Model suits a long panel better.

Usefulness of Panel Data

Although collection of data from a number of cross-sectional units, particularly firms, individuals, etc., at different points in time renders data collection process lengthy, expensive, and prone to the *problem of attrition* due to 'sample decay' or 'non-response' from some of the cross-sectional units at some points in time, panel data have some distinct advantages which are absent when data are only cross-sectional or time series. Some important advantages of panel data are mentioned below.

1. *Panel data can be used to deal with heterogeneity among the cross-sectional units.* Here heterogeneity means that the cross-sectional units are all different from one another. In reality, a number of unmeasured (or unobserved) explanatory variables generate such heterogeneity among the cross-sectional units. Leaving out such variables causes biased estimation of unknown parameters of the model. The same can be said about the omitted time series variables which influence the behaviour of cross-sectional units uniformly, but differently in each time point. *Panel data*

---

[2] Maddala and Lahiri (2009, 584) observed that one of the early uses of panel data in economics was in the context of estimation of production functions.

Table 9.1A   Incidence of Rural Poverty, Percentage of Rural Workers in Non-farm Employment and Rural Literacy Rate in 17 Major States of India

State	Year	POV	RNFW	LIT
Andhra Pradesh	1983	27.3	19.9	29.5
Assam	1983	41.9	20.1	41.8
Bihar	1983	64.9	16.4	29.0
Gujarat	1983	27.9	14.7	45.6
Haryana	1983	21.8	22.7	39.9
Himachal Pradesh	1983	17.8	12.9	51.6
Jammu & Kashmir	1983	25.2	25.3	28.8
Karnataka	1983	37.5	15.7	39.8
Kerala	1983	38.5	37.1	82.2
Madhya Pradesh	1983	48.2	9.1	30.7
Maharashtra	1983	45.0	14.2	47.8
Orissa	1983	67.5	20.8	39.4
Punjab	1983	14.3	17.2	44.1
Rajasthan	1983	37.7	13.2	24.1
Tamil Nadu	1983	56.2	25.7	47.1
Uttar Pradesh	1983	46.4	17.5	30.2
West Bengal	1983	61.6	26.3	42.4
Andhra Pradesh	1993–94	16.6	20.6	40.5
Assam	1993–94	44.4	20.8	52.4
Bihar	1993–94	57.2	15.6	36.5
Gujarat	1993–94	22.4	21.3	54.6
Haryana	1993–94	26.6	28.1	53.5
Himachal Pradesh	1993–94	29.3	19.8	65.2
Jammu & Kashmir	1993–94	19.7	24.0	39.1
Karnataka	1993–94	30.2	18.7	50.8
Kerala	1993–94	26.5	43.6	89.2
Madhya Pradesh	1993–94	40.4	10.1	41.1
Maharashtra	1993–94	37.7	17.6	59.5
Orissa	1993–94	50.1	19.2	49.3
Punjab	1993–94	13.7	25.4	56.0
Rajasthan	1993–94	26.9	20.1	36.1
Tamil Nadu	1993–94	33.0	29.6	57.8
Uttar Pradesh	1993–94	42.3	20.0	40.8
West Bengal	1993–94	37.4	36.6	54.0
Andhra Pradesh	2004–05	10.9	28.4	65.7
Assam	2004–05	23.1	25.3	66.1
Bihar	2004–05	43.1	25.1	49.3
Gujarat	2004–05	19.8	22.7	60.8

(Contd.)

Table 9.1A (*Contd.*)

State	Year	POV	RNFW	LIT
Haryana	2004–05	13.4	36.4	70.2
Himachal Pradesh	2004–05	12.5	30.4	79.8
Jammu & Kashmir	2004–05	4.8	36.1	53.9
Karnataka	2004–05	23.7	19.0	65.0
Kerala	2004–05	12.3	58.1	90.5
Madhya Pradesh	2004–05	38.2	17.0	69.9
Maharashtra	2004–05	30.4	20.1	77.8
Orissa	2004–05	47.8	31.1	67.4
Punjab	2004–05	9.6	33.3	70.6
Rajasthan	2004–05	19.9	27.1	70.7
Tamil Nadu	2004–05	23.0	34.8	72.0
Uttar Pradesh	2004–05	34.1	28.4	62.1
West Bengal	2004–05	28.5	37.3	70.2

Sources: (*i*) Dev and Ravi (2007) and (*ii*) NSSO, Reports on *Employment/Unemployment*, 1983 (38th round), 1993–94 (50th round), and 2004–05 (61st round).

Notes: (*i*) POV = incidence of rural poverty (headcount ratio), RNFE = percentage of rural workers in non-farm employment, and LIT = rural literacy rate; and (*ii*) Bihar includes Jharkhand, Madhya Pradesh includes Chhattisgarh, and Uttar Pradesh includes Uttaranchal.

can correct such types of *omitted variable problems*. Actually, the models that are estimated by using panel data (e.g., the fixed effects model and random effects model) are so specified that heterogeneity among the cross-sectional units is taken care of. This is viewed as the most attractive feature of the panel data models (Kennedy 2008, 282).

2. By combining time series with cross-sections, *panel data enhance both quantity and quality of data*. In this process, panel data *create more variability in the data, less collinearity among the variables, and more degrees of freedom*. As a consequence, *more efficient estimation of unknown parameters of the model becomes possible*.

3. Panel data can be used to examine issues that cannot be studied using cross-sectional or time series data alone. In particular, *panel data sets are better able to study complex issues of dynamic behaviour*. For example, with a cross-sectional data set one can estimate the rate of unemployment at a given point in time. Repeated cross-sections can show how this proportion changes over time. The panel data set alone can estimate what proportion of those who are unemployed in one period remained unemployed in another period. Similarly, answering questions such as whether the individuals' experiences of unemployment, malnutrition, illness, etc., are 'transitory' or 'chronic' in nature necessitates use of panel data.

4. *Panel data allow us to estimate more complicated behavioural models* which is not possible using only cross-sectional or time series data sets. For example, *phenomena*

such as economies of scale and technological change can be studied better by panel data rather than by pure cross-sectional or time series data.

5.   *Panel data are able to identify and measure effects that are simply not detectable in pure cross-sectional or time series data.* For example, to know whether union membership enhances wages of workers, we are required to analyse data on wages of a given set of workers at different points in time (e.g., before and after obtaining union membership). In a panel regression model, holding individual workers' characteristics constant, it is possible to examine whether union membership brings about any (statistically) significant change in workers' wages.

9.2 PANEL DATA MODELS

Any panel data set can be represented in terms of an algebraic model. Corresponding to the data given in Table 9.1A on three variables (rural headcount poverty ratio, proportion of rural workers in non-farm employment, and rural literacy rate), we may formulate the following linear regression model.

$$POV_{it} = \alpha + \beta_1 RNFW_{it} + \beta_2 LIT_{it} + \varepsilon_{it} \tag{9.1}$$

$$i = 1, 2, ..., 17$$
$$t = 1, 2, 3$$

In this model, all the variables have *it* as subscript. Here *i* and *t* refer to cross-sectional and time series aspects of data, respectively. As the number of cross-sectional units (N) is 17 and number of years (T) is 3, we have altogether 51 observations on each variable $(NT = 51)$. As usual, ε_{it} is the disturbance term that is assumed to be independently and identically distributed $[\varepsilon_{it} \sim i.\ i.\ d\ (0, \sigma^2)]$. For the purpose of hypothesis testing, we also assume that ε_{it} is normally distributed. Finally, all explanatory variables of the model are assumed to be non-stochastic, and none of these is correlated with the disturbance term.

Our next question is: How to estimate model (9.1)? In this context, there are three important approaches, which are known as the Constant Coefficients Model, Fixed Effects Model, and Random Effects Model. These models differ with regard to the assumptions that are made about the intercept, the slope coefficients and the disturbance term of model (9.1).

9.2.1 The Constant Coefficients Model (CCM)

The Constant Coefficients Model assumes that all coefficients (intercept and slope) remain unchanged across cross-sectional units, and over time. In other words, the CCM ignores the space and time dimensions of panel data set. Put differently, under the CCM, the cross-sectional units (states, in our example) are assumed to be homogeneous such that the values of intercept and slope coefficients are same irrespective of cross-sectional unit being considered. Accepting this *homogeneity assumption* (also called *pooling assumption*), the CCM uses the panel (or pooled) data set, and applies Ordinary Least Squares (OLS) method to estimate unknown parameters of the model. Thus, the CCM is nothing but straightforward application of OLS to a given panel or pooled data set to obtain estimates for unknown parameters of the model.

Limitation of Constant Coefficients Model

The main limitation of the Constant Coefficients Model is that, in reality, the homogeneity assumption may not be true, and different cross-sectional units may have different values for intercept and/or slope coefficients. To clarify this point, suppose that there are two categories of states in our sample: high-poverty states and low-poverty states. In this situation, the poverty equation if estimated by using data for high-poverty states would be different from the poverty equation for low-poverty states. This is because apart from the two variables which have been considered (RNFW and LIT) as determinants of rural poverty, there are many other factors (e.g., level of agricultural development, infrastructural facilities, credit availability, etc.) that cause low incidence of poverty in some states as opposed to others. Similarly, the poverty function may change over time in response to a major policy intervention by the government which is not captured by the explanatory variables considered in our model. Ignoring the differences between the states (caused by omission of other 'relevant' explanatory variables), and estimating a single poverty equation with pooled data is very likely to provide distorted results (i.e., incorrect estimates for unknown parameters of the model). Of course, one may think that the disturbance term captures the effect of omitted variables, if any. But then some of those omitted variables are also likely to be correlated with the explanatory variables included in the model. For example, an omitted variable like the level of agricultural development (which is represented by agricultural productivity) and infrastructures are likely to be correlated with RNFW.[3] In this situation, as the effects of these variables are captured by the disturbance term of the model, $Cov\,(RNFW_{it}, \varepsilon_{it}) \neq 0$ and there is violation of one important OLS assumption. This results in biased and inconsistent estimates for unknown parameters of our model (9.1).

However, the above-mentioned problem can be avoided if we follow the Fixed Effects Model or the Random Effects Model. As will be clear from the discussions below, both these models seek to make a more rational specification of the model such that the heterogeneity among the cross-sectional units is explicitly recognized, although their methods of doing so are different. In any case, these models are viewed as proper panel data models.

9.2.2 The Fixed-Effects Model

To understand the basic idea behind the Fixed Effects Model (FEM), suppose our objective is to examine the relationship between wages of workers and their education (years to schooling) by using data collected through a survey of a set of workers over a number of years. Now assuming that the relationship between wages and education is the same for all workers, we may formulate the following Constant Coefficients Model.

$$WAGE_{it} = \alpha + \beta\,EDU_{it} + \varepsilon_{it} \tag{9.2}$$

---

[3] It has been observed that the areas that are agriculturally developed and have better infrastructural facilities also have high percentage of rural workers in non-farm employment.

This model supposes that the values of α and β are same for all workers. This, however, appears to be unrealistic. As we know, α represents the wages when EDU is zero. Stated differently, α is the benchmark from which a worker's wages develop. This will usually be different for different workers. For example, holding education constant, the male worker probably obtains higher wages than the female worker.[4] This suggests that the value of intercept would vary across individual workers.

To illustrate the above point, suppose that we gathered data on wages and education (years of schooling) of two workers (one male and one female) for 15 time points. Such data have been plotted in Figure 9.1. Corresponding to the scatter plots of data for two workers, we can visualise two separate regression lines. It is shown that, at every level of education, the regression line of the male worker lies above the regression line of the female worker. This implies that even with the same level of education, the male worker gets higher wages than the female worker. This makes the value of intercept (α) different for two workers (although the slopes of the two lines are same). If we ignore this reality and estimate a single wage function (Equation 9.2) by using the pooled data set, we will have incorrect estimate of the intercept parameter of our model.

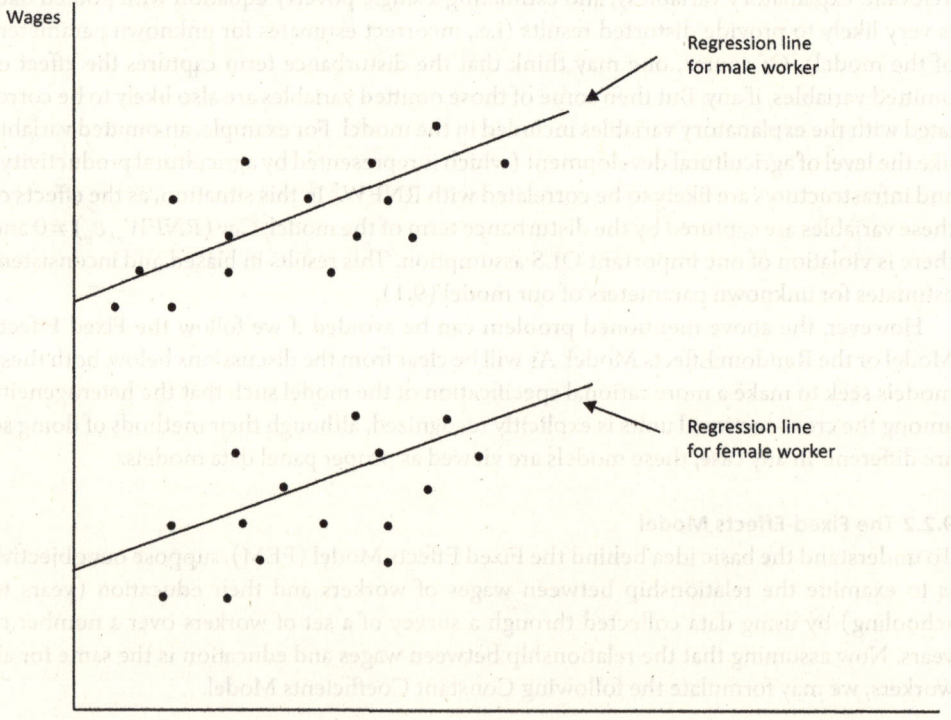

Figure 9.1   Relationship between Wages and Education of Two Workers—First Example

[4] Quite often we hear about gender discrimination in wages in the labour market.

To pursue this point a bit further, a more difficult situation arises if the data points for two workers are scattered in the manner shown in Figure 9.2. In this situation, as before, estimating two separate regressions gives different intercept values for two workers but the value of slope coefficient (β) is same and positive, which leads to the conclusion that returns to education is positive. However, if we pool all observations, the regression line corresponding to pooled data gives not only a different intercept but also turns the slope coefficient negative. This leads to a highly misleading conclusion that returns to education is negative.

The obvious implication of the above discussion is that if different individuals have different regression lines (i.e., 'individual effects' are present) we must take this into consideration to avoid such a misleading conclusion. In other words, the heterogeneity feature of the cross-sectional units (individuals) must be accommodated explicitly in the regression model while working with pooled or panel data set. The Fixed Effects Model does this by considering the intercept as a variable and uses dummy variables to account for differences among the individuals with regard to the value of intercept. Thus, if there are N

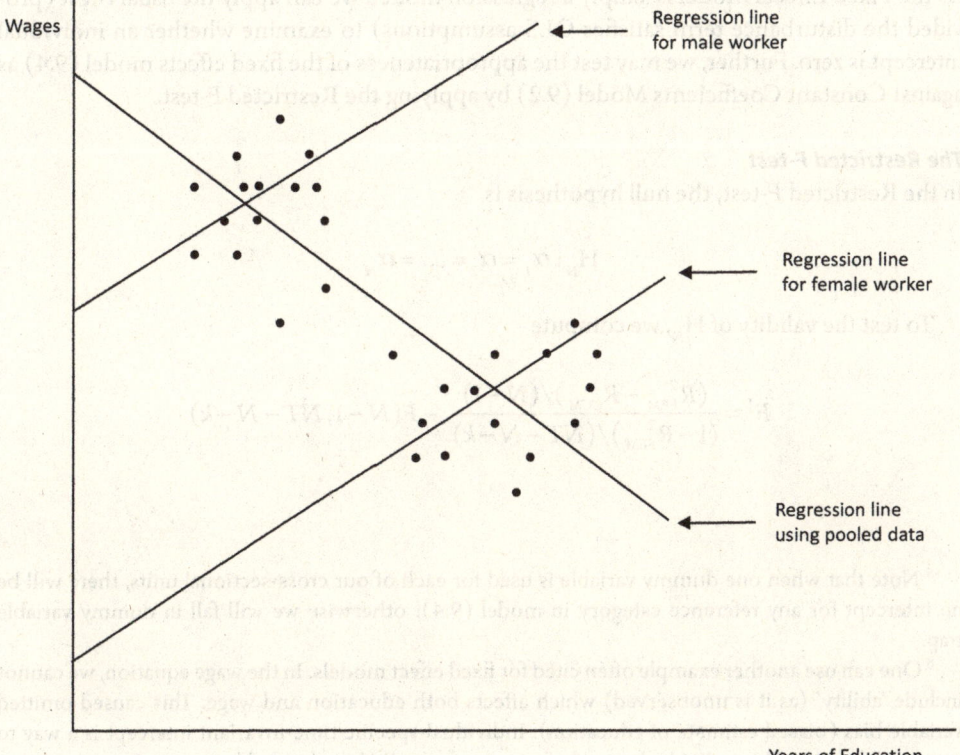

Figure 9.2   Relationship between Wages and Education of Two Workers—Second Example

cross-sectional units, we use N number of dummy variables[5] and the fixed effects model is written as

$$WAGE_{it} = \alpha_i + \beta\,EDU_{it} + \varepsilon_{it} \qquad (9.3)$$

Or

$$WAGE_{it} = \alpha_1 D_{1t} + \alpha_2 D_{2t} + ... + \alpha_N D_{Nt} + \beta\,EDU_{it} + \varepsilon_{it} \qquad (9.4)$$

Here the value of $D_{1t} = 1$ for first cross-sectional unit and 0 for all others, $D_{2t} = 1$ for second cross-sectional unit and 0 for all others, and so on. In this situation, α_1 is the intercept of first cross-sectional unit, α_2 is the intercept of second cross-sectional unit, and so on.

The model such as (9.3) or (9.4) is called Fixed Effects Model because although the intercept term is allowed to vary across cross-sectional units, for each cross-sectional unit the intercept is assumed to remain constant over time, i.e., the intercept of each cross-sectional unit is time-invariant.[6]

The fixed effects model is estimated by using the Ordinary Least Squares (OLS) method.[7] As the Fixed Effects Model is simply a regression model, we can apply the usual t-test (provided the disturbance term satisfies OLS assumptions) to examine whether an individual intercept is zero. Further, we may test the appropriateness of the fixed effects model (9.4) as against Constant Coefficients Model (9.2) by applying the Restricted F-test.

The Restricted F-test

In the Restricted F-test, the null hypothesis is

$$H_N : \alpha_1 = \alpha_2 = ... = \alpha_N$$

To test the validity of H_N, we compute

$$F^* = \frac{(R^2_{FEM} - R^2_{CCM})/(N-1)}{(1 - R^2_{FEM})/(NT-N-k)} \sim F(N-1, NT-N-k)$$

---

[5] Note that when one dummy variable is used for each of our cross-sectional units, there will be no intercept for any reference category in model (9.4); otherwise we will fall in dummy variable trap.

[6] One can use another example often cited for fixed effect models. In the wage equation, we cannot include 'ability' (as it is unobserved) which affects both education and wage. This caused omitted variable bias (biased estimate of education). Individual-specific time-invariant intercept is a way to get rid of this bias. This individual-specific factor is often called *unobserved heterogeneity*.

[7] That is why the fixed-effects model is also known as Fixed Effects Least Squares Dummy Variables (FELSDV) model, or simply as LSDV model.

where

R^2_{FEM} = computed R^2 value from the estimated Fixed Effects Model (called unrestricted regression)

R^2_{CCM} = computed R^2 value from the estimated Constant Coefficients Model (restricted regression)

N = number of intercepts in Fixed Effects Model (equal to number of cross-sectional units)

NT = total number of observations

k = number of explanatory variables in the Fixed Effects Model

The *decision rule* is: If $F^* > F_\lambda$ $(N-1, NT-N-k)$, i.e., computed-F is greater than the theoretical-F at a chosen level of significance λ and degrees of freedom $(N-1)$ for the numerator and $(NT-N-k)$ for the denominator, we reject the null hypothesis (H_N) and conclude that, compared with the Constant Coefficients Model, the Fixed Effects Model is more appropriate in the context of our pooled or panel data set. This also means that the fixed effects are present and the intercepts of cross-sectional units are statistically significantly different from each other.

One-Way and Two-Way Fixed Effects Models

Model (9.4) is known as *One-Way Fixed Effects Model* because we have allowed only the intercept to vary between cross-sectional units. However, we may also consider the period-effect if we believe that the intercept changes uniformly for all cross-sectional units over time (e.g., due to enforcement of minimum wages act by the government). To account for such a period-effect, we are required to add period dummies in model (9.4). The number of period dummies is determined by number of periods (T) for which data have been collected. The model that emerges eventually is called *Two-Way Fixed Effects Model* that considers both individual (cross-section) and period (time) effects. Further, if we wish to consider variation in the slope coefficient among cross-sectional units as well as over time, we shall have to extend the model further by introducing 'interaction or differential slope dummies', which are obtained by interacting N cross-section intercept-dummies and T time-dummies with the explanatory variable (EDU).

Limitations of Fixed Effects Model

Although easy to apply, the Fixed Effects Model suffers from following limitations.

1. Using too many dummy variables, we run up against degrees of freedom, and it becomes very difficult to obtain precise estimates for unknown parameters of our model.

2. By introducing many dummy variables, both individual and interactive, we invite the possibility of multicollinearity problem which also makes obtaining precise estimates for unknown parameters of our model difficult.

3. All the results in the Fixed Effects Model are based on the assumption that $\varepsilon_{it} \sim N$ $(0, \sigma^2)$. As the index i refers to cross-sectional units and t to time series observations, the disturbance term (ε_{it}) is likely to suffer from problems of heteroskedasticity and autocorrelation.

Within-Group and First-Difference Estimators

It may be noted that first two of above-mentioned problems can be avoided by adopting a simple trick. It is that either we express all the variables (including dummy variables) as deviations from their respective means or consider first-difference of the variables in the Fixed Effects Model. The former approach is known as *Within-Group Estimator* (WGE) while the latter is known as *First-Difference Estimator* (FDE). It is to be noted that such transformations of the variables are performed separately for each cross-sectional unit. The advantage of these approaches is that all the terms involving dummy variables are removed from the Fixed Effects Model. This helps to attain maximum economy of degrees of freedom and avoid the problem of multicollinearity (which is caused by correlations between the dummy variables).

However, there are some problems with these approaches: *(i)* In the process of transforming the variables, apart from dummy variables, the time-invariant explanatory variables[8] (e.g., the workers' caste, gender, parental education, etc.) get wiped out from the model;[9] *(ii)* Differencing leads to removal of long-run effects in the variables and we are left with only the short-run effects in the variables; and *(iii)* the disturbance term of the Fixed Effects First-Difference Model suffers from autocorrelation problem. These problems are avoided in the Random Effects Model which we discuss below.

9.2.3 The Random Effects Model

The Random Effects Model (REM) does not use dummy variables to capture the presence of 'individual effect'. It rather assumes that the individual effect (α_i) is a random variable with a mean value α_1. Then the intercept of ith cross-sectional unit can be expressed as

$$\alpha_i = \alpha_1 + u_i \qquad (9.5)$$

Actually, we are assuming that the cross-sectional units in our data set have been drawn from a much larger universe (population) and they have a common intercept α_1. The individual differences in the intercept values of cross-sectional units is reflected by the random error term, u_i. Thus, the Random Effects Model is specified as

$$WAGE_{it} = (\alpha_1 + u_i) + \beta EDU_{it} + \varepsilon_{it}$$
$$= \alpha_1 + \beta EDU_{it} + w_{it} \qquad (9.6)$$

Here w_{it} $(= u_i + \varepsilon_{it})$ is the composite random error term that has two components: *(i)* u_i, which represents the cross-section or individual-specific random error component, and *(ii)* ε_{it}, which is combined time series and cross-section random error component, sometimes called the *idiosyncratic random term* because it varies over cross-sectional units as well

---

[8] The values of these variables remain unchanged for a given cross-sectional unit at different points in time.

[9] For this reason, Fixed Effects Model is not attempted if there are time-invariant variables in the data set.

as over time. As this model considers individual effect (α_i) as a random variable, hence the name Random Effects Model.

The assumptions that are made with regard to u_i and ε_{it} are

$$u_i \sim N(0, \sigma_u^2)$$
$$\varepsilon_{it} \sim N(0, \sigma_\varepsilon^2)$$
$$E(u_i \varepsilon_{it}) = 0$$
$$E(u_i u_j) = 0 \quad \text{for } i \neq j$$
$$E(\varepsilon_{it} \varepsilon_{is}) = E(\varepsilon_{ij} \varepsilon_{jt}) = E(\varepsilon_{it} \varepsilon_{js}) = 0 \quad \text{for } i \neq j \text{ and } t \neq s$$

Here $\sigma_u^2 = Var(u_i)$ and $\sigma_\varepsilon^2 = Var(\varepsilon_{it})$.

These assumptions imply that individual error components are not correlated with each other and are not correlated across cross-section and time series units. Using these properties of u_i and ε_{it}, we can work out the properties of w_{it}.

$$E(w_{it}) = 0$$
$$Var(w_{it}) = \sigma_u^2 + \sigma_\varepsilon^2$$

It is observed that w_{it} has zero mean and constant variance (homoskedastic). However, it can be shown that w_{it} and w_{is} are correlated (i.e., the composite error term of a given cross-sectional unit at two different times are correlated). The value of such a correlation coefficient (ρ) is given by

$$\rho = \frac{\sigma_u^2}{\sigma_u^2 + \sigma_\varepsilon^2} \text{ for } t \neq s$$

If we ignore the above correlation structure and estimate the Random Effects Model (equation 9.6) by OLS method, the resulting estimators will be inefficient. The most appropriate method to estimate the Random Effects Model is the Generalised Least Squares (GLS) method.[10] For GLS procedure to have good properties, we should have large N and relatively small T (Wooldridge 2009, 490).

Another important point that needs mention is that the Random Effects Model supposes the composite error term w_{it} not to be correlated with any of the explanatory variables included in the model. However, since u_i is a component of w_{it}, sometimes w_{it} may be correlated with the explanatory variables included in the Random Effects Model.[11] In such a situation, Random Effects Model will result in inconsistent estimation of regression coefficients, and

---

[10] Formal discussion on GLS estimation of the REM is available in advanced textbooks on panel data econometrics. See, e.g., Wooldridge (2002, Chapter 10) and Baltagi (2008).

[11] This is because u_i captures the effect of omitted variables some of which may be correlated with the explanatory variable(s) of the REM.

we may have to fall back upon the Fixed Effects Model. Whether or not w_{it} is correlated with the explanatory variables in a given application is checked through the Hausman test.

Equation (9.6) represents One-Way Random Effects Model that considers only the cross-section effect. We may extend equation (9.6) to allow for a random error component to take into account the period effect. The model then becomes Two-Way Random Effects Model. The assumptions involved in the Two-Way Random Effects Model are different.

The EViews package uses GLS method to estimate the Random Effects Model. After estimation of the Random Effects Model, testing of hypothesis involving regression coefficients can be performed in the same manner as for any other regression model. The EViews conducts hypothesis tests (e.g., t-test and F-test) in standard ways using the appropriate estimate of the variance of the GLS estimator.

9.3 CHOOSING BETWEEN FEM AND REM: THE HAUSMAN TEST

In general, REM is considered suitable when the number of cross-sectional units (N) is large and the number of time series observations (T) is small. An intuitive explanation of this is that as the intercept (α_i) in the REM is a random variable, it must be allowed to assume a wide spectrum of values over $(-\infty, \infty)$. This is possible when N is sufficiently large. Thus, REM does not suit a data set satisfactorily with fewer cross-sectional units (i.e., long panels).[12] In such a situation, FEM that involves a lesser number of dummy variables (as N is small) appears suitable. FEM also enjoys computational convenience compared with the REM.

However, selection between FEM and REM is performed more rigorously by applying the Hausman test. As pointed out earlier, REM is not preferred if the composite error term (w_{it}) gets correlated with the explanatory variable(s) of the model, which at times becomes a possibility. Hausman adapted a test based on the idea that if there is no correlation between w_{it} and explanatory variable(s), both OLS and GLS are consistent but OLS is inefficient. On the other hand, if such correlation exists, OLS is consistent but GLS is not. More specifically, Hausman assumed that there are two estimators $\hat{\beta}^{FE}$ and $\hat{\beta}^{RE}$ of the parameter vector β and added two-hypothesis testing procedures. The hypotheses are

$$H_N : \text{Both } \hat{\beta}^{FE} \text{ and } \hat{\beta}^{RE} \text{ are consistent, but } \hat{\beta}^{FE} \text{ is inefficient}$$
$$H_A : \hat{\beta}^{FE} \text{ is consistent and efficient, but } \hat{\beta}^{RE} \text{ is inconsistent}$$

Here we actually test H_N (random effects are consistent and efficient) against H_A (random effects are inconsistent, as the fixed effects will always be consistent). Hausman takes $\hat{q} = (\hat{\beta}^{FE} - \hat{\beta}^{RE})$ as the basis for the relevant test statistic. The Hausman test statistic is given by

$$H = \hat{q}' [Var(\hat{\beta}^{FE}) - Var(\hat{\beta}^{RE})]^{-1} \hat{q} \sim \chi^2(k)$$

where k is the number of explanatory variables.

---

[12] This type of situation arises especially when the unit of observation is a large geographical area (say, states or provinces). In such a situation, one may attempt Fixed Effects Model rather than mechanically pursuing the Random Effects Model (Wooldridge 2009, 493).

The *decision rule* is: If computed value of Chi-square (χ^{2^*}) is greater than the theoretical Chi-square value at a chosen level of significance λ and degrees of freedom k, i.e., $\chi^{2^*} > \chi^2_\lambda(k)$ we reject H_N which says that the REM is consistent, and accept the Fixed Effects estimator. In contrast, we do not reject H_N if $\chi^{2^*} \leq \chi^2_\lambda(k)$ and prefer the Random Effects estimator.

9.4 ESTIMATION OF PANEL REGRESSION MODELS USING EVIEWS

We describe below the steps to be followed for estimating panel regression models using the EViews software package.

I. Organizing Data

As most of us are familiar with MS Excel, it is always convenient to enter the panel data (or any other data) in an Excel worksheet which can be easily imported in EViews. It is essential to arrange panel data in 'stacked by cross-section' format. This means that data for different cross-sections have to be stacked on top of one another, with all of the sequentially dated observations for a given cross-section grouped together. Note that state-level data presented in Table 9.1A are 'stacked by dates'. These data can be rearranged into 'stacked by cross-section' format by sorting. Another point to note is that our data do not belong to consecutive dates. Therefore, to appear them consecutively dated, we have to label the years 1983, 1994–95, and 2004–05 by 1, 2, and 3, respectively. We save the Excel file in any drive of our computer after this rearrangement (see Table 9.1B).

II. Importing Data from Excel Worksheet

The commands for importing the pooled data file from the Excel worksheet to the EViews worksheet are the same as mentioned in Chapter 2. As we import the data file in EViews, the 'Workfile' window as in Screenshot 9.1 opens.

III. Resetting the Workfile Structure

1. In the 'Workfile' window, double-click on **Range**, which will open the 'Workfile Structure' window like Screenshot 9.2.
2. In the 'Workfile Structure' window,
    (i)   Select the option **Dated Panel** (which is appropriate in the context of our data set) in 'Workfile structure type' edit box.
    (ii) In 'Panel identifier series' edit box, write **state** in 'Cross section ID series' box and **year** in 'Date series' box.
    (iii) Put **1** as 'Start date' and **3** as 'End date' in 'Observation inclusion/creation' edit box (as we have data for three time points, labelled as 1, 2 and 3).
3. Click **OK**.

IV. Estimating Panel Regression Models

1. In the main menu, click **Quick/Estimate Equation...** This opens the 'Equation Estimation' window as in Screenshot 9.3.

Table 9.1B   Data on Poverty and Other Variables in 'Stacked by Cross-Section' Format

State	Year	POV	RNFW	LIT
Andhra Pradesh	1	27.3	19.9	29.5
Andhra Pradesh	2	16.6	20.6	40.5
Andhra Pradesh	3	10.9	28.4	65.7
Assam	1	41.9	20.1	41.8
Assam	2	44.4	20.8	52.4
Assam	3	23.1	25.3	66.1
Bihar	1	64.9	16.4	29
Bihar	2	57.2	15.6	36.5
Bihar	3	43.1	25.1	49.3
Gujarat	1	27.9	14.7	45.6
Gujarat	2	22.4	21.3	54.6
Gujarat	3	19.8	22.7	60.8
Haryana	1	21.8	22.7	39.9
Haryana	2	26.6	28.1	53.5
Haryana	3	13.4	36.4	70.2
Himachal Pradesh	1	17.8	12.9	51.6
Himachal Pradesh	2	29.3	19.8	65.2
Himachal Pradesh	3	12.5	30.4	79.8
Jammu & Kashmir	1	25.2	25.3	28.8
Jammu & Kashmir	2	19.7	24	39.1
Jammu & Kashmir	3	4.8	36.1	53.9
Karnataka	1	37.5	15.7	39.8
Karnataka	2	30.2	18.7	50.8
Karnataka	3	23.7	19	65
Kerala	1	38.5	37.1	82.2
Kerala	2	26.5	43.6	89.2
Kerala	3	12.3	58.1	90.5
Madhya Pradesh	1	48.2	9.1	30.7
Madhya Pradesh	2	40.4	10.1	41.1
Madhya Pradesh	3	38.2	17	69.9
Maharashtra	1	45	14.2	47.8
Maharashtra	2	37.7	17.6	59.5
Maharashtra	3	30.4	20.1	77.8
Orissa	1	67.5	20.8	39.4
Orissa	2	50.1	19.2	49.3
Orissa	3	47.8	31.1	67.4
Punjab	1	14.3	17.2	44.1
Punjab	2	13.7	25.4	56
Punjab	3	9.6	33.3	70.6
Rajasthan	1	37.7	13.2	24.1

(*Contd.*)

Table 9.1B (*Contd.*)

State	Year	POV	RNFW	LIT
Rajasthan	2	26.9	20.1	36.1
Rajasthan	3	19.9	27.1	70.7
Tamil Nadu	1	56.2	25.7	47.1
Tamil Nadu	2	33	29.6	57.8
Tamil Nadu	3	23	34.8	72
Uttar Pradesh	1	46.4	17.5	30.2
Uttar Pradesh	2	42.3	20	40.8
Uttar Pradesh	3	34.1	28.4	62.1
West Bengal	1	61.6	26.3	42.4
West Bengal	2	37.4	36.6	54
West Bengal	3	28.5	37.3	70.2

Screenshot 9.1   Workfile Window for Panel Data Regression

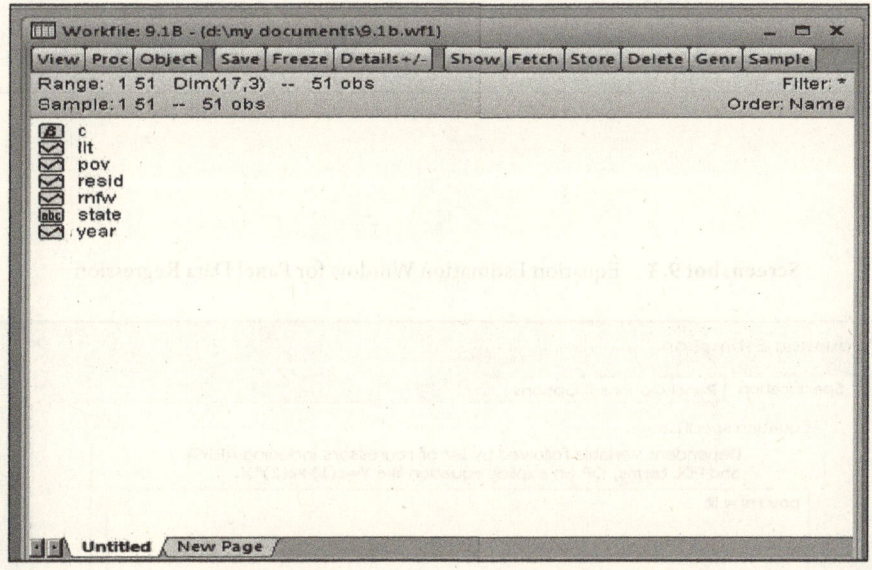

2.   In the 'Equation specification' edit box, write the specification of the equation (which, according to our data set is: **pov rnfw lit**).

3.   Click **Panel Options** and specify individual and period effects in two boxes of 'Effects specification'. By default, EViews assumes that there are no effects so that both the boxes are set to None. This may be changed to allow for either **Fixed** or **Random** effects in either the cross-section or period dimensions, or both.

4.   Click **OK** to obtain the regression output for the chosen model.

Screenshot 9.2   Workfile Structure Window for Panel Data Regression

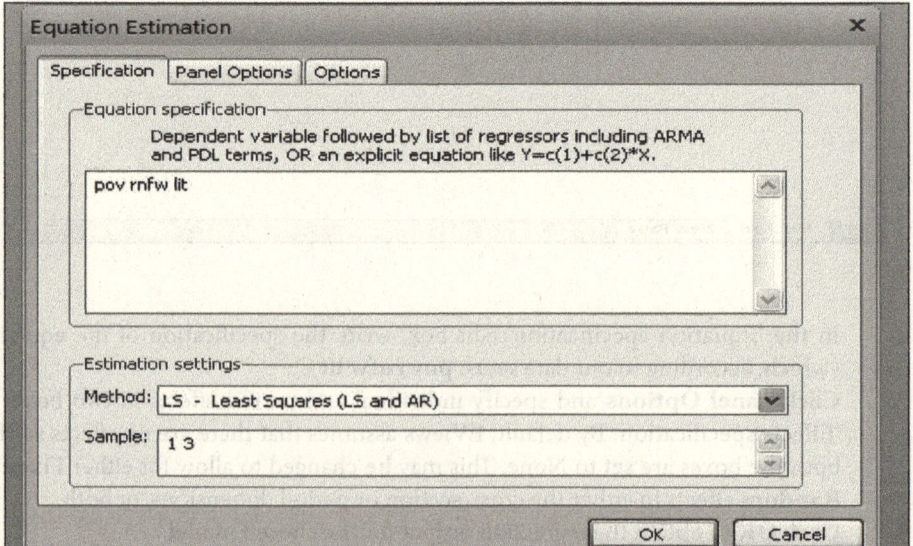

Screenshot 9.3   Equation Estimation Window for Panel Data Regression

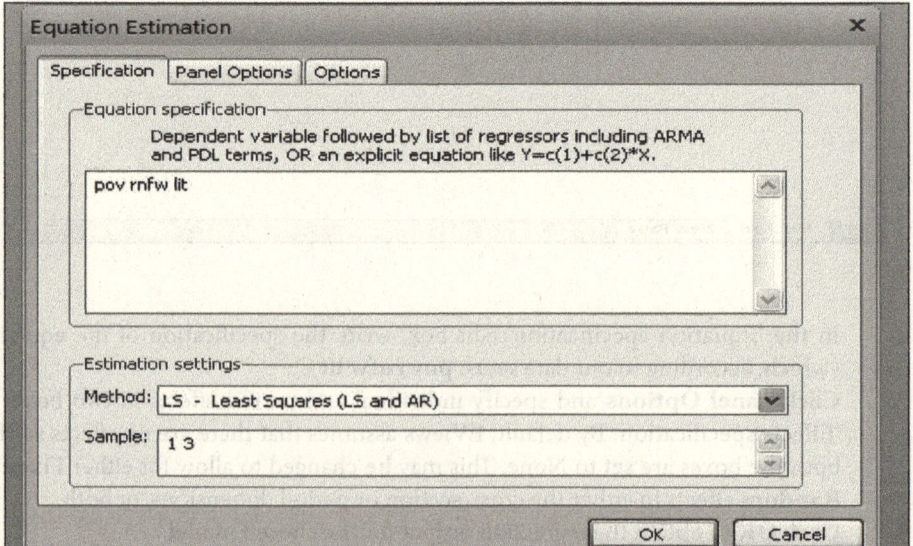

V. Obtaining Series for Fixed/Random Effects
After estimating the Fixed/Random Effects Model, to obtain the series for fixed/random effects, click the following: **View/Fixed/Random Effects/Cross-section Effects or Period Effects**.

VI. Choosing between OLS Model and Fixed Effects Model: Fixed Effects Testing
The fixed effects test is performed to choose between the results of OLS model (also called Constant Coefficients Model) and Fixed Effects Model. While using EViews, it is not necessary to separately estimate the OLS model using panel data. After estimating the Fixed Effects Model, as we conduct the fixed effects testing, the estimation results for OLS model are also provided along with the results of fixed effects testing.

To perform fixed effects testing, EViews employs two tests: (i) an F-test (which is same as the Restricted-F test mentioned earlier) and (ii) a Chi-square test. To perform this testing, click the following: **View/Fixed/Random Effects Testing/Redundant Fixed Effects–Likelihood Ratio**. The output window will provide the results of fixed effects testing.

VII. Estimating Random Effects Model
The procedure for estimation of random effects model is the same except that while selecting 'Effects specification' in the 'Equation Estimation' window, we choose **Random**.

VIII. Choosing between Fixed Effects Model and Random Effects Model
As mentioned earlier, we perform the Hausman test to choose between the Fixed Effects Model and Random Effects Model. To conduct this test, we must first estimate a model with random effects specification. Next, we select **View/Fixed/Random Effects Testing/Correlated Random Effects–Hausman Test**. The output window will provide the Hausman test result, followed by estimation results for the Fixed Effects Model.

9.5 INTERPRETATION OF PANEL REGRESSION RESULTS
We used data in Table 9.1B to estimate the Fixed Effects Model that considers only the cross-section effect. The results are presented in Table 9.2. It is found that there is a negative relationship between POV and RNFW. The same negative relationship holds between POV and LIT. Further, the estimated coefficients of both the variables are statistically significant at 5% level (p-values for computed t-statistics are greater than 0.01 but less than 0.05). Thus, it may be concluded that as the percentage of rural workers in non-farm employment and rural literacy rate increase, the incidence of rural poverty falls.

An important point to note is that, in the output table, 'C' is called the *common intercept* which is the average of all individual intercepts (i.e., average of estimated intercepts of 17 cross-sectional units/states). The EViews presents individual or fixed effects as deviations of individual intercepts from the common intercept.

The cross-section fixed effects (as deviations from common intercept) in the context of our model model are given in Table 9.3. Since all the cross-section fixed effects are non-zero, the presence of fixed effects is confirmed. Thus, compared with Constant Coefficients Model, Fixed Effects Model appears to have provided a better model specification in the context of our data set.

Table 9.2   Estimation Results for Fixed Effects Model

Method: Panel Least Squares
Date: 08/23/13 Time: 16:08
Sample: 1 3
Periods included: 3
Cross-sections included: 17
Total panel (balanced) observations: 51

Variable	Coefficient	Std. Error	t-Statistic	Prob.
C	63.17579	4.461375	14.16061	0.0000
RNFW	−0.656626	0.317247	−2.069761	0.0466
LIT	−0.287215	0.132758	−2.163440	0.0381
Effects Specification				
Cross-section fixed (dummy variables)				
R-squared	0.885900	Mean dependent var		31.94510
Adjusted R-squared	0.821719	S.D. dependent var		15.08201
S.E. of regression	6.368132	Akaike info criterion		6.819498
Sum squared resid	1297.699	Schwarz criterion		7.539197
Log likelihood	−154.8972	Hannan-Quinn criter.		7.094516
F-statistic	13.80309	Durbin-Watson stat		2.439116
Prob(F-statistic)	0.000000			

Source: This table represents the output obtained by the author after application of the EViews software.

Table 9.3   Cross-Section Fixed Effects Values

State	Effect
Andhra Pradesh	−16.83691
Assam	3.127292
Bihar	15.37943
Gujarat	−11.54726
Haryana	−7.827053
Himachal Pradesh	−10.67592
Jammu & Kashmir	−16.25623
Karnataka	−6.124284
Kerala	18.04467
Madhya Pradesh	0.580295
Maharashtra	3.605018
Orissa	22.46435
Punjab	−17.68727
Rajasthan	−9.256893
Tamil Nadu	10.88101
Uttar Pradesh	4.924213
West Bengal	17.20554

Source: Same as for Table 9.2.

However, to confirm this, we performed Redundant Fixed Effects Tests the results of which are presented in Table 9.4. The superiority of Fixed Effects Model over the Constant Coefficients Model is immediately reinforced. First, both computed-F and Chi-square values are statistically significant at 1% level. Secondly, the estimated coefficient of RNFE variable is found to be statistically insignificant in the Constant Coefficients Model (p-value being 0.3593). Thirdly, the computed value of Durbin-Watson statistic in the Constant Coefficients Model is 1.027028, which indicates presence of positive autocorrelation.[13] Thus, the Fixed Effects Model appears more satisfactory compared to the Constant Coefficients Model.

Table 9.4   Results of Redundant Fixed Effects Test

Redundant Fixed Effects Tests
Equation: Untitled
Test cross-section fixed effects

Effects Test	Statistic	d.f.	Prob.
Cross-section F	12.085139	(16,32)	0.0000
Cross-section Chi-square	99.550629	16	0.0000

Cross-section fixed effects test equation:
Dependent Variable: POV
Method: Panel Least Squares
Date: 08/23/13   Time: 16:10
Sample: 1 3
Periods included: 3
Cross-sections included: 17
Total panel (balanced) observations: 51

Variable	Coefficient	Std. Error	t-Statistic	Prob.
C	53.86041	6.718996	8.016140	0.0000
RNFW	−0.272544	0.294441	−0.925630	0.3593
LIT	−0.286311	0.163589	−1.750182	0.0865
R-squared	0.196443	Mean dependent var		31.94510
Adjusted R-squared	0.162961	S.D. dependent var		15.08201
S.E. of regression	13.79850	Akaike info criterion		8.144020
Sum squared resid	9139.137	Schwarz criterion		8.257657
Log likelihood	−204.6725	Hannan-Quinn criter.		8.187444
F-statistic	5.867186	Durbin-Watson stat		1.027028
Prob(F-statistic)	0.005253			

Source: Same as for Table 9.2.

[13] This becomes clear when we compare the value of computed-Durbin-Watson statistic with theoretical Durbin-Watson values (lower and upper).

However, it is also necessary to check the appropriateness of Fixed Effects Model as against Random Effects Model. This is particularly so as we have not been able to confirm absence of autocorrelation in the context of the Fixed Effects Model.[14] Thus, we estimated the Random Effects Model by invoking the cross-section effect, generated the series for cross-section random effects, and performed the Hausman test. The results are shown below in tables 9.5, 9.6, and 9.7, respectively.

Table 9.5 Estimation Results of Random Effects Model

Dependent Variable: POV
Method: Panel EGLS (Cross-section random effects)
Date: 08/23/13 Time: 16:11
Sample: 1 3
Periods included: 3
Cross-sections included: 17
Total panel (balanced) observations: 51
Swamy and Arora estimator of component variances

Variable	Coefficient	Std. Error	t-Statistic	Prob.
C	61.44857	5.255414	11.69243	0.0000
RNFW	−0.529278	0.274052	−1.931309	0.0594
LIT	−0.312326	0.120331	−2.595551	0.0125

Effects Specification		
	S.D.	Rho
Cross-section random	12.84410	0.8027
Idiosyncratic random	6.368132	0.1973

Weighted Statistics			
R-squared	0.518808	Mean dependent var	8.791245
Adjusted R-squared	0.498758	S.D. dependent var	8.949187
S.E. of regression	6.335885	Sum squared resid	1926.885
F-statistic	25.87611	Durbin-Watson stat	2.057605
Prob(F-statistic)	0.000000		

Unweighted Statistics			
R-squared	0.165263	Mean dependent var	31.94510
Sum squared resid	9493.754	Durbin-Watson stat	0.995170

Source: Same as for Table 9.2.

The following observations can be made here: Similar to Fixed Effects Model, both the slope coefficients of Random Effects Model have negative signs, and they are statistically significant. The presence of cross-section effects is also confirmed on the basis of non-zero values of cross-section random effects. The problem of autocorrelation is absent in the

---

[14] The computed value of Durbin-Watson statistic for the Fixed Effects Model is 2.439116, which fell in the 'inconclusive zone' when compared with theoretical Durbin-Watson values.

Table 9.6   Cross-Section Random Effects Values

State	Effect
Andhra Pradesh	−15.61879
Assam	3.129689
Bihar	14.45895
Gujarat	−10.13382
Haryana	−7.793433
Himachal Pradesh	−9.225687
Jammu & Kashmir	−15.83699
Karnataka	−4.955386
Kerala	14.85491
Madhya Pradesh	1.808724
Maharashtra	4.324152
Orissa	20.77752
Punjab	−16.40861
Rajasthan	−8.316482
Tamil Nadu	9.486900
Uttar Pradesh	4.591859
West Bengal	14.85650

Source: Same as for Table 9.2.

Random Effects Model as the computed value of Durbin-Watson statistic is 2.057605, which is greater than theoretical Durbin-Watson values (both lower and upper).[15] Above all, Random Effects Model gets accepted on the basis of Hausman test as the computed Chi-square (χ^{2*}) value is statistically insignificant. Thus, among the three alternative models, we prefer the Random Effects Model in the context of panel data in Table 9.1A.

9.6 QUESTIONS AND ASSIGNMENTS

A. Multiple-Choice Questions
Tick ($\sqrt{}$) the correct answer.
   (i)   The data set where the number of cross-sectional units is less than the number of
          time points is called
          (a)   Short panel
          (b)   Long panel
          (c)   Mixed panel
          (d)   Invalid panel

[15] For two explanatory variables and 51 observations, the lower and upper Durbin-Watson (theoretical) values are 1.462 and 1.628, respectively (at 5% significance level).

Table 9.7 Results of the Hausman Test

Correlated Random Effects - Hausman Test				
Equation: Untitled				
Test cross-section random effects				
Test Summary		Chi-Sq. Statistic	Chi-Sq. d.f.	Prob.
Cross-section random		1.515113	2	0.4688
Cross-section random effects test comparisons:				
Variable	Fixed	Random	Var(Diff.)	Prob.
RNFW	−0.656626	−0.529278	0.025542	0.4255
LIT	−0.287215	−0.312326	0.003145	0.6543

Cross-section random effects test equation:

Dependent Variable: POV

Method: Panel Least Squares

Date: 08/23/13 Time: 16:14

Sample: 1 3

Periods included: 3

Cross-sections included: 17

Total panel (balanced) observations: 51

Variable	Coefficient	Std. Error	t-Statistic	Prob.
C	63.17579	4.461375	14.16061	0.0000
RNFW	−0.656626	0.317247	−2.069761	0.0466
LIT	−0.287215	0.132758	−2.163440	0.0381
	Effects Specification			
Cross-section fixed (dummy variables)				
R-squared	0.885900	Mean dependent var		31.94510
Adjusted R-squared	0.821719	S.D. dependent var		15.08201
S.E. of regression	6.368132	Akaike info criterion		6.819498
Sum squared resid	1297.699	Schwarz criterion		7.539197
Log likelihood	−154.8972	Hannan-Quinn criter.		7.094516
F-statistic	13.80309	Durbin-Watson stat		2.439116
Prob(F-statistic)	0.000000			

Source: Same as for Table 9.2.

(ii) The Fixed Effects Model is more suitable for
   (a) Short panels
   (b) Medium panels
   (c) Long panels
   (d) None of the above
(iii) The omitted variable problem can be corrected by estimating a
   (a) Simple OLS model
   (b) Panel regression model
   (c) Auxiliary regression model
   (d) None of the above

(iv) The model that uses dummy variables to account for possible changes in parameter values in a regression model is known as
   (a) Simple regression model
   (b) Fixed Effects Model
   (c) Random Effects Model
   (d) None of the above

(v) The relevant test to choose between the Constant Coefficients Model and Fixed Effects Model is
   (a) Student's t-test
   (b) Chi-square test
   (c) Hausman test
   (d) Restricted F-test

(vi) The estimation procedure adopted by the Random Effects Model is
   (a) GLS
   (b) WLS
   (c) RLS
   (d) OLS

(vii) The relevant test to choose between the Fixed Effects Model and Random Effects Model is
   (a) Johansen test
   (b) Chi-square test
   (c) Restricted F-test
   (d) Hausman test

B. General Questions

(i) Define panel data.
(ii) Discuss the usefulness of panel data.
(iii) Distinguish between short panel and long panel.
(iv) What is the difference between balanced and unbalanced panels?
(v) Explain the features of the Constant Coefficients Model. What is its main limitation?
(vi) Discuss the Fixed Effects Model of panel data regression with suitable examples. How does it differ from the Constant Coefficients Model?
(vii) What is the difference between one-way and two-way fixed effects models?
(viii) What is 'within-group estimator' in the context of panel regression? What is the advantage of such an estimator? What is its disadvantage?
(ix) What is 'first-difference estimator' in the context of panel regression?
(x) Discuss the steps involved in the test that is performed to choose between the Constant Coefficients Model and Fixed Effects Model.
(xi) State the limitations of the Fixed Effects Model.
(xii) Discuss the Random Effects Model of panel data regression and point out its advantages over the Fixed Effects Model.
(xiii) How would you choose between the Fixed Effects Model and Random Effects Model for application to a particular problem?

(xiv) Point out the steps involved in application of EViews for estimation of panel regression models.

C. Computer Assignments

(i)   The supporters of neo-liberal economic policies viewed that poverty in a country like India (and also other developing countries) could be reduced at a faster rate through attainment of higher economic growth. To test empirical validity of this view, data have been compiled on percentage-point decline in poverty per year (DPOV) and growth of per capita net state domestic product (GPNSDP) for major states of India for two periods of time, which are presented in Table 9.8. Use these data to estimate an appropriate panel regression model to examine the importance of GPNSDP in accelerating the pace of poverty reduction in India. How would you justify appropriateness of your chosen model?

(ii) Table 9.9 gives data on cropping intensity, irrigation intensity and credit to agriculture by commercial banks for Karnataka and Punjab for the period 1989–90 to 2007–08. Use these data to estimate an appropriate panel regression model to understand importance of irrigation intensity and credit availability as determinants of cropping intensity. Justify your chosen model, and interpret the results obtained thereof.

(iii) Suppose you are asked to identify some determinants of productivity in Indian agriculture. From past literature on the subject, you learnt that agricultural productivity is high in the states that use more of modern inputs like irrigation, fertilisers, tractors and so on. It is also believed that agricultural productivity rises with rise in rural literacy rate. To examine the validity of these hypotheses, you compiled data on agricultural productivity (AGP), irrigation (IRRI), fertilizers consumption (FERT), tractors use (TRACT), and rural literacy rate (LIT) for 15 major states of India for three different periods. Such data are given in Table 9.10.

Specify an appropriate panel regression model to identify the main determinants of agricultural productivity. Estimate such a model and explain your results highlighting major determinants of agricultural productivity in India. How would you justify appropriateness of your specified model?

(iv) The researchers working on Indian labour markets observed existence of inter-state variation in the degree of casualisation of the workforce. They hypothesised that the degree of casualisation of workforce is positively related to variables such as unemployment rate, incidence of poverty, and degree of urbanization. To examine the empirical validity of their hypothesis, data have been collected on these variables for 15 major states of India at three points of time. Such data are presented in Table 9.11.

Estimate the 'fixed-effects' and 'random-effects' models of panel data regression using these data. Write down the results of both the models and interpret the results to indicate the validity of the hypothesis stated above. Which estimated model would you prefer ultimately, and why?

Table 9.8   Data on Change in Poverty Incidence and Growth of Per Capita NSDP in Major States of India

State	Period	DPOV	GPNSDP
Andhra Pradesh	1	1.36	6.07
Assam	1	1.58	2.56
Bihar	1	0.55	4.96
Chhattisgarh	1	0.14	4.22
Gujarat	1	0.56	5.83
Haryana	1	1.07	5.13
Himachal Pradesh	1	1.06	5.33
Jammu & Kashmir	1	1.20	2.48
Jharkhand	1	1.40	2.94
Karnataka	1	1.47	5.56
Kerala	1	1.06	6.31
Madhya Pradesh	1	−0.36	4.18
Maharashtra	1	0.87	6.02
Orissa	1	0.17	4.67
Punjab	1	0.14	3.72
Rajasthan	1	0.35	4.47
Tamil Nadu	1	1.38	5.90
Uttar Pradesh	1	0.68	2.91
Uttarakhand	1	−0.06	5.95
West Bengal	1	0.47	5.65
Andhra Pradesh	2	1.70	7.39
Assam	2	−0.70	3.62
Bihar	2	0.18	8.54
Chhattisgarh	2	0.14	4.86
Gujarat	2	1.72	7.59
Haryana	2	0.80	7.50
Himachal Pradesh	2	2.68	5.36
Jammu & Kashmir	2	0.74	3.09
Jharkhand	2	1.24	2.28
Karnataka	2	1.94	7.52
Kerala	2	1.52	8.06
Madhya Pradesh	2	2.38	5.52
Maharashtra	2	2.74	9.37
Orissa	2	4.04	6.82
Punjab	2	1.00	5.58
Rajasthan	2	1.92	4.13
Tamil Nadu	2	2.46	8.28
Uttar Pradesh	2	0.64	4.51
Uttarakhand	2	2.94	10.99
West Bengal	2	1.50	5.77

Source: Computed by the author using data available from the Planning Commission (Government of India) and RBI websites.

Note: DPOV = %-point decline in incidence of poverty per year; GPNSDP = annual growth of per capita NSDP; and Periods 1 and 2 refer to 1993–94 to 2004–05 and 2004–05 to 2009–10, respectively.

Table 9.9 Cropping Intensity (CRI), Irrigation Intensity (IRI), and Credit to Agriculture by
Scheduled Commercial Banks (CREDIT) in Karnataka and Punjab

State	Year	CRI	IRI	CREDIT
Karnataka	1989–90	1.13	1.23	1,318
Punjab	1989–90	1.76	1.77	1,365
Karnataka	1990–91	1.13	1.23	1,475
Punjab	1990–91	1.78	1.8	1,618
Karnataka	1991–92	1.16	1.23	1,493
Punjab	1991–92	1.78	1.81	1,719
Karnataka	1992–93	1.15	1.28	1,603
Punjab	1992–93	1.83	1.85	1,710
Karnataka	1993–94	1.15	1.28	1,756
Punjab	1993–94	1.81	1.84	1,851
Karnataka	1994–95	1.15	1.26	2,102
Punjab	1994–95	1.83	1.86	2,081
Karnataka	1995–96	1.15	1.24	2,365
Punjab	1995–96	1.87	1.91	2,155
Karnataka	1996–97	1.16	1.24	2,616
Punjab	1996–97	1.9	1.92	2,328
Karnataka	1997–98	1.16	1.23	3,107
Punjab	1997–98	1.85	1.87	2,278
Karnataka	1998–99	1.17	1.25	3,501
Punjab	1998–99	1.83	1.87	3,260
Karnataka	1999–2000	1.18	1.24	4,366
Punjab	1999–2000	1.94	1.87	3,758
Karnataka	2000–01	1.18	1.24	4,278
Punjab	2000–01	1.87	1.9	4,466
Karnataka	2001–02	1.16	1.2	5,737
Punjab	2001–02	1.87	1.89	5,066
Karnataka	2002–03	1.17	1.16	6,737
Punjab	2002–03	1.85	1.89	6,093
Karnataka	2003–04	1.17	1.13	8,438
Punjab	2003–04	1.87	1.88	7,073
Karnataka	2004–05	1.22	1.18	9,795
Punjab	2004–05	1.89	1.94	9,214
Karnataka	2005–06	1.24	1.22	11,976
Punjab	2005–06	1.88	1.94	11,197
Karnataka	2006–07	1.23	1.22	16,493
Punjab	2006–07	1.88	1.88	16,761
Karnataka	2007–08	1.24	1.21	18,999
Punjab	2007–08	1.88	1.87	19,507

Source: Centre for Monitoring Indian Economy (CMIE) reports for November 2000, March 2006,
and June 2010.
Note: Cropping intensity = gross cropped area/net sown area; Irrigation intensity = gross irrigated
area/net irrigated area; Credit to agriculture by commercial banks = amount of total credit advanced
(Rs)/gross cropped area (ha).

Table 9.10 Agricultural Productivity (AGP), Irrigation (IRRI), Fertilizers Consumption (FERT), Tractors Use (TRACT), and Rural Literacy Rate (LIT) in 15 Major States of India

State	Period	AGP	IRRI	FERT	TRACT	LIT
Andhra Pradesh	1980–83	6,276	36	56	19	29.5
Assam	1980–83	6,907	17	5	1	41.8
Bihar	1980–83	4,049	34	24	18	29.0
Gujarat	1980–83	5,693	23	41	29	45.6
Haryana	1980–83	6,229	62	71	170	39.9
Himachal Pradesh	1980–83	3,918	17	33	16	51.6
Jammu & Kashmir	1980–83	5,759	40	36	11	28.8
Karnataka	1980–83	4,990	13	37	20	39.8
Kerala	1980–83	12,334	13	49	6	82.2
Madhya Pradesh	1980–83	3,070	12	14	13	30.7
Maharashtra	1980–83	3,795	13	27	12	47.8
Orissa	1980–83	4,375	22	14	2	39.4
Punjab	1980–83	9,708	87	209	254	44.1
Rajasthan	1980–83	2,335	21	10	35	24.1
Tamil Nadu	1980–83	8,756	49	80	26	47.1
Uttar Pradesh	1980–83	5,808	47	75	82	30.2
West Bengal	1980–83	5,944	25	49	3	42.4
Andhra Pradesh	1990–93	8,728	40	137	52	40.5
Assam	1990–93	7,998	15	16	3	52.4
Bihar	1990–93	5,278	43	77	19	36.5
Gujarat	1990–93	6,640	29	75	70	54.6
Haryana	1990–93	9,682	76	175	444	53.5
Himachal Pradesh	1990–93	5,187	18	62	45	65.2
Jammu & Kashmir	1990–93	5,432	41	65	18	39.1
Karnataka	1990–93	6,342	23	82	37	50.8
Kerala	1990–93	14,655	12	111	9	89.2
Madhya Pradesh	1990–93	4,406	21	50	24	41.1
Maharashtra	1990–93	4,490	15	69	50	59.5
Orissa	1990–93	5,740	26	33	4	49.3
Punjab	1990–93	13,215	95	318	508	56.0
Rajasthan	1990–93	3,809	27	30	90	36.1
Tamil Nadu	1990–93	13,037	48	136	52	57.8
Uttar Pradesh	1990–93	8,355	62	129	201	40.8
West Bengal	1990–93	9,507	54	136	12	54.0
Andhra Pradesh	2003–06	11,537	39	185	85	65.7
Assam	2003–06	8,989	5	89	5	66.1
Bihar	2003–06	5,670	48	108	130	49.3
Gujarat	2003–06	11,836	37	120	150	60.8

(Contd.)

Table 9.10 (*Contd.*)

State	Period	AGP	IRRI	FERT	TRACT	LIT
Haryana	2003–06	11,569	84	307	549	70.2
Himachal Pradesh	2003–06	6,176	19	87	130	79.8
Jammu & Kashmir	2003–06	5,985	41	119	70	53.9
Karnataka	2003–06	6,994	25	118	60	65.0
Kerala	2003–06	13,858	15	98	10	90.5
Madhya Pradesh	2003–06	5,640	28	80	130	69.9
Maharashtra	2003–06	5,960	17	94	60	77.8
Orissa	2003–06	6,690	30	61	28	67.4
Punjab	2003–06	15,373	97	412	704	70.6
Rajasthan	2003–06	5,095	32	58	184	70.7
Tamil Nadu	2003–06	13,117	50	153	102	72.0
Uttar Pradesh	2003–06	9,894	70	205	397	62.1
West Bengal	2003–06	12,142	52	226	34	70.2

Sources: (1) For value of crop output and inputs data, G.S Bhalla and Gurmail Singh, 'Economic Liberalisation and Indian Agriculture', *Economic & Political Weekly*, 26 December 2009; and (2) For literacy rate, projected figures based on *Census of India* data.

Notes: (1) AGP = value of all crops output per ha of gross cropped area (Rs); IRRI = percentage of gross cropped area irrigated; FERT = fertilizers consumption (kg) per ha of gross cropped area; TRACT = number of tractors per ha of gross cropped area; and LIT = rural literacy rate; and (2) Bihar, Uttar Pradesh, and Madhya Pradesh include Jharkhand, Uttaranchal and Chhattisgarh, respectively.

Table 9.11   Percentage of Casual Workers to Total Workers (CASUAL), Unemployment Rate (UNEMP), Incidence of Poverty (POV), and Percentage of Urban Population (URBAN) in 15 Major States of India

State	Year	CASUAL	UNEMP	POV	URBAN
Andhra Pradesh	1983	39.6	1.25	28.91	24.12
Assam	1983	18.2	2.36	40.47	10.15
Bihar	1983	35.8	1.38	62.22	12.63
Gujarat	1983	30.7	1.43	32.79	31.88
Haryana	1983	17.9	2.84	21.37	22.5
Karnataka	1983	36.2	1.55	38.24	29.36
Kerala	1983	35.2	7.9	40.42	20.36
Madhya Pradesh	1983	25.7	0.6	49.78	20.94
Maharashtra	1983	34.5	1.81	43.44	35.87
Orissa	1983	36.8	0.6	65.29	12.15
Punjab	1983	14.9	2.34	16.18	28.11
Rajasthan	1983	11.6	0.73	34.46	21.46
Tamil Nadu	1983	42.3	3.1	51.66	33.23
Uttar Pradesh	1983	16	1.08	47.07	19.06

(*Contd.*)

Table 9.11 (*Contd.*)

State	Year	CASUAL	UNEMP	POV	URBAN
West Bengal	1983	31.5	4.11	54.85	27.12
Andhra Pradesh	1993–94	43.1	0.94	22.19	26.95
Assam	1993–94	26.2	5.7	40.86	11.54
Bihar	1993–94	41.1	2.2	54.96	13.2
Gujarat	1993–94	36.9	1.58	24.21	35.29
Haryana	1993–94	20.7	1.51	25.05	25.82
Karnataka	1993–94	34.8	1.42	33.16	31.77
Kerala	1993–94	40.7	7.77	25.43	26.27
Madhya Pradesh	1993–94	31.8	1.24	42.52	23.68
Maharashtra	1993–94	34.2	1.95	36.86	39.73
Orissa	1993–94	36.8	2.04	48.56	13.81
Punjab	1993–94	22.4	1.87	11.77	30.76
Rajasthan	1993–94	15.5	0.47	27.41	23.02
Tamil Nadu	1993–94	42.2	2.44	35.03	36.81
Uttar Pradesh	1993–94	19.7	1.11	40.85	20.17
West Bengal	1993–94	29.6	3.48	35.66	27.63
Andhra Pradesh	1999–2000	43.8	1.4	15.77	27.05
Assam	1999–2000	23.8	4.67	36.09	12.52
Bihar	1999–2000	41.1	2.43	42.6	13.33
Gujarat	1999–2000	35.2	0.87	14.07	37.01
Haryana	1999–2000	18.9	1.34	8.74	28.47
Karnataka	1999–2000	38.1	1.46	20.04	33.62
Kerala	1999–2000	40.1	8.62	12.72	26.02
Madhya Pradesh	1999–2000	36.4	1.04	37.43	24.76
Maharashtra	1999–2000	36.9	2.93	25.02	41.96
Orissa	1999–2000	44.1	2.51	47.15	14.78
Punjab	1999–2000	18.7	2.11	6.16	33.42
Rajasthan	1999–2000	14.9	0.78	15.28	23.32
Tamil Nadu	1999–2000	40.5	2.74	21.12	42.69
Uttar Pradesh	1999–2000	20.1	1.46	31.15	20.88
West Bengal	1999–2000	34.1	4.19	27.02	27.97

Sources: (1) NSSO reports on *Employment/Unemployment* for 1983 (38th round), 1993–94 (50th round) and 1999–2000 (55th round); and (2) Planning Commission (2001), *Human Development in India*.

Answers to Multiple-Choice Questions
(i) (b); (ii) (c) (iii) (b); (iv) (b); (v) (d); (vi) (a); (vii) (d).

10   Time Series Econometrics

The literature on time series econometrics has grown enormously over the past three decades or so. In this chapter, we introduce some important tools and techniques which are frequently used by the researchers working with time series data. After briefly describing the background that provoked recent advancements in this field, we define some important concepts of the time series econometrics literature. We discuss the tests of stationarity and cointegration, and explain the error correction mechanism. We discuss two important methods of forecasting, namely ARIMA and VAR. The tests of causality under Granger, Sims, and VAR methods have also been discussed. The issue of volatility in time series data has been discussed following ARCH/GARCH modelling approaches. A comprehensive section has been added to illustrate application of various tools to analyse time series data using the EViews software.

10.1 BACKGROUND

Methodological revolutions are not new in economics. We witnessed many revolutions in the past such as the Keynesian, monetarist, new classical, and so on. Each revolution called for a fundamental change in our way of thinking and also about how to model an economic phenomenon. However, since the mid-1980s both economics and econometrics have been passing through a new type of revolution, which is known as the 'unit root and cointegration revolution' (Rao 1994).

Prior to this new revolution, there was a consensus among the macroeconomists belonging to different schools over the fact that there was stability of long-run trend growth of output. The macroeconomists considered fluctuations from trend growth of output as temporary deviations. However, there was difference of opinion among them with regard to the efficacy of alternative short-run stabilization policies. The recent econometricians, led by Robert F. Engle and Clive W. J. Granger (winners of Nobel Prize in Economic Sciences in 2003), challenged this notion of stability of long-run trend growth of output.[1] They argued that the very data, which have been used to establish the so-called stability of long-run trend

---

[1] It needs mention that Nelson and Plosser (1982) in a provocative study using the US data observed that macroeconomic variables like GNP, exchange rate, interest rate, employment, money supply, stock prices, etc., behave like 'random walks'. As these series follow 'random walks', these are not 'trend-reverting'. Consequently, these economic variables do not revert back to long-run trend after a shock. This study paved the way for subsequent development of large literature in the field of macroeconometrics or time series econometrics.

growth of output, do not satisfy the stability requirement. According to them, an important stability requirement that the data should satisfy is that the means and variances of the variables, which are utilized to obtain the estimated relationship, should remain well-defined constants, and also independent of time. In other words, the variables have to be *stationary*.

The time series variables included in regression models need to be stationary because if their means and variances are changing, the computed t-statistics under the OLS regression fail to converge to their true values as sample size increases. In this situation, the conventional confidence intervals become invalid and hypothesis tests cannot be conducted as usual. Consequently, we might end up by accepting a wrong hypothesis that the variables have strong association between them although in reality there might not be any such association between the variables. This is known as the problem of 'spurious regression'.

Further, recent econometricians observed that most economic time series are non-stationary (i.e., they have unit roots), which renders the conclusion of stability of long-run trend growth of output in doubt. Thus, according to them, any applied macroeconometric work should start by examining the stationarity of the variables. The usual OLS technique can be applied to estimate the model only if the variables are stationary, i.e., they do not have unit roots. Otherwise, an alternative approach has to be followed, which is 'cointegration'.

Thus, stationarity, unit root, and cointegration are the fundamental concepts advanced by recent econometricians upon which further advancements of time series econometrics have taken place. So, in the next section, we clarify these and a few other concepts before we take up for discussion some select issues from the time series econometrics literature.

10.2 SOME IMPORTANT CONCEPTS

In this section, we define some concepts which arise frequently in the course of discussion on time series econometrics.

Stochastic Process

By a stochastic process, we mean a sequence of real valued random variables indexed by time. In time series, we suppose that for each time period we have a sample of size one (i.e., only one observation) on each of the random variables of the stochastic process. In other words, what we have is a *realization* of the stochastic process, which represents the sequence of observed data. Thus, the stochastic process may be viewed as the 'theoretical' or 'population' analogue of a time series, and, conversely, a time series may be considered a sample (or realization) from the stochastic process. For instance, the gross domestic product (GDP) of India (or any other country) for the years 1, 2, …, t may be viewed as a stochastic process in the sense that it is a sequence of random variables. The value of GDP that we observe in any particular year is a particular realization of all possible values. Therefore, we say that the GDP series is a stochastic process and the values of GDP observed over the years 1, 2, …, t are a particular realization (i.e., sample) of that process.

Stationary Stochastic Process

A stochastic process (time series) Y_t is said to be (*weakly* or *covariance*) stationary if its mean and variance are constant and independent of time and the covariances depend only upon the distance between two time periods, but not on time periods per se. So, Y_t is stationary when the following conditions hold.

$E(Y_t) = \mu$ = constant for all t;
$Var(Y_t) = \sigma^2$ = constant for all t; and
$Cov(Y_t, Y_{t-s}) = \gamma_s$ = constant for all $t \neq s$

These conditions imply that the mean and variance of the stationary series remain constant over time. In simple language, we say that these quantities remain same whether observations for the time series in Table 10.1 are for the period 1960 to 1985 or 1985 to 2010. If one or more of these conditions are violated, the time series is said to be non-stationary.

It has been found that the macroeconomic variables such as real interest rate, real exchange rate, growth rate of consumption, and growth rate of investment usually appear to be stationary. On the other hand, some examples of non-stationary series are nominal interest rate, inflation, unemployment rate, real money supply, nominal exchange rate, levels of GDP, consumption, and investment.

Table 10.1   Data on GDP and Consumption Expenditure for India

Year	CON	GDP	Year	CON	GDP	Year	CON	GDP
1960	54,456	63,108	1977	115,947	147,368	1994	246,724	322,203
1961	56,124	65,549	1978	117,497	155,781	1995	265,415	346,591
1962	57,377	67,602	1979	113,173	147,621	1996	288,577	372,784
1963	60,306	71,846	1980	122,014	157,577	1997	299,706	387,899
1964	64,923	77,189	1981	133,799	167,030	1998	327,867	411,923
1965	77,680	93,877	1982	139,328	172,819	1999	337,523	442,353
1966	76,683	93,843	1983	152,927	185,433	2000	353,228	460,182
1967	84,795	101,193	1984	154,360	192,523	2001	371,773	484,189
1968	87,657	104,607	1985	163,347	202,600	2002	370,454	502,428
1969	91,485	111,447	1986	174,478	212,260	2003	404,152	544,486
1970	96,252	117,192	1987	175,274	220,660	2004	408,187	589,559
1971	98,042	119,103	1988	190,431	241,926	2005	442,084	644,500
1972	96,911	118,449	1989	199,699	256,323	2006	473,873	704,256
1973	97,044	122,380	1990	203,065	270,495	2007	508,355	773,393
1974	99733	123,830	1991	214,370	273,372	2008	577,596	811,540
1975	109,166	135,157	1992	226,865	288,353	2009	610,838	885,430
1976	106,808	137,395	1993	238,108	302,101	2010	648,603	963,405

Source: World Bank, *National Accounts Data and OECD National Accounts Data File.*
Note: CON = consumption expenditure (in million $, 2000); and GDP = gross domestic product (in million $, 2000).

Purely Random or White Noise Stochastic Process

A purely random or *white noise* stochastic process is the one that has zero mean, constant variance, and is serially uncorrelated. On this basis, the error term in our classical linear regression model is *white noise* as we assume that it is independently and identically distributed with zero mean and constant variance.

Non-stationary Stochastic Process or Random Walk

Although we always wish to have stationary stochastic processes, quite often we obtain the non-stationary stochastic processes. An example of the non-stationary stochastic process is the *random walk* series. Good examples of *random walk* series from economics are stock prices and exchange rates.

Two types of random walks are usually observed in respect of economic time series, which are (*i*) random walk without drift, and (*ii*) random walk with drift.

Random Walk without Drift

Suppose u_t is a *white noise* error term with mean 0 and variance σ^2. Then the series Y_t is said to follow a random walk if

$$Y_t = Y_{t-1} + u_t \qquad (10.1)$$

This model shows that the value of Y at time t is equal to its value at time $t-1$ plus a random shock. This model does not have a constant term, and it takes the form of a first-order autoregressive [AR(1)] model.[2] It can be shown that although the mean does not vary over time for Y_t, the variance does, which violates one of the conditions of stationarity. To show this, we write

$$Y_1 = Y_0 + u_1$$
$$Y_2 = Y_1 + u_2 = Y_0 + u_1 + u_2$$
$$Y_3 = Y_2 + u_3 = Y_0 + u_1 + u_2 + u_3$$

In general, if the process started at some time 0 with a value of Y_0, we have

$$Y_t = Y_0 + \Sigma u_t \qquad (10.2)$$

Therefore,

$$E(Y_t) = E[Y_0 + \Sigma u_t] = Y_0 \qquad (10.3)$$

---

[2] An AR(1) model is the one where current value of a variable is determined by one-period lagged value of itself plus a *white noise* error term.

and

$$Var(Y_t) = E[Y_t - E(Y_t)]^2$$
$$= E[Y_0 + \Sigma u_t - Y_0]^2$$
$$= t.\sigma^2 \qquad (10.4)$$

It is clear that the mean of Y_t is equal to its initial value, which is constant. But variance of Y_t increases indefinitely with the progress of time (t). This violates the condition of stationarity. So we say that the random walk model (RWM) without drift represents a non-stationary stochastic process.

However, if we write (10.1) as

$$(Y_t - Y_{t-1}) = \Delta Y_t = u_t \qquad (10.5)$$

then ΔY_t becomes stationary because u_t is stationary. Thus, although Y_t is non-stationary, its first difference is stationary. So a random walk time series can be transformed into a stationary series by taking the first-difference of it.

Random Walk with Drift
Let us modify (10.1) as

$$Y_t = \theta + Y_{t-1} + u_t \qquad (10.6)$$

where θ is known as the 'drift parameter'.

The name drift comes from the fact that if we write the preceding equation as

$$Y_t - Y_{t-1} = \Delta Y_t = \theta + u_t \qquad (10.7)$$

then Y_t is shown to drift upward or downward depending upon θ being positive or negative. Model (10.6) is also an AR(1) model. For this model, we have

$$Y_1 = \theta + Y_0 + u_1$$
$$Y_2 = \theta + Y_1 + u_2 = \theta + \theta + Y_0 + u_1 + u_2$$
$$Y_3 = \theta + Y_2 + u_3 = \theta + \theta + \theta + Y_0 + u_1 + u_2 + u_3$$

In general, if the process started at some time 0 with a value of Y_0, then

$$Y_t = t.\theta + Y_0 + \Sigma u_t$$

Therefore,

$$E(Y_t) = E[t.\theta + Y_0 + \Sigma u_t] = t.\theta + Y_0 \qquad (10.8)$$

and

$$Var(Y_t) = E[Y_t - E(Y_t)]^2$$
$$= E[t.\theta + Y_0 + \Sigma u_t - t.\theta - Y_0]^2$$
$$= t.\sigma^2 \qquad (10.9)$$

It appears that for RWM with drift, both mean and variance increase over time, violating the conditions of weak stationarity.

Thus, it may be said that the random walk model, with or without drift, is a non-stationary stochastic process. Figure 10.1 graphically demonstrates two hypothetical random walk series—one with drift and another without drift.

Unit Root Stochastic Process

In time series literature, the random walk model is also known as the *unit root process*. If we rewrite the RWM (10.1) as

$$Y_t = \rho Y_{t-1} + u_t \qquad (10.10)$$

then model (10.10) transforms into a RWM without drift when $\rho = 1$. So when $\rho = 1$, we face what is known as the unit root problem, i.e., a situation of non-stationarity. We already

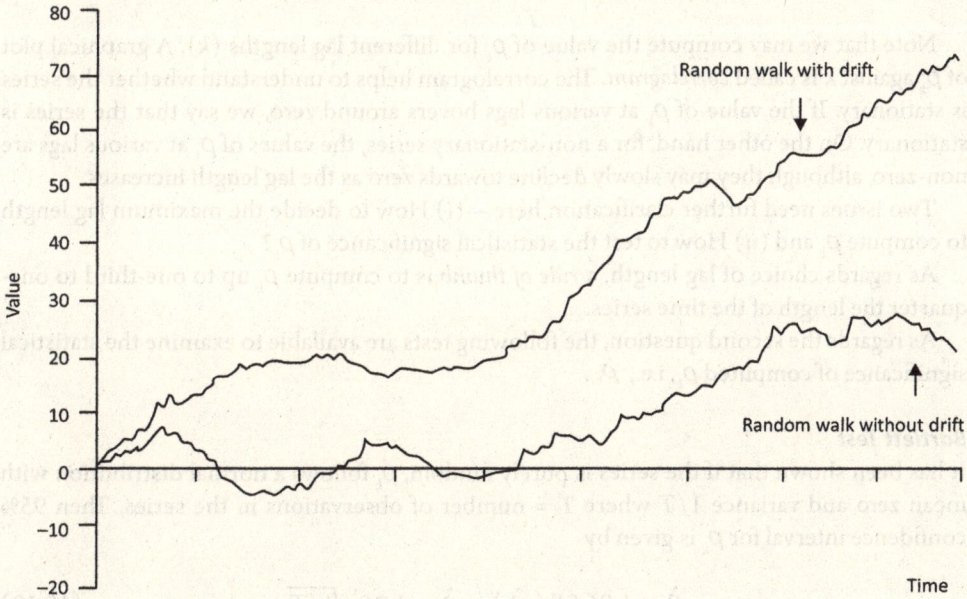

Figure 10.1   Random Walk Processes—With and Without Drift

Source: Author's own.

know that in this case the variance of Y_t changes over time. The name unit root is due to the fact that $\rho = 1$. Thus, the terms non-stationarity, random walk, and the unit root are used interchangeably.

10.3 TESTS FOR STATIONARITY

Graphical Approach
In general, stationarity of a series can be understood simply by plotting the series over time. If the series shows no tendency to drift upwards over time, it is stationary in mean. Otherwise, it is non-stationary in mean. Again, if a series starts to gyrate such that over time the amplitudes of the peaks and troughs increase, then the series is non-stationary in variance. Otherwise, it is stationary in variance.

Autocorrelation Function (ACF) and Correlogram
The stationarity of a given time series may by assessed by computing the value of its autocorrelation function (ρ). For the series Y_t, the value of ρ at lag k, denoted by ρ_k, is computed as[3]

$$\rho_k = \frac{\gamma_k}{\gamma_0} = \frac{Cov(Y_t, Y_{t-k})}{Var(Y_t)} \tag{10.11}$$

Note that we may compute the value of ρ_k for different lag lengths (k). A graphical plot of ρ_k against k is called *correlogram.* The correlogram helps to understand whether the series is stationary. If the value of ρ_k at various lags hovers around zero, we say that the series is stationary. On the other hand, for a non-stationary series, the values of ρ_k at various lags are non-zero, although they may slowly decline towards zero as the lag length increases.

Two issues need further clarification here—(i) How to decide the maximum lag length to compute ρ_k and (ii) How to test the statistical significance of ρ_k?

As regards choice of lag length, a *rule of thumb* is to compute ρ_k up to one-third to one-quarter the length of the time series.

As regards the second question, the following tests are available to examine the statistical significance of computed ρ_k, i.e., $\hat{\rho}_k$.

Bartlett Test
It has been shown that if the series is purely random, ρ_k follows a normal distribution with mean zero and variance $1/T$ where T = number of observations in the series. Then 95% confidence interval for ρ_k is given by

$$\hat{\rho}_k \pm 1.96 \, SE\,(\hat{\rho}_k) = \hat{\rho}_k \pm 1.96 \, \sqrt{1/T} \tag{10.12}$$

---

[3] As in practice where we work with sample data, this may be considered as sample autocorrelation function.

When ρ_k falls outside this interval, we reject the null hypothesis (H_N) that $\rho_k = 0$ and conclude that Y_t series is non-stationary. On the other hand, if ρ_k falls within this interval, we accept the H_N and conclude that Y_t is a stationary series. Stated differently, when the interval $\hat{\rho}_k \pm 1.96 SE(\hat{\rho}_k)$ does not include the value of 0 (zero), we reject the H_N: $\rho_k = 0$ at 95% level of confidence; otherwise, we accept it.

Box-Pierce Test

This test is applied to examine the validity of the null hypothesis (H_N) that all ρ_k's are simultaneously zero. Here we compute the Box-Pierce Q-statistic as

$$Q_{BP}^* = T \sum_{k=1}^{m} \hat{\rho}_k^2 \qquad (10.13)$$

where T = number of observations and m = maximum lag length.

It has been shown that Q_{BP}^* follows a Chi-square (χ^2) distribution with degrees of freedom = m. So when $Q_{BP}^* = \chi^{2*} > \chi^2$ at our chosen level of significance and given degrees of freedom, we reject the null hypothesis (H_N) that all ρ_k's are simultaneously zero, and conclude that the series is non-stationary.

Ljung-Box Test

This is a modified version of the Box-Pierce test. The modified Ljung-Box Q-statistic Q_{LB}^* is computed as

$$Q_{LB}^* = T(T+2) \sum_{k=1}^{m} \frac{\hat{\rho}_k^2}{T-k} \qquad (10.14)$$

Q_{LB}^* also follows a χ^2 distribution with degrees of freedom = m. Therefore, the *decision rule* is that when $Q_{LB}^* = \chi^{2*} > \chi^2$ at the chosen level of significance and degrees of freedom m, we reject the H_N that all ρ_k's are zero and conclude that there is non-stationarity.[4]

Unit Root Test

A more formal test of stationarity that has become widely popular is the unit root test. To understand this test, let us consider the following model [which is same as (10.10) above].

$$Y_t = \rho Y_{t-1} + u_t$$

where u_t is the *white noise* error term such that

$$E(u_t) = 0 \quad \text{for all } t$$
$$E(u_t^2) = \sigma^2 \quad \text{for all } t$$
$$E(u_t u_s) = 0 \quad t \neq s$$

[4] Comparing the Q_{BP}^* and Q_{LB}^* statistics, it has been observed that the former has poorer small sample properties compared with the latter, implying that it leads to the wrong decision too frequently for small samples.

We know that when $\rho = 1$, we face a non-stationary situation and conclude that Y_t has a unit root. This also implies that Y_t represents a random walk series. Therefore, one way to test if Y_t is non-stationary is to regress it on its one period lagged value, i.e., Y_{t-1}, and find out if $\hat{\rho}$ is statistically significantly equal to 1. If it is so, we conclude that Y_t is non-stationary.

Alternatively, we may rewrite the above model as

$$Y_t - Y_{t-1} = (\rho - 1)Y_{t-1} + u_t$$
$$\text{or} \quad \Delta Y_t = \delta Y_{t-1} + u_t \quad\quad\quad (10.15)$$
$$\text{where } \delta = (\rho - 1)$$

In practice, instead of estimating model (10.10), we estimate model (10.15) and test the validity of null hypothesis (H_N): $\delta = 0$. If $\delta = 0$, then $\rho = 1$, which means that Y_t has a unit root, and it is non-stationary.

To estimate model (10.15), we take first difference of Y_t and regress that on Y_{t-1}. In the next step, we test statistical significance of $\hat{\delta}$. An important point to note is that we cannot apply the conventional t-test here. This is because under the H_N: $\delta = 0$ (or $\rho = 1$), the computed-t of $\hat{\delta}$ does not have an approximate standard normal distribution even in large samples. In such a situation, we have to apply Dickey-Fuller (DF) or Augmented Dickey-Fuller (ADF) test.

Dickey-Fuller (1979) Test

Under the Dickey-Fuller (DF) test, after estimating model (10.15), we test the null hypothesis H_N: $\delta = 0$ (non-stationarity of Y_t). For this purpose, we compute the value of τ-statistic as

$$\tau_{\hat{\delta}}^{\cdot} = \frac{\hat{\delta} - \delta}{SE(\hat{\delta})} = \frac{\hat{\delta}}{SE(\hat{\delta})}$$

We then compare $\tau_{\hat{\delta}}^{\cdot}$ with critical-τ values, which have been initially tabulated by Dickey and Fuller using Monte Carlo experiments and subsequently extended by McKinnon (1991).

The results of the test are based on the following *decision rules*.

- If the absolute value of $\tau_{\hat{\delta}}^{\cdot}$ is greater than absolute value of critical-τ (alternatively, $\tau_{\hat{\delta}}^{\cdot}$ lies to the left of critical-τ, i.e., $\tau_{\hat{\delta}}^{\cdot}$ is more negative than critical-τ) at our chosen level of significance, we reject the H_N: $\delta = 0$ (or $\rho = 1$) and conclude that Y_t series is stationary.[5]

---

[5] Note that the Dickey-Fuller test is one-sided because the relevant alternative is that Y_t is stationary so that $\rho < 1$ or equivalently $\delta < 0$. It is also to be noted that the case of $\delta > 0$ is ruled out because in that case $\rho > 1$ and the series Y_t explodes.

- If $\tau_{\hat{\delta}}^{*}$ lies to the right of critical-τ (i.e., $\tau_{\hat{\delta}}^{*}$ is less negative than critical-τ) at our chosen level of significance, we accept the H_N: $\delta = 0$ (or $\rho = 1$) and conclude that the Y_t series has unit root, and hence non-stationary.

In practice, the Dickey-Fuller test is applied in two other forms:

$$\Delta Y_t = \alpha + \delta Y_{t-1} + u_t \qquad (10.16)$$

$$\Delta Y_t = \alpha + \beta t + \delta Y_{t-1} + u_t \qquad (10.17)$$

where α is a constant (drift) and t is a time trend. For all these models, the null hypothesis is H_N: $\delta = 0$ (presence of unit root or non-stationarity for Y_t). In practice, model (10.15) is considered if the time series has stochastic trend but no drift, model (10.16) is considered when the series has both stochastic trend and drift,[6] and model (10.17) is considered when the series has everything—drift, deterministic trend, and stochastic trend.

An important point to note is that the critical-τ values are different for these models. However, standard econometrics software packages like EViews provide proper critical values for the τ-statistic.

Augmented Dickey-Fuller (ADF) Test

The ADF test is same as the Dickey-Fuller test, except that the Dickey-Fuller regression equations [models (10.15) through (10.17)] are augmented by including m lags of the dependent variable (ΔY_t) to correct any serial correlation in the disturbance term. Here also we have three augmented models, which can be estimated and the null hypothesis H_N: $\delta = 0$ can be tested by using a τ-statistic. The models are

$$\Delta Y_t = \delta Y_{t-1} + \sum_{i=1}^{m} \gamma_i \, \Delta Y_{t-i} + u_t \qquad (10.18)$$

$$\Delta Y_t = \alpha + \delta Y_{t-1} + \sum_{i=1}^{m} \gamma_i \, \Delta Y_{t-i} + u_t \qquad (10.19)$$

$$\Delta Y_t = \alpha + \beta t + \delta Y_{t-1} + \sum_{i=1}^{m} \gamma_i \, \Delta Y_{t-i} + u_t \qquad (10.20)$$

where, as before, u_t is a white noise error term.

These equations incorporate difference terms $\Delta Y_{t-1} = (Y_{t-1} - Y_{t-2})$, $\Delta Y_{t-2} = (Y_{t-2} - Y_{t-3})$, etc. The number of difference terms to be included is determined by the frequency of data. Empirical researchers found that for annual data, one or two lags suffice in most cases, while

---

[6] While model (10.16) usually fits into the financial time series such as interest rates and exchange rates, model (10.17) fits into trending time series like asset prices or the levels of macroeconomic aggregates like real GDP.

twelve lags might be needed for monthly data. However, Schwert (1989) suggested the following *rule of thumb* to determine the maximum number of lagged terms (m) in the ADF test equations.[7]

$$m = \text{integer part of } \left[12.\left(\frac{T}{100}\right)^{\frac{1}{4}} \right]$$

where T = total time points for which data are available.

The *decision rules* under the ADF test are same as for the DF test.[8] As before, if $\tau_{\hat{\delta}}^{*}$ lies to the left of critical-τ at our chosen level of significance, we reject the null hypothesis (H_N: $\delta = 0$) and conclude that Y_t series is stationary.

While conducting the ADF test, quite often we are not sure about which of the three ADF models would be appropriate.[9] In the absence of any prior idea about the data-generating process (or stochastic properties) of the time series under consideration, we may follow the procedure suggested by Doldado, Jenkinson, and Sosvilla-Rivero [reported in Enders (2004, 212–14)], which starts from the estimation of the most general model given by (10.20) and then answering a set of questions regarding the appropriateness of each model and moving to the next model. This procedure has been illustrated in Figure 10.2 below.

However, although useful, this procedure should not be applied mechanically. Plotting the data and observing the graph is sometimes quite useful to obtain an idea about the presence or absence of drift (intercept), deterministic trend, and unit root (or stochastic trend) in the series.

Phillips-Perron (PP) Test

The DF/ADF tests are based on the assumptions that the error term is serially independent and has a constant variance. Thus, while using these tests, we have to ensure that these assumptions are valid.

Phillips and Perron (1988) developed a generalization of the ADF test procedure that allows for less restrictive assumptions concerning the distribution of error terms. The test regression here is also the AR(1) process:

$$\Delta Y_t = \delta Y_{t-1} + u_t$$

---

[7] Alternatively, we may determine the value of m by applying some information criteria (AIC, SIC, etc.). There is another method suggested by Ng and Perron (1995) in which a maximum value of m (m_{max}) is set first. Next the ADF model is estimated with $m = m_{max}$. If the absolute value of the t-statistic for testing the significance of the last lagged difference is greater than 1.6, then $m = m_{max}$ is accepted and the unit root test performed. Otherwise, the lag length is reduced by one and the process is repeated.

[8] The critical-τ values of the DF test are applicable under the ADF test.

[9] Note that the three ADF models represent three different data-generating processes.

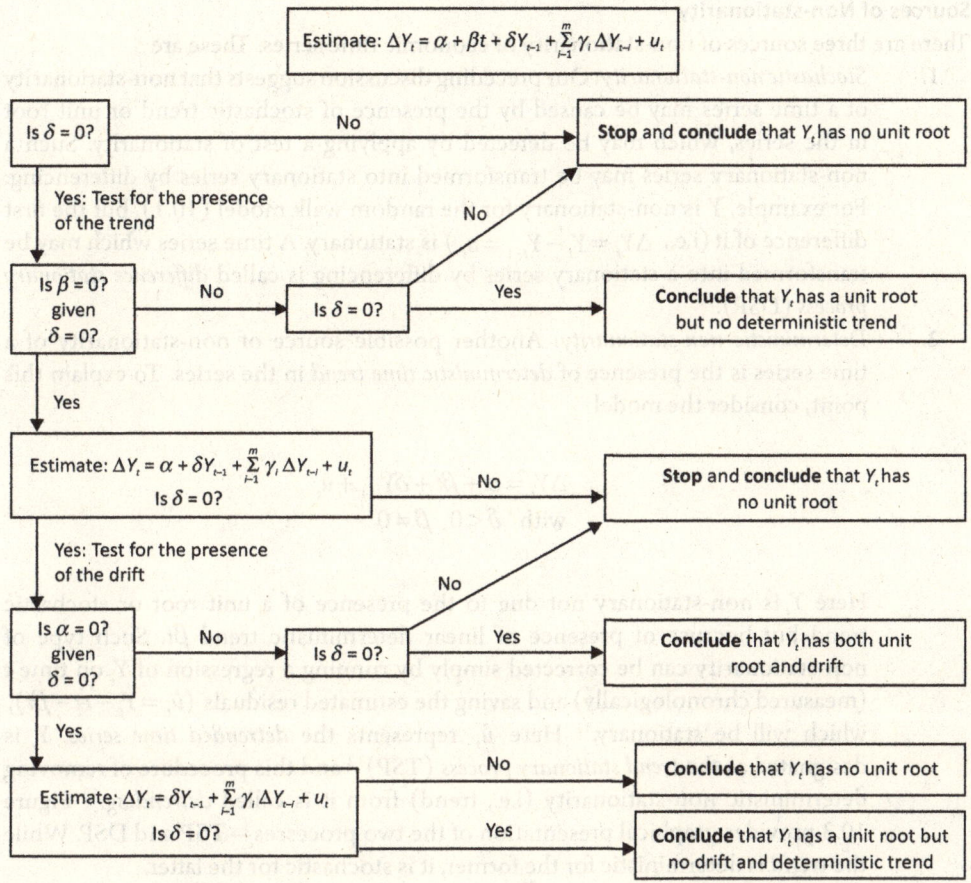

Figure 10.2   A Procedure to Test Unit Root by Applying the ADF Test

Source: Enders (2004, 213).

While the ADF test corrects for presence of serial correlation by adding lagged differenced terms on the right hand side of the above model, the PP test makes a correction to the computed τ-statistic of the estimated coefficient of δ to account for serial correlation in u_t. So the PP τ-statistic is just a modification of the ADF τ-statistic that takes into account the less restrictive nature of the error process. Further, it has been shown that asymptotic distribution of the PP τ-statistic is the same as the distribution of ADF τ-statistic. So the ADF critical values are still applicable here.

As with the ADF test, the PP test can be performed with the inclusion of a constant, a constant and linear trend, or neither in the test regression.

Sources of Non-stationarity

There are three sources of non-stationarity of economic time series. These are

1. *Stochastic non-stationarity*: Our preceding discussion suggests that non-stationarity of a time series may be caused by the presence of stochastic trend or unit root in the series, which may be detected by applying a test of stationarity. Such a non-stationary series may be transformed into stationary series by differencing. For example, Y_t is non-stationary for the random walk model (10.1), but the first difference of it (i.e., $\Delta Y_t = Y_t - Y_{t-1} = u_t$) is stationary. A time series which may be transformed into a stationary series by differencing is called *difference stationary process* (DSP).[10]

2. *Deterministic non-stationarity*: Another possible source of non-stationarity of a time series is the presence of *deterministic time trend* in the series. To explain this point, consider the model

$$\Delta Y_t = \alpha + \beta t + \delta Y_{t-1} + u_t$$
$$\text{with } \delta < 0, \ \beta \neq 0$$

Here Y_t is non-stationary not due to the presence of a unit root or stochastic trend but because of presence of linear deterministic trend βt. Such type of non-stationarity can be corrected simply by running a regression of Y_t on time t (measured chronologically) and saving the estimated residuals ($\hat{u}_t = Y_t - \hat{\alpha} - \hat{\beta} t$), which will be stationary.[11] Here $\hat{u}_t$ represents the *detrended time series*. Y_t is designated as the *trend stationary process* (TSP)[12] and this procedure of removing deterministic non-stationarity (i.e., trend) from it is called *detrending*.[13] Figure 10.3 provides graphical presentation of the two processes—TSP and DSP. While the trend is deterministic for the former, it is stochastic for the latter.

3. *Non-stationarity due to structural break*: A third type of non-stationarity may arise due to the presence of structural break in the series. A structural break appears

---

[10] Shocks to a difference stationary process has a permanent effect meaning that the level of the variable will be shifted permanently after the shock has occurred. But shocks to a stationary series are necessarily temporary such that the effects of the shocks dissipate and the series reverts to its long-run mean level. For this reason, the stationary series are needed for the purpose of forecasting.

[11] The other approach is to include t as an additional variable in the model that includes two trended variables (one dependent and other independent). This point is further discussed below.

[12] The mean of a TSP grows around a fixed (deterministic) trend. It tends to evolve around a steady, upward sloping, curve without a big swing away from that curve. Thus, the effects of shocks in a trend stationary series are temporary implying that the level of the variable is not influenced in the long run.

[13] It is clear that both TSP and DSP are 'trending' over time, and we need to follow a correct approach to make them stationary. If, mistakenly, we first difference the TSP, that will remove non-stationarity, but at the expense of introducing an MA(1) structure into the errors. On the other hand, if we attempt to detrend a series that is DSP, we will not remove non-stationarity.

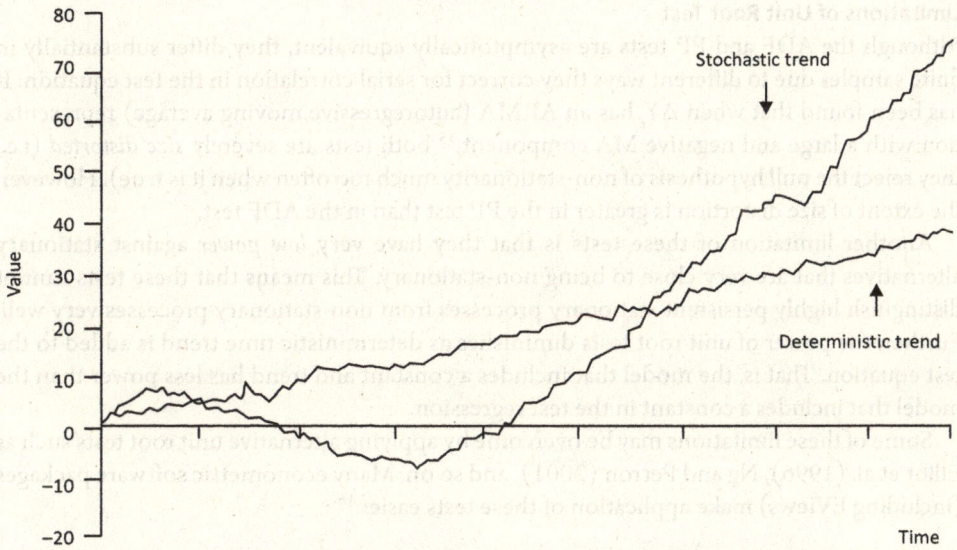

Figure 10.3 Time Series with Deterministic and Stochastic Trends

Source: Author's own.

when there is an unexpected shift in the series. This may happen for a variety of reasons such as changes in economic policy, changes in the structure of the economy, and so on. Existence of break in the time series not only makes the series non-stationary but also renders the standard tests of stationarity (e.g., DF/ADF and PP) ineffective. Moreover, a regression model that neglects such break (if any) may provide misleading basis for inference and forecasting. Therefore, while working with time series data, it is necessary to check the presence of structural break in the series.[14] Once the breakpoint has been identified, one may run the DF/ADF regression model again by incorporating a dummy variable to account for the break point. The result based on such a model is likely to be more reliable to understand stationarity of the series.

---

[14] Several breakpoint tests are available. For example, Perron's (1989) modified ADF unit root test includes dummy variable(s) to account for one exogenous (or known) breakpoint in the series. Another test that follows from Quandt (1960) and Andrews (1993), popularly known as the Quandt-Andrews test, seeks to determine the breakpoint in the time series endogenously. This methodology has been further extended by Bai and Perron (1998, 2003) to identify multiple structural breaks in the time series. We do not discuss these tests here as that is beyond the scope of this book. An introductory discussion on the breakpoint test in time series is available in Stock and Watson (2011, 556–61). A comprehensive review of literature on the methodologies to deal with structural breaks is provided by Perron (2006).

Limitations of Unit Root Test

Although the ADF and PP tests are asymptotically equivalent, they differ substantially in finite samples due to different ways they correct for serial correlation in the test equation. It has been found that when ΔY_t has an ARMA (autoregressive moving average) representation with a large and negative MA component,[15] both tests are severely *size distorted* (i.e., they reject the null hypothesis of non-stationarity much too often when it is true). However, the extent of size distortion is greater in the PP test than in the ADF test.

Another limitation of these tests is that they have very *low power* against stationary alternatives that are very close to being non-stationary. This means that these tests cannot distinguish highly persistent stationary processes from non-stationary processes very well. Further, the power of unit root tests diminishes as deterministic time trend is added to the test equation. That is, the model that includes a constant and trend has less power than the model that includes a constant in the test regression.

Some of these limitations may be overcome by applying alternative unit root tests such as Elliot et al. (1996), Ng and Perron (2001), and so on. Many econometric software packages (including EViews) make application of these tests easier.[16]

10.4 SPURIOUS REGRESSION PROBLEM

On the basis of our previous discussion, we can say that if Y_t and X_t are non-stationary variables, their means and/or variances are changing, i.e., they exhibit trends. In this situation, if we regress Y_t on X_t, we would have high R^2 value. Here high value of R^2 is obtained not necessarily because of strong relationship between the two variables, but because of common trends in the variables. This leads to a situation of 'spurious regression'.

Granger-Newbold suggested the following *rule of thumb* to diagnose the spurious regression result: if the value of R^2 is greater than the value of Durbin-Watson d-statistic or if $R^2 \simeq 1$, then we have reason to suspect that the regression result is spurious.

How to Avoid Spurious Regression Problem?

Two methods are suggested to avoid the problem of spurious regression. These are (*i*) inclusion of a trend term in the regression model and (*ii*) differencing.

Trend Term Inclusion

The common practice is to regress Y_t on X_t and t. The idea is that inclusion of the trend variable (t) would have the effect of detrending both Y_t and X_t. However, recent econometricians have criticized this method of detrending data. According to them, this is a valid practice if the trend is deterministic rather than stochastic (see Figure 10.3). If the trend is stochastic (i.e., variable), the practice of detrending data by a single trend variable will be misleading. In a situation of stochastic trend, we may observe one trend line for one sub-period while different trend line for the other. Whether or not the trend is deterministic or stochastic

---

[15] For meanings of ARMA and MA processes, refer to section 10.6.1 below.

[16] We do not discuss these tests here as that is outside the purview of this book.

may be known by applying the unit root test. If the time series has unit root, it indicates the presence of variable trend. In this situation, inclusion of a single trend term in the regression equation doesn't help.

Differencing

To understand the rationale of this method, consider the random walk model $Y_t = \rho Y_{t-1} + u_t$. It is clear that when $\rho = 1$, Y_t has a unit root and is non-stationary. Here, first-differencing of the series gives $\Delta Y_t = Y_t - Y_{t-1} = u_t$ which is *white noise* or stationary. So when both Y_t and X_t have unit roots, instead of regressing Y_t on X_t, it is better to regress ΔY_t on ΔX_t.

However, the main problem here is that using differenced variables instead of variables in levels leads to loss of valuable information in the data. Further, the model that uses differenced variables does not provide the long-run relationship between the two variables, which is provided by the model that considers the variables in levels. Moreover, using differenced variables, we are unable to connect the short-run and long-run dimensions of their relation. This is possible when we run the levels regression.

10.5 COINTEGRATION AND ERROR CORRECTION MECHANISM

Granger (1981) and Engle and Granger (1987) offered a solution to the spurious regression problem by introducing the concept of cointegration. Cointegration also offered a remedy to the problem of differencing mentioned above. Cointegrating regression retains the terms in levels but only in linear combinations that are stationary.[17]

To understand the idea of cointegration, let us clarify the notion of *integrated series*. Suppose we have data on Y_t which represents a non-stationary or random walk series. Now if Y_t is differenced once and the differenced series becomes stationary, we say that Y_t is integrated of order 1 [denoted by $Y_t \sim I(1)$]. If Y_t is differenced twice and the differenced series becomes stationary, then Y_t is integrated of order 2 $[Y_t \sim I(2)]$.[18] In general, if Y_t is differenced d times to make it stationary, then it is integrated of order d $[Y_t \sim I(d)]$.[19] In brief,

$$\begin{pmatrix} \text{Order of} \\ \text{integration} \\ \text{of a series} \end{pmatrix} = \begin{pmatrix} \text{Number of times the series} \\ \text{needs to be differenced in} \\ \text{order to make it stationary} \end{pmatrix} = \begin{pmatrix} \text{Number} \\ \text{of} \\ \text{unit roots} \end{pmatrix}$$

Now the Granger Theorem states that if both Y_t and X_t are $I(d)$, then there exists a linear combination of them that is integrated of order b, where $b < d$. It follows that when both Y_t

[17] The term cointegration has been coined by Clive W.J. Granger.

[18] Most economic data series are $I(1)$ which become stationary after first-differencing. A few exceptions are series for consumer price index, implicit price deflator, nominal money supply, nominal wages, and so on, which are usually $I(2)$.

[19] Needless to mention, if $d = 0$, the series is already stationary, i.e., $I(0)$ and it requires no differencing.

and X_t are $I(1)$, the linear combination of them is $I(0)$ or stationary. In this situation, we do not face the problem of spurious regression while estimating equation

$$Y_t = a + bX_t + \varepsilon_t \qquad (10.21)$$

Since $\varepsilon_t \sim I(0)$ or white noise, the linear combination of Y_t and X_t, i.e., $Y_t - a - bX_t$ is stationary. Thus, a meaningful (non-spurious) long-run relationship between Y_t and X_t is obtained by estimating equation (10.21). The estimated equation $\hat{Y}_t = \hat{a} + \hat{b}X_t$ represents the long-run relationship between the two variables. It is called the cointegrating regression and $(\hat{a}, \hat{b})$ is the cointegrating vector. The OLS estimates ($\hat{a}$ and $\hat{b}$) have efficiency and consistency properties. The estimated error ($\hat{\varepsilon}_t = Y_t - \hat{a} - \hat{b}X_t$) connects Y_t and X_t in the long run.

Some examples of cointegrated economic variables are short- and long-term interest rates, prices and wages, wholesale and retail prices, imports and exports, spot and future prices of a commodity, prices at home and prices abroad, household consumption and expenditures, and exchange rates determined in different markets. Although individually these variables are $I(1)$, a particular linear combination of them is likely to be $I(0)$.

10.5.1 Engle-Granger (EG) Cointegration Test

Engle and Granger (1987) provided a simple test to examine the presence of cointegrating relationship (i.e., long-run relationship) between the variables. The method runs through the following steps.

Step I: Test the variables for their order of integration by applying the DF/ADF test. There are different possibilities here.

(i)   If both variables are $I(0)$, it is not necessary to proceed to test the possibility of cointegration. Here one should continue with the OLS regression analysis since standard time series methods are applicable to the stationary variables.

(ii)   If the variables are integrated of different order, conclude that they are not cointegrated.[20]

(iii)   If both variables are integrated of same order, proceed to the next step.

Step II: If both the variables are $I(1)$ (which is usually the case for most economic time series), apply the OLS method to estimate equation (10.21) and generate the series of estimated residuals $\hat{\varepsilon}_t = Y_t - \hat{a} - \hat{b}X_t$.

Step III: Check stationarity of $\hat{\varepsilon}_t$ to determine if the variables were actually cointegrated. For this purpose, apply the ADF test. The form of the ADF test equation here is

$$\Delta\hat{\varepsilon}_t = \delta\hat{\varepsilon}_{t-1} + \sum_{i=1}^{m}\alpha_i\Delta\hat{\varepsilon}_{t-i} + v_t \qquad (10.22)$$

[20] Note that the autoregressive distributed lag (ARDL) model has been advocated recently to examine 'cointegration' among stochastic variables with different orders of integration.

Now testing the null hypothesis H_N: $\delta = 0$, we conclude whether $\hat{\varepsilon}_t$ is $I(0)$ (i.e., stationary) or not. When the H_N gets rejected, our conclusion is that $\hat{\varepsilon}_t \sim I(0)$ and the variables are cointegrated.[21]

Limitations of Engle-Granger Test

Although the EG method is very easy to understand and apply, it has many limitations.[22]

First, this test doesn't say anything about which of the variables (Y_t or X_t) is to be used as regressor and why. It has been shown that the result of cointegration may change depending upon which variable is used as the regressor, especially when we have a small sample. The situation becomes far more difficult when we have more than two variables.

Second, the most important problem of EG method is that when there are more than two variables, there remains a possibility of having more than one cointegrating relationship. The EG method cannot examine such a possibility and provides no information about the number of cointegrating vectors.

Third, under the EG test, we first estimate the model by OLS to generate the series for residuals whose stationarity is examined subsequently by applying the DF/ADF test. Hence any error introduced at the stage of generation of residual series (due to possible non-stationarity of the original series) is carried into the next step.

Fourth, structural breaks in the time series may also cause difficulties in cointegration analysis following the EG approach.

10.5.2 Error Correction Mechanism (ECM)[23]

It clearly emerges from our previous discussion that individually two series may be non-stationary, yet they may be cointegrated. The cointegrating equation gives long-run relationship between the two variables. However, cointegrating equation does not shed any light on short-run dynamics although its existence indicates that there must be some short-term forces that are responsible for keeping the long-run relationship intact. Thus, it is necessary to construct a more comprehensive model which combines short-run and long-run dynamics. This is done by the error correction model (ECM).

To understand the features of ECM, consider two series Y_t and X_t which are $I(1)$ so that their linear combination $\hat{\varepsilon}_t = Y_t - \hat{a} - \hat{b}X_t$ is $I(0)$. Then the long-run equilibrium relationship between the two variables is represented by $\hat{Y}_t = \hat{a} + \hat{b}X_t$. Corresponding to this long-run equilibrium relationship, we can write the ECM as

$$\Delta Y_t = \phi + \gamma \Delta X_t + \lambda \hat{\varepsilon}_{t-1} + w_t \qquad (10.23)$$

---

[21] It is to be noted that the critical values for testing stationarity of $\hat{\varepsilon}_t$ are different from the standard critical values of the ADF test used for testing stationarity of a variable. In fact, to have more robust conclusion regarding presence of cointegration, the critical values for testing stationarity of $\hat{\varepsilon}_t$ are required to be more negative.

[22] These limitations are avoided when Johansen's cointegration test is applied. However, we do not discuss Johansen's test as that is beyond the scope of this book. Interested readers may refer to Enders (2004, Chapter 6).

[23] Our discussion here follows Koop (2009, 173–5).

where $\hat{\varepsilon}_{t-1} = (Y_{t-1} - \hat{Y}_{t-1}) = (Y_{t-1} - \hat{a} - \hat{b}X_{t-1})$ is one-period lagged value of the error from the cointegrating regression and w_t is the error term in the ECM.

The ECM equation (10.23) states that ΔY_t depends not only on ΔX_t but also on the equilibrating error term $\hat{\varepsilon}_{t-1}$. Inclusion of $\hat{\varepsilon}_{t-1}$ is unique to the ECM and gives it its name. When $\hat{\varepsilon}_{t-1}$ is non-zero (positive or negative), there is disequilibrium in the short run. However, equilibrium will be restored in the long run if and only if $\lambda < 0$.[24] This point is clarified below.

Suppose $\Delta X_t = 0$ and $\hat{\varepsilon}_{t-1}$ is positive. In this situation, Y_{t-1} is too high to be in equilibrium, i.e., $Y_{t-1} > \hat{Y}_{t-1}$. But as $\lambda < 0$, the term $\lambda\hat{\varepsilon}_{t-1}$ is negative and so ΔY_t will be negative to restore equilibrium. Thus, if Y_{t-1} is above its equilibrium level, it will fall in the next period and the equilibrium error will be corrected in the model. Similarly, if $\hat{\varepsilon}_{t-1}$ is negative, i.e., $Y_{t-1} < \hat{Y}_{t-1}$, then $\lambda\hat{\varepsilon}_{t-1}$ will be positive, which will cause ΔY_t to be positive, leading Y_{t-1} to rise in period t.

Thus, the ECM has both long-run and short-run properties built into it. The long-run properties are embedded in the $\hat{\varepsilon}_{t-1}$ term. The short-run behaviour is partially captured by the equilibrium error term, which says that, if Y_t is out of equilibrium, it will be pulled towards it in the next period. Further aspects of short-run behaviour are captured by the inclusion of ΔX_t as an explanatory variable. This term implies that, if X_t changes, the equilibrium value of Y_t will also change and that Y_t will change accordingly. It is clear that γ captures the impact of short-run disturbances of X_t on Y_t, while λ captures the adjustment towards long-run equilibrium.

Statistical Properties of ECM
1.   We do not have to worry about the spurious regression problem. As Y_t and X_t are both $I(1)$, ΔY_t and ΔX_t are stationary.
2.   Since Y_t and X_t are cointegrated, the equilibrium error is stationary. Since all the variables in the ECM are stationary, we can estimate the ECM by OLS and conduct tests of significance of estimated coefficients using the usual t-test procedure.

10.6 ARIMA FORECASTING
An important purpose of constructing a time series model is to use that for the purpose of forecasting. A forecast is a quantitative estimate about possible future events which is developed on the basis of past and present information. Forecasts about future events are made by extrapolating the model beyond the period over which it has been estimated.

[24] This is the stability condition. Intuitively speaking, $\lambda < 0$ ensures that equilibrium errors are corrected. If $\lambda > 0$, then equilibrium errors will be magnified. Thus, when value of λ is negative and statistically significant, it implies that if there is any short-term disturbance from the long-run stable relationship, such a disturbance would be corrected over time and long-run stable relationship will be restored. On the other hand, if λ is positive and statistically significant, it implies that if there is any short-term disturbance, such a disturbance will not be corrected over time and long-run stable relationship will not be restored.

Indeed, the forecasts are frequently used as guides for private and public policymaking process. Governments, financial institutions, and policy organizations require forecasts of major economic variables such as gross domestic product, population growth, unemployment, interest rates, inflation, job growth, production, consumption, and so on. These forecasts are an integral part of the guidance behind monetary and fiscal policy and budgeting plans and decisions made by governments. They are instrumental in strategic planning decisions made by business organizations and financial institutions.

In this section, we discuss one of the most popular approaches towards econometric forecasting which is known as the Autoregressive Integrated Moving Average (ARIMA) forecasting method. Box and Jenkins (1976) introduced first the ARIMA models and hence this method is known as the Box-Jenkins methodology. Clearly, the term ARIMA has been derived from AR = autoregressive, I = integrated, and MA = moving average.

Before proceeding to discuss the ARIMA models, it is necessary to note that the forecasting methods that we are going to discuss assume that the underlying time series are stationary or they can be made stationary with appropriate transformations. Further, ARIMA models can be constructed both for a single time series as well as for multivariate time series. While the former is known as univariate ARIMA model, the latter is called multivariate ARIMA model. We discuss below the univariate ARIMA models.

10.6.1 AR, MA, and ARMA Modelling of Time Series Data

The question that we are faced with is—how the series for a time series variable, say Y_t, is generated? An answer to this question is that the process of generation of the series Y_t can be described or modelled in a variety of ways—as an autoregressive (AR) process or a moving average (MA) process or an autoregressive moving average (ARMA) process. Let us understand the features of these processes.

The AR Model

An autoregressive process (or model) is one where the current value of a variable Y_t depends upon only the value that the variable took in previous periods plus an error term. The simplest form of autoregressive model is the autoregressive model of order one, denoted by AR(1), which is written as

$$Y_t = \phi_1 Y_{t-1} + u_t \qquad (10.24)$$

In this model, we do not include a constant for simplicity, $|\phi_1|$ is assumed to be less than one to ensure stationarity of Y_t,[25] and u_t is the *white noise* error term. This equation implies that the value of Y at time t is some proportion $(=\phi_1)$ of its value at time $t-1$ plus a random shock or disturbance at time t. Here we say that Y_t follows a first-order autoregressive process, or it is AR(1).

---

[25] The case of $|\phi_1| > 1$ is also ruled out as in that case Y_t will tend to get bigger and bigger each period so that we have an explosive series.

The AR(p) model is a generalization of the AR(1) model. The number in the parenthesis indicates the order of the autoregressive process and hence the number of lagged dependent variables in the model. For example, the AR(2) model will have the form

$$Y_t = \phi_1 Y_{t-1} + \phi_2 Y_{t-2} + u_t \qquad (10.25)$$

and the AR(p) model will be

$$Y_t = \phi_1 Y_{t-1} + \phi_2 Y_{t-2} + \dots + \phi_p Y_{t-p} + u_t \qquad (10.26)$$

Note that in the preceding models only the current and past values of Y are involved and there are no other regressors.

PROPERTIES OF AR MODELS
The AR(1) model has the following properties.[26]

(i)   Mean of $Y_t = 0$ $\qquad\qquad\qquad\qquad\qquad\qquad\qquad\qquad\qquad$ (10.27)

(ii) $Var(Y_t) = \gamma_0 = \dfrac{\sigma_u^2}{(1 - \phi_1^2)}$ $\qquad\qquad\qquad\qquad\qquad\qquad$ (10.28)

(iii) $Cov(Y_t, Y_{t-1}) = \gamma_1 = \dfrac{\phi_1 \sigma_u^2}{(1 - \phi_1^2)}$ $\qquad\qquad\qquad\qquad\quad$ (10.29)

This is autocovariance at lag 1. We may compute the autocovariances for lags 2, 3, ..., p, denoted by $\gamma_2, \gamma_3, \dots, \gamma_p$, as

$$\gamma_2 = \frac{\phi_1^2 \sigma_u^2}{(1 - \phi_1^2)}, \gamma_3 = \frac{\phi_1^3 \sigma_u^2}{(1 - \phi_1^2)}, \dots, \gamma_p = \frac{\phi_1^p \sigma_u^2}{(1 - \phi_1^2)} \text{ respectively.}$$

(iv)   The autocorrelation function (ρ) of Y_t at various lags (p) is obtained by dividing the autocovariance by the variance of Y_t. Thus,

$$\rho_1 = \frac{\gamma_1}{\gamma_0} = \frac{\phi_1 \sigma_u^2}{(1 - \phi_1^2)} \bigg/ \frac{\sigma_u^2}{(1 - \phi_1^2)} = \phi_1$$

$$\rho_2 = \frac{\gamma_2}{\gamma_0} = \frac{\phi_1^2 \sigma_u^2}{(1 - \phi_1^2)} \bigg/ \frac{\sigma_u^2}{(1 - \phi_1^2)} = \phi_1^2$$

[26] For simple algebraic proofs of properties of both AR and MA models, refer to Enders (2004), Asteriou and Hall (2007), and Brooks (2008).

Similarly, the autocorrelation function at lag p is given by

$$\rho_p = \frac{\gamma_p}{\gamma_0} = \frac{\phi_1^p \sigma_u^2}{(1-\phi_1^2)} \bigg/ \frac{\sigma_u^2}{(1-\phi_1^2)} = \phi_1^p \qquad (10.30)$$

It follows from (10.30) that since $|\phi_1| < 1$, the autocorrelation function for the AR series will decay exponentially as the lag length (p) increases.

(v)   The partial autocorrelation function (PACF) of the AR process will be high and significant up to a certain lag, say k, and zero for lags beyond k. The PACF measures the correlation between an observation s periods ago and the current observation, after controlling for observations at intermediate lags, i.e., the correlation between Y_t and Y_{t-k}, after removing the effects of Y_{t-k+1}, Y_{t-k+2}, ..., Y_{t-1}.

The MA Model

The AR process is not the only mechanism that may have generated Y_t. In some situation, it might be possible to capture the process of generation of Y_t series by the following model.

$$Y_t = u_t + \theta u_{t-1} \qquad (10.31)$$

where, as before, u_t is a *white noise* error term. Model (10.31) implies that Y_t is determined as a moving average of the current and (immediate) past values of the error term. This model is called the first-order moving average or MA(1) model.

The general form of the MA model is an MA(q) model of the form

$$Y_t = u_t + \theta_1 u_{t-1} + \theta_2 u_{t-2} + ... + \theta_q u_{t-q} \qquad (10.32)$$

It appears that a moving average process is simply a linear combination of *white noise* processes, so that Y_t depends on the current and previous values of a *white noise* error term. Further, as long as q is finite, the MA(q) process is stationary as it is an average of q stationary *white noise* error terms which are stationary.

PROPERTIES OF MA MODELS

(i)   Mean of Y_t is zero as it is a moving average of white noise error terms.

(ii)   For the MA(1) model, $Var(Y_t) = (1 + \theta^2) \sigma_u^2$.

(iii) $Cov(Y_t, Y_{t-1}) = \theta \sigma_u^2$ for the MA(1) model but $Cov(Y_t, Y_{t-k}) = 0$ for $k > 1$ (since u_t is serially uncorrelated).

(iv)   The autocorrelation function for the MA model will be

$$\rho = \frac{Cov(Y_t, Y_{t-k})}{\sqrt{Var(Y_t)\,Var(Y_{t-k})}} = \begin{cases} \dfrac{\theta}{1+\theta^2} & \text{for } k=1 \\ 0 & \text{for } k>1 \end{cases}$$

(v)   The MA(1) process can be inverted into a convergent AR process with geometrically declining weights when $|\theta| < 1$. This is known as *invertibility property*. This property is important because the use of ACF and PACF for identification of the data generating process of the series implicitly assumes that it can be well approximated by an autoregressive model.

It is clear from property (v) that if we have an MA(q) model, we will expect the correlogram (the graph of the ACF) to have q spikes (i.e., significant ACF values) for $k = q$, and then the value of ACF goes down to zero immediately. Further, as the MA process can be represented by an AR process with geometrically declining weights, the PACF for an MA process should decline slowly as the lag length increases.

The ARMA Model

If we suppose that Y_t has characteristics of both AR and MA, then it is called an autoregressive moving average (ARMA) process. For example, an ARMA(1,1) model may be written as

$$Y_t = \phi_1 Y_{t-1} + u_t + \theta u_{t-1} \tag{10.33}$$

In general, an ARMA(p,q) process will have p autoregressive and q moving average terms. It is written as

$$Y_t = \phi_1 Y_{t-1} + \phi_2 Y_{t-2} + \ldots + \phi_p Y_{t-p} + u_t + \theta_1 u_{t-1} + \theta_2 u_{t-2} + \ldots + \theta_q u_{t-q} \tag{10.34}$$

THE ARIMA MODEL

If a time series is integrated of order d and we apply ARMA(p, q) model to it, then we say that the original time series is ARIMA(p, d, q), i.e., it is an autoregressive integrated moving average time series. Clearly, if a time series is ARIMA(2, 1, 2), it has to be differenced once to make it stationary and the stationary time series can be modelled as an ARMA(2, 2) process, i.e., it will have two AR and two MA terms. Similarly, an ARIMA(p, 0, q) series is same as ARMA(p, q) when the time series is stationary at the beginning. On the other hand, ARIMA(p, 0, 0) and ARIMA(0, 0, q) series represent AR(p) and MA(q) stationary processes, respectively. Thus, given the values of p, d, and q, one can say what process is being modelled.

10.6.2 The Box-Jenkins (BJ) Methodology

How do we know looking at a time series (say Y_t) whether it follows a purely AR process or a purely MA process or an ARMA process or an ARIMA process? The BJ methodology helps to obtain an answer to this question and eventually to perform the task of forecasting the future value of the variable.

The BJ forecasting method consists of following four steps.

1.   Identification of the model.
2.   Estimation of the chosen model.

3.   Diagnostic checking, i.e., finding out whether estimated residuals are *white noise*. If yes, go to the next step. If no, return to step 1.
4.   Forecasting.

(1) Model Identification

Identification consists of deciding on the values of p, d, and q. First, one has to decide d, i.e., the number of times the series should be differenced to achieve stationarity (in some cases the series may be already stationary such that $d = 0$). For this purpose, available tests of stationarity (such as DF/ADF, PP) may be applied.

Once a stationary series has been obtained, the next step is to decide how many autoregressive (p) and moving average (q) terms are needed to build an effective and *parsimonious* model of the process.[27] The main tools used in identification are the autocorrelation function (ACF) and partial autocorrelation function (PACF) and the resulting correlograms, which are simply the plots of ACFs and PACFs against the lag length.

For a pure MA(q) process, the ACF will show spikes (significant ACFs) up to lag q and will die down after the qth lag. The PACF for the MA(q) process will tend to die down quickly either by an exponential decay or a damped sinewave.

On the contrary, the pure AR(p) process will have an ACF which will tend to die down quickly either by an exponential decay or a damped sinewave, while the PACF will show spikes for lags up to p after which it will die down.

A mixed process is required when neither the ACF nor the PACF show a definite cut-off. Although identification of an appropriate model becomes difficult in this situation, it is not impossible.[28] For example, if both ACF and PACF show signs of exponential decay beginning at lag 1, an ARMA(1,1) model is likely to be appropriate. Similarly, if the ACF shows significant spikes at lags 1, 2, and 3 and then shows an exponential decay, while the PACF has a spike at lag 1 and then shows exponential decay, an ARMA(3,1) model may be considered. Table 10.2 suggests some possible combinations of ACF and PACF forms that may be helpful to decide the order of the ARMA processes.

(2) Estimation of the ARIMA Model

This stage is concerned with estimation of the parameters of the autoregressive and moving average terms included in the model. This can be done using the least squares or any other technique such as maximum likelihood, depending on the model. Almost every econometrics software package routinely does this.

---

[27] By *parsimonious* we mean that the model has the fewest parameters and greatest number of degrees of freedom among all possible models that fit the data.

[28] In practice, p or q are rarely taken to exceed 2, so that the number of possibilities that need to be tried out is limited.

Table 10.2   ACF and PACF Patterns of Some ARMA Models

Model	ACF	PACF
Pure white noise	All zero	All zero
AR(1)	Exponential or damped sinewave decay beginning at lag 1	Single positive spike at lag 1
MA(1)	Single positive spike at lag 1	Exponential or damped sinewave decay beginning at lag 1
ARMA(1,1)	Exponential or damped sinewave decay beginning at lag 1	Exponential or damped sinewave decay beginning at lag 1
ARMA(p,q)	Exponential or damped sinewave decay beginning at lag p	Exponential or damped sinewave decay beginning at lag q

Source: Author's own.

(3) Diagnostic Checking

In this step, we check whether the estimated model is good enough for the purpose of forecasting. This is also the point at which a choice is made between different ARMA representations, when more than one is possible.

Two criteria that come into play here are (*i*) the statistical properties of the estimated model and (*ii*) its simplicity and *parsimony*.

The first criterion encompasses answering the following questions.

- Are the residuals stationary or *white noise*?
- Are the parameters statistically significant?
- How good is the fit on past data?

To answer the first question, we examine the ACF and PACF of the residual series corresponding to the estimated model. Additionally, we may apply DF/ADF or some other test to examine stationarity of the residual series. The second question is answered by applying usual *t* or *z* tests to examine statistical significance of the parameters. The answer to the last question is *a priori* that the larger *p* and *q*, the better the fit. However, this goes against the criterion of *parsimony* because although it is easy to improve the model's fit on past data by adding additional explanatory variables (AR and/or MA terms), this presents the risk of the model breaking down when used in forecasting mode. With a more limited number of parameters, the chances are higher that the estimated model will be robust in forecasting. It is here some formal criteria (e.g., AIC or SBC) may be used to decide what is best, given this trade-off.

(4) Forecasting

Once the estimated model has been found adequate, it can be used for forecasting.

Steps in BJ Methodology

In sum, the steps to be followed sequentially while applying the BJ methodology are the following:

Step 1: Obtain the correlogram of the original series to study the ACF and PACF. Follow this up with application of the ADF test to confirm presence/absence of stationarity of the series. If the series is found to be stationary, go to step 3, if not, go to step 2.

Step 2: Take the first difference of the original series, study the ACF and PACF of it and apply the ADF test to see if it is stationary now.

Step 3: On the basis of the graphs of the ACF and PACF determine which models would be a good starting point.

Step 4: Estimate those models.

Step 5: For each of these models,

(a)   check if the parameter of the longest lag is significant. If not, then the model probably has too many parameters (and hence AR and MA terms), and the order of p and q should be decreased.

(b)   check the ACF and PACF of the residual series. If the model has at least enough parameters, then all ACFs and PACFs of the residuals will be insignificant.

(c)   check the values of AIC (Akaike Information Criterion) and SBC (Schwartz Bayesian Criterion) together with the adjusted-R^2 of alternative estimated models to find out the *parsimonious* model (i.e., the one that minimizes AIC and SBC and has highest value of adjusted-R^2).

Step 6: If changes in the original model are required, go back to step 4.

Merit and Demerit of the BJ Methodology

The main advantage of the BJ methodology is that it is easy to implement. This explains its popularity among the empirical researchers. Further, it has been found that, in many cases, the forecasts obtained by this method are more reliable than the traditional methods of forecasting (such as exponential smoothing), particularly for short-term forecasts.

However, the BJ approach shares the usual drawback of statistical models, namely, the absence of a straightforward economic interpretation of the model (what is the economic rationale for the chosen p and q?) and of the forecasts it produces.

10.7 VECTOR AUTOREGRESSIVE (VAR) MODEL

In simultaneous equations models, some variables are treated as endogenous and some as exogenous. This approach of classifying the variables is considered to be subjective and has been severely criticized by Christopher A. Sims (1980) who developed the vector autoregressive (VAR) model.

According to Sims, if there is simultaneity among a set a variables, then all these variables should be treated in the same way. In other words, there should not be *a priori* distinction between endogenous and exogenous variables. It is in this spirit that Sims developed his VAR model.

Thus, VAR represents a proper simultaneous-equations system in that all the variables in it are treated as endogenous. In VAR modelling, the value of a variable is expressed as a linear function of the past or lagged values of that variable and all other variables included in the model.

To illustrate VAR modelling, consider an example. Suppose our objective is to examine the variations in money supply (M) and income (Y). We assume that not only money supply affects income but also gets affected, in turn, by the income. In other words, there is simultaneity of relationship between M and Y. This type of situation is ideally suited for application of VAR.

Specification of the VAR Model

Under VAR modelling, the money supply equation includes, as explanatory variables, both lagged values of money supply and income plus an error term. Similarly, the income equation includes, as explanatory variables, both lagged values of money supply and income plus an error term. Since lagged values of the dependent variable are included on the right-hand side of the equation, the model is 'autoregressive'. The term 'vector' is due to dealing with a vector of two (or more) variables.

The VAR model corresponding to above example is specified as

$$M_t = \alpha_1 + \sum_{j=1}^{p} \beta_j M_{t-j} + \sum_{j=1}^{p} \gamma_j Y_{t-j} + u_{1t} \qquad (10.35)$$

$$Y_t = \alpha_2 + \sum_{j=1}^{p} \theta_j M_{t-j} + \sum_{j=1}^{p} \lambda_j Y_{t-j} + u_{2t} \qquad (10.36)$$

These two equations together represent the VAR system. We have assumed that each equation contains p lag values of M and Y and a stochastic error term, which is called impulses or innovations or shocks in the language of VAR. This model is known as a VAR(p) model.

Estimation of the VAR Model

Before estimating the VAR model, we have to ensure that both the variables are stationary. If they are non-stationary, we have to make them stationary by differencing, and differenced variables are to be used.

Another issue is determination of the value of p, i.e., the lag length. This is an empirical question. If we do not have adequate sample size, adding too many lagged terms will reduce the degrees of freedom. On the other hand, considering too few lagged terms might result in specification errors. As always, one way of resolving this issue is to use the model selection criteria like AIC and SBC. The model that shows up the lowest value of AIC/SBC may be chosen. In addition, the usual diagnostic checks need to be conducted to ensure that the VAR is well specified. In particular, a test like the LM test for autocorrelation should be applied.[29]

---

[29] The Durbin-Watson d-test cannot be used with a VAR as it contains lagged dependent variables as explanatory variables. Durbin's h-test may be applied here.

If there is evidence of autocorrelation, more lags should be added until autocorrelation has been removed.

If each equation of our VAR model contains the same number of lagged variables, it can be estimated by the OLS technique. Otherwise, we have to apply some systems method of estimation.

For the purpose of illustration, suppose that ours is a VAR(2) model, i.e., we have considered lags up to two periods in both the equations. Then our estimated equations are

$$\hat{M}_t = \hat{\alpha}_1 + \hat{\beta}_1 M_{t-1} + \hat{\beta}_2 M_{t-2} + \hat{\gamma}_1 Y_{t-1} + \hat{\gamma}_2 Y_{t-2} \tag{10.37}$$

$$\hat{Y}_t = \hat{\alpha}_2 + \hat{\theta}_1 M_{t-1} + \hat{\theta}_2 M_{t-2} + \hat{\lambda}_1 Y_{t-1} + \hat{\lambda}_2 Y_{t-2} \tag{10.38}$$

Forecasting with VAR

In practice, two types of forecasting are popular. First, we can make *ex ante* or *out-of-sample forecasting*. When we have data up to 2010 (say), we just put the values of M and Y in 2010 in our estimated VAR equations to obtain one-period-ahead forecasts of M and Y. Then we use those forecasts to compute two-period-ahead forecasts, and continue this process iteratively to the desired forecast horizon.[30]

There is another type of forecasting, known as *ex post* or *recursive forecasting*, which is done to assess forecasting performance of the VAR model. If we have data for $t = 1, 2, ..., T$, we could estimate the VAR model using data for $t = 1, 2, ..., n$ (where $n < T$) and then forecast. If we have tried many different values for n, we would have a series of forecasts. These forecasts may be compared with the actual observations to assess forecasting performance of the VAR model.

Vector Error Correction Model

In the preceding discussion of VAR, we assumed that all variables are stationary. Even if the variables were non-stationary at the beginning, they are made stationary through differencing and the differenced variables are used in the VAR model.

However, when the variables are non-stationary but cointegrated, we may use the vector error correction model (VECM). The VECM is a restricted VAR designed for use with non-stationary series that are known to be cointegrated. The VECM has cointegrating relations built into the specification so that it restricts the long-run behaviour of the endogenous variables to converge to their cointegrating relationships while allowing for short-run adjustment dynamics. The cointegrating term is known as error correction term since the deviation from long-run equilibrium is corrected gradually through a series of partial short-run dynamic adjustments.

[30] This method is also known as *iterated multi-period forecasting*.

In case of two variables, money supply (M) and income (Y), the VECM may be specified as

$$\Delta M_t = a_1 + b_1 \Delta M_{t-1} + ... + b_p \Delta M_{t-p} + c_1 \Delta Y_{t-1} + ... + c_p \Delta Y_{t-p} + \lambda_1 \hat{\varepsilon}_{t-1} + \varepsilon_{1t} \qquad (10.39)$$

$$\Delta Y_t = a_2 + g_1 \Delta M_{t-1} + ... + g_p \Delta M_{t-p} + h_1 \Delta Y_{t-1} + ... + h_p \Delta Y_{t-p} + \lambda_2 \hat{\varepsilon}_{t-1} + \varepsilon_{2t} \qquad (10.40)$$

As before, $\hat{\varepsilon}_{t-1}$ is the one-period lagged value of the error term from the cointegrating regression of M_t on Y_t, and $\lambda \hat{\varepsilon}_{t-1}$ is the error correction term. The VECM can be extended to the case of many variables. But the point to remember is that when there are more than two variables, it is possible to have more than one cointegrating relationships and hence more than one error correction term in each equation (e.g., instead of a single $\hat{\varepsilon}_{t-1}$, there will be $\hat{\varepsilon}_{1,t-1}$ and $\hat{\varepsilon}_{2,t-1}$ in the case of two cointegrating relationships). Most econometrics software packages enable us to carry out maximum likelihood estimation of the VECM, when there are more than two variables. However, for the two-variable case, we can still continue with the OLS method to estimate each equation of the VECM.

Impulse Response Analysis

When estimating VARs, the number of estimated parameters can in general be very large. This makes interpreting parameters difficult and understanding the properties of the estimated coefficients even more difficult. One way to circumvent this problem is using impulse responses. The impulse response functions (IRF) trace out the responses of the dependent variables in the VAR system to shocks in the error terms. In terms of our previous example, suppose u_{1t} in the money supply (M) equation (10.35) increases by a value of one standard deviation. Such a shock or change will change M in the current as well as future periods. But since M appears also in the income (Y) equation, the change in u_{1t} will also have an impact on Y. Similarly, a change of one standard deviation in u_{2t} in the income equation will have an impact on M. The impulse response functions trace out the effects of such shocks for several periods in future. If there are k variables in a VAR system, a total of k^2 impulse response functions could be generated. This is actually done by expressing the vector autoregressive model as a vector moving average model. If the system of equations is stable, any shock should gradually die away. On the other hand, an unstable system would produce an explosive time path.

Variance Decomposition

This is an alternative method to the impulse response functions for examining the effects of shocks to the dependent variables of the VAR system. This technique determines how much of the forecast error variance for any variable in the system is explained by innovations in each explanatory variable over a series of time horizons. Usually own series shocks explain most of the forecast error variance of the series in a VAR, although the shock will also affect other variables in the system.

Note that it is necessary to choose an ordering of the variables when computing impulse responses and variance decompositions. As in practice, the error terms of the equations in the VAR will be correlated, the result will be dependent on the order in which the equations in the model are estimated. Further, sometimes both impulse responses and variance decompositions become difficult to interpret accurately even though the confidence bands are constructed around these.

Merits and Demerits of VAR

Some advantages of the VAR model are

- It is very simple and the researcher does not have to worry about which variables are endogenous and which are exogenous.
- Estimation of the VAR model is very simple in the sense that each equation can be estimated separately using the usual OLS method.
- The forecasts obtained by this method are in many cases better than those obtained from more complex simultaneous-equations models.
- The VAR models can help interpret ongoing developments. By allowing comparison of results from the VAR with the actual developments, VAR-modelling identifies 'innovations'. This helps the researcher to reflect on how 'normal' the current situation is and if it does not appear to be so, to look for the special factors that may explain deviations from what the VAR predicts.
- One of the good features of the VAR model is that it allows us to test the direction of causality.[31] It highlights how the Granger causality runs.[32]

However, the VAR suffers from following criticisms.

- According to some critics, the VAR model is a-theoretic because it uses less prior information.
- Due to its emphasis on forecasting, VAR models are less suited for policy analysis.
- The biggest practical challenge in VAR modelling is that of choosing an appropriate lag length. As limited number of observations is generally available in most economic analyses, introduction of several lags of each variable can consume a lot of degrees of freedom.
- Strictly speaking, in an m-variable VAR model, all the m variables have to be stationary. If that is not the case, we will have to transform the data appropriately (i.e., by differencing). The most difficult situation arises when the model contains a mix of $I(0)$ and $I(1)$ variables (i.e., a mix of stationary and non-stationary variables).
- If there are several lags in each equation, it is not always easy to interpret each coefficient, especially if the signs of the coefficients alternate.

[31] In fact, initial objective of Sims towards developing the VAR model was to use it to test causality among the variables.

[32] This is further discussed in the next section.

10.8 CAUSALITY TESTS

In regression analysis, we examine dependence of one variable on other variable(s). But that does not necessarily imply causation. Existence of a relationship between variables does not necessarily prove causality, or direction of influence. Therefore, formal tests are needed to examine the direction of causality between the variables.

Granger Causality Test

Granger (1969) was the first econometrician to offer a formal test of the direction of causality between the variables.[33] It is basically a statistical test. Granger starts from the premise that the future cannot cause the present or the past (i.e., time does not run backward). If event B occurs after event A, we can say that that B cannot cause A. But, at the same time, if A occurs before B, it does not necessarily imply that A causes B. For instance, although the weatherman's prediction occurred before rain, it does not mean that the weatherman caused the rain.[34] In practice, we observe A and B as time series and we are interested to know whether A precedes B, or B precedes A, or they are contemporaneous. This is precisely understood by applying the Granger test. Clearly, it is not causality in the traditional sense of the term.

To understand the Granger causality test, suppose we want to answer the following question—is it that GDP causes money supply (written as GDP → M) or money supply causes GDP (M → GDP)? To answer this question, we may apply the Granger test that involves estimating the following pairs of equations.

$$GDP_t = a_1 + \sum_{i=1}^{n} \alpha_i M_{t-i} + \sum_{j=1}^{m} \beta_j GDP_{t-j} + \varepsilon_{1t} \tag{10.41}$$

$$M_t = a_2 + \sum_{i=1}^{n} \gamma_i M_{t-i} + \sum_{j=1}^{m} \delta_j GDP_{t-j} + \varepsilon_{2t} \tag{10.42}$$

where ε_{1t} and ε_{2t} are uncorrelated *white noise* error terms.

Equation (10.41) implies that GDP at time t depends on past values of itself and that of M. Equation (10.42) implies that M at time t depends on past values of itself and that of GDP.[35] In terms of this model, we can visualize four different cases.

1. $\hat{\alpha}_i s$ in (10.41) are statistically significantly different from zero (i.e., statistically significant) and $\hat{\delta}_j s$ in (10.42) are not statistically significantly different from zero

---

[33] Granger obtained the basic intuition behind this test from a paper by renowned mathematician Norbert Wiener. That is why some people call it the Wiener-Granger causality test.

[34] This example has been drawn from Maddala and Lahiri (2009, 390).

[35] Note that since we have two variables, we are dealing with bilateral causality. If we have more than two variables, we have to consider multi-variable causality, which is easily done following the vector autoregression.

(insignificant). In this case, there is *unidirectional causality* from M to GDP and we say that 'M (Granger) causes GDP'.

2. $\hat{\alpha}_i$s in (10.41) are not statistically significantly different from zero and $\hat{\delta}_j$s in (10.42) are statistically significantly different from zero. This shows *unidirectional causality* from GDP to M and we say that 'GDP (Granger) causes M'.

3. $\hat{\alpha}_i$s, $\hat{\beta}_j$s, $\hat{\gamma}_i$s, and $\hat{\delta}_j$s are statistically significantly different from zero (i.e., statistically significant). This represents the case of *bilateral* or *feedback causality*.

4. $\hat{\alpha}_i$s, $\hat{\beta}_j$s, $\hat{\gamma}_i$s, and $\hat{\delta}_j$s are not statistically significantly different from zero (statistically insignificant). This is the situation of *independence* where GDP and M are independent of each other.

To know which of the above cases holds, we apply Granger's test. The steps in this test are as follows.

Step 1: Regress current GDP on all lagged GDP terms but do not include the lagged M variables. This may be termed as the restricted regression model. Then obtain the RSS of this regression, which is labeled as RSS_R.

Step 2: Regress current GDP on all lagged GDP terms and also the lagged M variables. This is termed as the unrestricted regression model. The RSS of this regression is labeled as RSS_{UR}.

Step 3: Test the null hypothesis H_N: $\alpha_i = 0$ ($i = 1, 2, \ldots, n$). For this, calculate the F-statistic as

$$F^* = \frac{(RSS_R - RSS_{UR})/m}{RSS_{UR}/(n-k)}$$

where m = number of lagged M terms and k = number of parameters estimated in the unrestricted regression model (10.41).

Step 4: If the computed-F exceeds the critical-F value [i.e., $F^* > F_\lambda(m, n-k)$] then reject the H_N and conclude that 'M (Granger) causes GDP'.

Step 5: Repeat above steps to test for model (10.42) and know if GDP (Granger) causes M.

Important Points to Remember

1. Both GDP and M have to be stationary variables to apply this test. If they are non-stationary, we have to take first-difference of them to make them stationary and then apply this test on first-differenced variables.

2. Number of lagged terms to be included is a very important issue here. This issue may be resolved and an appropriate model may be chosen using the AIC or SBC.

3. It should be remembered that the direction of causality may depend critically on the number of lagged terms included.

4. If the disturbance terms ε_{1t} and ε_{2t} are correlated, appropriate transformation of the variables would be required.

5. Granger-causality is not necessarily transitive. Thus, when $M \rightarrow r$ (rate of interest) and $r \rightarrow$ GDP, it may or may not be true that $M \rightarrow$ GDP. So adequate caution needs

to be exercised against obtaining 'spurious causality' while using this test. If $M \to r \to GDP$ and we do not include r and say that $M \to GDP$, then the observed causality between M and GDP may be spurious. This problem may be overcome more conveniently by considering a multi-equation system such as the vector autoregression.

Sims Causality Test

Sims (1972) provided a test of causality which is somewhat similar to Granger except that the above equations are modified to include *leading values* of GDP and M apart from their lagged values.[36] Thus, Sims' equations are

$$GDP_t = a_1 + \sum_{i=1}^{n} \alpha_i M_{t-i} + \sum_{j=1}^{m} \beta_j GDP_{t-j} + \sum_{q=1}^{k} \eta_q M_{t+q} + \varepsilon_{1t} \qquad (10.43)$$

$$M_t = a_2 + \sum_{i=1}^{n} \gamma_i M_{t-i} + \sum_{j=1}^{m} \delta_j GDP_{t-j} + \sum_{q=1}^{k} \mu_q GDP_{t+q} + \varepsilon_{2t} \qquad (10.44)$$

Examining the first equation, if GDP causes M, then we will expect that there is some relationship between GDP and leading values of M. Therefore, instead of testing for lagged values of M, we test the validity of the null hypothesis (H_N) that all η_q's are zero. If H_N is rejected, then we say that causality runs from GDP to M as future cannot cause present. Similarly, while examining the second equation, the H_N is all μ_q's are zero, which, if rejected, would imply that causality runs from M to GDP.

To carry out this test, we estimate a model with no leading terms (which is the restricted regression model) and the same model including the leading terms (unrestricted regression) and compute the value of F-statistic in the manner described in the Granger test.

It needs mention here that it is not clear which of the two tests (Granger or Sims) is superior. Most researchers apply both and compare the results. However, one obvious limitation of Sims' test is that it uses more regressors (due to inclusion of leading terms) and suffers from low degrees of freedom.

Granger Causality in VAR

While discussing the VAR model, we mentioned that it allows us to test the direction of causality between the variables. The Granger causality test can be performed easily using the VAR equations. To understand how this is performed, consider the following VAR model.[37]

$$M_t = \alpha_1 + \alpha_2 M_{t-1} + \alpha_3 M_{t-2} + \alpha_4 Y_{t-1} + \alpha_5 Y_{t-2} + \alpha_6 R_{t-1} + \alpha_7 R_{t-2} + \varepsilon_{1t} \qquad (10.45)$$

$$Y_t = \beta_1 + \beta_2 M_{t-1} + \beta_3 M_{t-2} + \beta_4 Y_{t-1} + \beta_5 Y_{t-2} + \beta_6 R_{t-1} + \beta_7 R_{t-2} + \varepsilon_{2t} \qquad (10.46)$$

---

[36] The values of these variables at $t + 1$, $t + 2$, ... are called the leading values.

[37] For simplicity of discussion, we have considered lags up to two periods for each variable. Of course, in the ultimate analysis, this may be determined in terms of AIC/SBC values.

$$R_t = \gamma_1 + \gamma_2 M_{t-1} + \gamma_3 M_{t-2} + \gamma_4 Y_{t-1} + \gamma_5 Y_{t-2} + \gamma_6 R_{t-1} + \gamma_7 R_{t-2} + \varepsilon_{3t} \qquad (10.47)$$

where M = money supply, Y = income, R = rate of interest, and $\varepsilon_{1t}, \varepsilon_{2t}$, and ε_{3t} are error terms of money supply, income, and rate of interest equations, respectively.

Here the Granger causality tests are based on testing the joint significance of the lags of each variable in the system, apart from its own lags. Thus, a test that Y Granger causes M is given by testing hypotheses

$$H_N : \alpha_4 = \alpha_5 = 0 \text{ (no Granger causality)}$$
$$H_A : \text{at least one of the restrictions fails}$$

where the parameters α_i are defined in first equation (10.45) of the VAR. These hypotheses are commonly written as

$$H_N : Y \nrightarrow M$$
$$H_A : Y \rightarrow M$$

The reverse test that M Granger causes Y is given by testing the hypotheses

$$H_N : \beta_2 = \beta_3 = 0 \text{ (no Granger causality)}$$
$$H_A : \text{at least one of the restrictions fails}$$

where the parameters β_i are defined in the second equation (10.46) of the VAR. As before, these hypotheses are commonly written as

$$H_N : M \nrightarrow Y$$
$$H_A : M \rightarrow Y$$

These hypotheses can also be extended to test causality between interest rate (R) and money (M), as well as income (Y).

All these causality tests are performed after estimating the VAR system. The interpretation of Granger causality tests using a VAR has been illustrated using an example in the last section of this chapter.

10.9 ARCH/GARCH FOR MODELLING VOLATILITY

Financial time series such as stock prices, exchange rates, and inflation rates often exhibit the phenomenon of *volatility clustering*. This means that there are periods when these series show wide swings for an extended period followed by a period of relative calm. Knowledge of such volatility of time series is extremely important.

In fact, a great deal of macroeconometric work has been done to study variability of inflation over time. The decision makers do not consider inflation as such bad, but its variability is considered bad because that makes financial planning difficult. Similarly, variability in exchange rates might lead to huge losses or profits by the exporters and importers. The investors in the stock market are also likely to be affected by the volatility of stock prices as high volatility could mean huge losses or gains and hence greater uncertainty. Further, in the volatile capital market, it is difficult for the companies to raise capital. So the question is—How to model financial time series to forecast their values that might experience volatility?

Almost all financial time series are *random walks* in their level form, i.e., they are non-stationary, and they become stationary in the first-difference form. So one might think that while modelling financial time series, it would be better to use first-differenced variables. However, the problem is that these first-differenced series also often exhibit wide swings or volatility, which implies that the variance of financial time series varies over time. To model such 'varying variance', the so-called Autoregressive Conditional Heteroskedasticity (ARCH) model developed by Engle (1982) becomes useful.

The ARCH model assumes that heteroskedasticity or unequal variance has an autoregressive structure, which implies that heteroskedasticity observed over different periods is autocorrelated. When heteroskedasticity observed over different periods are autocorrelated, we say that the ARCH effect is present, i.e., there is *volatility clustering* in data.

The ARCH Model

Consider the k-variable linear model

$$Y_t = \beta_1 + \beta_2 X_{2t} + \beta_3 X_{3t} + ... + \beta_k X_{kt} + u_t \tag{10.48}$$

We assume that $u_t \sim N(0, \alpha_0 + \alpha_1 u_{t-1}^2)$, i.e., u_t is normally distributed with zero mean and variance $\alpha_0 + \alpha_1 u_{t-1}^2$. So the variance of u at time t depends on squared disturbance at $t - 1$ thereby giving the appearance of a serial correlation. Of course, the variance of u at time t may depend not only on one lagged squared disturbance term but also on several lagged squared disturbance terms as follows:

$$Var(u_t) = \sigma_t^2 = \alpha_0 + \alpha_1 u_{t-1}^2 + \alpha_2 u_{t-2}^2 + ... + \alpha_p u_{t-p}^2 \tag{10.49}$$

Equation (10.49) represents the ARCH model of order p. This equation is also named as the 'variance equation' while equation (10.48) is called the 'mean equation'.

Method of Testing the Presence of ARCH

The presence of ARCH is tested by examining the validity of the null hypothesis H_N: $\alpha_1 = \alpha_2 = ... = \alpha_p = 0$. To test this hypothesis, Engle proposed running the following auxiliary regression (since we do not directly observe σ_t^2).

$$e_t^2 = \alpha_0 + \alpha_1 e_{t-1}^2 + \alpha_2 e_{t-2}^2 + ... + \alpha_p e_{t-p}^2 \tag{10.50}$$

where $e_t = Y_t - \hat{Y_t}$ so that the series for e_t is obtained from OLS estimation of model (10.48).

The above null hypothesis may be tested by applying the usual F-test. Alternatively, we compute $T.R^2$, where R^2 is coefficient of determination from the auxiliary regression model

(10.50), and T is size of residuals (number of observations). It has been shown that, for large samples, $T.R^2 \sim \chi^2$ with degrees of freedom p, i.e., number of autoregressive terms in (10.50). Thus, if $T.R^2 = \chi^{2^*} > \chi^2$ at the chosen level of significance and degrees of freedom p, we reject the H_N and conclude that ARCH is present.

Although we described the procedure for testing ARCH by considering a time series regression model, the same technique applies to the purely autoregressive models and autoregressive distributed lag models.

The GARCH Model

One of the limitations of the ARCH specification (10.49) is that it looked more like a moving average specification than the autoregression. From this a new idea was born which was to include the lagged conditional variance terms as autoregressive terms. This idea was worked out by Bollerslev (1986) who advanced the GARCH (generalized autoregressive conditional heteroskedasticity) model.[38] The simplest GARCH (1, 1) model is written as

$$Var(u_t) = \sigma_t^2 = \alpha_0 + \alpha_1 u_{t-1}^2 + \alpha_2 \sigma_{t-1}^2 \qquad (10.51)$$

In this model, the conditional variance of u at time t depends not only on the squared error term in the previous period [as in ARCH(1)] but also on its conditional variance in the previous period.

This model can be generalized to a GARCH(p, q) model where there will be p lagged terms of squared error and q terms of the lagged conditional variances so that (10.51) becomes

$$Var(u_t) = \sigma_t^2 = \alpha_0 + \sum_{i=1}^{p} \alpha_i u_{t-i}^2 + \sum_{i=1}^{q} \beta_i \sigma_{t-i}^2 \qquad (10.52)$$

If we set $p = 1$ and $q = 0$, the first-order ARCH model is the same as GARCH (1, 0) model. Hence when all β_is are zero, the GARCH(p, q) model reduces to ARCH (p) model.

The advantage of the GARCH model is that it is much more flexible and more capable of matching a wide variety of patterns, in particular of financial volatility.

Estimation and Inference

The ARCH/GARCH models are estimated by the method of maximum likelihood (ML). The estimators of the ARCH/GARCH coefficients are normally distributed in large samples, so t-statistics in large samples have standard normal distributions and confidence intervals can be constructed as ML estimate $\pm$ standard errors.

---

[38] The GARCH model also got revised, subsequently, and we have models like GARCH-M (GARCH in mean), TGARCH (threshold GARCH), EGARCH (exponential GARCH), etc. We do not discuss these models here as that is beyond our scope. Interested readers may refer to Enders (2004) and Asteriou and Hall (2007).

10.10 APPLICATIONS USING EVIEWS

10.10.1 Stationarity Tests

To illustrate how to perform the test of stationarity of the time series using EViews, let us consider the GDP series in Table 10.1 above. We begin by a correlogram analysis, which is followed by application of ADF and PP tests to examine the presence of unit root (non-stationarity) in the GDP series.

Correlogram

To obtain correlogram of the GDP series using EViews, the following steps are performed.

1. Import data in EViews worksheet if that is provided in Excel or any other worksheet. That will open the 'Workfile' window (as in Screenshot 10.1).
2. Following the usual procedure, transform the GDP series in logs. This is done by clicking on 'Genr' on the main menu of 'Workfile' window, which will open the 'Generate Series by Equation' window (see Screenshot 10.1). In the 'Enter equation' box of the 'Generate Series by Equation' window, write **lgdp=log(gdp)** and click **OK**. This will generate the series for log GDP (labeled as lgdp), which will be added in the list of variables in 'Workfile' window.

Screenshot 10.1   Workfile of GDP and CON Series

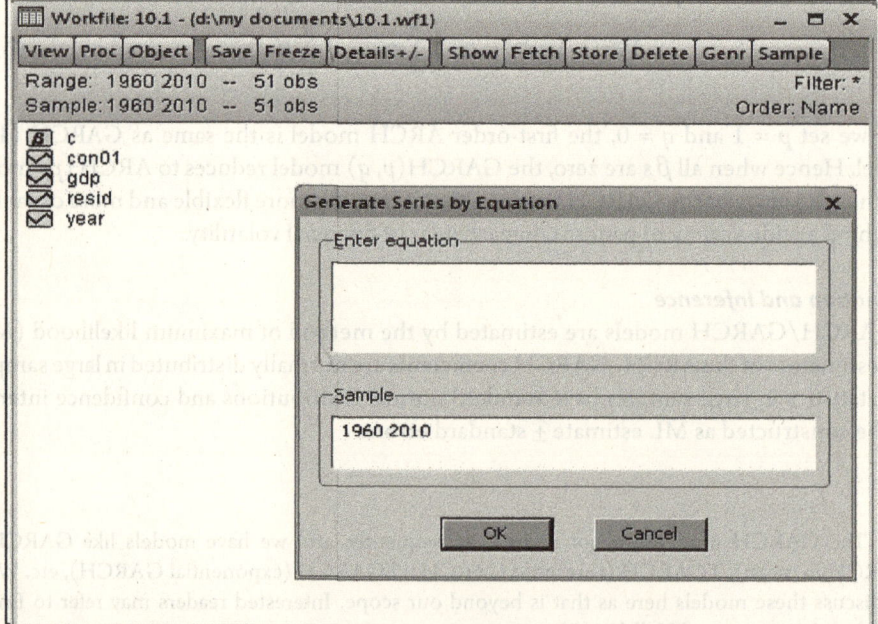

3. Double-click on **lgdp** from the 'Workfile' window which will open the data series in a new Window as shown in Screenshot 10.2. Also click on **View/Correlogram…** which will display 'Correlogram Specification' box.

4. The 'Correlogram Specification' box by default chooses to compute correlogram of the series in 'Level'. In addition, the number of lags to be considered needs to be selected. For our dataset, this is by default chosen as 24, but can be changed if necessary.

5. Click on **OK** in the 'Correlogram Specification' box, to obtain the output relating to correlogram of the lgdp series, which is shown in Screenshot 10.3.

INTERPRETATION OF CORRELOGRAM

The first two columns of the correlogram graphically display autocorrelations (AC) and partial autocorrelations (PAC) of the lgdp series at various lags; the corresponding numerical values of AC and PAC are reported in fourth and fifth columns, respectively. The computed AC and PAC, as a *rule of thumb*, are statistically significant if outside $\pm 1.96/\sqrt{T}$ band (shown by dotted lines), where T is the number of observations. The penultimate column gives the values of statistic resulting from a Ljung-Box (LB) test with number of lags provided in third column and p-values associated with computed LB-statistic in the last column.

Screenshot 10.2 View of the lgdp Series

Screenshot 10.3   Correlogram of the lgdp Series

| View | Proc | Object | Properties | | Print | Name | Freeze | | Samp |

Date: 08/23/13   Time: 16:26
Sample: 1960 2010
Included observations: 51

Autocorrelation	Partial Correlation		AC	PAC	Q-Stat	Prob
		1	0.931	0.931	46.844	0.000
		2	0.863	-0.028	87.908	0.000
		3	0.795	-0.032	123.52	0.000
		4	0.728	-0.035	154.00	0.000
		5	0.664	-0.013	179.93	0.000
		6	0.609	0.027	202.22	0.000
		7	0.554	-0.031	221.09	0.000
		8	0.503	-0.008	237.01	0.000
		9	0.453	-0.022	250.24	0.000
		10	0.405	-0.021	261.06	0.000
		11	0.358	-0.025	269.71	0.000
		12	0.309	-0.042	276.35	0.000
		13	0.261	-0.036	281.18	0.000
		14	0.213	-0.032	284.48	0.000
		15	0.164	-0.041	286.51	0.000
		16	0.120	-0.009	287.62	0.000
		17	0.077	-0.031	288.10	0.000
		18	0.038	-0.015	288.21	0.000
		19	-0.000	-0.028	288.21	0.000
		20	-0.041	-0.061	288.36	0.000
		21	-0.081	-0.038	288.95	0.000
		22	-0.119	-0.028	290.28	0.000
		23	-0.156	-0.028	292.62	0.000
		24	-0.187	-0.008	296.12	0.000

It appears from the correlogram that the AC starts from a very high value at lag 1, and declines gradually. Moreover, the ACs up to lag 12 are statistically significant. All these suggest that the lgdp series is non-stationary.

Augmented Dickey-Fuller (ADF) Test

We now examine presence of unit root or non-stationarity of the same lgdp series by applying the ADF test. To conduct this test in EViews, the first three steps are same as those for correlogram test. The subsequent steps are

1. From the data series window (Screenshot 10.2), click on **View/Unit Root Test...** This will open the 'Unit Root Test' dialog box.
2. In the 'Unit Root Test' dialog box, four things are to be specified.
    (i)   Type of test to perform (e.g., Augmented Dickey-Fuller, Phillips-Perron). By default, the Augmented Dickey-Fuller is chosen in the 'Test type' box. However, any other test can be chosen from the drop-down menu of 'Test type' box.
    (ii) In the 'Test for unit root in' box, we have to specify whether we want to test for a unit root in the 'level', 'first difference', or 'second difference' of the series. To begin with, we select 'level', and if we fail to reject the null hypothesis that lgdp has a unit root, then we continue with testing for the 'first difference', and so on.

(iii) From the 'Include in test equation' box, we have to specify which of the three models we wish to use (i.e., whether to include a constant, a constant and a linear trend, or neither in the test regression). For the model given by equation (10.18) above, select 'None', for model (10.19) select 'Intercept', and select 'Trend and intercept' for model (10.20). The choice of the model is very important since the distribution of the test statistic under the H_N will be different for these three cases.[39]

(iv) In the 'Lag length' box, we specify the number of lagged dependent variables to be included in the model to correct any possible autocorrelation. The EViews chooses a number here by default but it can be changed.

3. Click **OK** to obtain the test result, which is shown in Table 10.3A.

Table 10.3A   Results of ADF Test for lgdp

			t-Statistic	Prob.*
Null Hypothesis: LGDP has a unit root				
Exogenous: Constant				
Lag Length: 0 (Automatic—based on SIC, maxlag=10)				
Augmented Dickey-Fuller test statistic			1.505846	0.9991
Test critical values:	1% level		−3.568308	
	5% level		−2.921175	
	10% level		−2.598551	

*MacKinnon (1996) one-sided p-values.

Augmented Dickey-Fuller Test Equation
Dependent Variable: D(LGDP)
Method: Least Squares
Date: 08/23/13 Time: 16:30
Sample (adjusted): 1961 2010
Included observations: 50 after adjustments

Variable	Coefficient	Std. Error	t-Statistic	Prob.
LGDP(-1)	0.010209	0.006780	1.505846	0.1387
C	−0.070841	0.083390	−0.849517	0.3998
R-squared	0.045110	Mean dependent var		0.054513
Adjusted R-squared	0.025216	S.D. dependent var		0.035245
S.E. of regression	0.034798	Akaike info criterion		−3.839358
Sum squared resid	0.058122	Schwarz criterion		−3.762877
Log likelihood	97.98395	Hannan-Quinn criter.		−3.810234
F-statistic	2.267572	Durbin-Watson stat		2.207750
Prob(F-statistic)	0.138660			

Source: This table represents output obtained by the author after application of the EViews software.

[39] One method of choosing an appropriate model is described in Figure 10.2.

Table 10.3B   Results of ADF Test for First-Difference of lgdp

Null Hypothesis: D(LGDP) has a unit root

Exogenous: Constant

Lag Length: 0 (Automatic—based on SIC, maxlag=10)

		t-Statistic	Prob.*
Augmented Dickey-Fuller test statistic		−7.198202	0.0000
Test critical values:	1% level	−3.571310	
	5% level	−2.922449	
	10% level	−2.599224	

*MacKinnon (1996) one-sided p-values.

Augmented Dickey-Fuller Test Equation

Dependent Variable: D(LGDP,2)

Method: Least Squares

Date: 08/23/13 Time: 16:31

Sample (adjusted): 1962 2010

Included observations: 49 after adjustments

Variable	Coefficient	Std. Error	t-Statistic	Prob.
D(LGDP(−1))	−1.053960	0.146420	−7.198202	0.0000
C	0.057759	0.009409	6.138944	0.0000
R-squared	0.524359	Mean dependent var		0.000948
Adjusted R-squared	0.514239	S.D. dependent var		0.051441
S.E. of regression	0.035852	Akaike info criterion		−3.778858
Sum squared resid	0.060413	Schwarz criterion		−3.701641
Log likelihood	94.58202	Hannan-Quinn criter.		−3.749562
F-statistic	51.81411	Durbin-Watson stat		1.970303
Prob(F-statistic)	0.000000			

Source: Same as for Table 10.3A.

INTERPRETATION OF ADF TEST RESULTS

It is observed that the value of computed τ-statistic is 1.505846 (with p-value 0.9991), which is greater than (or lies to the right of) all critical τ-statistic values. Hence we accept the null hypothesis and conclude that lgdp has a unit root, and is non-stationary. Now to check whether the first difference of lgdp series has a unit root, we have to repeat the above steps except that in the 'Test for unit root in' box, we select 'first difference'. The results of unit root test for the first difference of lgdp series ($\Delta lgdp$) are provided in Table 10.3B above. It is observed that the computed τ-statistic (−7.198202) for $\Delta lgdp$ is lower than (or lies to the left of) all critical τ-statistic values. This implies that the lgdp series in first-difference form is stationary.

Phillips-Perron (PP) Test

To perform the PP test, we repeat the above-mentioned steps again except that we put 'Phillips-Perron' in 'Test type' box of the 'Test for unit root in' box [Step 2(i) above]. The results of PP test for the $\Delta lgdp$ series are shown in Table 10.4. The *decision rules* here are the

Table 10.4   Results of PP Test for First-Difference of lgdp

Null Hypothesis: D(LGDP) has a unit root

Exogenous: Constant

Bandwidth: 2 (Newey-West automatic) using Bartlett kernel

		Adj. *t*-Stat	Prob.*
Phillips-Perron test statistic		−7.198964	0.0000
Test critical values:	1% level	−3.571310	
	5% level	−2.922449	
	10% level	−2.599224	

*MacKinnon (1996) one-sided *p*-values.

Residual variance (no correction)			0.001233
HAC corrected variance (Bartlett kernel)			0.001367

Phillips-Perron Test Equation

Dependent Variable: D(LGDP,2)

Method: Least Squares

Date: 08/23/13 Time: 16:32

Sample (adjusted): 1962 2010

Included observations: 49 after adjustments

Variable	Coefficient	Std. Error	*t*-Statistic	Prob.
D(LGDP(-1))	−1.053960	0.146420	−7.198202	0.0000
C	0.057759	0.009409	6.138944	0.0000
R-squared	0.524359	Mean dependent var		0.000948
Adjusted *R*-squared	0.514239	S.D. dependent var		0.051441
S.E. of regression	0.035852	Akaike info criterion		−3.778858
Sum squared resid	0.060413	Schwarz criterion		−3.701641
Log likelihood	94.58202	Hannan-Quinn criter.		−3.749562
F-statistic	51.81411	Durbin-Watson stat		1.970303
Prob(*F*-statistic)	0.000000			

Source: Same as for Table 10.3A.

same as in ADF test. It is found that the hypothesis of a unit root for $\Delta lgdp$ series is rejected under PP test also. Thus, the PP test reinforces our previous conclusion that the lgdp series in first-difference form does not have a unit root and is stationary.

10.10.2 Estimation of Cointegrating Regression and the ECM

We consider data given in Table 10.1 to examine cointegration between consumption expenditure (CON) and income (GDP) in India following the Engle-Granger (EG) method. The steps to be followed are

1.   Transform CON and GDP in logs and examine their stationarity by applying the ADF test. We observed earlier that log of GDP (lgdp) is non-stationary in level but stationary in first-difference, i.e., lgdp ~ $I(1)$. It may be checked that the same is true about log of CON (lcon), i.e., lcon ~ $I(1)$.

2.   Since both the variables are $I(1)$, we run a simple OLS regression of lcon on lgdp using the 'Estimate Equation...' dialog box in EViews. The results of such regression are in Table 10.5.

3.   Generate the series for residuals whose stationarity needs to be examined to know whether the cointegration is valid. To generate the residuals series, click on **Proc/ Make Residual Series.../OK** from the output window of above regression. This will generate the residuals series which is saved with variable name 'res' (say). To save 'res', click on **Object/Store to DB.../OK**.

4.   Check the stationarity of the 'res' series by applying the ADF test again. The results are given in Table 10.6, which show that the residual series is stationary in level (the null hypothesis of a unit root is rejected at 5% level). This implies that the cointegration between lcon and lgdp variables is valid.

5.   Since cointegration has become possible, we proceed to estimate the error correction model (ECM) using the 'Estimate Equation...' dialog box again. To estimate an ECM like $\Delta lcon = \varphi + \gamma \Delta lgdp + \lambda (res)_{t-1} + \varepsilon_t$, write **d(lcon) c d(lgdp) res(-1)** in the 'Equation specification' box of the 'Estimate Equation...' dialog box, and click **OK**. The resulting output is presented in Table 10.7.

INTERPRETATION OF COINTEGRATION TEST RESULTS

On the basis of the results presented in Table 10.5, we may write the estimated cointegrating relationship as

$$\widehat{lcon} = 0.692828 + 0.923569 \, lgdp$$
$$t: (9.673087) \ (158.9964^*)$$
$$R^2: 0.998065 \ \text{D-W}: 0.666227$$
$$^*\text{implies significance at 1\% level}$$

Table 10.5   Results of Regression of lcon on lgdp

Dependent Variable: LCON
Method: Least Squares
Date: 08/23/13 Time: 16:35
Sample: 1960 2010
Included observations: 51

Variable	Coefficient	Std. Error	t-Statistic	Prob.
C	0.692829	0.071624	9.673087	0.0000
LGDP	0.923569	0.005809	158.9964	0.0000
R-squared	0.998065	Mean dependent var		12.05987
Adjusted R-squared	0.998026	S.D. dependent var		0.698547
S.E. of regression	0.031037	Akaike info criterion		−4.068878
Sum squared resid	0.047200	Schwarz criterion		−3.993120
Log likelihood	105.7564	Hannan-Quinn criter.		−4.039929
F-statistic	25279.85	Durbin-Watson stat		0.666227
Prob(F-statistic)	0.000000			

Source: Same as for Table 10.3A.

Table 10.6 Results of ADF Test for Residual (res) Series

Null Hypothesis: RES has a unit root
Exogenous: Constant
Lag Length: 0 (Automatic—based on SIC, maxlag=10)

		t-Statistic	Prob.*
Augmented Dickey-Fuller test statistic		−2.996659	0.0420
Test critical values:	1% level	−3.568308	
	5% level	−2.921175	
	10% level	−2.598551	

*MacKinnon (1996) one-sided p-values.

Augmented Dickey-Fuller Test Equation
Dependent Variable: D(RES)
Method: Least Squares
Date: 08/23/13   Time: 16:37
Sample (adjusted): 1961 2010
Included observations: 50 after adjustments

Variable	Coefficient	Std. Error	t-Statistic	Prob.
RES(−1)	−0.328344	0.109570	−2.996659	0.0043
C	−0.000565	0.003322	−0.170122	0.8656
R-squared	0.157599	Mean dependent var		−0.000798
Adjusted R-squared	0.140049	S.D. dependent var		0.025320
S.E. of regression	0.023480	Akaike info criterion		−4.626142
Sum squared resid	0.026463	Schwarz criterion		−4.549661
Log likelihood	117.6535	Hannan-Quinn criter.		−4.597017
F-statistic	8.979966	Durbin-Watson stat		2.187595
Prob(F-statistic)	0.004311			

Source: Same as for Table 10.3A.

Table 10.7 Results of Estimated ECM

Dependent Variable: D(LCON)
Method: Least Squares
Date: 08/23/13   Time: 16:39
Sample (adjusted): 1961 2010
Included observations: 50 after adjustments

Variable	Coefficient	Std. Error	t-Statistic	Prob.
C	0.001914	0.006211	0.308238	0.7593
D(LGDP)	0.878086	0.095950	9.151515	0.0000
RES(-1)	−0.328351	0.110466	−2.972421	0.0046
R-squared	0.663306	Mean dependent var		0.049549
Adjusted R-squared	0.648978	S.D. dependent var		0.039955
S.E. of regression	0.023672	Akaike info criterion		−4.590911
Sum squared resid	0.026337	Schwarz criterion		−4.476190
Log likelihood	117.7728	Hannan-Quinn criter.		−4.547225
F-statistic	46.29626	Durbin-Watson stat		2.209558
Prob(F-statistic)	0.000000			

Source: Same as for Table 10.3A.

The above equation provides the long-run relationship between lcon and lgdp variables. Since both the variables are in logs, the estimated slope coefficient (0.923569) represents long-run elasticity of consumption expenditure to change in GDP.

As the above cointegrating relationship has been validated by the ADF unit root test for residuals[40], we look into the results of estimated ECM, which are summarized as

$$d(\widehat{lcon}) = 0.001914 + 0.878086\,d(lgdp) - 0.328351\,(res)_{t-1}$$
$$t : (0.308238)\ (9.151515^*)\qquad (-2.972421^*)$$
$$R^2 : 0.663306 \qquad \text{D-W} : 2.209558$$
$$^*\text{implies significance at 1\% level}$$

These results are quite satisfactory especially because $\hat{\lambda}\,(=-0.328351)$ is negative and statistically significant, which implies that if there were any short-term disturbance from the long-run stable relationship (as represented by the cointegrating regression), such a disturbance would be corrected over time and the long-run stable relationship would be restored. Here, $\hat{\gamma} = 0.878086$ gives short-run elasticity of consumption expenditure with respect to change in GDP. This is expectedly lower than the long-run elasticity.

10.10.3 ARIMA (BJ) Forecasting

Consider the data series on wheat production for the period 1970–71 to 2010–11 in India, presented in Table 10.8. Suppose we want to forecast the levels of wheat production for three years beyond 2010–11 using this data series and applying the ARIMA (BJ) methodology.

Our steps are the following.

1. We obtain the correlogram of the series labeled 'Wheat', which is shown in Table 10.9. It is observed that the ACF of the series exhibits a dying-out pattern of the spikes (significant ACF values) and there exists one significant spike for PACF at lag 1. These observations indicate that Wheat series is non-stationary. Application of the ADF test further confirms this conclusion.[41]

2. Since wheat series is non-stationary, we now obtain the correlogram of first-differenced series for wheat $[d(wheat)]$ to see if that is stationary. Such correlogram (Table 10.10) shows that ACF of the $d(wheat)$ series has a significant spike at lag 1 but shows no clear pattern of spikes after that point. On the other hand, PACF contains significant spikes at lags 1 and 10. On the basis of these patterns

---

[40] Although $R^2 > DW$ – statistic for the cointegrating regression, it may still be acceptable as its residuals series is stationary. However, in a situation like this, one should apply another test (e.g., Johansen's test) and see whether the same conclusion follows.

[41] We have not presented the results of ADF test to save space.

Table 10.8   Data on Production (Million Tons) of Wheat, Rice, and
Total Foodgrains (TFG) in India

Year	Wheat	Rice	TFG	Year	Wheat	Rice	TFG
1970–71	23.83	42.22	108.42	1991–92	55.69	74.68	168.38
1971–72	26.41	43.07	105.17	1992–93	57.21	72.86	179.48
1972–73	24.74	39.24	97.03	1993–94	59.84	80.30	184.26
1973–74	21.78	44.05	104.67	1994–95	65.77	81.81	191.50
1974–75	24.10	39.58	99.83	1995–96	62.10	76.98	180.42
1975–76	28.84	48.74	121.03	1996–97	69.35	81.73	199.43
1976–77	29.01	41.92	111.17	1997–98	66.35	82.54	193.12
1977–78	31.75	52.67	126.41	1998–99	71.29	86.08	203.61
1978–79	35.51	53.77	131.90	1999–2000	76.37	89.68	209.80
1979–80	31.83	42.33	109.70	2000–01	69.68	84.98	196.81
1980–81	36.31	53.63	129.59	2001–02	72.77	93.34	212.85
1981–82	37.45	53.25	133.30	2002–03	65.76	71.82	174.78
1982–83	42.79	47.12	129.52	2003–04	72.15	88.53	213.19
1983–84	45.48	60.10	152.37	2004–05	68.64	83.13	198.36
1984–85	44.07	58.34	145.54	2005–06	69.35	91.79	208.59
1985–86	47.05	63.83	150.44	2006–07	75.81	93.35	217.28
1986–87	44.32	60.56	143.42	2007–08	78.57	96.69	230.78
1987–88	46.17	56.86	140.35	2008–09	80.68	99.18	234.47
1988–89	54.11	70.49	169.92	2009–10	80.80	89.13	218.11
1989–90	49.85	73.57	171.04	2010–11	85.93	95.32	241.56
1990–91	55.14	74.29	176.39				

Source: RBI, *Handbook of Statistics on Indian Economy 2011–12.*

of ACF and PACF, we may say that $d(wheat)$ series is stationary. This is again
confirmed by the ADF test the results which are presented in Table 10.11.

3. We now identify the ARIMA structure of the $d(wheat)$ series. Inspection of
    ACF and PACF for $d(wheat)$ series suggests that it might be modeled as an
    ARIMA(1,10) structure.

4. Before estimating such a model, we have to *resize* the sample range from the
    'Workfile' window (Screenshot 10.4 displayed on page 306). For this, double click
    on **Range**, which will open 'Workfile Structure' window. Select 'Unstructured/
    Undated' in the 'Workfile structure type' box and put 44 in 'Data range' box (since
    the initial Wheat series has 41 observations and we want forecasts for three years
    beyond 41st year) of 'Workfile Structure' window and click **OK**.

5. Now estimate an ARIMA(1,10) model using the 'Estimate Equation…' dialog
    box of EViews. We write **d(wheat) c ar(1) ma(10)** in the 'Equation specification'

Table 10.9   Correlogram of the Series of Wheat

Date: 08/23/13 Time: 16.44
Sample: 1 41
Included observations: 41

Autocorrelation	Partial Correlation		AC	PAC	Q-Stat	Prob
		1	0.911	0.911	36.555	0.000
		2	0.852	0.133	69.377	0.000
		3	0.776	−0.104	97.344	0.000
		4	0.693	−0.118	120.21	0.000
		5	0.622	0.017	139.17	0.000
		6	0.562	0.051	155.06	0.000
		7	0.506	0.007	168.34	0.000
		8	0.439	−0.122	178.62	0.000
		9	0.390	0.035	187.02	0.000
		10	0.317	−0.142	192.72	0.000
		11	0.257	−0.003	196.61	0.000
		12	0.173	−0.179	198.43	0.000
		13	0.112	0.050	199.22	0.000
		14	0.057	0.021	199.43	0.000
		15	−0.012	−0.126	199.44	0.000
		16	−0.057	0.005	199.67	0.000
		17	−0.131	−0.183	200.93	0.000
		18	−0.185	0.001	203.54	0.000
		19	−0.225	0.098	207.59	0.000
		20	−0.274	0.130	213.90	0.000

Source: Same as for Table 10.3A.

box of 'Estimate Equation' dialog box,[42] and click **OK**. The resulting output is displayed in Screenshot 10.5A.

6. To obtain required forecasts, click **Forecast** from output window which will open the 'Forecast' dialog box (see Screenshot 10.5B). In the 'Forecast' dialog box, specify the following.

   (i)   Series to forecast, i.e., whether forecasted series should be in level or first-difference form (obviously, we prefer level).

   (ii) Name for the forecast series, which is to be put in the 'Series name' box (this has been chosen as 'wheatf' by default).

   (iii) Method of forecast (we select 'Dynamic forecast'), and

---

[42] If we choose to estimate an ARMA(1,0) model, we shall write the specification of equation as **d(wheat) c ar(1)**, for an ARMA(2,0) **d(wheat) c ar(1) ar(2)**, for an ARMA(0,10) model **d(wheat) c ma(10)**, and so on.

Table 10.10 Correlogram of First-Differenced Series of Wheat

Date: 08/23/13 Time: 16.43

Sample: 1 41

Included observations: 40

Autocorrelation	Partial Correlation		AC	PAC	Q-Stat	Prob
		1	−0.503	−0.503	10.833	0.001
		2	0.194	−0.079	12.538	0.002
		3	0.005	0.094	12.539	0.006
		4	−0.211	−0.212	14.626	0.006
		5	0.224	0.018	17.045	0.004
		6	−0.210	0.051	19.229	0.004
		7	0.102	−0.077	19.761	0.006
		8	−0.046	−0.045	19.872	0.011
		9	−0.085	−0.063	20.261	0.016
		10	−0.090	−0.117	20.713	0.023
		11	0.152	−0.329	22.047	0.024
		12	−0.154	0.020	23.466	0.024
		13	0.168	−0.104	25.224	0.022
		14	−0.033	−0.000	25.294	0.032
		15	−0.139	0.010	26.586	0.032
		16	0.255	−0.184	31.133	0.013
		17	−0.183	0.066	33.566	0.010
		18	0.128	−0.056	34.826	0.010
		19	−0.005	−0.028	34.828	0.015
		20	−0.132	−0.116	36.294	0.014

Source: Same as for Table 10.3A.

(iv) Output format, i.e., whether 'Forecast graph' and 'Forecast evaluation' statistics are needed. These are selected by default.

7. Click **OK**. The forecast series will be graphically displayed along with some forecast evaluation statistics as in Screenshot 10.6. The forecast series has also been saved in the 'Workfile' with series name 'wheatf'.

8. To obtain the forecast levels of wheat production for three years beyond 2010–11, we return to the 'Workfile' window and double click on 'wheatf'. The entire forecast series will be displayed, as in Screenshot 10.7.

Forecasts

From Screenshot 10.7, we gather the forecast values of wheat production in India for 2011–12, 2012–13, and 2013–14, which are 88.56233, 90.21612, and 91.86991 (in million tonnes), respectively.

Table 10.11　　ADF Test Results for First-Differenced Series of Wheat

Null Hypothesis: D(WHEAT) has a unit root

Exogenous: Constant

Lag Length: 0 (Automatic—based on SIC, maxlag=9)

		t-Statistic	Prob.*
Augmented Dickey-Fuller test statistic		−10.59044	0.0000
Test critical values:	1% level	−3.610453	
	5% level	−2.938987	
	10% level	−2.607932	

*MacKinnon (1996) one-sided p-values.

Augmented Dickey-Fuller Test Equation

Dependent Variable: D(WHEAT,2)

Method: Least Squares

Date: 05/15/12　Time: 12:31

Sample (adjusted): 3 41

Included observations: 39 after adjustments

Variable	Coefficient	Std. Error	t-Statistic	Prob.
D(WHEAT(−1))	−1.514427	0.143000	−10.59044	0.0000
C	2.277614	0.583868	3.900905	0.0004
R-squared	0.751940	Mean dependent var		0.065385
Adjusted R-squared	0.745236	S.D. dependent var		6.745843
S.E. of regression	3.404910	Akaike info criterion		5.338235
Sum squared resid	428.9563	Schwarz criterion		5.423545
Log likelihood	−102.0956	Hannan-Quinn criter.		5.368843
F-statistic	112.1574	Durbin-Watson stat		2.035308
Prob(F-statistic)	0.000000			

Source: Same as for Table 10.3A.

Screenshot 10.4　　Workfile Window of Wheat Series

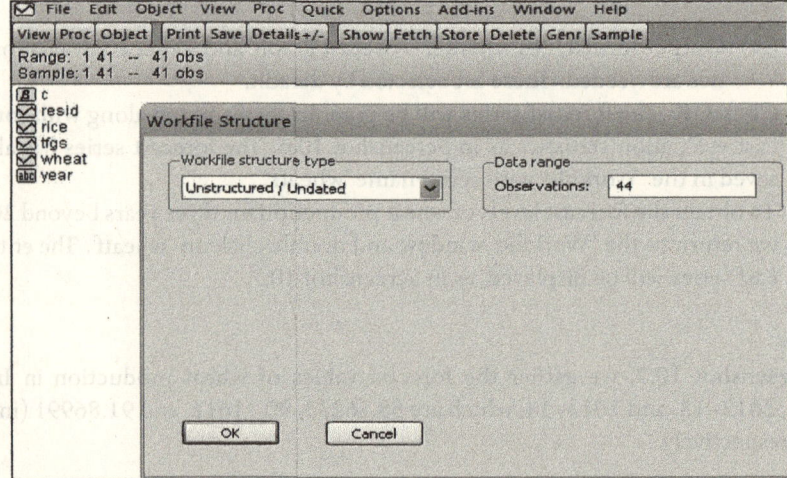

Screenshot 10.5A Output Window of d(wheat)

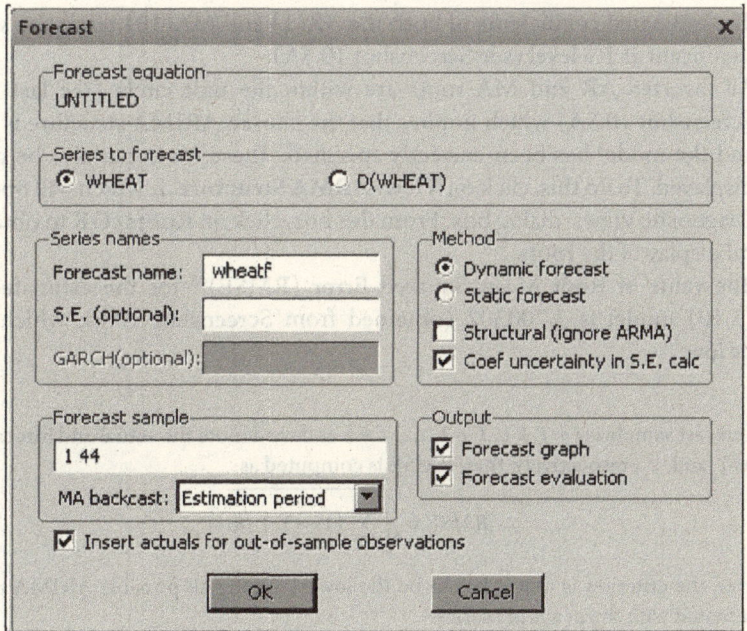

```
☑   File   Edit   Object   View   Proc   Quick   Options
View  Proc  Object    Print  Name  Freeze     Estimate  Foreca
```

Dependent Variable: D(WHEAT)
Method: Least Squares
Date: 08/23/13   Time: 17:41
Sample (adjusted): 3 41
Included observations: 39 after adjustments
Convergence achieved after 9 iterations
MA Backcast: -7 2

Variable	Coefficient	Std. Error	t-Statistic	Prob.
C	1.653790	0.256404	6.449941	0.0000
AR(1)	-0.526141	0.139464	-3.772589	0.0006
MA(10)	-0.848735	0.042274	-20.07678	0.0000

R-squared	0.490535	Mean dependent var	1.526154
Adjusted R-squared	0.462231	S.D. dependent var	3.903408
S.E. of regression	2.862475	Akaike info criterion	5.015053
Sum squared resid	294.9754	Schwarz criterion	5.143020
Log likelihood	-94.79354	Hannan-Quinn criter.	5.060967
F-statistic	17.33118	Durbin-Watson stat	2.220880
Prob(F-statistic)	0.000005		

Inverted AR Roots	-.53			
Inverted MA Roots	.98	.80+.58i	.80-.58i	.30-.94i
	.30+.94i	-.30-.94i	-.30+.94i	-.80-.58i
	-.80+.58i	-.98		

Screenshot 10.5B Forecast Dialog Box

Forecast   X

┌─Forecast equation─────────────────────────────────┐
│ UNTITLED   │
└───┘

┌─Series to forecast────────────────────────────────┐
│ ⦿ WHEAT   ○ D(WHEAT)   │
└───┘

┌─Series names───────────────┐ ┌─Method──────────────┐
│ Forecast name: wheatf   │ │ ⦿ Dynamic forecast   │
│   │ │ ○ Static forecast   │
│ S.E. (optional):   │ │   │
│   │ │ ☐ Structural (ignore ARMA) │
│ GARCH(optional):   │ │ ☑ Coef uncertainty in S.E. calc │
└────────────────────────────┘ └──────────────────────┘

┌─Forecast sample────────────┐ ┌─Output──────────────┐
│ 1 44   │ │ ☑ Forecast graph   │
│   │ │ ☑ Forecast evaluation │
│ MA backcast: Estimation period ▼ │ └──────────────────┘
└────────────────────────────┘

☑ Insert actuals for out-of-sample observations

        OK   Cancel

Screenshot 10.6   Graphical Display of Forecast Series for Wheat

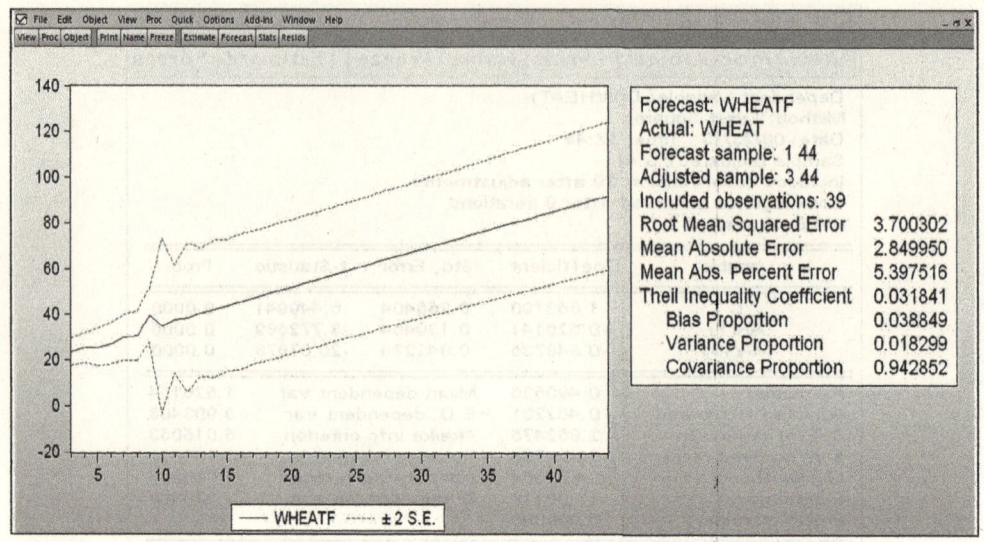

Evaluation of Forecasts

Some idea about the reliability of our forecasts may be obtained on the basis of the following aspects.

1. The estimated coefficients of both the AR(1) and MA(10) terms are statistically significant at 1% level (see Screenshot 10.5A).
2. All inverted AR and MA roots are within the unit circle (see last section of Screenshot 10.5A) which implies that the chosen ARIMA structure is stationary and the model has been correctly specified. These roots can also be graphically displayed. To do this, click on **View/ARMA Structure...** which will open 'ARMA Diagnostic Views' dialog box. From this box, click on **Roots/OK** to obtain graphical display of the roots.
3. The value of Root Mean Squared Error (RMSE)[43] for the estimated ARIMA (1,10) model is 3.700302 (obtained from Screenshot 10.6), which seems to be low.[44]

---

[43] If the forecast sample is $j = T + 1, T + 2, ..., T + h$ and we denote the actual and forecasted values in period t as Y_t and $\hat{Y}_t$, respectively, then RMSE is computed as:

$$RMSE = \sqrt{\sum_{t=T+1}^{T+h} (\hat{Y}_t - Y_t) \Big/ h}$$

[44] However, the criterion is that it has to be the lowest among all possible ARIMA models that might be estimated with the $d(wheat)$ series.

Screenshot 10.7   Forecast Levels of Wheat Production in India

File	Edit	Object	View	Proc	Quick	Options	A
View	Proc	Object	Properties		Print	Name	Freeze	Defau

2	NA			
3	23.76800			
4	25.46834			
5	25.59684			
6	27.14575			
7	30.05043			
8	30.68983			
9	39.60458			
10	34.90593			
11	38.01846			
12	38.56798			
13	40.80273			
14	42.15080			
15	43.96544			
16	45.53460			
17	47.23292			
18	48.86328			
19	50.52940			
20	52.17670			
21	53.83391			
22	55.48590			
23	57.14064			
24	58.79393			
25	60.44798			
26	62.10164			
27	63.75550			
28	65.40925			
29	67.06306			
30	68.71684			
31	70.37064			
32	72.02442			
33	73.67822			
34	75.33201			
35	76.98580			
36	78.63959			
37	80.29338			
38	81.94717			
39	83.60096			
40	85.26475			
41	86.90854			
42	88.56233			
43	90.21612			
44	91.86991			

4.   The values of 'bias proportion', 'variance proportion', and 'covariance proportion' are 0.038849, 0.018299, and 0.942852, respectively.[45] Since the values of bias and variance proportions are low and that of covariance proportion is high, our forecasts may be considered satisfactory.

[45] These are computed by decomposing $RMSE^2$ = MSE (Mean Squared Error). The 'bias proportion' tells us how far the mean of the forecast is from the mean of the actual series, the 'variance proportion' conveys how far the variation of the forecast is from the variation of the actual series, and the 'covariance proportion' measures the remaining unsystematic forecasting error. If the 'forecast' is good, the bias and variance proportions should be small so that most of the bias should be concentrated on the covariance proportion.

10.10.4 Estimation of VAR Model

Suppose we want to estimate the following VAR(1) model using data given in Table 10.12.

$$
\left.
\begin{aligned}
LM_t &= \alpha_1 + \alpha_2 LM_{t-1} + \alpha_3 LY_{t-1} + \alpha_4 LR_{t-1} + \varepsilon_{1t} \\
LY_t &= \beta_1 + \beta_2 LM_{t-1} + \beta_3 LY_{t-1} + \beta_4 LR_{t-1} + \varepsilon_{2t} \\
LR_t &= \gamma_1 + \gamma_2 LM_{t-1} + \gamma_3 LY_{t-1} + \gamma_4 LR_{t-1} + \varepsilon_{3t}
\end{aligned}
\right\}
\qquad (10.53)
$$

Using EViews, our steps are the following.

1. Transform the variables (M, Y, and R) in logs following the procedure mentioned earlier. The transformed variables are labeled as LM, LY and LR, respectively.
2. Examine the stochastic properties of these log-transformed variables. Applying the ADF test, we found that all the log-transformed variables are non-stationary in 'level' but stationary in 'first-difference' form. Therefore, while estimating the

Table 10.12 Data on Income (Y), Money Supply (M), and Rate of Interest (R) in India

Year	Y	M	R	Year	Y	M	R
1970–71	474,131	768	7.75	1991–92	1,099,072	3,781	16.50
1971–72	478,918	838	8.50	1992–93	1,158,025	3,944	19.00
1972–73	477,392	901	8.50	1993–94	1,223,816	4,311	19.00
1973–74	499,120	879	8.75	1994–95	1,302,076	4,686	15.00
1974–75	504,914	779	11.25	1995–96	1,396,974	4,928	16.50
1975–76	550,379	906	14.00	1996–97	1,508,378	5,472	14.50
1976–77	557,258	1,097	14.00	1997–98	1,573,263	6,185	14.00
1977–78	598,885	1,235	13.00	1998–99	1,678,410	6,972	13.00
1978–79	631,839	1,505	13.00	1999–2000	1,786,525	7,737	12.00
1979–80	598,974	1,513	16.50	2000–01	1,864,301	8,434	11.50
1980–81	641,921	1,511	16.50	2001–02	1,972,606	9,289	11.50
1981–82	678,033	1,555	16.50	2002–03	2,048,286	10,300	10.75
1982–83	697,861	1,729	16.50	2003–04	2,222,758	1,1402	10.25
1983–84	752,669	1,901	16.50	2004–05	2,388,768	11,990	10.25
1984–85	782,484	2,124	16.50	2005–06	2,616,101	13,894	10.25
1985–86	815,049	2,359	16.50	2006–07	2,871,120	15,864	12.25
1986–87	850,217	2,645	16.50	2007–08	3,129,717	18,398	12.25
1987–88	880,267	2,837	16.50	2008–09	3,339,375	20,317	12.25
1988–89	969,702	3,109	16.50	2009-10	3,605,108	22,869	11.75
1989–90	1,029,178	3,454	16.50	2010-11	3,913,251	24,216	8.25
1990–91	1,083,572	3,605	16.50				

Source: RBI, *Handbook of Statistics on Indian Economy 2011–12.*

Note: Y = GDP at factor cost (Rs Crore, Base Year: 1999–2000 = 100); M = real money supply (Rs Crore) = broad money (M_3)/wholesale price index (all commodities, Base: 1993–94 = 100); and R = lending rate of the State Bank of India.

VAR model, we shall use first-difference of these variables. Note that the log-transformed variables in first-difference form provide annual growth rates of these variables (as we have yearly data).

3. To estimate the VAR model, click on **Quick/Estimate VAR ...** from the main menu of EViews. This opens the 'VAR Specification' dialog box, as shown in Screenshot 10.8.
4. From the 'VAR Specification' dialog box,
    (i)   select **Unrestricted VAR** from 'VAR Type' box,
    (ii) write **d(LM) d(LY) d(LR)** in the 'Endogenous Variables' box, and
    (iii) write **1 1** in the 'Lag Intervals for Endogenous:' box (as we intend to estimate a VAR(1) model that considers one period lag for right-hand side variables)[46].
5. Click **OK** to obtain the VAR estimation output, which is shown in Table 10.13.

Screenshot 10.8   VAR Specification Dialog Box

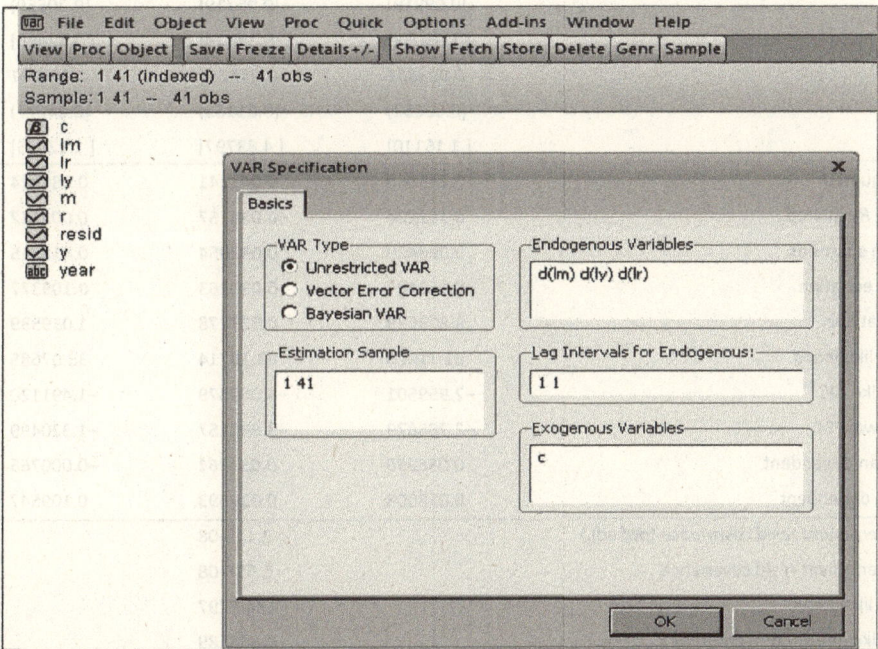

Interpretation of VAR Results

In Table 10.13, the second column corresponds to results relating to money supply equation, the third to income equation and the fourth to rate of interest equation. In each of these columns, apart from estimated coefficient has each right-hand side variable its standard error and computed value have been reported. On the basis of our results, it can be said

---

[46] For estimating a VAR(2) model, we shall write here **1 2**, we shall write **1 3** for VAR(3) model, and so on.

Table 10.13 Estimation Output for VAR(1) Model

Vector Autoregression Estimates
Date: 08/23/13 Time: 18:09
Sample (adjusted): 3 41
Included observations: 39 after adjustments
Standard errors in ( ) & t-statistics in [ ]

	D(LM)	D(LY)	D(LR)
D(LM(−1))	0.251088	−0.112575	−0.437633
	(0.16451)	(0.09485)	(0.34280)
	[1.52628]	[−1.18689]	[−1.27663]
D(LY(−1))	0.742301	0.127117	−0.218009
	(0.30867)	(0.17796)	(0.64320)
	[2.40484]	[0.71429]	[−0.33894]
D(LR(−1))	0.183539	−0.019058	0.067104
	(0.09919)	(0.05719)	(0.20669)
	[1.85038]	[−0.33326]	[0.32466]
C	0.023831	0.057249	0.047941
	(0.02052)	(0.01183)	(0.04277)
	[1.16110]	[4.83797]	[1.12095]
R-squared	0.245865	0.043241	0.081814
Adj. R-squared	0.181224	−0.038767	0.003112
Sum sq. resids	0.096429	0.032054	0.418715
S.E. equation	0.052489	0.030263	0.109377
F-statistic	3.803589	0.527278	1.039539
Log likelihood	61.71026	83.18714	33.07685
Akaike AIC	−2.959501	−4.060879	−1.491120
Schwarz SC	−2.788879	−3.890257	−1.320499
Mean dependent	0.086250	0.053861	−0.000765
S.D. dependent	0.058008	0.029693	0.109547
Determinant resid covariance (dof adj.)		2.11E-08	
Determinant resid covariance		1.53E-08	
Log likelihood		184.9297	
Akaike information criterion		−8.868189	
Schwarz criterion		−8.356324	

Source: Same as for Table 10.3A.

columns, apart from estimated coefficient for each right-hand side variable, its standard error and computed-*t* value have been reported. On the basis of our results, it can be said that higher growth of income $[d(LY)]$ during period $t-1$ leads to higher growth of money supply $[d(LM)]$ in period t. This is revealed by statistical significance of computed-*t* for the estimated coefficient of $d[LY(-1)]$.[47] The same relation holds between growth of interest rate $[d(LR(-1)]$ and growth of money supply (computed-t being 1.85038). However, no other estimated coefficient appears to be statistically significant in any of the equations.

Testing Granger Causality in VAR Model

We may conduct a Granger Causality test to understand the direction of causality between three endogenous variables of our VAR model. For this, click on **View/Lag Structure/Granger Causality/Block Exogeneity Wald Test** from the VAR output window to obtain the results of the test, which are shown in Table 10.14.

The following conclusions follow from the results of the Causality Test here.[48]

(i)   Money supply growth result
        $D(LY) \to D(LM) \Rightarrow D(LY)$ Granger causes $D(LM)$
        $D(LR) \to D(LM) \Rightarrow D(LR)$ Granger causes $D(LM)$
        $D(LY), D(LR) \to D(LM) \Rightarrow D(LY)$ & $D(LR)$ jointly Granger cause $D(LM)$

Table 10.14   Results of VAR Granger Causality Test

VAR Granger Causality/Block Exogeneity Wald Tests
Date: 08/23/13 Time: 18:15
Sample: 1 41
Included observations: 39

Dependent variable: D(LM)			
Excluded	Chi-sq	Df	Prob.
D(LY)	5.783268	1	0.0162
D(LR)	3.423900	1	0.0643
All	7.752272	2	0.0207
Dependent variable: D(LY)			
Excluded	Chi-sq	df	Prob.
D(LM)	1.408708	1	0.2353
D(LR)	0.111059	1	0.7389
All	1.408731	2	0.4944
Dependent variable: D(LR)			
Excluded	Chi-sq	df	Prob.
D(LM)	1.629772	1	0.2017
D(LY)	0.114882	1	0.7347
All	2.155347	2	0.3404

Source: Same as for Table 10.3A.

[47] Note that the EViews output on VAR does not provide the significance levels of computed-t values. However, this should not prevent us from using the *rule of thumb* that, for a large sample ($n \geq 30$), the critical-t value at 5% significance level becomes ≥ 1.697 (in one-tailed test). Thus, if computed-t is found to be ≥ 1.697, it may be viewed as statistically significant at 5% level. However, if the sample is small, we must use the specific critical-t values given in the table for t distribution as this *rule of thumb* is not safe to apply.

[48] We focus on the p-values reported in the last column of the table to draw our conclusion regarding direction of causality between the variables.

(ii) Income growth result

$D(LM) \nrightarrow D(LY) \Rightarrow D(LM)$ doesn't Granger cause $D(LY)$

$D(LR) \nrightarrow D(LY) \Rightarrow D(LR)$ doesn't Granger cause $D(LY)$

$D(LM), D(LR) \nrightarrow D(LY) \Rightarrow D(LM)$ & $D(LR)$ do not jointly Granger cause $D(LY)$

(iii) Interest rate growth result

$D(LM) \nrightarrow D(LR) \Rightarrow D(LM)$ doesn't Granger cause $D(LR)$

$D(LY) \nrightarrow D(LR) \Rightarrow D(LY)$ doesn't Granger cause $D(LR)$

$D(LM), D(LY) \nrightarrow D(LR) \Rightarrow D(LM)$ & $D(LY)$ do not jointly Granger cause $D(LR)$

The conclusion drawn from the causality test is same as the conclusion that follows from the VAR estimation result, which is that both income growth and growth of rate of interest in India in one period lead to growth of money supply in the next period. Thus, causality runs from income growth to money supply growth, and from interest rate growth to money supply growth.

Usefulness of Estimated VAR Model

To assess the usefulness of our estimated VAR model, we consider the following.

(i) *Inverse roots of AR characteristic polynomial in table/graph*: The estimated VAR is considered to be stable if all roots have modulus less than one and lie inside the unit circle. The number of such roots is $k.p$ where k is the number of endogenous variables and p is the largest lag. To obtain these roots, click on **View/Lag Structure/AR Roots Table or AR Roots Graph** from the main menu of the VAR output window. For our estimated VAR model, the table of AR roots is shown below (Table 10.15). It is found that our estimated VAR model satisfies the stability condition.

Table 10.15 Results of VAR Stability Condition Check

Roots of Characteristic Polynomial
Endogenous variables: D(LM) D(LY) D(LR)
Exogenous variables: C
Lag specification: 1 1
Date: 08/23/13 Time: 18:18

Root	Modulus
0.142022 − 0.388655i	0.413791
0.142022 + 0.388655i	0.413791
0.161265	0.161265

No root lies outside the unit circle.
VAR satisfies the stability condition.

Source: Same as for Table 10.3A.

(ii)   *Lag Length Selection*: Whether or not we have selected the maximum lag length appropriately for our VAR model may be checked in terms of criteria like AIC, SBC, HQC, and so on. The model that shows up lowest values of these criteria is chosen. To compute these values at various lags, again click **View/ Lag Structure/Lag Length Criteria...** from the main menu of VAR output window which will display the 'Lag Specification' box. Select a lag length and click **OK**. If we select maximum lag length 3, the result displayed in Table 10.16 is obtained.

It appears that values of AIC, SIC, and HQC are all minimum at lag 0. This justifies selection of minimum possible lag (one-period) for the right-hand side variables of our VAR model.[49]

(iii)   *Autocorrelation LM Test*: To examine possible presence of autocorrelation in our VAR model, we have to conduct the Autocorrelation LM test. To do this, click on **View/Residual Tests/ Autocorrelation LM Test...** from the VAR output window which will open the 'Lag Specification' box. Select the number of lags to include in the VAR model and click **OK**. As we selected 6 lags, the output presented in Table 10.17 is obtained.

The result shows that the computed LM-statistic (which follows a Chi-square distribution) is statistically insignificant (as $p > 0.10$) even for lag 1 which leads to acceptance of the null hypothesis of absence of serial correlation in the VAR model that we have estimated.

Table 10.16   Results of Lag Length Selection Test

VAR Lag Order Selection Criteria
Endogenous variables: D(LM) D(LY) D(LR)
Exogenous variables: C
Date: 08/23/13 Time: 18:20
Sample: 1 41
Included observations: 37

Lag	LogL	LR	FPE	AIC	SC	HQ
0	167.4756	NA*	2.76e-08*	−8.890571*	−8.759956*	−8.844523*
1	176.0071	15.21843	2.84e-08	−8.865249	−8.342789	−8.681057
2	180.3230	6.998701	3.70e-08	−8.612052	−7.697747	−8.289717
3	185.7598	7.934850	4.61e-08	−8.419449	−7.113299	−7.958970

* indicates lag order selected by the criterion
LR: sequential modified LR test statistic (each test at 5% level)
FPE: Final prediction error
AIC: Akaike information criterion
SC: Schwarz information criterion
HQ: Hannan-Quinn information criterion

Source: Same as for Table 10.3A.

[49] It is to be noted that sometimes the values of AIC, SBC, and HQC may not be uniformly minimum at a particular lag length. In that situation, we may rely on the HQC value. This is because, in general, AIC chooses a long lag structure, SBC chooses a very short lag structure, and HQC falls in-between.

Table 10.17   Results of VAR Residual Serial Correlation LM Tests

VAR Residual Serial Correlation LM Tests
Null Hypothesis: no serial correlation at lag order h
Date: 08/23/13 Time: 18:21
Sample: 1 41
Included observations: 39

Lags	LM-Stat	Prob
1	10.08161	0.3439
2	3.915474	0.9169
3	6.444158	0.6948
4	10.50377	0.3113
5	14.58633	0.1029
6	7.331186	0.6027

Probs from Chi-square with 9 *df*.

Source: Same as for Table 10.3A.

(iv)   *Impulse Responses*: To obtain impulse responses for the estimated VAR model, click on **View/Impulse Response…** from the VAR output window which will open 'Impulse Responses' dialog box, as shown in Screenshot 10.9. From this dialog box, select 'Display Format' and 'Periods' for which responses to shocks are to be obtained, and click **OK**. For instance, if we select 'Multiple Graphs' as 'Display Format' and 20 'Periods', the impulse responses will be displayed graphically as in Screenshot 10.10. Here responses of different endogenous variables to shocks are shown by solid lines. The dotted lines provide plus/minus two standard error bands about impulse responses. Studying these impulse responses, we understand the time required by each endogenous variable to revert back to the long-run equilibrium base following shocks.

(v)   *Variance Decomposition*: As we know, this reflects the proportion of the forecast error variance of a variable which is explained by an unanticipated change (shock) in itself as opposed to that proportion attributable to change in other interrelated variables. To obtain variance decomposition results for the estimated VAR model, click on **View/Variance Decomposition…** from the output window which will open 'VAR Variance Decompositions' dialog box, as shown in Screenshot 10.11. From this dialog box, select 'Display Format', 'Periods' for which decompositions are to be obtained, and click **OK**.

For instance, when we select 'Multiple Graphs' as 'Display Format' and 20 'Periods', variance decompositions are displayed graphically as in Screenshot 10.12. However, if we select 'Table' as the 'Display Format', quantitative information regarding variance decompositions are obtained, as shown in Table 10.18. The variance decomposition results show that for each endogenous variable of the model, 79% or more of forecast error variance is accounted for by own shock even in the 20th year.

Screenshot 10.9 Impulse Response Dialog Box

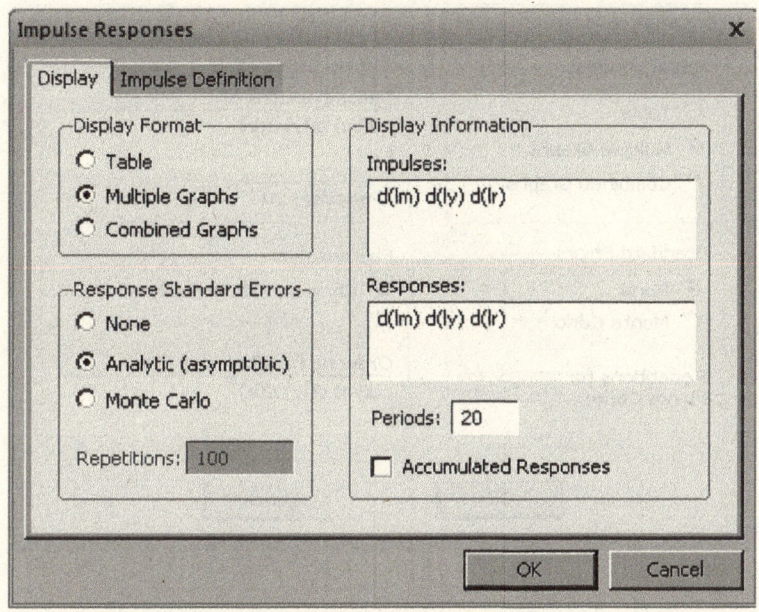

Screenshot 10.10 Graphical Display of Impulse Responses

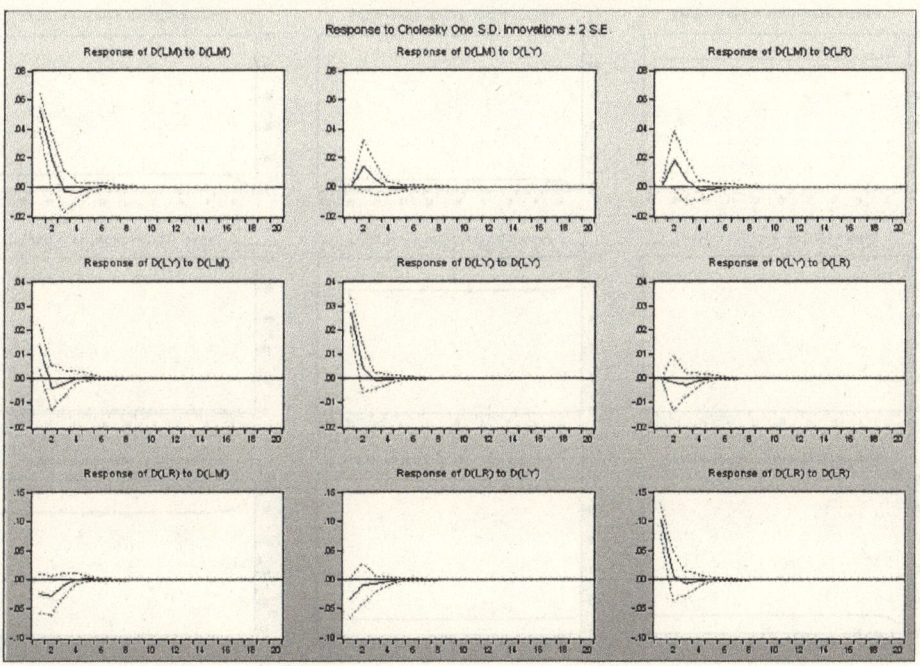

Screenshot 10.11   VAR Variance Decompositions Dialog Box

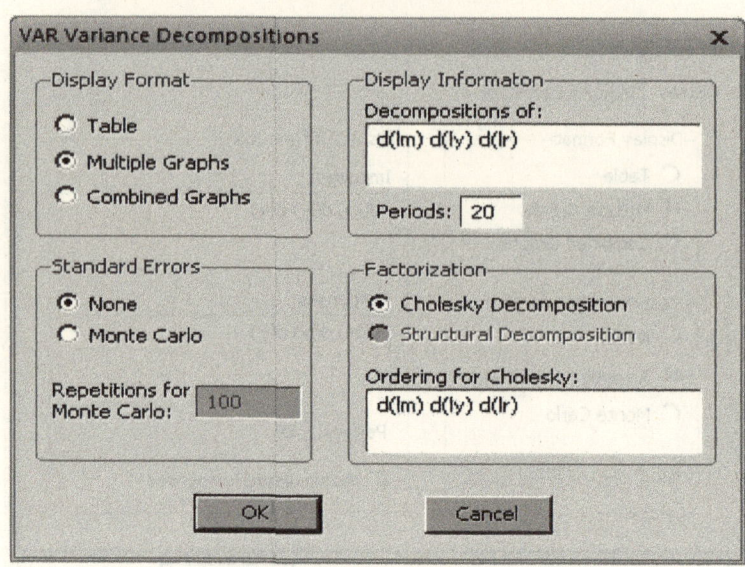

Screenshot 10.12   Graphical Display of Variance Decompositions

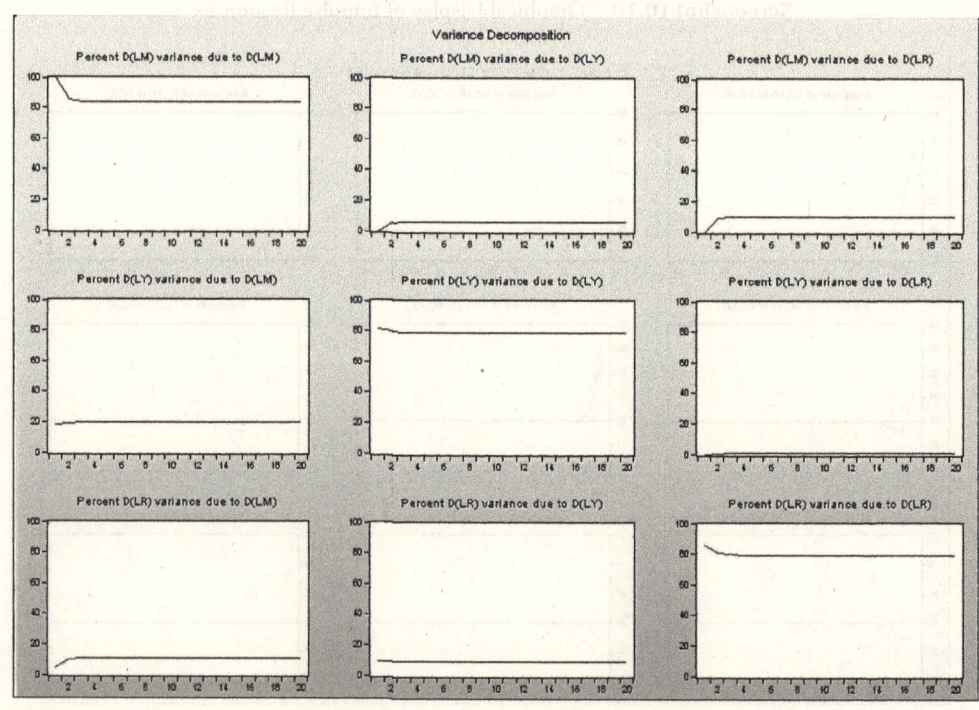

Table 10.18 Variance Decomposition Results for Estimated VAR Model

Variance Decomposition of D(LM):

Period	S.E.	D(LM)	D(LY)	D(LR)
1	0.052489	100.0000	0.000000	0.000000
2	0.060359	84.97956	5.511239	9.509205
3	0.060826	83.96079	6.130871	9.908343
4	0.060996	83.92081	6.114054	9.965134
5	0.061023	83.85399	6.139515	10.00649
6	0.061026	83.85454	6.139729	10.00573
7	0.061027	83.85327	6.140030	10.00670
8	0.061027	83.85306	6.140135	10.00681
9	0.061027	83.85306	6.140131	10.00681
10	0.061027	83.85305	6.140135	10.00682
11	0.061027	83.85305	6.140135	10.00682
12	0.061027	83.85305	6.140135	10.00682
13	0.061027	83.85305	6.140135	10.00682
14	0.061027	83.85305	6.140135	10.00682
15	0.061027	83.85305	6.140135	10.00682
16	0.061027	83.85305	6.140135	10.00682
17	0.061027	83.85305	6.140135	10.00682
18	0.061027	83.85305	6.140135	10.00682
19	0.061027	83.85305	6.140135	10.00682
20	0.061027	83.85305	6.140135	10.00682

Variance Decomposition of D(LY):

Period	S.E.	D(LM)	D(LY)	D(LR)
1	0.030263	18.57267	81.42733	0.000000
2	0.030835	19.40359	80.20355	0.392865
3	0.031015	19.61154	79.36552	1.022946
4	0.031028	19.60240	79.32741	1.070195
5	0.031032	19.61934	79.30738	1.073271
6	0.031033	19.61917	79.30497	1.075860
7	0.031033	19.61939	79.30474	1.075875
8	0.031033	19.61945	79.30462	1.075931
9	0.031033	19.61944	79.30462	1.075940
10	0.031033	19.61945	79.30461	1.075940
11	0.031033	19.61945	79.30461	1.075940
12	0.031033	19.61945	79.30461	1.075940
13	0.031033	19.61945	79.30461	1.075940
14	0.031033	19.61945	79.30461	1.075940
15	0.031033	19.61945	79.30461	1.075940
16	0.031033	19.61945	79.30461	1.075940

(Contd.)

Table 10.18 (Contd.)

Period	S.E.	D(LM)	D(LY)	D(LR)
17	0.031033	19.61945	79.30461	1.075940
18	0.031033	19.61945	79.30461	1.075940
19	0.031033	19.61945	79.30461	1.075940
20	0.031033	19.61945	79.30461	1.075940
Variance Decomposition of D(LR):				
Period	S.E.	D(LM)	D(LY)	D(LR)
1	0.109377	4.798774	9.236246	85.96498
2	0.113263	10.33683	9.135384	80.52779
3	0.114116	10.81778	9.448172	79.73405
4	0.114167	10.81989	9.489443	79.69066
5	0.114185	10.84053	9.487182	79.67229
6	0.114188	10.84051	9.488414	79.67108
7	0.114188	10.84086	9.488415	79.67072
8	0.114188	10.84094	9.488425	79.67064
9	0.114188	10.84094	9.488430	79.67063
10	0.114188	10.84094	9.488430	79.67063
11	0.114188	10.84094	9.488430	79.67063
12	0.114188	10.84094	9.488430	79.67063
13	0.114188	10.84094	9.488430	79.67063
14	0.114188	10.84094	9.488430	79.67063
15	0.114188	10.84094	9.488430	79.67063
16	0.114188	10.84094	9.488430	79.67063
17	0.114188	10.84094	9.488430	79.67063
18	0.114188	10.84094	9.488430	79.67063
19	0.114188	10.84094	9.488430	79.67063
20	0.114188	10.84094	9.488430	79.67063
Cholesky Ordering: D(LM) D(LY) D(LR)				

Source: Same as for Table 10.3A.

Forecasting with VAR Model

Suppose we want to make *ex ante* forecasts of the values of LM, LY, and LR for two years beyond 41st year. This can be done easily using EViews. The steps involved are the following.

1.   Expand the sample range of the data before estimating the specified VAR model. For this, double click on **Range**, which will open 'Workfile Structure' window. Select 'Unstructured/Undated' in the 'Workfile structure type' box and put 43 in 'Data range' box (since the initial series has 41 observations and we want forecasts for two years beyond 41st year) of 'Workfile Structure' window and click **OK**.

2.   Estimate the VAR model by following the steps mentioned earlier.

Screenshot 10.13   Model Solution Dialog Box of Estimated VAR Model

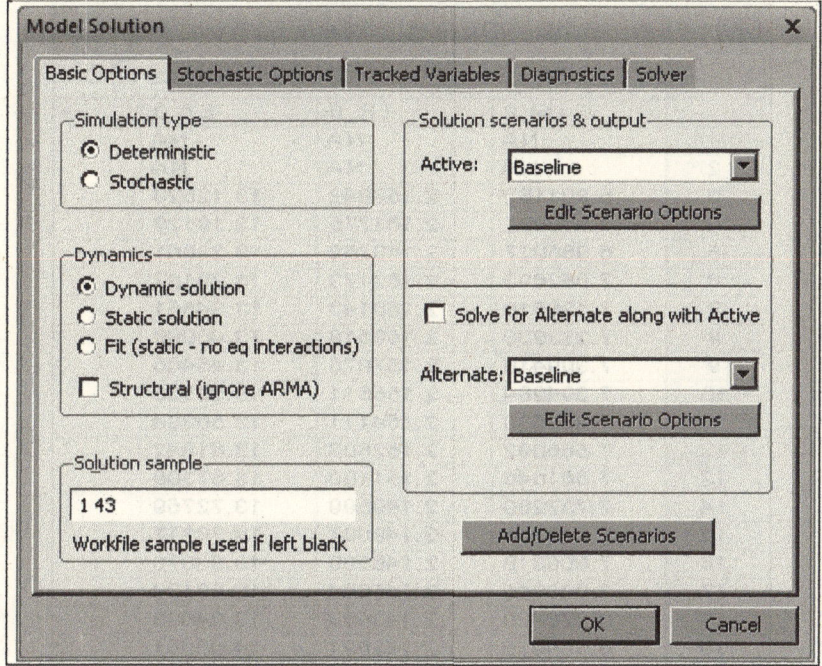

3.   From the VAR output window, click on **Proc/Make Model/Proc/Solve Model...**
        which will open the 'Model Solution' dialog box as shown in Screenshot 10.13.
4.   In the 'Model Solution' dialog box,
        (i)   select 'Deterministic' from 'Simulation type' box,
        (ii)   select 'Dynamic solution' from 'Dynamics' box,
        (iii) write 1 43 in 'Solution sample' box, and
        (iv)   click **OK**.
5.   Now click on **Proc/Make Group/Table...** which will open 'Make Group/Table'
        dialog box. Click **OK** from this box which will display the forecasted series as
        shown in Screenshot 10.14. From here we gather the forecasted values (in logs) of
        three endogenous variables of our VAR model for the 42nd and 43rd years.

10.10.5 Testing of ARCH Effect

Graphical Presentation of Volatility Clustering

Suppose we want to examine the presence of ARCH or *volatility clustering* in the series for
daily percentage changes in SENSEX index (labeled as SEN) in India, presented in Table
10.19. To have a graphical display of volatility clustering in the series (if any) we obtain the
data in the EViews workfile. In the next step, double click on SEN which will open the 'SEN

Screenshot 10.14   Forecasted Series from VAR Estimation

var File Edit Object View Proc Quick		
View | Proc | Object | Print | Name | Freeze | Def		
	LM_0	LR_0	LY_0

	LM_0	LR_0	LY_0
1	NA	NA	NA
2	NA	NA	NA
3	6.801162	2.153842	13.12623
4	6.879981	2.161775	13.18129
5	6.965927	2.163752	13.23651
6	7.052693	2.162173	13.29107
7	7.138516	2.160143	13.34551
8	7.223938	2.158519	13.40006
9	7.309410	2.157075	13.45466
10	7.394964	2.155611	13.50925
11	7.480533	2.154111	13.56384
12	7.566092	2.152603	13.61842
13	7.651646	2.151100	13.67300
14	7.737200	2.149599	13.72759
15	7.822755	2.148097	13.78217
16	7.908310	2.146596	13.83676
17	7.993865	2.145094	13.89134
18	8.079420	2.143593	13.94593
19	8.164975	2.142091	14.00051
20	8.250531	2.140590	14.05510
21	8.336086	2.139088	14.10968
22	8.421641	2.137587	14.16427
23	8.507196	2.136085	14.21885
24	8.592751	2.134583	14.27344
25	8.678306	2.133082	14.32802
26	8.763861	2.131580	14.38261
27	8.849416	2.130079	14.43719
28	8.934971	2.128577	14.49178
29	9.020526	2.127076	14.54636
30	9.106081	2.125574	14.60095
31	9.191636	2.124073	14.65553
32	9.277192	2.122571	14.71011
33	9.362747	2.121070	14.76470
34	9.448302	2.119568	14.81928
35	9.533857	2.118066	14.87387
36	9.619412	2.116565	14.92845
37	9.704967	2.115063	14.98304
38	9.790522	2.113562	15.03762
39	9.876077	2.112060	15.09221
40	9.961632	2.110559	15.14679
41	10.04719	2.109057	15.20138
42	10.13274	2.107556	15.25596
43	10.21830	2.106054	15.31055

Table 10.19   Daily Percentage Changes in Exchange Rate and SENSEX Index in India

(Period: 01.01.2008 to 30.11.2010)

Obs.	ER	SEN	Obs.	ER	SEN	Obs.	ER	SEN	Obs.	ER	SEN	Obs.	ER	SEN
1	0.011	0.029	23	-0.044	-0.270	45	0.368	-2.285	67	0.098	-0.470	89	0.175	0.581
2	0.011	0.351	24	-0.033	1.437	46	0.032	-0.889	68	0.000	0.562	90	0.072	0.949
3	0.022	-0.256	25	0.022	0.983	47	0.000	0.534	69	-0.076	-0.263	91	0.245	0.203
4	-0.143	0.723	26	0.055	0.007	48	0.258	-1.514	70	-0.011	0.310	92	0.031	-0.513
5	-0.044	0.263	27	0.187	-1.236	49	0.150	-0.141	71	0.022	0.940	93	0.051	0.033
6	-0.011	0.126	28	-0.132	-1.492	50	-0.214	0.541	72	0.000	0.243	94	0.435	-0.855
7	0.022	-0.007	29	0.077	-0.154	51	-0.118	0.013	73	-0.076	1.304	95	-0.313	-0.666
8	0.000	-0.603	30	0.197	-2.125	52	0.086	-2.126	74	0.054	0.115	96	-0.285	-0.793
9	0.000	0.515	31	-0.088	-0.060	53	0.011	1.125	75	0.011	-0.223	97	0.335	-0.194
10	0.000	-0.208	32	0.033	0.883	54	0.342	-2.703	76	0.098	0.060	98	-0.041	0.661
11	-0.022	-1.011	33	-0.033	2.046	55	-0.160	0.070	77	0.152	1.039	99	-0.081	-0.553
12	0.000	-0.829	34	0.011	0.844	56	-0.182	0.470	78	-0.043	-0.280	100	-0.183	0.264
13	0.022	-0.367	35	0.000	-0.161	57	-0.118	0.845	79	0.086	0.915	101	-0.358	-0.942
14	-0.022	-1.542	36	0.229	0.066	58	-0.237	2.559	80	0.258	-0.228	102	0.297	-0.273
15	0.121	-3.342	37	0.304	-1.115	59	0.022	-0.351	81	0.203	0.779	103	0.102	-1.236
16	0.384	-2.215	38	-0.087	0.288	60	0.011	-0.193	82	-0.107	-0.270	104	0.234	0.708
17	-0.186	2.187	39	-0.098	-0.955	61	-0.054	0.954	83	0.150	-0.294	105	-0.071	-0.547
18	-0.143	-0.929	40	0.076	0.748	62	-0.141	-1.972	84	0.541	-0.084	106	0.101	-1.435
19	-0.033	2.783	41	-0.152	0.381	63	0.011	0.293	85	0.618	-0.653	107	0.000	-0.513
20	0.077	-0.497	42	-0.196	0.048	64	-0.033	0.226	86	-0.428	-0.882	108	0.000	0.855
21	-0.077	-0.146	43	0.087	-0.004	65	0.022	-1.364	87	0.314	0.320	109	-0.081	0.185
22	0.033	-0.808	44	0.120	-0.603	66	-0.043	1.156	88	0.497	-0.279	110	0.061	-0.173

(Contd.)

Table 10.19 (Contd.)

Obs.	ER	SEN	Obs.	ER	SEN	Obs.	ER	SEN	Obs.	ER	SEN	Obs.	ER	SEN
111	0.030	0.586	135	-0.162	1.700	159	0.200	0.147	183	0.474	-1.712	207	-0.402	2.424
112	0.020	0.841	136	-0.071	0.678	160	0.486	0.096	184	0.019	1.558	208	0.247	-2.970
113	-0.020	-0.766	137	0.000	0.790	161	-0.336	-0.560	185	-0.074	-1.798	209	1.082	-1.360
114	0.030	-0.952	138	-0.388	2.507	162	0.000	-0.761	186	0.534	-2.588	210	0.592	-0.693
115	0.040	-1.513	139	-0.381	-0.483	163	0.060	1.567	187	0.500	-0.394	211	-0.415	-0.439
116	0.000	-0.836	140	0.279	-1.501	164	0.415	-0.197	188	0.655	-1.384	212	0.607	-1.686
117	-0.030	-0.571	141	0.072	0.225	165	0.049	1.621	189	-0.018	-3.183	213	0.052	-0.801
118	-0.122	0.348	142	0.246	-1.721	166	0.186	-0.437	190	-0.520	3.109	214	0.676	-1.628
119	-0.091	0.612	143	-0.072	1.533	167	-0.078	-1.228	191	-0.390	0.664	215	-0.423	2.322
120	0.061	-1.907	144	0.020	0.208	168	-0.108	1.361	192	0.651	-2.628	216	0.052	-0.059
121	0.162	-1.085	145	-0.123	0.901	169	0.614	-0.129	193	0.384	-0.924	217	-0.104	-1.025
122	0.322	-1.644	146	0.031	-0.234	170	0.222	-0.700	194	-0.160	-2.562	218	-0.104	1.623
123	0.070	2.294	147	-0.123	1.127	171	0.307	-1.014	195	0.134	1.065	219	-0.009	0.316
124	-0.040	-1.852	148	-0.289	0.325	172	0.314	-0.992	196	0.407	-0.227	220	0.217	-1.225
125	-0.090	1.178	149	-0.114	0.126	173	0.161	-1.481	197	0.438	-1.735	221	0.371	-0.497
126	-0.091	0.232	150	0.320	0.145	174	0.647	-0.040	198	0.139	-5.040	222	-0.536	0.041
127	0.251	-0.570	151	-0.206	0.952	175	-0.271	-0.830	199	0.122	-0.967	223	-0.096	2.331
128	-0.241	1.955	152	0.412	-0.825	176	0.345	0.172	200	-0.278	2.648	224	-0.087	-1.263
129	0.030	-0.118	153	0.276	-0.341	177	-0.364	2.308	201	-0.456	3.431	225	-0.413	0.946
130	-0.445	-1.447	154	0.152	-1.075	178	-0.871	-0.147	202	-0.256	2.373	226	-0.088	2.273
131	0.102	-0.452	155	0.414	-0.232	179	0.305	-1.338	203	-0.303	1.216	227	-0.534	-0.042
132	0.354	-2.186	156	0.489	0.096	180	0.104	0.389	204	-1.306	-2.140	228	0.170	0.200
133	0.000	-0.345	157	-0.139	-1.305	181	0.396	-0.463	205	0.449	-1.688	229	-0.692	0.633
134	-0.232	1.813	158	-0.200	0.478	182	0.169	-1.451	206	0.082	1.015	230	-0.109	0.634

(Contd.)

Table 10.19 (Contd.)

Obs.	ER	SEN	Obs.	ER	SEN	Obs.	ER	SEN	Obs.	ER	SEN	Obs.	ER	SEN
231	−0.447	−1.154	255	−0.168	0.171	279	0.865	−1.412	303	0.017	1.239	327	−0.283	−1.013
232	−0.046	1.585	256	0.230	−0.693	280	−0.076	−0.917	304	−0.341	−1.318	328	−0.193	0.474
233	−0.184	0.101	257	−0.301	1.620	281	0.226	0.099	305	0.193	0.299	329	0.028	0.081
234	0.285	−0.744	258	0.018	1.205	282	0.109	−1.297	306	0.209	−0.172	330	0.375	−1.023
235	0.997	−1.070	259	0.027	−0.100	283	−0.461	0.672	307	0.355	−0.323	331	0.036	1.632
236	0.446	−0.532	260	0.106	0.875	284	0.244	−0.872	308	−0.138	−0.322	332	0.146	0.570
237	−0.986	−1.102	261	−0.009	−1.680	285	−0.084	0.965	309	0.017	1.256	333	−0.493	0.989
238	0.782	0.942	262	−0.186	0.394	286	−0.025	2.097	310	−0.243	0.750	334	−0.276	0.635
239	−0.232	0.824	263	−0.134	0.249	287	−0.076	0.917	311	0.035	0.164	335	0.138	0.100
240	−0.045	−0.309	264	0.151	−0.527	288	−0.279	−0.389	312	0.398	−1.437	336	−0.277	−0.012
241	0.250	1.138	265	−0.080	0.992	289	0.085	0.549	313	−0.190	1.557	337	0.296	0.401
242	0.142	0.239	266	−0.116	1.302	290	−0.493	0.121	314	−0.470	2.700	338	−0.074	0.274
243	−0.464	1.363	267	0.089	0.287	291	−0.542	−0.170	315	−0.026	−0.013	339	0.276	−1.277
244	0.277	0.254	268	0.107	−0.130	292	0.328	2.160	316	−0.131	−0.643	340	0.192	1.344
245	−0.062	−3.267	269	−0.089	−0.695	293	−0.181	0.216	317	−0.035	0.593	341	−0.293	0.965
246	0.276	−0.825	270	0.000	0.768	294	0.447	0.893	318	−0.185	−0.871	342	0.138	−0.156
247	−0.285	−1.391	271	0.000	−1.510	295	−0.248	1.480	319	−0.018	−0.713	343	−0.009	−0.492
248	0.276	−0.185	272	0.390	−1.281	296	0.462	−1.931	320	0.316	1.731	344	0.483	−1.045
249	−0.187	1.409	273	0.605	−0.095	297	−0.111	0.632	321	−0.219	−0.497	345	−0.163	0.240
250	0.338	−1.527	274	0.000	0.132	298	−0.558	2.774	322	0.429	−0.533	346	0.136	−1.282
251	−0.275	1.309	275	0.035	−1.072	299	−0.260	0.774	323	−0.245	1.086	347	0.136	−0.776
252	−0.187	0.028	276	−0.061	0.394	300	0.458	0.847	324	−1.227	6.944	348	0.063	0.774
253	0.383	−1.079	277	0.511	0.254	301	−0.536	0.248	325	−0.617	0.054	349	0.234	−0.589
254	0.115	−1.561	278	0.275	−0.308	302	−0.044	0.652	326	0.201	−0.739	350	0.464	−0.007

(Contd.)

Table 10.19 (Contd.)

Obs.	ER	SEN	Obs.	ER	SEN	Obs.	ER	SEN	Obs.	ER	SEN	Obs.	ER	SEN
351	-0.339	0.298	375	0.000	-0.122	399	-0.133	-0.321	423	0.206	-0.521	447	0.151	0.046
352	0.000	-0.233	376	0.234	-0.451	400	0.293	-0.234	424	0.075	0.991	448	0.009	-0.132
353	-0.018	1.250	377	0.018	0.610	401	-0.160	-0.195	425	-0.393	0.518	449	0.141	-0.548
354	-0.278	0.062	378	-0.297	0.790	402	0.009	0.812	426	-0.236	-0.091	450	0.159	0.607
355	-0.298	-0.866	379	-0.262	0.698	403	-0.125	0.896	427	0.339	0.321	451	-0.084	0.402
356	0.199	0.452	380	-0.300	-0.255	404	-0.089	0.290	428	-0.216	-0.251	452	0.103	-0.124
357	-0.272	0.039	381	0.119	0.199	405	-0.161	0.161	429	0.376	-0.543	453	-0.243	0.172
358	0.181	0.748	382	-0.082	-1.078	406	-0.090	0.089	430	0.205	-0.564	454	-0.066	-0.877
359	0.208	-2.609	383	0.255	-1.002	407	0.126	0.127	431	-0.196	0.054	455	0.504	-0.578
360	0.269	0.391	384	-0.045	-0.433	408	0.170	-0.134	432	0.121	-0.182	456	-0.307	0.762
361	0.357	-1.248	385	0.118	0.187	409	-0.116	0.639	433	0.232	-1.016	457	-0.028	0.692
362	0.000	-0.037	386	0.370	-0.157	410	-0.188	0.584	434	0.296	-0.186	458	-0.169	-0.072
363	-0.205	-0.807	387	-0.189	1.417	411	-0.352	0.089	435	0.339	-0.620	459	-0.047	0.040
364	0.629	-0.335	388	0.117	-0.300	412	0.190	0.078	436	-0.515	-0.425	460	0.028	-0.213
365	-0.495	1.445	389	0.367	-1.803	413	-0.009	0.375	437	0.074	-1.364	461	0.178	-0.302
366	-0.107	1.235	390	0.053	0.729	414	-0.190	-0.431	438	0.083	1.407	462	0.215	0.621
367	0.018	-0.009	391	-0.036	-0.066	415	0.127	0.161	439	0.000	0.412	463	0.093	-0.259
368	-0.045	1.482	392	0.036	0.656	416	-0.108	-0.229	440	-0.287	0.254	464	-0.046	0.162
369	-0.233	1.294	393	-0.214	1.092	417	0.054	0.414	441	-0.223	0.906	465	-0.186	-0.178
370	-0.144	-0.369	394	0.259	0.166	418	-0.163	0.720	442	-0.047	-0.153	466	0.131	-0.055
371	0.090	-0.637	395	0.036	0.225	419	-0.300	-0.685	443	0.037	1.067	467	-0.019	-0.563
372	0.063	1.120	396	0.133	0.031	420	-0.339	0.237	444	-0.065	-0.398	468	0.037	0.092
373	-0.054	0.420	397	-0.098	0.387	421	-0.314	-0.391	445	0.000	0.396	469	0.093	-0.048
374	-0.153	-0.011	398	0.009	-0.703	422	-0.504	0.095	446	-0.385	0.471	470	0.065	-0.451

(Contd.)

Table 10.19 (Contd.)

Obs.	ER	SEN	Obs.	ER	SEN	Obs.	ER	SEN	Obs.	ER	SEN	Obs.	ER	SEN
471	-0.046	-0.309	497	-0.028	-0.005	523	0.057	0.176	549	0.088	0.296	575	0.224	-0.966
472	0.000	0.237	498	-0.084	-0.514	524	-0.019	-0.003	550	-0.205	0.125	576	0.463	0.443
473	0.046	1.380	499	-0.198	0.885	525	0.124	-0.004	551	0.117	-0.134	577	-0.621	0.722
474	-0.084	0.325	500	0.047	-0.720	526	-0.162	0.815	552	0.146	-0.769	578	0.140	0.243
475	-0.065	0.102	501	0.441	-1.178	527	0.076	0.072	553	-0.029	0.307	579	0.564	-0.863
476	0.037	-0.144	502	0.233	0.396	528	-0.010	0.146	554	-0.127	0.137	580	-0.304	-0.426
477	-0.046	0.302	503	-0.121	0.289	529	0.010	-0.416	555	0.117	-0.429	581	0.028	0.106
478	-0.158	0.233	504	-0.112	-0.326	530	0.067	0.101	556	0.000	-0.626	582	0.000	0.683
479	-0.290	0.314	505	-0.093	0.624	531	0.067	0.268	557	0.301	-0.125	583	-0.148	0.365
480	-0.075	0.037	506	-0.075	-0.308	532	-0.277	0.212	558	0.510	-0.256	584	-0.233	0.690
481	-0.236	-0.210	507	-0.188	0.507	533	-0.250	0.164	559	0.172	-0.562	585	0.149	0.187
482	-0.066	-0.186	508	-0.151	0.538	534	-0.135	-0.298	560	-0.595	1.430	586	-0.355	0.125
483	-0.419	-0.034	509	0.188	-0.268	535	0.193	-0.154	561	0.174	-0.476	587	0.140	0.381
484	0.038	-0.259	510	0.234	-0.364	536	-0.396	0.999	562	0.182	0.137	588	-0.338	-0.113
485	0.267	0.217	511	-0.291	0.122	537	-0.273	0.014	563	-0.327	0.177	589	-0.473	0.749
486	-0.191	0.186	512	-0.028	0.132	538	-0.029	0.069	564	0.106	-0.688	590	0.379	-0.309
487	0.181	-0.076	513	0.113	-0.081	539	0.263	-0.622	565	0.593	-0.408	591	0.254	0.015
488	-0.010	0.214	514	0.103	-0.005	540	-0.332	0.533	566	-0.162	0.104	592	-0.066	-0.063
489	-0.038	-0.383	515	-0.122	0.466	541	0.000	-0.195	567	0.427	-1.219	593	0.281	-0.383
490	0.313	-0.029	516	-0.198	0.897	542	0.264	-0.076	568	0.702	0.293	594	-0.356	0.491
491	0.019	-1.065	517	-0.113	0.585	543	-0.234	-0.448	569	0.185	-0.195	595	0.337	-0.591
492	0.189	-0.490	518	-0.076	-0.072	544	0.108	-0.119	570	-0.260	0.063	596	0.075	0.411
493	0.009	-0.205	519	-0.038	0.058	545	0.107	-0.473	571	0.674	-1.195	597	0.074	-0.473
494	0.103	-1.289	520	-0.333	0.275	546	0.010	0.149	572	0.155	0.979	598	0.000	-0.120
495	0.019	0.045	521	0.105	-0.127	547	-0.195	0.030	573	-0.951	1.241	599	0.009	-0.049
496	0.056	0.136	522	-0.124	0.116	548	0.039	0.251	574	-0.084	0.210	600	0.102	0.429

(Contd.)

Table 10.19 (Contd.)

Obs.	ER	SEN	Obs.	ER	SEN	Obs.	ER	SEN	Obs.	ER	SEN	Obs.	ER	SEN
601	0.259	−0.355	621	0.000	0.245	641	−0.083	0.077	661	−0.302	0.065	681	−0.117	0.695
602	−0.213	0.447	622	0.009	−0.106	642	−0.102	−0.040	662	0.341	−0.145	682	0.010	−0.021
603	−0.093	0.445	623	−0.198	−0.069	643	−0.177	0.800	663	−0.410	0.287	683	−0.068	0.256
604	−0.019	0.252	624	0.047	0.342	644	0.214	0.198	664	−0.020	−0.484	684	−0.039	0.899
605	0.185	0.118	625	0.216	−0.161	645	−0.009	0.050	665	0.098	−0.139	685	−0.059	−0.086
606	−0.279	−0.115	626	0.225	−0.359	646	−0.130	0.308	666	−0.078	0.192	686	0.137	0.167
607	0.102	−0.070	627	0.372	0.009	647	−0.234	0.934	667	0.429	−0.293	687	−0.010	−0.118
608	0.056	0.112	628	−0.334	0.223	648	0.056	0.312	668	−0.234	1.029	688	−0.137	−0.600
609	0.259	−0.066	629	0.186	−0.279	649	0.000	0.347	669	−0.313	−0.401	689	0.381	−0.921
610	0.018	−0.122	630	−0.093	−0.005	650	−0.066	−0.189	670	−0.148	−0.797	690	0.484	0.328
611	0.138	0.240	631	−0.037	0.498	651	−0.311	0.395	671	0.226	0.095	691	0.077	−0.961
612	0.073	0.327	632	−0.056	0.343	652	−0.341	0.685	672	0.196	−0.402	692	0.220	0.143
613	−0.304	0.043	633	0.028	0.018	653	0.114	0.208	673	−0.166	−0.242	693	−0.182	−0.759
614	−0.130	−0.267	634	0.167	−0.231	654	−0.190	−0.130	674	0.069	0.841	694	0.029	0.817
615	−0.093	0.139	635	0.130	−0.314	655	0.057	−0.176	675	0.098	−0.204	695	0.306	−0.582
616	−0.177	−0.290	636	−0.111	0.111	656	−0.048	0.401	676	−0.098	0.295	696	0.048	−0.515
617	0.056	0.084	637	0.046	−0.547	657	−0.479	0.156	677	0.068	−0.175	697	−0.019	−0.317
618	−0.159	−0.300	638	−0.019	0.081	658	0.087	−0.027	678	0.088	−0.466	698	0.095	−0.410
619	−0.253	0.514	639	0.222	−0.147	659	−0.203	−0.322	679	−0.029	−0.140	699	0.066	0.605
620	0.028	0.081	640	−0.194	0.564	660	−0.233	1.051	680	0.049	0.198	700	0.218	0.259

Source: Computed by the author using data downloaded from *www.rbi.org.in* and *www.bse.org.in*, last accessed on 12 May 2012.

Note: ER = daily percentage changes in exchange rate and SEN = daily percentage changes in SENSEX index (closing value).

Workfile'. From here click on **View/Graph…** which will open the 'Graph Options' dialog box. Click **OK** to obtain the graph, as shown in Figure 10.4.

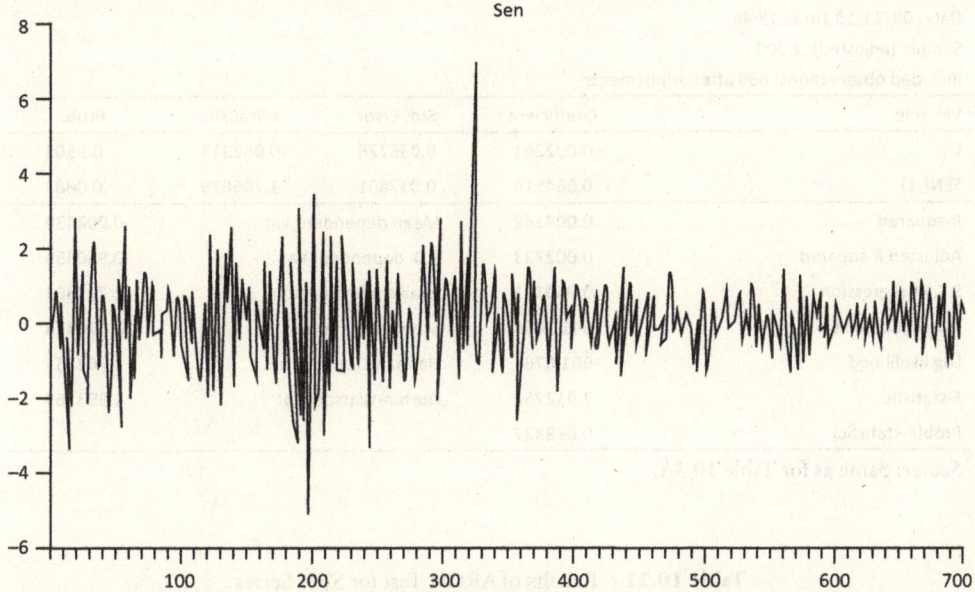

Sen

Figure 10.4   Daily Percentage Changes in SENSEX Index in India, 1 January 2008 to
30 November 2010

It clearly emerges that daily percentage changes in SENSEX index exhibit volatility clustering, in which there are some periods of high volatility such as between 180th and 220th days, and other periods of relative calm or tranquility, such as between 590th and 640th days.

Estimation of ARCH Model

To examine the presence of ARCH effect in SEN series, we estimate an AR(1) model (as the 'mean' equation, for simplicity). To do this, click on **Quick/Estimate Equation…** which opens the 'Equation Estimation' dialog box. Write **sen c sen(–1)** in the 'Equation specification' box of the 'Equation Estimation' dialog box and click **OK**. This gives the output as shown in Table 10.20.

Now to know whether there is ARCH effect in the residuals of the estimated AR(1) model, we perform the ARCH test. To do this, click on **View/Residual Diagnostics/ Heteroskedasticity Tests…** from the output window, which opens 'Heteroskedasticity Tests' dialog box. From this box select 'ARCH' as 'Specification' and the number of lag terms to include. If we are interested about ARCH(1), we shall put 1 in the 'Number of lags' box, and click **OK** to obtain the results, as shown in Table 10.21.

It appears that $T.R^2$ statistic (or Obs*R-squared as presented by EViews) is 6.862783 with p-value less than 0.01. Thus, we reject the null hypothesis of homoskedasticity and conclude that ARCH(1) effects are present in the series for SEN.

Table 10.20   Estimated AR(1) Model for SEN Series

Dependent Variable: SEN
Method: Least Squares
Date: 08/23/13 Time: 18:46
Sample (adjusted): 2 700
Included observations: 699 after adjustments

Variable	Coefficient	Std. Error	t-Statistic	Prob.
C	−0.002261	0.036278	−0.062313	0.9503
SEN(-1)	0.064514	0.037801	1.706679	0.0883
R-squared	0.004162	Mean dependent var		−0.002439
Adjusted R-squared	0.002733	S.D. dependent var		0.960455
S.E. of regression	0.959141	Akaike info criterion		2.757301
Sum squared resid	641.2066	Schwarz criterion		2.770318
Log likelihood	−961.6765	Hannan-Quinn criter.		2.762333
F-statistic	2.912752	Durbin-Watson stat		1.993765
Prob(F-statistic)	0.088327			

Source: Same as for Table 10.3A.

Table 10.21   Results of ARCH Test for SEN Series

Heteroskedasticity Test: ARCH

F-statistic	6.911069	Prob. F(1,696)		0.0088
Obs*R-squared	6.862783	Prob. Chi-Square(1)		0.0088

Test Equation:
Dependent Variable: RESID^2
Method: Least Squares
Date: 08/23/13 Time: 18:47
Sample (adjusted): 3 700
Included observations: 698 after adjustments

Variable	Coefficient	Std. Error	t-Statistic	Prob.
C	0.827374	0.100843	8.204592	0.0000
RESID^2(-1)	0.099158	0.037719	2.628891	0.0088
R-squared	0.009832	Mean dependent var		0.918457
Adjusted R-squared	0.008409	S.D. dependent var		2.512640
S.E. of regression	2.502052	Akaike info criterion		4.674961
Sum squared resid	4357.145	Schwarz criterion		4.687993
Log likelihood	−1629.561	Hannan-Quinn criter.		4.679999
F-statistic	6.911069	Durbin-Watson stat		2.020802
Prob(F-statistic)	0.008755			

Source: Same as for Table 10.3A.

Estimation of GARCH Model

To estimate the GARCH model, click on **Quick/Estimate Equation…** to open the 'Equation Estimation' dialog box. Change the estimation method by clicking on the down arrow in the 'Method' box of 'Estimation settings' and choose 'ARCH-Autoregressive Conditional Heteroskedasticity' option. This will open the 'Equation Estimation' dialog box as in Screenshot 10.15. In order to estimate a GARCH(1,1) model, write **sen c sen(−1)** in the 'Mean equation' box, and in the small boxes write 1 for the 'Order:ARCH' and 1 for the 'GARCH' and click **OK**. The resulting output is displayed in Table 10.22.

The result of the estimated GARCH model shows that the coefficients on both the lagged squared residual and lagged conditional variance terms in the conditional variance equation are highly statistically significant (p-value = 0.00). This indicates presence of volatility clustering in the series for SEN. Also, the sum of the coefficients on the lagged squared

Screenshot 10.15   Equation Estimation Dialog Box for the GARCH Model

Table 10.22   Results of GARCH(1,1) Model

Dependent Variable: SEN
Method: ML-ARCH (Marquardt)—Normal distribution
Date: 08/23/13 Time: 18:52
Sample (adjusted): 2 700
Included observations: 699 after adjustments
Convergence achieved after 18 iterations
Presample variance: backcast (parameter = 0.7)
GARCH = C(3) + C(4)*RESID(−1)^2 + C(5)*GARCH(−1)

Variable	Coefficient	Std. Error	z-Statistic	Prob.
C	0.042894	0.024279	1.766678	0.0773
SEN(−1)	0.032224	0.042891	0.751296	0.4525
Variance Equation				
C	0.006661	0.002763	2.410629	0.0159
RESID(−1)^2	0.136544	0.019259	7.089846	0.0000
GARCH(−1)	0.868725	0.016337	53.17633	0.0000
R-squared	0.000897	Mean dependent var		−0.002439
Adjusted R-squared	−0.000537	S.D. dependent var		0.960455
S.E. of regression	0.960712	Akaike info criterion		2.393252
Sum squared resid	643.3087	Schwarz criterion		2.425796
Log likelihood	−831.4417	Hannan-Quinn criter.		2.405833
Durbin-Watson stat	1.927818			

Source: Same as for Table 10.3A.

residual (0.136544) and lagged conditional variance (0.868725) is very close to unity which implies that volatility shocks in the SEN series are quite persistent.

10.11 QUESTIONS AND ASSIGNMENTS

A. Multiple-Choice Questions
Tick ($\sqrt{}$) the correct answer.

    (i)   The term cointegration has been coined by
        (a) F.M. Fisher
        (b) R. Frisch
        (c) C.W.J. Granger
        (d) Christopher A. Sims

    (ii)   An I(0) series becomes stationary after
        (a) one-time differencing
        (b) two-time differencing
        (c) three-time differencing
        (d) no differencing is required

(iii)   The cointegrating regression represents
    (a)   short-run relationship between the dependent and explanatory variable
    (b)   long-run relationship between the dependent and explanatory variable
    (c)   dynamic relationship between the dependent and explanatory variable
    (d)   none of the above
(iv)   The ARIMA forecasting method is developed by
    (a)   Engle and Granger
    (b)   Dickey and Fuller
    (c)   Box and Jenkins
    (d)   Sims and Sargent
(v)   The VAR model has been developed by
    (a)   C.W.J. Granger
    (b)   Christopher A. Sims
    (c)   D. McFadden
    (d)   Robert F. Engle
(vi)   The ARCH model has been proposed by
    (a)   J.J. Heckman
    (b)   L.R. Klein
    (c)   Robert F. Engle
    (d)   Thomas J. Sargent
(vii)   The clustering of volatility is more frequently observed in
    (a)   cross-section data
    (b)   panel data
    (c)   financial time-series data
    (d)   Census data

B. General Questions

(i)   Narrate briefly the background that led to the 'unit root and cointegration revolution' in economics since early 1980s.
(ii)   Distinguish between the stationary and non-stationary processes.
(iii)   Distinguish between the white noise and random walk series.
(iv)   What is the random walk model? How does the random walk model with drift differ from the random walk model without drift? Show that the random walk model, with or without drift, is a non-stationary process.
(v)   Give examples of economic variables which are usually non-stationary. How can such variables be made stationary?
(vi)   Why it is necessary to ensure stationarity of the time-series variables involved in regression analysis?
(vii)   What does a 'unit root' mean?
(viii)   What is the autocorrelation function (ACF)? What is correlogram? Explain how the correlogram is used to understand the stationarity of the time series.

(ix)   Explain how you would examine stationarity of time-series data using the Augmented Dickey-Fuller (ADF) test. What are main limitations of this test?

(x)   State the difference between the Dickey-Fuller and Phillips-Perron tests of stationarity.

(xi)   What is meant by the 'spurious regression' problem? When does such a problem arise?

(xii)   Distinguish between a series that is 'difference stationary' and a series that is 'trend stationary'. Are shocks persistent in the latter?

(xiii) What is meant by 'cointegration'? Explain the steps in Engle-Granger test of cointegration between two time-series variables. What are the limitations of this test?

(xiv)   What is the 'error correction mechanism' (ECM)? Explain how the ECM reconciles the short-run behaviour of an economic variable with its long-run behaviour.

(xv)   Distinguish between the autoregressive (AR) and moving average (MA) processes. State the properties of the AR and MA processes.

(xvi)   What is the autoregressive integrated moving average (ARIMA) process?

(xvii) What is the difference between *ex ante* and *ex post* forecasts?

(xviii) Define an ARIMA process. Discuss the steps involved in Box-Jenkins (BJ) methodology for ARIMA model selection. How you would assess the reliability of forecasts obtained through application of BJ methodology?

(xix)   Construct a vector autoregressive (VAR) model and explain how you would examine causality between the variables using this model. What are the advantages and disadvantages of the VAR modelling?

(xx)   What is the vector error correction model (VECM)? When such a model is used?

(xxi)   Explain the steps involved in forecasting the values of the variables in the VAR model. How you assess appropriateness of your estimated VAR model?

(xxii) Explain the steps involved in Granger test for causality. How does Granger causality test differ from Sims' causality test?

(xxiii) What is meant by the 'ARCH effect'? Explain Engle's procedure of examining the presence of ARCH(p) effects in time-series data.

(xxiv) What is the difference between the ARCH and GARCH models? Which one of these is superior? Why?

(xxv)   Indicate whether the following statements are true (T), false (F), or uncertain (U) and give brief explanation.

(a)   The random walk model represents a stationary stochastic process.

(b)   The mean of the random walk series without drift changes over time.

(c)   Both mean and variance of random walk series with drift change over time.

(d)   The trend in a non-stationary series is constant.

(e)   For a non-stationary series, the values of autocorrelation function (ACF) are all insignificant.

(f)   Non-stationarity of a series may arise due to structural break in the series.

(g) Detrending method is employed to run a regression that involves time-series variables which are difference-stationary.

(h) Differencing method is employed to run a regression that involves time-series variables which are trend-stationary.

C. Computer Assignments

(i) Draw correlograms using the data on rice and total foodgrains production (million tonnes) in India during 1970–71 to 2010–11 presented in Table 10.8 above and state whether these series are stationary. Also apply the ADF and PP tests to confirm the validity of your conclusions based on correlogram analyses. If the series were non–stationary, do they become stationary after differencing?

(ii) Consider the data on GDP and SAVINGS in India for the period 1970–71 to 2009–10, presented in Table 10.23. Test for cointegration between these variables by applying the Engle-Granger test. Also estimate the error correction model and interpret the results. What are the values of short- and long-run elasticities of SAVINGS with respect to GDP?

(iii) Consider the data on wholesale price index (WPI) and consumer price index (CPI) in India for the period 1970–71 to 2009–10, presented in Table 10.23. Test for cointegration between these variables by applying the Engle–Granger test.

(iv) Consider the data on total foodgrains production (TFG) (million tonnes) in India during 1970–71 to 2010–11, presented in Table 10.8 above. Using these data, forecast the levels of foodgrains production in India for three years beyond 2010–11. Are your forecasts reliable? Justify your answer.

(v) Consider the data on daily percentage changes in exchange rate (ER) and SENSEX Index (SEN) in India for the period 01.01.2008 to 30.11.2010, presented in Table 10.19 above. Examine the causality between these variables by estimating an appropriately specified VAR model. What is your conclusion regarding the direction of causality between these variables?

(vi) There is an exhaustive literature on the causal relation between government revenue (REV) and expenditure (EXP). To examine such a causal relation in the Indian context, estimate an appropriately specified VAR model using data on central government revenue and expenditure in India for the period 1970–71 to 2009–10, presented in Table 10.23. What is your conclusion regarding direction of causality between government revenue and expenditure in India?

(vii) Consider the data on GDP and EXPORT in India for the period 1970–71 to 2009–10, presented in Table 10.23. Construct a VAR model and estimate such a model to forecast the levels of GDP and EXPORT for India for 2010–11 and 2011–12. Also provide an assessment of reliability of your forecasts.

(viii) Consider the data on daily percentage changes in exchange rate (ER) in India for the period 01.01.2008 to 30.11.2010, presented in Table 10.19 above. Does the series for ER exhibit presence of ARCH/GARCH effect? Interpret your test results.

Table 10.23   Some Macroeconomic Data for India, 1970–71 to 2009–10

Year	GDP	SAVINGS	EXPORT	REV	EXP	WPI	CPI
1970–71	474,131	6,571	1,535	5,339	5,624	14	17
1971–72	478,918	7,281	1,608	6,372	6,892	15	18
1972–73	477,392	7,788	1,972	6,987	7,857	17	19
1973–74	499,120	10,912	2,523	7,890	8,218	20	24
1974–75	504,914	12,298	3,329	9,216	9,936	25	32
1975–76	550,379	14,196	4,036	12,013	12,379	25	31
1976–77	557,258	17,320	5,143	13,526	13,657	25	26
1977–78	598,885	19,995	5,408	14,573	15,506	27	29
1978–79	631,839	23,601	5,726	17,259	18,766	27	28
1979–80	598,974	24,213	6,418	16,529	18,962	31	31
1980–81	641,921	26,881	6,711	20,291	22,768	37	35
1981–82	678,033	30,896	7,806	23,873	25,265	40	40
1982–83	697,861	33,787	8,803	29,135	30,791	42	42
1983–84	752,669	38,091	9,771	34,117	35,534	46	47
1984–85	782,484	45,453	11,744	39,887	43,632	48	47
1985–86	815,049	53,389	10,895	47,350	52,666	51	49
1986–87	850,217	58,036	12,452	54,655	62,916	54	51
1987–88	880,267	72,264	15,674	62,445	68,261	58	56
1988–89	969,702	87,166	20,232	73,469	79,111	62	64
1989–90	1,029,178	1,06,092	27,658	82,316	92,908	67	67
1990–91	1,083,572	1,30,010	32,558	93,951	105,298	74	72
1991–92	1,099,072	1,41,089	44,042	104,558	111,414	84	86
1992–93	1,158,025	1,59,682	53,688	110,306	122,618	92	97
1993–94	1,223,816	1,89,933	69,751	130,893	141,853	100	100
1994–95	1,302,076	2,47,462	82,674	159,778	160,739	113	112
1995–96	1,396,974	291,002	106,353	168,468	178,275	122	124
1996–97	1,508,378	313,068	118,817	187,823	201,007	127	131
1997–98	1,573,263	363,506	130,101	232,963	232,053	133	136
1998–99	1,678,410	389,747	139,753	279,549	279,340	141	150
1999–2000	1,786,525	484,256	159,561	297,189	298,053	145	157
2000–01	1,864,301	499,033	203,571	326,789	325,592	156	157
2001–02	1,972,606	534,885	209,018	363,806	362,310	161	159
2002–03	2,048,286	646,521	255,137	411,365	413,248	167	164
2003–04	2,222,758	820,685	293,367	475,146	471,203	176	170
2004–05	2,388,768	997,873	375,340	506,382	498,252	187	175
2005–06	2,616,101	1,228,026	456,418	526,626	505,738	196	181

(Contd.)

Table 10.23 (*Contd.*)

Year	GDP	SAVINGS	EXPORT	REV	EXP	WPI	CPI
2006–07	2,871,120	1,475,108	571,779	583,387	583,387	209	195
2007–08	3,129,717	1,779,614	655,864	712,671	712,671	218	210
2008–09	3,339,375	1,798,347	840,755	883,956	883,956	236	231
2009–10	3,605,108	2,207,423	845,534	1,024,487	1,024,487	245	263

Source: RBI, *Handbook of Statistics on Indian Economy 2010–11*.

Note: GDP = GDP at Factor Cost (Rs. Crore) [Base Year: 1999–2000]; SAVINGS = Gross Domestic Savings (Rs. Crore) [Base Year: 1999–2000]; EXPORT = Exports (Rs. Crore); REV = Central Govt. Revenue (total) [Rs. Crore]; EXP = Central Government Expenditure (total) [Rs. Crore]; WPI = Wholesale Price Index (Base: 1993–94 = 100) for all commodities, annual average; CPI = Consumer Price Index (Base: 1993–94 = 100) for agricultural labourers, annual average.

Answers to Multiple-Choice Questions

(i) (c); (ii) (d); (iii) (b); (iv) (c); (v) (b); (vi) (c); (vii) (c).

11 Simultaneous Equations System

The purpose of this chapter is to provide a brief introduction to the simultaneous equations system. We note the difference between the single and simultaneous equations systems, and point out the main features of a simultaneous equations system. The consequence of applying OLS to estimate an equation of a simultaneous equations system is discussed next. This is followed by a discussion on identification problem and the rules of identification. We discuss two methods of estimation of the simultaneous equations system, which are ILS and 2SLS. Application of EViews software for 2SLS estimation has been explained.

11.1 SINGLE EQUATION VERSUS SIMULTANEOUS EQUATIONS SYSTEMS

Under the single equation system, one variable is expressed as a function of one or more variables. For example, let us suppose that Y depends on $X_1, X_2, ..., X_k$. The relationship between Y and the X's can be expressed by writing out a single equation. Here we suppose that variation or change in the X's cause variation or change in Y variable. Thus, the cause and effect runs from X's to Y; variation in the values of X's is the cause while variation in the values of Y is the effect. It is also clear that in this formulation, there is a 'one-way causation' in the sense that changes in X's cause change in Y, but not the other way round.

However, we might have circumstances where this one-way or unidirectional causation does not work. This means that not only do the X's influence Y, but also Y in turn influences some of the X's. The simultaneous equations system recognizes this two-way or simultaneous relationship between Y and some of the X's.

Features of a Simultaneous Equations System

The main features of a simultaneous equations system are:

(i) Presence of more than one equation. The number of equations is equal to the number of mutually or jointly determined variables, which are called the *endogenous variables* of the system. The endogenous variables are stochastic. Their values are determined within the system.

(ii) The endogenous variable of one equation may become an explanatory variable in another equation. Presence of such 'endogenous explanatory variable' creates difficulty to distinguish between the dependent and explanatory variables of the system. Further, being stochastic, the endogenous explanatory variable gets correlated with the disturbance term of the equation in which it appears. Our discussion below would show that in this situation, any attempt to estimate an equation of the simultaneous equations system by the OLS method produces biased and inconsistent estimates for unknown parameters.

(iii)   The simultaneous equations system also includes other variables called the *predetermined* or *exogenous variables*. These variables are non-stochastic and their values are determined outside the system.

An Example of Simultaneous Equations System (SES)

Let us consider the simple Keynesian model of income determination

$$C_t = \alpha + \beta Y_t + \varepsilon_t \tag{11.1}$$

$$Y_t = C_t + I_t \tag{11.2}$$

where C, Y, and I denote consumption, income, and investment, respectively. The subscript t refers to time. By assumption, β (the marginal propensity to consume) is greater than zero but less than 1. It is observed that, while C_t is an endogenous variable in equation (11.1), it becomes an explanatory variable in equation (11.2). Similarly Y_t which is an explanatory variable in (11.1) becomes endogenous variable in (11.2). Thus, C_t and Y_t are the two endogenous or jointly-determined variables of this system while I_t is an exogenous or predetermined variable. The model comprising equations (11.1) and (11.2) represents a simultaneous equations system.

Simultaneous versus Recursive Systems

It is necessary to distinguish between the simultaneous equations model and a 'recursive model'. Like the simultaneous equations model, the recursive model is also a multi-equation model. But there is no simultaneity in the recursive model. In other words, there is no expression of two-way relationship between the variables in a recursive model. The following is an example of recursive model.

$$Y_{1t} = \alpha_0 + \alpha_1 X_{1t} + u_{1t} \tag{11.3}$$

$$Y_{2t} = \beta_0 + \beta_1 Y_{1t} + \beta_2 X_{1t} + u_{2t} \tag{11.4}$$

Although this system looks like a simultaneous equations system, it is actually a recursive system. In equation (11.3), the endogenous variable Y_1 is solely a function of the exogenous variable X_1 and no endogenous variable appears on the right hand side of the equation. Therefore, this equation may be treated separately from others. The same is true of equation (11.4) where the endogenous variable Y_2 is a function of Y_1 and exogenous variable X_1 and there is no equation where Y_1 is a function of Y_2. This system is called 'recursive' because each equation can be estimated in sequential order. The OLS method can be applied in a straightforward manner to estimate a recursive system. However, this method is not appropriate for the simultaneous equations system as will be clear from the discussion in next section.

11.2 OLS ESTIMATION OF SES: CONSEQUENCE OF IGNORING SIMULTANEITY

In the Keynesian model of income determination considered above, ε_t influences C_t, which in turn influences Y_t. This means that Y_t and ε_t become correlated, which violates an important assumption of the classical linear regression model. In this situation, we will have biased and inconsistent estimates for unknown parameters of the model if equation (11.1) is treated as a separate single equation model and estimated by applying the OLS method. This is shown below.

We assume that

(i) $E(\varepsilon_t) = 0$;

(ii) $E(\varepsilon_t^2) = \sigma_\varepsilon^2$ constant for all t;

(iii) $E(\varepsilon_t \varepsilon_s) = 0$ for $t \neq s$; and

(iv) $Cov(I_t, \varepsilon_t) = E(I_t \varepsilon_t) = 0$ as I_t is exogenous.

After substituting $Y_t = C_t + I_t$ in equation (11.1) and making some algebraic manipulations, we obtain

$$C_t = \frac{\alpha}{1-\beta} + \frac{\beta}{1-\beta} I_t + \frac{1}{1-\beta} \varepsilon_t \qquad (11.5)$$

$$Y_t = \frac{\alpha}{1-\beta} + \frac{1}{1-\beta} I_t + \frac{1}{1-\beta} \varepsilon_t \qquad (11.6)$$

Now

$$Cov(Y_t, \varepsilon_t) = E(Y_t \varepsilon_t)$$

$$= E\left[\frac{\alpha}{1-\beta} \varepsilon_t + \frac{1}{1-\beta} I_t \varepsilon_t + \frac{1}{1-\beta} \varepsilon_t^2 \right]$$

$$= \frac{1}{1-\beta} \sigma_\varepsilon^2 \neq 0 \qquad\qquad [\because E(\varepsilon_t) = 0 \text{ and } E(I_t \varepsilon_t) = 0]$$

This shows that for the above simultaneous equations system, $Cov(Y_t, \varepsilon_t) \neq 0$.

Let us now examine the consequence of applying the OLS method to estimate unknown parameters of the consumption function.

We know that $\hat{\beta}$, the OLS estimator of β, is given by

$$\hat{\beta} = \frac{\sum (C_t - \bar{C}_t)(Y_t - \bar{Y}_t)}{\sum (Y_t - \bar{Y}_t)^2}$$

$$= \frac{\sum (C_t - \bar{C}_t) y_t}{\sum y_t^2} \qquad [y_t = Y_t - \bar{Y}_t]$$

$$= \frac{\sum C_t y_t}{\sum y_t^2} \qquad \left[\because \bar{C}_t \sum y_t = 0 \right]$$

$$= \frac{\sum (\alpha + \beta Y_t + \varepsilon_t) y_t}{\sum y_t^2}$$

$$= \frac{\alpha \sum y_t + \beta \sum Y_t y_t + \sum y_t \varepsilon_t}{\sum y_t^2}$$

$$= \beta + \frac{\sum y_t \varepsilon_t}{\sum y_t^2} \qquad \left[\begin{array}{l} \because (i) \sum y_t = \sum (Y_t - \bar{Y}) = 0 \text{ and} \\ (ii) \ y_t = Y_t - \bar{Y}_t \Rightarrow Y_t = y_t + \bar{Y}_t ; \text{so} \ \dfrac{\sum (y_t + \bar{Y}_t) y_t}{\sum y_t^2} = 1 \end{array} \right]$$

$$= \beta + \frac{\sum y_t \varepsilon_t / n}{\sum y_t^2 / n}$$

Note that $\sum y_t \varepsilon_t / n$ is sample covariance between Y_t and ε_t. When sample size increases indefinitely, $\sum y_t \varepsilon_t / n$ approaches to population covariance between Y_t and ε_t.

Therefore,

$$\underset{n \to \infty}{p \lim} \left(\frac{\sum y_t \varepsilon_t}{n} \right) = \frac{1}{1-\beta} \sigma_\varepsilon^2$$

Further, $\sum y_t^2 / n$ represents sample variance of Y_t, which approaches to its population variance as sample size increases indefinitely, i.e.,

$$\underset{n \to \infty}{p \lim} \left(\frac{\sum y_t^2}{n} \right) = \sigma_Y^2$$

Therefore,

$$\underset{n \to \infty}{p \lim} \hat{\beta} = \beta + \frac{1}{1-\beta} \frac{\sigma_\varepsilon^2}{\sigma_Y^2} \neq \beta$$

This shows that $\hat{\beta}$ is asymptotically biased and hence inconsistent.

The direction of asymptotic bias becomes clear when we apply the information that $0 < \beta < 1$. As σ_ε^2 and σ_Y^2 are positive, $\underset{n \to \infty}{p \lim} \hat{\beta} > \beta$ and $\hat{\beta}$ provides an overestimate of β. This bias does not disappear no matter how large the sample size is. This is called the 'simultaneous equations bias'. This bias has been generated because of ignoring simultaneity among the variables and applying OLS method to estimate an equation that belonged to a family of simultaneous equations system.

11.3 STRUCTURAL AND REDUCED-FORM EQUATIONS

In the context of simultaneous equations system, it is important to distinguish between the structural and reduced-form equations. A structural equation is any equation of the simultaneous equations system where one endogenous variable is expressed as a function of other endogenous variable(s), predetermined variable(s), and stochastic disturbance term. The structural equation may also take the form of an identity. Often the structural equations express the structure of the economy or the behaviour of an economic agent. That is why the structural equations are also called the behavioural equations. The coefficients of the structural equation are called *structural coefficients*.

A reduced-form equation expresses an endogenous variable solely in terms of predetermined variables and stochastic disturbance. The reduced-form equations are obtained by solving the structural equations for the endogenous variables. The coefficients of the reduced-form equations are called *reduced-form coefficients*, which are actually combinations of the structural coefficients. There are as many reduced-form equations as there are endogenous variables in the system. The equations (11.5) and (11.6) above are reduced-form equations for structural equations (11.1) and (11.2), respectively.

To illustrate the ideas of structural and reduced-form equations more clearly, let us consider the general G equations simultaneous equations model given by

$$\beta_{11}Y_{1t} + \beta_{12}Y_{2t} + \ .... \ + \beta_{1G}Y_{Gt} + \gamma_{11}X_{1t} + \gamma_{12}X_{2t} + \ .... \ + \gamma_{1k}X_{kt} = u_{1t}$$
$$\beta_{21}Y_{1t} + \beta_{22}Y_{2t} + \ .... \ + \beta_{2G}Y_{Gt} + \gamma_{21}X_{1t} + \gamma_{22}X_{2t} + \ .... \ + \gamma_{2k}X_{kt} = u_{2t}$$

$$\beta_{G1}Y_{1t} + \beta_{G2}Y_{2t} + \ .... \ + \beta_{GG}Y_{Gt} + \gamma_{G1}X_{1t} + \gamma_{G2}X_{2t} + \ .... \ + \gamma_{Gk}X_{kt} = u_{Gt}$$

In the above model, there are G number of endogenous variables $(Y_1, Y_2, ..., Y_G)$, k exogenous or predetermined variables $(X_1, X_2, ..., X_k)$ and G stochastic disturbance terms $(u_1, u_2, ..., u_G)$. However, all endogenous and predetermined variables might not appear in every equation, as some of the βs and γs would be zero. Further, in each equation, one of the βs is taken to be unity. This means that one of the endogenous variables serves as the 'dependent' variable when the equation is written out as a standard regression equation. Again, if there is a constant term in any one of the equations, one of the Xs will be equal to unity. It should also be noted that some of the equations might actually be identities, which means that all their coefficients are known and they contain no disturbance term. The subscript t refers to time.

Using matrix notations, we may write above simultaneous equations system as

$$\begin{bmatrix} \beta_{11} & \beta_{12} & .... & \beta_{1G} \\ \beta_{21} & \beta_{22} & .... & \beta_{2G} \\ . & & & \\ . & & & \\ . & & & \\ \beta_{G1} & \beta_{G2} & .... & \beta_{GG} \end{bmatrix} \begin{bmatrix} Y_{1t} \\ Y_{2t} \\ . \\ . \\ . \\ Y_{Gt} \end{bmatrix} + \begin{bmatrix} \gamma_{11} & \gamma_{12} & ... & \gamma_{1k} \\ \gamma_{21} & \gamma_{22} & ... & \gamma_{2k} \\ . & & & \\ . & & & \\ . & & & \\ \gamma_{G1} & \gamma_{G2} & ... & \gamma_{Gk} \end{bmatrix} \begin{bmatrix} X_{1t} \\ X_{2t} \\ . \\ . \\ . \\ X_{kt} \end{bmatrix} = \begin{bmatrix} u_{1t} \\ u_{2t} \\ . \\ . \\ . \\ u_{Gt} \end{bmatrix}$$

More compactly,

$$BY_t + \Gamma X_t = u_t \tag{11.7}$$

where B is $(G \times G)$ matrix of parameters associated with G endogenous variables; Y_t is $(G \times 1)$ vector of G endogenous variables; Γ is $(G \times K)$ matrix of parameters associated with K predetermined variables; X_t is $(K \times 1)$ vector of K predetermined variables; and u_t is $(G \times 1)$ vector of stochastic disturbances.

The equations appearing in (11.7) are called the *structural* or *behavioural* equations. The parameters βs and γs are *structural parameters* or *structural coefficients*. As regards stochastic disturbances, we assume that they are normally distributed with zero means and constant variances, i.e., $u_t \sim N(0, \phi)$, where ϕ is variance–covariance matrix of structural disturbances of order $(G \times G)$. It is also assumed that there are no correlations between different observations of disturbances, both within equations and across different equations [i.e., $E(u_t u_s') = 0$, where $t, s = 1, 2, ..., n$ and $t \neq s$].

To obtain the reduced-form equations, we solve the structural form equations for values of the endogenous variables. This means that in reduced-form equations, the endogenous variables (Y's) will be expressed solely in terms of the predetermined variables (X's) and the stochastic disturbances (u's). This may be done in the following manner:

$$Y_t = -B^{-1}\Gamma X_t + B^{-1}u_t$$
$$\Rightarrow Y_t = \Pi X_t + v_t \tag{11.8}$$

where $\Pi = -B^{-1}\Gamma$ and $v_t = B^{-1}u_t$.

Expression (11.8) is the reduced-form of the simultaneous equations system (11.7). The parameters in Π are the *reduced-form parameters* and the disturbances in v_t are *reduced-form disturbances*. Writing out (11.8) in full, we have the following reduced-form equations:

$$Y_{1t} = \pi_{11}X_{1t} + \pi_{12}X_{2t} + ... + \pi_{1k}X_{kt} + v_{1t}$$
$$Y_{2t} = \pi_{21}X_{1t} + \pi_{22}X_{2t} + ... + \pi_{2k}X_{kt} + v_{2t}$$

$$Y_{Gt} = \pi_{G1}X_{1t} + \pi_{G2}X_{2t} + ... + \pi_{Gk}X_{kt} + v_{Gt}$$

11.4 IDENTIFICATION PROBLEM

Before estimating any structural equation of a simultaneous equations system, it is necessary to check whether it would be possible to estimate the parameters of the equation given the data set. Identification does this by determining whether the parameters of a particular equation can be estimated meaningfully. Here we are not talking about whether estimation result will be good or bad, but rather whether estimation can in principle be carried out at all. If it is not possible to estimate the parameters of a particular structural equation, we say that the structural equation is *unidentified* or *under-identified*. However, if the parameters of the equation can be estimated, we say that the equation is *identified*. An identified equation may be either *exactly* or *just identified* or *over-identified*. It is *exactly identified* when unique numerical values of the parameters of the structural equation are obtained. A structural equation is *over-identified* when more than one numerical value is obtained for some of the parameters.

To illustrate the identification problem further, let us consider the following demand–supply model:

Demand function:

$$Q_t^d = \alpha_0 + \alpha_1 P_t + u_{1t} \qquad (11.9)$$

Supply function:

$$Q_t^s = \beta_0 + \beta_1 P_t + u_{2t} \qquad (11.10)$$

Equilibrium condition:

$$Q_t = Q_t^d = Q_t^s \qquad (11.11)$$

where Q_t^d is quantity demanded in period t, Q_t^s is quantity supplied in period t, αs and βs are structural parameters, and u_{1t} and u_{2t} are stochastic disturbances. By assumption, the demand function is downward sloping ($\alpha_1 < 0$) and the supply function is upward sloping ($\beta_1 > 0$).

An important feature of this model is that price and quantity are jointly determined because of equilibrium condition. Now, given data on price (P_t) and quantity (Q_t), and no other information, it is not possible to say whether we have estimated the demand function or the supply function. Our data points (P_t, Q_t), as shown in the scatter diagram (Figure 11.1), actually represent the points of intersection of various demand and supply curves because of the equilibrium condition. Even a single data point might represent intersection of various demand and supply curves (Figure 11.2). In other words, considering one single point, we cannot say which demand and supply curve of a whole family of such curves generated that point. In such a situation, if we estimate any equation using data on P_t and Q_t, we will not be able to say whether we have estimated the demand or supply function. Both the demand and supply functions of the model are *unidentified*.

An alternative way of expressing the above problem is to say that as the equations (11.9) and (11.10) are unidentified, it would not be possible to obtain solutions (or numerical estimates) for their structural parameters. We may further clarify this point algebraically.

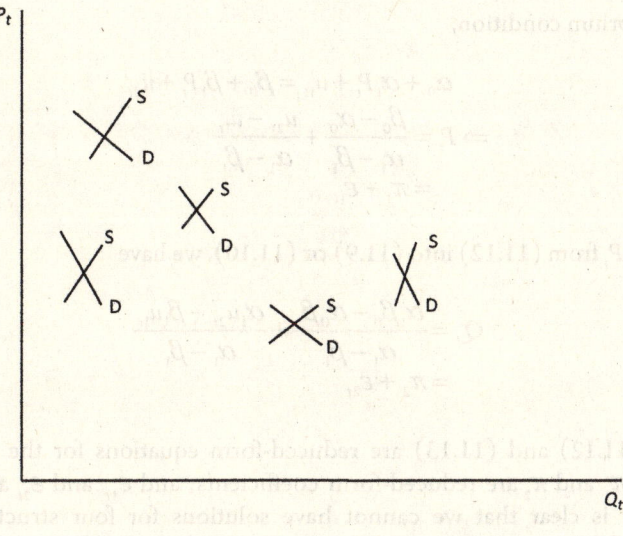

Figure 11.1   Scatter Plot of Data on P_t and Q_t

Source: Author's own.

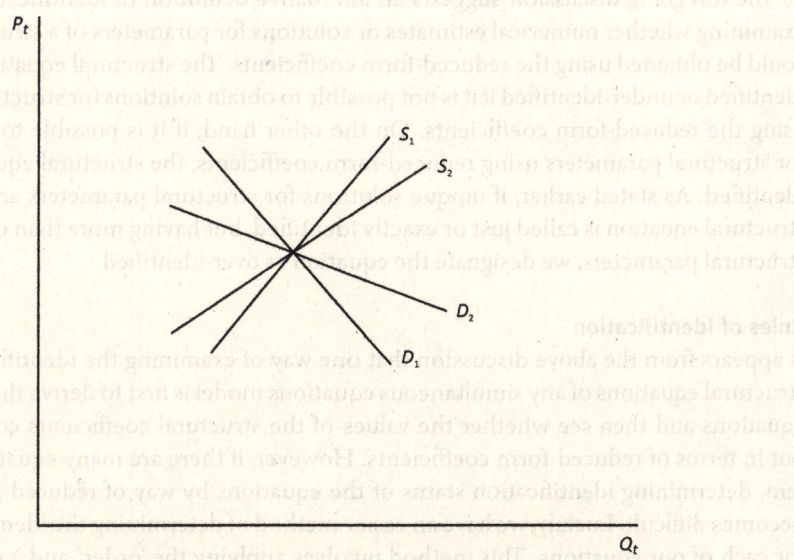

Figure 11.2   Plot of a Data Point on P_t and Q_t

Source: Author's own.

Using equilibrium condition,

$$\alpha_0 + \alpha_1 P_t + u_{1t} = \beta_0 + \beta_1 P_t + u_{2t}$$

$$\Rightarrow P_t = \frac{\beta_0 - \alpha_0}{\alpha_1 - \beta_1} + \frac{u_{2t} - u_{1t}}{\alpha_1 - \beta_1}$$

$$= \pi_1 + \varepsilon_{1t} \tag{11.12}$$

Substituting P_t from (11.12) into (11.9) or (11.10), we have

$$Q_t = \frac{\alpha_1 \beta_0 - \alpha_0 \beta_1}{\alpha_1 - \beta_1} + \frac{\alpha_1 u_{2t} - \beta_1 u_{1t}}{\alpha_1 - \beta_1}$$

$$= \pi_2 + \varepsilon_{2t} \tag{11.13}$$

Equations (11.12) and (11.13) are reduced-form equations for the above demand–supply model; π_1 and π_2 are reduced-form coefficients; and ε_{1t} and ε_{2t} are reduced-form disturbances. It is clear that we cannot have solutions for four structural coefficients $(\alpha_0, \alpha_1, \beta_0, \text{and } \beta_1)$ from two reduced-form coefficients $(\pi_1 \text{ and } \pi_2)$. Here the reduced-form coefficients contain all the structural coefficients. Obviously, we require four independent equations to have solutions for four unknowns (structural coefficients). As we are unable to obtain solutions for the structural coefficients using the reduced-form coefficients, we say that the structural equations of the model are unidentified or under-identified.

The foregoing discussion suggests an alternative definition of identification. It is about examining whether numerical estimates or solutions for parameters of a structural equation could be obtained using the reduced-form coefficients. The structural equation is called unidentified or under-identified if it is not possible to obtain solutions for structural parameters using the reduced-form coefficients. On the other hand, if it is possible to have solutions for structural parameters using reduced-form coefficients, the structural equation becomes identified. As stated earlier, if unique solutions for structural parameters are obtained, the structural equation is called just or exactly identified, but having more than one solution for structural parameters, we designate the equation as over-identified.

Rules of Identification

It appears from the above discussion that one way of examining the identification status of structural equations of any simultaneous equations model is first to derive the reduced-form equations and then see whether the values of the structural coefficients could be worked out in terms of reduced-form coefficients. However, if there are many equations in the system, determining identification status of the equations by way of reduced-form equations becomes difficult. Luckily, we have an easier method of determining the identification status for each of our equations. This method involves applying the 'order' and 'rank' conditions, which are stated below.[1]

---

[1] The formal derivation of these conditions is provided in the Appendix 11.1.

- *Order or necessary condition*: It requires that the number of variables (endogenous and predetermined) excluded from an equation but included in other equations must be greater than or equal to the total number of equations (i.e., the number of endogenous variables in the system) less one. Symbolically, for g^{th} equation of a simultaneous equations system, $G^{\Delta\Delta} + K^{**} \geq G - 1$ where $G^{\Delta\Delta}$ and K^{**} are respectively the numbers of endogenous and predetermined variables excluded from the gth equation and G is the total number of endogenous variables in the system. The status of a structural equation on the basis of this condition is summarized in Table 11.1.

Table 11.1   Status of a Structural Equation on the Basis of Order Condition Alone

Status	Number of Excluded Variables ($G^{\Delta\Delta} + K^{**}$)
Unidentified or under-identified	$< G - 1$
Just or exactly identified	$= G - 1$
Over-identified	$> G - 1$

Source: Author's own.

- *Rank or sufficient condition*: A sufficient condition of identification is the rank condition. It is possible for an equation to be identified on the basis of order condition, but may fail to be identified by the rank condition. Hence, it is important to look into this condition as well. The rank condition for identification is that the rank of the matrix containing structural coefficients of variables excluded from the equation (say g^{th}) but included in the system must be equal to number of endogenous variables in the system less one. Symbolically, *rank* $\Delta = G - 1$ (or *rank* $\Delta - G^{\Delta\Delta} = G^{\Delta} - 1$) where Δ is the matrix of structural coefficients of endogenous and predetermined variables excluded from the gth equation but included in the system, and G is the number of endogenous variables in the system.

Considering both order and rank conditions, we determine identification status of a structural equation as follows.[2]

Table 11.2   Status of a Structural Equation on the Basis of Both Order and Rank Conditions

Status	Number of Excluded Variables ($G^{\Delta\Delta} + K^{**}$)	Rank of Matrix Δ
Unidentified or under-identified	$\geq G - 1$	$< G - 1$
Just or exactly identified	$= G - 1$	$= G - 1$
Over-identified	$> G - 1$	$= G - 1$

Source: Author's own.

[2] Note that if an equation fails to satisfy the order condition, there is no need to check fulfillment of rank condition. In fact, the rank condition is checked for the equation that satisfied the order condition first.

An Application of Rules of Identification

Consider the following structural model

$$Y_{1i} = 3Y_{2i} - 2X_{1i} + X_{2i} + u_{1i}$$
$$Y_{2i} = Y_{3i} + X_{3i} + u_{2i}$$
$$Y_{3i} = Y_{1i} - Y_{2i} - 2X_{3i} + u_{3i}$$

where Y's are endogenous variables and X's are predetermined variables. Our objective is to determine the identification status of the equations by applying the order and rank conditions.

The conditions of identification are

(i)　*Order condition*: For an equation, the number of excluded variables (endogenous and exogenous) $[G^{\Delta\Delta} + K^{**}]$ must be greater or equal to total number of endogenous variables in the system (G) less one.

(ii)　*Rank condition*: The rank of the matrix (Δ) containing structural coefficients of variables excluded from the equation but included in the system must be equal to number of endogenous variables in the system less one. Symbolically, *rank* $\Delta = G - 1$ (or *rank* $\Delta - G^{\Delta\Delta} = G^{\Delta} - 1$).

Examining the Order Condition

In the above system, we have altogether three endogenous and three predetermined variables, i.e., $G = 3$ and $K = 3$. Now,

- For the first equation, $(G^{\Delta\Delta} + K^{**}) = 2 = (G - 1)$. So the order condition has been satisfied.
- For the second equation, $(G^{\Delta\Delta} + K^{**}) = 3 > (G - 1) = 2$. This shows that the order condition has been over-fulfilled.
- For the third equation, $(G^{\Delta\Delta} + K^{**}) = 2 = (G - 1) = 2$. So the order condition has been satisfied.

Examining the Rank Condition

To examine the rank condition, we rewrite the structural equations as

$$-Y_{1i} + 3Y_{2i} + 0Y_{3i} - 2X_{1i} + X_{2i} + 0X_{3i} + u_{1i} = 0$$
$$0Y_{1i} - Y_{2i} + Y_{3i} + 0X_{1i} + 0X_{2i} + X_{3i} + u_{2i} = 0$$
$$Y_{1i} - Y_{2i} - Y_{3i} + 0X_{1i} + 0X_{2i} - 2X_{3i} + u_{3i} = 0$$

The coefficients of the variables may be tabulated, ignoring the disturbances, as:

Equation No.	Coefficients of the Variables					
	Y_{1i}	Y_{2i}	Y_{3i}	X_{1i}	X_{2i}	X_{3i}
1	−1	3	0	−2	1	0
2	0	−1	1	0	0	1
3	1	−1	−1	0	0	−2

- For the first equation,

$$G^\Delta = 2 \text{ and } G^{\Delta\Delta} = 1$$

$$\Delta = \begin{bmatrix} 1 & 1 \\ -1 & -2 \end{bmatrix} \text{ and } |\Delta| \neq 0$$

$$\therefore rank \, \Delta = 2 \text{ and } rank \, \Delta - G^{\Delta\Delta} = 1$$

$$\Rightarrow (rank \, \Delta - G^{\Delta\Delta}) = 1 = (G^\Delta - 1). \text{ So, the rank condition is satisfied.}$$

As both the order and rank conditions are satisfied, the first equation is just-identified.

- For the second equation,

$$G^\Delta = 2 \text{ and } G^{\Delta\Delta} = 1$$

$$\Delta = \begin{bmatrix} -1 & -2 & 1 \\ 1 & 0 & 0 \end{bmatrix} \text{ and } |\Delta_1| = \begin{vmatrix} -1 & -2 \\ 1 & 0 \end{vmatrix} \neq 0$$

$$\therefore rank \, \Delta = 2 \text{ and } rank \, \Delta - G^{\Delta\Delta} = 1$$

$$\Rightarrow (rank \, \Delta - G^{\Delta\Delta}) = 1 = (G^\Delta - 1), \text{ which satisfies the rank condition.}$$

As the order condition is over-fulfilled and rank condition is satisfied, the second equation is over-identified.

- For the third equation,

$$G^\Delta = 3 \text{ and } G^{\Delta\Delta} = 0$$

$$\Delta = \begin{bmatrix} -2 & 1 \\ 0 & 0 \end{bmatrix} \text{ and } |\Delta| = 0$$

But $rank \, \Delta = 1$ as there are non-zero elements in Δ matrix.

Here $rank \, \Delta - G^{\Delta\Delta} = 1 - 0 = 1$ and $G^\Delta - 1 = 2$

$$\Rightarrow rank \, \Delta - G^{\Delta\Delta} < G^\Delta - 1, \text{ which violated the rank condition.}$$

Although the order condition was satisfied, the third equation is an unidentified equation as the rank condition is violated.

11.5 ESTIMATION OF SIMULTANEOUS EQUATIONS SYSTEM

There are two categories of methods available to estimate the structural equations of the simultaneous equations system. These are called 'single equation methods' and the 'system methods'. The single equation methods are designed to estimate a single structural equation with limited reference to the rest of the system. The examples are indirect least squares (ILS), two-stage least squares (2SLS), instrumental variable method (IV), and k-class estimators. Under system methods, however, all equations of the system are estimated simultaneously.

The examples of system methods are three-stage least squares (3SLS) and full information maximum likelihood method (FIML).

We discuss below two of the single equation methods, namely the ILS and 2SLS. The systems methods are not discussed as those are outside the purview of the present book.

Indirect Least Squares (ILS)

This method is applied to estimate an exact or just identified equation of a simultaneous equations system. As the name suggests, here we continue with the least squares method to obtain estimates for unknown parameters of the exactly identified equation, but that is done indirectly using estimates of reduced-form coefficients. There are three steps in this method.

First, we derive the reduced-form equations for our model.

Second, we apply OLS method to the reduced-form equations individually to obtain estimates of reduced-form coefficients.

Finally, estimates for structural coefficients are computed using estimated reduced-from coefficients.

An Illustration

We consider the following structural model to illustrate the method of indirect least squares.

$$Y_{1t} = \alpha Y_{2t} + \delta X_t + u_{1t}$$

$$Y_{2t} = \beta Y_{1t} + u_{2t}$$

In this model, Y_{1t} and Y_{2t} are the endogenous variables, X_t is the predetermined variable, and u_{1t} and u_{2t} are structural disturbances.

Applying the rules of identification, it will be found that while the first equation is unidentified, the second equation is exactly identified. Therefore, it will not be possible to estimate the parameters of first equation although we may apply the ILS method to obtain an estimate of the unknown parameter β of the second equation. To estimate the structural parameter in the second equation above by applying the ILS method, the steps to be followed are given below.

Step 1: Derive the reduced-form equations as

$$Y_{1t} = \alpha(\beta Y_{1t} + u_{2t}) + \delta X_t + u_{1t}$$
$$= \frac{\delta}{1-\alpha\beta}X_t + \frac{u_{1t} + \alpha u_{2t}}{1-\alpha\beta}$$
$$= \pi_1 X_t + v_{1t}$$

where $\pi_1 = \delta/(1-\alpha\beta)$ and $v_{1t} = (u_{1t} + \alpha u_{2t})/(1-\alpha\beta)$.

Again,

$$Y_{2t} = \beta\left(\frac{\delta}{1-\alpha\beta}X_t + \frac{u_{1t} + \alpha u_{2t}}{1-\alpha\beta}\right) + u_{2t}$$

$$= \frac{\beta\delta}{1-\alpha\beta}X_t + \frac{\beta u_{1t} + u_{2t}}{1-\alpha\beta}$$

$$= \pi_2 X_t + v_{2t}$$

where $\pi_2 = \beta\delta/(1-\alpha\beta)$ and $v_{2t} = (\beta u_{1t} + u_{2t})/(1-\alpha\beta)$.

Step 2: Having obtained the two reduced-form equations, we now apply the OLS method to obtain estimates for two reduced-form parameters π_1 and π_2. Suppose these are denoted by $\hat{\pi}_1$ and $\hat{\pi}_2$, respectively.

Step 3: Now we use $\hat{\pi}_1$ and $\hat{\pi}_2$ to obtain the estimate for structural coefficient β, which is

$$\hat{\beta} = \frac{\hat{\pi}_2}{\hat{\pi}_1}.$$

What Happens If the ILS Is Applied to Estimate an Over-identified Equation?

We have pointed out that the ILS method is suitable for estimating parameters of an exactly identified equation. Let us now examine the consequence of applying this method to estimate an over-identified equation.

$$Y_{1t} = \beta_{12}Y_{2t} + \gamma_{11}X_{1t} + \gamma_{12}X_{2t} + u_{1t}$$

$$Y_{2t} = \beta_{21}Y_{1t} + u_{2t}$$

where, as before, Y's are endogenous variables, X's are predetermined variables, and u's are structural disturbances.

In this system of simultaneous equations, the first equation is unidentified and second equation is over-identified. Suppose we apply the ILS method to estimate the structural parameter of this over-identified equation. Following the ILS steps, we first derive the reduced-form equations, which are

$$Y_{1t} = \frac{\gamma_{11}}{1-\beta_{12}\beta_{21}}X_{1t} + \frac{\gamma_{12}}{1-\beta_{12}\beta_{21}}X_{2t} + \frac{u_{1t} + \beta_{12}u_{2t}}{1-\beta_{12}\beta_{21}}$$

$$= \pi_{11}X_{1t} + \pi_{12}X_{2t} + v_{1t} \tag{11.14}$$

$$Y_{2t} = \frac{\beta_{21}\gamma_{11}}{1-\beta_{12}\beta_{21}}X_{1t} + \frac{\beta_{21}\gamma_{12}}{1-\beta_{12}\beta_{21}}X_{2t} + \frac{\beta_{21}u_{1t} + u_{2t}}{1-\beta_{12}\beta_{21}}$$

$$= \pi_{21}X_{1t} + \pi_{22}X_{2t} + v_{2t} \tag{11.15}$$

In the second step, applying the OLS method, estimated reduced-form equations are obtained as

$$\hat{Y}_{1t} = \hat{\pi}_{11}X_{1t} + \hat{\pi}_{12}X_{2t}$$

$$\hat{Y}_{2t} = \hat{\pi}_{21}X_{1t} + \hat{\pi}_{22}X_{2t}$$

Finally, the estimate for the structural coefficient of the over-identified equation (β_{21}) is computed using estimated reduced-form coefficients in the manner stated below.

$$\frac{\hat{\pi}_{21}}{\hat{\pi}_{11}} = \frac{\hat{\beta}_{21}\hat{\gamma}_{11}}{1 - \hat{\beta}_{12}\hat{\beta}_{21}} \bigg/ \frac{\hat{\gamma}_{11}}{1 - \hat{\beta}_{12}\hat{\beta}_{21}} = \hat{\beta}_{21}$$

$$\frac{\hat{\pi}_{22}}{\hat{\pi}_{12}} = \frac{\hat{\beta}_{21}\hat{\gamma}_{12}}{1 - \hat{\beta}_{12}\hat{\beta}_{21}} \bigg/ \frac{\hat{\gamma}_{12}}{1 - \hat{\beta}_{12}\hat{\beta}_{21}} = \hat{\beta}_{21}$$

It appears that application of ILS method failed to provide a unique solution for the structural parameter of the over-identified equation. This creates a problem of choosing between these two estimates. Hence, *the ILS method is not suitable for estimating the structural parameters of an over-identified equation*. This is one of the limitations of this method. Another limitation of this method is that it does not give the standard error of the estimates of structural parameters and it is rather complicated to calculate them.

Two-Stage Least Squares (2SLS)

We have noted that the ILS technique is not appropriate to estimate an over-identified equation. However, the reality is that most simultaneous equation models tend to be over-identified. For estimating an over-identified equation of a simultaneous equations system, an appropriate technique is the two-stage least squares (2SLS) proposed independently by Basmann (1957) and Theil (1954, 1958).

The basic idea behind the 2SLS method is to replace the 'endogenous explanatory variables' or stochastic regressors (which are correlated with the disturbance term causing simultaneous equations bias) with one that is non-stochastic and hence independent of the disturbance term. This involves the following two stages (hence the name 2SLS).

Stage 1: Regress each endogenous variable on all the exogenous and lagged exogenous variables (if any) of the system by using OLS method and obtain the fitted or estimated values of the endogenous variables from these regressions (i.e., $\hat{Y}$).

Stage 2: Use the fitted values from stage 1 as proxies or 'instruments' for the 'endogenous explanatory variables' in the original (structural form) equation and estimate the model again by using OLS.

One condition here is that the values of R^2 and F-statistics from first-stage regression should be sufficiently high to ensure that $\hat{Y}$ and Y are highly correlated so that $\hat{Y}$ is a good instrument (or proxy) for Y. Here Stock and Watson (2011, 439) suggested a *rule of thumb* to check the strength of the instruments. According to them, a first-stage F-statistic less than 10 indicates weak instruments, and using such instruments will make 2SLS estimates biased even in large samples and the corresponding t-statistics and confidence intervals will become unreliable.

Advantages of 2SLS Method

(i) The 2SLS method is very simple and easy to apply.

(ii) An important advantage of this method over the ILS is that it can be used to obtain consistent structural parameter estimates for the over-identified as well as the exactly identified equation. However, it needs to be noted that the 2SLS and ILS estimates are identical for an exactly identified equation.

(iii) Unlike the ILS, 2SLS gives the standard errors of the estimates of structural parameters directly.

11.6 APPLICATION OF 2SLS USING EVIEWS[3]

To understand application of 2SLS method in EViews, consider the following GDP-money supply model which we want to estimate using yearly data for the Indian economy, presented in Table 11.3.

$$GDP_t = \beta_{10} + \beta_{11} MS_t + \gamma_{11} INV_t + \gamma_{12} CE_t + u_{1t} \tag{11.16}$$

$$MS_t = \beta_{20} + \beta_{21} GDP_t + \gamma_{21} GDP_{t-1} + \gamma_{22} MS_{t-1} + u_{2t} \tag{11.17}$$

where GDP = gross domestic product; MS = money supply; INV= investment; and CE = private final consumption expenditure. The subscript t refers to time.

In this system, the GDP and MS are the two endogenous variables and the exogenous variables are INV and CE. The second equation also includes two lagged endogenous variables (GDP_{t-1} and MS_{t-1}). It can be verified that both the equations are over-identified. So we will apply the 2SLS method to estimate the structural parameters of the two equations of our system. Our steps here are the following.

(1) Obtain the data in EViews workfile.

(2) From the main menu, click **Quick/Estimate Equation…** which opens the 'Equation Estimation' window. From this window, change the 'Method' from default LS—Least Squares (NLS and ARMA) to TSLS—Two Stage Least Squares (TSNLS and ARMA) which opens a new 'Equation Estimation' window as shown in Screenshot 11.1.

---

[3] Note that under the ILS method, we derive the reduced-form equations which are to be estimated by applying the OLS method. The steps to be followed for estimating the reduced-form equations by the OLS method are same as those described in Chapter 3.

Table 11.3 Some Macroeconomic Data for India, 1950–51 to 2009–10

Year	CE	INV	GDP	MS	Year	CE	INV	GDP	MS
1950–51	2,07,559	24,643	2,24,786	2021	1980–81	5,60,718	1,49,728	6,41,921	23,424
1951–52	2,20,752	31,265	2,30,034	1812	1981–82	5,83,839	1,44,196	6,78,033	24,937
1952–53	2,29,660	23,030	2,36,562	1764	1982–83	5,88,909	1,43,958	6,97,861	28,535
1953–54	2,43,467	26,312	2,50,960	1828	1983–84	6,35,334	1,51,247	7,52,669	33,398
1954–55	2,51,454	29,508	2,61,615	1955	1984–85	6,51,495	1,63,269	7,82,484	39,915
1955–56	2,53,858	39,798	2,68,316	2217	1985–86	6,80,420	1,78,991	8,15,049	44,095
1956–57	2,65,088	48,223	2,83,589	2342	1986–87	6,98,991	1,79,971	8,50,217	51,516
1957–58	2,59,851	44,927	2,80,160	2413	1987–88	7,21,499	2,05,216	8,80,267	58,555
1958–59	2,83,706	44,633	3,01,422	2526	1988–89	7,69,480	2,33,728	9,69,702	66,786
1959–60	2,86,933	44,355	3,08,018	2720	1989–90	8,04,428	2,49,711	10,29,178	81,060
1960–61	3,03,255	52,500	3,29,825	2869	1990–91	8,43,556	2,91,611	10,83,572	92,892
1961–62	3,08,425	51,617	3,40,060	3049	1991–92	8,60,869	2,46,099	10,99,072	1,14,406
1962–63	3,12,443	58,725	3,47,253	3317	1992–93	8,79,689	2,69,647	11,58,025	1,24,066
1963–64	3,24,066	63,651	3,64,834	3752	1993–94	9,18,944	2,86,305	12,23,816	1,50,778
1964–65	3,43,425	69,412	3,92,503	4080	1994–95	9,61,346	3,49,266	13,02,076	1,92,257
1965–66	3,43,729	77,792	3,78,157	4529	1995–96	10,18,423	3,75,888	13,96,974	2,14,835
1966–67	3,48,196	84,686	3,82,006	4951	1996–97	10,97,390	3,74,006	15,08,378	2,40,615
1967–68	3,67,895	79,229	4,13,094	5350	1997–98	11,22,195	4,19,378	15,73,263	2,67,844
1968–69	3,77,559	77,235	4,23,874	5779	1998–99	11,90,267	4,19,885	16,78,410	3,09,068
1969–70	3,91,582	87,852	4,51,496	6536	1999–2000	12,57,541	5,06,244	17,86,525	3,41,796
1970–71	4,04,880	89,870	4,74,131	7374	2000–01	13,00,494	4,88,658	18,64,301	3,79,450
1971–72	4,12,758	94,318	4,78,918	8323	2001–02	13,77,316	4,74,449	19,72,606	4,22,843
1972–73	4,15,523	93,933	4,77,392	9700	2002–03	14,13,594	5,54,044	20,48,286	4,73,581
1973–74	4,25,720	1,11,567	4,99,120	11200	2003–04	15,01,974	6,51,346	22,22,758	5,78,716

(Contd.)

Table 11.3 (Contd.)

Year	CE	INV	GDP	MS	Year	CE	INV	GDP	MS
1974–75	4,25,399	1,00,075	5,04,914	11975	2004–05	15,84,690	7,93,545	23,88,768	6,49,790
1975–76	4,49,557	1,03,685	5,50,379	13325	2005–06	16,92,194	9,22,637	26,16,101	8,26,415
1976–77	4,58,521	1,17,640	5,57,258	16024	2006–07	18,00,874	10,46,065	28,71,120	9,67,955
1977–78	4,95,910	1,29,808	5,98,885	14388	2007–08	19,46,780	12,36,511	31,29,717	11,55,837
1978–79	5,26,219	1,56,955	6,31,839	17292	2008–09	20,85,582	11,67,158	33,39,375	12,59,707
1979–80	5,14,416	1,41,769	5,98,974	20000	2009–10	22,39,317	13,86,159	36,05,108	14,89,301

Source: Reserve Bank of India, *Handbook of Statistics on Indian Economy 2010–11.*

Note: CE = private final consumption expenditure; INV = gross capital formation; GDP = gross domestic product; and MS = M_2 money supply [all figures in Rs. Crore and at constant 1999–2000 prices].

Screenshot 11.1   Equation Estimation Window for 2SLS

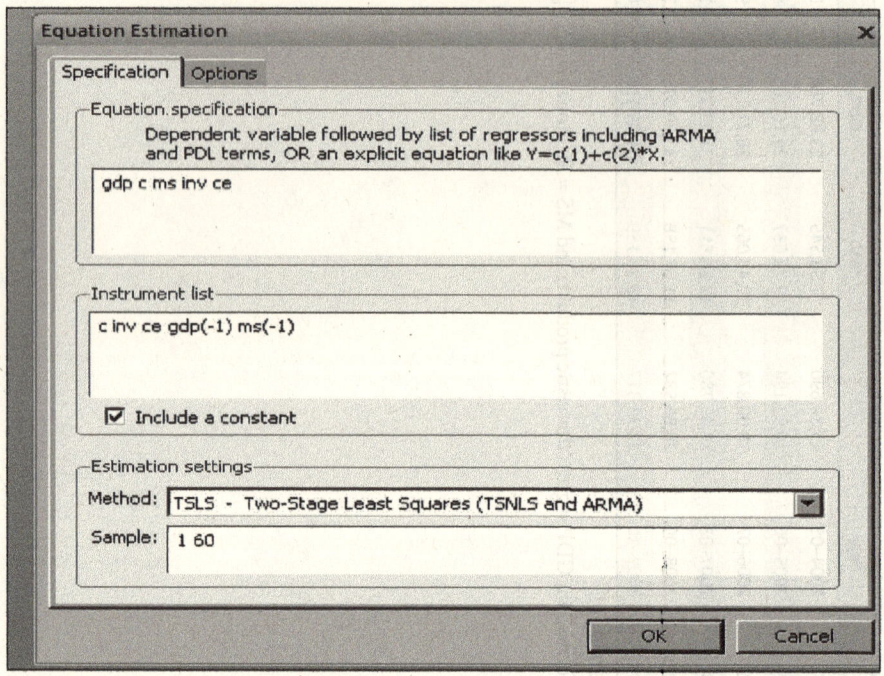

(3)   In the new 'Equation Estimation' window, we have to put two things: (*i*) In the 'Equation specification' box, we put the specification of first equation by writing: **gdp c ms inv ce**; and (*ii*) In the 'Instrument list' box, we write the names of all exogenous and lagged endogenous variables: **c inv ce gdp(–1) ms(–1)**.

(4)   Click **OK** to obtain results of 2SLS estimation for the GDP equation. These are shown in Table 11.4.

Following similar steps, we obtain results of 2SLS estimation for the money supply (MS) equation, which are presented in Table 11.5.

Interpretation of Results

It appears that, for the GDP equation, the estimated coefficients of all explanatory variables have expected positive signs. Further, all of them (except INV) have statistical significance. Thus, it may be concluded that increases in money supply and consumption expenditure lead to expansion of GDP in India.

All the estimated coefficients from the MS equation are also statistically significant. Here, we find that the current period GDP and one-period lagged MS positively influence MS in the current period. However, the impact of one-period lagged GDP on current period MS is

Table 11.4   Results of 2SLS Estimation of the GDP Equation

Dependent Variable: GDP
Method: Two-Stage Least Squares
Date: 08/23/13 Time: 19:02
Sample (adjusted): 2 60
Included observations: 59 after adjustments
Instrument specification: C INV CE GDP(−1) MS(−1)

Variable	Coefficient	Std. Error	t-Statistic	Prob.
C	−73599.46	7121.722	−10.33450	0.0000
MS	0.463407	0.060280	7.687621	0.0000
INV	0.111909	0.092811	1.205766	0.2331
CE	1.295792	0.025298	51.22160	0.0000
R-squared	0.999531	Mean dependent var		1009851.
Adjusted R-squared	0.999505	S.D. dependent var		855470.3
S.E. of regression	19029.04	Sum squared resid		1.99E+10
F-statistic	39054.42	Durbin-Watson stat		0.562536
Prob(F-statistic)	0.000000	Second-Stage SSR		2.08E+10
J-statistic	18.83571	Instrument rank		5
Prob(J-statistic)	0.000014			

Source: This table reports the output obtained by the auother after application of the EViews software.

Table 11.5   Results of 2SLS Estimation of the MS Equation

Dependent Variable: MS
Method: Two-Stage Least Squares
Date: 08/23/13 Time: 19:04
Sample (adjusted): 2 60
Included observations: 59 after adjustments
Instrument specification: C INV CE GDP(−1) MS(−1)

Variable	Coefficient	Std. Error	t-Statistic	Prob.
C	1085.073	5263.759	0.206140	0.8374
GDP	0.511699	0.122531	4.176092	0.0001
GDP(−1)	−0.534816	0.128760	−4.153581	0.0001
MS(−1)	1.105492	0.026782	41.27777	0.0000
R-squared	0.997972	Mean dependent var		184707.8
Adjusted R-squared	0.997861	S.D. dependent var		336380.5
S.E. of regression	15555.77	Sum squared resid		1.33E+10
F-statistic	9022.666	Durbin-Watson stat		2.873747
Prob(F-statistic)	0.000000	Second-Stage SSR		1.28E+10
J-statistic	14.27583	Instrument rank		5
Prob(J-statistic)	0.000158			

Source: Same as for Table 11.4.

negative, which is the result often observed while estimating the GDP-money supply model that we have considered.

To assess the strength of the instrument (which is $\widehat{MS}$) used in the second stage while estimating the first model by 2SLS, we run another OLS regression of MS on INV, CE, one-period lagged GDP, and one-period lagged MS. From the result of such regression, the value of computed-F is found to be very high (9423.111) and statistically significant,[4] which implies that $\widehat{MS}$ served as a satisfactory instrument for the MS variable in the first equation. Likewise, the strength of the instrument $\widehat{GDP}$ used in the second stage of 2SLS estimation of second equation is assessed by running another OLS regression of GDP on INV, CE, one-period lagged GDP, and one-period lagged MS which also provided a very high (41005.06) and statistically significant value for computed-F thereby suggesting that $\widehat{GDP}$ served as a satisfactory instrument for GDP in the second equation.

11.7 QUESTIONS AND ASSIGNMENTS

A. Multiple-Choice Questions
Tick ($\sqrt{}$) the correct answer.
(i)　The simultaneous equations bias
　　(a)　refers to the bias of the researcher towards using his chosen model
　　(b)　refers to the bias in the estimated parameters that disappears when sample size becomes large
　　(c)　refers to the bias in the estimated parameters that does not disappear when sample size becomes large
　　(d)　means the error terms are biased positively in small samples
(ii)　In simultaneous equations models, the OLS can be applied if
　　(a)　it is a recursive model
　　(b)　order condition is satisfied
　　(c)　rank condition is satisfied
　　(d)　both order and rank conditions are satisfied
(iii)　An appropriate method to estimate an over-identified equation is
　　(a)　OLS
　　(b)　ILS
　　(c)　2SLS
　　(d)　Ridge regression
(iv)　In the context of a system of linear simultaneous equations
　　(a)　The rank condition is both necessary and sufficient for identification of any particular equation
　　(b)　The rank condition is the necessary condition and order condition is the sufficient condition for identification

---

[4] The detailed results have not been presented to save space. However, interested scholars may check this by running such a regression.

    (c)   The order condition is necessary for the rank condition to hold
    (d)   Both (a) and (c)

(v)   There is no such thing as R^2 for the simultaneous equations model as a whole—the statement is
    (a)   Fully true
    (b)   Partially true
    (c)   False
    (d)   Uncertain

B. General Questions

(i)   Define the following.
    (a)   Endogenous variables
    (b)   Exogenous variables
    (c)   Structural equations
    (d)   Reduced-form equations
    (e)   Structural coefficients
    (f)   Reduced-form coefficients
    (g)   Recursive simultaneous equations system
    (h)   Simultaneous equations bias
    (i)   Order condition of identification
    (j)   Rank condition of identification
    (k)   Indirect least squares
    (l)   Two-stage least squares

(ii)   Indicate whether the following statements are true (T), false (F) or uncertain (U) and give a brief explanation.
    (a)   The problem of simultaneity does not arise in a recursive simultaneous equations model.
    (b)   The purpose of identification is to examine whether estimation result for a simultaneous equations system is good or bad.
    (c)   If an equation is exactly identified, the ILS and 2SLS give identical results.
    (d)   The OLS method is not applicable to estimate an equation from the simultaneous equations system.
    (e)   In simultaneous equations system, the greater the number of exogenous variables the better.

(iii)   Distinguish between the single equation system and the simultaneous equations system.

(iv)   Is it possible to estimate by OLS method an equation that belongs to a simultaneous equations system? If not, why not?

(v)   Explain the consequence of applying the indirect least squares method to estimate structural parameters of an equation that is over-identified.

(vi)   What is meant by identification? Explain why identification problem arises in a simultaneous equations system.

(vii) State the rules of identification. When is an equation of a system unidentified, exactly identified, and over-identified?

(viii) Derive the order and rank conditions for identification of an equation in a simultaneous equations system.

(ix) Consider the following macro-model.

$$C_t = a_0 + a_1 Y_t + u_t$$
$$Y_t = C_t + I_t + G_t$$

where C = consumption, Y = income, I = Investment, G = government spending, u_t = stochastic disturbance and t = time. In this model, the two endogenous variables are C and Y while the exogenous variables are I and G.

Derive the reduced-form equations for the two structural equations of above model.

(x) The structure of a model with three endogenous and three exogenous variables is given below (1 indicates presence and 0 absence of the variable in the equation).

1	0	1	1	1	0
0	1	1	0	0	1
1	1	1	0	0	1

Which of the three equations are identified?

(xi) Explain the 2SLS method. When is it applied? What are the advantages of this method?

(xii) Consider the following system of equations.

$$C_t = \alpha + \beta Y_t + \varepsilon_t$$
$$Y_t = C_t + I_t$$

where C, Y, and I denote consumption, income and investment respectively, and subscript t refers to time. Can you estimate the unknown parameters (α and β) by applying the OLS method? If not, why not? Which method do you think will be appropriate here?

(xiii) Determine the identification status of the equations in the following macro-model. Consumption function

$$C_t = \alpha_0 + \alpha_1 Y_t + \alpha_2 C_{t-1} + u_{1t}$$

Investment function

$$I_t = \beta_0 + \beta_1 r_t + \beta_2 I_{t-1} + u_{2t}$$

Interest rate function

$$r_t = \gamma_0 + \gamma_1 Y_t + \gamma_2 M_t + u_{3t}$$

Income identity

$$Y_t = C_t + I_t + G_t$$

where C = consumption expenditure, Y= income, I = investment, r = rate of interest, G = government expenditure, and u's are the disturbance terms.

(xiv) Determine the identification status of the equations in the following demand–supply model.

Demand function

$$Q_t = \alpha_1 + \alpha_2 P_t + \alpha_3 Y_t + u_{1t}$$

Supply function

$$Q_t = \beta_1 + \beta_2 P_t + u_{2t}$$

where Q, P and Y represent quantity, price and income respectively, t refers to time, and u_{1t} and u_{2t} are the structural disturbances.

Is it possible to estimate the structural parameters of the above model? If yes, state the estimation procedure and the steps therein.

(xv) Consider the following modified Keynesian model of income determination.

$$C_t = \alpha_0 + \alpha_1 Y_t + \alpha_2 C_{t-1} + u_{1t}$$
$$I_t = \beta_0 + \beta_1 Y_t + \beta_2 Y_{t-1} + u_{2t}$$
$$Y_t = C_t + I_t + G_t$$

where C = consumption expenditure, Y= income, G = government expenditure, and u_{1t} and u_{2t} are the disturbance terms. G_t and Y_{t-1} are assumed predetermined.

(a) Obtain the reduced-form equations and determine which of the structural equations is identified (just/over).

(b) Which method would you use to estimate the parameters of the over identified and just-identified equations? Justify your answer.

B. Computer Assignments

(i) Consider the following model

$$CE_t = \alpha + \beta GDP_t + \varepsilon_t$$
$$GDP_t = CE_t + INV_t$$

where CE = private final consumption expenditure, GDP = gross domestic product and INV = investment expenditure measured by gross capital formation. The subscript t refers to time.

Use data on these variables given in Table 11.3 above to estimate the consumption equation by applying both the ILS and 2SLS methods and interpret the results. Do you find any difference in results from these methods? If not, why?

(ii)   Consider the following model

$$R_t = \alpha_1 + \alpha_2 M_t + \alpha_3 M_{t-1} + \alpha_4 Y_t + \varepsilon_{1t}$$
$$Y_t = \beta_1 + \beta_2 R_t + \beta_3 I_t + \varepsilon_{2t}$$

where R = rate of interest; M = money supply; Y = GDP; and I = investment. The subscript t refers to time.

(a)   Examine the identification status of the equations of above model.

(b)   Use data in Table 11.6 to estimate the structural parameters of the second equation by applying an appropriate method and interpret the result.

Table 11.6   Data on GDP (Y), Money Supply (M), Rate of Interest (R), and Investment (I) for India

Year	Y	M	R	I
1970–71	474,131	7,374	7.8	89,870
1971–72	478,918	8,323	8.5	94,318
1972–73	477,392	9,700	8.5	93,933
1973–74	499,120	11,200	8.8	111,567
1974–75	504,914	11,975	11.3	100,075
1975–76	550,379	13,325	14.0	103,685
1976–77	557,258	16,024	14.0	117,640
1977–78	598,885	14,388	13.0	129,808
1978–79	631,839	17,292	13.0	156,955
1979–80	598,974	20,000	16.5	141,769
1980–81	641,921	23,424	16.5	149,728
1981–82	678,033	24,937	16.5	144,196
1982–83	697,861	28,535	16.5	143,958
1983–84	752,669	33,398	16.5	151,247
1984–85	782,484	39,915	16.5	163,269
1985–86	815,049	44,095	16.5	178,991
1986–87	850,217	51,516	16.5	179,971
1987–88	880,267	58,555	16.5	205,216
1988–89	969,702	66,786	16.5	233,728
1989–90	1,029,178	81,060	16.5	249,711
1990–91	1,083,572	92,892	16.5	291,611
1991–92	1,099,072	114,406	16.5	246,099
1992–93	1,158,025	124,066	19.0	269,647
1993–94	1,223,816	150,778	19.0	286,305

(Contd.)

Table 11.6 (*Contd.*)

Year	Y	M	R	I
1994–95	1,302,076	192,257	15.0	349,266
1995–96	1,396,974	214,835	16.5	375,888
1996–97	1,508,378	240,615	14.5	374,006
1997–98	1,573,263	267,844	14.0	419,378
1998–99	1,678,410	309,068	13.0	419,885
1999–2000	1,786,525	341,796	12.0	506,244
2000–01	1,864,301	379,450	11.5	488,658
2001–02	1,972,606	422,843	11.5	474,449
2002–03	2,048,286	473,581	10.8	554,044
2003–04	2,222,758	578,716	10.3	651,346
2004–05	2,388,768	649,790	10.3	793,545
2005–06	2,616,101	826,415	10.3	922,637
2006–07	2,871,120	967,955	12.3	1,046,065
2007–08	3,129,717	1,155,837	12.3	1,236,511
2008–09	3,339,375	1,259,707	12.3	1,167,158
2009–10	3,605,108	1,489,301	11.8	1,386,159

Source: Reserve Bank of India, *Handbook of Statistics on Indian Economy 2010–11*.

Note: Y = GDP at 1999–2000 prices (Rs. Crore); $M = M_2$ money supply at 1999–2000 prices (Rs. Crore); R = rate of interest proxied by lending rate of the State Bank of India; and I = gross domestic capital formation at 1999–2000 prices (Rs. Crore).

Answers to Multiple-Choice Questions
(i) (c); (ii) (a) (iii) (c); (iv) (d); (v) (a).

APPENDIX 11.1: ALGEBRAIC DERIVATION OF RULES OF IDENTIFICATION[5]
Consider the structural equations

$$BY_t = \Gamma X_t + u_t$$

where $B = \begin{bmatrix} \beta_{11} & \beta_{12} & \cdots & \beta_{1G} \\ \beta_{21} & \beta_{22} & \cdots & \beta_{2G} \\ \cdot & & & \\ \cdot & & & \\ \cdot & & & \\ \beta_{G1} & \beta_{G2} & \cdots & \beta_{GG} \end{bmatrix}$, $\Gamma = \begin{bmatrix} \gamma_{11} & \gamma_{12} & \cdots & \gamma_{1k} \\ \gamma_{21} & \gamma_{22} & \cdots & \gamma_{2k} \\ \cdot & & & \\ \cdot & & & \\ \cdot & & & \\ \gamma_{G1} & \gamma_{G2} & \cdots & \gamma_{Gk} \end{bmatrix}$, $Y_t = \begin{bmatrix} Y_{1t} \\ Y_{2t} \\ \cdot \\ \cdot \\ \cdot \\ Y_{Gt} \end{bmatrix}$, $X_t = \begin{bmatrix} X_{1t} \\ X_{2t} \\ \cdot \\ \cdot \\ \cdot \\ X_{kt} \end{bmatrix}$ and $u_t = \begin{bmatrix} u_{1t} \\ u_{2t} \\ \cdot \\ \cdot \\ \cdot \\ u_{Gt} \end{bmatrix}$

The corresponding reduced-form equations are

$$Y_t = \Pi X_t + v_t$$

[5] Here we follow the approach of Kmenta (1986, 662–66).

$$\text{where } \Pi = -B^{-1}\Gamma = \begin{bmatrix} \pi_{11} & \pi_{12} & \cdots & \pi_{1k} \\ \pi_{21} & \pi_{22} & \cdots & \pi_{2k} \\ \cdot \\ \cdot \\ \cdot \\ \pi_{G1} & \pi_{G2} & \cdots & \pi_{Gk} \end{bmatrix} \text{ and } v_t = B^{-1}u_t = \begin{bmatrix} v_{1t} \\ v_{2t} \\ \cdot \\ \cdot \\ \cdot \\ v_{Gt} \end{bmatrix}$$

By substituting the reduced-form equations into the structural form, we obtain

$$B\Pi X_t + Bv_t + \Gamma X_t = u_t$$
$$\Rightarrow B\Pi X_t + BB^{-1}u_t + \Gamma X_t = u_t$$
$$\Rightarrow B\Pi = -\Gamma$$

This is the relation used for determining the identification status of the structural equations. Writing out the matrices in full, we have

$$\begin{bmatrix} \beta_{11} & \beta_{12} & \cdots & \beta_{1G} \\ \beta_{21} & \beta_{22} & \cdots & \beta_{2G} \\ \cdot \\ \cdot \\ \cdot \\ \beta_{G1} & \beta_{G2} & \cdots & \beta_{GG} \end{bmatrix} \begin{bmatrix} \pi_{11} & \pi_{12} & \cdots & \pi_{1k} \\ \pi_{21} & \pi_{22} & \cdots & \pi_{2k} \\ \cdot \\ \cdot \\ \cdot \\ \pi_{G1} & \pi_{G2} & \cdots & \pi_{Gk} \end{bmatrix} = - \begin{bmatrix} \gamma_{11} & \gamma_{12} & \cdots & \gamma_{1k} \\ \gamma_{21} & \gamma_{22} & \cdots & \gamma_{2k} \\ \cdot \\ \cdot \\ \cdot \\ \gamma_{G1} & \gamma_{G2} & \cdots & \gamma_{Gk} \end{bmatrix}$$

For a single equation of the system, say g^{th}, this becomes

$$\begin{bmatrix} \beta_{g1} & \beta_{g2} & \cdots & \beta_{gG} \end{bmatrix} \begin{bmatrix} \pi_{11} & \pi_{12} & \cdots & \pi_{1k} \\ \pi_{21} & \pi_{22} & \cdots & \pi_{2k} \\ \cdot \\ \cdot \\ \cdot \\ \pi_{G1} & \pi_{G2} & \cdots & \pi_{Gk} \end{bmatrix} = - \begin{bmatrix} \gamma_{g1} & \gamma_{g2} & \cdots & \gamma_{gk} \end{bmatrix}$$

$$\Rightarrow \beta_g \Pi = -\gamma_g \tag{A11.1}$$

where $\beta_g = \begin{bmatrix} \beta_{g1} & \beta_{g2} & \cdots & \beta_{gG} \end{bmatrix}$ and $\gamma_g = \begin{bmatrix} \gamma_{g1} & \gamma_{g2} & \cdots & \gamma_{gk} \end{bmatrix}$

If all the endogenous and predetermined variables of the system do not appear in the gth equation, then some of the βs and γs would be zero.

Let us suppose

G^Δ = number of endogenous variables appearing in the gth equation (i.e., number of non-zero elements in β_g);

$G^{\Delta\Delta} = G - G^{\Delta}$;

K^{*} = number of predetermined variables appearing in the gth equation (i.e., number of non-zero elements in γ_g); and

$K^{**} = K - K^{*}$

Assume that the elements of β_g and γ_g are arranged in such a way that the non-zero elements appear first, followed by the zero elements. Then we can partition β_g and γ_g as

$$\left.\begin{array}{l} \beta_g = \begin{bmatrix} \beta_\Delta & 0_{\Delta\Delta} \end{bmatrix} \\ \gamma_g = \begin{bmatrix} \gamma_\cdot & 0_{\cdot\cdot} \end{bmatrix} \end{array}\right\} \qquad\qquad\text{(A11.2)}$$

where

$$\beta_\Delta = [\beta_{g1} \ \beta_{g2} \ \cdots \ \beta_{gG^\Delta}]_{(1 \times G^\Delta)}$$

$$0_{\Delta\Delta} = [0 \ 0 \ \cdots \ 0]_{(1 \times G^{\Delta\Delta})}$$

$$\gamma_\cdot = [\gamma_{g1} \ \gamma_{g2} \ \cdots \ \gamma_{gk^*}]_{(1 \times k^*)}$$

$$0_{\cdot\cdot} = [0 \ 0 \ \cdots \ 0]_{(1 \times k^{**})}$$

The matrix Π can also be partitioned in the corresponding manner.

$$\Pi = \begin{bmatrix} \Pi_{\Delta\cdot} & \Pi_{\Delta\cdot\cdot} \\ \\ \Pi_{\Delta\Delta\cdot} & \Pi_{\Delta\Delta\cdot\cdot} \end{bmatrix} \qquad\qquad\text{(A11.3)}$$

where $\qquad\quad$ $\Pi_{\Delta\cdot}$ is a sub-matrix of order $G^\Delta \times K^*$;

$\qquad\qquad\qquad$ $\Pi_{\Delta\cdot\cdot}$ is a sub-matrix of order $G^\Delta \times K^{**}$;

$\qquad\qquad\qquad$ $\Pi_{\Delta\Delta\cdot}$ is a sub-matrix of order $G^{\Delta\Delta} \times K^*$; and

$\qquad\qquad\qquad$ $\Pi_{\Delta\Delta\cdot\cdot}$ is a sub-matrix of order $G^{\Delta\Delta} \times K^{**}$.

Using (A11.2) and (A11.3), we can write (A11.1) as

$$\begin{bmatrix} \beta_\Delta & 0_{\Delta\Delta} \end{bmatrix} \begin{bmatrix} \Pi_{\Delta\cdot} & \Pi_{\Delta\cdot\cdot} \\ \\ \Pi_{\Delta\Delta\cdot} & \Pi_{\Delta\Delta\cdot\cdot} \end{bmatrix} = -\begin{bmatrix} \gamma_\cdot & 0_{\cdot\cdot} \end{bmatrix} \qquad\qquad\text{(A11.4)}$$

This leads to the following equalities:

$$\underset{(1 \times G^\Delta)}{\beta_\Delta} \ \underset{(G^\Delta \times K^*)}{\Pi_{\Delta\cdot}} = -\underset{(1 \times K^*)}{\gamma_\cdot} \qquad\qquad\text{(A11.5)}$$

$$\underset{(1 \times G^\Delta)}{\beta_\Delta} \ \underset{(G^\Delta \times K^{**})}{\Pi_{\Delta\cdot\cdot}} = \underset{(1 \times K^{**})}{0_{\cdot\cdot}} \qquad\qquad\text{(A11.6)}$$

Since one of the βs in structural equation is unity, the equalities (A11.5) and (A11.6) involve $G^\Delta - 1$ unknown βs and K^* unknown γs. The equality (A11.6) is particularly important since it does not involve any γs. If we can solve (A11.6) for β_Δ, we can easily solve for γ from (A11.5). Note that equality (A11.6) contains altogether K^{**} equations, one for each element of $1 \times K^{**}$ vector. Therefore, if we want to obtain solution for the $G^\Delta - 1$ unknown elements of β_Δ, we need at least $G^\Delta - 1$ equations. This means that we require

$$K^{**} \geq G^\Delta - 1$$
$$\Rightarrow K^{**} \geq G - G^{\Delta\Delta} - 1$$
$$\Rightarrow K^{**} + G^{\Delta\Delta} \geq G - 1 \qquad \text{(A11.7)}$$

This is known as the 'order condition' of identification. It states that number of predetermined and endogenous variables excluded from the gth equation must be greater than or equal to number of endogenous variables in the system less one. However, this is only a necessary condition and not a sufficient condition because K^{**} equations in (A11.6) may not be independent. The sufficient condition, also called the 'rank condition', is that the number of independent equations in (A11.6) is $G^\Delta - 1$. This happens when the order of the largest non-zero determinant that can be formed from all square sub-matrices of $\Pi_{\Delta^{**}}$ is $G^\Delta - 1$, i.e.,

$$rank\, \Pi_{\Delta^{**}} = G^\Delta - 1 \qquad \text{(A11.8a)}$$

It can further be shown that

$$rank\, \Pi_{\Delta^{**}} = rank\, \Delta - G^{\Delta\Delta} \qquad \text{(A11.8b)}$$
$$\Delta = [B_{\Delta\Delta} \quad \Gamma_{**}]$$

Here, $B_{\Delta\Delta}$ and Γ_{**} are matrices of the structural coefficients for the variables omitted from the gth equation but included in other structural equations. Then the rank condition becomes

$$rank\, \Delta - G^{\Delta\Delta} = G^\Delta - 1 \qquad \text{(A11.9)}$$
$$\Rightarrow rank\, \Delta = G - 1 \qquad [\because\ G^\Delta + G^{\Delta\Delta} = G]$$

General Appendix

Review of Some Statistical Concepts

The pre-requisite for this book is some introductory idea about probability theory and statistical inference. In most cases, a course on these precedes the course on introductory econometrics at the level of undergraduate studies. For this reason, we do not enter into a detailed discussion on these aspects in this book.[1] The purpose of this appendix is just to recapitulate a few concepts of probability and statistics that are frequently referred to in this book while discussing various issues in econometrics. It is hoped that it would help the readers to refresh their memories and appreciate the econometric issues discussed in this book.

G1. SUMMATION AND PRODUCT OPERATORS

Summation Operator

The summation operator is useful shorthand for manipulating expressions involving the sum of many numbers. The Greek capital letter Σ (sigma) is used to indicate summation. If $x_1, x_2, ..., x_n$ denotes a sequence of n numbers, then the sum of these numbers is written as

$$\sum_{i=1}^{n} x_i = x_1 + x_2 + ... + x_n$$

Some important properties of the summation operator are

(i)   For any constant c,

$$\sum_{i=1}^{n} c = nc$$

(ii)   For any constant c,

$$\sum_{i=1}^{n} cx_i = c\sum_{i=1}^{n} x_i$$

---

[1] For detailed discussion on probability theory and statistical inference, one may refer to other introductory texts like Hoel, Port, and Stone (1971), Mood, Graybill, and Boes (1974), Bowen and Starr (1982), Mansfield (1994), and Spiegel and Stephens (2010).

(iii)　For a and b as constants,

$$\sum_{i=1}^{n}(a+bx_i)=na+b\sum_{i=1}^{n}x_i$$

(iv)　If $[(x, y_i): i = 1, 2, ..., n]$ is a set of n pairs of numbers and a and b are constants, then,

$$\sum_{i=1}^{n}(x_i + y_i)=\sum_{i=1}^{n}x_i +\sum_{i=1}^{n}y_i; \text{ and}$$
$$\sum_{i=1}^{n}(ax_i + by_i)=a\sum_{i=1}^{n}x_i +b\sum_{i=1}^{n}y_i$$

Product Operator

For the sequence of n numbers $x_1, x_2, ..., x_n$, the product operator Π is defined as

$$\prod_{i=1}^{n}x_i = x_1.x_2....x_n$$

G2. RANDOM VARIABLES AND PROBABILITY DISTRIBUTIONS

Sample Space and Events

The concept of probability is applied to experiments that have somewhat uncertain outcomes. For instance, we cannot say what will be the sex of the person we meet next or whether we will observe head (H) up or tail (T) up if a (fair) coin is tossed. Suppose we plan to toss a coin repeatedly and record the results. Then, this act of tossing the coin is called the *experiment*. Put differently, an *experiment* is the process of collecting information or data relevant to a phenomenon that shows variation in its outcomes. The result of a particular experiment is called an *event* or *outcome*. Thus, in repeated experiments of tossing a coin, the events could be $H\,H\,T\,H\,H\,T\,T$ .... All events or outcomes of an experiment constitute the *sample space*. So an event is a subset of the sample space.

Random Variable

A random variable is a variable whose values cannot be predicted exactly. The values of the random variable are determined by chance, i.e., by the outcome of an experiment. In the coin-tossing example, the number of heads observed in 10 tosses is an example of a random variable. Before we toss the coin 10 times, it is not known how many times the coin will show up heads. Once we toss the coin 10 times, and count the number of heads, we obtain the outcome of the random variable for this particular trial of the experiment. Another trial can produce a different outcome.

　　Some random variables are *discrete* and some are *continuous*. As the name suggests, a discrete random variable takes on only a discrete set of values like 0, 1, 2, 3, ... For example, the number of sixes observed in the throwing of a die five times may be represented by a discrete random variable taking values 0, 1, 2, 3, 4, and 5. The simplest example of a discrete random variable is the *Bernoulli random variable* that takes only two values, 0 and 1. A continuous random variable, on the other hand, is one that takes on a continuum of possible values. For example, the heights of a group of students drawn randomly in a college may be represented by a continuous random variable.

Probability Distribution

If we tabulate all possible values of the random variable and their corresponding probabilities, then the table of values is called the *probability distribution* of the random variable. For a discrete random variable, the probability distribution shows all possible values of the variable and their corresponding probabilities. Obviously, the sum of these probabilities is equal to 1. A hypothetical probability distribution of the number of sixes in the throwing of a die five times is displayed in Table A.1. According to this probability distribution, the probability of observing no sixes is 0.10 or 10%, that of observing 1 six is 0.20 or 20%, that of observing 2 sixes is 0.30 or 30%, and so on.

Table A.1 Probability Distribution of Number of Sixes (X) in Throwing a Die Five Times

	Outcome (Number of Sixes)					
	0	1	2	3	4	5
Probability	0.10	0.20	0.30	0.35	0.05	0.00
Cumulative Probability	0.10	0.30	0.60	0.95	1.00	1.00

We can compute the probability of an event from the probability distribution. For example, the probability of the event of two or three sixes is the sum of the probabilities of the constituent outcomes: $P(X = 2 \text{ or } X = 3) = P(X = 2) + P(X = 3) = 0.30 + 0.35 = 0.65$ or 65%.

Cumulative Probability Distribution

The cumulative probability distribution is the probability of the value of the random variable being less than or equal to a particular value. The last row of above table provides the cumulative probability distribution of the discrete random variable X. It shows that the probability of observing at most two heads (i.e., $X \leq 2$) is 0.60 or 60%. A cumulative probability distribution is also called the *cumulative distribution function* (CDF).

The cumulative probability distribution of a continuous random variable is defined in the same way as that for a discrete random variable. It shows the probability of the continuous random variable having a value which is less than or equal to a particular value. As mentioned earlier, the heights (Y) of a group of students drawn randomly in a college is a continuous random variable. A hypothetical cumulative probability distribution for this variable is shown in Figure A1. It shows that $Pr(Y \leq 64 \text{ inches}) = 0.65$ or 65% and $Pr(Y \leq 66 \text{ inches}) = 0.90$ or 90%. It means that the probability of the height of the students being less than or equal to 64 inches is 0.65 or 65% and that of 66 inches is 0.90 or 90%.

This further means that as much as 25% (90%–65%) of the students have heights between 64 and 66 inches.

Probability Density Function

As a continuous random variable takes on a continuum of possible values, the probability distribution used for a discrete random variable, which lists the probability of each possible value of it, cannot be used. Instead, the probability is summarized by the *probability density function* (PDF). The area under the probability density function between any two points is the probability that the continuous random variable falls between those two points. Figure A.2 plots the probability density function of heights of the students. The probability that the height of the students is between 62 and 64 inches is given by the area under the PDF between 62 and 64 inches, which is 0.35 or 35%. It is obvious that the total area under the PDF is equal to 1. However, the probability that a continuous random variable is precisely equal to a particular value is zero since the area under the PDF at this particular value is a line with zero width.

Expected Value of a Random Variable

The expected value of a discrete random variable (X), denoted by $E(X)$, is the weighted mean of the possible values that the random variable can assume, where the weights attached

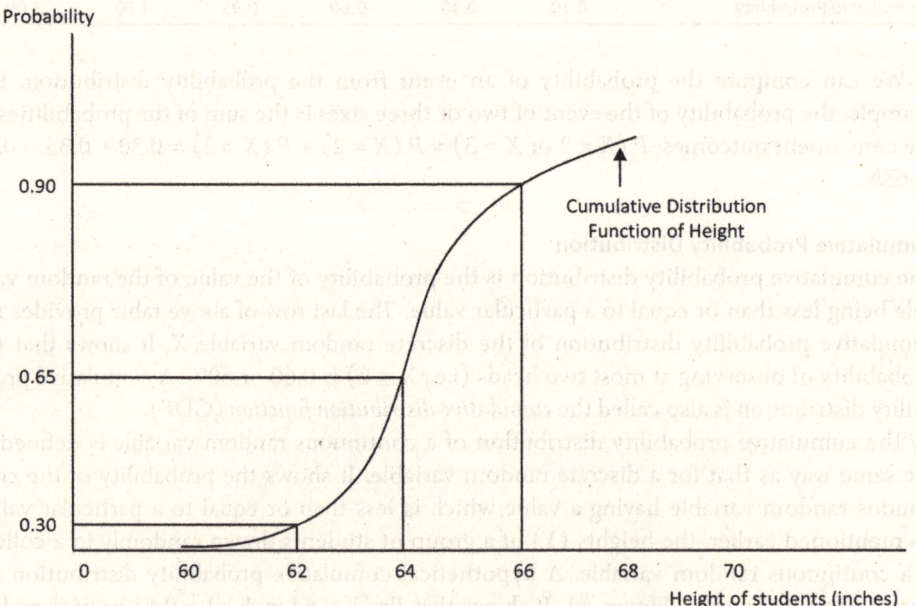

Figure A.1   Cumulative Probability Distribution of Heights of the Students

Source: Author's own.

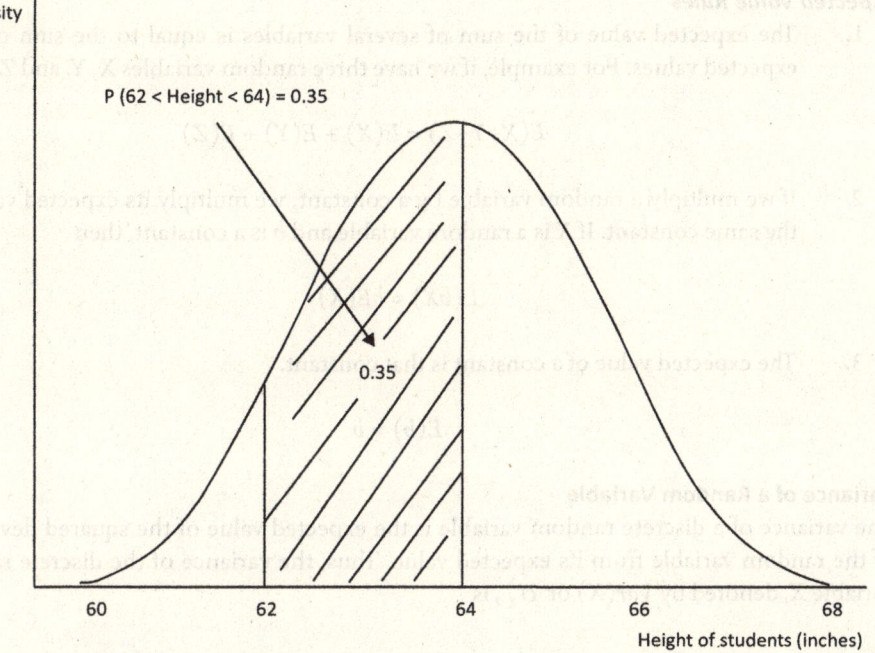

P (62 < Height < 64) = 0.35

0.35

60   62   64   66   68

Height of students (inches)

Density

Figure A.2 Probability Density Function of Heights of the Students

Source: Author's own.

to each value is the probability that the random variable will assume this value. If the discrete random variable X assumes n values, $x_1, x_2, \ldots, x_n$, and the corresponding probabilities of these values are $P(x_1), P(x_2), \ldots, P(x_n)$, then

$$E(X) = \sum_{i=1}^{n} x_i P(x_i)$$

The expected value of a continuous random variable is also the probability-weighted average of the possible values of the random variable. However, as a continuous random variable takes on a continuum of possible values, the formal mathematical expression of it involves calculus. If Y is a continuous random variable and $f(y)$ is its probability density function, then expected value of Y is given by

$$E(Y) = \int y f(y) dy$$

where the range of the integration is the range of values for which $f(y)$ is non-zero.

Expected Value Rules

1. The expected value of the sum of several variables is equal to the sum of their expected values. For example, if we have three random variables X, Y, and Z, then

$$E(X+Y+Z) = E(X) + E(Y) + E(Z)$$

2. If we multiply a random variable by a constant, we multiply its expected value by the same constant. If X is a random variable and b is a constant, then

$$E(bX) = bE(X)$$

3. The expected value of a constant is that constant.

$$E(b) = b$$

Variance of a Random Variable

The variance of a discrete random variable is the expected value of the squared deviations of the random variable from its expected value. Thus, the variance of the discrete random variable X, denoted by $Var(X)$ or σ_X^2, is

$$Var(X) = \sigma_X^2 = E[X - E(X)]^2 = \sum_{i=1}^{n} [x_i - E(X)]^2 P(x_i)$$

On the other hand, the variance of the continuous random variable Y, denoted by $Var(Y)$ or σ_Y^2, is given by

$$Var(Y) = \sigma_Y^2 = \int [y - E(Y)]^2 f(y) dy$$

Some Variance Rules

1. If $X = Y + Z$, then $Var(X) = Var(Y) + Var(Z) + 2Cov(Y, Z)$
2. If $X = bY$, where b is a constant, then $Var(X) = b^2 Var(Y)$
3. If $X = b$, where b is a constant, then $Var(X) = 0$

Standard Deviation of a Random Variable

The standard deviation of a random variable is the positive square root of its variance. Thus, the standard deviation of a (discrete) random variable X, denoted by σ_X is

$$\sigma_X = \sqrt{E[X - E(X)]^2} = \sqrt{\sum_{i=1}^{n} [x_i - E(X)]^2 P(x_i)}$$

Joint, Marginal, and Conditional Probability Distributions

Joint probability is defined as the probability of joint occurrence of two or more events. For example, suppose that two coins (A and B) are each tossed once. Let X be the random variable corresponding to the number of times coin A shows up heads, and let Y be the number of times coin B shows up tails. Then, Table A.2 shows the joint probability distribution for X and Y. The joint probabilities in the table show the probabilities that X and Y assume particular values. For example, the probability that $X = 0$ and $Y = 1$, denoted by $P(X = 0$ and $Y = 1) = 1/4$.

The row and column totals in the joint probability table are the marginal probabilities. The row totals in Table A.2 corresponds to $P(x)$ and constitute the marginal probability distribution of X. On the other hand, the column totals in the same table correspond to $P(y)$ and constitute the marginal probability distribution of Y. Table A.3 shows the marginal probability distributions of X and Y.

Table A.2 Joint Probability Distribution for X and Y

Value of X	Value of Y		Total (Marginal Probabilities)
	0 (no heads)	1 (one head)	
0 (no heads)	1/4	1/4	1/2
1 (one head)	1/4	1/4	1/2
Total (marginal probabilities)	1/2	1/2	1

Table A.3 Marginal Probability Distributions of X and Y

Marginal Probability Distribution of X		Marginal Probability Distribution of Y	
Value of X	Probability	Value of Y	Probability
0	1/2	0	1/2
1	1/2	1	1/2
Total	1	Total	1

To obtain the *conditional probability* that X assumes a particular value (say 1) given that Y assumes a particular value (say 0), we divide the joint probability that $X = 1$ and $Y = 0$ by the marginal probability of $Y = 0$. Thus,

$$P(X = 1 | Y = 0) = \frac{P(X = 1 \text{ and } Y = 0)}{P(Y = 0)} = \frac{1/4}{1/2} = \frac{1}{2} = 0.5$$

Again, the conditional probability that $X = 0$ given that $Y = 0$ is obtained as:

$$P(X = 0 | Y = 0) = \frac{P(X = 0 \text{ and } Y = 0)}{P(Y = 0)} = \frac{1/4}{1/2} = \frac{1}{2} = 0.5$$

Table A.4 shows the conditional probability distribution of X given that $Y = 0$.

Table A.4 Conditional Probability Distributions of X

Conditional Probability Distribution of X Given That $Y = 0$		Conditional Probability Distribution of X Given That $Y = 1$	
Value of X	Probability	Value of X	Probability
0	1/2	0	1/2
1	1/2	1	1/2
Total	1	Total	1

We may derive the conditional probability distribution of Y given that X assumes a particular value in a similar way. To obtain the conditional probability that $Y = 1$, given $X = 1$, we divide the joint probability that $Y = 1$ and $X = 1$ by the marginal probability that $X = 1$. Thus,

$$P(Y=1|X=1) = \frac{P(Y=1 \text{ and } X=1)}{P(X=1)} = \frac{1/4}{1/2} = \frac{1}{2} = 0.5$$

Again, to obtain the conditional probability that $Y = 0$, given $X = 1$, we divide the joint probability that $Y = 0$ and $X = 1$ by the marginal probability that $X = 1$ so that

$$P(Y=0|X=1) = \frac{P(Y=0 \text{ and } X=1)}{P(X=1)} = \frac{1/4}{1/2} = \frac{1}{2} = 0.5$$

The conditional probability distribution of Y given that $X = 1$ is shown in Table A.5.

Table A.5 Conditional Probability Distributions of Y

Conditional Probability Distribution of Y Given That $X = 0$		Conditional Probability Distribution of Y Given That $X = 1$	
Value of X	Probability	Value of X	Probability
0	1/2	0	1/2
1	1/2	1	1/2
Total	1	Total	1

Statistical Independence of Random Variables

Two random variables X and Y are statistically independent if the conditional probability distribution of X, given any value of Y, is identical to the marginal probability distribution of X, and if the conditional probability distribution of Y, given any value of X, is identical to the marginal probability distribution of Y. In the context of two coins tossing example, it is found that X and Y are independent. This is because both conditional probability distributions of Y in Table A.4 are identical to the marginal probability distribution of Y in Table A.3, and both conditional probability distributions of X in Table A.5 are identical to the marginal probability distribution of X in Table A.3.

Conditional Expectation and Variance

The conditional expectation of Y given X is the mean of the conditional distribution of Y given X. It is computed using the conditional distribution of Y given X (i.e., for a specified value of X). If Y takes on n values, $y_1, y_2, \dots, y_n$, given that $X = x$, then the conditional mean of Y is

$$E(Y|X=x) = \sum_{i=1}^{n} y_i \, Pr(Y_i = y_i | X = x)$$

The conditional variance of Y given X is the variance of the conditional distribution of Y given X, which is expressed as

$$Var(Y|X=x) = \sum_{i=1}^{n} [y_i - E(Y|X=x)]^2 \, Pr(Y_i = y_i | X = x)$$

Covariance and Correlation between Two Random Variables

The covariance between the random variables X and Y, denoted by σ_{XY}, is a numerical measure of their joint variation and is defined as the expected value of the product $[\{X - E(X)\}\{Y - E(Y)\}]$. If X takes on m values and Y takes on n values, then the covariance is computed as

$$Cov(X,Y) = \sigma_{XY} = E[\{X - E(X)\}\{Y - E(Y)\}]$$
$$= \sum_{i=1}^{m} \sum_{j=1}^{n} \{X - E(X)\}\{Y - E(Y)\} Pr(X = x_i, Y = y_j)$$

The correlation coefficient between X and Y is given by

$$Cor(X,Y) = \frac{Cov(X,Y)}{\sqrt{Var(X)Var(Y)}} = \frac{\sigma_{XY}}{\sigma_X \sigma_Y}$$

where σ_X and σ_Y are standard deviations of X and Y, respectively.

G3. SOME IMPORTANT PROBABILITY DISTRIBUTIONS

Normal Distribution

Normal distribution is the most widely used continuous probability distribution. It is the cornerstone in the application of statistical inference based on random samples of data. The normal density function is a symmetric, bell-shaped curve that has a dense concentration around the central value and tails off without bound to the left and to the right (see Figure A.3). The mathematical expression for the probability density function of a normal random variable (X) is given by

$$f(x) = \frac{1}{\sigma\sqrt{2\pi}} e^{-\frac{1}{2}\left(\frac{x-\mu}{\sigma}\right)^2} \tag{A1}$$

where μ is the random variable's expected value or mean, σ is its standard deviation, e is approximately 2.71828 and is the base of the natural logarithms, and π is approximately 3.14159. Regardless of the values of μ and σ, the probability that the value of a normal random variable will lie within one standard deviation of its mean (i.e., within $\mu \pm \sigma$) is 68.2%, the probability that it will lie within $\mu \pm 2\sigma$ is 95.4%, and within $\mu \pm 3\sigma$ is 99.7%.

The location and shape of the normal density function (or normal curve) can vary considerably depending upon its mean (μ) and standard deviation (σ). The location of the normal curve on the horizontal axis is determined entirely by its mean while its standard deviation determines the amount of spread. If σ increases, its spread widens and if σ decreases, its spread narrows.

The symmetrical feature of the normal curve implies that its height at a value that is a certain amount below the mean is equal to its height at a value that is the same amount above the mean. This means that the area under the normal curve between μ and $\mu - \sigma$ is the same as the area under the curve between μ and $\mu + \sigma$ (see Figure A.3). As the normal curve is

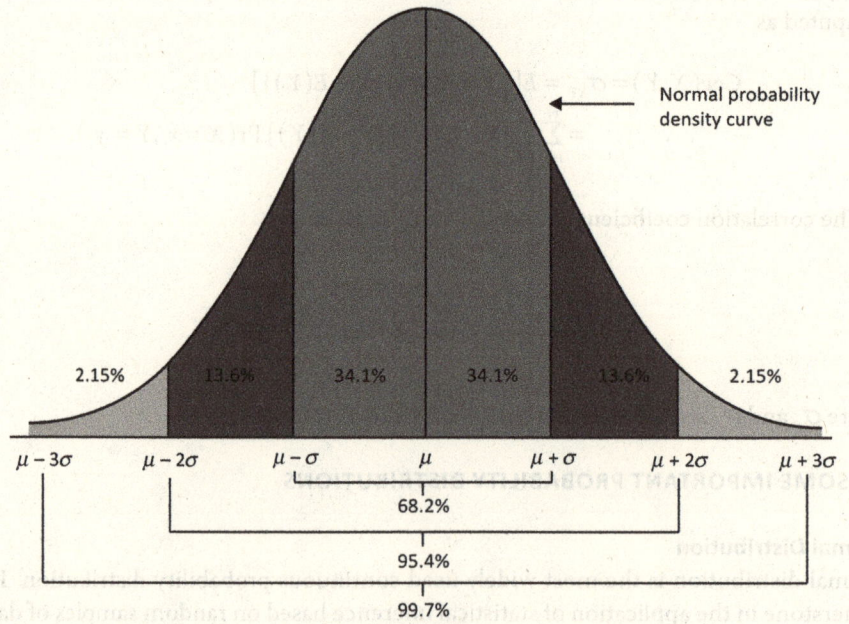

Figure A.3   The Normal Probability Density Curve

Source: Author's own.

symmetrical, its mean equals both median and mode. A normal random variable can assume values ranging from $-\infty$ to $+\infty$.

We denote a normally distributed random variable compactly as

$$X \sim N(\mu, \sigma^2)$$

where $\sim$ means 'is distributed as', N stands for the normal distribution, and μ and σ^2 are mean and variance, which are the two parameters of the normal distribution.

Standard Normal Curve

If we express any normal random variable as a deviation from its mean, and measure these deviations in units of its standard deviation, the resulting random variable is called a *standard normal variable*, and its probability distribution is called the *standard normal curve*. Thus, if X is normally distributed, then

$$Z = \frac{X - \mu}{\sigma}$$

has the standard normal distribution regardless of the values of μ and σ. The mean of the standard normal distribution is zero and its standard deviation is 1, i.e., $Z \sim N(0, 1)$. The probability density function of the standardized normal variable (Z) is given by

$$f(Z) = \frac{1}{\sqrt{2\pi}} e^{-\frac{1}{2}z^2}$$

Multivariate Normal Distribution

The multivariate normal distribution describes the joint distribution of a set of random variables. When only two random variables are considered, it becomes the bivariate normal distribution. The bivariate normal probability density function for the two variables X and Y, denoted by $g(x, y)$, is

$$g(x,y) = \frac{1}{2\pi\sigma_X\sigma_Y\sqrt{1-\rho_{XY}^2}} e^{\left\{-\frac{1}{2(1-\rho_{XY}^2)}\left[\left(\frac{x-\mu_X}{\sigma_X}\right)^2 - 2\rho_{XY}\left(\frac{x-\mu_X}{\sigma_X}\right)\left(\frac{y-\mu_Y}{\sigma_Y}\right)+\left(\frac{y-\mu_Y}{\sigma_Y}\right)^2\right]\right\}}$$

where ρ_{XY} is the correlation between X and Y.

If X and Y are jointly distributed but uncorrelated (i.e., $\rho_{XY} = 0$), then they are independently distributed. This means that

$$g(x, y) = f(x)f(y)$$

where f is the normal density given in (A1) above.

X^2 (Chi-square) Distribution

If $Z_1, Z_2, \ldots, Z_k$ are k independently and identically distributed (*i.i.d*) standardized normal variables (i.e., they all have zero mean and unit variance), then the random variable

$$Z = \sum_{i=1}^{k} Z_i^2$$

is said to follow a Chi-square distribution with k degrees of freedom. This distribution is denoted by χ_k^2 where the subscript k denotes the degrees of freedom.

For relatively low degrees of freedom (k), the χ^2 distribution becomes skewed to the right, but as the value of k increases, it tends to become symmetrical. The mean of the χ^2 distribution is k and the variance is $2k$. Another important property is that if S_1 and S_2 are two independent χ^2 variables with k_1 and k_2 degrees of freedom respectively, then $S_1 + S_2$ is also a χ^2 variable with degrees of freedom $k_1 + k_2$.

Student's *t* Distribution

Let X_1 be a standardized normal variable [i.e., $X_1 \sim N(0, 1)$], X_2 variable follows the Chi-square distribution with k degrees of freedom, and X_1 and X_2 are independently distributed. Then the random variable defined as

$$t = \frac{X_1}{\sqrt{X_2 / k}}$$

follows Student's *t*-distribution with k degrees of freedom.

Two important properties of *t*-distribution are

1. Although the *t*-distribution is also symmetrical like normal distribution, it is flatter than the normal distribution. However, as the degrees of freedom increases, the *t*-distribution approximates the normal distribution, and

2. The mean of the *t*-distribution is zero and its variance is $k/(k-2)$.

The *F*-Distribution

Let W_1 and W_2 be independently distributed random variables with Chi-square (χ^2) distributions with k_1 and k_2 degrees of freedom respectively. Then the random variable

$$F = \frac{W_1 / k_1}{W_2 / k_2}$$

follows an *F*-distribution with k_1 and k_2 degrees of freedom. An *F*-distributed variable is denoted by F_{k_1, k_2} where k_1 is the degrees of freedom for the numerator and k_2 is the degrees of freedom for the denominator.

Important properties of the F-distribution are

1. Like the χ^2 distribution, the F-distribution is skewed to the right. But as k_1 and k_2 become large, the F-distribution approaches to the normal distribution.
2. When k_2 is fairly large, the F_{k_1, k_2} distribution is well approximated by a $\chi^2_{k_1}$ distribution divided by k_1, and
3. The square of a t-distributed random variable with k degrees of freedom has an F-distribution with 1 and k degrees of freedom, i.e.,

$$t^2 = F_{1,k}$$

G4. STATISTICAL INFERENCE

Two aspects of classical statistical inference used throughout in econometrics are *estimation* and *hypothesis testing*. Estimation is the process of estimating or inferring about a population parameter using the corresponding statistic of a sample drawn from the population. Hypothesis testing is the process of determining, on the basis of sample information, whether to accept or reject a hypothesis or assumption with regard to the value of the population parameter. Depending on the test results, inferences or conclusions may be drawn on the relationship between the dependent and independent variables in probability terms.

To be valid, estimation should be done by drawing a *representative sample*, which is ensured when the *random sampling* procedure is followed. In random sampling, each item of the population has equal chance of being picked in the sample.

Point Estimation and Interval Estimation

There are two types of estimation—*point estimation* and *interval estimation*. Point estimation provides a single-point estimate of the population parameter. On the other hand, the interval estimation provides a range of values within which the true value of the parameter is likely to fall. For example, if we draw a random sample (denoted by Y_1) from a population whose parameter values (mean, standard deviation, etc.) are not known and the sample observations are 1, 3, 6, 7, and 8, then the sample mean $\bar{Y}_1 = 5$ represents the point estimate of the unknown population mean. However, if we say that the true population mean lies between $\bar{Y}_1 - 1$ and $\bar{Y}_1 + 1$, i.e., between 4 and 6, then the range of values from 4 to 6 becomes an interval estimate of true population mean.

Methods of Estimation

Some important methods of estimation are least squares, maximum likelihood and moment (also its extension, the generalized method of moments). We have discussed in detail the least squares estimation method in chapters 2 and 3, and outlined the maximum likelihood method in Appendix 3.2 of Chapter 3. We have not discussed the moment method as that is outside the purview of this book.

The Difference between Estimator and Estimate

It is necessary to note the difference between an estimator and an estimate. An estimator is a general rule, usually just a formula, for estimating an unknown population parameter given the sample data. Once we have obtained a specific sample, we use it to obtain a specific number which we call the estimate. Thus, the estimator is a formula whereas the estimate is a number. If we take repeated samples, the estimator will be the same, but the estimate will vary from sample to sample.

Statistical Properties of Estimators

The desirable statistical properties for estimators fall into two categories—small sample (or finite sample) properties and large sample (or asymptotic) properties. Underlying both these sets of properties is the notion that an estimator has a sampling or probability distribution (this concept is clarified below). These properties have been explained in section 2.5 of Chapter 2.

Probability Distribution of an Estimator

Suppose we take repeated random samples of same size, $Y_1, Y_2, ..., Y_n$, from a population and measure the mean of each sample. It is quite obvious that all such means, i.e., $\bar{Y}_1, \bar{Y}_2, ..., \bar{Y}_n$, would differ from each other. The probability distribution of these sample means is called the *sampling distribution of mean*.

Two important theorems relate the sampling distribution of the mean to the parent population.

1. When repeated random samples of size n are drawn from the population, then mean ($\mu_{\bar{Y}}$) and standard deviation or standard error ($\sigma_{\bar{Y}}$) of the sampling distribution of the mean are

$$\mu_{\bar{Y}} = \mu \text{ and } \sigma_{\bar{Y}} = \sigma/\sqrt{n}$$

   where μ and σ are true (population) mean and standard deviation.

2. As the sample size n increases (i.e., $n \to \infty$), the sampling distribution of the mean approaches to normal distribution irrespective of the shape of the parent population. This approximation is sufficiently good for $n \geq 30$. This is known as the *central limit theorem*.[2]

---

[2] More specifically, the central limit theorem states that if Y has a distribution with mean μ and standard deviation σ_Y for which moment generating function exists, then the distribution of $\dfrac{(\bar{Y} - \mu)}{\sigma_Y/\sqrt{n}}$ has a distribution that approaches standard normal distribution as the sample size (n) becomes infinite. In other words, the distribution of $\bar{Y}$ in large samples is approximately normal with mean μ, and variance σ_Y^2/n or standard deviation $\sigma_Y/\sqrt{n}$.

Hypothesis Testing

Null and Alternative Hypotheses

The starting point of statistical hypotheses testing is specifying the hypothesis to be tested, called the *null hypothesis* (denoted by H_N or H_0). Hypothesis testing entails using data to test the null hypothesis against a second hypothesis, called *alternative hypothesis* (denoted by H_A or H_1).

For instance, the null hypothesis that the population mean $E(Y)$ takes on a specific value (μ_0) is expressed as

$$H_N: E(Y) = \mu_0$$

The alternative hypothesis specifies what is true if the null hypothesis is not true. The most general alternative hypothesis is

$$H_A: E(Y) \neq \mu_0$$

This is called the *two-sided alternative hypothesis,* or composite hypothesis.

Type I and Type II Errors

A statistical hypothesis test can make two types of mistakes or errors. A Type I error occurs when a null hypothesis is rejected when in fact it is true. On the other hand, a Type II error occurs when the null hypothesis is not rejected when in fact it is false. The probability of a Type I error is designated as α, and it is called the *level of significance*. The probability of a Type II error is designated as β, and it is called the *power of a test*. Thus, the power of a test is its ability to reject a false null hypothesis.

The p-value or Exact Level of Significance

Instead of preselecting α at arbitrary levels such as 1%, 5%, or 10%, we may obtain the p (probability) value or exact level of significance of a test statistic. The p-value is defined as the lowest significance level at which a null hypothesis can be rejected. Almost all software packages now routinely report the p-value of the estimated test statistic.

The Critical Value

The *critical value* of the test statistic is the value of the statistic for which the test just rejects the null hypothesis at the given significance level. The set of values of the test statistic for which the test rejects the null hypothesis is the *rejection region,* and the values of the test statistic for which it does not reject the null hypothesis is the *acceptance region.*

Confidence Intervals

Because of random sampling error, it is impossible to know the exact value of the population parameter using only the information in the sample. However, we may use data from a random sample to construct a set of values that contains the population parameter with a certain pre-specified probability. Such a set is called a *confidence set*, and the pre-specified probability that the population parameter is contained in this set is called the *confidence level*. The confidence set for the population parameter turns out to be all the possible values of the population parameter between a lower and an upper limit, so that the confidence set is an interval, called a *confidence interval*.

Statistical Tables

Table A.6   *t* Distribution: Critical Values of *t*

			Tail Probabilities			
One-tailed test →	0.10	0.05	0.025	0.01	0.005	0.001
Two-tailed test →	0.20	0.10	0.05	0.02	0.01	0.002
1	3.078	6.314	12.706	31.821	63.657	318.309
2	1.886	2.920	4.303	6.965	9.925	22.327
3	1.638	2.353	3.182	4.541	5.841	10.215
4	1.533	2.132	2.776	3.747	4.604	7.173
5	1.476	2.015	2.571	3.365	4.032	5.893
6	1.440	1.943	2.447	3.143	3.707	5.208
7	1.415	1.894	2.365	2.998	3.499	4.785
8	1.397	1.860	2.306	2.896	3.355	4.501
9	1.383	1.833	2.262	2.821	3.250	4.297
10	1.372	1.812	2.228	2.764	3.169	4.144
11	1.363	1.796	2.201	2.718	3.106	4.025
12	1.356	1.782	2.179	2.681	3.055	3.930
13	1.350	1.771	2.160	2.650	3.012	3.852
14	1.345	1.761	2.145	2.624	2.977	3.787
15	1.341	1.753	2.131	2.602	2.947	3.733
16	1.337	1.746	2.120	2.583	2.921	3.686
17	1.333	1.740	2.110	2.567	2.898	3.646
18	1.330	1.734	2.101	2.552	2.878	3.610
19	1.328	1.729	2.093	2.539	2.861	3.579
20	1.325	1.725	2.086	2.528	2.845	3.552
21	1.323	1.721	2.080	2.518	2.831	3.527
22	1.321	1.717	2.074	2.508	2.819	3.505
23	1.319	1.714	2.069	2.500	2.807	3.485
24	1.318	1.711	2.064	2.492	2.797	3.467
25	1.316	1.708	2.060	2.485	2.787	3.450
26	1.315	1.706	2.056	2.479	2.779	3.435
27	1.314	1.703	2.052	2.473	2.771	3.421
28	1.313	1.701	2.048	2.467	2.763	3.408
29	1.311	1.699	2.045	2.462	2.756	3.396
30	1.310	1.697	2.042	2.457	2.750	3.385
32	1.309	1.694	2.037	2.449	2.738	3.365
34	1.307	1.691	2.032	2.441	2.728	3.348
36	1.306	1.688	2.028	2.434	2.719	3.333
38	1.304	1.686	2.024	2.429	2.712	3.319
40	1.303	1.684	2.021	2.423	2.704	3.307
42	1.302	1.682	2.018	2.418	2.698	3.296
44	1.301	1.680	2.015	2.414	2.692	3.286
46	1.300	1.679	2.013	2.410	2.687	3.277
48	1.299	1.677	2.011	2.407	2.682	3.269
50	1.299	1.676	2.009	2.403	2.678	3.261
60	1.296	1.671	2.000	2.390	2.660	3.232
70	1.294	1.667	1.994	2.381	2.648	3.211
80	1.292	1.664	1.990	2.374	2.639	3.195
90	1.291	1.662	1.987	2.368	2.632	3.183
100	1.290	1.660	1.984	2.364	2.626	3.174
120	1.289	1.658	1.980	2.358	2.617	3.160
150	1.287	1.655	1.976	2.351	2.609	3.145
200	1.286	1.653	1.972	2.345	2.601	3.131

Degrees of freedom

Table A.7: *F*-distribution: Critical Values of *F* (1% Significance Level)

					Degrees of freedom for numerator							
	1	2	3	4	5	6	7	8	9	10	12	14
1	4052.18	4999.50	5403.35	5624.58	5763.65	5858.99	5928.36	5981.07	6022.47	6055.85	6106.32	6142.67
2	98.50	99.00	99.17	99.25	99.30	99.33	99.36	99.37	99.39	99.40	99.42	99.43
3	34.12	30.82	29.46	28.71	28.24	27.91	27.67	27.49	27.35	27.23	27.05	26.92
4	21.20	18.00	16.69	15.98	15.52	15.21	14.98	14.80	14.66	14.55	14.37	14.25
5	16.26	13.27	12.06	11.39	10.97	10.67	10.46	10.29	10.16	10.05	9.89	9.77
6	13.75	10.92	9.78	9.15	8.75	8.47	8.26	8.10	7.98	7.87	7.72	7.60
7	12.25	9.55	8.45	7.85	7.46	7.19	6.99	6.84	6.72	6.62	6.47	6.36
8	11.26	8.65	7.59	7.01	6.63	6.37	6.18	6.03	5.91	5.81	5.67	5.56
9	10.56	8.02	6.99	6.42	6.06	5.80	5.61	5.47	5.35	5.26	5.11	5.01
10	10.04	7.56	6.55	5.99	5.64	5.39	5.20	5.06	4.94	4.85	4.71	4.60
11	9.65	7.21	6.22	5.67	5.32	5.07	4.89	4.74	4.63	4.54	4.40	4.29
12	9.33	6.93	5.95	5.41	5.06	4.82	4.64	4.50	4.39	4.30	4.16	4.05
13	9.07	6.70	5.74	5.21	4.86	4.62	4.44	4.30	4.19	4.10	3.96	3.86
14	8.86	6.51	5.56	5.04	4.69	4.46	4.28	4.14	4.03	3.94	3.80	3.70
15	8.68	6.36	5.42	4.89	4.56	4.32	4.14	4.00	3.89	3.80	3.67	3.56
16	8.53	6.23	5.29	4.77	4.44	4.20	4.03	3.89	3.78	3.69	3.55	3.45
17	8.40	6.11	5.18	4.67	4.34	4.10	3.93	3.79	3.68	3.59	3.46	3.35
18	8.29	6.01	5.09	4.58	4.25	4.01	3.84	3.71	3.60	3.51	3.37	3.27
19	8.18	5.93	5.01	4.50	4.17	3.94	3.77	3.63	3.52	3.43	3.30	3.19
20	8.10	5.85	4.94	4.43	4.10	3.87	3.70	3.56	3.46	3.37	3.23	3.13
21	8.02	5.78	4.87	4.37	4.04	3.81	3.64	3.51	3.40	3.31	3.17	3.07
22	7.95	5.72	4.82	4.31	3.99	3.76	3.59	3.45	3.35	3.26	3.12	3.02
23	7.88	5.66	4.76	4.26	3.94	3.71	3.54	3.41	3.30	3.21	3.07	2.97
24	7.82	5.61	4.72	4.22	3.90	3.67	3.50	3.36	3.26	3.17	3.03	2.93
25	7.77	5.57	4.68	4.18	3.85	3.63	3.46	3.32	3.22	3.13	2.99	2.89
26	7.72	5.53	4.64	4.14	3.82	3.59	3.42	3.29	3.18	3.09	2.96	2.86
27	7.68	5.49	4.60	4.11	3.78	3.56	3.39	3.26	3.15	3.06	2.93	2.82
28	7.64	5.45	4.57	4.07	3.75	3.53	3.36	3.23	3.12	3.03	2.90	2.79
29	7.60	5.42	4.54	4.04	3.73	3.50	3.33	3.20	3.09	3.00	2.87	2.77
30	7.56	5.39	4.51	4.02	3.70	3.47	3.30	3.17	3.07	2.98	2.84	2.74
35	7.42	5.27	4.40	3.91	3.59	3.37	3.20	3.07	2.96	2.88	2.74	2.64
40	7.31	5.18	4.31	3.83	3.51	3.29	3.12	2.99	2.89	2.80	2.66	2.56
50	7.17	5.06	4.20	3.72	3.41	3.19	3.02	2.89	2.78	2.70	2.56	2.46
60	7.08	4.98	4.13	3.65	3.34	3.12	2.95	2.82	2.72	2.63	2.50	2.39
70	7.01	4.92	4.07	3.60	3.29	3.07	2.91	2.78	2.67	2.59	2.45	2.35
80	6.96	4.88	4.04	3.56	3.26	3.04	2.87	2.74	2.64	2.55	2.42	2.31
90	6.93	4.85	4.01	3.53	3.23	3.01	2.84	2.72	2.61	2.52	2.39	2.29
100	6.90	4.82	3.98	3.51	3.21	2.99	2.82	2.69	2.59	2.50	2.37	2.27
120	6.85	4.79	3.95	3.48	3.17	2.96	2.79	2.66	2.56	2.47	2.34	2.23
150	6.81	4.75	3.91	3.45	3.14	2.92	2.76	2.63	2.53	2.44	2.31	2.20
200	6.76	4.71	3.88	3.41	3.11	2.89	2.73	2.60	2.50	2.41	2.27	2.17
250	6.74	4.69	3.86	3.40	3.09	2.87	2.71	2.58	2.48	2.39	2.26	2.15
300	6.72	4.68	3.85	3.38	3.08	2.86	2.70	2.57	2.47	2.38	2.24	2.14
400	6.70	4.66	3.83	3.37	3.06	2.85	2.68	2.56	2.45	2.37	2.23	2.13
500	6.69	4.65	3.82	3.36	3.05	2.84	2.68	2.55	2.44	2.36	2.22	2.12
600	6.68	4.64	3.81	3.35	3.05	2.83	2.67	2.54	2.44	2.35	2.21	2.11
750	6.67	4.63	3.81	3.34	3.04	2.83	2.66	2.53	2.43	2.34	2.21	2.11
1000	6.66	4.63	3.80	3.34	3.04	2.82	2.66	2.53	2.43	2.34	2.20	2.10

Degrees of freedom for denominator

(Contd.)

Table A.7 (*Contd.*)

	Degrees of freedom for numerator												
	16	18	20	25	30	35	40	50	60	75	100	150	200
1	6170.10	6191.53	6208.73	6239.83	6260.65	6275.57	6286.78	6302.52	6313.03	6323.56	6334.11	6344.68	6349.97
2	99.44	99.44	99.45	99.46	99.47	99.47	99.47	99.48	99.48	99.49	99.49	99.49	99.49
3	26.83	26.75	26.69	26.58	26.50	26.45	26.41	26.35	26.32	26.28	26.24	26.20	26.18
4	14.15	14.08	14.02	13.91	13.84	13.79	13.75	13.69	13.65	13.61	13.58	13.54	13.52
5	9.68	9.61	9.55	9.45	9.38	9.33	9.29	9.24	9.20	9.17	9.13	9.09	9.08
6	7.52	7.45	7.40	7.30	7.23	7.18	7.14	7.09	7.06	7.02	6.99	6.95	6.93
7	6.28	6.21	6.16	6.06	5.99	5.94	5.91	5.86	5.82	5.79	5.75	5.72	5.70
8	5.48	5.41	5.36	5.26	5.20	5.15	5.12	5.07	5.03	5.00	4.96	4.93	4.91
9	4.92	4.86	4.81	4.71	4.65	4.60	4.57	4.52	4.48	4.45	4.41	4.38	4.36
10	4.52	4.46	4.41	4.31	4.25	4.20	4.17	4.12	4.08	4.05	4.01	3.98	3.96
11	4.21	4.15	4.10	4.01	3.94	3.89	3.86	3.81	3.78	3.74	3.71	3.67	3.66
12	3.97	3.91	3.86	3.76	3.70	3.65	3.62	3.57	3.54	3.50	3.47	3.43	3.41
13	3.78	3.72	3.66	3.57	3.51	3.46	3.43	3.38	3.34	3.31	3.27	3.24	3.22
14	3.62	3.56	3.51	3.41	3.35	3.30	3.27	3.22	3.18	3.15	3.11	3.08	3.06
15	3.49	3.42	3.37	3.28	3.21	3.17	3.13	3.08	3.05	3.01	2.98	2.94	2.92
16	3.37	3.31	3.26	3.16	3.10	3.05	3.02	2.97	2.93	2.90	2.86	2.83	2.81
17	3.27	3.21	3.16	3.07	3.00	2.96	2.92	2.87	2.83	2.80	2.76	2.73	2.71
18	3.19	3.13	3.08	2.98	2.92	2.87	2.84	2.78	2.75	2.71	2.68	2.64	2.62
19	3.12	3.05	3.00	2.91	2.84	2.80	2.76	2.71	2.67	2.64	2.60	2.57	2.55
20	3.05	2.99	2.94	2.84	2.78	2.73	2.69	2.64	2.61	2.57	2.54	2.50	2.48
21	2.99	2.93	2.88	2.79	2.72	2.67	2.64	2.58	2.55	2.51	2.48	2.44	2.42
22	2.94	2.88	2.83	2.73	2.67	2.62	2.58	2.53	2.50	2.46	2.42	2.38	2.36
23	2.89	2.83	2.78	2.69	2.62	2.57	2.54	2.48	2.45	2.41	2.37	2.34	2.32
24	2.85	2.79	2.74	2.64	2.58	2.53	2.49	2.44	2.40	2.37	2.33	2.29	2.27
25	2.81	2.75	2.70	2.60	2.54	2.49	2.45	2.40	2.36	2.33	2.29	2.25	2.23
26	2.78	2.72	2.66	2.57	2.50	2.45	2.42	2.36	2.33	2.29	2.25	2.21	2.19
27	2.75	2.68	2.63	2.54	2.47	2.42	2.38	2.33	2.29	2.26	2.22	2.18	2.16
28	2.72	2.65	2.60	2.51	2.44	2.39	2.35	2.30	2.26	2.23	2.19	2.15	2.13
29	2.69	2.63	2.57	2.48	2.41	2.36	2.33	2.27	2.23	2.20	2.16	2.12	2.10
30	2.66	2.60	2.55	2.45	2.39	2.34	2.30	2.25	2.21	2.17	2.13	2.09	2.07
35	2.56	2.50	2.44	2.35	2.28	2.23	2.19	2.14	2.10	2.06	2.02	1.98	1.96
40	2.48	2.42	2.37	2.27	2.20	2.15	2.11	2.06	2.02	1.98	1.94	1.90	1.87
50	2.38	2.32	2.27	2.17	2.10	2.05	2.01	1.95	1.91	1.87	1.82	1.78	1.76
60	2.31	2.25	2.20	2.10	2.03	1.98	1.94	1.88	1.84	1.79	1.75	1.70	1.68
70	2.27	2.20	2.15	2.05	1.98	1.93	1.89	1.83	1.78	1.74	1.70	1.65	1.62
80	2.23	2.17	2.12	2.01	1.94	1.89	1.85	1.79	1.75	1.70	1.65	1.61	1.58
90	2.21	2.14	2.09	1.99	1.92	1.86	1.82	1.76	1.72	1.67	1.62	1.57	1.55
100	2.19	2.12	2.07	1.97	1.89	1.84	1.80	1.74	1.69	1.65	1.60	1.55	1.52
120	2.15	2.09	2.03	1.93	1.86	1.81	1.76	1.70	1.66	1.61	1.56	1.51	1.48
150	2.12	2.06	2.00	1.90	1.83	1.77	1.73	1.66	1.62	1.57	1.52	1.46	1.43
200	2.09	2.03	1.97	1.87	1.79	1.74	1.69	1.63	1.58	1.53	1.48	1.42	1.39
250	2.07	2.01	1.95	1.85	1.77	1.72	1.67	1.61	1.56	1.51	1.46	1.40	1.36
300	2.06	1.99	1.94	1.84	1.76	1.70	1.66	1.59	1.55	1.50	1.44	1.38	1.35
400	2.05	1.98	1.92	1.82	1.75	1.69	1.64	1.58	1.53	1.48	1.42	1.36	1.32
500	2.04	1.97	1.92	1.81	1.74	1.68	1.63	1.57	1.52	1.47	1.41	1.34	1.31
600	2.03	1.96	1.91	1.80	1.73	1.67	1.63	1.56	1.51	1.46	1.40	1.34	1.30
750	2.02	1.96	1.90	1.80	1.72	1.66	1.62	1.55	1.50	1.45	1.39	1.33	1.29
1000	2.02	1.95	1.90	1.79	1.72	1.66	1.61	1.54	1.50	1.44	1.38	1.32	1.28

Table A.8 F-distribution: Critical Values of F (5% Significance Level)

	1	2	3	4	5	6	7	8	9	10	12	14
	— Degrees of freedom for numerator											
1	161.45	199.50	215.71	224.58	230.16	233.99	236.77	238.88	240.54	241.88	243.91	245.36
2	18.51	19.00	19.16	19.25	19.30	19.33	19.35	19.37	19.38	19.40	19.41	19.42
3	10.13	9.55	9.28	9.12	9.01	8.94	8.89	8.85	8.81	8.79	8.74	8.71
4	7.71	6.94	6.59	6.39	6.26	6.16	6.09	6.04	6.00	5.96	5.91	5.87
5	6.61	5.79	5.41	5.19	5.05	4.95	4.88	4.82	4.77	4.74	4.68	4.64
6	5.99	5.14	4.76	4.53	4.39	4.28	4.21	4.15	4.10	4.06	4.00	3.96
7	5.59	4.74	4.35	4.12	3.97	3.87	3.79	3.73	3.68	3.64	3.57	3.53
8	5.32	4.46	4.07	3.84	3.69	3.58	3.50	3.44	3.39	3.35	3.28	3.24
9	5.12	4.26	3.86	3.63	3.48	3.37	3.29	3.23	3.18	3.14	3.07	3.03
10	4.96	4.10	3.71	3.48	3.33	3.22	3.14	3.07	3.02	2.98	2.91	2.86
11	4.84	3.98	3.59	3.36	3.20	3.09	3.01	2.95	2.90	2.85	2.79	2.74
12	4.75	3.89	3.49	3.26	3.11	3.00	2.91	2.85	2.80	2.75	2.69	2.64
13	4.67	3.81	3.41	3.18	3.03	2.92	2.83	2.77	2.71	2.67	2.60	2.55
14	4.60	3.74	3.34	3.11	2.96	2.85	2.76	2.70	2.65	2.60	2.53	2.48
15	4.54	3.68	3.29	3.06	2.90	2.79	2.71	2.64	2.59	2.54	2.48	2.42
16	4.49	3.63	3.24	3.01	2.85	2.74	2.66	2.59	2.54	2.49	2.42	2.37
17	4.45	3.59	3.20	2.96	2.81	2.70	2.61	2.55	2.49	2.45	2.38	2.33
18	4.41	3.55	3.16	2.93	2.77	2.66	2.58	2.51	2.46	2.41	2.34	2.29
19	4.38	3.52	3.13	2.90	2.74	2.63	2.54	2.48	2.42	2.38	2.31	2.26
20	4.35	3.49	3.10	2.87	2.71	2.60	2.51	2.45	2.39	2.35	2.28	2.22
21	4.32	3.47	3.07	2.84	2.68	2.57	2.49	2.42	2.37	2.32	2.25	2.20
22	4.30	3.44	3.05	2.82	2.66	2.55	2.46	2.40	2.34	2.30	2.23	2.17
23	4.28	3.42	3.03	2.80	2.64	2.53	2.44	2.37	2.32	2.27	2.20	2.15
24	4.26	3.40	3.01	2.78	2.62	2.51	2.42	2.36	2.30	2.25	2.18	2.13
25	4.24	3.39	2.99	2.76	2.60	2.49	2.40	2.34	2.28	2.24	2.16	2.11
26	4.22	3.37	2.98	2.74	2.59	2.47	2.39	2.32	2.27	2.22	2.15	2.09
27	4.21	3.35	2.96	2.73	2.57	2.46	2.37	2.31	2.25	2.20	2.13	2.08
28	4.20	3.34	2.95	2.71	2.56	2.45	2.36	2.29	2.24	2.19	2.12	2.06
29	4.18	3.33	2.93	2.70	2.55	2.43	2.35	2.28	2.22	2.18	2.10	2.05
30	4.17	3.32	2.92	2.69	2.53	2.42	2.33	2.27	2.21	2.16	2.09	2.04
35	4.12	3.27	2.87	2.64	2.49	2.37	2.29	2.22	2.16	2.11	2.04	1.99
40	4.08	3.23	2.84	2.61	2.45	2.34	2.25	2.18	2.12	2.08	2.00	1.95
50	4.03	3.18	2.79	2.56	2.40	2.29	2.20	2.13	2.07	2.03	1.95	1.89
60	4.00	3.15	2.76	2.53	2.37	2.25	2.17	2.10	2.04	1.99	1.92	1.86
70	3.98	3.13	2.74	2.50	2.35	2.23	2.14	2.07	2.02	1.97	1.89	1.84
80	3.96	3.11	2.72	2.49	2.33	2.21	2.13	2.06	2.00	1.95	1.88	1.82
90	3.95	3.10	2.71	2.47	2.32	2.20	2.11	2.04	1.99	1.94	1.86	1.80
100	3.94	3.09	2.70	2.46	2.31	2.19	2.10	2.03	1.97	1.93	1.85	1.79
120	3.92	3.07	2.68	2.45	2.29	2.18	2.09	2.02	1.96	1.91	1.83	1.78
150	3.90	3.06	2.66	2.43	2.27	2.16	2.07	2.00	1.94	1.89	1.82	1.76
200	3.89	3.04	2.65	2.42	2.26	2.14	2.06	1.98	1.93	1.88	1.80	1.74
250	3.88	3.03	2.64	2.41	2.25	2.13	2.05	1.98	1.92	1.87	1.79	1.73
300	3.87	3.03	2.63	2.40	2.24	2.13	2.04	1.97	1.91	1.86	1.78	1.72
400	3.86	3.02	2.63	2.39	2.24	2.12	2.03	1.96	1.90	1.85	1.78	1.72
500	3.86	3.01	2.62	2.39	2.23	2.12	2.03	1.96	1.90	1.85	1.77	1.71
600	3.86	3.01	2.62	2.39	2.23	2.11	2.02	1.95	1.90	1.85	1.77	1.71
750	3.85	3.01	2.62	2.38	2.23	2.11	2.02	1.95	1.89	1.84	1.77	1.70
1000	3.85	3.00	2.61	2.38	2.22	2.11	2.02	1.95	1.89	1.84	1.76	1.70

Degrees of freedom for denominator

(Contd.)

Table A.8 (*Contd.*)

					Degrees of freedom for numerator								
	16	18	20	25	30	35	40	50	60	75	100	150	200
1	246.46	247.32	248.01	249.26	250.10	250.69	251.14	251.77	252.20	252.62	253.04	253.46	253.68
2	19.43	19.44	19.45	19.46	19.46	19.47	19.47	19.48	19.48	19.48	19.49	19.49	19.49
3	8.69	8.67	8.66	8.63	8.62	8.60	8.59	8.58	8.57	8.56	8.55	8.54	8.54
4	5.84	5.82	5.80	5.77	5.75	5.73	5.72	5.70	5.69	5.68	5.66	5.65	5.65
5	4.60	4.58	4.56	4.52	4.50	4.48	4.46	4.44	4.43	4.42	4.41	4.39	4.39
6	3.92	3.90	3.87	3.83	3.81	3.79	3.77	3.75	3.74	3.73	3.71	3.70	3.69
7	3.49	3.47	3.44	3.40	3.38	3.36	3.34	3.32	3.30	3.29	3.27	3.26	3.25
8	3.20	3.17	3.15	3.11	3.08	3.06	3.04	3.02	3.01	2.99	2.97	2.96	2.95
9	2.99	2.96	2.94	2.89	2.86	2.84	2.83	2.80	2.79	2.77	2.76	2.74	2.73
10	2.83	2.80	2.77	2.73	2.70	2.68	2.66	2.64	2.62	2.60	2.59	2.57	2.56
11	2.70	2.67	2.65	2.60	2.57	2.55	2.53	2.51	2.49	2.47	2.46	2.44	2.43
12	2.60	2.57	2.54	2.50	2.47	2.44	2.43	2.40	2.38	2.37	2.35	2.33	2.32
13	2.51	2.48	2.46	2.41	2.38	2.36	2.34	2.31	2.30	2.28	2.26	2.24	2.23
14	2.44	2.41	2.39	2.34	2.31	2.28	2.27	2.24	2.22	2.21	2.19	2.17	2.16
15	2.38	2.35	2.33	2.28	2.25	2.22	2.20	2.18	2.16	2.14	2.12	2.10	2.10
16	2.33	2.30	2.28	2.23	2.19	2.17	2.15	2.12	2.11	2.09	2.07	2.05	2.04
17	2.29	2.26	2.23	2.18	2.15	2.12	2.10	2.08	2.06	2.04	2.02	2.00	1.99
18	2.25	2.22	2.19	2.14	2.11	2.08	2.06	2.04	2.02	2.00	1.98	1.96	1.95
19	2.21	2.18	2.16	2.11	2.07	2.05	2.03	2.00	1.98	1.96	1.94	1.92	1.91
20	2.18	2.15	2.12	2.07	2.04	2.01	1.99	1.97	1.95	1.93	1.91	1.89	1.88
21	2.16	2.12	2.10	2.05	2.01	1.98	1.96	1.94	1.92	1.90	1.88	1.86	1.84
22	2.13	2.10	2.07	2.02	1.98	1.96	1.94	1.91	1.89	1.87	1.85	1.83	1.82
23	2.11	2.08	2.05	2.00	1.96	1.93	1.91	1.88	1.86	1.84	1.82	1.80	1.79
24	2.09	2.05	2.03	1.97	1.94	1.91	1.89	1.86	1.84	1.82	1.80	1.78	1.77
25	2.07	2.04	2.01	1.96	1.92	1.89	1.87	1.84	1.82	1.80	1.78	1.76	1.75
26	2.05	2.02	1.99	1.94	1.90	1.87	1.85	1.82	1.80	1.78	1.76	1.74	1.73
27	2.04	2.00	1.97	1.92	1.88	1.86	1.84	1.81	1.79	1.76	1.74	1.72	1.71
28	2.02	1.99	1.96	1.91	1.87	1.84	1.82	1.79	1.77	1.75	1.73	1.70	1.69
29	2.01	1.97	1.94	1.89	1.85	1.83	1.81	1.77	1.75	1.73	1.71	1.69	1.67
30	1.99	1.96	1.93	1.88	1.84	1.81	1.79	1.76	1.74	1.72	1.70	1.67	1.66
35	1.94	1.91	1.88	1.82	1.79	1.76	1.74	1.70	1.68	1.66	1.63	1.61	1.60
40	1.90	1.87	1.84	1.78	1.74	1.72	1.69	1.66	1.64	1.61	1.59	1.56	1.55
50	1.85	1.81	1.78	1.73	1.69	1.66	1.63	1.60	1.58	1.55	1.52	1.50	1.48
60	1.82	1.78	1.75	1.69	1.65	1.62	1.59	1.56	1.53	1.51	1.48	1.45	1.44
70	1.79	1.75	1.72	1.66	1.62	1.59	1.57	1.53	1.50	1.48	1.45	1.42	1.40
80	1.77	1.73	1.70	1.64	1.60	1.57	1.54	1.51	1.48	1.45	1.43	1.39	1.38
90	1.76	1.72	1.69	1.63	1.59	1.55	1.53	1.49	1.46	1.44	1.41	1.38	1.36
100	1.75	1.71	1.68	1.62	1.57	1.54	1.52	1.48	1.45	1.42	1.39	1.36	1.34
120	1.73	1.69	1.66	1.60	1.55	1.52	1.50	1.46	1.43	1.40	1.37	1.33	1.32
150	1.71	1.67	1.64	1.58	1.54	1.50	1.48	1.44	1.41	1.38	1.34	1.31	1.29
200	1.69	1.66	1.62	1.56	1.52	1.48	1.46	1.41	1.39	1.35	1.32	1.28	1.26
250	1.68	1.65	1.61	1.55	1.50	1.47	1.44	1.40	1.37	1.34	1.31	1.27	1.25
300	1.68	1.64	1.61	1.54	1.50	1.46	1.43	1.39	1.36	1.33	1.30	1.26	1.23
400	1.67	1.63	1.60	1.53	1.49	1.45	1.42	1.38	1.35	1.32	1.28	1.24	1.22
500	1.66	1.62	1.59	1.53	1.48	1.45	1.42	1.38	1.35	1.31	1.28	1.23	1.21
600	1.66	1.62	1.59	1.52	1.48	1.44	1.41	1.37	1.34	1.31	1.27	1.23	1.20
750	1.66	1.62	1.58	1.52	1.47	1.44	1.41	1.37	1.34	1.30	1.26	1.22	1.20
1000	1.65	1.61	1.58	1.52	1.47	1.43	1.41	1.36	1.33	1.30	1.26	1.22	1.19

Table A.9 Upper-tail Critical Values of Chi-Square Distribution

Degrees of freedom	Level of significance			
	0.10	0.05	0.01	0.00
1	2.706	3.841	6.635	10.828
2	4.605	5.991	9.210	13.816
3	6.251	7.815	11.345	16.266
4	7.779	9.488	13.277	18.467
5	9.236	11.070	15.086	20.516
6	10.645	12.592	16.812	22.458
7	12.017	14.067	18.475	24.322
8	13.362	15.507	20.090	26.125
9	14.684	16.919	21.666	27.878
10	15.987	18.307	23.209	29.589
11	17.275	19.675	24.725	31.265
12	18.549	21.026	26.217	32.910
13	19.812	22.362	27.688	34.529
14	21.064	23.685	29.141	36.124
15	22.307	24.996	30.578	37.698
16	23.542	26.296	32.000	39.253
17	24.769	27.587	33.409	40.791
18	25.989	28.869	34.805	42.314
19	27.204	30.144	36.191	43.821
20	28.412	31.410	37.566	45.315
21	29.615	32.671	38.932	46.798
22	30.813	33.924	40.289	48.269
23	32.007	35.172	41.639	49.729
24	33.196	36.415	42.980	51.180
25	34.382	37.653	44.314	52.620
26	35.563	38.885	45.642	54.053
27	36.741	40.113	46.963	55.477
28	37.916	41.337	48.278	56.894
29	39.087	42.557	49.588	58.302
30	40.256	43.773	50.892	59.704
40	51.805	55.759	63.691	73.403
50	63.167	67.505	76.154	86.662
60	74.397	79.082	88.380	99.609
70	85.527	90.531	100.425	112.319
80	96.578	101.880	112.329	124.842
90	107.565	113.145	124.117	137.211
100	118.498	124.342	135.807	149.452

Table A.10 Durbin-Watson d statistic: 1% Significance Points of d_L and d_U

No. of obs. (n) ↓	1		2		3		4		5	
	d_L	d_U	d_L	d_U	d_L	d_U	d_L	d_U	d_L	d_U
6	0.390	1.142	–	–	–	–	–	–	–	–
7	0.435	1.036	0.294	1.676	–	–	–	–	–	–
8	0.497	1.003	0.345	1.489	0.229	2.102	–	–	–	–
9	0.554	0.998	0.408	1.389	0.279	1.875	0.183	2.433	–	–
10	0.604	1.001	0.466	1.333	0.340	1.733	0.230	2.193	0.150	2.690
11	0.653	1.010	0.519	1.297	0.396	1.640	0.286	2.030	0.193	2.453
12	0.697	1.023	0.569	1.274	0.449	1.575	0.339	1.913	0.244	2.280
13	0.738	1.038	0.616	1.261	0.499	1.526	0.391	1.826	0.294	2.150
14	0.776	1.054	0.660	1.254	0.547	1.490	0.441	1.757	0.343	2.049
15	0.811	1.070	0.700	1.252	0.591	1.465	0.487	1.705	0.390	1.967
16	0.844	1.086	0.738	1.253	0.633	1.447	0.532	1.664	0.437	1.901
17	0.873	1.102	0.773	1.255	0.672	1.432	0.574	1.631	0.481	1.847
18	0.902	1.118	0.805	1.259	0.708	1.422	0.614	1.604	0.522	1.803
19	0.928	1.133	0.835	1.264	0.742	1.416	0.650	1.583	0.561	1.767
20	0.952	1.147	0.862	1.270	0.774	1.410	0.684	1.567	0.598	1.736
21	0.975	1.161	0.889	1.276	0.803	1.408	0.718	1.554	0.634	1.712
22	0.997	1.174	0.915	1.284	0.832	1.407	0.748	1.543	0.666	1.691
23	1.017	1.186	0.938	1.290	0.858	1.407	0.777	1.535	0.699	1.674
24	1.037	1.199	0.959	1.298	0.881	1.407	0.805	1.527	0.728	1.659
25	1.055	1.210	0.981	1.305	0.906	1.408	0.832	1.521	0.756	1.645
26	1.072	1.222	1.000	1.311	0.928	1.410	0.855	1.517	0.782	1.635
27	1.088	1.232	1.019	1.318	0.948	1.413	0.878	1.514	0.808	1.625
28	1.104	1.244	1.036	1.325	0.969	1.414	0.901	1.512	0.832	1.618
29	1.119	1.254	1.053	1.332	0.988	1.418	0.921	1.511	0.855	1.611
30	1.134	1.264	1.070	1.339	1.006	1.421	0.941	1.510	0.877	1.606
31	1.147	1.274	1.085	1.345	1.022	1.425	0.960	1.509	0.897	1.601
32	1.160	1.283	1.100	1.351	1.039	1.428	0.978	1.509	0.917	1.597
33	1.171	1.291	1.114	1.358	1.055	1.432	0.995	1.510	0.935	1.594
34	1.184	1.298	1.128	1.364	1.070	1.436	1.012	1.511	0.954	1.591
35	1.195	1.307	1.141	1.370	1.085	1.439	1.028	1.512	0.971	1.589
36	1.205	1.315	1.153	1.376	1.098	1.442	1.043	1.513	0.987	1.587
37	1.217	1.322	1.164	1.383	1.112	1.446	1.058	1.514	1.004	1.585
38	1.227	1.330	1.176	1.388	1.124	1.449	1.072	1.515	1.019	1.584
39	1.237	1.337	1.187	1.392	1.137	1.452	1.085	1.517	1.033	1.583
40	1.246	1.344	1.197	1.398	1.149	1.456	1.098	1.518	1.047	1.583
45	1.288	1.376	1.245	1.424	1.201	1.474	1.156	1.528	1.111	1.583
50	1.324	1.403	1.285	1.445	1.245	1.491	1.206	1.537	1.164	1.587
55	1.356	1.428	1.320	1.466	1.284	1.505	1.246	1.548	1.209	1.592
60	1.382	1.449	1.351	1.484	1.317	1.520	1.283	1.559	1.248	1.598
65	1.407	1.467	1.377	1.500	1.346	1.534	1.314	1.568	1.283	1.604
70	1.429	1.485	1.400	1.514	1.372	1.546	1.343	1.577	1.313	1.611
75	1.448	1.501	1.422	1.529	1.395	1.557	1.368	1.586	1.340	1.617
80	1.465	1.514	1.440	1.541	1.416	1.568	1.390	1.595	1.364	1.624
85	1.481	1.529	1.458	1.553	1.434	1.577	1.411	1.603	1.386	1.630
90	1.496	1.541	1.474	1.563	1.452	1.587	1.429	1.611	1.406	1.636
95	1.510	1.552	1.489	1.573	1.468	1.596	1.446	1.618	1.425	1.641
100	1.522	1.562	1.502	1.582	1.482	1.604	1.461	1.625	1.441	1.647
150	1.611	1.637	1.598	1.651	1.584	1.665	1.571	1.679	1.557	1.693
200	1.664	1.684	1.653	1.693	1.643	1.704	1.633	1.715	1.623	1.725

(Contd.)

Table A.10   (Contd.)

No. of obs. (n) ↓	6 d_L	6 d_U	7 d_L	7 d_U	8 d_L	8 d_U	9 d_L	9 d_U	10 d_L	10 d_U
6	–	–	–	–	–	–	–	–	–	–
7	–	–	–	–	–	–	–	–	–	–
8	–	–	–	–	–	–	–	–	–	–
9	–	–	–	–	–	–	–	–	–	–
10	–	–	–	–	–	–	–	–	–	–
11	0.124	2.892	–	–	–	–	–	–	–	–
12	0.164	2.665	0.105	3.053	–	–	–	–	–	–
13	0.211	2.490	0.140	2.838	0.090	3.182	–	–	–	–
14	0.257	2.354	0.183	2.667	0.122	2.981	0.078	3.287	–	–
15	0.303	2.244	0.226	2.530	0.161	2.817	0.107	3.101	0.068	3.374
16	0.349	2.153	0.269	2.416	0.200	2.681	0.142	2.944	0.094	3.201
17	0.393	2.078	0.313	2.319	0.241	2.566	0.179	2.811	0.127	3.053
18	0.435	2.015	0.355	2.238	0.282	2.467	0.216	2.697	0.160	2.925
19	0.476	1.963	0.396	2.169	0.322	2.381	0.255	2.597	0.196	2.813
20	0.515	1.918	0.436	2.110	0.362	2.308	0.294	2.510	0.232	2.174
21	0.552	1.881	0.474	2.059	0.400	2.244	0.331	2.434	0.268	2.625
22	0.587	1.849	0.510	2.015	0.437	2.188	0.368	2.367	0.304	2.548
23	0.620	1.821	0.545	1.977	0.473	2.140	0.404	2.308	0.340	2.479
24	0.652	1.797	0.578	1.944	0.507	2.097	0.439	2.255	0.375	2.417
25	0.682	1.776	0.610	1.915	0.540	2.059	0.473	2.209	0.409	2.362
26	0.711	1.759	0.640	1.889	0.572	2.026	0.505	2.168	0.441	2.313
27	0.738	1.743	0.669	1.867	0.602	1.997	0.536	2.131	0.473	2.269
28	0.764	1.729	0.696	1.847	0.630	1.970	0.566	2.098	0.504	2.229
29	0.788	1.718	0.723	1.830	0.658	1.947	0.595	2.068	0.533	2.193
30	0.812	1.707	0.748	1.814	0.684	1.925	0.622	2.041	0.562	2.160
31	0.834	1.698	0.772	1.800	0.710	1.906	0.649	2.017	0.589	2.131
32	0.856	1.690	0.794	1.788	0.734	1.889	0.674	1.995	0.615	2.104
33	0.876	1.683	0.816	1.776	0.757	1.874	0.698	1.975	0.641	2.080
34	0.896	1.677	0.837	1.766	0.779	1.860	0.722	1.957	0.665	2.057
35	0.914	1.671	0.857	1.757	0.800	1.847	0.744	1.940	0.689	2.037
36	0.932	1.666	0.877	1.749	0.821	1.836	0.766	1.925	0.711	2.018
37	0.950	1.662	0.895	1.742	0.841	1.825	0.787	1.911	0.733	2.001
38	0.966	1.658	0.913	1.735	0.860	1.816	0.807	1.899	0.754	1.985
39	0.982	1.655	0.930	1.729	0.878	1.807	0.826	1.887	0.774	1.970
40	0.997	1.652	0.946	1.724	0.895	1.799	0.844	1.876	0.749	1.956
45	1.065	1.643	1.019	1.704	0.974	1.768	0.927	1.834	0.881	1.902
50	1.123	1.639	1.081	1.692	1.039	1.748	0.997	1.805	0.955	1.864
55	1.172	1.638	1.134	1.685	1.095	1.734	1.057	1.785	1.018	1.837
60	1.214	1.639	1.179	1.682	1.144	1.726	1.108	1.771	1.072	1.817
65	1.251	1.642	1.218	1.680	1.186	1.720	1.153	1.761	1.120	1.802
70	1.283	1.645	1.253	1.680	1.223	1.716	1.192	1.754	1.162	1.792
75	1.313	1.649	1.284	1.682	1.256	1.714	1.227	1.748	1.199	1.783
80	1.338	1.653	1.312	1.683	1.285	1.714	1.259	1.745	1.232	1.777
85	1.362	1.657	1.337	1.685	1.312	1.714	1.287	1.743	1.262	1.773
90	1.383	1.661	1.360	1.687	1.336	1.714	1.312	1.741	1.288	1.769
95	1.403	1.666	1.381	1.690	1.358	1.715	1.336	1.741	1.313	1.767
100	1.421	1.670	1.400	1.693	1.378	1.717	1.357	1.741	1.335	1.765
150	1.543	1.708	1.530	1.722	1.515	1.737	1.501	1.752	1.486	1.767
200	1.613	1.735	1.603	1.746	1.592	1.757	1.582	1.768	1.571	1.779

Table A.11 Durbin-Watson d statistic: 5% Significance Points of d_L and d_U

No. of obs. (n)	The number of regressors excluding the intercept (k)									
	1		2		3		4		5	
↓	d_L	d_U	d_L	d_U	d_L	d_U	d_L	d_U	d_L	d_U
6	0.610	1.400	–	–	–	–	–	–	–	–
7	0.700	1.356	0.467	1.896	–	–	–	–	–	–
8	0.763	1.332	0.559	1.777	0.367	2.287	–	–	–	–
9	0.824	1.320	0.629	1.699	0.455	2.128	0.296	2.588	–	–
10	0.879	1.320	0.697	1.641	0.525	2.016	0.376	2.414	0.243	2.822
11	0.927	1.324	0.758	1.604	0.595	1.928	0.444	2.283	0.315	2.645
12	0.971	1.331	0.812	1.579	0.658	1.864	0.512	2.177	0.380	2.506
13	1.010	1.340	0.861	1.562	0.715	1.816	0.574	2.094	0.444	2.390
14	1.045	1.350	0.905	1.551	0.767	1.779	0.632	2.030	0.505	2.296
15	1.077	1.361	0.946	1.543	0.814	1.750	0.685	1.977	0.562	2.220
16	1.106	1.371	0.982	1.539	0.857	1.728	0.734	1.935	0.615	2.157
17	1.133	1.381	1.015	1.536	0.897	1.710	0.779	1.900	0.664	2.104
18	1.158	1.391	1.046	1.535	0.933	1.696	0.820	1.872	0.710	2.060
19	1.180	1.401	1.074	1.536	0.967	1.685	0.859	1.848	0.752	2.023
20	1.201	1.411	1.100	1.537	0.998	1.676	0.894	1.828	0.792	1.991
21	1.221	1.420	1.125	1.538	1.026	1.669	0.927	1.812	0.829	1.964
22	1.239	1.429	1.147	1.541	1.053	1.664	0.958	1.797	0.863	1.940
23	1.257	1.437	1.168	1.543	1.078	1.660	0.986	1.785	0.895	1.920
24	1.273	1.446	1.188	1.546	1.101	1.656	1.013	1.775	0.925	1.902
25	1.288	1.454	1.206	1.550	1.123	1.654	1.038	1.767	0.953	1.886
26	1.302	1.461	1.224	1.553	1.143	1.652	1.062	1.759	0.979	1.873
27	1.316	1.469	1.240	1.556	1.162	1.651	1.084	1.753	1.004	1.861
28	1.328	1.476	1.255	1.560	1.181	1.650	1.104	1.747	1.028	1.850
29	1.341	1.483	1.270	1.563	1.198	1.650	1.124	1.743	1.050	1.841
30	1.352	1.489	1.284	1.567	1.214	1.650	1.143	1.739	1.071	1.833
31	1.363	1.496	1.297	1.570	1.229	1.650	1.160	1.735	1.090	1.825
32	1.373	1.502	1.309	1.574	1.244	1.650	1.177	1.732	1.109	1.819
33	1.383	1.508	1.321	1.577	1.258	1.651	1.193	1.730	1.127	1.813
34	1.393	1.514	1.333	1.580	1.271	1.652	1.208	1.728	1.144	1.808
35	1.402	1.519	1.343	1.584	1.283	1.653	1.222	1.726	1.160	1.803
36	1.411	1.525	1.354	1.587	1.295	1.654	1.236	1.724	1.175	1.799
37	1.419	1.530	1.364	1.590	1.307	1.655	1.249	1.723	1.190	1.795
38	1.427	1.535	1.373	1.594	1.318	1.656	1.261	1.722	1.204	1.792
39	1.435	1.540	1.382	1.597	1.328	1.658	1.273	1.722	1.218	1.789
40	1.442	1.544	1.391	1.600	1.338	1.659	1.285	1.721	1.230	1.786
45	1.475	1.566	1.430	1.615	1.383	1.666	1.336	1.720	1.287	1.776
50	1.503	1.585	1.462	1.628	1.421	1.674	1.378	1.721	1.335	1.771
55	1.528	1.601	1.490	1.641	1.452	1.681	1.414	1.724	1.374	1.768
60	1.549	1.616	1.514	1.652	1.480	1.689	1.444	1.727	1.408	1.767
65	1.567	1.629	1.536	1.662	1.503	1.696	1.471	1.731	1.438	1.767
70	1.583	1.641	1.554	1.672	1.525	1.703	1.494	1.735	1.464	1.768
75	1.598	1.652	1.571	1.680	1.543	1.709	1.515	1.739	1.487	1.770
80	1.611	1.662	1.586	1.688	1.560	1.715	1.534	1.743	1.507	1.772
85	1.624	1.671	1.600	1.696	1.575	1.721	1.550	1.747	1.525	1.774
90	1.635	1.679	1.612	1.703	1.589	1.726	1.566	1.751	1.542	1.776
95	1.645	1.687	1.623	1.709	1.602	1.732	1.579	1.755	1.557	1.778
100	1.654	1.694	1.634	1.715	1.613	1.736	1.592	1.758	1.571	1.780
150	1.720	1.747	1.706	1.760	1.693	1.774	1.679	1.788	1.665	1.802
200	1.758	1.779	1.748	1.789	1.738	1.799	1.728	1.809	1.718	1.820

(Contd.)

Table A.11 (Contd.)

No. of obs. (n)	The number of regressors excluding the intercept (k)									
	6		7		8		9		10	
↓	d_L	d_U	d_L	d_U	d_L	d_U	d_L	d_U	d_L	d_U
6	–	–	–	–	–	–	–	–	–	–
7	–	–	–	–	–	–	–	–	–	–
8	–	–	–	–	–	–	–	–	–	–
9	–	–	–	–	–	–	–	–	–	–
10	–	–	–	–	–	–	–	–	–	–
11	0.203	3.004	–	–	–	–	–	–	–	–
12	0.268	2.832	0.171	3.149	–	–	–	–	–	–
13	0.328	2.692	0.230	2.985	0.147	3.266	–	–	–	–
14	0.389	2.572	0.286	2.848	0.200	3.111	0.127	3.360	–	–
15	0.447	2.471	0.343	2.727	0.251	2.979	0.175	3.216	0.111	3.438
16	0.502	2.388	0.398	2.624	0.304	2.860	0.222	3.090	0.155	3.304
17	0.554	2.318	0.451	2.537	0.356	2.757	0.272	2.975	0.198	3.184
18	0.603	2.258	0.502	2.461	0.407	2.668	0.321	2.873	0.244	3.073
19	0.649	2.206	0.549	2.396	0.456	2.589	0.369	2.783	0.290	2.974
20	0.691	2.162	0.595	2.339	0.502	2.521	0.416	2.704	0.336	2.885
21	0.731	2.124	0.637	2.290	0.546	2.461	0.461	2.633	0.380	2.806
22	0.769	2.090	0.677	2.246	0.588	2.407	0.504	2.571	0.424	2.735
23	0.804	2.061	0.715	2.208	0.628	2.360	0.545	2.514	0.465	2.670
24	0.837	2.035	0.750	2.174	0.666	2.318	0.584	2.464	0.506	2.613
25	0.868	2.013	0.784	2.144	0.702	2.280	0.621	2.419	0.544	2.560
26	0.897	1.992	0.816	2.117	0.735	2.246	0.657	2.379	0.581	2.513
27	0.925	1.974	0.845	2.093	0.767	2.216	0.691	2.342	0.616	2.470
28	0.951	1.959	0.874	2.071	0.798	2.188	0.723	2.309	0.649	2.431
29	0.975	1.944	0.900	2.052	0.826	2.164	0.753	2.278	0.681	2.396
30	0.998	1.931	0.926	2.034	0.854	2.141	0.782	2.251	0.712	2.363
31	1.020	1.920	0.950	2.018	0.879	2.120	0.810	2.226	0.741	2.333
32	1.041	1.909	0.972	2.004	0.904	2.102	0.836	2.203	0.769	2.306
33	1.061	1.900	0.994	1.991	0.927	2.085	0.861	2.181	0.796	2.281
34	1.079	1.891	1.015	1.978	0.950	2.069	0.885	2.162	0.821	2.257
35	1.097	1.884	1.034	1.967	0.971	2.054	0.908	2.144	0.845	2.236
36	1.114	1.876	1.053	1.957	0.991	2.041	0.930	2.127	0.868	2.216
37	1.131	1.870	1.071	1.948	1.011	2.029	0.951	2.112	0.891	2.197
38	1.146	1.864	1.088	1.939	1.029	2.017	0.970	2.098	0.912	2.180
39	1.161	1.859	1.104	1.932	1.047	2.007	0.990	2.085	0.932	2.164
40	1.175	1.854	1.120	1.924	1.064	1.997	1.008	2.072	0.952	2.149
45	1.238	1.835	1.189	1.895	1.139	1.958	1.089	2.022	1.038	2.088
50	1.291	1.822	1.246	1.875	1.201	1.930	1.156	1.986	1.110	2.044
55	1.334	1.814	1.294	1.861	1.253	1.909	1.212	1.959	1.170	2.010
60	1.372	1.808	1.335	1.850	1.298	1.894	1.260	1.939	1.222	1.984
65	1.404	1.805	1.370	1.843	1.336	1.882	1.301	1.923	1.266	1.964
70	1.433	1.802	1.401	1.838	1.369	1.874	1.337	1.910	1.305	1.948
75	1.458	1.801	1.428	1.834	1.399	1.867	1.369	1.901	1.339	1.935
80	1.480	1.801	1.453	1.831	1.425	1.861	1.397	1.893	1.369	1.925
85	1.500	1.801	1.474	1.829	1.448	1.857	1.422	1.886	1.396	1.916
90	1.518	1.801	1.494	1.827	1.469	1.854	1.445	1.881	1.420	1.909
95	1.535	1.802	1.512	1.827	1.489	1.852	1.465	1.877	1.442	1.903
100	1.550	1.803	1.528	1.826	1.506	1.850	1.484	1.874	1.462	1.898
150	1.651	1.817	1.637	1.832	1.622	1.846	1.608	1.862	1.593	1.877
200	1.707	1.831	1.697	1.841	1.686	1.852	1.675	1.863	1.665	1.874

Table A.12   Critical Values for Pearson's Correlation Coefficient

	Significance level					
One-sided →	0.250	0.100	0.050	0.025	0.010	0.005
Two-sided →	0.500	0.200	0.100	0.050	0.020	0.010
1	0.707	0.951	0.988	0.997	1.000	1.000
2	0.500	0.800	0.900	0.950	0.980	0.990
3	0.404	0.687	0.805	0.878	0.934	0.959
4	0.347	0.608	0.729	0.811	0.882	0.917
5	0.309	0.551	0.669	0.755	0.833	0.875
6	0.281	0.507	0.622	0.707	0.789	0.834
7	0.260	0.472	0.582	0.666	0.750	0.798
8	0.242	0.443	0.549	0.632	0.716	0.765
9	0.228	0.419	0.521	0.602	0.685	0.735
10	0.216	0.398	0.497	0.576	0.658	0.708
11	0.206	0.380	0.476	0.553	0.634	0.684
12	0.197	0.365	0.458	0.532	0.612	0.661
13	0.189	0.351	0.441	0.514	0.592	0.641
14	0.182	0.338	0.426	0.497	0.574	0.623
15	0.176	0.327	0.412	0.482	0.558	0.606
16	0.170	0.317	0.400	0.468	0.543	0.590
17	0.165	0.308	0.389	0.456	0.529	0.575
18	0.160	0.299	0.378	0.444	0.516	0.561
19	0.156	0.291	0.369	0.433	0.503	0.549
20	0.152	0.284	0.360	0.423	0.492	0.537
21	0.148	0.277	0.352	0.413	0.482	0.526
22	0.145	0.271	0.344	0.404	0.472	0.515
23	0.142	0.265	0.337	0.396	0.462	0.505
24	0.138	0.260	0.330	0.388	0.453	0.496
25	0.136	0.255	0.323	0.381	0.445	0.487
26	0.133	0.250	0.317	0.374	0.437	0.479
27	0.131	0.245	0.312	0.367	0.430	0.471
28	0.128	0.241	0.306	0.361	0.423	0.463
29	0.126	0.237	0.301	0.355	0.416	0.456
30	0.124	0.233	0.296	0.349	0.409	0.449
35	0.114	0.216	0.275	0.325	0.381	0.418
40	0.107	0.202	0.257	0.304	0.358	0.393
45	0.101	0.190	0.243	0.288	0.338	0.372
50	0.096	0.181	0.231	0.273	0.322	0.354
55	0.091	0.172	0.220	0.261	0.307	0.339
60	0.087	0.165	0.211	0.250	0.295	0.325
65	0.084	0.159	0.203	0.240	0.284	0.313
70	0.081	0.153	0.195	0.232	0.274	0.302
75	0.078	0.148	0.189	0.224	0.265	0.292
80	0.076	0.143	0.183	0.217	0.257	0.283
85	0.073	0.139	0.178	0.211	0.249	0.275
90	0.071	0.135	0.173	0.205	0.242	0.267
95	0.069	0.131	0.168	0.200	0.236	0.260
100	0.068	0.128	0.164	0.195	0.230	0.254

The left margin of the data rows (1 to 100) is labelled: **Degrees of freedom**

Note: For testing the significance of correlation coefficient computed from n pairs of observation, the appropriate degrees of freedom are $n-2$. For testing the significance of a partial correlation coefficient between two variables after eliminating k independent variables, computed from observations on n individuals (i.e., on n sets of observations) the degrees of freedom are $n-2-k$.

References

Agung, I. Gusti Ngurah. 2011. *Cross Section and Experimental Data Analysis Using EViews*. Singapore: John Wiley & Sons.

Amemiya, T. 1981. 'Qualitative Response Models: A Survey', *Journal of Economic Literature*, 19(4): 1483–536.

Andrews, D.W.K. 1993. 'Tests for Parameter Instability and Structural Change with Unknown Change Point', *Econometrica*, 61(4): 821–56.

Asteriou, Dimitrios and Stephen G. Hall. 2007. *Applied Econometrics: A Modern Approach Using EViews and Microfit*. New York: Palgrave Macmillan.

Bai, Jushan and Pierre Perron. 1998. 'Estimating and Testing Linear Models with Multiple Structural Changes', *Econometrica*, 66(1): 47–78.

———. 2003. 'Computation and Analysis of Multiple Structural Change Models', *Journal of Applied Econometrics*, 18(1): 1–22.

Baltagi, Badi H. 2008. *Econometrics*, 4th Edition. Berlin: Springer-Verlag.

———. 2008. *Econometric Analysis of Panel Data*, 4th Edition. United Kingdom: John Wiley & Sons.

Basmann, Robert L. 1957. 'A Generalized Classical Method of Linear Estimation of Coefficients in a Structural Equation ', *Econometrica*, 25(1): 77–83.

Belsley, D.A., E. Kuh, and R.E. Welsch. 2004. *Regression Diagnostics: Identifying Influential Data and Sources of Collinearity*. USA: John Wiley & Sons.

Bhalla, G.S. and Gurmail Singh. 2009 'Economic Liberalisation and Indian Agriculture', *Economic & Political Weekly*, 26 December, 44(52): 34–44.

Bollerslev, T. 1986. 'Generalised Autoregressive Conditional Heteroskedasticity', *Journal of Econometrics*, 31(3): 307–27.

Bowen, Earl K. and Martin K. Starr. 1982. *Basic Statistics for Business and Economics*. Singapore: McGraw-Hill Book Co.

Box, G.E.P. and G.M. Jenkins. 1976. *Time Series Analysis: Forecasting and Control*, Revised Edition. San Francisco: Holden Day.

Breusch, T. 1978. 'Testing for Autocorrelation in Dynamic Linear Models ', *Australian Economic Papers*, 17(31): 334–55.

Breusch, T. and A. Pagan. 1979. 'A Simple Test for Heteroskedasticity and Random Coefficient Variation', *Econometrica*, 47(5): 1278–94.

Brooks, Chris. 2008. *Introductory Econometrics for Finance*, 2nd Edition. Cambridge: Cambridge University Press.

Cagan, P. 1956. 'The Monetary Dynamics of Hyper Inflations', in M. Friedman (ed.), *Studies in the Quantity Theory of Money*. Chicago: University of Chicago Press.

Chatterjee, Samprit and Ali S. Hadi. 2006. *Regression Analysis by Example*, 4th Edition. USA: John Wiley & Sons.

Cochrane, D. and G. Orcutt. 1949. 'Application of Least Squares Regression to Relationships Containing Autocorrelated Error Terms', *Journal of the American Statistical Association*, 44(245): 32–61.

Desai, Vandana and Robert B. Porter (eds). 2006. *Doing Development Research*. New Delhi: Vistaar Publications.

Dev, S. Mahendra and C. Ravi. 2007. 'Poverty and Inequality: All-India and States, 1983-2005', *Economic & Political Weekly*, 42(6): 509–21.

Devereux, Stephen and John Hoddinott (eds). 1993. *Fieldwork in Developing Countries*. Boulder, Colorado: Lynne Rienner Publishers.

Dickey, D.A. and W.A. Fuller. 1979. 'Distribution of the Estimators for Autoregressive Time Series with a Unit Root', *Journal of the American Statistical Association*, 74(366a): 427–31.

Dolado, J., T. Jenkinson, and S. Sosvilla-Rivero. 1990. 'Cointegration and Unit Roots', *Journal of Economic Surveys*, 4(3): 249–73.

Dougherty, Christopher. 2011. *Introduction to Econometrics*, 4th Edition. Oxford: Oxford University Press.

Durbin, J. 1970. 'Testing for Serial Correlation in Least Squares Regression: When Some the Variables are Lagged Dependent Variables ', *Econometrica*, 38(3): 410–21.

Durbin, J. and G.S. Watson. 1951. 'Testing for Serial Correlation in Least–Squares Regression', *Biometrika*, 38(1–2): 159–71.

Elliot, Graham, Thomas J. Rothenberg, and James H. Stock. 1996. 'Efficient Tests for an Autoregressive Unit Root', *Econometrica*, 64(4): 813–36.

Enders, Walter. 2004. *Applied Econometric Time Series*, 2nd Edition. USA: John Wiley & Sons.

Engle, Robert F. 1982. 'Autoregressive Conditional Heteroskedasticity with Estimates of the Variance of UK Inflation', *Econometrica*, 50(4): 987–1008.

Engle, Robert F. and Clive W.J. Granger. 1987. 'Cointegration and Error Correction: Representation, Estimation and Testing', *Econometrica*, 55(2): 251–76.

Engle, Robert F. and Daniel L. McFadden (eds). 1994. *Handbook of Econometrics*, Vol. 4. Amsterdam, The Netherlands: Elsevier Science BV.

Frisch, Ragnar. 1933. 'Editorial Note', *Econometrica*, 1(1). Available at https://www.econometricsociety.org/issue.asp?ref=0012-9682&vid=1&iid=1&oc=&s= (accessed on 21 August 2014).

Geweke, John, Joel Horowitz, and Hashem Pesaran. 2008. 'Econometrics', in Steven N. Durlauf and Lawrence E. Blume (eds), *The New Palgrave Dictionary of Economics*, pp. 609–32. New York: Palgrave Macmillan.

Glejser, H. 1969. 'A New Test for Heteroskedasticity', *Journal of the American Statistical Association*, 64(325): 316–23.

Godfrey, L.G. 1978. 'Testing for Higher Order Serial Correlation in Regression Equations when the Regressions Contain Lagged Dependent Variables', *Econometrica*, 46(6): 1303–10.

Goldberger, Arthur S. 1964. *Econometric Theory*. New York: John Wiley & Sons.

Goldfeld, S. and R. Quandt. 1965. 'Some Tests for Heteroskedasticity', *Journal of the American Statistical Association*, 60(310): 539–47.

Granger, C.W.J. 1969. 'Investigating Causal Relations by Econometric Models and Cross-Spectral Methods', *Econometrica*, 37(3): 424–38.

Granger, C.W.J. 1981. 'Some Properties of Time Series Data and Their Use in Econometric Model Specification', *Journal of Econometrics*, 16(1): 121–30.

Greene, William H. 2003. *Econometric Analysis*, 5th Edition. New Delhi: Pearson Education.

Griliches, Zvi and Michael D. Intriligator (eds). 1983. *Handbook of Econometrics*, Vol. 1. Amsterdam, The Netherlands: Elsevier Science BV.

———. 1984. *Handbook of Econometrics*, Vol. 2. Amsterdam, The Netherlands: Elsevier Science BV.

———. 1986. *Handbook of Econometrics*, Vol. 3. Amsterdam, The Netherlands: Elsevier Science BV.

Gujarati, Damodar N. and Dawn C. Porter. 2009. *Basic Econometrics*, 5th Edition. New York: McGraw Hill.

Haavelmo, Trygve. 1944. 'The Probability Approach in Econometrics', *Econometrica*, 12(Suppl.): 1–118.

Heckman, James J. and Edward E. Leamer (eds). 2001. *Handbook of Econometrics*, Vol. 5. Amsterdam, The Netherlands: Elsevier Science BV.

———. 2007. *Handbook of Econometrics*, Vol. 6, Parts A and B. Amsterdam, The Netherlands: Elsevier Science BV.

Hildreth, G. and J.Y. Lu. 1960. 'Demand Relations with Autocorrelated Disturbances', Technical Bulletin No. 276, Michigan State University Agricultural Experiment Station, November, Michigan State University.

Hoel, Paul G., Sidney C. Port, and Charles J. Stone. 1971, *Introduction to Probability Theory*. New Delhi: Universal Book Stall.

Johnston, Jack and John Dinardo. 1997. *Econometric Methods*, 4th Edition. New York: McGraw-Hill.

Judge, George G., R. Carter Hill, William E. Griffiths, Helmut Lutkepohl, and Tsoung-Chao Lee. 1982. *Introduction to the Theory and Practice of Econometrics*. New York: John Wiley & Sons.

Kennedy, Peter. 2008. *A Guide to Econometrics*, 6th Edition. USA: Blackwell Publishing.

Klein, Lawrence R. 1962. *An Introduction to Econometrics*. Englewood Cliffs, NJ: Prentice Hall.

Kmenta, Jan. 1986. *Elements of Econometrics*, 2nd Edition. New York: Macmillan Publishing Co.

Koop, Gary. 2008. *Introduction to Econometrics*. England: John Wiley & Sons.

———. 2009. *Analysis of Economic Data*. England: John Wiley & Sons.

Koyck, L.M. 1954. *Distributed Lags and Investment Analysis*. New York: North-Holland.

Lange, Oskar. 1962. *Introduction to Econometrics*. Oxford: Pergamon Press.

Longley, J.W. 1967. 'An Appraisal of Least Squares Programs for the Electronic Computer from the Point of the User', *Journal of the American Statistical Association*, 62(319): 819–41.

Maddala, G.S. and Kajal Lahiri. 2009. *Introduction to Econometrics*, 4th Edition. England: John Wiley & Sons.

Mansfield, Edwin. 1994. *Statistics for Business and Economics: Methods and Applications*, 5th Edition. London: W.W. Norton & Co.

Marschak, J. 1948. *Introduction to Econometrics*. Buffalo: University of Buffalo.

McCulloch, J. Huston. 1985. 'Miscellanea: On Heteros*edasticity', *Econometrica*, 53(2): 483.

McKinnon, J.G. 1991. 'Critical Values for Cointegration Tests', in R.F. Engle and C.W.J. Granger (eds), *Long-Run Economic Relationships: Readings in Cointegration*, pp. 267–76. Oxford: Oxford University Press.

Meyers, Lawrence S., Glenn Gamst, and A.J. Guarino. 2006. *Applied Multivariate Research: Design and Interpretation*. Thousand Oaks, California: Sage Publications.

Mood, Alexander M., Franklin A. Graybill, and Duane C.C. Boes. 1974. *Introduction to the Theory of Statistics*, 3rd Edition. New York: McGraw Hill.

National Sample Survey Organisation (NSSO). 2011. *Key Indicators of Household Consumer Expenditure in India 2009–10*, Ministry of Statistics & Programme Implementation, Government of India.

Nelson, C.R. and C.I. Plosser. 1982. 'Trends and Random Walks in Macroeconomic Time Series', *Journal of Monetary Economics*, 10(2): 139–62.

Nerlove, Marc. 1958. *Distributed Lags and Demand Analysis for Agricultural and Other Commodities*, Agricultural Handbook No. 141, U.S. Department of Agriculture, June.

Newey, W.K. and K. West. 1987. 'A Simple Positive Semi-Definite Heteroskedasticity and Autocorrelation Consistent Covariance Matrix', *Econometrica*, 55(3): 703–8.

Ng, S. and P. Perron. 1995. 'Unit Root Tests in ARMA Models with Data-Dependent Methods for the Selection of the Truncation Lag', *Journal of the American Statistical Association*, 90(429): 268–81.

———. 2001. 'Lag Length Selection and the Construction of Unit Root Tests with Good Size and Power', *Econometrica*, 69(6): 1519–54.

Patterson, Kerry. 2000. *An Introduction to Applied Econometrics: A Time Series Approach*. New York: Palgrave Macmillan.

Perron, P. 1989. 'The Great Crash, the Oil Price Shock, and the Unit Root Hypothesis', *Econometrica*, 57(6): 1361–401.

———. 2006. 'Dealing with Structural Breaks', in Terence C. Mills and Kerry Patterson (eds), *Palgrave Handbook of Econometrics*, Volume 1: Econometric Theory, pp. 278–352. New York: Palgrave Macmillan.

Phillips, P.C.B and Pierre Perron. 1988. 'Testing for Unit Root in Tine Series Regression', *Biometrika*, 75(2): 335–46.

Quandt, R.E. 1960. 'Tests of the Hypothesis that a Linear Regression System Obeys Two Separate Regimes', *Journal of the American Statistical Association*, 55(290): 324–30.

Rao, B. Bhaskara. 1994. *Cointegration for the Applied Economist*. New York: St. Martin's Press.

Rao, Potluri and Roger LeRoy L. Miller. 1972. *Applied Econometrics*. New Delhi: Prentice-Hall India.

Reserve Bank of India (RBI). 2011. *Handbook of Statistics on Indian Economy 2010–11*, Mumbai: Reserve Bank of India.

———. 2012. *Handbook of Statistics on Indian Economy 2011–12*, Mumbai: Reserve Bank of India.

Rudra, Ashok. 1989. 'Field Survey Methods', in Pranab Bardhan (ed.), *Conversations Between Economists and Anthropologists*. New Delhi: Oxford University Press.

Ryan, Thomas P. 2008. *Modern Regression Methods*. 2nd Edition, New York: John Wiley & Sons.

Samuelson, P.A., T.C. Koopmans, and J.R.N. Stone. 1954. 'The Report of the Evaluative Committee for Econometrica', *Econometrica*, 22(2): 141–6.

Schwert, G.W. 1989. 'Tests for Unit Roots: A Monte Carlo Investigation', *Journal of Business & Economic Statistics*, 7(2): 147–58.

Sims, Christopher A. 1972. 'Money, Income and Causality', *American Economic Review*, 62(4): 540–52.

———. 1980, 'Macroeconomics and Reality', *Econometrica*, 48(1): 1–48.

Sowey, Eric R. 1983. 'The University Teaching of Econometrics: A Personal View', *Econometric Reviews*, 2(2): 255–89.

Spanos, Aris. 2006, 'Econometrics in Retrospect and Prospect', in Terence C. Mills and Kerry Patterson (eds), *Palgrave Handbook of Econometrics*, Volume 1: Econometric Theory, pp. 3–58. New York: Palgrave Macmillan.

Spiegel, Murray R. and Larry J. Stephens. 2010, *Statistics*, 4th Edition. New Delhi: Tata McGraw-Hill Education Pvt. Ltd.

Stigler, Stephen M. 1986. *The History of Statistics: The Measurement of Uncertainty Before 1900*. Cambridge, MA: The Belknap Press of Harvard University Press.

Stock, James H. and Mark W. Watson. 2011. *Introduction to Econometrics*, USA: Pearson Education Inc., 3rd Edition.

Theil, Henri. 1954. 'Estimation of Parameters of Econometric Models', *Bulletin of International Statistical Institute*, 34(Part II): 122–9.

———. 1958. *Economic Forecasts and Policy*, 2nd Edition. Amsterdam: North-Holland.

Thomas, R.L. 1993. *Introductory Econometrics*, 2nd Edition. New York: Longman.

Tintner, G. 1953. 'The Definition of Econometrics', *Econometrica*, 21(1): 31–40.

White, H. 1980. 'A Heteroskedasticity-Consistent Covariance Matrix Estimator and a Direct Test for Heteroskedasticity', *Econometrica*, 48(4): 871–38.

Wooldridge, Jeffrey M. 2002. *Econometric Analysis of Cross Section and Panel Data*. Cambridge, MA: The MIT Press.

———. 2009. *Introductory Econometrics: A Modern Approach*, 4th Edition. USA: South-Western Cengage Learning.

World Bank. (N.A.). *National Accounts Data and OECD National Accounts Data File* downloaded from http://data.worldbank.org/indicator/NY.GDP.MKTP.CD, accessed on 10 May 2012.

Index

About the Author

Sankar Kumar Bhaumik is Professor in the Department of Economics, University of Calcutta. He has more than 32 years of teaching and research experience. His fields of specialization are econometrics, agricultural economics, Indian economic development, and research methodology. He has been teaching econometrics to post-graduate students for the past three decades or so. He has also done extensive research in the areas of agrarian relations, agricultural development, rural credit, and globalization and employment. His previous publications include *Tenancy Relations and Agrarian Development: A Study of West Bengal* (1993) and *Reforming Indian Agriculture: Towards Employment Generation and Poverty Reduction* (2008). He has to his credit more than 30 research papers published in refereed journals/edited books. He has so far completed 5 research projects, and supervised 10 PhD theses and 11 MPhil dissertations.